The C Standard++

The C++ Standard
Incorporating Technical Corrigendum 1

BS ISO/IEC 14882: 2003 (Second Edition)

WILEY

John Wiley & Sons, Ltd

Published in 2003 by John Wiley & Sons Ltd,
John Wiley & Sons Ltd, The Atrium, Southern Gate, Chichester,
West Sussex PO19 8SQ, England
Telephone   (+44) 1243 779777

Email (for orders and customer service enquiries): cs-books@wiley.co.uk
Visit our Home Page on www.wileyeurope.com or www.wiley.com

Other Wiley Editorial Offices

John Wiley & Sons Inc., 111 River Street, Hoboken, NJ 07030, USA

Jossey-Bass, 989 Market Street, San Francisco, CA 94103-1741, USA

Wiley-VCH Verlag GmbH, Boschstr. 12, D-69469 Weinheim, Germany

John Wiley & Sons Australia Ltd, 33 Park Road, Milton, Queensland 4064, Australia

John Wiley & Sons (Asia) Pte Ltd, 2 Clementi Loop #02-01, Jin Xing Distripark, Singapore 129809

John Wiley & Sons Canada Ltd, 22 Worcester Road, Etobicoke, Ontario, Canada M9W 1L1

Library of Congress Cataloging-in-Publication Data

The C++ standard / British Standards Institute.æ 2nd ed.
    p. cm.
    ISBN 0-470-84674-7 (Cloth : alk. paper)
    1. C++ (Computer program language) I. British Standards Institute.
    QA76.73.C153C16 2003
    005.13'3ædc21

                                          2003014730

British Library Cataloguing in Publication Data

ISBN: 0-470-84674-7

A catalogue record for this book is available from the British Library

Printed and bound in Great Britain by Antony Rowe Ltd, Chippenham
This book is printed on acid-free paper responsibly manufactured from sustainable forestry
in which at least two trees are planted for each one used for paper production

Contents

Contents

Contents

Contents

Contents

Contents

Contents

Contents

Contents

Contents

Contents

Foreword

The ISO standard is the culmination of the early years of C++ and the basis for its further evolution. This foreword examines the role of the standards committee in the life of C++ and ponders the future of Standard C++. C++ is a general-purpose programming language with a bias toward systems programming. By design and necessity it is a language that can — and often does — provide run-time performance unmatched by anything but carefully handcrafted assembly code. Similarly, by design and necessity it is a language that is available on a wide variety of platforms from the tiniest processors to the most ambitious supercomputers. In addition, C++'s abstraction mechanisms — such as classes and templates — effectively serve users for whom high performance is merely a fringe benefit. The result has been an extraordinary diversity of application areas and user communities.

This widespread and diverse use implies centrifugal forces that could tear the language apart into competing dialects, thus destroying the portability and shared community that are among the most valuable benefits of a common general-purpose language. This danger is made more acute because C++ lacks conventional centralizing forces such as a corporation with legal ownership (and a deep war chest for marketing and development), a dominant implementation, or a centralized users' organization.

The C++ community's response to this challenge was to establish the ISO C++ standards committee (and its national counterparts) and to support its work for more than a decade. The honor of taking the initiative goes to people from DEC, HP, and IBM, who — led by Larry Rosler and Dmitry Lenkov — in late 1988 contacted me about starting ANSI standardization of C++. It took them a couple of hours to convince me, but once convinced I started to prepare. The ARM (''The Annotated C++ Reference Manual'') was the first and most visible result. The ARM, or rather the reference manual in ''The C++ Programming Language (2nd edition)'', became the base document for the ANSI standardization of C++. AT&T deserves special praise for contributing this reference manual to the standards effort. A less enlightened company might have tried to retain C++ as a proprietary language.

The first and most significant effect of forming the ANSI C++ group was as obvious as it was unexpected to people unfamiliar with standardization. Suddenly, the community had an open forum where people from different parts of the community could meet to discuss all topics of importance to the language and its users. Commercial allies could talk without falling foul of cartel rules, commercial competitors could settle technical issues without getting into trouble with corporate rules, and there now was a place and time for people to meet face to face. In the committee, I finally met people I had known for years via email.

The C++ standardization always involved people from many countries. Even the ARM was reviewed by more than 100 people from half a dozen countries, and the first organizational meeting of what was to become the ANSI C++ committee (in Washington D.C. in December of 1989) had participants from several countries. In 1991, this international aspect of C++ was formalized by making the standardization an ISO process.

In retrospect, the committee's role as an open forum and as a focus of the C++ community was at least as important as the final standard. The C++ standards committee is the center of the C++ community. Had the members not left their commercial rivalries at the committee door and focused on technical issues, the C++ standards effort would have failed. I am told that this consistently civil, civic, and often friendly behavior is uncommon in a standards committee. One of the things that have made the C++ standards process worth while for me personally and professionally is that only in the rarest of cases have members interpreted their obligations narrowly or destructively. I cannot think of a meeting where I didn't learn something worthwhile. The C++ committee has been the source of many long-term friendships.

The committee membership was always large enough and dedicated enough to keep alive communication with the community at large. The image of a handful of experts meeting in some ''isolated, small, dark, smoke-filled room'' is about as far from the reality of the C++ committee as you can get. I once counted

102 people in the meeting room. There are rarely fewer than 50 people attending a meeting and something like 200 people participate between meetings using email and websites. I have seen people providing real-time reports to newsgroups from the meeting room. In addition, several nations have their own groups and meetings. From this extended group of members, information flows to and from the rest of the C++ community through email, newsgroups, presentations, papers, and books. This open, two-way, communication has been essential for the development of C++.

The result of the committee's work so far and the basis of all future work on C++ is the current standard. Code written against this standard will work for years and even decades to come. The virtues of the standard document are completeness and precision. For most readers, its problems are that it is hard to read, contains no rationale, and gives only few hints at implementation techniques. The standard is not a tutorial, not even a tutorial for experts. There are textbooks covering that need, and people who try to learn C++ from the standard usually have a terrible time figuring out the language features and — like anyone trying to learn C++ from a manual — fail to appreciate the programming techniques those features exist to support. The closest thing we have to a rationale for C++ is my ''The Design and Evolution of C++'' which discusses the motivation behind most of the major design decisions.

A standard is just a heap of paper (or a bag of bits) until someone takes it seriously enough to provide implementations that approximate it as closely as can be done given real-world constraints. The C++ community is now fortunate enough to have several high-quality implementations that closely approximate the standard and at least one that passes all conformance tests with flying colors. These implementations and their numerous ports cover more platforms than I could possibly know of. The community owes thanks to the compiler and standard-library writers — many of whom are members of the committee or represented there by colleagues. Standard C++ is not an easy language to implement, yet for a given platform there is often a choice of good compilers and standard-library implementations. One implication of this wide availability is a high degree of practical portability (if that's your aim) across an astounding range of systems.

The committee was never just backwards looking. Naturally, much of its effort is concerned with the detailed, tedious, and necessary work of clearly stating existing rules and resolving compatibility problems. However, a living language cannot be static and unchanging, so C++ has evolved to meet challenges. For example, in my 1990 C++ reference manual, exceptions and templates were labeled ''experimental,'' yet they were obviously essential parts of what C++ was supposed to be. Today, through the work of the committee, the efforts of implementers, and the creative ideas of users, templates and exceptions are the key to some of the most powerful and innovative uses of C++.

Library development has always been one of the most vital driving forces of C++. One of my earliest principles for C++ was to prefer facilities that ease or enable library building over facilities that merely solve specific problems. This idea was sorely tested by the lack of a good standard container library. C++ was expressive enough to define a good string class, a good complex number library, and good specific vector, list, and associative-array classes, but by 1992, nobody had come up with a sufficiently general, flexible, and efficient container framework. Most ideas were derivatives of the original Simula containers-of-objects design. However, such containers cannot hold built-in types or classes not specifically derived from the container element base class (usually called ''Object'' or ''Link''), require ugly and inefficient casting when retrieving objects from a container, lead to overuse of heap storage, and lack any effective notion of container interchangeability; see the discussion in chapter 16 of ''The C++ Programming Language (3rd edition)''. Clearly, templates held the key to a better solution, but until Alex Stepanov came forward with his STL, nobody had constructed a sufficiently general, elegant, and efficient solution to the standard container problem.

The STL evolved into the containers, iterators, and algorithms part of the C++ standard library. Through that evolution, it became the inspiration for a generation of C++ programmers and the starting point for modern generic and generative programming. This inspiration had repercussions beyond the C++ community. The success of templates and STL-style containers have been one of the major reasons for the inclusion of simple generics into Java and C# and for the work on comprehensive support for generic programming in dialects of functional programming languages such as Haskell and ML. In this, the impact of C++'s generic programming facilities and techniques resemble the impact that C++'s object-oriented programming facilities and techniques had on the programming community as a whole a decade before. Then, C++'s mainstream acceptance helped inspire CORBA, COM, Java, and even object-oriented facilities for Fortran and Cobol.

So where does the C++ standards process take us from here? The current standard describing both language and library is a better approximation of my original aims for C++ than any previous version. However, we can obviously do better still and the standards committee intends to meet that challenge. Unfortunately, there are things that a committee cannot do well. Among the most obvious of those are innovation and design. The current standard contains a few obvious and embarrassing examples of design by committee in both the core language and in the standard library, but I consider those blemishes, potentially correctable, and non-critical. As the work on the next standard begins, the committee must and will try even harder to avoid that trap.

The most successful additions to C++ were developed outside the committee and appeared as well-developed ideas combining features and a philosophy of use. The best example is again the STL. In contrast, less successful developments tend to be minor technical enhancements that grew as the committee tried to compensate for a lack of clear vision. Examples are `std::string` and some of the details of templates. What the committee seems to do well is to refine facilities given a clearly articulated vision and concrete code examples.

What directions might the committee take? That's for the committee to decide, so I can only guess and I hope that we'll again be surprised by some brilliant new insight or library that can disrupt the regular proceedings and set C++ on a new and more productive track. However, in the absence of such an exciting breakthrough, the predictable directions are

— Improve the support for generic programming.

— Improve the support for library building and use.

— Make the language more regular, predictable, and teachable.

— Standardize libraries that will make C++ a better platform for systems programming.

These directions will eventually become reasonably well specified and backed by specific language proposals, library proposals, explanations of programming techniques, and concrete examples. Ideally, the size and number of core-language extensions will be low because facilities provided as libraries can be more easily and more thoroughly tested before their inclusion in the standard. Compatibility with the current C++ standard, improvements in the degree of static type safety, and adherence to the zero-overhead principle (''what you don't explicitly ask for, you don't pay for'') are considered very important.

These directions affirm the original guiding principles for C++, distinguish C++ among programming languages, and will serve the diverse C++ community well.

Bjarne Stroustrup
Texas A&M University and AT&T Labs
`bs@cs.tamu.edu`

Introduction

You are holding a copy of the International Standard for the C++ programming language. This most recent revision merges the first C++ standard, officially known as BS ISO/IEC 14882:1998, with updates (Technical Corrigendum 1) adopted between 1997 (when the standard was ratified) and 2001. These updates correct places where the original standard was found to be ambiguous, self-contradictory, or unclear.

In order to achieve maximum precision, much of the C++ standard is written in prose that only a language lawyer could love—but the standard is important to everyone who writes programs in C++, whether computing professional or amateur. A programming language standard is a contract between the programmer and the vendor who supplies his or her compiler. Another way of looking at it is to say that the standard defines a floor for features the vendor must provide and a ceiling for features a programmer can definitely rely on. The vendor knows what syntax the compiler is expected to handle, what the acceptable constructs mean, and what standard libraries must be provided. Given that base, a vendor can concentrate on quality-of-implementation issues such as optimising code, rather than on adding features which will be incompatible with other compilers. The programmer can be assured that a conforming program will compile and run anywhere and produce its required results. ''Anywhere'' means not just your current machine, but the next one you buy, those belonging to your customers or friends, and even computers not yet invented.

This standard is the result of more than a decade of work by many talented people. It is not perfect, but it is a stable base for C++ compiler implementers and users. There are still some blemishes left, which the international committee is working to remedy. In addition to merely correcting defects, the committee is hard at work preparing the next version of the Standard, still several years away. These are its objectives: to make C++ easier to learn and teach, to improve its usefulness for systems programming and library creation, better to support generic programming, and to add significant new features to the Standard Library.

You and every other programmer can do your bit to improve the language. The first way is to participate in the activities of your national standards organisation. In Britain this is the British Standards Institution (BSI), in the USA it is the American National Standards Institute (ANSI), and there are equivalent national bodies in most other countries. All of these bodies are members of ISO, the International Organization for Standardization, and many of them send delegations to meetings of the international C++ committee, formally known as Working Group 21 of Sub-Committee 22 of the Joint Technical Commission 1 between ISO and the International Electrotechnical Commission (IEC) — or ISO/IEC JTC1/SC22/WG21 for short.

Special mention should be made of the C++ standards committee in ANSI, known as J16. This group is so large and so important that it meets jointly with WG21 in week-long sessions twice a year. The UK C++ panel is, after ANSI J16, the largest and most active national delegation. It meets four to six times a year, usually in London, though much of its work is carried out through email discussions.

http://www.iso.ch/iso/en/aboutiso/isomembers/MemberCountryList.MemberCountryList contains a complete list of ISO members. The following are the national bodies who are most active in WG21 activities:

USA (ANSI)	http://www.ansi.org
UK (BSI)	http://www.bsi-global.com
Australia (SAI)	http://www.standards.com.au
Canada (SCC)	http://www.scc.ca
Denmark (DS)	http://www.ds.dk
France (AFNOR)	http://www.afnor.fr
Germany (DIN)	http://www.din.de
Ireland (NSAI)	http://www.nsai.ie
Japan (JISC)	http://www.jisc.go.jp
Netherlands (NEN)	http://www.nen.nl

Norway (NSF)   `http://www.standard.no`
Switzerland (SNV)   `http://www.snv.ch`

Some national bodies charge a fee to individuals or companies for standardisation activities. Furthermore, these people or their employers expend significant amounts of time and expense on unremunerated standards work. Why do they do it? Besides the personal satisfaction of contributing to the long-term benefit of the industry, they know there is no better way to gain in-depth understanding of C++ and its capabilities.

But even if lack of time, membership fees, or travel expenses prevent you from attending committee meetings, there are other ways to join in the work and realise these benefits for the community and for yourself.

If you identify a place where the standard is ambiguous or unclear, or contradicts some other part of the standard, you can suggest it as a potential defect report. Any national body can raise a defect report, so contacting your national standards committee is one route—but WG21 also looks for input from unofficial channels such as the newsgroups `comp.std.c++` and `comp.lang.c++.moderated`. Moderators of these groups work with WG21 and will forward significant issues raised in newsgroup discussions.

Much of the preliminary work on new C++ Library facilities goes on under the umbrella of an organization named Boost (`http://www.boost.org`). This site provides free peer-reviewed libraries written in portable C++. Anyone can make a submission to the Boost collection.

The UK C++ panel serves as a channel for submitting comments and new ideas to WG21. If your national standards body does not participate in the C++ committee, you can write to `standards@accu.org` to have your ideas considered.

Issues and technical papers which the C++ committee is considering are published on the committee's official website at `http://www.dkuug.dk/jtc1/sc22/wg21`. You can help WG21 to establish future directions for C++. Read, study, think, and debate current C++ issues in news groups. Members of the standards committee follow and participate in news group discussions.

Another way to educate yourself and influence the standards process is to join professional organisations such as ACCU (`http://www.accu.org`), which helps to underwrite standards activities in the UK.

Finally, there is one more way you can contribute to the development of C++: simply to write the best code you possibly can. Write clean, elegant, robust, portable, and maintainable code displaying the unmatched power and expressiveness of C++. Don't settle for anything less and you'll have something that will amaze and inspire other programmers. Most languages force you to choose between elegance and efficiency — with Standard C++ you can have both!

Lois Goldthwaite
Convenor of BSI C++ panel, IST5/–/21
`standards@accu.org`

1 General [intro]

1.1 Scope [intro.scope]

1   This International Standard specifies requirements for implementations of the C++ programming language. The first such requirement is that they implement the language, and so this International Standard also defines C++. Other requirements and relaxations of the first requirement appear at various places within this International Standard.

2   C++ is a general purpose programming language based on the C programming language as described in ISO/IEC 9899:1990 *Programming languages – C* (1.2). In addition to the facilities provided by C, C++ provides additional data types, classes, templates, exceptions, namespaces, inline functions, operator overloading, function name overloading, references, free store management operators, and additional library facilities.

1.2 Normative references [intro.refs]

1   The following standards contain provisions which, through reference in this text, constitute provisions of this International Standard. At the time of publication, the editions indicated were valid. All standards are subject to revision, and parties to agreements based on this International Standard are encouraged to investigate the possibility of applying the most recent editions of the standards indicated below. Members of IEC and ISO maintain registers of currently valid International Standards.

— ISO/IEC 2382 (all parts), *Information technology – Vocabulary*

— ISO/IEC 9899:1990, *Programming languages – C*

— ISO/IEC 9899/Amd.1:1995, *Programming languages – C, AMENDMENT 1: C Integrity*

— ISO/IEC 10646-1:1993 *Information technology – Universal Multiple-Octet Coded Character Set (UCS) – Part 1: Architecture and Basic Multilingual Plane*

2   The library described in clause 7 of ISO/IEC 9899:1990 and clause 7 of ISO/IEC 9899/Amd.1:1995 is hereinafter called the *Standard C Library*.[1]

1.3 Definitions [intro.defs]

1   For the purposes of this International Standard, the definitions given in ISO/IEC 2382 and the following definitions apply. 17.1 defines additional terms that are used only in clauses 17 through 27.

2   Terms that are used only in a small portion of this International Standard are defined where they are used and italicized where they are defined.

1.3.1 argument [defns.argument]

an expression in the comma-separated list bounded by the parentheses in a function call expression, a sequence of preprocessing tokens in the comma-separated list bounded by the parentheses in a function-like macro invocation, the operand of `throw`, or an expression, *type-id* or *template-name* in the comma-separated list bounded by the angle brackets in a template instantiation. Also known as an *actual argument* or *actual parameter*.

---

[1] With the qualifications noted in clauses 17 through 27, and in C.2, the Standard C library is a subset of the Standard C++ library.

1.3.2 diagnostic message   **[defns.diagnostic]**
a message belonging to an implementation-defined subset of the implementation's output messages.

1.3.3 dynamic type   **[defns.dynamic.type]**
the type of the most derived object (1.8) to which the lvalue denoted by an lvalue expression refers. [*Example:* if a pointer (8.3.1) p whose static type is "pointer to class B" is pointing to an object of class D, derived from B (clause 10), the dynamic type of the expression *p is "D." References (8.3.2) are treated similarly.] The dynamic type of an rvalue expression is its static type.

1.3.4 ill-formed program   **[defns.ill.formed]**
input to a C++ implementation that is not a well-formed program (1.3.14).

1.3.5 implementation-defined behavior   **[defns.impl.defined]**
behavior, for a well-formed program construct and correct data, that depends on the implementation and that each implementation shall document.

1.3.6 implementation limits   **[defns.impl.limits]**
restrictions imposed upon programs by the implementation.

1.3.7 locale-specific behavior   **[defns.locale.specific]**
behavior that depends on local conventions of nationality, culture, and language that each implementation shall document.

1.3.8 multibyte character   **[defns.multibyte]**
a sequence of one or more bytes representing a member of the extended character set of either the source or the execution environment. The extended character set is a superset of the basic character set (2.2).

1.3.9 parameter   **[defns.parameter]**
an object or reference declared as part of a function declaration or definition, or in the catch clause of an exception handler, that acquires a value on entry to the function or handler; an identifier from the comma-separated list bounded by the parentheses immediately following the macro name in a function-like macro definition; or a *template-parameter*. Parameters are also known as *formal arguments* or *formal parameters*.

1.3.10 signature   **[defns.signature]**
the information about a function that participates in overload resolution (13.3): the types of its parameters and, if the function is a class member, the *cv-* qualifiers (if any) on the function itself and the class in which the member function is declared.[2] The signature of a function template specialization includes the types of its template arguments (14.5.5.1).

1.3.11 static type   **[defns.static.type]**
the type of an expression (3.9), which type results from analysis of the program without considering execution semantics. The static type of an expression depends only on the form of the program in which the expression appears, and does not change while the program is executing.

---

[2] Function signatures do not include return type, because that does not participate in overload resolution.

1.3.12 undefined behavior [defns.undefined]

behavior, such as might arise upon use of an erroneous program construct or erroneous data, for which this International Standard imposes no requirements. Undefined behavior may also be expected when this International Standard omits the description of any explicit definition of behavior. [*Note:* permissible undefined behavior ranges from ignoring the situation completely with unpredictable results, to behaving during translation or program execution in a documented manner characteristic of the environment (with or without the issuance of a diagnostic message), to terminating a translation or execution (with the issuance of a diagnostic message). Many erroneous program constructs do not engender undefined behavior; they are required to be diagnosed.]

1.3.13 unspecified behavior [defns.unspecified]

behavior, for a well-formed program construct and correct data, that depends on the implementation. The implementation is not required to document which behavior occurs. [*Note:* usually, the range of possible behaviors is delineated by this International Standard.]

1.3.14 well-formed program [defns.well.formed]

a C++ program constructed according to the syntax rules, diagnosable semantic rules, and the One Definition Rule (3.2).

1.4 Implementation compliance [intro.compliance]

1 The set of *diagnosable rules* consists of all syntactic and semantic rules in this International Standard except for those rules containing an explicit notation that "no diagnostic is required" or which are described as resulting in "undefined behavior."

2 Although this International Standard states only requirements on C++ implementations, those requirements are often easier to understand if they are phrased as requirements on programs, parts of programs, or execution of programs. Such requirements have the following meaning:

— If a program contains no violations of the rules in this International Standard, a conforming implementation shall, within its resource limits, accept and correctly execute[3] that program.

— If a program contains a violation of any diagnosable rule, a conforming implementation shall issue at least one diagnostic message, except that

— If a program contains a violation of a rule for which no diagnostic is required, this International Standard places no requirement on implementations with respect to that program.

3 For classes and class templates, the library clauses specify partial definitions. Private members (clause 11) are not specified, but each implementation shall supply them to complete the definitions according to the description in the library clauses.

4 For functions, function templates, objects, and values, the library clauses specify declarations. Implementations shall supply definitions consistent with the descriptions in the library clauses.

5 The names defined in the library have namespace scope (7.3). A C++ translation unit (2.1) obtains access to these names by including the appropriate standard library header (16.2).

6 The templates, classes, functions, and objects in the library have external linkage (3.5). The implementation provides definitions for standard library entities, as necessary, while combining translation units to form a complete C++ program (2.1).

7 Two kinds of implementations are defined: *hosted* and *freestanding*. For a hosted implementation, this International Standard defines the set of available libraries. A freestanding implementation is one in which execution may take place without the benefit of an operating system, and has an implementation-defined set of libraries that includes certain language-support libraries (17.4.1.3).

---

[3] "Correct execution" can include undefined behavior, depending on the data being processed; see 1.3 and 1.9.

8   A conforming implementation may have extensions (including additional library functions), provided they do not alter the behavior of any well-formed program. Implementations are required to diagnose programs that use such extensions that are ill-formed according to this International Standard. Having done so, however, they can compile and execute such programs.

1.5 Structure of this International Standard   [intro.structure]

1   Clauses 2 through 16 describe the C++ programming language. That description includes detailed syntactic specifications in a form described in 1.6. For convenience, Annex A repeats all such syntactic specifications.

2   Clauses 17 through 27 (the *library clauses*) describe the Standard C++ library, which provides definitions for the following kinds of entities: macros (16.3), values (clause 3), types (8.1, 8.3), templates (clause 14), classes (clause 9), functions (8.3.5), and objects (clause 7).

3   Annex B recommends lower bounds on the capacity of conforming implementations.

4   Annex C summarizes the evolution of C++ since its first published description, and explains in detail the differences between C++ and C. Certain features of C++ exist solely for compatibility purposes; Annex D describes those features.

5   Finally, Annex E says what characters are valid in universal-character names in C++ identifiers (2.10).

6   Throughout this International Standard, each example is introduced by "[*Example:*" and terminated by "]". Each note is introduced by "[*Note:*" and terminated by "]". Examples and notes may be nested.

1.6 Syntax notation   [syntax]

1   In the syntax notation used in this International Standard, syntactic categories are indicated by *italic* type, and literal words and characters in `constant width` type. Alternatives are listed on separate lines except in a few cases where a long set of alternatives is presented on one line, marked by the phrase "one of." An optional terminal or nonterminal symbol is indicated by the subscript "*opt*," so

   { *expression*$_{opt}$ }

indicates an optional expression enclosed in braces.

2   Names for syntactic categories have generally been chosen according to the following rules:

   — *X-name* is a use of an identifier in a context that determines its meaning (e.g. *class-name*, *typedef-name*).

   — *X-id* is an identifier with no context-dependent meaning (e.g. *qualified-id*).

   — *X-seq* is one or more *X*'s without intervening delimiters (e.g. *declaration-seq* is a sequence of declarations).

   — *X-list* is one or more *X*'s separated by intervening commas (e.g. *expression-list* is a sequence of expressions separated by commas).

1.7 The C++ memory model   [intro.memory]

1   The fundamental storage unit in the C++ memory model is the *byte*. A byte is at least large enough to contain any member of the basic execution character set and is composed of a contiguous sequence of bits, the number of which is implementation-defined. The least significant bit is called the *low-order* bit; the most significant bit is called the *high-order* bit. The memory available to a C++ program consists of one or more sequences of contiguous bytes. Every byte has a unique address.

2   [*Note:* the representation of types is described in 3.9.]

1.8 The C++ object model   [intro.object]

1   The constructs in a C++ program create, destroy, refer to, access, and manipulate objects. An *object* is a region of storage. [*Note:* A function is not an object, regardless of whether or not it occupies storage in the way that objects do.] An object is created by a *definition* (3.1), by a *new-expression* (5.3.4) or by the implementation (12.2) when needed. The properties of an object are determined when the object is created. An object can have a *name* (clause 3). An object has a *storage duration* (3.7) which influences its *lifetime* (3.8). An object has a *type* (3.9). The term *object type* refers to the type with which the object is created. Some objects are *polymorphic* (10.3); the implementation generates information associated with each such object that makes it possible to determine that object's type during program execution. For other objects, the interpretation of the values found therein is determined by the type of the *expression*s (clause 5) used to access them.

2   Objects can contain other objects, called *sub-objects*. A sub-object can be a *member sub-object* (9.2), a *base class sub-object* (clause 10), or an array element. An object that is not a sub-object of any other object is called a *complete object*.

3   For every object x, there is some object called *the complete object of* x, determined as follows:

— If x is a complete object, then x is the complete object of x.

— Otherwise, the complete object of x is the complete object of the (unique) object that contains x.

4   If a complete object, a data member (9.2), or an array element is of class type, its type is considered the *most derived* class, to distinguish it from the class type of any base class subobject; an object of a most derived class type is called a *most derived object*.

5   Unless it is a bit-field (9.6), a most derived object shall have a non-zero size and shall occupy one or more bytes of storage. Base class sub-objects may have zero size. An object of POD[4] type (3.9) shall occupy contiguous bytes of storage.

6   [*Note:* C++ provides a variety of built-in types and several ways of composing new types from existing types (3.9).]

1.9 Program execution   [intro.execution]

1   The semantic descriptions in this International Standard define a parameterized nondeterministic abstract machine. This International Standard places no requirement on the structure of conforming implementations. In particular, they need not copy or emulate the structure of the abstract machine. Rather, conforming implementations are required to emulate (only) the observable behavior of the abstract machine as explained below.[5]

2   Certain aspects and operations of the abstract machine are described in this International Standard as implementation-defined (for example, `sizeof(int)`). These constitute the parameters of the abstract machine. Each implementation shall include documentation describing its characteristics and behavior in these respects. Such documentation shall define the instance of the abstract machine that corresponds to that implementation (referred to as the ''corresponding instance'' below).

3   Certain other aspects and operations of the abstract machine are described in this International Standard as unspecified (for example, order of evaluation of arguments to a function). Where possible, this International Standard defines a set of allowable behaviors. These define the nondeterministic aspects of the abstract machine. An instance of the abstract machine can thus have more than one possible execution sequence for a given program and a given input.

---

[4] The acronym POD stands for "plain old data."

[5] This provision is sometimes called the "as-if" rule, because an implementation is free to disregard any requirement of this International Standard as long as the result is *as if* the requirement had been obeyed, as far as can be determined from the observable behavior of the program. For instance, an actual implementation need not evaluate part of an expression if it can deduce that its value is not used and that no side effects affecting the observable behavior of the program are produced.

4   Certain other operations are described in this International Standard as undefined (for example, the effect of dereferencing the null pointer). [*Note:* this International Standard imposes no requirements on the behavior of programs that contain undefined behavior.]

5   A conforming implementation executing a well-formed program shall produce the same observable behavior as one of the possible execution sequences of the corresponding instance of the abstract machine with the same program and the same input. However, if any such execution sequence contains an undefined operation, this International Standard places no requirement on the implementation executing that program with that input (not even with regard to operations preceding the first undefined operation).

6   The observable behavior of the abstract machine is its sequence of reads and writes to `volatile` data and calls to library I/O functions.[6)]

7   Accessing an object designated by a `volatile` lvalue (3.10), modifying an object, calling a library I/O function, or calling a function that does any of those operations are all *side effects*, which are changes in the state of the execution environment. Evaluation of an expression might produce side effects. At certain specified points in the execution sequence called *sequence points*, all side effects of previous evaluations shall be complete and no side effects of subsequent evaluations shall have taken place.[7)]

8   Once the execution of a function begins, no expressions from the calling function are evaluated until execution of the called function has completed.[8)]

9   When the processing of the abstract machine is interrupted by receipt of a signal, the values of objects with type other than `volatile sig_atomic_t` are unspecified, and the value of any object not of `volatile sig_atomic_t` that is modified by the handler becomes undefined.

10   An instance of each object with automatic storage duration (3.7.2) is associated with each entry into its block. Such an object exists and retains its last-stored value during the execution of the block and while the block is suspended (by a call of a function or receipt of a signal).

11   The least requirements on a conforming implementation are:

      — At sequence points, volatile objects are stable in the sense that previous evaluations are complete and subsequent evaluations have not yet occurred.

      — At program termination, all data written into files shall be identical to one of the possible results that execution of the program according to the abstract semantics would have produced.

      — The input and output dynamics of interactive devices shall take place in such a fashion that prompting messages actually appear prior to a program waiting for input. What constitutes an interactive device is implementation-defined.

      [*Note:* more stringent correspondences between abstract and actual semantics may be defined by each implementation.]

12   A *full-expression* is an expression that is not a subexpression of another expression. If a language construct is defined to produce an implicit call of a function, a use of the language construct is considered to be an expression for the purposes of this definition.

13   [*Note:* certain contexts in C++ cause the evaluation of a full-expression that results from a syntactic construct other than *expression* (5.18). For example, in 8.5 one syntax for *initializer* is

---

[6)] An implementation can offer additional library I/O functions as an extension. Implementations that do so should treat calls to those functions as "observable behavior" as well.

[7)] Note that some aspects of sequencing in the abstract machine are unspecified; the preceding restriction upon side effects applies to that particular execution sequence in which the actual code is generated. Also note that when a call to a library I/O function returns, the side effect is considered complete, even though some external actions implied by the call (such as the I/O itself) may not have completed yet.

[8)] In other words, function executions do not interleave with each other.

(*expression-list*)

but the resulting construct is a function call upon a constructor function with *expression-list* as an argument list; such a function call is a full-expression. For example, in 8.5, another syntax for *initializer* is

= *initializer-clause*

but again the resulting construct might be a function call upon a constructor function with one *assignment-expression* as an argument; again, the function call is a full-expression.]

14 [*Note:* the evaluation of a full-expression can include the evaluation of subexpressions that are not lexically part of the full-expression. For example, subexpressions involved in evaluating default argument expressions (8.3.6) are considered to be created in the expression that calls the function, not the expression that defines the default argument.]

15 [*Note:* operators can be regrouped according to the usual mathematical rules only where the operators really are associative or commutative.[9] For example, in the following fragment

```
int a, b;
/*...*/
a = a + 32760 + b + 5;
```

the expression statement behaves exactly the same as

```
a = (((a + 32760) + b) + 5);
```

due to the associativity and precedence of these operators. Thus, the result of the sum (a + 32760) is next added to b, and that result is then added to 5 which results in the value assigned to a. On a machine in which overflows produce an exception and in which the range of values representable by an int is [−32768,+32767], the implementation cannot rewrite this expression as

```
a = ((a + b) + 32765);
```

since if the values for a and b were, respectively, −32754 and −15, the sum a + b would produce an exception while the original expression would not; nor can the expression be rewritten either as

```
a = ((a + 32765) + b);
```

or

```
a = (a + (b + 32765));
```

since the values for a and b might have been, respectively, 4 and −8 or −17 and 12. However on a machine in which overflows do not produce an exception and in which the results of overflows are reversible, the above expression statement can be rewritten by the implementation in any of the above ways because the same result will occur.]

16 There is a sequence point at the completion of evaluation of each full-expression[10].

17 When calling a function (whether or not the function is inline), there is a sequence point after the evaluation of all function arguments (if any) which takes place before execution of any expressions or statements in the function body. There is also a sequence point after the copying of a returned value and before the execution of any expressions outside the function[11]. Several contexts in C++ cause evaluation of a function call, even though no corresponding function call syntax appears in the translation unit. [*Example:* evaluation of a new expression invokes one or more allocation and constructor functions; see 5.3.4. For another example, invocation of a conversion function (12.3.2) can arise in contexts in which no function call syntax

---

[9] Overloaded operators are never assumed to be associative or commutative.
[10] As specified in 12.2, after the "end-of-full-expression" sequence point, a sequence of zero or more invocations of destructor functions for temporary objects takes place, usually in reverse order of the construction of each temporary object.
[11] The sequence point at the function return is not explicitly specified in ISO C, and can be considered redundant with sequence points at full-expressions, but the extra clarity is important in C++. In C++, there are more ways in which a called function can terminate its execution, such as the throw of an exception.

appears.] The sequence points at function-entry and function-exit (as described above) are features of the function calls as evaluated, whatever the syntax of the expression that calls the function might be.

18   In the evaluation of each of the expressions

```
a && b
a || b
a ? b : c
a , b
```

using the built-in meaning of the operators in these expressions (5.14, 5.15, 5.16, 5.18), there is a sequence point after the evaluation of the first expression[12].

1.10 Acknowledgments   [intro.ack]

1   The C++ programming language as described in this International Standard is based on the language as described in Chapter R (Reference Manual) of Stroustrup: *The C++ Programming Language* (second edition, Addison-Wesley Publishing Company, ISBN 0–201–53992–6, copyright © 1991 AT&T). That, in turn, is based on the C programming language as described in Appendix A of Kernighan and Ritchie: *The C Programming Language* (Prentice-Hall, 1978, ISBN 0–13–110163–3, copyright © 1978 AT&T).

2   Portions of the library clauses of this International Standard are based on work by P.J. Plauger, which was published as *The Draft Standard C++ Library* (Prentice-Hall, ISBN 0–13–117003–1, copyright © 1995 P.J. Plauger).

3   All rights in these originals are reserved.

---

[12] The operators indicated in this paragraph are the built-in operators, as described in clause 5. When one of these operators is overloaded (clause 13) in a valid context, thus designating a user-defined operator function, the expression designates a function invocation, and the operands form an argument list, without an implied sequence point between them.

2 Lexical conventions [lex]

1   The text of the program is kept in units called *source files* in this International Standard. A source file together with all the headers (17.4.1.2) and source files included (16.2) via the preprocessing directive `#include`, less any source lines skipped by any of the conditional inclusion (16.1) preprocessing directives, is called a *translation unit*. [*Note:* a C++ program need not all be translated at the same time.]

2   [*Note:* previously translated translation units and instantiation units can be preserved individually or in libraries. The separate translation units of a program communicate (3.5) by (for example) calls to functions whose identifiers have external linkage, manipulation of objects whose identifiers have external linkage, or manipulation of data files. Translation units can be separately translated and then later linked to produce an executable program. (3.5).]

2.1 Phases of translation [lex.phases]

1   The precedence among the syntax rules of translation is specified by the following phases.[13]

1. Physical source file characters are mapped, in an implementation-defined manner, to the basic source character set (introducing new-line characters for end-of-line indicators) if necessary. Trigraph sequences (2.3) are replaced by corresponding single-character internal representations. Any source file character not in the basic source character set (2.2) is replaced by the universal-character-name that designates that character. (An implementation may use any internal encoding, so long as an actual extended character encountered in the source file, and the same extended character expressed in the source file as a universal-character-name (i.e. using the `\uXXXX` notation), are handled equivalently.)

2. Each instance of a new-line character and an immediately preceding backslash character is deleted, splicing physical source lines to form logical source lines. If, as a result, a character sequence that matches the syntax of a universal-character-name is produced, the behavior is undefined. If a source file that is not empty does not end in a new-line character, or ends in a new-line character immediately preceded by a backslash character, the behavior is undefined.

3. The source file is decomposed into preprocessing tokens (2.4) and sequences of white-space characters (including comments). A source file shall not end in a partial preprocessing token or partial comment[14]. Each comment is replaced by one space character. New-line characters are retained. Whether each nonempty sequence of white-space characters other than new-line is retained or replaced by one space character is implementation-defined. The process of dividing a source file's characters into preprocessing tokens is context-dependent. [*Example:* see the handling of < within a `#include` preprocessing directive.]

4. Preprocessing directives are executed and macro invocations are expanded. If a character sequence that matches the syntax of a universal-character-name is produced by token concatenation (16.3.3), the behavior is undefined. A `#include` preprocessing directive causes the named header or source file to be processed from phase 1 through phase 4, recursively.

5. Each source character set member, escape sequence, or universal-character-name in character literals and string literals is converted to a member of the execution character set (2.13.2, 2.13.4).

6. Adjacent ordinary string literal tokens are concatenated. Adjacent wide string literal tokens are concatenated.

---

[13] Implementations must behave as if these separate phases occur, although in practice different phases might be folded together.

[14] A partial preprocessing token would arise from a source file ending in the first portion of a multi-character token that requires a terminating sequence of characters, such as a *header-name* that is missing the closing " or >. A partial comment would arise from a source file ending with an unclosed /* comment.

7   White-space characters separating tokens are no longer significant. Each preprocessing token is converted into a token. (2.6). The resulting tokens are syntactically and semantically analyzed and translated. [*Note:* Source files, translation units and translated translation units need not necessarily be
stored as files, nor need there be any one-to-one correspondence between these entities and any external
representation. The description is conceptual only, and does not specify any particular implementation.
]

8   Translated translation units and instantiation units are combined as follows: [*Note:* some or all of these
may be supplied from a library.] Each translated translation unit is examined to produce a list of
required instantiations. [*Note:* this may include instantiations which have been explicitly requested
(14.7.2).] The definitions of the required templates are located. It is implementation-defined whether
the source of the translation units containing these definitions is required to be available. [*Note:* an
implementation could encode sufficient information into the translated translation unit so as to ensure
the source is not required here.] All the required instantiations are performed to produce *instantiation
units*. [*Note:* these are similar to translated translation units, but contain no references to uninstantiated
templates and no template definitions.] The program is ill-formed if any instantiation fails.

9   All external object and function references are resolved. Library components are linked to satisfy external references to functions and objects not defined in the current translation. All such translator output
is collected into a program image which contains information needed for execution in its execution
environment.

2.2 Character sets   [lex.charset]

1   The *basic source character set* consists of 96 characters: the space character, the control characters representing horizontal tab, vertical tab, form feed, and new-line, plus the following 91 graphical characters:[15]

```
a b c d e f g h i j k l m n o p q r s t u v w x y z
A B C D E F G H I J K L M N O P Q R S T U V W X Y Z
0 1 2 3 4 5 6 7 8 9
_ { } [ ] # ( ) < > % : ; . ? * + - / ^ & | ~ ! = , \ " '
```

2   The *universal-character-name* construct provides a way to name other characters.

> *hex-quad:*
>> *hexadecimal-digit hexadecimal-digit hexadecimal-digit hexadecimal-digit*

> *universal-character-name:*
>> \u *hex-quad*
>> \U *hex-quad hex-quad*

The character designated by the universal-character-name \UNNNNNNNN is that character whose character
short name in ISO/IEC 10646 is NNNNNNNN; the character designated by the universal-character-name
\uNNNN is that character whose character short name in ISO/IEC 10646 is 0000NNNN. If the hexadecimal
value for a universal character name is less than 0x20 or in the range 0x7F-0x9F (inclusive), or if the universal character name designates a character in the basic source character set, then the program is ill-
formed.

3   The *basic execution character set* and the *basic execution wide-character set* shall each contain all the
members of the basic source character set, plus control characters representing alert, backspace, and car-
riage return, plus a *null character* (respectively, *null wide character*), whose representation has all zero bits.
For each basic execution character set, the values of the members shall be non-negative and distinct from
one another. In both the source and execution basic character sets, the value of each character after 0 in the

---

[15] The glyphs for the members of the basic source character set are intended to identify characters from the subset of ISO/IEC 10646
which corresponds to the ASCII character set. However, because the mapping from source file characters to the source character set
(described in translation phase 1) is specified as implementation-defined, an implementation is required to document how the basic
source characters are represented in source files.

above list of decimal digits shall be one greater than the value of the previous. The *execution character set* and the *execution wide-character set* are supersets of the basic execution character set and the basic execution wide-character set, respectively. The values of the members of the execution character sets are implementation-defined, and any additional members are locale-specific.

2.3 Trigraph sequences   [lex.trigraph]

1   Before any other processing takes place, each occurrence of one of the following sequences of three characters ("*trigraph sequences*") is replaced by the single character indicated in Table 1.

Table 1—trigraph sequences

trigraph	replacement	trigraph	replacement	trigraph	replacement
??=	#	??(	[	??<	{
??/	\	??)	]	??>	}
??'	^	??!	|	??-	~

2   [*Example:*

        ??=define arraycheck(a,b) a??(b??) ??!??! b??(a??)

becomes

        #define arraycheck(a,b) a[b] || b[a]

   —*end example*]

3   No other trigraph sequence exists. Each ? that does not begin one of the trigraphs listed above is not changed.

2.4 Preprocessing tokens   [lex.pptoken]

> *preprocessing-token:*
> > *header-name*
> > *identifier*
> > *pp-number*
> > *character-literal*
> > *string-literal*
> > *preprocessing-op-or-punc*
> > each non-white-space character that cannot be one of the above

1   Each preprocessing token that is converted to a token (2.6) shall have the lexical form of a keyword, an identifier, a literal, an operator, or a punctuator.

2   A *preprocessing token* is the minimal lexical element of the language in translation phases 3 through 6. The categories of preprocessing token are: *header names*, *identifiers*, *preprocessing numbers*, *character literals*, *string literals*, *preprocessing-op-or-punc*, and single non-white-space characters that do not lexically match the other preprocessing token categories. If a ' or a " character matches the last category, the behavior is undefined. Preprocessing tokens can be separated by *white space*; this consists of comments (2.7), or *white-space characters* (space, horizontal tab, new-line, vertical tab, and form-feed), or both. As described in clause 16, in certain circumstances during translation phase 4, white space (or the absence thereof) serves as more than preprocessing token separation. White space can appear within a preprocessing token only as part of a header name or between the quotation characters in a character literal or string literal.

3   If the input stream has been parsed into preprocessing tokens up to a given character, the next preprocessing token is the longest sequence of characters that could constitute a preprocessing token, even if that would cause further lexical analysis to fail.

4   [*Example:* The program fragment `1Ex` is parsed as a preprocessing number token (one that is not a valid floating or integer literal token), even though a parse as the pair of preprocessing tokens `1` and `Ex` might produce a valid expression (for example, if `Ex` were a macro defined as `+1`). Similarly, the program fragment `1E1` is parsed as a preprocessing number (one that is a valid floating literal token), whether or not `E` is a macro name.]

5   [*Example:* The program fragment `x+++++y` is parsed as `x ++ ++ + y`, which, if `x` and `y` are of built-in types, violates a constraint on increment operators, even though the parse `x ++ + ++ y` might yield a correct expression.]

2.5 Alternative tokens   [lex.digraph]

1   Alternative token representations are provided for some operators and punctuators[16].

2   In all respects of the language, each alternative token behaves the same, respectively, as its primary token, except for its spelling[17]. The set of alternative tokens is defined in Table 2.

Table 2—alternative tokens

alternative	primary	alternative	primary	alternative	primary
`<%`	`{`	`and`	`&&`	`and_eq`	`&=`
`%>`	`}`	`bitor`	`|`	`or_eq`	`|=`
`<:`	`[`	`or`	`||`	`xor_eq`	`^=`
`:>`	`]`	`xor`	`^`	`not`	`!`
`%:`	`#`	`compl`	`~`	`not_eq`	`!=`
`%:%:`	`##`	`bitand`	`&`		

2.6 Tokens   [lex.token]

token:
    identifier
    keyword
    literal
    operator
    punctuator

1   There are five kinds of tokens: identifiers, keywords, literals,[18] operators, and other separators. Blanks, horizontal and vertical tabs, newlines, formfeeds, and comments (collectively, "white space"), as described below, are ignored except as they serve to separate tokens. [*Note:* Some white space is required to separate otherwise adjacent identifiers, keywords, numeric literals, and alternative tokens containing alphabetic characters.]

---

[16] These include "digraphs" and additional reserved words. The term "digraph" (token consisting of two characters) is not perfectly descriptive, since one of the alternative preprocessing-tokens is `%:%:` and of course several primary tokens contain two characters. Nonetheless, those alternative tokens that aren't lexical keywords are colloquially known as "digraphs".

[17] Thus the "stringized" values (16.3.2) of `[` and `<:` will be different, maintaining the source spelling, but the tokens can otherwise be freely interchanged.

[18] Literals include strings and character and numeric literals.

2.7 Comments [lex.comment]

1   The characters /* start a comment, which terminates with the characters */. These comments do not nest.
The characters // start a comment, which terminates with the next new-line character. If there is a form-
feed or a vertical-tab character in such a comment, only white-space characters shall appear between it and
the new-line that terminates the comment; no diagnostic is required. [*Note:* The comment characters //,
/*, and */ have no special meaning within a // comment and are treated just like other characters. Similarly, the comment characters // and /* have no special meaning within a /* comment.]

2.8 Header names   [lex.header]

> *header-name:*
>> *<h-char-sequence>*
>> *"q-char-sequence"*
>
> *h-char-sequence:*
>> *h-char*
>> *h-char-sequence h-char*
>
> *h-char:*
>> any member of the source character set except
>>> new-line and >
>
> *q-char-sequence:*
>> *q-char*
>> *q-char-sequence q-char*
>
> *q-char:*
>> any member of the source character set except
>>> new-line and "

1   Header name preprocessing tokens shall only appear within a #include preprocessing directive (16.2).
The sequences in both forms of *header-name*s are mapped in an implementation-defined manner to headers
or to external source file names as specified in 16.2.

2   If either of the characters ' or \, or either of the character sequences /* or // appears in a *q-char-
sequence* or a *h-char-sequence*, or the character " appears in a *h-char-sequence*, the behavior is undefined.[19]

2.9 Preprocessing numbers   [lex.ppnumber]

> *pp-number:*
>> *digit*
>> *. digit*
>> *pp-number digit*
>> *pp-number nondigit*
>> *pp-number* e *sign*
>> *pp-number* E *sign*
>> *pp-number* .

1   Preprocessing number tokens lexically include all integral literal tokens (2.13.1) and all floating literal
tokens (2.13.3).

2   A preprocessing number does not have a type or a value; it acquires both after a successful conversion (as
part of translation phase 7, 2.1) to an integral literal token or a floating literal token.

---

[19] Thus, sequences of characters that resemble escape sequences cause undefined behavior.

2.10 Identifiers [lex.name]

> *identifier:*
>> *nondigit*
>> *identifier nondigit*
>> *identifier digit*
>
> *nondigit* : one of
>> *universal-character-name*
>> _ a b c d e f g h i j k l m
>> n o p q r s t u v w x y z
>> A B C D E F G H I J K L M
>> N O P Q R S T U V W X Y Z
>
> *digit* : one of
>> 0 1 2 3 4 5 6 7 8 9

1   An identifier is an arbitrarily long sequence of letters and digits. Each universal-character-name in an identifier shall designate a character whose encoding in ISO 10646 falls into one of the ranges specified in Annex E. Upper- and lower-case letters are different. All characters are significant.[20]

2   In addition, some identifiers are reserved for use by C++ implementations and standard libraries (17.4.3.1.2) and shall not be used otherwise; no diagnostic is required.

2.11 Keywords [lex.key]

1   The identifiers shown in Table 3 are reserved for use as keywords (that is, they are unconditionally treated as keywords in phase 7):

Table 3—keywords

asm	do	if	return	typedef
auto	double	inline	short	typeid
bool	dynamic_cast	int	signed	typename
break	else	long	sizeof	union
case	enum	mutable	static	unsigned
catch	explicit	namespace	static_cast	using
char	export	new	struct	virtual
class	extern	operator	switch	void
const	false	private	template	volatile
const_cast	float	protected	this	wchar_t
continue	for	public	throw	while
default	friend	register	true	
delete	goto	reinterpret_cast	try	

2   Furthermore, the alternative representations shown in Table 4 for certain operators and punctuators (2.5) are reserved and shall not be used otherwise:

---

[20] On systems in which linkers cannot accept extended characters, an encoding of the universal-character-name may be used in forming valid external identifiers. For example, some otherwise unused character or sequence of characters may be used to encode the \u in a universal-character-name. Extended characters may produce a long external identifier, but C++ does not place a translation limit on significant characters for external identifiers. In C++, upper- and lower-case letters are considered different for all identifiers, including external identifiers.

Table 4—alternative representations

and	and_eq	bitand	bitor	compl	not
not_eq	or	or_eq	xor	xor_eq	

2.12 Operators and punctuators   [lex.operators]

1   The lexical representation of C++ programs includes a number of preprocessing tokens which are used in the syntax of the preprocessor or are converted into tokens for operators and punctuators:

preprocessing-op-or-punc :   one of

```
{       }       [       ]       #       ##      (       )
<:      :>      <%      %>      %:      %:%:    ;       :       . . .
new     delete  ?       ::      .       .*
+       -       *       /       %       ^       &       |       ~
!       =       <       >       +=      -=      *=      /=      %=
^=      &=      |=      <<      >>      >>=     <<=     ==      !=
<=      >=      &&      ||      ++      --      ,       ->*     ->
and     and_eq  bitand  bitor   compl   not     not_eq
or      or_eq   xor     xor_eq
```

Each *preprocessing-op-or-punc* is converted to a single token in translation phase 7 (2.1).

2.13 Literals   [lex.literal]

1   There are several kinds of literals.[21]

> *literal:*
> > *integer-literal*
> > *character-literal*
> > *floating-literal*
> > *string-literal*
> > *boolean-literal*

2.13.1 Integer literals   [lex.icon]

> *integer-literal:*
> > *decimal-literal integer-suffix$_{opt}$*
> > *octal-literal integer-suffix$_{opt}$*
> > *hexadecimal-literal integer-suffix$_{opt}$*

> *decimal-literal:*
> > *nonzero-digit*
> > *decimal-literal digit*

> *octal-literal:*
> > 0
> > *octal-literal octal-digit*

> *hexadecimal-literal:*
> > 0x *hexadecimal-digit*
> > 0X *hexadecimal-digit*
> > *hexadecimal-literal hexadecimal-digit*

---

[21] The term "literal" generally designates, in this International Standard, those tokens that are called "constants" in ISO C.

nonzero-digit: one of
    1   2   3   4   5   6   7   8   9

octal-digit: one of
    0   1   2   3   4   5   6   7

hexadecimal-digit: one of
    0   1   2   3   4   5   6   7   8   9
    a   b   c   d   e   f
    A   B   C   D   E   F

integer-suffix:
    unsigned-suffix long-suffix$_{opt}$
    long-suffix unsigned-suffix$_{opt}$

unsigned-suffix: one of
    u   U

long-suffix: one of
    l   L

1   An integer literal is a sequence of digits that has no period or exponent part. An integer literal may have a prefix that specifies its base and a suffix that specifies its type. The lexically first digit of the sequence of digits is the most significant. A *decimal* integer literal (base ten) begins with a digit other than 0 and consists of a sequence of decimal digits. An *octal* integer literal (base eight) begins with the digit 0 and consists of a sequence of octal digits.[22] A *hexadecimal* integer literal (base sixteen) begins with 0x or 0X and consists of a sequence of hexadecimal digits, which include the decimal digits and the letters a through f and A through F with decimal values ten through fifteen. [*Example:* the number twelve can be written 12, 014, or 0XC.]

2   The type of an integer literal depends on its form, value, and suffix. If it is decimal and has no suffix, it has the first of these types in which its value can be represented: int, long int; if the value cannot be represented as a long int, the behavior is undefined. If it is octal or hexadecimal and has no suffix, it has the first of these types in which its value can be represented: int, unsigned int, long int, unsigned long int. If it is suffixed by u or U, its type is the first of these types in which its value can be represented: unsigned int, unsigned long int. If it is suffixed by l or L, its type is the first of these types in which its value can be represented: long int, unsigned long int. If it is suffixed by ul, lu, uL, Ul, lU, UL, or LU, its type is unsigned long int.

3   A program is ill-formed if one of its translation units contains an integer literal that cannot be represented by any of the allowed types.

2.13.2 Character literals   [lex.ccon]

character-literal:
    ' *c-char-sequence* '
    L' *c-char-sequence* '

c-char-sequence:
    c-char
    c-char-sequence c-char

---

[22] The digits 8 and 9 are not octal digits.

c-char:

      any member of the source character set except
            the single-quote ', backslash \, or new-line character
      escape-sequence
      universal-character-name

escape-sequence:

      simple-escape-sequence
      octal-escape-sequence
      hexadecimal-escape-sequence

simple-escape-sequence: one of
      \' \" \? \\
      \a \b \f \n \r \t \v

octal-escape-sequence:

      \ *octal-digit*
      \ *octal-digit octal-digit*
      \ *octal-digit octal-digit octal-digit*

hexadecimal-escape-sequence:

      \x *hexadecimal-digit*
      hexadecimal-escape-sequence hexadecimal-digit

1   A character literal is one or more characters enclosed in single quotes, as in 'x', optionally preceded by the letter L, as in L'x'. A character literal that does not begin with L is an ordinary character literal, also referred to as a narrow-character literal. An ordinary character literal that contains a single *c-char* has type char, with value equal to the numerical value of the encoding of the *c-char* in the execution character set. An ordinary character literal that contains more than one *c-char* is a *multicharacter literal*. A multicharacter literal has type int and implementation-defined value.

2   A character literal that begins with the letter L, such as L'x', is a wide-character literal. A wide-character literal has type wchar_t.[23] The value of a wide-character literal containing a single *c-char* has value equal to the numerical value of the encoding of the *c-char* in the execution wide-character set. The value of a wide-character literal containing multiple *c-char*s is implementation-defined.

3   Certain nongraphic characters, the single quote ', the double quote ", the question mark ?, and the backslash \, can be represented according to Table 5.

---

[23] They are intended for character sets where a character does not fit into a single byte.

Table 5—escape sequences

new-line	NL (LF)	\n
horizontal tab	HT	\t
vertical tab	VT	\v
backspace	BS	\b
carriage return	CR	\r
form feed	FF	\f
alert	BEL	\a
backslash	\	\\
question mark	?	\?
single quote	'	\'
double quote	"	\"
octal number	*ooo*	*ooo*
hex number	*hhh*	\x*hhh*

The double quote " and the question mark ?, can be represented as themselves or by the escape sequences \" and \? respectively, but the single quote ' and the backslash \ shall be represented by the escape sequences \' and \\ respectively. If the character following a backslash is not one of those specified, the behavior is undefined. An escape sequence specifies a single character.

4   The escape *ooo* consists of the backslash followed by one, two, or three octal digits that are taken to specify the value of the desired character. The escape \x*hhh* consists of the backslash followed by x followed by one or more hexadecimal digits that are taken to specify the value of the desired character. There is no limit to the number of digits in a hexadecimal sequence. A sequence of octal or hexadecimal digits is terminated by the first character that is not an octal digit or a hexadecimal digit, respectively. The value of a character literal is implementation-defined if it falls outside of the implementation-defined range defined for char (for ordinary literals) or wchar_t (for wide literals).

5   A universal-character-name is translated to the encoding, in the execution character set, of the character named. If there is no such encoding, the universal-character-name is translated to an implementation-defined encoding. [*Note:* in translation phase 1, a universal-character-name is introduced whenever an actual extended character is encountered in the source text. Therefore, all extended characters are described in terms of universal-character-names. However, the actual compiler implementation may use its own native character set, so long as the same results are obtained.]

2.13.3 Floating literals   [lex.fcon]

> *floating-literal:*
> > *fractional-constant exponent-part$_{opt}$ floating-suffix$_{opt}$*
> > *digit-sequence exponent-part floating-suffix$_{opt}$*

> *fractional-constant:*
> > *digit-sequence$_{opt}$. digit-sequence*
> > *digit-sequence .*

> *exponent-part:*
> > e *sign$_{opt}$ digit-sequence*
> > E *sign$_{opt}$ digit-sequence*

> *sign:* one of
> > +   –

digit-sequence:
>   *digit*
>   *digit-sequence digit*

floating-suffix: one of
>   f   l   F   L

1   A floating literal consists of an integer part, a decimal point, a fraction part, an e or E, an optionally signed integer exponent, and an optional type suffix. The integer and fraction parts both consist of a sequence of decimal (base ten) digits. Either the integer part or the fraction part (not both) can be omitted; either the decimal point or the letter e (or E) and the exponent (not both) can be omitted. The integer part, the optional decimal point and the optional fraction part form the *significant part* of the floating literal. The exponent, if present, indicates the power of 10 by which the significant part is to be scaled. If the scaled value is in the range of representable values for its type, the result is the scaled value if representable, else the larger or smaller representable value nearest the scaled value, chosen in an implementation-defined manner. The type of a floating literal is double unless explicitly specified by a suffix. The suffixes f and F specify float, the suffixes l and L specify long double. If the scaled value is not in the range of representable values for its type, the program is ill-formed.

2.13.4 String literals   [lex.string]

string-literal:
>   " *s-char-sequence*$_{opt}$ "
>   L" *s-char-sequence*$_{opt}$ "

s-char-sequence:
>   *s-char*
>   *s-char-sequence s-char*

s-char:
>   any member of the source character set except
>>   the double-quote ", backslash \, or new-line character
>   *escape-sequence*
>   *universal-character-name*

1   A string literal is a sequence of characters (as defined in 2.13.2) surrounded by double quotes, optionally beginning with the letter L, as in "..." or L"...". A string literal that does not begin with L is an ordinary string literal, also referred to as a narrow string literal. An ordinary string literal has type "array of *n* const char" and *static* storage duration (3.7), where *n* is the size of the string as defined below, and is initialized with the given characters. A string literal that begins with L, such as L"asdf", is a wide string literal. A wide string literal has type "array of *n* const wchar_t" and has static storage duration, where *n* is the size of the string as defined below, and is initialized with the given characters.

2   Whether all string literals are distinct (that is, are stored in nonoverlapping objects) is implementation-defined. The effect of attempting to modify a string literal is undefined.

3   In translation phase 6 (2.1), adjacent narrow string literals are concatenated and adjacent wide string literals are concatenated. If a narrow string literal token is adjacent to a wide string literal token, the behavior is undefined. Characters in concatenated strings are kept distinct. [*Example:*

```
"\xA" "B"
```

contains the two characters '\xA' and 'B' after concatenation (and not the single hexadecimal character '\xAB').]

4   After any necessary concatenation, in translation phase 7 (2.1), '\0' is appended to every string literal so that programs that scan a string can find its end.

5 　Escape sequences and universal-character-names in string literals have the same meaning as in character literals (2.13.2), except that the single quote ′ is representable either by itself or by the escape sequence \′, and the double quote " shall be preceded by a \. In a narrow string literal, a universal-character-name may map to more than one `char` element due to *multibyte encoding*. The size of a wide string literal is the total number of escape sequences, universal-character-names, and other characters, plus one for the terminating `L′\0′`. The size of a narrow string literal is the total number of escape sequences and other characters, plus at least one for the multibyte encoding of each universal-character-name, plus one for the terminating `′\0′`.

2.13.5 Boolean literals　　　　　　　　　　　　　　　　　　　　　　　　　　**[lex.bool]**

> *boolean-literal:*
> 　　　　`false`
> 　　　　`true`

1 　The Boolean literals are the keywords `false` and `true`. Such literals have type `bool`. They are not lvalues.

3 Basic concepts   [basic]

1   [*Note:* this clause presents the basic concepts of the C++ language. It explains the difference between an *object* and a *name* and how they relate to the notion of an *lvalue.* It introduces the concepts of a *declaration* and a *definition* and presents C++'s notion of *type, scope, linkage,* and *storage duration.* The mechanisms for starting and terminating a program are discussed. Finally, this clause presents the fundamental types of the language and lists the ways of constructing *compound* types from these.

2   This clause does not cover concepts that affect only a single part of the language. Such concepts are discussed in the relevant clauses.]

3   An *entity* is a value, object, subobject, base class subobject, array element, variable, function, instance of a function, enumerator, type, class member, template, or namespace.

4   A *name* is a use of an identifier (2.10) that denotes an entity or *label* (6.6.4, 6.1). A *variable* is introduced by the declaration of an object. The variable's name denotes the object.

5   Every name that denotes an entity is introduced by a *declaration.* Every name that denotes a label is introduced either by a `goto` statement (6.6.4) or a *labeled-statement* (6.1).

6   Some names denote types, classes, enumerations, or templates. In general, it is necessary to determine whether or not a name denotes one of these entities before parsing the program that contains it. The process that determines this is called *name lookup* (3.4).

7   Two names are *the same* if

— they are identifiers composed of the same character sequence; or

— they are the names of overloaded operator functions formed with the same operator; or

— they are the names of user-defined conversion functions formed with the same type.

8   An identifier used in more than one translation unit can potentially refer to the same entity in these translation units depending on the linkage (3.5) of the identifier specified in each translation unit.

3.1 Declarations and definitions   [basic.def]

1   A declaration (clause 7) introduces names into a translation unit or redeclares names introduced by previous declarations. A declaration specifies the interpretation and attributes of these names.

2   A declaration is a *definition* unless it declares a function without specifying the function's body (8.4), it contains the `extern` specifier (7.1.1) or a *linkage-specification*[24] (7.5) and neither an *initializer* nor a *function-body,* it declares a static data member in a class declaration (9.4), it is a class name declaration (9.1), or it is a `typedef` declaration (7.1.3), a *using-declaration* (7.3.3), or a *using-directive* (7.3.4).

---

[24] Appearing inside the braced-enclosed *declaration-seq* in a *linkage-specification* does not affect whether a declaration is a definition.

3   [*Example:* all but one of the following are definitions:

```
int a;                              // defines a
extern const int c = 1;             // defines c
int f(int x) { return x+a; }        // defines f and defines x
struct S { int a; int b; };         // defines S, S::a, and S::b
struct X {                          // defines X
    int x;                          // defines nonstatic data member x
    static int y;                   // declares static data member y
    X(): x(0) { }                   // defines a constructor of X
};
int X::y = 1;                       // defines X::y
enum { up, down };                  // defines up and down
namespace N { int d; }              // defines N and N::d
namespace N1 = N;                   // defines N1
X anX;                              // defines anX
```

whereas these are just declarations:

```
extern int a;                       // declares a
extern const int c;                 // declares c
int f(int);                         // declares f
struct S;                           // declares S
typedef int Int;                    // declares Int
extern X anotherX;                  // declares anotherX
using N::d;                         // declares N::d
```

—*end example*]

4   [*Note:* in some circumstances, C++ implementations implicitly define the default constructor (12.1), copy
         constructor (12.8), assignment operator (12.8), or destructor (12.4) member functions. [*Example:* given

```
struct C {
    string s;                       // string is the standard library class (clause 21)
};

int main()
{
    C a;
    C b = a;
    b = a;
}
```

the implementation will implicitly define functions to make the definition of C equivalent to

```
struct C {
    string s;
    C(): s() { }
    C(const C& x): s(x.s) { }
    C& operator=(const C& x) { s = x.s; return *this; }
    ~C() { }
};
```

—*end example*] —*end note*]

5   [*Note:* a class name can also be implicitly declared by an *elaborated-type-specifier* (3.3.1).]

6   A program is ill-formed if the definition of any object gives the object an incomplete type (3.9).

3.2 One definition rule

[basic.def.odr]

1   No translation unit shall contain more than one definition of any variable, function, class type, enumeration type or template.

2   An expression is *potentially evaluated* unless it appears where an integral constant expression is required (see 5.19), is the operand of the `sizeof` operator (5.3.3), or is the operand of the `typeid` operator and the expression does not designate an lvalue of polymorphic class type (5.2.8). An object or non-overloaded function is *used* if its name appears in a potentially-evaluated expression. A virtual member function is used if it is not pure. An overloaded function is used if it is selected by overload resolution when referred to from a potentially-evaluated expression. [*Note:* this covers calls to named functions (5.2.2), operator overloading (clause 13), user-defined conversions (12.3.2), allocation function for placement new (5.3.4), as well as non-default initialization (8.5). A copy constructor is used even if the call is actually elided by the implementation.] An allocation or deallocation function for a class is used by a new expression appearing in a potentially-evaluated expression as specified in 5.3.4 and 12.5. A deallocation function for a class is used by a delete expression appearing in a potentially-evaluated expression as specified in 5.3.5 and 12.5. A copy-assignment function for a class is used by an implicitly-defined copy-assignment function for another class as specified in 12.8. A default constructor for a class is used by default initialization as specified in 8.5. A constructor for a class is used as specified in 8.5. A destructor for a class is used as specified in 12.4.

3   Every program shall contain exactly one definition of every non-inline function or object that is used in that program; no diagnostic required. The definition can appear explicitly in the program, it can be found in the standard or a user-defined library, or (when appropriate) it is implicitly defined (see 12.1, 12.4 and 12.8). An inline function shall be defined in every translation unit in which it is used.

4   Exactly one definition of a class is required in a translation unit if the class is used in a way that requires the class type to be complete. [*Example:* the following complete translation unit is well-formed, even though it never defines X:

```
struct X;              // declare X as a struct type
struct X* x1;          // use X in pointer formation
X* x2;                 // use X in pointer formation
```

—*end example*] [*Note:* the rules for declarations and expressions describe in which contexts complete class types are required. A class type T must be complete if:

— an object of type T is defined (3.1, 5.3.4), or

— an lvalue-to-rvalue conversion is applied to an lvalue referring to an object of type T (4.1), or

— an expression is converted (either implicitly or explicitly) to type T (clause 4, 5.2.3, 5.2.7, 5.2.9, 5.4), or

— an expression that is not a null pointer constant, and has type other than `void *`, is converted to the type pointer to T or reference to T using an implicit conversion (clause 4), a `dynamic_cast` (5.2.7) or a `static_cast` (5.2.9), or

— a class member access operator is applied to an expression of type T (5.2.5), or

— the `typeid` operator (5.2.8) or the `sizeof` operator (5.3.3) is applied to an operand of type T, or

— a function with a return type or argument type of type T is defined (3.1) or called (5.2.2), or

— an lvalue of type T is assigned to (5.17).]

5   There can be more than one definition of a class type (clause 9), enumeration type (7.2), inline function with external linkage (7.1.2), class template (clause 14), non-static function template (14.5.5), static data member of a class template (14.5.1.3), member function of a class template (14.5.1.1), or template specialization for which some template parameters are not specified (14.7, 14.5.4) in a program provided that each definition appears in a different translation unit, and provided the definitions satisfy the following requirements. Given such an entity named D defined in more than one translation unit, then

— each definition of D shall consist of the same sequence of tokens; and

— in each definition of D, corresponding names, looked up according to 3.4, shall refer to an entity defined within the definition of D, or shall refer to the same entity, after overload resolution (13.3) and after matching of partial template specialization (14.8.3), except that a name can refer to a const object with internal or no linkage if the object has the same integral or enumeration type in all definitions of D, and the object is initialized with a constant expression (5.19), and the value (but not the address) of the object is used, and the object has the same value in all definitions of D; and

— in each definition of D, the overloaded operators referred to, the implicit calls to conversion functions, constructors, operator new functions and operator delete functions, shall refer to the same function, or to a function defined within the definition of D; and

— in each definition of D, a default argument used by an (implicit or explicit) function call is treated as if its token sequence were present in the definition of D; that is, the default argument is subject to the three requirements described above (and, if the default argument has sub-expressions with default arguments, this requirement applies recursively).[25]

— if D is a class with an implicitly-declared constructor (12.1), it is as if the constructor was implicitly defined in every translation unit where it is used, and the implicit definition in every translation unit shall call the same constructor for a base class or a class member of D. [*Example:*

```
// translation unit 1:
struct X {
        X(int);
        X(int, int);
};
X::X(int = 0) { }
class D: public X { };
D d2;                                   // X(int) called by D()

// translation unit 2:
struct X {
        X(int);
        X(int, int);
};
X::X(int = 0, int = 0) { }
class D: public X { };                  // X(int, int) called by D();
                                        // D()'s implicit definition
                                        // violates the ODR
```

—*end example*] If D is a template, and is defined in more than one translation unit, then the last four requirements from the list above shall apply to names from the template's enclosing scope used in the template definition (14.6.3), and also to dependent names at the point of instantiation (14.6.2). If the definitions of D satisfy all these requirements, then the program shall behave as if there were a single definition of D. If the definitions of D do not satisfy these requirements, then the behavior is undefined.

3.3 Declarative regions and scopes   [basic.scope]

1   Every name is introduced in some portion of program text called a *declarative region*, which is the largest part of the program in which that name is *valid*, that is, in which that name may be used as an unqualified name to refer to the same entity. In general, each particular name is valid only within some possibly discontiguous portion of program text called its *scope*. To determine the scope of a declaration, it is sometimes convenient to refer to the *potential scope* of a declaration. The scope of a declaration is the same as its potential scope unless the potential scope contains another declaration of the same name. In that case, the potential scope of the declaration in the inner (contained) declarative region is excluded from the scope

---

[25] 8.3.6 describes how default argument names are looked up.

of the declaration in the outer (containing) declarative region.

2   [*Example:* in

```
int j = 24;
int main()
{
        int i = j, j;
        j = 42;
}
```

the identifier j is declared twice as a name (and used twice). The declarative region of the first j includes the entire example. The potential scope of the first j begins immediately after that j and extends to the end of the program, but its (actual) scope excludes the text between the , and the }. The declarative region of the second declaration of j (the j immediately before the semicolon) includes all the text between { and }, but its potential scope excludes the declaration of i. The scope of the second declaration of j is the same as its potential scope.]

3   The names declared by a declaration are introduced into the scope in which the declaration occurs, except that the presence of a `friend` specifier (11.4), certain uses of the *elaborated-type-specifier* (3.3.1), and *using-directive*s (7.3.4) alter this general behavior.

4   Given a set of declarations in a single declarative region, each of which specifies the same unqualified name,

— they shall all refer to the same entity, or all refer to functions and function templates; or

— exactly one declaration shall declare a class name or enumeration name that is not a typedef name and the other declarations shall all refer to the same object or enumerator, or all refer to functions and function templates; in this case the class name or enumeration name is hidden (3.3.7). [*Note:* a namespace name or a class template name must be unique in its declarative region (7.3.2, clause 14).]

[*Note:* these restrictions apply to the declarative region into which a name is introduced, which is not necessarily the same as the region in which the declaration occurs. In particular, *elaborated-type-specifier*s (3.3.1) and friend declarations (11.4) may introduce a (possibly not visible) name into an enclosing namespace; these restrictions apply to that region. Local extern declarations (3.5) may introduce a name into the declarative region where the declaration appears and also introduce a (possibly not visible) name into an enclosing namespace; these restrictions apply to both regions.]

5   [*Note:* the name lookup rules are summarized in 3.4.]

3.3.1 Point of declaration   [basic.scope.pdecl]

1   The *point of declaration* for a name is immediately after its complete declarator (clause 8) and before its *initializer* (if any), except as noted below. [*Example:*

```
int x = 12;
{ int x = x; }
```

Here the second x is initialized with its own (indeterminate) value.]

2   [*Note:* a nonlocal name remains visible up to the point of declaration of the local name that hides it. [*Example:*

```
const int  i = 2;
{ int  i[i]; }
```

declares a local array of two integers.]]

3   The point of declaration for an enumerator is immediately after its *enumerator-definition*. [*Example:*

```
const int x = 12;
{ enum { x = x }; }
```

Here, the enumerator x is initialized with the value of the constant x, namely 12.]

4   After the point of declaration of a class member, the member name can be looked up in the scope of its class. [*Note:* this is true even if the class is an incomplete class. For example,

```
struct X {
        enum E { z = 16 };
        int b[X::z];                    // OK
};
```

—*end note*]

5   The point of declaration of a class first declared in an *elaborated-type-specifier* is as follows:

— for an *elaborated-type-specifier* of the form

     class-key identifier ;

the *elaborated-type-specifier* declares the *identifier* to be a *class-name* in the scope that contains the declaration, otherwise

— for an *elaborated-type-specifier* of the form

     class-key identifier

if the *elaborated-type-specifier* is used in the *decl-specifier-seq* or *parameter-declaration-clause* of a function defined in namespace scope, the *identifier* is declared as a *class-name* in the namespace that contains the declaration; otherwise, except as a friend declaration, the *identifier* is declared in the smallest non-class, non-function-prototype scope that contains the declaration. [*Note:* if the *elaborated-type-specifier* designates an enumeration, the *identifier* must refer to an already declared *enum-name*. If the *identifier* in the *elaborated-type-specifier* is a *qualified-id*, it must refer to an already declared *class-name* or *enum-name*. See 3.4.4.]

6   [*Note:* friend declarations refer to functions or classes that are members of the nearest enclosing namespace, but they do not introduce new names into that namespace (7.3.1.2). Function declarations at block scope and object declarations with the extern specifier at block scope refer to delarations that are members of an enclosing namespace, but they do not introduce new names into that scope.]

7   [*Note:* For point of instantiation of a template, see 14.6.4.1 .]

3.3.2 Local scope   [basic.scope.local]

1   A name declared in a block (6.3) is local to that block. Its potential scope begins at its point of declaration (3.3.1) and ends at the end of its declarative region.

2   The potential scope of a function parameter name in a function definition (8.4) begins at its point of declaration. If the function has a *function-try-block* the potential scope of a parameter ends at the end of the last associated handler, else it ends at the end of the outermost block of the function definition. A parameter name shall not be redeclared in the outermost block of the function definition nor in the outermost block of any handler associated with a *function-try-block*.

3   The name in a catch exception-declaration is local to the handler and shall not be redeclared in the outermost block of the handler.

4   Names declared in the *for-init-statement*, and in the *condition* of if, while, for, and switch statements are local to the if, while, for, or switch statement (including the controlled statement), and shall not be redeclared in a subsequent condition of that statement nor in the outermost block (or, for the if statement, any of the outermost blocks) of the controlled statement; see 6.4.

3.3.3 Function prototype scope   [basic.scope.proto]

1   In a function declaration, or in any function declarator except the declarator of a function definition (8.4),
names of parameters (if supplied) have function prototype scope, which terminates at the end of the nearest
enclosing function declarator.

3.3.4 Function scope   [basic.funscope]

1   Labels (6.1) have *function scope* and may be used anywhere in the function in which they are declared.
Only labels have function scope.

3.3.5 Namespace scope   [basic.scope.namespace]

1   The declarative region of a *namespace-definition* is its *namespace-body*. The potential scope denoted by an
original-namespace-name is the concatenation of the declarative regions established by each of the
namespace-definitions in the same declarative region with that *original-namespace-name*. Entities declared
in a *namespace-body* are said to be *members* of the namespace, and names introduced by these declarations
into the declarative region of the namespace are said to be *member names* of the namespace. A namespace
member name has namespace scope. Its potential scope includes its namespace from the name's point of
declaration (3.3.1) onwards; and for each *using-directive* (7.3.4) that nominates the member's namespace,
the member's potential scope includes that portion of the potential scope of the *using-directive* that follows
the member's point of declaration. [*Example:*

```
namespace N {
        int i;
        int g(int a) { return a; }
        int j();
        void q();
}
namespace { int l=1; }
// the potential scope of l is from its point of declaration
// to the end of the translation unit

namespace N {
        int g(char a)           // overloads N::g(int)
        {
                return l+a;     // l is from unnamed namespace
        }

        int i;                  // error: duplicate definition
        int j();                // OK: duplicate function declaration

        int j()                 // OK: definition of N::j()
        {
                return g(i);    // calls N::g(int)
        }
        int q();                // error: different return type
}
```

—*end example*]

2   A namespace member can also be referred to after the `::` scope resolution operator (5.1) applied to the
name of its namespace or the name of a namespace which nominates the member's namespace in a *using-
directive;* see 3.4.3.2.

3   The outermost declarative region of a translation unit is also a namespace, called the *global namespace*. A
name declared in the global namespace has *global namespace scope* (also called *global scope*). The potential scope of such a name begins at its point of declaration (3.3.1) and ends at the end of the translation unit
that is its declarative region. Names with global namespace scope are said to be *global*.

3.3.6 Class scope

1   The following rules describe the scope of names declared in classes.

1) The potential scope of a name declared in a class consists not only of the declarative region following the name's declarator, but also of all function bodies, default arguments, and constructor *ctor-initializers* in that class (including such things in nested classes).

2) A name N used in a class S shall refer to the same declaration in its context and when re-evaluated in the completed scope of S. No diagnostic is required for a violation of this rule.

3) If reordering member declarations in a class yields an alternate valid program under (1) and (2), the program is ill-formed, no diagnostic is required.

4) A name declared within a member function hides a declaration of the same name whose scope extends to or past the end of the member function's class.

5) The potential scope of a declaration that extends to or past the end of a class definition also extends to the regions defined by its member definitions, even if the members are defined lexically outside the class (this includes static data member definitions, nested class definitions, member function definitions (including the member function body and, for constructor functions (12.1), the ctor-initializer (12.6.2)) and any portion of the declarator part of such definitions which follows the identifier, including a *parameter-declaration-clause* and any default arguments (8.3.6). [*Example:*

```
typedef int   c;
enum { i = 1 };

class X {
    char  v[i];              // error: i refers to ::i
                             // but when reevaluated is X::i
    int  f() { return sizeof(c); }    // OK: X::c
    char  c;
    enum { i = 2 };
};

typedef char*  T;
struct Y {
    T   a;                  // error: T refers to ::T
                             // but when reevaluated is Y::T
    typedef long  T;
    T  b;
};

typedef int I;
class D {
    typedef I I;            // error, even though no reordering involved
};
```

—*end example*]

2   The name of a class member shall only be used as follows:

— in the scope of its class (as described above) or a class derived (clause 10) from its class,

— after the . operator applied to an expression of the type of its class (5.2.5) or a class derived from its class,

— after the -> operator applied to a pointer to an object of its class (5.2.5) or a class derived from its class,

— after the :: scope resolution operator (5.1) applied to the name of its class or a class derived from its class.

3.3.7 Name hiding [basic.scope.hiding]

1 A name can be hidden by an explicit declaration of that same name in a nested declarative region or derived class (10.2).

2 A class name (9.1) or enumeration name (7.2) can be hidden by the name of an object, function, or enumerator declared in the same scope. If a class or enumeration name and an object, function, or enumerator are declared in the same scope (in any order) with the same name, the class or enumeration name is hidden wherever the object, function, or enumerator name is visible.

3 In a member function definition, the declaration of a local name hides the declaration of a member of the class with the same name; see 3.3.6. The declaration of a member in a derived class (clause 10) hides the declaration of a member of a base class of the same name; see 10.2.

4 During the lookup of a name qualified by a namespace name, declarations that would otherwise be made visible by a *using-directive* can be hidden by declarations with the same name in the namespace containing the *using-directive;* see (3.4.3.2).

5 If a name is in scope and is not hidden it is said to be *visible.*

3.4 Name lookup [basic.lookup]

1 The name lookup rules apply uniformly to all names (including *typedef-names* (7.1.3), *namespace-names* (7.3) and *class-names* (9.1)) wherever the grammar allows such names in the context discussed by a particular rule. Name lookup associates the use of a name with a declaration (3.1) of that name. Name lookup shall find an unambiguous declaration for the name (see 10.2). Name lookup may associate more than one declaration with a name if it finds the name to be a function name; the declarations are said to form a set of overloaded functions (13.1). Overload resolution (13.3) takes place after name lookup has succeeded. The access rules (clause 11) are considered only once name lookup and function overload resolution (if applicable) have succeeded. Only after name lookup, function overload resolution (if applicable) and access checking have succeeded are the attributes introduced by the name's declaration used further in expression processing (clause 5).

2 A name "looked up in the context of an expression" is looked up as an unqualified name in the scope where the expression is found.

3 The injected-class-name of a class (clause 9) is also considered to be a member of that class for the purposes of name hiding and lookup.

4 [*Note:* 3.5 discusses linkage issues. The notions of scope, point of declaration and name hiding are discussed in 3.3.]

3.4.1 Unqualified name lookup [basic.lookup.unqual]

1 In all the cases listed in 3.4.1, the scopes are searched for a declaration in the order listed in each of the respective categories; name lookup ends as soon as a declaration is found for the name. If no declaration is found, the program is ill-formed.

2 The declarations from the namespace nominated by a *using-directive* become visible in a namespace enclosing the *using-directive;* see 7.3.4. For the purpose of the unqualified name lookup rules described in 3.4.1, the declarations from the namespace nominated by the *using-directive* are considered members of that enclosing namespace.

3 The lookup for an unqualified name used as the *postfix-expression* of a function call is described in 3.4.2. [*Note:* for purposes of determining (during parsing) whether an expression is a *postfix-expression* for a function call, the usual name lookup rules apply. The rules in 3.4.2 have no effect on the syntactic interpretation of an expression. For example,

```
typedef int f;
struct A {
        friend void f(A &);
        operator int();
        void g(A a) {
                f(a);
        }
};
```

The expression f(a) is a *cast-expression* equivalent to int(a). Because the expression is not a function call, the argument-dependent name lookup (3.4.2) does not apply and the friend function f is not found.]

4   A name used in global scope, outside of any function, class or user-declared namespace, shall be declared before its use in global scope.

5   A name used in a user-declared namespace outside of the definition of any function or class shall be declared before its use in that namespace or before its use in a namespace enclosing its namespace.

6   A name used in the definition of a function following the function's *declarator-id*[26] that is a member of namespace N (where, only for the purpose of exposition, N could represent the global scope) shall be declared before its use in the block in which it is used or in one of its enclosing blocks (6.3) or, shall be declared before its use in namespace N or, if N is a nested namespace, shall be declared before its use in one of N's enclosing namespaces.
[*Example:*

```
namespace A {
        namespace N {
                void f();
        }
}
void A::N::f() {
        i = 5;
        // The following scopes are searched for a declaration of i:
        // 1) outermost block scope of A::N::f, before the use of i
        // 2) scope of namespace N
        // 3) scope of namespace A
        // 4) global scope, before the definition of A::N::f
}
```

—*end example*]

7   A name used in the definition of a class X outside of a member function body or nested class definition[27] shall be declared in one of the following ways:

— before its use in class X or be a member of a base class of X (10.2), or

— if X is a nested class of class Y (9.7), before the definition of X in Y, or shall be a member of a base class of Y (this lookup applies in turn to Y's enclosing classes, starting with the innermost enclosing class),[28] or

— if X is a local class (9.8) or is a nested class of a local class, before the definition of class X in a block enclosing the definition of class X, or

— if X is a member of namespace N, or is a nested class of a class that is a member of N, or is a local class

---

[26] This refers to unqualified names that occur, for instance, in a type or default argument expression in the *parameter-declaration-clause* or used in the function body.
[27] This refers to unqualified names following the class name; such a name may be used in the *base-clause* or may be used in the class definition.
[28] This lookup applies whether the definition of X is nested within Y's definition or whether X's definition appears in a namespace scope enclosing Y's definition (9.7).

or a nested class within a local class of a function that is a member of N, before the definition of class X in namespace N or in one of N's enclosing namespaces.

[*Example:*

```
namespace M {
        class B { };
}

namespace N {
        class Y : public M::B {
                class X {
                        int a[i];
                };
        };
}
```

```
// The following scopes are searched for a declaration of i:
// 1) scope of class N::Y::X, before the use of i
// 2) scope of class N::Y, before the definition of N::Y::X
// 3) scope of N::Y's base class M::B
// 4) scope of namespace N, before the definition of N::Y
// 5) global scope, before the definition of N
```

—*end example*] [*Note:* when looking for a prior declaration of a class or function introduced by a friend declaration, scopes outside of the innermost enclosing namespace scope are not considered; see 7.3.1.2.] [*Note:* 3.3.6 further describes the restrictions on the use of names in a class definition. 9.7 further describes the restrictions on the use of names in nested class definitions. 9.8 further describes the restrictions on the use of names in local class definitions.]

8   A name used in the definition of a member function (9.3) of class X following the function's *declarator-id*[29] shall be declared in one of the following ways:

— before its use in the block in which it is used or in an enclosing block (6.3), or

— shall be a member of class X or be a member of a base class of X (10.2), or

— if X is a nested class of class Y (9.7), shall be a member of Y, or shall be a member of a base class of Y (this lookup applies in turn to Y's enclosing classes, starting with the innermost enclosing class),[30] or

— if X is a local class (9.8) or is a nested class of a local class, before the definition of class X in a block enclosing the definition of class X, or

— if X is a member of namespace N, or is a nested class of a class that is a member of N, or is a local class or a nested class within a local class of a function that is a member of N, before the member function definition, in namespace N or in one of N's enclosing namespaces.

[*Example:*

---

[29] That is, an unqualified name that occurs, for instance, in a type or default argument expression in the *parameter-declaration-clause*, in the function body, or in an expression of a *mem-initializer* in a constructor definition.
[30] This lookup applies whether the member function is defined within the definition of class X or whether the member function is defined in a namespace scope enclosing X's definition.

```
class B { };
namespace M {
        namespace N {
                class X : public B {
                        void f();
                };
        }
}
void M::N::X::f() {
        i = 16;
}
```

// *The following scopes are searched for a declaration of* i :
// *1) outermost block scope of* M::N::X::f, *before the use of* i
// *2) scope of class* M::N::X
// *3) scope of* M::N::X*'s base class* B
// *4) scope of namespace* M::N
// *5) scope of namespace* M
// *6) global scope, before the definition of* M::N::X::f

—*end example*] [*Note:* 9.3 and 9.4 further describe the restrictions on the use of names in member function definitions. 9.7 further describes the restrictions on the use of names in the scope of nested classes. 9.8 further describes the restrictions on the use of names in local class definitions.]

9   Name lookup for a name used in the definition of a friend function (11.4) defined inline in the class granting friendship shall proceed as described for lookup in member function definitions. If the friend function is not defined in the class granting friendship, name lookup in the friend function definition shall proceed as described for lookup in namespace member function definitions.

10   In a friend declaration naming a member function, a name used in the function declarator and not part of a *template-argument* in a *template-id* is first looked up in the scope of the member function's class. If it is not found, or if the name is part of a *template-argument* in a *template-id*, the look up is as described for unqualified names in the definition of the class granting friendship. [*Example:*

```
struct A {
        typedef int AT;
        void f1(AT);
        void f2(float);
};
struct B {
        typedef float BT;
        friend void A::f1(AT);    // parameter type is A::AT
        friend void A::f2(BT);    // parameter type is B::BT
};
```

—*end example*]

11   During the lookup for a name used as a default argument (8.3.6) in a function *parameter-declaration-clause* or used in the *expression* of a *mem-initializer* for a constructor (12.6.2), the function parameter names are visible and hide the names of entities declared in the block, class or namespace scopes containing the function declaration. [*Note:* 8.3.6 further describes the restrictions on the use of names in default arguments. 12.6.2 further describes the restrictions on the use of names in a *ctor-initializer*.]

12   A name used in the definition of a static data member of class X (9.4.2) (after the *qualified-id* of the static member) is looked up as if the name was used in a member function of X. [*Note:* 9.4.2 further describes the restrictions on the use of names in the definition of a static data member.]

13   A name used in the handler for a *function-try-block* (clause 15) is looked up as if the name was used in the outermost block of the function definition. In particular, the function parameter names shall not be redeclared in the *exception-declaration* nor in the outermost block of a handler for the *function-try-block*.

Names declared in the outermost block of the function definition are not found when looked up in the scope of a handler for the *function-try-block*. [*Note:* but function parameter names are found.]

14   [*Note:* the rules for name lookup in template definitions are described in 14.6.]

3.4.2 Argument-dependent name lookup   **[basic.lookup.koenig]**

1   When an unqualified name is used as the *postfix-expression* in a function call (5.2.2), other namespaces not considered during the usual unqualified lookup (3.4.1) may be searched, and namespace-scope friend function declarations (11.4) not otherwise visible may be found. These modifications to the search depend on the types of the arguments (and for template template arguments, the namespace of the template argument).

2   For each argument type T in the function call, there is a set of zero or more associated namespaces and a set of zero or more associated classes to be considered. The sets of namespaces and classes is determined entirely by the types of the function arguments (and the namespace of any template template argument). Typedef names and *using-declaration*s used to specify the types do not contribute to this set. The sets of namespaces and classes are determined in the following way:

— If T is a fundamental type, its associated sets of namespaces and classes are both empty.

— If T is a class type (including unions), its associated classes are: the class itself; the class of which it is a member, if any; and its direct and indirect base classes. Its associated namespaces are the namespaces in which its associated classes are defined.

— If T is an enumeration type, its associated namespace is the namespace in which it is defined. If it is class member, its associated class is the member's class; else it has no associated class.

— If T is a pointer to U or an array of U, its associated namespaces and classes are those associated with U.

— If T is a function type, its associated namespaces and classes are those associated with the function parameter types and those associated with the return type.

— If T is a pointer to a member function of a class X, its associated namespaces and classes are those associated with the function parameter types and return type, together with those associated with X.

— If T is a pointer to a data member of class X, its associated namespaces and classes are those associated with the member type together with those associated with X.

— If T is a *template-id*, its associated namespaces and classes are the namespace in which the template is defined; for member templates, the member template's class; the namespaces and classes associated with the types of the template arguments provided for template type parameters (excluding template template parameters); the namespaces in which any template template arguments are defined; and the classes in which any member templates used as template template arguments are defined. [*Note:* non-type template arguments do not contribute to the set of associated namespaces.]

In addition, if the argument is the name or address of a set of overloaded functions and/or function templates, its associated classes and namespaces are the union of those associated with each of the members of the set: the namespace in which the function or function template is defined and the classes and namespaces associated with its (non-dependent) parameter types and return type.

2a   If the ordinary unqualified lookup of the name finds the declaration of a class member function, the associated namespaces and classes are not considered. Otherwise the set of declarations found by the lookup of the function name is the union of the set of declarations found using ordinary unqualified lookup and the set of declarations found in the namespaces and classes associated with the argument types. [*Note:* the namespaces and classes associated with the argument types can include namespaces and classes already considered by the ordinary unqualified lookup.] [*Example:*

```
namespace NS {
    class T { };
    void f(T);
}
NS::T parm;
int main() {
    f(parm);                        // OK: calls NS::f
}
```

—*end example*]

3   When considering an associated namespace, the lookup is the same as the lookup performed when the associated namespace is used as a qualifier (3.4.3.2) except that:

— Any *using-directive*s in the associated namespace are ignored.

— Any namespace-scope friend functions declared in associated classes are visible within their respective namespaces even if they are not visible during an ordinary lookup (11.4).

3.4.3 Qualified name lookup   [basic.lookup.qual]

1   The name of a class or namespace member can be referred to after the :: scope resolution operator (5.1) applied to a *nested-name-specifier* that nominates its class or namespace. During the lookup for a name preceding the :: scope resolution operator, object, function, and enumerator names are ignored. If the name found is not a *class-name* (clause 9) or *namespace-name* (7.3.1), the program is ill-formed. [*Example:*

```
class A {
public:
        static int n;
};
int main()
{
        int A;
        A::n = 42;              // OK
        A b;                    // ill-formed: A does not name a type
}
```

—*end example*]

2   [*Note:* Multiply qualified names, such as N1::N2::N3::n, can be used to refer to members of nested classes (9.7) or members of nested namespaces.]

3   In a declaration in which the *declarator-id* is a *qualified-id*, names used before the *qualified-id* being declared are looked up in the defining namespace scope; names following the *qualified-id* are looked up in the scope of the member's class or namespace. [*Example:*

```
class X { };
class C {
        class X { };
        static const int number = 50;
        static X arr[number];
};
X C::arr[number];              // ill-formed:
                              // equivalent to: ::X C::arr[C::number];
                              // not to: C::X C::arr[C::number];
```

—*end example*]

4   A name prefixed by the unary scope operator :: (5.1) is looked up in global scope, in the translation unit where it is used. The name shall be declared in global namespace scope or shall be a name whose declaration is visible in global scope because of a *using-directive* (3.4.3.2). The use of :: allows a global name to

be referred to even if its identifier has been hidden (3.3.7).

5　If a *pseudo-destructor-name* (5.2.4) contains a *nested-name-specifier*, the *type-name*s are looked up as types in the scope designated by the *nested-name-specifier*. In a *qualified-id* of the form:

> : : *opt* *nested-name-specifier* ˜ *class-name*

where the *nested-name-specifier* designates a namespace scope, and in a *qualified-id* of the form:

> : : *opt* *nested-name-specifier* *class-name* : : ˜ *class-name*

the *class-name*s are looked up as types in the scope designated by the *nested-name-specifier*. [*Example:*

```
struct C {
        typedef int I;
};
typedef int I1, I2;
extern int* p;
extern int* q;
p->C::I::~I();                // I is looked up in the scope of C
q->I1::~I2();                 // I2 is looked up in the scope of
                              // the postfix-expression


struct A {
        ~A();
};
typedef A AB;
int main()
{
        AB *p;
        p->AB::~AB();         // explicitly calls the destructor for A
}
```

—*end example*] [*Note:* 3.4.5 describes how name lookup proceeds after the . and -> operators.]

3.4.3.1 Class members 　　　　　　　　　　　　　　　　　　　　　　　 **[class.qual]**

1　If the *nested-name-specifier* of a *qualified-id* nominates a class, the name specified after the *nested-name-specifier* is looked up in the scope of the class (10.2), except for the cases listed below. The name shall represent one or more members of that class or of one of its base classes (clause 10). [*Note:* a class member can be referred to using a *qualified-id* at any point in its potential scope (3.3.6).] The exceptions to the name lookup rule above are the following:

— a destructor name is looked up as specified in 3.4.3;

— a *conversion-type-id* of an *operator-function-id* is looked up both in the scope of the class and in the context in which the entire *postfix-expression* occurs and shall refer to the same type in both contexts;

— the *template-arguments* of a *template-id* are looked up in the context in which the entire *postfix-expression* occurs.

1a　If the *nested-name-specifier* nominates a class C, and the name specified after the *nested-name-specifier*, when looked up in C, is the injected-class-name of C (clause 9), the name is instead considered to name the constructor of class C. Such a constructor name shall be used only in the *declarator-id* of a constructor definition that appears outside of the class definition. [*Example:*

```
struct A { A(); };
struct B: public A { B(); };

A::A() { }
B::B() { }

B::A ba;                                  // object of type A
A::A a;                                   // error, A::A is not a type name
```

—*end example*]

2   A class member name hidden by a name in a nested declarative region or by the name of a derived class member can still be found if qualified by the name of its class followed by the : : operator.

3.4.3.2 Namespace members   [namespace.qual]

1   If the *nested-name-specifier* of a *qualified-id* nominates a namespace, the name specified after the *nested-name-specifier* is looked up in the scope of the namespace, except that the *template-arguments* of a *template-id* are looked up in the context in which the entire *postfix-expression* occurs.

2   Given X::m (where X is a user-declared namespace), or given ::m (where X is the global namespace), let S be the set of all declarations of m in X and in the transitive closure of all namespaces nominated by *using-directive*s in X and its used namespaces, except that *using-directive*s are ignored in any namespace, including X, directly containing one or more declarations of m. No namespace is searched more than once in the lookup of a name. If S is the empty set, the program is ill-formed. Otherwise, if S has exactly one member, or if the context of the reference is a *using-declaration* (7.3.3), S is the required set of declarations of m. Otherwise if the use of m is not one that allows a unique declaration to be chosen from S, the program is ill-formed. [*Example:*

```
int x;
namespace Y {
        void f(float);
        void h(int);
}

namespace Z {
        void h(double);
}

namespace A {
        using namespace Y;
        void f(int);
        void g(int);
        int i;
}

namespace B {
        using namespace Z;
        void f(char);
        int i;
}

namespace AB {
        using namespace A;
        using namespace B;
        void g();
}
```

```
void h()
{
        AB::g();                // g is declared directly in AB,
                                // therefore S is { AB::g() } and AB::g() is chosen
        AB::f(1);               // f is not declared directly in AB so the rules are
                                // applied recursively to A and B;
                                // namespace Y is not searched and Y::f(float)
                                // is not considered;
                                // S is { A::f(int), B::f(char) } and overload
                                // resolution chooses A::f(int)
        AB::f('c');             // as above but resolution chooses B::f(char)

        AB::x++;                // x is not declared directly in AB, and
                                // is not declared in A or B, so the rules are
                                // applied recursively to Y and Z,
                                // S is { } so the program is ill-formed
        AB::i++;                // i is not declared directly in AB so the rules are
                                // applied recursively to A and B,
                                // S is { A::i, B::i } so the use is ambiguous
                                // and the program is ill-formed
        AB::h(16.8);            // h is not declared directly in AB and
                                // not declared directly in A or B so the rules are
                                // applied recursively to Y and Z,
                                // S is { Y::h(int), Z::h(double) } and overload
                                // resolution chooses Z::h(double)
}
```

3   The same declaration found more than once is not an ambiguity (because it is still a unique declaration). For example:

```
namespace A {
        int a;
}

namespace B {
        using namespace A;
}

namespace C {
        using namespace A;
}

namespace BC {
        using namespace B;
        using namespace C;
}

void f()
{
        BC::a++;                // OK: S is { A::a, A::a }
}

namespace D {
        using A::a;
}
```

```
namespace BD {
        using namespace B;
        using namespace D;
}

void g()
{
        BD::a++;                        // OK: S is { A::a, A::a }
}
```

4   Because each referenced namespace is searched at most once, the following is well-defined:

```
namespace B {
        int b;
}

namespace A {
        using namespace B;
        int a;
}

namespace B {
        using namespace A;
}

void f()
{
        A::a++;          // OK: a declared directly in A, S is { A::a }
        B::a++;          // OK: both A and B searched (once), S is { A::a }
        A::b++;          // OK: both A and B searched (once), S is { B::b }
        B::b++;          // OK: b declared directly in B, S is { B::b }
}
```

—*end example*]

5   During the lookup of a qualified namespace member name, if the lookup finds more than one declaration of the member, and if one declaration introduces a class name or enumeration name and the other declarations either introduce the same object, the same enumerator or a set of functions, the non-type name hides the class or enumeration name if and only if the declarations are from the same namespace; otherwise (the declarations are from different namespaces), the program is ill-formed. [*Example:*

```
namespace A {
        struct x { };
        int x;
        int y;
}

namespace B {
        struct y {};
}

namespace C {
        using namespace A;
        using namespace B;
        int i = C::x;          // OK, A::x (of type int)
        int j = C::y;          // ambiguous, A::y or B::y
}
```

—*end example*]

6   In a declaration for a namespace member in which the *declarator-id* is a *qualified-id*, given that the *qualified-id* for the namespace member has the form

        nested-name-specifier unqualified-id

the *unqualified-id* shall name a member of the namespace designated by the *nested-name-specifier*. [*Example:*

```
namespace A {
        namespace B {
                void f1(int);
        }
        using namespace B;
}
void A::f1(int) { }                    // ill-formed, f1 is not a member of A
```

—*end example*] However, in such namespace member declarations, the *nested-name-specifier* may rely on *using-directive*s to implicitly provide the initial part of the *nested-name-specifier*. [*Example:*

```
namespace A {
        namespace B {
                void f1(int);
        }
}

namespace C {
        namespace D {
                void f1(int);
        }
}

using namespace A;
using namespace C::D;
void B::f1(int){}                      // OK, defines A::B::f1(int)
```

—*end example*]

3.4.4   Elaborated type specifiers   [basic.lookup.elab]

1   An *elaborated-type-specifier* may be used to refer to a previously declared *class-name* or *enum-name* even though the name has been hidden by a non-type declaration (3.3.7). The *class-name* or *enum-name* in the *elaborated-type-specifier* may either be a simple *identifer* or be a *qualified-id*.

2   If the name in the *elaborated-type-specifier* is a simple *identifer*, and unless the *elaborated-type-specifier* has the following form:

        class-key identifier ;

the *identifier* is looked up according to 3.4.1 but ignoring any non-type names that have been declared. If this name lookup finds a *typedef-name*, the *elaborated-type-specifier* is ill-formed. If the *elaborated-type-specifier* refers to an *enum-name* and this lookup does not find a previously declared *enum-name*, the *elaborated-type-specifier* is ill-formed. If the *elaborated-type-specifier* refers to an *class-name* and this lookup does not find a previously declared *class-name*, or if the *elaborated-type-specifier* has the form:

        class-key identifier ;

the *elaborated-type-specifier* is a declaration that introduces the *class-name* as described in 3.3.1.

3   If the name is a *qualified-id*, the name is looked up according its qualifications, as described in 3.4.3, but ignoring any non-type names that have been declared. If this name lookup finds a *typedef-name,* the *elaborated-type-specifier* is ill-formed. If this name lookup does not find a previously declared *class-name* or *enum-name*, the *elaborated-type-specifier* is ill-formed. [*Example:*

```
struct Node {
        struct Node* Next;          // OK: Refers to Node at global scope
        struct Data* Data;          // OK: Declares type Data
                                    // at global scope and member Data
};

struct Data {
        struct Node* Node;          // OK: Refers to Node at global scope
        friend struct ::Glob;       // error: Glob is not declared
                                    // cannot introduce a qualified type (7.1.5.3)
        friend struct Glob;         // OK: Refers to (as yet) undeclared Glob
                                    // at global scope.
        /* ... */
};

struct Base {
        struct Data;                        // OK: Declares nested Data
        struct ::Data*      thatData;       // OK: Refers to ::Data
        struct Base::Data* thisData;        // OK: Refers to nested Data
        friend class ::Data;                // OK: global Data is a friend
        friend class Data;                  // OK: nested Data is a friend
        struct Data { /* ... */ };          // Defines nested Data
};

struct Data;                        // OK: Redeclares Data at global scope
struct ::Data;                      // error: cannot introduce a qualified type (7.1.5.3)
struct Base::Data;                  // error: cannot introduce a qualified type (7.1.5.3)
struct Base::Datum;                 // error: Datum undefined
struct Base::Data* pBase;           // OK: refers to nested Data
```

—*end example*]

3.4.5 Class member access   [basic.lookup.classref]

1   In a class member access expression (5.2.5), if the . or -> token is immediately followed by an *identifier* followed by a <, the identifier must be looked up to determine whether the < is the beginning of a template argument list (14.2) or a less-than operator. The identifier is first looked up in the class of the object expression. If the identifier is not found, it is then looked up in the context of the entire *postfix-expression* and shall name a class or function template. If the lookup in the class of the object expression finds a template, the name is also looked up in the context of the entire *postfix-expression* and

— if the name is not found, the name found in the class of the object expression is used, otherwise

— if the name is found in the context of the entire *postfix-expression* and does not name a class template, the name found in the class of the object expression is used, otherwise

— if the name found is a class template, it must refer to the same entity as the one found in the class of the object expression, otherwise the program is ill-formed.

2   If the *id-expression* in a class member access (5.2.5) is an *unqualified-id*, and the type of the object expression is of a class type C (or of pointer to a class type C), the *unqualified-id* is looked up in the scope of class C. If the type of the object expression is of pointer to scalar type, the *unqualified-id* is looked up in the context of the complete *postfix-expression*.

3   If the *unqualified-id* is ˜*type-name*, and the type of the object expression is of a class type C (or of pointer to a class type C), the *type-name* is looked up in the context of the entire *postfix-expression* and in the scope of class C. The *type-name* shall refer to a *class-name*. If *type-name* is found in both contexts, the name shall refer to the same class type. If the type of the object expression is of scalar type, the *type-name* is looked up in the scope of the complete *postfix-expression*.

4   If the *id-expression* in a class member access is a *qualified-id* of the form

```
class-name-or-namespace-name::...
```

the *class-name-or-namespace-name* following the `.` or `->` operator is looked up both in the context of the entire *postfix-expression* and in the scope of the class of the object expression. If the name is found only in the scope of the class of the object expression, the name shall refer to a *class-name*. If the name is found only in the context of the entire *postfix-expression*, the name shall refer to a *class-name* or *namespace-name*. If the name is found in both contexts, the *class-name-or-namespace-name* shall refer to the same entity. [*Note:* the result of looking up the *class-name-or-namespace-name* is not required to be a unique base class of the class type of the object expression, as long as the entity or entities named by the *qualified-id* are members of the class type of the object expression and are not ambiguous according to 10.2.

```
struct A {
        int a;
};
struct B: virtual A { };
struct C: B { };
struct D: B { };
struct E: public C, public D { };
struct F: public A { };

void f() {
        E e;
        e.B::a = 0;              // OK, only one A::a in E

        F f;
        f.A::a = 1;              // OK, A::a is a member of F
}
```

—*end note*]

5   If the *qualified-id* has the form

```
::class-name-or-namespace-name::...
```

the *class-name-or-namespace-name* is looked up in global scope as a *class-name* or *namespace-name*.

6   If the *nested-name-specifier* contains a class *template-id* (14.2), its *template-argument*s are evaluated in the context in which the entire *postfix-expression* occurs.

7   If the *id-expression* is a *conversion-function-id*, its *conversion-type-id* shall denote the same type in both the context in which the entire *postfix-expression* occurs and in the context of the class of the object expression (or the class pointed to by the pointer expression).

3.4.6 Using-directives and namespace aliases   [basic.lookup.udir]

1   When looking up a *namespace-name* in a *using-directive* or *namespace-alias-definition*, only namespace names are considered.

3.5 Program and linkage   [basic.link]

1   A *program* consists of one or more *translation units* (clause 2) linked together. A translation unit consists of a sequence of declarations.

> *translation-unit:*
> *declaration-seq*$_{opt}$

2   A name is said to have *linkage* when it might denote the same object, reference, function, type, template, namespace or value as a name introduced by a declaration in another scope:

— When a name has *external linkage*, the entity it denotes can be referred to by names from scopes of other translation units or from other scopes of the same translation unit.

— When a name has *internal linkage*, the entity it denotes can be referred to by names from other scopes in the same translation unit.

— When a name has *no linkage*, the entity it denotes cannot be referred to by names from other scopes.

3   A name having namespace scope (3.3.5) has internal linkage if it is the name of

— an object, reference, function or function template that is explicitly declared `static` or,

— an object or reference that is explicitly declared `const` and neither explicitly declared `extern` nor previously declared to have external linkage; or

— a data member of an anonymous union.

4   A name having namespace scope has external linkage if it is the name of

— an object or reference, unless it has internal linkage; or

— a function, unless it has internal linkage; or

— a named class (clause 9), or an unnamed class defined in a typedef declaration in which the class has the typedef name for linkage purposes (7.1.3); or

— a named enumeration (7.2), or an unnamed enumeration defined in a typedef declaration in which the enumeration has the typedef name for linkage purposes (7.1.3); or

— an enumerator belonging to an enumeration with external linkage; or

— a template, unless it is a function template that has internal linkage (clause 14); or

— a namespace (7.3), unless it is declared within an unnamed namespace.

5   In addition, a member function, static data member, class or enumeration of class scope has external linkage if the name of the class has external linkage.

6   The name of a function declared in block scope, and the name of an object declared by a block scope `extern` declaration, have linkage. If there is a visible declaration of an entity with linkage having the same name and type, ignoring entities declared outside the innermost enclosing namespace scope, the block scope declaration declares that same entity and receives the linkage of the previous declaration. If there is more than one such matching entity, the program is ill-formed. Otherwise, if no matching entity is found, the block scope entity receives external linkage.
[*Example:*

```
static void f();
static int i = 0;                     //1
void g() {
        extern void f();              // internal linkage
        int i;                        //2: i has no linkage
        {
                extern void f();      // internal linkage
                extern int i;         //3: external linkage
        }
}
```

There are three objects named i in this program. The object with internal linkage introduced by the declaration in global scope (line `//1`), the object with automatic storage duration and no linkage introduced by the declaration on line `//2`, and the object with static storage duration and external linkage introduced by the declaration on line `//3`.]

7   When a block scope declaration of an entity with linkage is not found to refer to some other declaration, then that entity is a member of the innermost enclosing namespace. However such a declaration does not introduce the member name in its namespace scope. [*Example:*

```
namespace X {
        void p()
        {
                q();                    // error: q not yet declared
                extern void q();        // q is a member of namespace X
        }

        void middle()
        {
                q();                    // error: q not yet declared
        }

        void q() { /* ... */ }          // definition of X::q
}

void q() { /* ... */ }                  // some other, unrelated q
```
—*end example*]

8   Names not covered by these rules have no linkage. Moreover, except as noted, a name declared in a local scope (3.3.2) has no linkage. A name with no linkage (notably, the name of a class or enumeration declared in a local scope (3.3.2)) shall not be used to declare an entity with linkage. If a declaration uses a typedef name, it is the linkage of the type name to which the typedef refers that is considered. [*Example:*

```
void f()
{
    struct A { int x; };        // no linkage
    extern A a;                 // ill-formed
    typedef A B;
    extern B b;                 // ill-formed
}
```
—*end example*] This implies that names with no linkage cannot be used as template arguments (14.3).

9   Two names that are the same (clause 3) and that are declared in different scopes shall denote the same object, reference, function, type, enumerator, template or namespace if

— both names have external linkage or else both names have internal linkage and are declared in the same translation unit; and

— both names refer to members of the same namespace or to members, not by inheritance, of the same class; and

— when both names denote functions, the function types are identical for purposes of overloading; and

— when both names denote function templates, the signatures (14.5.5.1) are the same.

10   After all adjustments of types (during which typedefs (7.1.3) are replaced by their definitions), the types specified by all declarations referring to a given object or function shall be identical, except that declarations for an array object can specify array types that differ by the presence or absence of a major array bound (8.3.4). A violation of this rule on type identity does not require a diagnostic.

11   [*Note:* linkage to non-C++ declarations can be achieved using a *linkage-specification* (7.5).]

3.6 Start and termination   **[basic.start]**

3.6.1 Main function   **[basic.start.main]**

1   A program shall contain a global function called `main`, which is the designated start of the program. It is implementation-defined whether a program in a freestanding environment is required to define a `main` function. [*Note:* in a freestanding environment, start-up and termination is implementation-defined; start-up contains the execution of constructors for objects of namespace scope with static storage duration; termination contains the execution of destructors for objects with static storage duration.]

2   An implementation shall not predefine the `main` function. This function shall not be overloaded. It shall have a return type of type `int`, but otherwise its type is implementation-defined. All implementations shall allow both of the following definitions of `main`:

```
int main() { /* ... */ }
```

and

```
int main(int argc, char* argv[]) { /* ... */ }
```

In the latter form `argc` shall be the number of arguments passed to the program from the environment in which the program is run. If `argc` is nonzero these arguments shall be supplied in `argv[0]` through `argv[argc-1]` as pointers to the initial characters of null-terminated multibyte strings (NTMBSs) (17.3.2.1.3.2) and `argv[0]` shall be the pointer to the initial character of a NTMBS that represents the name used to invoke the program or `""`. The value of `argc` shall be nonnegative. The value of `argv[argc]` shall be 0. [*Note:* it is recommended that any further (optional) parameters be added after `argv`.]

3   The function `main` shall not be used (3.2) within a program. The linkage (3.5) of `main` is implementation-defined. A program that declares `main` to be `inline` or `static` is ill-formed. The name `main` is not otherwise reserved. [*Example:* member functions, classes, and enumerations can be called `main`, as can entities in other namespaces.]

4   Calling the function

```
void exit(int);
```

declared in `<cstdlib>` (18.3) terminates the program without leaving the current block and hence without destroying any objects with automatic storage duration (12.4). If `exit` is called to end a program during the destruction of an object with static storage duration, the program has undefined behavior.

5   A return statement in `main` has the effect of leaving the main function (destroying any objects with automatic storage duration) and calling `exit` with the return value as the argument. If control reaches the end of `main` without encountering a `return` statement, the effect is that of executing

```
return 0;
```

3.6.2 Initialization of non-local objects   **[basic.start.init]**

1   Objects with static storage duration (3.7.1) shall be zero-initialized (8.5) before any other initialization takes place. Zero-initialization and initialization with a constant expression are collectively called *static initialization*; all other initialization is *dynamic initialization*. Objects of POD types (3.9) with static storage duration initialized with constant expressions (5.19) shall be initialized before any dynamic initialization takes place. Objects with static storage duration defined in namespace scope in the same translation unit and dynamically initialized shall be initialized in the order in which their definition appears in the translation unit. [*Note:* 8.5.1 describes the order in which aggregate members are initialized. The initialization of local static objects is described in 6.7.]

2   An implementation is permitted to perform the initialization of an object of namespace scope with static storage duration as a static initialization even if such initialization is not required to be done statically,

provided that

— the dynamic version of the initialization does not change the value of any other object of namespace scope with static storage duration prior to its initialization, and

— the static version of the initialization produces the same value in the initialized object as would be produced by the dynamic initialization if all objects not required to be initialized statically were initialized dynamically.

[*Note:* as a consequence, if the initialization of an object `obj1` refers to an object `obj2` of namespace scope with static storage duration potentially requiring dynamic initialization and defined later in the same translation unit, it is unspecified whether the value of `obj2` used will be the value of the fully initialized `obj2` (because `obj2` was statically initialized) or will be the value of `obj2` merely zero-initialized. For example,

```
inline double fd() { return 1.0; }
extern double d1;
double d2 = d1;            // unspecified:
                           // may be statically initialized to 0.0 or
                           // dynamically initialized to 1.0
double d1 = fd();          // may be initialized statically to 1.0
```

—*end note*]

3   It is implementation-defined whether or not the dynamic initialization (8.5, 9.4, 12.1, 12.6.1) of an object of namespace scope is done before the first statement of `main`. If the initialization is deferred to some point in time after the first statement of `main`, it shall occur before the first use of any function or object defined in the same translation unit as the object to be initialized.[31] [*Example:*

```
// – File 1 –
#include "a.h"
#include "b.h"
B b;
A::A(){
        b.Use();
}

// – File 2 –
#include "a.h"
A a;

// – File 3 –
#include "a.h"
#include "b.h"
extern A a;
extern B b;

int main() {
        a.Use();
        b.Use();
}
```

It is implementation-defined whether either a or b is initialized before `main` is entered or whether the initializations are delayed until a is first used in `main`. In particular, if a is initialized before `main` is entered, it is not guaranteed that b will be initialized before it is used by the initialization of a, that is, before A::A is called. If, however, a is initialized at some point after the first statement of `main`, b will be initialized prior to its use in A::A.]

---

[31] An object defined in namespace scope having initialization with side-effects must be initialized even if it is not used (3.7.1).

4   If construction or destruction of a non-local static object ends in throwing an uncaught exception, the result is to call `terminate` (18.6.3.3).

3.6.3 Termination   [basic.start.term]

1   Destructors (12.4) for initialized objects of static storage duration (declared at block scope or at namespace scope) are called as a result of returning from `main` and as a result of calling `exit` (18.3). These objects are destroyed in the reverse order of the completion of their constructor or of the completion of their dynamic initialization. If an object is initialized statically, the object is destroyed in the same order as if the object was dynamically initialized. For an object of array or class type, all subobjects of that object are destroyed before any local object with static storage duration initialized during the construction of the sub-objects is destroyed.

2   If a function contains a local object of static storage duration that has been destroyed and the function is called during the destruction of an object with static storage duration, the program has undefined behavior if the flow of control passes through the definition of the previously destroyed local object.

3   If a function is registered with `atexit` (see `<cstdlib>`, 18.3) then following the call to `exit`, any objects with static storage duration initialized prior to the registration of that function shall not be destroyed until the registered function is called from the termination process and has completed. For an object with static storage duration constructed after a function is registered with `atexit`, then following the call to `exit`, the registered function is not called until the execution of the object's destructor has completed. If `atexit` is called during the construction of an object, the complete object to which it belongs shall be destroyed before the registered function is called.

4   Calling the function

         void abort();

declared in `<cstdlib>` terminates the program without executing destructors for objects of automatic or static storage duration and without calling the functions passed to `atexit()`.

3.7 Storage duration   [basic.stc]

1   Storage duration is the property of an object that defines the minimum potential lifetime of the storage containing the object. The storage duration is determined by the construct used to create the object and is one of the following:

— static storage duration

— automatic storage duration

— dynamic storage duration

2   Static and automatic storage durations are associated with objects introduced by declarations (3.1) and implicitly created by the implementation (12.2). The dynamic storage duration is associated with objects created with `operator new` (5.3.4).

3   The storage class specifiers `static` and `auto` are related to storage duration as described below.

4   The storage duration categories apply to references as well. The lifetime of a reference is its storage duration.

3.7.1 Static storage duration [basic.stc.static]

1   All objects which neither have dynamic storage duration nor are local have *static storage duration*. The storage for these objects shall last for the duration of the program (3.6.2, 3.6.3).

2   If an object of static storage duration has initialization or a destructor with side effects, it shall not be eliminated even if it appears to be unused, except that a class object or its copy may be eliminated as specified in 12.8.

3   The keyword `static` can be used to declare a local variable with static storage duration. [*Note:* 6.7 describes the initialization of local `static` variables; 3.6.3 describes the destruction of local `static` variables.]

4   The keyword `static` applied to a class data member in a class definition gives the data member static storage duration.

3.7.2 Automatic storage duration [basic.stc.auto]

1   Local objects explicitly declared `auto` or `register` or not explicitly declared `static` or `extern` have *automatic storage duration*. The storage for these objects lasts until the block in which they are created exits.

2   [*Note:* these objects are initialized and destroyed as described in 6.7.]

3   If a named automatic object has initialization or a destructor with side effects, it shall not be destroyed before the end of its block, nor shall it be eliminated as an optimization even if it appears to be unused, except that a class object or its copy may be eliminated as specified in 12.8.

3.7.3 Dynamic storage duration [basic.stc.dynamic]

1   Objects can be created dynamically during program execution (1.9), using *new-expression*s (5.3.4), and destroyed using *delete-expression*s (5.3.5). A C++ implementation provides access to, and management of, dynamic storage via the global *allocation functions* `operator new` and `operator new[]` and the global *deallocation functions* `operator delete` and `operator delete[]`.

2   The library provides default definitions for the global allocation and deallocation functions. Some global allocation and deallocation functions are replaceable (18.4.1). A C++ program shall provide at most one definition of a replaceable allocation or deallocation function. Any such function definition replaces the default version provided in the library (17.4.3.4). The following allocation and deallocation functions (18.4) are implicitly declared in global scope in each translation unit of a program

```
void* operator new(std::size_t) throw(std::bad_alloc);
void* operator new[](std::size_t) throw(std::bad_alloc);
void operator delete(void*) throw();
void operator delete[](void*) throw();
```

These implicit declarations introduce only the function names `operator new`, `operator new[]`, `operator delete`, `operator delete[]`. [*Note:* the implicit declarations do not introduce the names `std`, `std::bad_alloc`, and `std::size_t`, or any other names that the library uses to declare these names. Thus, a *new-expression*, *delete-expression* or function call that refers to one of these functions without including the header `<new>` is well-formed. However, referring to `std`, `std::bad_alloc`, and `std::size_t` is ill-formed unless the name has been declared by including the appropriate header.] Allocation and/or deallocation functions can also be declared and defined for any class (12.5).

3   Any allocation and/or deallocation functions defined in a C++ program, including the default versions in the library, shall conform to the semantics specified in 3.7.3.1 and 3.7.3.2.

3.7.3.1 Allocation functions   [basic.stc.dynamic.allocation]

1   An allocation function shall be a class member function or a global function; a program is ill-formed if an allocation function is declared in a namespace scope other than global scope or declared static in global scope. The return type shall be `void*`. The first parameter shall have type `size_t` (18.1). The first parameter shall not have an associated default argument (8.3.6). The value of the first parameter shall be interpreted as the requested size of the allocation. An allocation function can be a function template. Such a template shall declare its return type and first parameter as specified above (that is, template parameter types shall not be used in the return type and first parameter type). Template allocation functions shall have two or more parameters.

2   The allocation function attempts to allocate the requested amount of storage. If it is successful, it shall return the address of the start of a block of storage whose length in bytes shall be at least as large as the requested size. There are no constraints on the contents of the allocated storage on return from the allocation function. The order, contiguity, and initial value of storage allocated by successive calls to an allocation function is unspecified. The pointer returned shall be suitably aligned so that it can be converted to a pointer of any complete object type and then used to access the object or array in the storage allocated (until the storage is explicitly deallocated by a call to a corresponding deallocation function). Even if the size of the space requested is zero, the request can fail. If the request succeeds, the value returned shall be a non-null pointer value (4.10) p0 different from any previously returned value p1, unless that value p1 was subsequently passed to an `operator delete`. The effect of dereferencing a pointer returned as a request for zero size is undefined.[32]

3   An allocation function that fails to allocate storage can invoke the currently installed `new_handler` (18.4.2.2), if any. [*Note:* A program-supplied allocation function can obtain the address of the currently installed `new_handler` using the `set_new_handler` function (18.4.2.3).] If an allocation function declared with an empty *exception-specification* (15.4), `throw()`, fails to allocate storage, it shall return a null pointer. Any other allocation function that fails to allocate storage shall only indicate failure by throwing an exception of class `std::bad_alloc` (18.4.2.1) or a class derived from `std::bad_alloc`.

4   A global allocation function is only called as the result of a new expression (5.3.4), or called directly using the function call syntax (5.2.2), or called indirectly through calls to the functions in the C++ standard library. [*Note:* in particular, a global allocation function is not called to allocate storage for objects with static storage duration (3.7.1), for objects of type `type_info` (5.2.8), for the copy of an object thrown by a `throw` expression (15.1).]

3.7.3.2 Deallocation functions   [basic.stc.dynamic.deallocation]

1   Deallocation functions shall be class member functions or global functions; a program is ill-formed if deallocation functions are declared in a namespace scope other than global scope or declared static in global scope.

2   Each deallocation function shall return `void` and its first parameter shall be `void*`. A deallocation function can have more than one parameter. If a class T has a member deallocation function named `operator delete` with exactly one parameter, then that function is a usual (non-placement) deallocation function. If class T does not declare such an `operator delete` but does declare a member deallocation function named `operator delete` with exactly two parameters, the second of which has type `std::size_t` (18.1), then this function is a usual deallocation function. Similarly, if a class T has a member deallocation function named `operator delete[]` with exactly one parameter, then that function is a usual (non-placement) deallocation function. If class T does not declare such an `operator delete[]` but does declare a member deallocation function named `operator delete[]` with exactly two parameters, the second of which has type `std::size_t`, then this function is a usual deallocation function. A deallocation function can be an instance of a function template. Neither the first parameter nor the return type shall

---

[32] The intent is to have `operator new()` implementable by calling `malloc()` or `calloc()`, so the rules are substantially the same. C++ differs from C in requiring a zero request to return a non-null pointer.

depend on a template parameter. [*Note:* that is, a deallocation function template shall have a first parameter of type `void*` and a return type of `void` (as specified above).] A deallocation function template shall have two or more function parameters. A template instance is never a usual deallocation function, regardless of its signature.

3   The value of the first argument supplied to one of the deallocation functions provided in the standard library may be a null pointer value; if so, the call to the deallocation function has no effect. Otherwise, the value supplied to `operator delete(void*)` in the standard library shall be one of the values returned by a previous invocation of either `operator new(size_t)` or `operator new(size_t, const std::nothrow_t&)` in the standard library, and the value supplied to `operator delete[](void*)` in the standard library shall be one of the values returned by a previous invocation of either `operator new[](size_t)` or `operator new[](size_t, const std::nothrow_t&)` in the standard library.

4   If the argument given to a deallocation function in the standard library is a pointer that is not the null pointer value (4.10), the deallocation function shall deallocate the storage referenced by the pointer, rendering invalid all pointers referring to any part of the *deallocated storage.* The effect of using an invalid pointer value (including passing it to a deallocation function) is undefined.[33)

3.7.4 Duration of sub-objects   [basic.stc.inherit]

1   The storage duration of member subobjects, base class subobjects and array elements is that of their complete object (1.8).

3.8 Object Lifetime   [basic.life]

1   The *lifetime* of an object is a runtime property of the object. The lifetime of an object of type `T` begins when:

— storage with the proper alignment and size for type `T` is obtained, and

— if `T` is a class type with a non-trivial constructor (12.1), the constructor call has completed.

The lifetime of an object of type `T` ends when:

— if `T` is a class type with a non-trivial destructor (12.4), the destructor call starts, or

— the storage which the object occupies is reused or released.

2   [*Note:* the lifetime of an array object or of an object of POD type (3.9) starts as soon as storage with proper size and alignment is obtained, and its lifetime ends when the storage which the array or object occupies is reused or released. 12.6.2 describes the lifetime of base and member subobjects.]

3   The properties ascribed to objects throughout this International Standard apply for a given object only during its lifetime. [*Note:* in particular, before the lifetime of an object starts and after its lifetime ends there are significant restrictions on the use of the object, as described below, in 12.6.2 and in 12.7. Also, the behavior of an object under construction and destruction might not be the same as the behavior of an object whose lifetime has started and not ended. 12.6.2 and 12.7 describe the behavior of objects during the construction and destruction phases.]

4   A program may end the lifetime of any object by reusing the storage which the object occupies or by explicitly calling the destructor for an object of a class type with a non-trivial destructor. For an object of a class type with a non-trivial destructor, the program is not required to call the destructor explicitly before the storage which the object occupies is reused or released; however, if there is no explicit call to the destructor or if a *delete-expression* (5.3.5) is not used to release the storage, the destructor shall not be implicitly called and any program that depends on the side effects produced by the destructor has undefined behavior.

[33) On some implementations, it causes a system-generated runtime fault.

5 Before the lifetime of an object has started but after the storage which the object will occupy has been allocated[34] or, after the lifetime of an object has ended and before the storage which the object occupied is reused or released, any pointer that refers to the storage location where the object will be or was located may be used but only in limited ways. Such a pointer refers to allocated storage (3.7.3.2), and using the pointer as if the pointer were of type void*, is well-defined. Such a pointer may be dereferenced but the resulting lvalue may only be used in limited ways, as described below. If the object will be or was of a class type with a non-trivial destructor, and the pointer is used as the operand of a *delete-expression*, the program has undefined behavior. If the object will be or was of a non-POD class type, the program has undefined behavior if:

— the pointer is used to access a non-static data member or call a non-static member function of the object, or

— the pointer is implicitly converted (4.10) to a pointer to a base class type, or

— the pointer is used as the operand of a static_cast (5.2.9) (except when the conversion is to void*, or to void* and subsequently to char*, or unsigned char*).

— the pointer is used as the operand of a dynamic_cast (5.2.7). [*Example:*

```
struct B {
        virtual void f();
        void mutate();
        virtual ~B();
};

struct D1 : B { void f(); };
struct D2 : B { void f(); };

void B::mutate() {
        new (this) D2;          // reuses storage – ends the lifetime of *this
        f();                    // undefined behavior
        ... = this;             // OK, this points to valid memory
}

void g() {
        void* p = malloc(sizeof(D1) + sizeof(D2));
        B* pb = new (p) D1;
        pb->mutate();
        &pb;                    // OK: pb points to valid memory
        void* q = pb;           // OK: pb points to valid memory
        pb->f();                // undefined behavior, lifetime of *pb has ended
}
```

—*end example*]

6 Similarly, before the lifetime of an object has started but after the storage which the object will occupy has been allocated or, after the lifetime of an object has ended and before the storage which the object occupied is reused or released, any lvalue which refers to the original object may be used but only in limited ways. Such an lvalue refers to allocated storage (3.7.3.2), and using the properties of the lvalue which do not depend on its value is well-defined. If an lvalue-to-rvalue conversion (4.1) is applied to such an lvalue, the program has undefined behavior; if the original object will be or was of a non-POD class type, the program has undefined behavior if:

— the lvalue is used to access a non-static data member or call a non-static member function of the object, or

— the lvalue is implicitly converted (4.10) to a reference to a base class type, or

---

[34] For example, before the construction of a global object of non-POD class type (12.7).

— the lvalue is used as the operand of a `static_cast` (5.2.9) (except when the conversion is ultimately to `char&` or `unsigned char&`), or

— the lvalue is used as the operand of a `dynamic_cast` (5.2.7) or as the operand of `typeid`.

7 If, after the lifetime of an object has ended and before the storage which the object occupied is reused or released, a new object is created at the storage location which the original object occupied, a pointer that pointed to the original object, a reference that referred to the original object, or the name of the original object will automatically refer to the new object and, once the lifetime of the new object has started, can be used to manipulate the new object, if:

— the storage for the new object exactly overlays the storage location which the original object occupied, and

— the new object is of the same type as the original object (ignoring the top-level cv-qualifiers), and

— the type of the original object is not const-qualified, and, if a class type, does not contain any non-static data member whose type is const-qualified or a reference type, and

— the original object was a most derived object (1.8) of type `T` and the new object is a most derived object of type `T` (that is, they are not base class subobjects). [*Example:*

```
struct C {
        int i;
        void f();
        const C& operator=( const C& );
};

const C& C::operator=( const C& other)
{
        if ( this != &other ) {
                this->~C();              // lifetime of *this ends
                new (this) C(other);     // new object of type C created
                f();                     // well-defined
        }
        return *this;
}

C c1;
C c2;
c1 = c2;                                 // well-defined
c1.f();                                  // well-defined; c1 refers to a new object of type C
```

—*end example*]

8 If a program ends the lifetime of an object of type `T` with static (3.7.1) or automatic (3.7.2) storage duration and if `T` has a non-trivial destructor,[35] the program must ensure that an object of the original type occupies that same storage location when the implicit destructor call takes place; otherwise the behavior of the program is undefined. This is true even if the block is exited with an exception. [*Example:*

```
class T { };
struct B {
        ~B();
};
```

---

[35] that is, an object for which a destructor will be called implicitly—either either upon exit from the block for an object with automatic storage duration or upon exit from the program for an object with static storage duration.

```
void h() {
        B b;
        new (&b) T;
}                                    // undefined behavior at block exit
```
—end example]

9   Creating a new object at the storage location that a `const` object with static or automatic storage duration occupies or, at the storage location that such a `const` object used to occupy before its lifetime ended results in undefined behavior. [*Example:*

```
struct B {
        B();
        ~B();
};

const B b;

void h() {
        b.~B();
        new (&b) const B;          // undefined behavior
}
```
—end example]

3.9 Types   **[basic.types]**

1   [*Note:* 3.9 and the subclauses thereof impose requirements on implementations regarding the representation of types. There are two kinds of types: fundamental types and compound types. Types describe objects (1.8), references (8.3.2), or functions (8.3.5).]

2   For any object (other than a base-class subobject) of POD type T, whether or not the object holds a valid value of type T, the underlying bytes (1.7) making up the object can be copied into an array of `char` or `unsigned char`.[36] If the content of the array of `char` or `unsigned char` is copied back into the object, the object shall subsequently hold its original value. [*Example:*

```
#define N sizeof(T)
char buf[N];
T obj;                         // obj initialized to its original value
memcpy(buf, &obj, N);          // between these two calls to memcpy,
                               // obj might be modified
memcpy(&obj, buf, N);          // at this point, each subobject of obj of scalar type
                               // holds its original value
```
—end example]

3   For any POD type T, if two pointers to T point to distinct T objects obj1 and obj2, where neither obj1 nor obj2 is a base-class subobject, if the value of obj1 is copied into obj2, using the `memcpy` library function, obj2 shall subsequently hold the same value as obj1. [*Example:*

```
T* t1p;
T* t2p;
                               // provided that t2p points to an initialized object ...
memcpy(t1p, t2p, sizeof(T));   // at this point, every subobject of POD type in *t1p contains
                               // the same value as the corresponding subobject in *t2p
```
—end example]

---

[36] By using, for example, the library functions (17.4.1.2) memcpy or memmove.

4   The *object representation* of an object of type T is the sequence of N unsigned char objects taken up by the object of type T, where N equals sizeof(T). The *value representation* of an object is the set of bits that hold the value of type T. For POD types, the value representation is a set of bits in the object representation that determines a *value*, which is one discrete element of an implementation-defined set of values.[37]

5   Object types have *alignment requirements* (3.9.1, 3.9.2). The *alignment* of a complete object type is an implementation-defined integer value representing a number of bytes; an object is allocated at an address that meets the alignment requirements of its object type.

6   A class that has been declared but not defined, or an array of unknown size or of incomplete element type, is an incompletely-defined object type.[38] Incompletely-defined object types and the void types are incomplete types (3.9.1). Objects shall not be defined to have an incomplete type.

7   A class type (such as "class X") might be incomplete at one point in a translation unit and complete later on; the type "class X" is the same type at both points. The declared type of an array object might be an array of incomplete class type and therefore incomplete; if the class type is completed later on in the translation unit, the array type becomes complete; the array type at those two points is the same type. The declared type of an array object might be an array of unknown size and therefore be incomplete at one point in a translation unit and complete later on; the array types at those two points ("array of unknown bound of T" and "array of N T") are different types. The type of a pointer to array of unknown size, or of a type defined by a typedef declaration to be an array of unknown size, cannot be completed. [*Example:*

```
class X;                    // X is an incomplete type
extern X* xp;               // xp is a pointer to an incomplete type
extern int arr[];           // the type of arr is incomplete
typedef int UNKA[];         // UNKA is an incomplete type
UNKA* arrp;                 // arrp is a pointer to an incomplete type
UNKA** arrpp;

void foo()
{
    xp++;                   // ill-formed: X is incomplete
    arrp++;                 // ill-formed: incomplete type
    arrpp++;                // OK: sizeof UNKA* is known
}

struct X { int i; };        // now X is a complete type
int  arr[10];               // now the type of arr is complete

X x;
void bar()
{
    xp = &x;                // OK; type is "pointer to X"
    arrp = &arr;            // ill-formed: different types
    xp++;                   // OK: X is complete
    arrp++;                 // ill-formed: UNKA can't be completed
}
```

—*end example*]

8   [*Note:* the rules for declarations and expressions describe in which contexts incomplete types are prohibited.]

9   An *object type* is a (possibly cv-qualified) type that is not a function type, not a reference type, and not a void type.

---

[37] The intent is that the memory model of C++ is compatible with that of ISO/IEC 9899 Programming Language C.

[38] The size and layout of an instance of an incompletely-defined object type is unknown.

10   Arithmetic types (3.9.1), enumeration types, pointer types, and pointer to member types (3.9.2), and *cv-qualified* versions of these types (3.9.3) are collectively called *scalar types*. Scalar types, POD-struct types, POD-union types (clause 9), arrays of such types and *cv-qualified* versions of these types (3.9.3) are collectively called *POD types*.

11   If two types T1 and T2 are the same type, then T1 and T2 are *layout-compatible* types. [*Note:* Layout-compatible enumerations are described in 7.2. Layout-compatible POD-structs and POD-unions are described in 9.2.]

3.9.1 Fundamental types   [basic.fundamental]

1   Objects declared as characters (char) shall be large enough to store any member of the implementation's basic character set. If a character from this set is stored in a character object, the integral value of that character object is equal to the value of the single character literal form of that character. It is implementation-defined whether a char object can hold negative values. Characters can be explicitly declared unsigned or signed. Plain char, signed char, and unsigned char are three distinct types. A char, a signed char, and an unsigned char occupy the same amount of storage and have the same alignment requirements (3.9); that is, they have the same object representation. For character types, all bits of the object representation participate in the value representation. For unsigned character types, all possible bit patterns of the value representation represent numbers. These requirements do not hold for other types. In any particular implementation, a plain char object can take on either the same values as a signed char or an unsigned char; which one is implementation-defined.

2   There are four *signed integer types*: "signed char", "short int", "int", and "long int." In this list, each type provides at least as much storage as those preceding it in the list. Plain ints have the natural size suggested by the architecture of the execution environment[39]; the other signed integer types are provided to meet special needs.

3   For each of the signed integer types, there exists a corresponding (but different) *unsigned integer type*: "unsigned char", "unsigned short int", "unsigned int", and "unsigned long int," each of which occupies the same amount of storage and has the same alignment requirements (3.9) as the corresponding signed integer type[40]; that is, each signed integer type has the same object representation as its corresponding unsigned integer type. The range of nonnegative values of a *signed integer* type is a subrange of the corresponding *unsigned integer* type, and the value representation of each corresponding signed/unsigned type shall be the same.

4   Unsigned integers, declared unsigned, shall obey the laws of arithmetic modulo 2^n where n is the number of bits in the value representation of that particular size of integer.[41]

5   Type wchar_t is a distinct type whose values can represent distinct codes for all members of the largest extended character set specified among the supported locales (22.1.1). Type wchar_t shall have the same size, signedness, and alignment requirements (3.9) as one of the other integral types, called its *underlying type*.

6   Values of type bool are either true or false.[42] [*Note:* there are no signed, unsigned, short, or long bool types or values.] As described below, bool values behave as integral types. Values of type bool participate in integral promotions (4.5).

---

[39] that is, large enough to contain any value in the range of INT_MIN and INT_MAX, as defined in the header <climits>.
[40] See 7.1.5.2 regarding the correspondence between types and the sequences of *type-specifiers* that designate them.
[41] This implies that unsigned arithmetic does not overflow because a result that cannot be represented by the resulting unsigned integer type is reduced modulo the number that is one greater than the largest value that can be represented by the resulting unsigned integer type.
[42] Using a bool value in ways described by this International Standard as "undefined," such as by examining the value of an uninitialized automatic variable, might cause it to behave as if it is neither true nor false.

7   Types bool, char, wchar_t, and the signed and unsigned integer types are collectively called *integral* types.[43] A synonym for integral type is *integer type*. The representations of integral types shall define values by use of a pure binary numeration system.[44] [*Example:* this International Standard permits 2's complement, 1's complement and signed magnitude representations for integral types.]

8   There are three *floating point* types: float, double, and long double. The type double provides at least as much precision as float, and the type long double provides at least as much precision as double. The set of values of the type float is a subset of the set of values of the type double; the set of values of the type double is a subset of the set of values of the type long double. The value representation of floating-point types is implementation-defined. *Integral* and *floating* types are collectively called *arithmetic* types. Specializations of the standard template numeric_limits (18.2) shall specify the maximum and minimum values of each arithmetic type for an implementation.

9   The void type has an empty set of values. The void type is an incomplete type that cannot be completed. It is used as the return type for functions that do not return a value. Any expression can be explicitly converted to type *cv* void (5.4). An expression of type void shall be used only as an expression statement (6.2), as an operand of a comma expression (5.18), as a second or third operand of ? : (5.16), as the operand of typeid, or as the expression in a return statement (6.6.3) for a function with the return type void.

10   [*Note:* even if the implementation defines two or more basic types to have the same value representation, they are nevertheless different types.]

3.9.2 Compound types   [basic.compound]

1   Compound types can be constructed in the following ways:

— *arrays* of objects of a given type, 8.3.4;

— *functions*, which have parameters of given types and return void or references or objects of a given type, 8.3.5;

— *pointers* to void or objects or functions (including static members of classes) of a given type, 8.3.1;

— *references* to objects or functions of a given type, 8.3.2;

— *classes* containing a sequence of objects of various types (clause 9), a set of types, enumerations and functions for manipulating these objects (9.3), and a set of restrictions on the access to these entities (clause 11);

— *unions*, which are classes capable of containing objects of different types at different times, 9.5;

— *enumerations*, which comprise a set of named constant values. Each distinct enumeration constitutes a different *enumerated type*, 7.2;

— *pointers to non-static*[45] *class members*, which identify members of a given type within objects of a given class, 8.3.3.

2   These methods of constructing types can be applied recursively; restrictions are mentioned in 8.3.1, 8.3.4, 8.3.5, and 8.3.2.

3   A pointer to objects of type T is referred to as a "pointer to T." [*Example:* a pointer to an object of type int is referred to as "pointer to int" and a pointer to an object of class X is called a "pointer to X."] Except for pointers to static members, text referring to "pointers" does not apply to pointers to members. Pointers to

---

[43] Therefore, enumerations (7.2) are not integral; however, enumerations can be promoted to int, unsigned int, long, or unsigned long, as specified in 4.5.

[44] A positional representation for integers that uses the binary digits 0 and 1, in which the values represented by successive bits are additive, begin with 1, and are multiplied by successive integral power of 2, except perhaps for the bit with the highest position. (Adapted from the *American National Dictionary for Information Processing Systems*.)

[45] Static class members are objects or functions, and pointers to them are ordinary pointers to objects or functions.

incomplete types are allowed although there are restrictions on what can be done with them (3.9). A valid value of an object pointer type represents either the address of a byte in memory (1.7) or a null pointer (4.10). If an object of type T is located at an address A, a pointer of type *cv* T* whose value is the address A is said to *point to* that object, regardless of how the value was obtained. [*Note:* for instance, the address one past the end of an array (5.7) would be considered to point to an unrelated object of the array's element type that might be located at that address.] The value representation of pointer types is implementation-defined. Pointers to cv-qualified and cv-unqualified versions (3.9.3) of layout-compatible types shall have the same value representation and alignment requirements (3.9).

4   Objects of cv-qualified (3.9.3) or cv-unqualified type void* (pointer to void), can be used to point to objects of unknown type. A void* shall be able to hold any object pointer. A cv-qualified or cv-unqualified (3.9.3) void* shall have the same representation and alignment requirements as a cv-qualified or cv-unqualified char*.

3.9.3 CV-qualifiers   [basic.type.qualifier]

1   A type mentioned in 3.9.1 and 3.9.2 is a *cv-unqualified type*. Each type which is a cv-unqualified complete or incomplete object type or is void (3.9) has three corresponding cv-qualified versions of its type: a *const-qualified* version, a *volatile-qualified* version, and a *const-volatile-qualified* version. The term *object type* (1.8) includes the cv-qualifiers specified when the object is created. The presence of a const specifier in a *decl-specifier-seq* declares an object of *const-qualified object type*; such object is called a *const object*. The presence of a volatile specifier in a *decl-specifier-seq* declares an object of *volatile-qualified object type*; such object is called a *volatile object*. The presence of both *cv-qualifiers* in a *decl-specifier-seq* declares an object of *const-volatile-qualified object type*; such object is called a *const volatile object*. The cv-qualified or cv-unqualified versions of a type are distinct types; however, they shall have the same representation and alignment requirements (3.9).[46]

2   A compound type (3.9.2) is not cv-qualified by the cv-qualifiers (if any) of the types from which it is compounded. Any cv-qualifiers applied to an array type affect the array element type, not the array type (8.3.4).

3   Each non-static, non-mutable, non-reference data member of a const-qualified class object is const-qualified, each non-static, non-reference data member of a volatile-qualified class object is volatile-qualified and similarly for members of a const-volatile class. See 8.3.5 and 9.3.2 regarding cv-qualified function types.

4   There is a (partial) ordering on cv-qualifiers, so that a type can be said to be *more cv-qualified* than another. Table 6 shows the relations that constitute this ordering.

Table 6—relations on const and volatile

no cv-qualifier	<	const
no cv-qualifier	<	volatile
no cv-qualifier	<	const volatile
const	<	const volatile
volatile	<	const volatile

5   In this International Standard, the notation *cv* (or *cv1*, *cv2*, etc.), used in the description of types, represents an arbitrary set of cv-qualifiers, i.e., one of {const}, {volatile}, {const, volatile}, or the empty set. Cv-qualifiers applied to an array type attach to the underlying element type, so the notation "*cv* T," where T is an array type, refers to an array whose elements are so-qualified. Such array types can be said to be more (or less) cv-qualified than other types based on the cv-qualification of the underlying

---

[46] The same representation and alignment requirements are meant to imply interchangeability as arguments to functions, return values from functions, and members of unions.

element types.

3.10 Lvalues and rvalues [basic.lval]

1   Every expression is either an *lvalue* or an *rvalue*.

2   An lvalue refers to an object or function. Some rvalue expressions—those of class or cv-qualified class type—also refer to objects.[47]

3   [*Note:* some built-in operators and function calls yield lvalues. [*Example:* if E is an expression of pointer type, then `*E` is an lvalue expression referring to the object or function to which E points. As another example, the function

```
int& f();
```

yields an lvalue, so the call `f()` is an lvalue expression.]]

4   [*Note:* some built-in operators expect lvalue operands. [*Example:* built-in assignment operators all expect their left hand operands to be lvalues.] Other built-in operators yield rvalues, and some expect them. [*Example:* the unary and binary + operators expect rvalue arguments and yield rvalue results.] The discussion of each built-in operator in clause 5 indicates whether it expects lvalue operands and whether it yields an lvalue.]

5   The result of calling a function that does not return a reference is an rvalue. User defined operators are functions, and whether such operators expect or yield lvalues is determined by their parameter and return types.

6   An expression which holds a temporary object resulting from a cast to a nonreference type is an rvalue (this includes the explicit creation of an object using functional notation (5.2.3)).

7   Whenever an lvalue appears in a context where an rvalue is expected, the lvalue is converted to an rvalue; see 4.1, 4.2, and 4.3.

8   The discussion of reference initialization in 8.5.3 and of temporaries in 12.2 indicates the behavior of lvalues and rvalues in other significant contexts.

9   Class rvalues can have cv-qualified types; non-class rvalues always have cv-unqualified types. Rvalues shall always have complete types or the `void` type; in addition to these types, lvalues can also have incomplete types.

10   An lvalue for an object is necessary in order to modify the object except that an rvalue of class type can also be used to modify its referent under certain circumstances. [*Example:* a member function called for an object (9.3) can modify the object.]

11   Functions cannot be modified, but pointers to functions can be modifiable.

12   A pointer to an incomplete type can be modifiable. At some point in the program when the pointed to type is complete, the object at which the pointer points can also be modified.

13   The referent of a `const`-qualified expression shall not be modified (through that expression), except that if it is of class type and has a `mutable` component, that component can be modified (7.1.5.1).

14   If an expression can be used to modify the object to which it refers, the expression is called *modifiable*. A program that attempts to modify an object through a nonmodifiable lvalue or rvalue expression is ill-formed.

15   If a program attempts to access the stored value of an object through an lvalue of other than one of the following types the behavior is undefined[48]:

---

[47] Expressions such as invocations of constructors and of functions that return a class type refer to objects, and the implementation can invoke a member function upon such objects, but the expressions are not lvalues.
[48] The intent of this list is to specify those circumstances in which an object may or may not be aliased.

— the dynamic type of the object,

— a cv-qualified version of the dynamic type of the object,

— a type that is the signed or unsigned type corresponding to the dynamic type of the object,

— a type that is the signed or unsigned type corresponding to a cv-qualified version of the dynamic type of the object,

— an aggregate or union type that includes one of the aforementioned types among its members (including, recursively, a member of a subaggregate or contained union),

— a type that is a (possibly cv-qualified) base class type of the dynamic type of the object,

— a `char` or `unsigned char` type.

4 Standard conversions [conv]

1   Standard conversions are implicit conversions defined for built-in types. Clause 4 enumerates the full set of such conversions. A *standard conversion sequence* is a sequence of standard conversions in the following order:

— Zero or one conversion from the following set: lvalue-to-rvalue conversion, array-to-pointer conversion, and function-to-pointer conversion.

— Zero or one conversion from the following set: integral promotions, floating point promotion, integral conversions, floating point conversions, floating-integral conversions, pointer conversions, pointer to member conversions, and boolean conversions.

— Zero or one qualification conversion.

[*Note:* a standard conversion sequence can be empty, i.e., it can consist of no conversions.] A standard conversion sequence will be applied to an expression if necessary to convert it to a required destination type.

2   [*Note:* expressions with a given type will be implicitly converted to other types in several contexts:

— When used as operands of operators. The operator's requirements for its operands dictate the destination type (clause 5).

— When used in the condition of an `if` statement or iteration statement (6.4, 6.5). The destination type is `bool`.

— When used in the expression of a `switch` statement. The destination type is integral (6.4).

— When used as the source expression for an initialization (which includes use as an argument in a function call and use as the expression in a `return` statement). The type of the entity being initialized is (generally) the destination type. See 8.5, 8.5.3.

—*end note*]

3   An expression e can be *implicitly converted* to a type `T` if and only if the declaration "`T t=e;`" is well-formed, for some invented temporary variable `t` (8.5). The effect of the implicit conversion is the same as performing the declaration and initialization and then using the temporary variable as the result of the conversion. The result is an lvalue if `T` is a reference type (8.3.2), and an rvalue otherwise. The expression e is used as an lvalue if and only if the initialization uses it as an lvalue.

4   [*Note:* For user-defined types, user-defined conversions are considered as well; see 12.3. In general, an implicit conversion sequence (13.3.3.1) consists of a standard conversion sequence followed by a user-defined conversion followed by another standard conversion sequence.

5   There are some contexts where certain conversions are suppressed. For example, the lvalue-to-rvalue conversion is not done on the operand of the unary & operator. Specific exceptions are given in the descriptions of those operators and contexts.]

4.1 Lvalue-to-rvalue conversion   [conv.lval]

1   An lvalue (3.10) of a non-function, non-array type T can be converted to an rvalue. If T is an incomplete type, a program that necessitates this conversion is ill-formed. If the object to which the lvalue refers is not an object of type T and is not an object of a type derived from T, or if the object is uninitialized, a program that necessitates this conversion has undefined behavior. If T is a non-class type, the type of the rvalue is the cv-unqualified version of T. Otherwise, the type of the rvalue is T. [49]

2   The value contained in the object indicated by the lvalue is the rvalue result. When an lvalue-to-rvalue conversion occurs within the operand of sizeof (5.3.3) the value contained in the referenced object is not accessed, since that operator does not evaluate its operand.

3   [*Note:* See also 3.10.]

4.2 Array-to-pointer conversion   [conv.array]

1   An lvalue or rvalue of type "array of N T" or "array of unknown bound of T" can be converted to an rvalue of type "pointer to T." The result is a pointer to the first element of the array.

2   A string literal (2.13.4) that is not a wide string literal can be converted to an rvalue of type "pointer to char"; a wide string literal can be converted to an rvalue of type "pointer to wchar_t". In either case, the result is a pointer to the first element of the array. This conversion is considered only when there is an explicit appropriate pointer target type, and not when there is a general need to convert from an lvalue to an rvalue. [*Note:* this conversion is deprecated. See Annex D.] For the purpose of ranking in overload resolution (13.3.3.1.1), this conversion is considered an array-to-pointer conversion followed by a qualification conversion (4.4). [*Example:* "abc" is converted to "pointer to const char" as an array-to-pointer conversion, and then to "pointer to char" as a qualification conversion.]

4.3 Function-to-pointer conversion   [conv.func]

1   An lvalue of function type T can be converted to an rvalue of type "pointer to T." The result is a pointer to the function.[50]

2   [*Note:* See 13.4 for additional rules for the case where the function is overloaded.]

4.4 Qualification conversions   [conv.qual]

1   An rvalue of type "pointer to *cv1* T" can be converted to an rvalue of type "pointer to *cv2* T" if "*cv2* T" is more cv-qualified than "*cv1* T."

2   An rvalue of type "pointer to member of X of type *cv1* T" can be converted to an rvalue of type "pointer to member of X of type *cv2* T" if "*cv2* T" is more cv-qualified than "*cv1* T."

3   [*Note:* Function types (including those used in pointer to member function types) are never cv-qualified (8.3.5).]

4   A conversion can add cv-qualifiers at levels other than the first in multi-level pointers, subject to the following rules:[51]

Two pointer types T1 and T2 are *similar* if there exists a type *T* and integer $n > 0$ such that:

$$T1 \text{ is } cv_{1,0} \text{ pointer to } cv_{1,1} \text{ pointer to } \cdots cv_{1,n-1} \text{ pointer to } cv_{1,n} \ T$$

and

---

[49] In C++ class rvalues can have cv-qualified types (because they are objects). This differs from ISO C, in which non-lvalues never have cv-qualified types.

[50] This conversion never applies to nonstatic member functions because an lvalue that refers to a nonstatic member function cannot be obtained.

[51] These rules ensure that const-safety is preserved by the conversion.

$T2$ is $cv_{2,0}$ pointer to $cv_{2,1}$ pointer to $\cdots$ $cv_{2,n-1}$ pointer to $cv_{2,n}$ T

where each $cv_{i,j}$ is const, volatile, const volatile, or nothing. The n-tuple of cv-qualifiers after the first in a pointer type, e.g., $cv_{1,1}$, $cv_{1,2}$, $\cdots$, $cv_{1,n}$ in the pointer type T1, is called the *cv-qualification signature* of the pointer type. An expression of type $T1$ can be converted to type $T2$ if and only if the following conditions are satisfied:

— the pointer types are similar.

— for every $j > 0$, if const is in $cv_{1,j}$ then const is in $cv_{2,j}$, and similarly for volatile.

— if the $cv_{1,j}$ and $cv_{2,j}$ are different, then const is in every $cv_{2,k}$ for $0 < k < j$.

[*Note:* if a program could assign a pointer of type T** to a pointer of type const T** (that is, if line //1 below was allowed), a program could inadvertently modify a const object (as it is done on line //2). For example,

```
int main() {
        const char c = 'c';
        char* pc;
        const char** pcc = &pc;         //1: not allowed
        *pcc = &c;
        *pc = 'C';                      //2: modifies a const object
}
```

—*end note*]

5   A *multi-level* pointer to member type, or a *multi-level mixed* pointer and pointer to member type has the form:

$$cv_0 P_0 \text{ to } cv_1 P_1 \text{ to } \cdots cv_{n-1} P_{n-1} \text{ to } cv_n T$$

where P_i is either a pointer or pointer to member and where T is not a pointer type or pointer to member type.

6   Two multi-level pointer to member types or two multi-level mixed pointer and pointer to member types T1 and T2 are *similar* if there exists a type T and integer $n > 0$ such that:

$$T1 \text{ is } cv_{1,0} P_0 \text{ to } cv_{1,1} P_1 \text{ to } \cdots cv_{1,n-1} P_{n-1} \text{ to } cv_{1,n} T$$

and

$$T2 \text{ is } cv_{2,0} P_0 \text{ to } cv_{2,1} P_1 \text{ to } \cdots cv_{2,n-1} P_{n-1} \text{ to } cv_{2,n} T$$

7   For similar multi-level pointer to member types and similar multi-level mixed pointer and pointer to member types, the rules for adding cv-qualifiers are the same as those used for similar pointer types.

4.5 Integral promotions   [conv.prom]

1   An rvalue of type char, signed char, unsigned char, short int, or unsigned short int can be converted to an rvalue of type int if int can represent all the values of the source type; otherwise, the source rvalue can be converted to an rvalue of type unsigned int.

2   An rvalue of type wchar_t (3.9.1) or an enumeration type (7.2) can be converted to an rvalue of the first of the following types that can represent all the values of its underlying type: int, unsigned int, long, or unsigned long.

3   An rvalue for an integral bit-field (9.6) can be converted to an rvalue of type int if int can represent all the values of the bit-field; otherwise, it can be converted to unsigned int if unsigned int can represent all the values of the bit-field. If the bit-field is larger yet, no integral promotion applies to it. If the bit-field has an enumerated type, it is treated as any other value of that type for promotion purposes.

4   An rvalue of type `bool` can be converted to an rvalue of type `int`, with `false` becoming zero and `true` becoming one.

5   These conversions are called *integral promotions*.

4.6 Floating point promotion   [conv.fpprom]

1   An rvalue of type `float` can be converted to an rvalue of type `double`. The value is unchanged.

2   This conversion is called *floating point promotion*.

4.7 Integral conversions   [conv.integral]

1   An rvalue of an integer type can be converted to an rvalue of another integer type. An rvalue of an enumeration type can be converted to an rvalue of an integer type.

2   If the destination type is unsigned, the resulting value is the least unsigned integer congruent to the source integer (modulo 2^n where n is the number of bits used to represent the unsigned type). [*Note:* In a two's complement representation, this conversion is conceptual and there is no change in the bit pattern (if there is no truncation).]

3   If the destination type is signed, the value is unchanged if it can be represented in the destination type (and bit-field width); otherwise, the value is implementation-defined.

4   If the destination type is `bool`, see 4.12. If the source type is `bool`, the value `false` is converted to zero and the value `true` is converted to one.

5   The conversions allowed as integral promotions are excluded from the set of integral conversions.

4.8 Floating point conversions   [conv.double]

1   An rvalue of floating point type can be converted to an rvalue of another floating point type. If the source value can be exactly represented in the destination type, the result of the conversion is that exact representation. If the source value is between two adjacent destination values, the result of the conversion is an implementation-defined choice of either of those values. Otherwise, the behavior is undefined.

2   The conversions allowed as floating point promotions are excluded from the set of floating point conversions.

4.9 Floating-integral conversions   [conv.fpint]

1   An rvalue of a floating point type can be converted to an rvalue of an integer type. The conversion truncates; that is, the fractional part is discarded. The behavior is undefined if the truncated value cannot be represented in the destination type. [*Note:* If the destination type is `bool`, see 4.12.]

2   An rvalue of an integer type or of an enumeration type can be converted to an rvalue of a floating point type. The result is exact if possible. Otherwise, it is an implementation-defined choice of either the next lower or higher representable value. [*Note:* loss of precision occurs if the integral value cannot be represented exactly as a value of the floating type.] If the source type is `bool`, the value `false` is converted to zero and the value `true` is converted to one.

4.10 Pointer conversions [conv.ptr]

1   A *null pointer constant* is an integral constant expression (5.19) rvalue of integer type that evaluates to zero. A null pointer constant can be converted to a pointer type; the result is the *null pointer value* of that type and is distinguishable from every other value of pointer to object or pointer to function type. Two null pointer values of the same type shall compare equal. The conversion of a null pointer constant to a pointer to cv-qualified type is a single conversion, and not the sequence of a pointer conversion followed by a qualification conversion (4.4).

2   An rvalue of type "pointer to *cv* T," where T is an object type, can be converted to an rvalue of type "pointer to *cv* void." The result of converting a "pointer to *cv* T" to a "pointer to *cv* void" points to the start of the storage location where the object of type T resides, as if the object is a most derived object (1.8) of type T (that is, not a base class subobject).

3   An rvalue of type "pointer to *cv* D," where D is a class type, can be converted to an rvalue of type "pointer to *cv* B," where B is a base class (clause 10) of D. If B is an inaccessible (clause 11) or ambiguous (10.2) base class of D, a program that necessitates this conversion is ill-formed. The result of the conversion is a pointer to the base class sub-object of the derived class object. The null pointer value is converted to the null pointer value of the destination type.

4.11 Pointer to member conversions [conv.mem]

1   A null pointer constant (4.10) can be converted to a pointer to member type; the result is the *null member pointer value* of that type and is distinguishable from any pointer to member not created from a null pointer constant. Two null member pointer values of the same type shall compare equal. The conversion of a null pointer constant to a pointer to member of cv-qualified type is a single conversion, and not the sequence of a pointer to member conversion followed by a qualification conversion (4.4).

2   An rvalue of type "pointer to member of B of type *cv* T," where B is a class type, can be converted to an rvalue of type "pointer to member of D of type *cv* T," where D is a derived class (clause 10) of B. If B is an inaccessible (clause 11), ambiguous (10.2) or virtual (10.1) base class of D, a program that necessitates this conversion is ill-formed. The result of the conversion refers to the same member as the pointer to member before the conversion took place, but it refers to the base class member as if it were a member of the derived class. The result refers to the member in D's instance of B. Since the result has type "pointer to member of D of type *cv* T," it can be dereferenced with a D object. The result is the same as if the pointer to member of B were dereferenced with the B sub-object of D. The null member pointer value is converted to the null member pointer value of the destination type.[52]

4.12 Boolean conversions [conv.bool]

1   An rvalue of arithmetic, enumeration, pointer, or pointer to member type can be converted to an rvalue of type bool. A zero value, null pointer value, or null member pointer value is converted to false; any other value is converted to true.

---

[52] The rule for conversion of pointers to members (from pointer to member of base to pointer to member of derived) appears inverted compared to the rule for pointers to objects (from pointer to derived to pointer to base) (4.10, clause 10). This inversion is necessary to ensure type safety. Note that a pointer to member is not a pointer to object or a pointer to function and the rules for conversions of such pointers do not apply to pointers to members. In particular, a pointer to member cannot be converted to a void*.

5 Expressions [expr]

1   [*Note:* Clause 5 defines the syntax, order of evaluation, and meaning of expressions. An expression is a sequence of operators and operands that specifies a computation. An expression can result in a value and can cause side effects.

2   Operators can be overloaded, that is, given meaning when applied to expressions of class type (clause 9) or enumeration type (7.2). Uses of overloaded operators are transformed into function calls as described in 13.5. Overloaded operators obey the rules for syntax specified in clause 5, but the requirements of operand type, lvalue, and evaluation order are replaced by the rules for function call. Relations between operators, such as ++a meaning a+=1, are not guaranteed for overloaded operators (13.5), and are not guaranteed for operands of type bool. —*end note*]

3   Clause 5 defines the effects of operators when applied to types for which they have not been overloaded. Operator overloading shall not modify the rules for the *built-in operators*, that is, for operators applied to types for which they are defined by this Standard. However, these built-in operators participate in overload resolution, and as part of that process user-defined conversions will be considered where necessary to convert the operands to types appropriate for the built-in operator. If a built-in operator is selected, such conversions will be applied to the operands before the operation is considered further according to the rules in clause 5; see 13.3.1.2, 13.6.

4   Except where noted, the order of evaluation of operands of individual operators and subexpressions of individual expressions, and the order in which side effects take place, is unspecified.[53] Between the previous and next sequence point a scalar object shall have its stored value modified at most once by the evaluation of an expression. Furthermore, the prior value shall be accessed only to determine the value to be stored. The requirements of this paragraph shall be met for each allowable ordering of the subexpressions of a full expression; otherwise the behavior is undefined. [*Example:*

```
i = v[i++];          // the behavior is unspecified
i = 7, i++, i++;     // i becomes 9

i = ++i + 1;         // the behavior is unspecified
i = i + 1;           // the value of i is incremented
```

—*end example*]

5   If during the evaluation of an expression, the result is not mathematically defined or not in the range of representable values for its type, the behavior is undefined, unless such an expression is a constant expression (5.19), in which case the program is ill-formed. [*Note:* most existing implementations of C++ ignore integer overflows. Treatment of division by zero, forming a remainder using a zero divisor, and all floating point exceptions vary among machines, and is usually adjustable by a library function.]

6   If an expression initially has the type "reference to T" (8.3.2, 8.5.3), the type is adjusted to "T" prior to any further analysis, the expression designates the object or function denoted by the reference, and the expression is an lvalue.

7   An expression designating an object is called an *object-expression*.

8   Whenever an lvalue expression appears as an operand of an operator that expects an rvalue for that operand, the lvalue-to-rvalue (4.1), array-to-pointer (4.2), or function-to-pointer (4.3) standard conversions are applied to convert the expression to an rvalue. [*Note:* because cv-qualifiers are removed from the type of an expression of non-class type when the expression is converted to an rvalue, an lvalue expression of type

---

[53] The precedence of operators is not directly specified, but it can be derived from the syntax.

`const int` can, for example, be used where an rvalue expression of type `int` is required.]

9   Many binary operators that expect operands of arithmetic or enumeration type cause conversions and yield result types in a similar way. The purpose is to yield a common type, which is also the type of the result. This pattern is called the *usual arithmetic conversions*, which are defined as follows:

— If either operand is of type `long double`, the other shall be converted to `long double`.

— Otherwise, if either operand is `double`, the other shall be converted to `double`.

— Otherwise, if either operand is `float`, the other shall be converted to `float`.

— Otherwise, the integral promotions (4.5) shall be performed on both operands.[54]

— Then, if either operand is `unsigned long` the other shall be converted to `unsigned long`.

— Otherwise, if one operand is a `long int` and the other `unsigned int`, then if a `long int` can represent all the values of an `unsigned int`, the `unsigned int` shall be converted to a `long int`; otherwise both operands shall be converted to `unsigned long int`.

— Otherwise, if either operand is `long`, the other shall be converted to `long`.

— Otherwise, if either operand is `unsigned`, the other shall be converted to `unsigned`.

[*Note:* otherwise, the only remaining case is that both operands are `int`]

10   The values of the floating operands and the results of floating expressions may be represented in greater precision and range than that required by the type; the types are not changed thereby.[55]

5.1 Primary expressions   [expr.prim]

1   Primary expressions are literals, names, and names qualified by the scope resolution operator : :.

> *primary-expression:*
>   *literal*
>   `this`
>   (*expression*)
>   *id-expression*
>
> *id-expression:*
>   *unqualified-id*
>   *qualified-id*
>
> *unqualified-id:*
>   *identifier*
>   *operator-function-id*
>   *conversion-function-id*
>   ˜ *class-name*
>   *template-id*

2   A *literal* is a primary expression. Its type depends on its form (2.13). A string literal is an lvalue; all other literals are rvalues.

3   The keyword `this` names a pointer to the object for which a nonstatic member function (9.3.2) is invoked. The keyword `this` shall be used only inside a nonstatic class member function body (9.3) or in a constructor *mem-initializer* (12.6.2). The type of the expression is a pointer to the function's class (9.3.2), possibly with cv-qualifiers on the class type. The expression is an rvalue.

---

[54] As a consequence, operands of type `bool`, `wchar_t`, or an enumerated type are converted to some integral type.
[55] The cast and assignment operators must still perform their specific conversions as described in 5.4, 5.2.9 and 5.17.

4   The operator : : followed by an *identifier*, a *qualified-id*, or an *operator-function-id* is a *primary-expression*. Its type is specified by the declaration of the identifier, *qualified-id*, or *operator-function-id*. The result is the entity denoted by the identifier, *qualified-id*, or *operator-function-id*. The result is an lvalue if the entity is a function or variable. The identifier, *qualified-id*, or *operator-function-id* shall have global namespace scope or be visible in global scope because of a *using-directive* (7.3.4). [*Note:* the use of : : allows a type, an object, a function, an enumerator, or a namespace declared in the global namespace to be referred to even if its identifier has been hidden (3.4.3).]

5   A parenthesized expression is a primary expression whose type and value are identical to those of the enclosed expression. The presence of parentheses does not affect whether the expression is an lvalue. The parenthesized expression can be used in exactly the same contexts as those where the enclosed expression can be used, and with the same meaning, except as otherwise indicated.

6   An *id-expression* is a restricted form of a *primary-expression*. [*Note:* an *id-expression* can appear after . and - > operators (5.2.5).]

7   An *identifier* is an *id-expression* provided it has been suitably declared (clause 7). [*Note:* for *operator-function-id*s, see 13.5; for *conversion-function-id*s, see 12.3.2; for *template-id*s, see 14.2. A *class-name* prefixed by ~ denotes a destructor; see 12.4. Within the definition of a nonstatic member function, an *identifier* that names a nonstatic member is transformed to a class member access expression (9.3.1).] The type of the expression is the type of the *identifier*. The result is the entity denoted by the identifier. The result is an lvalue if the entity is a function, variable, or data member.

    qualified-id:
        : :*opt nested-name-specifier* template*opt unqualified-id*
        : : *identifier*
        : : *operator-function-id*
        : : *template-id*

    nested-name-specifier:
        class-or-namespace-name : : *nested-name-specifier*opt
        class-or-namespace-name : : template *nested-name-specifier*

    class-or-namespace-name:
        class-name
        namespace-name

A *nested-name-specifier* that names a class, optionally followed by the keyword template (14.2), and then followed by the name of a member of either that class (9.2) or one of its base classes (clause 10), is a *qualified-id*; 3.4.3.1 describes name lookup for class members that appear in *qualified-ids*. The result is the member. The type of the result is the type of the member. The result is an lvalue if the member is a static member function or a data member. [*Note:* a class member can be referred to using a *qualified-id* at any point in its potential scope (3.3.6).] Where *class-name* : : *class-name* is used, and the two *class-name*s refer to the same class, this notation names the constructor (12.1). Where *class-name* : : ~ *class-name* is used, the two *class-name*s shall refer to the same class; this notation names the destructor (12.4). [*Note:* a *typedef-name* that names a class is a *class-name* (7.1.3). Except as the *identifier* in the declarator for a constructor or destructor definition outside of a class *member-specification* (12.1, 12.4), a *typedef-name* that names a class may be used in a *qualified-id* to refer to a constructor or destructor.]

8   A *nested-name-specifier* that names a namespace (7.3), followed by the name of a member of that namespace (or the name of a member of a namespace made visible by a *using-directive*) is a *qualified-id*; 3.4.3.2 describes name lookup for namespace members that appear in *qualified-ids*. The result is the member. The type of the result is the type of the member. The result is an lvalue if the member is a function or a variable.

9   In a *qualified-id*, if the *id-expression* is a *conversion-function-id*, its *conversion-type-id* shall denote the same type in both the context in which the entire *qualified-id* occurs and in the context of the class denoted by the *nested-name-specifier*.

10   An *id-expression* that denotes a nonstatic data member or nonstatic member function of a class can only be used:

— as part of a class member access (5.2.5) in which the object-expression refers to the member's class or a class derived from that class, or

— to form a pointer to member (5.3.1), or

— in the body of a nonstatic member function of that class or of a class derived from that class (9.3.1), or

— in a *mem-initializer* for a constructor for that class or for a class derived from that class (12.6.2).

11   A *template-id* shall be used as an *unqualified-id* only as specified in 14.7.2, 14.7, and 14.5.4.

5.2 Postfix expressions   **[expr.post]**

1   Postfix expressions group left-to-right.

> *postfix-expression:*
>> *primary-expression*
>> *postfix-expression* [*expression*]
>> *postfix-expression* (*expression-list$_{opt}$*)
>> *simple-type-specifier* (*expression-list$_{opt}$*)
>> typename : :$_{opt}$ *nested-name-specifier identifier* (*expression-list$_{opt}$*)
>> typename : :$_{opt}$ *nested-name-specifier* template$_{opt}$ *template-id* (*expression-list$_{opt}$*)
>> *postfix-expression* . template$_{opt}$ *id-expression*
>> *postfix-expression* -> template$_{opt}$ *id-expression*
>> *postfix-expression* . *pseudo-destructor-name*
>> *postfix-expression* -> *pseudo-destructor-name*
>> *postfix-expression* ++
>> *postfix-expression* --
>> dynamic_cast < *type-id* > (*expression*)
>> static_cast < *type-id* > (*expression*)
>> reinterpret_cast < *type-id* > (*expression*)
>> const_cast < *type-id* > (*expression*)
>> typeid (*expression*)
>> typeid (*type-id*)
>
> *expression-list:*
>> *assignment-expression*
>> *expression-list* , *assignment-expression*
>
> *pseudo-destructor-name:*
>> : :$_{opt}$ *nested-name-specifier$_{opt}$ type-name* : : ~ *type-name*
>> : :$_{opt}$ *nested-name-specifier* template *template-id* : : ~ *type-name*
>> : :$_{opt}$ *nested-name-specifier$_{opt}$* ~ *type-name*

5.2.1 Subscripting   **[expr.sub]**

1   A postfix expression followed by an expression in square brackets is a postfix expression. One of the expressions shall have the type "pointer to T" and the other shall have enumeration or integral type. The result is an lvalue of type "T." The type "T" shall be a completely-defined object type.[56] The expression E1[E2] is identical (by definition) to * ((E1)+(E2)). [*Note:* see 5.3 and 5.7 for details of * and + and 8.3.4 for details of arrays.]

---

[56] This is true even if the subscript operator is used in the following common idiom: &x[0].

5.2.2 Function call   **[expr.call]**

1   There are two kinds of function call: ordinary function call and member function[57] (9.3) call. A function call is a postfix expression followed by parentheses containing a possibly empty, comma-separated list of expressions which constitute the arguments to the function. For an ordinary function call, the postfix expression shall be either an lvalue that refers to a function (in which case the function-to-pointer standard conversion (4.3) is suppressed on the postfix expression), or it shall have pointer to function type. Calling a function through an expression whose function type has a language linkage that is different from the language linkage of the function type of the called function's definition is undefined (7.5). For a member function call, the postfix expression shall be an implicit (9.3.1, 9.4) or explicit class member access (5.2.5) whose *id-expression* is a function member name, or a pointer-to-member expression (5.5) selecting a function member. The first expression in the postfix expression is then called the *object expression*, and the call is as a member of the object pointed to or referred to. In the case of an implicit class member access, the implied object is the one pointed to by `this`. [*Note:* a member function call of the form `f()` is interpreted as `(*this).f()` (see 9.3.1).] If a function or member function name is used, the name can be overloaded (clause 13), in which case the appropriate function shall be selected according to the rules in 13.3. The function called in a member function call is normally selected according to the static type of the object expression (clause 10), but if that function is `virtual` and is not specified using a *qualified-id* then the function actually called will be the final overrider (10.3) of the selected function in the dynamic type of the object expression [*Note:* the dynamic type is the type of the object pointed or referred to by the current value of the object expression. 12.7 describes the behavior of virtual function calls when the object-expression refers to an object under construction or destruction.]

2   If no declaration of the called function is visible from the scope of the call the program is ill-formed.

3   The type of the function call expression is the return type of the statically chosen function (i.e., ignoring the `virtual` keyword), even if the type of the function actually called is different. This type shall be a complete object type, a reference type or the type `void`.

4   When a function is called, each parameter (8.3.5) shall be initialized (8.5, 12.8, 12.1) with its corresponding argument. If the function is a nonstatic member function, the "`this`" parameter of the function (9.3.2) shall be initialized with a pointer to the object of the call, converted as if by an explicit type conversion (5.4). [*Note:* There is no access checking on this conversion; the access checking is done as part of the (possibly implicit) class member access operator. See 11.2.] When a function is called, the parameters that have object type shall have completely-defined object type. [*Note:* this still allows a parameter to be a pointer or reference to an incomplete class type. However, it prevents a passed-by-value parameter to have an incomplete class type.] During the initialization of a parameter, an implementation may avoid the construction of extra temporaries by combining the conversions on the associated argument and/or the construction of temporaries with the initialization of the parameter (see 12.2). The lifetime of a parameter ends when the function in which it is defined returns. The initialization and destruction of each parameter occurs within the context of the calling function. [*Example:* the access of the constructor, conversion functions or destructor is checked at the point of call in the calling function. If a constructor or destructor for a function parameter throws an exception, the search for a handler starts in the scope of the calling function; in particular, if the function called has a *function-try-block* (clause 15) with a handler that could handle the exception, this handler is not considered.] The value of a function call is the value returned by the called function except in a virtual function call if the return type of the final overrider is different from the return type of the statically chosen function, the value returned from the final overrider is converted to the return type of the statically chosen function.

5   [*Note:* a function can change the values of its non-const parameters, but these changes cannot affect the values of the arguments except where a parameter is of a reference type (8.3.2); if the reference is to a const-qualified type, `const_cast` is required to be used to cast away the constness in order to modify the argument's value. Where a parameter is of `const` reference type a temporary object is introduced if

---

[57] A static member function (9.4) is an ordinary function.

needed (7.1.5, 2.13, 2.13.4, 8.3.4, 12.2). In addition, it is possible to modify the values of nonconstant objects through pointer parameters.]

6   A function can be declared to accept fewer arguments (by declaring default arguments (8.3.6)) or more arguments (by using the ellipsis, . . . 8.3.5) than the number of parameters in the function definition (8.4). [*Note:* this implies that, except where the ellipsis (. . .) is used, a parameter is available for each argument.]

7   When there is no parameter for a given argument, the argument is passed in such a way that the receiving function can obtain the value of the argument by invoking va_arg (18.7). The lvalue-to-rvalue (4.1), array-to-pointer (4.2), and function-to-pointer (4.3) standard conversions are performed on the argument expression. After these conversions, if the argument does not have arithmetic, enumeration, pointer, pointer to member, or class type, the program is ill-formed. If the argument has a non-POD class type (clause 9), the behavior is undefined. If the argument has integral or enumeration type that is subject to the integral promotions (4.5), or a floating point type that is subject to the floating point promotion (4.6), the value of the argument is converted to the promoted type before the call. These promotions are referred to as the *default argument promotions*.

8   The order of evaluation of arguments is unspecified. All side effects of argument expression evaluations take effect before the function is entered. The order of evaluation of the postfix expression and the argument expression list is unspecified.

9   Recursive calls are permitted, except to the function named main (3.6.1).

10   A function call is an lvalue if and only if the result type is a reference.

5.2.3 Explicit type conversion (functional notation)   [expr.type.conv]

1   A *simple-type-specifier* (7.1.5) followed by a parenthesized *expression-list* constructs a value of the specified type given the expression list. If the expression list is a single expression, the type conversion expression is equivalent (in definedness, and if defined in meaning) to the corresponding cast expression (5.4). If the *simple-type-specifier* specifies a class type, the class type shall be complete. If the expression list specifies more than a single value, the type shall be a class with a suitably declared constructor (8.5, 12.1), and the expression T(x1, x2, ...) is equivalent in effect to the declaration T t(x1, x2, ...); for some invented temporary variable t, with the result being the value of t as an rvalue.

2   The expression T(), where T is a simple-type-specifier (7.1.5.2) for a non-array complete object type or the (possibly cv-qualified) void type, creates an rvalue of the specified type, which is value-initialized (8.5; no initialization is done for the void() case). [*Note:* if T is a non-class type that is *cv-qualified*, the cv-qualifiers are ignored when determining the type of the resulting rvalue (3.10).]

5.2.4 Pseudo destructor call   [expr.pseudo]

1   The use of a *pseudo-destructor-name* after a dot . or arrow -> operator represents the destructor for the non-class type named by *type-name*. The result shall only be used as the operand for the function call operator (), and the result of such a call has type void. The only effect is the evaluation of the *postfix-expression* before the dot or arrow.

2   The left hand side of the dot operator shall be of scalar type. The left hand side of the arrow operator shall be of pointer to scalar type. This scalar type is the object type. The type designated by the *pseudo-destructor-name* shall be the same as the object type. Furthermore, the two *type-name*s in a *pseudo-destructor-name* of the form

          :: *opt* *nested-name-specifier* *opt* *type-name* : : ˜ *type-name*

shall designate the same scalar type. The *cv*-unqualified versions of the object type and of the type designated by the *pseudo-destructor-name* shall be the same type.

5.2.5 Class member access [expr.ref]

1   A postfix expression followed by a dot `.` or an arrow `->`, optionally followed by the keyword `template` (14.8.1), and then followed by an *id-expression*, is a postfix expression. The postfix expression before the dot or arrow is evaluated;[58] the result of that evaluation, together with the *id-expression*, determine the result of the entire postfix expression.

2   For the first option (dot) the type of the first expression (the *object expression*) shall be "class object" (of a complete type). For the second option (arrow) the type of the first expression (the *pointer expression*) shall be "pointer to class object" (of a complete type). In these cases, the *id-expression* shall name a member of the class or of one of its base classes. [*Note:* because the name of a class is inserted in its class scope (clause 9), the name of a class is also considered a nested member of that class.] [*Note:* 3.4.5 describes how names are looked up after the `.` and `->` operators.]

3   If `E1` has the type "pointer to class `X`," then the expression `E1->E2` is converted to the equivalent form `(*(E1)).E2`; the remainder of 5.2.5 will address only the first option (dot)[59]. Abbreviating *object-expression.id-expression* as `E1.E2`, then the type and lvalue properties of this expression are determined as follows. In the remainder of 5.2.5, *cq* represents either `const` or the absence of `const`; *vq* represents either `volatile` or the absence of `volatile`. *cv* represents an arbitrary set of cv-qualifiers, as defined in 3.9.3.

4   If `E2` is declared to have type "reference to `T`", then `E1.E2` is an lvalue; the type of `E1.E2` is `T`. Otherwise, one of the following rules applies.

— If `E2` is a static data member, and the type of `E2` is `T`, then `E1.E2` is an lvalue; the expression designates the named member of the class. The type of `E1.E2` is `T`.

— If `E2` is a non-static data member, and the type of `E1` is "*cq1 vq1* `X`", and the type of `E2` is "*cq2 vq2* `T`", the expression designates the named member of the object designated by the first expression. If `E1` is an lvalue, then `E1.E2` is an lvalue. Let the notation *vq12* stand for the "union" of *vq1* and *vq2* ; that is, if *vq1* or *vq2* is `volatile`, then *vq12* is `volatile`. Similarly, let the notation *cq12* stand for the "union" of *cq1* and *cq2*; that is, if *cq1* or *cq2* is `const`, then *cq12* is `const`. If `E2` is declared to be a `mutable` member, then the type of `E1.E2` is "*vq12* `T`". If `E2` is not declared to be a `mutable` member, then the type of `E1.E2` is "*cq12 vq12* `T`".

— If `E2` is a (possibly overloaded) member function, function overload resolution (13.3) is used to determine whether `E1.E2` refers to a static or a non-static member function.

    — If it refers to a static member function, and the type of `E2` is "function of (parameter type list) returning `T`", then `E1.E2` is an lvalue; the expression designates the static member function. The type of `E1.E2` is the same type as that of `E2`, namely "function of (parameter type list) returning `T`".

    — Otherwise, if `E1.E2` refers to a non-static member function, and the type of `E2` is "function of (parameter type list) *cv* returning `T`", then `E1.E2` is *not* an lvalue. The expression designates a non-static member function. The expression can be used only as the left-hand operand of a member function call (9.3). [*Note:* any redundant set of parentheses surrounding the expression is ignored (5.1).] The type of `E1.E2` is "function of (parameter type list) *cv* returning `T`".

— If `E2` is a nested type, the expression `E1.E2` is ill-formed.

— If `E2` is a member enumerator, and the type of `E2` is `T`, the expression `E1.E2` is not an lvalue. The type of `E1.E2` is `T`.

---

[58] This evaluation happens even if the result is unnecessary to determine the value of the entire postfix expression, for example if the *id-expression* denotes a static member.
[59] Note that if `E1` has the type "pointer to class `X`", then `(*(E1))` is an lvalue.

5   [*Note:* "class objects" can be structures (9.2) and unions (9.5). Classes are discussed in clause 9.]

5.2.6 Increment and decrement   [expr.post.incr]

1   The value obtained by applying a postfix ++ is the value that the operand had before applying the operator. [*Note:* the value obtained is a copy of the original value] The operand shall be a modifiable lvalue. The type of the operand shall be an arithmetic type or a pointer to a complete object type. After the result is noted, the value of the object is modified by adding 1 to it, unless the object is of type `bool`, in which case it is set to `true`. [*Note:* this use is deprecated, see annex D.] The result is an rvalue. The type of the result is the cv-unqualified version of the type of the operand. See also 5.7 and 5.17.

2   The operand of postfix -- is decremented analogously to the postfix ++ operator, except that the operand shall not be of type `bool`. [*Note:* For prefix increment and decrement, see 5.3.2.]

5.2.7 Dynamic cast   [expr.dynamic.cast]

1   The result of the expression `dynamic_cast<T>(v)` is the result of converting the expression v to type T. T shall be a pointer or reference to a complete class type, or "pointer to *cv* `void`". Types shall not be defined in a `dynamic_cast`. The `dynamic_cast` operator shall not cast away constness (5.2.11).

2   If T is a pointer type, v shall be an rvalue of a pointer to complete class type, and the result is an rvalue of type T. If T is a reference type, v shall be an lvalue of a complete class type, and the result is an lvalue of the type referred to by T.

3   If the type of v is the same as the required result type (which, for convenience, will be called R in this description), or it is the same as R except that the class object type in R is more cv-qualified than the class object type in v, the result is v (converted if necessary).

4   If the value of v is a null pointer value in the pointer case, the result is the null pointer value of type R.

5   If T is "pointer to *cv1* B" and v has type "pointer to *cv2* D" such that B is a base class of D, the result is a pointer to the unique B sub-object of the D object pointed to by v. Similarly, if T is "reference to *cv1* B" and v has type "*cv2* D" such that B is a base class of D, the result is an lvalue for the unique[60] B sub-object of the D object referred to by v. In both the pointer and reference cases, *cv1* shall be the same cv-qualification as, or greater cv-qualification than, *cv2*, and B shall be an accessible unambiguous base class of D. [*Example:*

```
struct B {};
struct D : B {};
void foo(D* dp)
{
    B*  bp = dynamic_cast<B*>(dp);      // equivalent to B* bp = dp;
}
```

—*end example*]

6   Otherwise, v shall be a pointer to or an lvalue of a polymorphic type (10.3).

7   If T is "pointer to *cv* `void`," then the result is a pointer to the most derived object pointed to by v. Otherwise, a run-time check is applied to see if the object pointed or referred to by v can be converted to the type pointed or referred to by T.

8   The run-time check logically executes as follows:

— If, in the most derived object pointed (referred) to by v, v points (refers) to a `public` base class sub-object of a T object, and if only one object of type T is derived from the sub-object pointed (referred) to by v, the result is a pointer (an lvalue referring) to that T object.

---

[60] The most derived object (1.8) pointed or referred to by v can contain other B objects as base classes, but these are ignored.

— Otherwise, if v points (refers) to a `public` base class sub-object of the most derived object, and the type of the most derived object has a base class, of type T, that is unambiguous and `public`, the result is a pointer (an lvalue referring) to the T sub-object of the most derived object.

— Otherwise, the run-time check *fails*.

9 The value of a failed cast to pointer type is the null pointer value of the required result type. A failed cast to reference type throws `bad_cast` (18.5.2).
[*Example:*

```
class A { virtual void f(); };
class B { virtual void g(); };
class D : public virtual A, private B {};
void g()
{
    D    d;
    B*   bp = (B*)&d;                      // cast needed to break protection
    A*   ap = &d;                          // public derivation, no cast needed
    D&   dr = dynamic_cast<D&>(*bp);       // fails
    ap = dynamic_cast<A*>(bp);             // fails
    bp = dynamic_cast<B*>(ap);             // fails
    ap = dynamic_cast<A*>(&d);             // succeeds
    bp = dynamic_cast<B*>(&d);             // fails
}

class E : public D, public B {};
class F : public E, public D {};
void h()
{
    F    f;
    A*   ap  = &f;                         // succeeds: finds unique A
    D*   dp  = dynamic_cast<D*>(ap);       // fails: yields 0
                                           // f has two D sub-objects
    E*   ep  = (E*)ap;                     // ill-formed:
                                           // cast from virtual base
    E*   ep1 = dynamic_cast<E*>(ap);       // succeeds
}
```

—*end example*] [*Note:* 12.7 describes the behavior of a `dynamic_cast` applied to an object under construction or destruction.]

5.2.8 Type identification   [expr.typeid]

1 The result of a `typeid` expression is an lvalue of static type `const std::type_info` (18.5.1) and dynamic type `const std::type_info` or `const` *name* where *name* is an implementation-defined class derived from `std::type_info` which preserves the behavior described in 18.5.1.[61] The lifetime of the object referred to by the lvalue extends to the end of the program. Whether or not the destructor is called for the `type_info` object at the end of the program is unspecified.

2 When `typeid` is applied to an lvalue expression whose type is a polymorphic class type (10.3), the result refers to a `type_info` object representing the type of the most derived object (1.8) (that is, the dynamic type) to which the lvalue refers. If the lvalue expression is obtained by applying the unary `*` operator to a pointer[62] and the pointer is a null pointer value (4.10), the `typeid` expression throws the `bad_typeid` exception (18.5.3).

---
[61] The recommended name for such a class is `extended_type_info`.
[62] If p is an expression of pointer type, then *p, (*p), *(p), ((*p)), *((p)), and so on all meet this requirement.

3   When `typeid` is applied to an expression other than an lvalue of a polymorphic class type, the result refers to a `type_info` object representing the static type of the expression. Lvalue-to-rvalue (4.1), array-to-pointer (4.2), and function-to-pointer (4.3) conversions are not applied to the expression. If the type of the expression is a class type, the class shall be completely-defined. The expression is not evaluated.

4   When `typeid` is applied to a *type-id*, the result refers to a `type_info` object representing the type of the *type-id*. If the type of the *type-id* is a reference type, the result of the `typeid` expression refers to a `type_info` object representing the referenced type. If the type of the *type-id* is a class type or a reference to a class type, the class shall be completely-defined. Types shall not be defined in the *type-id*.

5   The top-level cv-qualifiers of the lvalue expression or the *type-id* that is the operand of `typeid` are always ignored. [*Example:*

```
class D { ... };
D d1;
const D d2;

typeid(d1)  ==  typeid(d2);          // yields true
typeid(D)   ==  typeid(const D);     // yields true
typeid(D)   ==  typeid(d2);          // yields true
typeid(D)   ==  typeid(const D&);    // yields true
```

—*end example*]

6   If the header `<typeinfo>` (18.5.1) is not included prior to a use of `typeid`, the program is ill-formed.

7   [*Note:* 12.7 describes the behavior of `typeid` applied to an object under construction or destruction.]

5.2.9 Static cast   [expr.static.cast]

1   The result of the expression `static_cast<T>(v)` is the result of converting the expression `v` to type `T`. If `T` is a reference type, the result is an lvalue; otherwise, the result is an rvalue. Types shall not be defined in a `static_cast`. The `static_cast` operator shall not cast away constness (5.2.11).

2   An expression `e` can be explicitly converted to a type `T` using a `static_cast` of the form `static_cast<T>(e)` if the declaration "`T t(e);`" is well-formed, for some invented temporary variable `t` (8.5). The effect of such an explicit conversion is the same as performing the declaration and initialization and then using the temporary variable as the result of the conversion. The result is an lvalue if `T` is a reference type (8.3.2), and an rvalue otherwise. The expression `e` is used as an lvalue if and only if the initialization uses it as an lvalue.

3   Otherwise, the `static_cast` shall perform one of the conversions listed below. No other conversion shall be performed explicitly using a `static_cast`.

4   Any expression can be explicitly converted to type "*cv* void." The expression value is discarded. [*Note:* however, if the value is in a temporary variable (12.2), the destructor for that variable is not executed until the usual time, and the value of the variable is preserved for the purpose of executing the destructor.] The lvalue-to-rvalue (4.1), array-to-pointer (4.2), and function-to-pointer (4.3) standard conversions are not applied to the expression.

5   An lvalue of type "*cv1* B", where B is a class type, can be cast to type "reference to *cv2* D", where D is a class derived (clause 10) from B, if a valid standard conversion from "pointer to D" to "pointer to B" exists (4.10), *cv2* is the same cv-qualification as, or greater cv-qualification than, *cv1*, and B is not a virtual base class of D. The result is an lvalue of type "*cv2* D." If the lvalue of type "*cv1* B" is actually a sub-object of an object of type D, the lvalue refers to the enclosing object of type D. Otherwise, the result of the cast is undefined. [*Example:*

```
struct B {};
struct D : public B {};
D d;
B &br = d;

static_cast<D&>(br);          // produces lvalue to the original d object
```

—end example]

6   The inverse of any standard conversion sequence (clause 4), other than the lvalue-to-rvalue (4.1), array-to-pointer (4.2), function-to-pointer (4.3), and boolean (4.12) conversions, can be performed explicitly using `static_cast`. The lvalue-to-rvalue (4.1), array-to-pointer (4.2), and function-to-pointer (4.3) conversions are applied to the operand. Such a `static_cast` is subject to the restriction that the explicit conversion does not cast away constness (5.2.11), and the following additional rules for specific cases:

7   A value of integral or enumeration type can be explicitly converted to an enumeration type. The value is unchanged if the original value is within the range of the enumeration values (7.2). Otherwise, the resulting enumeration value is unspecified.

8   An rvalue of type "pointer to *cv1* B", where B is a class type, can be converted to an rvalue of type "pointer to *cv2* D", where D is a class derived (clause 10) from B, if a valid standard conversion from "pointer to D" to "pointer to B" exists (4.10), *cv2* is the same cv-qualification as, or greater cv-qualification than, *cv1*, and B is not a virtual base class of D. The null pointer value (4.10) is converted to the null pointer value of the destination type. If the rvalue of type "pointer to *cv1* B" points to a B that is actually a sub-object of an object of type D, the resulting pointer points to the enclosing object of type D. Otherwise, the result of the cast is undefined.

9   An rvalue of type "pointer to member of D of type *cv1* T" can be converted to an rvalue of type "pointer to member of B of type *cv2* T", where B is a base class (clause 10) of D, if a valid standard conversion from "pointer to member of B of type T" to "pointer to member of D of type T" exists (4.11), and *cv2* is the same cv-qualification as, or greater cv-qualification than, *cv1*.[63] The null member pointer value (4.11) is converted to the null member pointer value of the destination type. If class B contains the original member, or is a base or derived class of the class containing the original member, the resulting pointer to member points to the original member. Otherwise, the result of the cast is undefined. [*Note:* although class B need not contain the original member, the dynamic type of the object on which the pointer to member is dereferenced must contain the original member; see 5.5.]

10   An rvalue of type "pointer to *cv1* `void`" can be converted to an rvalue of type "pointer to *cv2* T," where T is an object type and *cv2* is the same cv-qualification as, or greater cv-qualification than, *cv1*. A value of type pointer to object converted to "pointer to *cv* `void`" and back to the original pointer type will have its original value.

5.2.10 Reinterpret cast   [expr.reinterpret.cast]

1   The result of the expression `reinterpret_cast<T>(v)` is the result of converting the expression v to type T. If T is a reference type, the result is an lvalue; otherwise, the result is an rvalue and the lvalue-to-rvalue (4.1), array-to-pointer (4.2), and function-to-pointer (4.3) standard conversions are performed on the the expression v. Types shall not be defined in a `reinterpret_cast`. Conversions that can be performed explicitly using `reinterpret_cast` are listed below. No other conversion can be performed explicitly using `reinterpret_cast`.

2   The `reinterpret_cast` operator shall not cast away constness. [*Note:* see 5.2.11 for the definition of "casting away constness". Subject to the restrictions in this section, an expression may be cast to its own type using a `reinterpret_cast` operator.]

---

[63] Function types (including those used in pointer to member function types) are never cv-qualified; see 8.3.5 .

3   The mapping performed by `reinterpret_cast` is implementation-defined. [*Note:* it might, or might not, produce a representation different from the original value.]

4   A pointer can be explicitly converted to any integral type large enough to hold it. The mapping function is implementation-defined [*Note:* it is intended to be unsurprising to those who know the addressing structure of the underlying machine.]

5   A value of integral type or enumeration type can be explicitly converted to a pointer.[64] A pointer converted to an integer of sufficient size (if any such exists on the implementation) and back to the same pointer type will have its original value; mappings between pointers and integers are otherwise implementation-defined.

6   A pointer to a function can be explicitly converted to a pointer to a function of a different type. The effect of calling a function through a pointer to a function type (8.3.5) that is not the same as the type used in the definition of the function is undefined. Except that converting an rvalue of type "pointer to T1" to the type "pointer to T2" (where T1 and T2 are function types) and back to its original type yields the original pointer value, the result of such a pointer conversion is unspecified. [*Note:* see also 4.10 for more details of pointer conversions.]

7   A pointer to an object can be explicitly converted to a pointer to an object of different type.[65] Except that converting an rvalue of type "pointer to T1" to the type "pointer to T2" (where T1 and T2 are object types and where the alignment requirements of T2 are no stricter than those of T1) and back to its original type yields the original pointer value, the result of such a pointer conversion is unspecified.

8   The null pointer value (4.10) is converted to the null pointer value of the destination type.

9   An rvalue of type "pointer to member of X of type T1" can be explicitly converted to an rvalue of type "pointer to member of Y of type T2" if T1 and T2 are both function types or both object types.[66] The null member pointer value (4.11) is converted to the null member pointer value of the destination type. The result of this conversion is unspecified, except in the following cases:

— converting an rvalue of type "pointer to member function" to a different pointer to member function type and back to its original type yields the original pointer to member value.

— converting an rvalue of type "pointer to data member of X of type T1" to the type "pointer to data member of Y of type T2" (where the alignment requirements of T2 are no stricter than those of T1) and back to its original type yields the original pointer to member value.

10   An lvalue expression of type T1 can be cast to the type "reference to T2" if an expression of type "pointer to T1" can be explicitly converted to the type "pointer to T2" using a `reinterpret_cast`. That is, a reference cast `reinterpret_cast<T&>(x)` has the same effect as the conversion `*reinterpret_cast<T*>(&x)` with the built-in & and * operators. The result is an lvalue that refers to the same object as the source lvalue, but with a different type. No temporary is created, no copy is made, and constructors (12.1) or conversion functions (12.3) are not called.[67]

---

[64] Converting an integral constant expression (5.19) with value zero always yields a null pointer (4.10), but converting other expressions that happen to have value zero need not yield a null pointer.

[65] The types may have different cv-qualifiers, subject to the overall restriction that a `reinterpret_cast` cannot cast away constness.

[66] T1 and T2 may have different cv-qualifiers, subject to the overall restriction that a `reinterpret_cast` cannot cast away constness.

[67] This is sometimes referred to as a *type pun*.

5.2.11 Const cast [expr.const.cast]

1 The result of the expression const_cast<T>(v) is of type T. If T is a reference type, the result is an lvalue; otherwise, the result is an rvalue and, the lvalue-to-rvalue (4.1), array-to-pointer (4.2), and function-to-pointer (4.3) standard conversions are performed on the expression v. Types shall not be defined in a const_cast. Conversions that can be performed explicitly using const_cast are listed below. No other conversion shall be performed explicitly using const_cast.

2 [*Note:* Subject to the restrictions in this section, an expression may be cast to its own type using a const_cast operator.]

3 For two pointer types T1 and T2 where

$$T1 \text{ is } cv_{1,0} \text{ pointer to } cv_{1,1} \text{ pointer to } \cdots cv_{1,n-1} \text{ pointer to } cv_{1,n} T$$

and

$$T2 \text{ is } cv_{2,0} \text{ pointer to } cv_{2,1} \text{ pointer to } \cdots cv_{2,n-1} \text{ pointer to } cv_{2,n} T$$

where T is any object type or the void type and where $cv_{1,k}$ and $cv_{2,k}$ may be different cv-qualifications, an rvalue of type T1 may be explicitly converted to the type T2 using a const_cast. The result of a pointer const_cast refers to the original object.

4 An lvalue of type T1 can be explicitly converted to an lvalue of type T2 using the cast const_cast<T2&> (where T1 and T2 are object types) if a pointer to T1 can be explicitly converted to the type pointer to T2 using a const_cast. The result of a reference const_cast refers to the original object.

5 For a const_cast involving pointers to data members, multi-level pointers to data members and multi-level mixed pointers and pointers to data members (4.4), the rules for const_cast are the same as those used for pointers; the "member" aspect of a pointer to member is ignored when determining where the cv-qualifiers are added or removed by the const_cast. The result of a pointer to data member const_cast refers to the same member as the original (uncast) pointer to data member.

6 A null pointer value (4.10) is converted to the null pointer value of the destination type. The null member pointer value (4.11) is converted to the null member pointer value of the destination type.

7 [*Note:* Depending on the type of the object, a write operation through the pointer, lvalue or pointer to data member resulting from a const_cast that casts away a const-qualifier[68] may produce undefined behavior (7.1.5.1).]

8 The following rules define the process known as *casting away constness*. In these rules Tn and Xn represent types. For two pointer types:

$$X1 \text{ is } T1 cv_{1,1} * \cdots cv_{1,N} * \quad \text{where } T1 \text{ is not a pointer type}$$
$$X2 \text{ is } T2 cv_{2,1} * \cdots cv_{2,M} * \quad \text{where } T2 \text{ is not a pointer type}$$
$$K \text{ is } min(N,M)$$

casting from X1 to X2 casts away constness if, for a non-pointer type T there does not exist an implicit conversion (clause 4) from:

$$Tcv_{1,(N-K+1)} * cv_{1,(N-K+2)} * \cdots cv_{1,N} *$$

to

$$Tcv_{2,(M-K+1)} * cv_{2,(M-K+2)} * \cdots cv_{2,M} *$$

---

[68] const_cast is not limited to conversions that cast away a const-qualifier.

9   Casting from an lvalue of type T1 to an lvalue of type T2 using a reference cast casts away constness if a
     cast from an rvalue of type "pointer to T1" to the type "pointer to T2" casts away constness.

10   Casting from an rvalue of type "pointer to data member of X of type T1" to the type "pointer to data mem-
     ber of Y of type T2" casts away constness if a cast from an rvalue of type "pointer to T1" to the type
     "pointer to T2" casts away constness.

11   For multi-level pointer to members and multi-level mixed pointers and pointer to members (4.4), the
     "member" aspect of a pointer to member level is ignored when determining if a const cv-qualifier has
     been cast away.

12   [*Note:* some conversions which involve only changes in cv-qualification cannot be done using
     const_cast. For instance, conversions between pointers to functions are not covered because such
     conversions lead to values whose use causes undefined behavior. For the same reasons, conversions
     between pointers to member functions, and in particular, the conversion from a pointer to a const member
     function to a pointer to a non-const member function, are not covered.]

5.3 Unary expressions   [expr.unary]

1   Expressions with unary operators group right-to-left.

> *unary-expression:*
> > *postfix-expression*
> > ++ *cast-expression*
> > -- *cast-expression*
> > *unary-operator cast-expression*
> > sizeof *unary-expression*
> > sizeof (*type-id*)
> > *new-expression*
> > *delete-expression*
>
> *unary-operator:* one of
> > *   &   +   -   !   ~

5.3.1 Unary operators   [expr.unary.op]

1   The unary * operator performs *indirection*: the expression to which it is applied shall be a pointer to an
     object type, or a pointer to a function type and the result is an lvalue referring to the object or function to
     which the expression points. If the type of the expression is "pointer to T," the type of the result is "T."
     [*Note:* a pointer to an incomplete type (other than *cv* void) can be dereferenced. The lvalue thus obtained
     can be used in limited ways (to initialize a reference, for example); this lvalue must not be converted to an
     rvalue, see 4.1.]

2   The result of the unary & operator is a pointer to its operand. The operand shall be an lvalue or a *qualified-
     id*. In the first case, if the type of the expression is "T," the type of the result is "pointer to T." In particular,
     the address of an object of type "*cv* T" is "pointer to *cv* T," with the same cv-qualifiers. For a *qualified-id*,
     if the member is a static member of type "T", the type of the result is plain "pointer to T." If the member is
     a nonstatic member of class C of type T, the type of the result is "pointer to member of class C of type
     T." [*Example:*

```
struct A { int i; };
struct B : A { };
... &B::i ...                    // has type int A::*
```

     —*end example*] [*Note:* a pointer to member formed from a mutable nonstatic data member (7.1.1) does
     not reflect the mutable specifier associated with the nonstatic data member.]

3   A pointer to member is only formed when an explicit & is used and its operand is a *qualified-id* not
     enclosed in parentheses. [*Note:* that is, the expression &(qualified-id), where the *qualified-id* is

enclosed in parentheses, does not form an expression of type "pointer to member." Neither does `qualified-id`, because there is no implicit conversion from a *qualified-id* for a nonstatic member function to the type "pointer to member function" as there is from an lvalue of function type to the type "pointer to function" (4.3). Nor is `&unqualified-id` a pointer to member, even within the scope of the *unqualified-id*'s class.]

4   The address of an object of incomplete type can be taken, but if the complete type of that object is a class type that declares `operator&()` as a member function, then the behavior is undefined (and no diagnostic is required). The operand of `&` shall not be a bit-field.

5   The address of an overloaded function (clause 13) can be taken only in a context that uniquely determines which version of the overloaded function is referred to (see 13.4). [*Note:* since the context might determine whether the operand is a static or nonstatic member function, the context can also affect whether the expression has type "pointer to function" or "pointer to member function."]

6   The operand of the unary + operator shall have arithmetic, enumeration, or pointer type and the result is the value of the argument. Integral promotion is performed on integral or enumeration operands. The type of the result is the type of the promoted operand.

7   The operand of the unary - operator shall have arithmetic or enumeration type and the result is the negation of its operand. Integral promotion is performed on integral or enumeration operands. The negative of an unsigned quantity is computed by subtracting its value from 2^n, where n is the number of bits in the promoted operand. The type of the result is the type of the promoted operand.

8   The operand of the logical negation operator `!` is implicitly converted to `bool` (clause 4); its value is `true` if the converted operand is `false` and `false` otherwise. The type of the result is `bool`.

9   The operand of `~` shall have integral or enumeration type; the result is the one's complement of its operand. Integral promotions are performed. The type of the result is the type of the promoted operand. There is an ambiguity in the *unary-expression* `~X()`, where X is a *class-name*. The ambiguity is resolved in favor of treating `~` as a unary complement rather than treating `~X` as referring to a destructor.

5.3.2 Increment and decrement   [expr.pre.incr]

1   The operand of prefix `++` is modified by adding 1, or set to `true` if it is `bool` (this use is deprecated). The operand shall be a modifiable lvalue. The type of the operand shall be an arithmetic type or a pointer to a completely-defined object type. The value is the new value of the operand; it is an lvalue. If x is not of type `bool`, the expression `++x` is equivalent to `x+=1`. [*Note:* see the discussions of addition (5.7) and assignment operators (5.17) for information on conversions.]

2   The operand of prefix `--` is modified by subtracting 1. The operand shall not be of type `bool`. The requirements on the operand of prefix `--` and the properties of its result are otherwise the same as those of prefix `++`. [*Note:* For postfix increment and decrement, see 5.2.6.]

5.3.3 Sizeof   [expr.sizeof]

1   The `sizeof` operator yields the number of bytes in the object representation of its operand. The operand is either an expression, which is not evaluated, or a parenthesized *type-id*. The `sizeof` operator shall not be applied to an expression that has function or incomplete type, or to an enumeration type before all its enumerators have been declared, or to the parenthesized name of such types, or to an lvalue that designates a bit-field. `sizeof(char)`, `sizeof(signed char)` and `sizeof(unsigned char)` are 1; the result of `sizeof` applied to any other fundamental type (3.9.1) is implementation-defined. [*Note:* in particular, `sizeof(bool)` and `sizeof(wchar_t)` are implementation-defined.[69]] [*Note:* See 1.7 for the definition of *byte* and 3.9 for the definition of *object representation*.]

---

[69] `sizeof(bool)` is not required to be 1.

2   When applied to a reference or a reference type, the result is the size of the referenced type. When applied to a class, the result is the number of bytes in an object of that class including any padding required for placing objects of that type in an array. The size of a most derived class shall be greater than zero (1.8). The result of applying `sizeof` to a base class subobject is the size of the base class type.[70] When applied to an array, the result is the total number of bytes in the array. This implies that the size of an array of *n* elements is *n* times the size of an element.

3   The `sizeof` operator can be applied to a pointer to a function, but shall not be applied directly to a function.

4   The lvalue-to-rvalue (4.1), array-to-pointer (4.2), and function-to-pointer (4.3) standard conversions are not applied to the operand of `sizeof`.

5   Types shall not be defined in a `sizeof` expression.

6   The result is a constant of type `size_t`. [*Note:* `size_t` is defined in the standard header `<cstddef>`(18.1).]

5.3.4 New [expr.new]

1   The *new-expression* attempts to create an object of the *type-id* (8.1) or *new-type-id* to which it is applied. The type of that object is the *allocated type*. This type shall be a complete object type, but not an abstract class type or array thereof (1.8, 3.9, 10.4). [*Note:* because references are not objects, references cannot be created by *new-expressions*.] [*Note:* the *type-id* may be a cv-qualified type, in which case the object created by the *new-expression* has a cv-qualified type.]

> *new-expression:*
>   `::`*opt* `new` *new-placement*opt *new-type-id new-initializer*opt
>   `::`*opt* `new` *new-placement*opt (*type-id*) *new-initializer*opt
>
> *new-placement:*
>   (*expression-list*)
>
> *new-type-id:*
>   *type-specifier-seq new-declarator*opt
>
> *new-declarator:*
>   *ptr-operator new-declarator*opt
>   *direct-new-declarator*
>
> *direct-new-declarator:*
>   [*expression*]
>   *direct-new-declarator* [*constant-expression*]
>
> *new-initializer:*
>   (*expression-list*opt)

Entities created by a *new-expression* have dynamic storage duration (3.7.3). [*Note:* the lifetime of such an entity is not necessarily restricted to the scope in which it is created.] If the entity is a non-array object, the *new-expression* returns a pointer to the object created. If it is an array, the *new-expression* returns a pointer to the initial element of the array.

2   The *new-type-id* in a *new-expression* is the longest possible sequence of *new-declarators*. [*Note:* this prevents ambiguities between declarator operators &, *, [], and their expression counterparts.] [*Example:*

---

[70] The actual size of a base class subobject may be less than the result of applying `sizeof` to the subobject, due to virtual base classes and less strict padding requirements on base class subobjects.

```
new int * i;                  // syntax error: parsed as (new int*) i
                              //        not as (new int)*i
```

The * is the pointer declarator and not the multiplication operator.]

3   [*Note:* parentheses in a *new-type-id* of a *new-expression* can have surprising effects. [*Example:*

```
new int(*[10])();             // error
```

is ill-formed because the binding is

```
(new int) (*[10])();          // error
```

Instead, the explicitly parenthesized version of the new operator can be used to create objects of compound types (3.9.2):

```
new (int (*[10])());
```

allocates an array of 10 pointers to functions (taking no argument and returning int).]]

4   The *type-specifier-seq* shall not contain class declarations, or enumeration declarations.

5   When the allocated object is an array (that is, the *direct-new-declarator* syntax is used or the *new-type-id* or *type-id* denotes an array type), the *new-expression* yields a pointer to the initial element (if any) of the array. [*Note:* both new int and new int[10] have type int* and the type of new int[i][10] is int (*)[10].]

6   Every *constant-expression* in a *direct-new-declarator* shall be an integral constant expression (5.19) and evaluate to a strictly positive value. The *expression* in a *direct-new-declarator* shall have integral or enumeration type (3.9.1) with a non-negative value. [*Example:* if n is a variable of type int, then new float[n][5] is well-formed (because n is the *expression* of a *direct-new-declarator*), but new float[5][n] is ill-formed (because n is not a *constant-expression*). If n is negative, the effect of new float[n][5] is undefined.]

7   When the value of the *expression* in a *direct-new-declarator* is zero, the allocation function is called to allocate an array with no elements.

8   A *new-expression* obtains storage for the object by calling an *allocation function* (3.7.3.1). If the *new-expression* terminates by throwing an exception, it may release storage by calling a deallocation function (3.7.3.2). If the allocated type is a non-array type, the allocation function's name is operator new and the deallocation function's name is operator delete. If the allocated type is an array type, the allocation function's name is operator new[] and the deallocation function's name is operator delete[]. [*Note:* an implementation shall provide default definitions for the global allocation functions (3.7.3, 18.4.1.1, 18.4.1.2). A C++ program can provide alternative definitions of these functions (17.4.3.4) and/or class-specific versions (12.5).]

9   If the *new-expression* begins with a unary :: operator, the allocation function's name is looked up in the global scope. Otherwise, if the allocated type is a class type T or array thereof, the allocation function's name is looked up in the scope of T. If this lookup fails to find the name, or if the allocated type is not a class type, the allocation function's name is looked up in the global scope.

10 A *new-expression* passes the amount of space requested to the allocation function as the first argument of type std::size_t. That argument shall be no less than the size of the object being created; it may be greater than the size of the object being created only if the object is an array. For arrays of char and unsigned char, the difference between the result of the *new-expression* and the address returned by the allocation function shall be an integral multiple of the most stringent alignment requirement (3.9) of any object type whose size is no greater than the size of the array being created. [*Note:* Because allocation functions are assumed to return pointers to storage that is appropriately aligned for objects of any type, this constraint on array allocation overhead permits the common idiom of allocating character arrays into which objects of other types will later be placed.]

11   The *new-placement* syntax is used to supply additional arguments to an allocation function. If used, over-load resolution is performed on a function call created by assembling an argument list consisting of the amount of space requested (the first argument) and the expressions in the *new-placement* part of the *new-expression* (the second and succeeding arguments). The first of these arguments has type `size_t` and the remaining arguments have the corresponding types of the expressions in the *new-placement*.

12   [*Example:*

— `new T` results in a call of `operator new(sizeof(T))`,

— `new(2,f) T` results in a call of `operator new(sizeof(T),2,f)`,

— `new T[5]` results in a call of `operator new[](sizeof(T)*5+x)`, and

— `new(2,f) T[5]` results in a call of `operator new[](sizeof(T)*5+y,2,f)`.

Here, `x` and `y` are non-negative unspecified values representing array allocation overhead; the result of the *new-expression* will be offset by this amount from the value returned by `operator new[]`. This over-head may be applied in all array *new-expression*s, including those referencing the library function `operator new[](std::size_t, void*)` and other placement allocation functions. The amount of overhead may vary from one invocation of `new` to another.]

13   [*Note:* unless an allocation function is declared with an empty *exception-specification* (15.4), `throw()`, it indicates failure to allocate storage by throwing a *bad_alloc* exception (clause 15, 18.4.2.1); it returns a non-null pointer otherwise. If the allocation function is declared with an empty *exception-specification*, `throw()`, it returns null to indicate failure to allocate storage and a non-null pointer otherwise.] If the allocation function returns null, initialization shall not be done, the deallocation function shall not be called, and the value of the *new-expression* shall be null.

14   [*Note:* when the allocation function returns a value other than null, it must be a pointer to a block of storage in which space for the object has been reserved. The block of storage is assumed to be appropriately aligned and of the requested size. The address of the created object will not necessarily be the same as that of the block if the object is an array.]

15   A *new-expression* that creates an object of type `T` initializes that object as follows:

— If the *new-initializer* is omitted:

  — If `T` is a (possibly cv-qualified) non-POD class type (or array thereof), the object is default-initialized (8.5). If `T` is a const-qualified type, the underlying class type shall have a user-declared default constructor.

  — Otherwise, the object created has indeterminate value. If `T` is a const-qualified type, or a (possibly cv-qualified) POD class type (or array thereof) containing (directly or indirectly) a member of const-qualified type, the program is ill-formed;

— If the *new-initializer* is of the form `()`, the item is value-initialized (8.5);

— If the *new-initializer* is of the form (*expression-list*) and `T` is a class type, the appropriate constructor is called, using *expression-list* as the arguments (8.5);

— If the *new-initializer* is of the form (*expression-list*) and `T` is an arithmetic, enumeration, pointer, or pointer-to-member type and *expression-list* comprises exactly one expression, then the object is initialized to the (possibly converted) value of the expression (8.5);

— Otherwise the *new-expression* is ill-formed.

16   If the *new-expression* creates an object or an array of objects of class type, access and ambiguity control are done for the allocation function, the deallocation function (12.5), and the constructor (12.1). If the new expression creates an array of objects of class type, access and ambiguity control are done for the destructor (12.4).

17   If any part of the object initialization described above[71]) terminates by throwing an exception and a suitable
      deallocation function can be found, the deallocation function is called to free the memory in which the
      object was being constructed, after which the exception continues to propagate in the context of the *new-
      expression*. If no unambiguous matching deallocation function can be found, propagating the exception
      does not cause the object's memory to be freed. [*Note:* This is appropriate when the called allocation func-
      tion does not allocate memory; otherwise, it is likely to result in a memory leak.]

18   If the *new-expression* begins with a unary : : operator, the deallocation function's name is looked up in the
      global scope. Otherwise, if the allocated type is a class type T or an array thereof, the deallocation
      function's name is looked up in the scope of T. If this lookup fails to find the name, or if the allocated type
      is not a class type or array thereof, the deallocation function's name is looked up in the global scope.

19   A declaration of a placement deallocation function matches the declaration of a placement allocation func-
      tion if it has the same number of parameters and, after parameter transformations (8.3.5), all parameter
      types except the first are identical. Any non-placement deallocation function matches a non-placement
      allocation function. If the lookup finds a single matching deallocation function, that function will be called;
      otherwise, no deallocation function will be called.

20   If a *new-expression* calls a deallocation function, it passes the value returned from the allocation function
      call as the first argument of type void*. If a placement deallocation function is called, it is passed the
      same additional arguments as were passed to the placement allocation function, that is, the same arguments
      as those specified with the *new-placement* syntax. If the implementation is allowed to make a copy of any
      argument as part of the call to the allocation function, it is allowed to make a copy (of the same original
      value) as part of the call to the deallocation function or to reuse the copy made as part of the call to the allo-
      cation function. If the copy is elided in one place, it need not be elided in the other.

21   Whether the allocation function is called before evaluating the constructor arguments or after evaluating the
      constructor arguments but before entering the constructor is unspecified. It is also unspecified whether the
      arguments to a constructor are evaluated if the allocation function returns the null pointer or exits using an
      exception.

5.3.5 Delete   **[expr.delete]**

1   The *delete-expression* operator destroys a most derived object (1.8) or array created by a *new-expression*.

          delete-expression:
                : : *opt* delete *cast-expression*
                : : *opt* delete [ ] *cast-expression*

      The first alternative is for non-array objects, and the second is for arrays. The operand shall have a pointer
      type, or a class type having a single conversion function (12.3.2) to a pointer type. The result has type
      void.

2   If the operand has a class type, the operand is converted to a pointer type by calling the above-mentioned
      conversion function, and the converted operand is used in place of the original operand for the remainder of
      this section. In either alternative, if the value of the operand of delete is the null pointer the operation
      has no effect. In the first alternative (*delete object*), the value of the operand of delete shall be a pointer
      to a non-array object or a pointer to a sub-object (1.8) representing a base class of such an object (clause
      10). If not, the behavior is undefined. In the second alternative (*delete array*), the value of the operand of
      delete shall be the pointer value which resulted from a previous array *new-expression*.[72]) If not, the
      behavior is undefined. [*Note:* this means that the syntax of the *delete-expression* must match the type of the
      object allocated by new, not the syntax of the *new-expression*.] [*Note:* a pointer to a const type can be
      the operand of a *delete-expression*; it is not necessary to cast away the constness (5.2.11) of the pointer

---

71) This may include evaluating a *new-initializer* and/or calling a constructor.
72) For non-zero-length arrays, this is the same as a pointer to the first element of the array created by that *new-expression*. Zero-
length arrays do not have a first element.

expression before it is used as the operand of the *delete-expression.*]

3   In the first alternative (*delete object*), if the static type of the operand is different from its dynamic type, the static type shall be a base class of the operand's dynamic type and the static type shall have a virtual destructor or the behavior is undefined. In the second alternative (*delete array*) if the dynamic type of the object to be deleted differs from its static type, the behavior is undefined.[73)]

4   The *cast-expression* in a *delete-expression* shall be evaluated exactly once. If the *delete-expression* calls the implementation deallocation function (3.7.3.2), and if the operand of the delete expression is not the null pointer constant, the deallocation function will deallocate the storage referenced by the pointer thus rendering the pointer invalid. [*Note:* the value of a pointer that refers to deallocated storage is indeterminate.]

5   If the object being deleted has incomplete class type at the point of deletion and the complete class has a non-trivial destructor or a deallocation function, the behavior is undefined.

6   The *delete-expression* will invoke the destructor (if any) for the object or the elements of the array being deleted. In the case of an array, the elements will be destroyed in order of decreasing address (that is, in reverse order of the completion of their constructor; see 12.6.2).

7   The *delete-expression* will call a *deallocation function* (3.7.3.2).

8   [*Note:* An implementation provides default definitions of the global deallocation functions `operator delete()` for non-arrays (18.4.1.1) and `operator delete[]()` for arrays (18.4.1.2). A C++ program can provide alternative definitions of these functions (17.4.3.4), and/or class-specific versions (12.5).] When the keyword `delete` in a *delete-expression* is preceded by the unary `::` operator, the global deallocation function is used to deallocate the storage.

9   Access and ambiguity control are done for both the deallocation function and the destructor (12.4, 12.5).

5.4 Explicit type conversion (cast notation)   [expr.cast]

1   The result of the expression (T) *cast-expression* is of type T. The result is an lvalue if T is a reference type, otherwise the result is an rvalue. [*Note:* if T is a non-class type that is *cv-qualified*, the *cv-qualifiers* are ignored when determining the type of the resulting rvalue; see 3.10.]

2   An explicit type conversion can be expressed using functional notation (5.2.3), a type conversion operator (`dynamic_cast`, `static_cast`, `reinterpret_cast`, `const_cast`), or the *cast* notation.

>   *cast-expression:*
>   *unary-expression*
>   (*type-id*) *cast-expression*

3   Types shall not be defined in casts.

4   Any type conversion not mentioned below and not explicitly defined by the user (12.3) is ill-formed.

5   The conversions performed by

— a `const_cast` (5.2.11),

— a `static_cast` (5.2.9),

— a `static_cast` followed by a `const_cast`,

— a `reinterpret_cast` (5.2.10), or

— a `reinterpret_cast` followed by a `const_cast`,

can be performed using the cast notation of explicit type conversion. The same semantic restrictions and

---

[73)] This implies that an object cannot be deleted using a pointer of type `void*` because there are no objects of type `void`.

behaviors apply. If a conversion can be interpreted in more than one of the ways listed above, the interpretation that appears first in the list is used, even if a cast resulting from that interpretation is ill-formed. If a conversion can be interpreted in more than one way as a `static_cast` followed by a `const_cast`, the conversion is ill-formed. [*Example:*

```
struct A {};
struct I1 : A {};
struct I2 : A {};
struct D : I1, I2 {};
A *foo( D *p ) {
        return (A*)( p );          // ill-formed static_cast interpretation
}
```

—*end example*]

6   The operand of a cast using the cast notation can be an rvalue of type "pointer to incomplete class type". The destination type of a cast using the cast notation can be "pointer to incomplete class type". In such cases, even if there is a inheritance relationship between the source and destination classes, whether the `static_cast` or `reinterpret_cast` interpretation is used is unspecified.

7   In addition to those conversions, the following `static_cast` and `reinterpret_cast` operations (optionally followed by a `const_cast` operation) may be performed using the cast notation of explicit type conversion, even if the base class type is not accessible:

— a pointer to an object of derived class type or an lvalue of derived class type may be explicitly converted to a pointer or reference to an unambiguous base class type, respectively;

— a pointer to member of derived class type may be explicitly converted to a pointer to member of an unambiguous non-virtual base class type;

— a pointer to an object of non-virtual base class type, an lvalue of non-virtual base class type, or a pointer to member of non-virtual base class type may be explicitly converted to a pointer, a reference, or a pointer to member of a derived class type, respectively.

5.5 Pointer-to-member operators   [expr.mptr.oper]

1   The pointer-to-member operators `->*` and `.*` group left-to-right.

> *pm-expression:*
> > *cast-expression*
> > *pm-expression* `.*` *cast-expression*
> > *pm-expression* `->*` *cast-expression*

2   The binary operator `.*` binds its second operand, which shall be of type "pointer to member of T" (where T is a completely-defined class type) to its first operand, which shall be of class T or of a class of which T is an unambiguous and accessible base class. The result is an object or a function of the type specified by the second operand.

3   The binary operator `->*` binds its second operand, which shall be of type "pointer to member of T" (where T is a completely-defined class type) to its first operand, which shall be of type "pointer to T" or "pointer to a class of which T is an unambiguous and accessible base class." The result is an object or a function of the type specified by the second operand.

4   If the dynamic type of the object does not contain the member to which the pointer refers, the behavior is undefined.

5   The restrictions on *cv*-qualification, and the manner in which the *cv*-qualifiers of the operands are combined to produce the *cv*-qualifiers of the result, are the same as the rules for E1.E2 given in 5.2.5. [*Note:* it is not possible to use a pointer to member that refers to a `mutable` member to modify a `const` class object. For example,

```
struct S {
        mutable int i;
};
const S cs;
int S::* pm = &S::i;              // pm refers to mutable member S::i
cs.*pm = 88;                      // ill-formed: cs is a const object
```

]

6   If the result of .* or ->* is a function, then that result can be used only as the operand for the function call operator (). [*Example:*

```
(ptr_to_obj->*ptr_to_mfct)(10);
```

calls the member function denoted by ptr_to_mfct for the object pointed to by ptr_to_obj.] The result of a .* expression is an lvalue only if its first operand is an lvalue and its second operand is a pointer to data member. The result of an ->* expression is an lvalue only if its second operand is a pointer to data member. If the second operand is the null pointer to member value (4.11), the behavior is undefined.

5.6 Multiplicative operators   [expr.mul]

1   The multiplicative operators *, /, and % group left-to-right.

> *multiplicative-expression:*
>   *pm-expression*
>   *multiplicative-expression* * *pm-expression*
>   *multiplicative-expression* / *pm-expression*
>   *multiplicative-expression* % *pm-expression*

2   The operands of * and / shall have arithmetic or enumeration type; the operands of % shall have integral or enumeration type. The usual arithmetic conversions are performed on the operands and determine the type of the result.

3   The binary * operator indicates multiplication.

4   The binary / operator yields the quotient, and the binary % operator yields the remainder from the division of the first expression by the second. If the second operand of / or % is zero the behavior is undefined; otherwise (a/b)*b + a%b is equal to a. If both operands are nonnegative then the remainder is nonnegative; if not, the sign of the remainder is implementation-defined[74].

5.7 Additive operators   [expr.add]

1   The additive operators + and - group left-to-right. The usual arithmetic conversions are performed for operands of arithmetic or enumeration type.

> *additive-expression:*
>   *multiplicative-expression*
>   *additive-expression* + *multiplicative-expression*
>   *additive-expression* - *multiplicative-expression*

For addition, either both operands shall have arithmetic or enumeration type, or one operand shall be a pointer to a completely defined object type and the other shall have integral or enumeration type.

2   For subtraction, one of the following shall hold:

— both operands have arithmetic or enumeration type; or

---

[74] According to work underway toward the revision of ISO C, the preferred algorithm for integer division follows the rules defined in the ISO Fortran standard, ISO/IEC 1539:1991, in which the quotient is always rounded toward zero.

— both operands are pointers to cv-qualified or cv-unqualified versions of the same completely defined object type; or

— the left operand is a pointer to a completely defined object type and the right operand has integral or enumeration type.

3   The result of the binary + operator is the sum of the operands. The result of the binary - operator is the difference resulting from the subtraction of the second operand from the first.

4   For the purposes of these operators, a pointer to a nonarray object behaves the same as a pointer to the first element of an array of length one with the type of the object as its element type.

5   When an expression that has integral type is added to or subtracted from a pointer, the result has the type of the pointer operand. If the pointer operand points to an element of an array object, and the array is large enough, the result points to an element offset from the original element such that the difference of the subscripts of the resulting and original array elements equals the integral expression. In other words, if the expression P points to the i-th element of an array object, the expressions (P)+N (equivalently, N+(P)) and (P)-N (where N has the value n) point to, respectively, the $i+n$-th and $i-n$-th elements of the array object, provided they exist. Moreover, if the expression P points to the last element of an array object, the expression (P)+1 points one past the last element of the array object, and if the expression Q points one past the last element of an array object, the expression (Q)-1 points to the last element of the array object. If both the pointer operand and the result point to elements of the same array object, or one past the last element of the array object, the evaluation shall not produce an overflow; otherwise, the behavior is undefined.

6   When two pointers to elements of the same array object are subtracted, the result is the difference of the subscripts of the two array elements. The type of the result is an implementation-defined signed integral type; this type shall be the same type that is defined as ptrdiff_t in the <cstddef> header (18.1). As with any other arithmetic overflow, if the result does not fit in the space provided, the behavior is undefined. In other words, if the expressions P and Q point to, respectively, the i-th and j-th elements of an array object, the expression (P)-(Q) has the value $i-j$ provided the value fits in an object of type ptrdiff_t. Moreover, if the expression P points either to an element of an array object or one past the last element of an array object, and the expression Q points to the last element of the same array object, the expression ((Q)+1)-(P) has the same value as ((Q)-(P))+1 and as -((P)-((Q)+1)), and has the value zero if the expression P points one past the last element of the array object, even though the expression (Q)+1 does not point to an element of the array object. Unless both pointers point to elements of the same array object, or one past the last element of the array object, the behavior is undefined.[75]

7   If the value 0 is added to or subtracted from a pointer value, the result compares equal to the original pointer value. If two pointers point to the same object or both point one past the end of the same array or both are null, and the two pointers are subtracted, the result compares equal to the value 0 converted to the type ptrdiff_t.

---

[75] Another way to approach pointer arithmetic is first to convert the pointer(s) to character pointer(s): In this scheme the integral value of the expression added to or subtracted from the converted pointer is first multiplied by the size of the object originally pointed to, and the resulting pointer is converted back to the original type. For pointer subtraction, the result of the difference between the character pointers is similarly divided by the size of the object originally pointed to.

When viewed in this way, an implementation need only provide one extra byte (which might overlap another object in the program) just after the end of the object in order to satisfy the "one past the last element" requirements.

5.8 Shift operators   [expr.shift]

1   The shift operators `<<` and `>>` group left-to-right.

> *shift-expression:*
>   *additive-expression*
>   *shift-expression* `<<` *additive-expression*
>   *shift-expression* `>>` *additive-expression*

The operands shall be of integral or enumeration type and integral promotions are performed. The type of the result is that of the promoted left operand. The behavior is undefined if the right operand is negative, or greater than or equal to the length in bits of the promoted left operand.

2   The value of `E1 << E2` is `E1` (interpreted as a bit pattern) left-shifted `E2` bit positions; vacated bits are zero-filled. If `E1` has an unsigned type, the value of the result is `E1` multiplied by the quantity 2 raised to the power `E2`, reduced modulo `ULONG_MAX+1` if `E1` has type unsigned long, `UINT_MAX+1` otherwise. [*Note:* the constants `ULONG_MAX` and `UINT_MAX` are defined in the header `<climits>`).]

3   The value of `E1 >> E2` is `E1` right-shifted `E2` bit positions. If `E1` has an unsigned type or if `E1` has a signed type and a nonnegative value, the value of the result is the integral part of the quotient of `E1` divided by the quantity 2 raised to the power `E2`. If `E1` has a signed type and a negative value, the resulting value is implementation-defined.

5.9 Relational operators   [expr.rel]

1   The relational operators group left-to-right. [*Example:* `a<b<c` means `(a<b)<c` and *not* `(a<b)&&(b<c)`.]

> *relational-expression:*
>   *shift-expression*
>   *relational-expression* `<` *shift-expression*
>   *relational-expression* `>` *shift-expression*
>   *relational-expression* `<=` *shift-expression*
>   *relational-expression* `>=` *shift-expression*

The operands shall have arithmetic, enumeration or pointer type. The operators `<` (less than), `>` (greater than), `<=` (less than or equal to), and `>=` (greater than or equal to) all yield `false` or `true`. The type of the result is `bool`.

2   The usual arithmetic conversions are performed on operands of arithmetic or enumeration type. Pointer conversions (4.10) and qualification conversions (4.4) are performed on pointer operands (or on a pointer operand and a null pointer constant) to bring them to their *composite pointer type*. If one operand is a null pointer constant, the composite pointer type is the type of the other operand. Otherwise, if one of the operands has type "pointer to *cv1* `void`", then the other has type "pointer to *cv2 T*" and the composite pointer type is "pointer to *cv12* `void`", where *cv12* is the union of *cv1* and *cv2*. Otherwise, the composite pointer type is a pointer type similar (4.4) to the type of one of the operands, with a cv-qualification signature (4.4) that is the union of the cv-qualification signatures of the operand types. [*Note:* this implies that any pointer can be compared to a null pointer constant and that any object pointer can be compared to a pointer to (possibly cv-qualified) `void`.] [*Example:*

```
void *p;
const int *q;
int **pi;
const int *const *pci;
void ct()
{
    p <= q;          // Both converted to const void * before comparison
    pi <= pci;       // Both converted to const int *const * before comparison
}
```

—*end example*] Pointers to objects or functions of the same type (after pointer conversions) can be compared, with a result defined as follows:

— If two pointers p and q of the same type point to the same object or function, or both point one past the end of the same array, or are both null, then p<=q and p>=q both yield `true` and p<q and p>q both yield `false`.

— If two pointers p and q of the same type point to different objects that are not members of the same object or elements of the same array or to different functions, or if only one of them is null, the results of p<q, p>q, p<=q, and p>=q are unspecified.

— If two pointers point to nonstatic data members of the same object, or to subobjects or array elements of such members, recursively, the pointer to the later declared member compares greater provided the two members are not separated by an *access-specifier* label (11.1) and provided their class is not a union.

— If two pointers point to nonstatic data members of the same object separated by an *access-specifier* label (11.1) the result is unspecified.

— If two pointers point to data members of the same union object, they compare equal (after conversion to `void*`, if necessary). If two pointers point to elements of the same array or one beyond the end of the array, the pointer to the object with the higher subscript compares higher.

— Other pointer comparisons are unspecified.

5.10 Equality operators   [expr.eq]

> *equality-expression:*
> > *relational-expression*
> > *equality-expression* == *relational-expression*
> > *equality-expression* != *relational-expression*

1   The == (equal to) and the != (not equal to) operators have the same semantic restrictions, conversions, and result type as the relational operators except for their lower precedence and truth-value result. [*Note:* a<b == c<d is `true` whenever a<b and c<d have the same truth-value.] Pointers to objects or functions of the same type (after pointer conversions) can be compared for equality. Two pointers of the same type compare equal if and only if they are both null, both point to the same function, or both represent the same address (3.9.2).

2   In addition, pointers to members can be compared, or a pointer to member and a null pointer constant. Pointer to member conversions (4.11) and qualification conversions (4.4) are performed to bring them to a common type. If one operand is a null pointer constant, the common type is the type of the other operand. Otherwise, the common type is a pointer to member type similar (4.4) to the type of one of the operands, with a cv-qualification signature (4.4) that is the union of the cv-qualification signatures of the operand types. [*Note:* this implies that any pointer to member can be compared to a null pointer constant.] If both operands are null, they compare equal. Otherwise if only one is null, they compare unequal. Otherwise if either is a pointer to a virtual member function, the result is unspecified. Otherwise they compare equal if and only if they would refer to the same member of the same most derived object (1.8) or the same subobject if they were dereferenced with a hypothetical object of the associated class type. [*Example:*

```
struct B {
        int f();
};
struct L : B { };
struct R : B { };
struct D : L, R { };
```

```
int (B::*pb)() = &B::f;
int (L::*pl)() = pb;
int (R::*pr)() = pb;
int (D::*pdl)() = pl;
int (D::*pdr)() = pr;
bool x = (pdl == pdr);              // false
```

—*end example*]

5.11 Bitwise AND operator   [expr.bit.and]

> *and-expression:*
> > *equality-expression*
> > *and-expression* & *equality-expression*

1   The usual arithmetic conversions are performed; the result is the bitwise AND function of the operands. The operator applies only to integral or enumeration operands.

5.12 Bitwise exclusive OR operator   [expr.xor]

> *exclusive-or-expression:*
> > *and-expression*
> > *exclusive-or-expression* ^ *and-expression*

1   The usual arithmetic conversions are performed; the result is the bitwise exclusive OR function of the operands. The operator applies only to integral or enumeration operands.

5.13 Bitwise inclusive OR operator   [expr.or]

> *inclusive-or-expression:*
> > *exclusive-or-expression*
> > *inclusive-or-expression* | *exclusive-or-expression*

1   The usual arithmetic conversions are performed; the result is the bitwise inclusive OR function of its operands. The operator applies only to integral or enumeration operands.

5.14 Logical AND operator   [expr.log.and]

> *logical-and-expression:*
> > *inclusive-or-expression*
> > *logical-and-expression* && *inclusive-or-expression*

1   The && operator groups left-to-right. The operands are both implicitly converted to type bool (clause 4). The result is true if both operands are true and false otherwise. Unlike &, && guarantees left-to-right evaluation: the second operand is not evaluated if the first operand is false.

2   The result is a bool. All side effects of the first expression except for destruction of temporaries (12.2) happen before the second expression is evaluated.

5.15 Logical OR operator   [expr.log.or]

> *logical-or-expression:*
> > *logical-and-expression*
> > *logical-or-expression* || *logical-and-expression*

1   The || operator groups left-to-right. The operands are both implicitly converted to bool (clause 4). It returns true if either of its operands is true, and false otherwise. Unlike |, || guarantees left-to-right evaluation; moreover, the second operand is not evaluated if the first operand evaluates to true.

2   The result is a `bool`. All side effects of the first expression except for destruction of temporaries (12.2) happen before the second expression is evaluated.

5.16 Conditional operator   [expr.cond]

> *conditional-expression:*
> > *logical-or-expression*
> > *logical-or-expression* ? *expression* : *assignment-expression*

1   Conditional expressions group right-to-left. The first expression is implicitly converted to `bool` (clause 4). It is evaluated and if it is `true`, the result of the conditional expression is the value of the second expression, otherwise that of the third expression. All side effects of the first expression except for destruction of temporaries (12.2) happen before the second or third expression is evaluated. Only one of the second and third expressions is evaluated.

2   If either the second or the third operand has type (possibly cv-qualified) `void`, then the lvalue-to-rvalue (4.1), array-to-pointer (4.2), and function-to-pointer (4.3) standard conversions are performed on the second and third operands, and one of the following shall hold:

— The second or the third operand (but not both) is a *throw-expression* (15.1); the result is of the type of the other and is an rvalue.

— Both the second and the third operands have type `void`; the result is of type `void` and is an rvalue. [*Note:* this includes the case where both operands are *throw-expression*s.]

3   Otherwise, if the second and third operand have different types, and either has (possibly cv-qualified) class type, an attempt is made to convert each of those operands to the type of the other. The process for determining whether an operand expression `E1` of type `T1` can be converted to match an operand expression `E2` of type `T2` is defined as follows:

— If `E2` is an lvalue: `E1` can be converted to match `E2` if `E1` can be implicitly converted (clause 4) to the type "reference to `T2`", subject to the constraint that in the conversion the reference must bind directly (8.5.3) to `E1`.

— If `E2` is an rvalue, or if the conversion above cannot be done:

— if `E1` and `E2` have class type, and the underlying class types are the same or one is a base class of the other: `E1` can be converted to match `E2` if the class of `T2` is the same type as, or a base class of, the class of `T1`, and the cv-qualification of `T2` is the same cv-qualification as, or a greater cv-qualification than, the cv-qualification of `T1`. If the conversion is applied, `E1` is changed to an rvalue of type `T2` that still refers to the original source class object (or the appropriate subobject thereof). [*Note:* that is, no copy is made.]

— Otherwise (i.e., if `E1` or `E2` has a nonclass type, or if they both have class types but the underlying classes are not either the same or one a base class of the other): `E1` can be converted to match `E2` if `E1` can be implicitly converted to the type that expression `E2` would have if `E2` were converted to an rvalue (or the type it has, if `E2` is an rvalue).

Using this process, it is determined whether the second operand can be converted to match the third operand, and whether the third operand can be converted to match the second operand. If both can be converted, or one can be converted but the conversion is ambiguous, the program is ill-formed. If neither can be converted, the operands are left unchanged and further checking is performed as described below. If exactly one conversion is possible, that conversion is applied to the chosen operand and the converted operand is used in place of the original operand for the remainder of this section.

4   If the second and third operands are lvalues and have the same type, the result is of that type and is an lvalue.

5   Otherwise, the result is an rvalue. If the second and third operand do not have the same type, and either has (possibly cv-qualified) class type, overload resolution is used to determine the conversions (if any) to be applied to the operands (13.3.1.2, 13.6). If the overload resolution fails, the program is ill-formed. Otherwise, the conversions thus determined are applied, and the converted operands are used in place of the original operands for the remainder of this section.

6   Lvalue-to-rvalue (4.1), array-to-pointer (4.2), and function-to-pointer (4.3) standard conversions are performed on the second and third operands. After those conversions, one of the following shall hold:

— The second and third operands have the same type; the result is of that type.

— The second and third operands have arithmetic or enumeration type; the usual arithmetic conversions are performed to bring them to a common type, and the result is of that type.

— The second and third operands have pointer type, or one has pointer type and the other is a null pointer constant; pointer conversions (4.10) and qualification conversions (4.4) are performed to bring them to their composite pointer type (5.9). The result is of the composite pointer type.

— The second and third operands have pointer to member type, or one has pointer to member type and the other is a null pointer constant; pointer to member conversions (4.11) and qualification conversions (4.4) are performed to bring them to a common type, whose cv-qualification shall match the cv-qualification of either the second or the third operand. The result is of the common type.

5.17 Assignment operators   [expr.ass]

1   There are several assignment operators, all of which group right-to-left. All require a modifiable lvalue as their left operand, and the type of an assignment expression is that of its left operand. The result of the assignment operation is the value stored in the left operand after the assignment has taken place; the result is an lvalue.

> *assignment-expression:*
>> *conditional-expression*
>> *logical-or-expression   assignment-operator   assignment-expression*
>> *throw-expression*

> *assignment-operator* :   one of
>>   =   *=   /=   %=   +=   -=   >>=   <<=   &=   ^= |=

2   In simple assignment (=), the value of the expression replaces that of the object referred to by the left operand.

3   If the left operand is not of class type, the expression is implicitly converted (clause 4) to the cv-unqualified type of the left operand.

4   If the left operand is of class type, the class shall be complete. Assignment to objects of a class is defined by the copy assignment operator (12.8, 13.5.3).

5   [*Note:* For class objects, assignment is not in general the same as initialization (8.5, 12.1, 12.6, 12.8).]

6   When the left operand of an assignment operator denotes a reference to T, the operation assigns to the object of type T denoted by the reference.

7   The behavior of an expression of the form E1 *op*= E2 is equivalent to E1 = E1 *op* E2 except that E1 is evaluated only once. In += and -=, E1 shall either have arithmetic type or be a pointer to a possibly cv-qualified completely defined object type. In all other cases, E1 shall have arithmetic type.

8   If the value being stored in an object is accessed from another object that overlaps in any way the storage of the first object, then the overlap shall be exact and the two objects shall have the same type, otherwise the behavior is undefined.

1   The comma operator groups left-to-right.

> *expression:*
> > *assignment-expression*
> > *expression* , *assignment-expression*

A pair of expressions separated by a comma is evaluated left-to-right and the value of the left expression is discarded. The lvalue-to-rvalue (4.1), array-to-pointer (4.2), and function-to-pointer (4.3) standard conversions are not applied to the left expression. All side effects (1.9) of the left expression, except for the destruction of temporaries (12.2), are performed before the evaluation of the right expression. The type and value of the result are the type and value of the right operand; the result is an lvalue if its right operand is.

2   In contexts where comma is given a special meaning, [*Example:* in lists of arguments to functions (5.2.2) and lists of initializers (8.5)] the comma operator as described in clause 5 can appear only in parentheses. [*Example:*

```
f(a, (t=3, t+2), c);
```

has three arguments, the second of which has the value 5.]

5.19 Constant expressions   **[expr.const]**

1   In several places, C++ requires expressions that evaluate to an integral or enumeration constant: as array bounds (8.3.4, 5.3.4), as `case` expressions (6.4.2), as bit-field lengths (9.6), as enumerator initializers (7.2), as static member initializers (9.4.2), and as integral or enumeration non-type template arguments (14.3).

> *constant-expression:*
> > *conditional-expression*

An *integral constant-expression* can involve only literals (2.13), enumerators, `const` variables or static data members of integral or enumeration types initialized with constant expressions (8.5), non-type template parameters of integral or enumeration types, and `sizeof` expressions. Floating literals (2.13.3) can appear only if they are cast to integral or enumeration types. Only type conversions to integral or enumeration types can be used. In particular, except in `sizeof` expressions, functions, class objects, pointers, or references shall not be used, and assignment, increment, decrement, function-call, or comma operators shall not be used.

2   Other expressions are considered *constant-expression*s only for the purpose of non-local static object initialization (3.6.2). Such constant expressions shall evaluate to one of the following:

— a null pointer value (4.10),

— a null member pointer value (4.11),

— an arithmetic constant expression,

— an address constant expression,

— a reference constant expression,

— an address constant expression for a complete object type, plus or minus an integral constant expression, or

— a pointer to member constant expression.

3   An *arithmetic constant expression* shall satisfy the requirements for an integral constant expression, except that

— floating literals need not be cast to integral or enumeration type, and

— conversions to floating point types are permitted.

4   An *address constant expression* is a pointer to an lvalue designating an object of static storage duration, a
     string literal (2.13.4), or a function. The pointer shall be created explicitly, using the unary & operator, or
     implicitly using a non-type template parameter of pointer type, or using an expression of array (4.2) or
     function (4.3) type. The subscripting operator [] and the class member access . and -> operators, the &
     and * unary operators, and pointer casts (except dynamic_casts, 5.2.7) can be used in the creation of an
     address constant expression, but the value of an object shall not be accessed by the use of these operators.
     If the subscripting operator is used, one of its operands shall be an integral constant expression. An expres-
     sion that designates the address of a subobject of a non-POD class object (clause 9) is not an address con-
     stant expression (12.7). Function calls shall not be used in an address constant expression, even if the func-
     tion is inline and has a reference return type.

5   A *reference constant expression* is an lvalue designating an object of static storage duration, a non-type
     template parameter of reference type, or a function. The subscripting operator [], the class member access
     . and -> operators, the & and * unary operators, and reference casts (except those invoking user-defined
     conversion functions (12.3.2) and except dynamic_casts (5.2.7)) can be used in the creation of a refer-
     ence constant expression, but the value of an object shall not be accessed by the use of these operators. If
     the subscripting operator is used, one of its operands shall be an integral constant expression. An lvalue
     expression that designates a member or base class of a non-POD class object (clause 9) is not a reference
     constant expression (12.7). Function calls shall not be used in a reference constant expression, even if the
     function is inline and has a reference return type.

6   A *pointer to member constant expression* shall be created using the unary & operator applied to a *qualified-
     id* operand (5.3.1), optionally preceded by a pointer to member cast (5.2.9).

6 Statements **[stmt.stmt]**

1   Except as indicated, statements are executed in sequence.

> *statement:*
> > *labeled-statement*
> > *expression-statement*
> > *compound-statement*
> > *selection-statement*
> > *iteration-statement*
> > *jump-statement*
> > *declaration-statement*
> > *try-block*

6.1 Labeled statement **[stmt.label]**

1   A statement can be labeled.

> *labeled-statement:*
> > *identifier* : *statement*
> > `case` *constant-expression* : *statement*
> > `default` : *statement*

An identifier label declares the identifier. The only use of an identifier label is as the target of a `goto`. The scope of a label is the function in which it appears. Labels shall not be redeclared within a function. A label can be used in a `goto` statement before its definition. Labels have their own name space and do not interfere with other identifiers.

2   Case labels and default labels shall occur only in switch statements.

6.2 Expression statement **[stmt.expr]**

1   Expression statements have the form

> *expression-statement:*
> > *expression$_{opt}$* `;`

The expression is evaluated and its value is discarded. The lvalue-to-rvalue (4.1), array-to-pointer (4.2), and function-to-pointer (4.3) standard conversions are not applied to the expression. All side effects from an expression statement are completed before the next statement is executed. An expression statement with the expression missing is called a null statement. [*Note:* Most statements are expression statements— usually assignments or function calls. A null statement is useful to carry a label just before the } of a compound statement and to supply a null body to an iteration statement such as a `while` statement (6.5.1).]

6.3 Compound statement or block **[stmt.block]**

1   So that several statements can be used where one is expected, the compound statement (also, and equivalently, called "block") is provided.

> *compound-statement:*
> > { *statement-seq$_{opt}$* }
>
> *statement-seq:*
> > *statement*
> > *statement-seq statement*

A compound statement defines a local scope (3.3). [*Note:* a declaration is a *statement* (6.7).]

6.4 Selection statements

1   Selection statements choose one of several flows of control.

> *selection-statement:*
> > if (*condition*) *statement*
> > if (*condition*) *statement* else *statement*
> > switch (*condition*) *statement*

> *condition:*
> > *expression*
> > *type-specifier-seq declarator* = *assignment-expression*

In clause 6, the term *substatement* refers to the contained *statement* or *statement*s that appear in the syntax notation. The substatement in a *selection-statement* (each substatement, in the else form of the if statement) implicitly defines a local scope (3.3). If the substatement in a selection-statement is a single statement and not a *compound-statement,* it is as if it was rewritten to be a compound-statement containing the original substatement. [*Example:*

```
if (x)
    int i;
```

can be equivalently rewritten as

```
if (x) {
    int i;
}
```

Thus after the if statement, i is no longer in scope.]

2   The rules for *condition*s apply both to *selection-statement*s and to the for and while statements (6.5). The *declarator* shall not specify a function or an array. The *type-specifier-seq* shall not contain typedef and shall not declare a new class or enumeration.

3   A name introduced by a declaration in a *condition* (either introduced by the *type-specifier-seq* or the *declarator* of the condition) is in scope from its point of declaration until the end of the substatements controlled by the condition. If the name is re-declared in the outermost block of a substatement controlled by the condition, the declaration that re-declares the name is ill-formed. [*Example:*

```
if (int x = f()) {
        int x;                  // ill-formed, redeclaration of x
}
else {
        int x;                  // ill-formed, redeclaration of x
}
```

—*end example*]

4   The value of a *condition* that is an initialized declaration in a statement other than a switch statement is the value of the declared variable implicitly converted to type bool. If that conversion is ill-formed, the program is ill-formed. The value of a *condition* that is an initialized declaration in a switch statement is the value of the declared variable if it has integral or enumeration type, or of that variable implicitly converted to integral or enumeration type otherwise. The value of a *condition* that is an expression is the value of the expression, implicitly converted to bool for statements other than switch; if that conversion is ill-formed, the program is ill-formed. The value of the condition will be referred to as simply "the condition" where the usage is unambiguous.

5   If a *condition* can be syntactically resolved as either an expression or the declaration of a local name, it is interpreted as a declaration.

6.4.1 The `if` statement
[stmt.if]

1   If the condition (6.4) yields `true` the first substatement is executed. If the `else` part of the selection statement is present and the condition yields `false`, the second substatement is executed. In the second form of `if` statement (the one including `else`), if the first substatement is also an `if` statement then that inner `if` statement shall contain an `else` part.[76)

6.4.2 The `switch` statement
[stmt.switch]

1   The `switch` statement causes control to be transferred to one of several statements depending on the value of a condition.

2   The condition shall be of integral type, enumeration type, or of a class type for which a single conversion function to integral or enumeration type exists (12.3). If the condition is of class type, the condition is converted by calling that conversion function, and the result of the conversion is used in place of the original condition for the remainder of this section. Integral promotions are performed. Any statement within the `switch` statement can be labeled with one or more case labels as follows:

> `case` *constant-expression* `:`

where the *constant-expression* shall be an integral *constant-expression*. The integral constant-expression (5.19) is implicitly converted to the promoted type of the switch condition. No two of the case constants in the same switch shall have the same value after conversion to the promoted type of the switch condition.

3   There shall be at most one label of the form

> `default :`

within a `switch` statement.

4   Switch statements can be nested; a `case` or `default` label is associated with the smallest switch enclosing it.

5   When the `switch` statement is executed, its condition is evaluated and compared with each case constant. If one of the case constants is equal to the value of the condition, control is passed to the statement following the matched case label. If no case constant matches the condition, and if there is a `default` label, control passes to the statement labeled by the default label. If no case matches and if there is no `default` then none of the statements in the switch is executed.

6   `case` and `default` labels in themselves do not alter the flow of control, which continues unimpeded across such labels. To exit from a switch, see `break`, 6.6.1. [*Note:* usually, the substatement that is the subject of a switch is compound and `case` and `default` labels appear on the top-level statements contained within the (compound) substatement, but this is not required. Declarations can appear in the substatement of a *switch-statement*.]

6.5 Iteration statements
[stmt.iter]

1   Iteration statements specify looping.

> *iteration-statement:*
>   `while (` *condition* `)` *statement*
>   `do` *statement* `while (` *expression* `) ;`
>   `for (` *for-init-statement* *condition*$_{opt}$ `;` *expression*$_{opt}$ `)` *statement*

> *for-init-statement:*
>   *expression-statement*
>   *simple-declaration*

[*Note:* a *for-init-statement* ends with a semicolon.]

[76) In other words, the `else` is associated with the nearest un-elsed `if`.

2   The substatement in an *iteration-statement* implicitly defines a local scope (3.3) which is entered and exited each time through the loop.

3   If the substatement in an iteration-statement is a single statement and not a *compound-statement,* it is as if it was rewritten to be a compound-statement containing the original statement. [*Example:*

```
while (--x >= 0)
    int i;
```

can be equivalently rewritten as

```
while (--x >= 0) {
    int i;
}
```

Thus after the `while` statement, `i` is no longer in scope.]

4   [*Note:* The requirements on *condition*s in iteration statements are described in 6.4.   —*end note*]

6.5.1 The `while` statement   [stmt.while]

1   In the `while` statement the substatement is executed repeatedly until the value of the condition (6.4) becomes `false`. The test takes place before each execution of the substatement.

2   When the condition of a while statement is a declaration, the scope of the variable that is declared extends from its point of declaration (3.3.1) to the end of the while *statement*. A while statement of the form

```
while (T t = x) statement
```

is equivalent to

```
label:
{                                       // start of condition scope
    T t = x;
    if (t) {
        statement
        goto label;
    }
}                                       // end of condition scope
```

The object created in a condition is destroyed and created with each iteration of the loop. [*Example:*

```
struct A {
    int val;
    A(int i) : val(i) { }
    ~A() { }
    operator bool() { return val != 0; }
};
int i = 1;
while (A a = i) {
    //...
    i = 0;
}
```

In the while-loop, the constructor and destructor are each called twice, once for the condition that succeeds and once for the condition that fails.]

6.5.2 The do statement [stmt.do]

1   The expression is implicitly converted to `bool`; if that is not possible, the program is ill-formed.

2   In the do statement the substatement is executed repeatedly until the value of the expression becomes `false`. The test takes place after each execution of the statement.

6.5.3 The for statement   [stmt.for]

1   The `for` statement

         for (*for-init-statement condition*_{opt} ; *expression*_{opt}) *statement*

is equivalent to

```
{
        for-init-statement
        while ( condition ) {
                statement
                expression ;
        }
}
```

except that names declared in the *for-init-statement* are in the same declarative-region as those declared in the *condition*, and except that a `continue` in *statement* (not enclosed in another iteration statement) will execute *expression* before re-evaluating *condition*. [*Note:* Thus the first statement specifies initialization for the loop; the condition (6.4) specifies a test, made before each iteration, such that the loop is exited when the condition becomes `false`; the expression often specifies incrementing that is done after each iteration.]

2   Either or both of the condition and the expression can be omitted. A missing *condition* makes the implied `while` clause equivalent to `while(true)`.

3   If the *for-init-statement* is a declaration, the scope of the name(s) declared extends to the end of the *for-statement*. [*Example:*

```
int i = 42;
int a[10];

for (int i = 0; i < 10; i++)
        a[i] = i;

int j = i;                          // j = 42
```

—*end example*]

6.6 Jump statements   [stmt.jump]

1   Jump statements unconditionally transfer control.

```
jump-statement:
        break ;
        continue ;
        return expressionopt ;
        goto identifier ;
```

2   On exit from a scope (however accomplished), destructors (12.4) are called for all constructed objects with automatic storage duration (3.7.2) (named objects or temporaries) that are declared in that scope, in the reverse order of their declaration. Transfer out of a loop, out of a block, or back past an initialized variable with automatic storage duration involves the destruction of variables with automatic storage duration that are in scope at the point transferred from but not at the point transferred to. (See 6.7 for transfers into blocks). [*Note:* However, the program can be terminated (by calling `exit()` or `abort()`(18.3), for

example) without destroying class objects with automatic storage duration.]

6.6.1 The break statement   [stmt.break]

1   The break statement shall occur only in an *iteration-statement* or a switch statement and causes termination of the smallest enclosing *iteration-statement* or switch statement; control passes to the statement following the terminated statement, if any.

6.6.2 The continue statement   [stmt.cont]

1   The continue statement shall occur only in an *iteration-statement* and causes control to pass to the loop-continuation portion of the smallest enclosing *iteration-statement*, that is, to the end of the loop. More precisely, in each of the statements

```
while (foo) {        do {               for (;;) {
  {                    {                  {
  // ...               // ...             // ...
  }                    }                  }
contin: ;            contin: ;          contin: ;
}                    } while (foo);     }
```

a continue not contained in an enclosed iteration statement is equivalent to goto contin.

6.6.3 The return statement   [stmt.return]

1   A function returns to its caller by the return statement.

2   A return statement without an expression can be used only in functions that do not return a value, that is, a function with the return type void, a constructor (12.1), or a destructor (12.4). A return statement with an expression of non-void type can be used only in functions returning a value; the value of the expression is returned to the caller of the function. The expression is implicitly converted to the return type of the function in which it appears. A return statement can involve the construction and copy of a temporary object (12.2). Flowing off the end of a function is equivalent to a return with no value; this results in undefined behavior in a value-returning function.

3   A return statement with an expression of type "*cv* void" can be used only in functions with a return type of *cv* void; the expression is evaluated just before the function returns to its caller.

6.6.4 The goto statement   [stmt.goto]

1   The goto statement unconditionally transfers control to the statement labeled by the identifier. The identifier shall be a label (6.1) located in the current function.

6.7 Declaration statement   [stmt.dcl]

1   A declaration statement introduces one or more new identifiers into a block; it has the form

> *declaration-statement:*
>   *block-declaration*

If an identifier introduced by a declaration was previously declared in an outer block, the outer declaration is hidden for the remainder of the block, after which it resumes its force.

2   Variables with automatic storage duration (3.7.2) are initialized each time their *declaration-statement* is executed. Variables with automatic storage duration declared in the block are destroyed on exit from the block (6.6).

3   It is possible to transfer into a block, but not in a way that bypasses declarations with initialization. A program that jumps[77] from a point where a local variable with automatic storage duration is not in scope to a

---

[77] The transfer from the condition of a switch statement to a case label is considered a jump in this respect.

point where it is in scope is ill-formed unless the variable has POD type (3.9) and is declared without an *initializer* (8.5).
[*Example:*

```
    void f()
    {
        // ...
        goto lx;                    // ill-formed: jump into scope of a
        // ...
    ly:
        X a = 1;
        // ...
    lx:
        goto ly;                    // OK, jump implies destructor
                                    // call for a followed by construction
                                    // again immediately following label ly

    }
```

—*end example*]

4   The zero-initialization (8.5) of all local objects with static storage duration (3.7.1) is performed before any other initialization takes place. A local object of POD type (3.9) with static storage duration initialized with *constant-expression*s is initialized before its block is first entered. An implementation is permitted to perform early initialization of other local objects with static storage duration under the same conditions that an implementation is permitted to statically initialize an object with static storage duration in namespace scope (3.6.2). Otherwise such an object is initialized the first time control passes through its declaration; such an object is considered initialized upon the completion of its initialization. If the initialization exits by throwing an exception, the initialization is not complete, so it will be tried again the next time control enters the declaration. If control re-enters the declaration (recursively) while the object is being initialized, the behavior is undefined. [*Example:*

```
    int foo(int i)
    {
        static int s = foo(2*i);    // recursive call – undefined
        return i+1;
    }
```

—*end example*]

5   The destructor for a local object with static storage duration will be executed if and only if the variable was constructed. [*Note:* 3.6.3 describes the order in which local objects with static storage duration are destroyed.]

6.8 Ambiguity resolution   [stmt.ambig]

1   There is an ambiguity in the grammar involving *expression-statement*s and *declaration*s: An *expression-statement* with a function-style explicit type conversion (5.2.3) as its leftmost subexpression can be indistinguishable from a *declaration* where the first *declarator* starts with a (. In those cases the *statement* is a *declaration*. [*Note:* To disambiguate, the whole *statement* might have to be examined to determine if it is an *expression-statement* or a *declaration*. This disambiguates many examples. [*Example:* assuming T is a *simple-type-specifier* (7.1.5),

```
        T(a)->m = 7;            // expression-statement
        T(a)++;                 // expression-statement
        T(a,5)<<c;              // expression-statement
```

```
T(*d)(int);              // declaration
T(e)[5];                 // declaration
T(f) = { 1, 2 };         // declaration
T(*g)(double(3));        // declaration
```

In the last example above, g, which is a pointer to T, is initialized to `double(3)`. This is of course ill-formed for semantic reasons, but that does not affect the syntactic analysis.   —*end example*]

2   The remaining cases are *declaration*s. [*Example:*

```
class T {
        // ...
public:
        T();
        T(int);
        T(int, int);
};
T(a);                    // declaration
T(*b)();                 // declaration
T(c)=7;                  // declaration
T(d),e,f=3;              // declaration
extern int h;
T(g)(h,2);               // declaration
```

—*end example*] —*end note*]

3   The disambiguation is purely syntactic; that is, the meaning of the names occurring in such a statement, beyond whether they are *type-name*s or not, is not generally used in or changed by the disambiguation. Class templates are instantiated as necessary to determine if a qualified name is a *type-name*. Disambigua-tion precedes parsing, and a statement disambiguated as a declaration may be an ill-formed declaration. If, during parsing, a name in a template parameter is bound differently than it would be bound during a trial parse, the program is ill-formed. No diagnostic is required. [*Note:* This can occur only when the name is declared earlier in the declaration.] [*Example:*

```
struct T1 {
        T1 operator()(int x) { return T1(x); }
        int operator=(int x) { return x; }
        T1(int) { }
};
struct T2 { T2(int){ } };
int a, (*(*b)(T2))(int), c, d;

void f() {
        // disambiguation requires this to be parsed
        // as a declaration
        T1(a) = 3,
        T2(4),                    // T2 will be declared as
        (*(*b)(T2(c)))(int(d));   // a variable of type T1
                                  // but this will not allow
                                  // the last part of the
                                  // declaration to parse
                                  // properly since it depends
                                  // on T2 being a type-name
}
```

—*end example*]

7   Declarations   [dcl.dcl]

1   Declarations specify how names are to be interpreted. Declarations have the form

> *declaration-seq:*
> > *declaration*
> > *declaration-seq declaration*

> *declaration:*
> > *block-declaration*
> > *function-definition*
> > *template-declaration*
> > *explicit-instantiation*
> > *explicit-specialization*
> > *linkage-specification*
> > *namespace-definition*

> *block-declaration:*
> > *simple-declaration*
> > *asm-definition*
> > *namespace-alias-definition*
> > *using-declaration*
> > *using-directive*

> *simple-declaration:*
> > *decl-specifier-seq$_{opt}$ init-declarator-list$_{opt}$;*

[*Note: asm-definition*s are described in 7.4, and *linkage-specification*s are described in 7.5. *Function-definition*s are described in 8.4 and *template-declaration*s are described in clause 14. *Namespace-definition*s are described in 7.3.1, *using-declaration*s are described in 7.3.3 and *using-directive*s are described in 7.3.4.] The *simple-declaration*

> *decl-specifier-seq$_{opt}$ init-declarator-list$_{opt}$;*

is divided into two parts: *decl-specifier*s, the components of a *decl-specifier-seq*, are described in 7.1 and *declarator*s, the components of an *init-declarator-list*, are described in clause 8.

2   A declaration occurs in a scope (3.3); the scope rules are summarized in 3.4. A declaration that declares a function or defines a class, namespace, template, or function also has one or more scopes nested within it. These nested scopes, in turn, can have declarations nested within them. Unless otherwise stated, utterances in clause 7 about components in, of, or contained by a declaration or subcomponent thereof refer only to those components of the declaration that are *not* nested within scopes nested within the declaration.

3   In a *simple-declaration*, the optional *init-declarator-list* can be omitted only when declaring a class (clause 9) or enumeration (7.2), that is, when the *decl-specifier-seq* contains either a *class-specifier*, an *elaborated-type-specifier* with a *class-key* (9.1), or an *enum-specifier*. In these cases and whenever a *class-specifier* or *enum-specifier* is present in the *decl-specifier-seq*, the identifiers in these specifiers are among the names being declared by the declaration (as *class-name*s, *enum-name*s, or *enumerator*s, depending on the syntax). In such cases, and except for the declaration of an unnamed bit-field (9.6), the *decl-specifier-seq* shall introduce one or more names into the program, or shall redeclare a name introduced by a previous declaration. [*Example:*

```
enum { };                   // ill-formed
typedef class { };          // ill-formed
```

—*end example*]

4   Each *init-declarator* in the *init-declarator-list* contains exactly one *declarator-id*, which is the name declared by that *init-declarator* and hence one of the names declared by the declaration. The *type-specifiers* (7.1.5) in the *decl-specifier-seq* and the recursive *declarator* structure of the *init-declarator* describe a type (8.3), which is then associated with the name being declared by the *init-declarator*.

5   If the *decl-specifier-seq* contains the `typedef` specifier, the declaration is called a *typedef declaration* and the name of each *init-declarator* is declared to be a *typedef-name*, synonymous with its associated type (7.1.3). If the *decl-specifier-seq* contains no `typedef` specifier, the declaration is called a *function declaration* if the type associated with the name is a function type (8.3.5) and an *object declaration* otherwise.

6   Syntactic components beyond those found in the general form of declaration are added to a function declaration to make a *function-definition*. An object declaration, however, is also a definition unless it contains the `extern` specifier and has no initializer (3.1). A definition causes the appropriate amount of storage to be reserved and any appropriate initialization (8.5) to be done.

7   Only in function declarations for constructors, destructors, and type conversions can the *decl-specifier-seq* be omitted.[78]

7.1 Specifiers   [dcl.spec]

1   The specifiers that can be used in a declaration are

        decl-specifier:
                storage-class-specifier
                type-specifier
                function-specifier
                `friend`
                `typedef`

        decl-specifier-seq:
                decl-specifier-seq$_{opt}$ decl-specifier

2   The longest sequence of *decl-specifiers* that could possibly be a type name is taken as the *decl-specifier-seq* of a *declaration*. The sequence shall be self-consistent as described below. [*Example:*

```
typedef char* Pc;
static Pc;                      // error: name missing
```

Here, the declaration `static Pc` is ill-formed because no name was specified for the static variable of type `Pc`. To get a variable called `Pc`, a *type-specifier* (other than `const` or `volatile`) has to be present to indicate that the *typedef-name* `Pc` is the name being (re)declared, rather than being part of the *decl-specifier* sequence. For another example,

```
void f(const Pc);               // void f(char* const) (not const char*)
void g(const int Pc);           // void g(const int)
```

—*end example*]

3   [*Note:* since `signed`, `unsigned`, `long`, and `short` by default imply `int`, a *type-name* appearing after one of those specifiers is treated as the name being (re)declared. [*Example:*

```
void h(unsigned Pc);            // void h(unsigned int)
void k(unsigned int Pc);        // void k(unsigned int)
```

—*end example*] —*end note*]

---

[78] The "implicit int" rule of C is no longer supported.

7.1.1 Storage class specifiers

1   The storage class specifiers are

> *storage-class-specifier:*
> > auto
> > register
> > static
> > extern
> > mutable

At most one *storage-class-specifier* shall appear in a given *decl-specifier-seq*. If a *storage-class-specifier* appears in a *decl-specifier-seq*, there can be no typedef specifier in the same *decl-specifier-seq* and the *init-declarator-list* of the declaration shall not be empty (except for global anonymous unions, which shall be declared static (9.5)). The *storage-class-specifier* applies to the name declared by each *init-declarator* in the list and not to any names declared by other specifiers. A *storage-class-specifier* shall not be specified in an explicit specialization (14.7.3) or an explicit instantiation (14.7.2) directive.

2   The auto or register specifiers can be applied only to names of objects declared in a block (6.3) or to function parameters (8.4). They specify that the named object has automatic storage duration (3.7.2). An object declared without a *storage-class-specifier* at block scope or declared as a function parameter has automatic storage duration by default. [*Note:* hence, the auto specifier is almost always redundant and not often used; one use of auto is to distinguish a *declaration-statement* from an *expression-statement* (6.8) explicitly. —*end note*]

3   A register specifier has the same semantics as an auto specifier together with a hint to the implementation that the object so declared will be heavily used. [*Note:* the hint can be ignored and in most implementations it will be ignored if the address of the object is taken. —*end note*]

4   The static specifier can be applied only to names of objects and functions and to anonymous unions (9.5). There can be no static function declarations within a block, nor any static function parameters. A static specifier used in the declaration of an object declares the object to have static storage duration (3.7.1). A static specifier can be used in declarations of class members; 9.4 describes its effect. For the linkage of a name declared with a static specifier, see 3.5.

5   The extern specifier can be applied only to the names of objects and functions. The extern specifier cannot be used in the declaration of class members or function parameters. For the linkage of a name declared with an extern specifier, see 3.5.

6   A name declared in a namespace scope without a *storage-class-specifier* has external linkage unless it has internal linkage because of a previous declaration and provided it is not declared const. Objects declared const and not explicitly declared extern have internal linkage.

7   The linkages implied by successive declarations for a given entity shall agree. That is, within a given scope, each declaration declaring the same object name or the same overloading of a function name shall imply the same linkage. Each function in a given set of overloaded functions can have a different linkage, however. [*Example:*

```
static char* f();              // f() has internal linkage
char* f()                      // f() still has internal linkage
    { /* ... */ }

char* g();                     // g() has external linkage
static char* g()               // error: inconsistent linkage
    { /* ... */ }

void h();
inline void h();               // external linkage
```

```
inline void l();
void l();                              // external linkage

inline void m();
extern void m();                       // external linkage

static void n();
inline void n();                       // internal linkage

static int a;                          // a has internal linkage
int a;                                 // error: two definitions

static int b;                          // b has internal linkage
extern int b;                          // b still has internal linkage

int c;                                 // c has external linkage
static int c;                          // error: inconsistent linkage

extern int d;                          // d has external linkage
static int d;                          // error: inconsistent linkage
```
—*end example*]

8   The name of a declared but undefined class can be used in an `extern` declaration. Such a declaration can only be used in ways that do not require a complete class type. [*Example:*

```
struct S;
extern S a;
extern S f();
extern void g(S);

void h()
{
    g(a);                              // error: S is incomplete
    f();                               // error: S is incomplete
}
```

—*end example*] The `mutable` specifier can be applied only to names of class data members (9.2) and cannot be applied to names declared `const` or `static`, and cannot be applied to reference members. [*Example:*

```
class X {
        mutable const int* p;     // OK
        mutable int* const q;     // ill-formed
};
```

—*end example*]

9   The `mutable` specifier on a class data member nullifies a `const` specifier applied to the containing class object and permits modification of the mutable class member even though the rest of the object is *const* (7.1.5.1).

7.1.2 Function specifiers [dcl.fct.spec]

1 *Function-specifiers* can be used only in function declarations.

> *function-specifier:*
>> `inline`
>> `virtual`
>> `explicit`

2 A function declaration (8.3.5, 9.3, 11.4) with an `inline` specifier declares an *inline function*. The inline specifier indicates to the implementation that inline substitution of the function body at the point of call is to be preferred to the usual function call mechanism. An implementation is not required to perform this inline substitution at the point of call; however, even if this inline substitution is omitted, the other rules for inline functions defined by 7.1.2 shall still be respected.

3 A function defined within a class definition is an inline function. The `inline` specifier shall not appear on a block scope function declaration.[79]

4 An inline function shall be defined in every translation unit in which it is used and shall have exactly the same definition in every case (3.2). [*Note:* a call to the inline function may be encountered before its definition appears in the translation unit.] If a function with external linkage is declared inline in one translation unit, it shall be declared inline in all translation units in which it appears; no diagnostic is required. An `inline` function with external linkage shall have the same address in all translation units. A `static` local variable in an `extern inline` function always refers to the same object. A string literal in an `extern inline` function is the same object in different translation units.

5 The `virtual` specifier shall only be used in declarations of nonstatic class member functions that appear within a *member-specification* of a class declaration; see 10.3.

6 The `explicit` specifier shall be used only in declarations of constructors within a class declaration; see 12.3.1.

7.1.3 The `typedef` specifier [dcl.typedef]

1 Declarations containing the *decl-specifier* `typedef` declare identifiers that can be used later for naming fundamental (3.9.1) or compound (3.9.2) types. The `typedef` specifier shall not be used in a *function-definition* (8.4), and it shall not be combined in a *decl-specifier-seq* with any other kind of specifier except a *type-specifier*.

> *typedef-name:*
>> *identifier*

A name declared with the `typedef` specifier becomes a *typedef-name*. Within the scope of its declaration, a *typedef-name* is syntactically equivalent to a keyword and names the type associated with the identifier in the way described in clause 8. A *typedef-name* is thus a synonym for another type. A *typedef-name* does not introduce a new type the way a class declaration (9.1) or enum declaration does. [*Example:* after

```
typedef int MILES, *KLICKSP;
```

the constructions

```
MILES distance;
extern KLICKSP metricp;
```

are all correct declarations; the type of `distance` is `int`; that of `metricp` is "pointer to `int`."]

2 In a given non-class scope, a `typedef` specifier can be used to redefine the name of any type declared in that scope to refer to the type to which it already refers. [*Example:*

---

[79] The inline keyword has no effect on the linkage of a function.

```
typedef struct s { /* ... */ } s;
typedef int I;
typedef int I;
typedef I I;
```

—*end example*]

3   In a given scope, a `typedef` specifier shall not be used to redefine the name of any type declared in that scope to refer to a different type. [*Example:*

```
class complex { /* ... */ };
typedef int complex;            // error: redefinition
```

—*end example*] Similarly, in a given scope, a class or enumeration shall not be declared with the same name as a *typedef-name* that is declared in that scope and refers to a type other than the class or enumeration itself. [*Example:*

```
typedef int complex;
class complex { /* ... */ };    // error: redefinition
```

—*end example*]

4   A *typedef-name* that names a class is a *class-name* (9.1). If a *typedef-name* is used following the *class-key* in an *elaborated-type-specifier* (7.1.5.3) or in the *class-head* of a class declaration (9), or is used as the *identifier* in the declarator for a constructor or destructor declaration (12.1, 12.4), the program is ill-formed. [*Example:*

```
struct S {
    S();
    ~S();
};

typedef struct S T;

S a = T();            // OK
struct T * p;         // error
```

—*end example*]

5   If the typedef declaration defines an unnamed class (or enum), the first *typedef-name* declared by the declaration to be that class type (or enum type) is used to denote the class type (or enum type) for linkage purposes only (3.5). [*Example:*

```
typedef struct { } *ps, S;      // S is the class name for linkage purposes
```

—*end example*] [*Note:* if the *typedef-name* is used where a *class-name* (or *enum-name*) is required, the program is ill-formed. For example,

```
typedef struct {
    S();                        // error: requires a return type because S is
                                // an ordinary member function, not a constructor
} S;
```

—*end note*]

7.1.4 The `friend` specifier   **[dcl.friend]**

1   The `friend` specifier is used to specify access to class members; see 11.4.

7.1.5 Type specifiers   **[dcl.type]**

1   The type-specifiers are

> *type-specifier:*
>> *simple-type-specifier*
>> *class-specifier*
>> *enum-specifier*
>> *elaborated-type-specifier*
>> *cv-qualifier*

As a general rule, at most one *type-specifier* is allowed in the complete *decl-specifier-seq* of a *declaration*. The only exceptions to this rule are the following:

— `const` or `volatile` can be combined with any other *type-specifier*. However, redundant cv-qualifiers are prohibited except when introduced through the use of typedefs (7.1.3) or template type arguments (14.3), in which case the redundant cv-qualifiers are ignored.

— `signed` or `unsigned` can be combined with `char`, `long`, `short`, or `int`.

— `short` or `long` can be combined with `int`.

— `long` can be combined with `double`.

2   At least one *type-specifier* that is not a *cv-qualifier* is required in a declaration unless it declares a constructor, destructor or conversion function.[80)

3   [*Note: class-specifier*s and *enum-specifier*s are discussed in clause 9 and 7.2, respectively. The remaining *type-specifier*s are discussed in the rest of this section.]

7.1.5.1 The *cv-qualifiers*   **[dcl.type.cv]**

1   There are two *cv-qualifiers*, `const` and `volatile`. If a *cv-qualifier* appears in a *decl-specifier-seq*, the *init-declarator-list* of the declaration shall not be empty. [*Note:* 3.9.3 describes how cv-qualifiers affect object and function types.]

2   An object declared in namespace scope with a const-qualified type has internal linkage unless it is explicitly declared `extern` or unless it was previously declared to have external linkage. A variable of non-volatile const-qualified integral or enumeration type initialized by an integral constant expression can be used in integral constant expressions (5.19). [*Note:* as described in 8.5, the definition of an object or subobject of const-qualified type must specify an initializer or be subject to default-initialization.]

3   A pointer or reference to a cv-qualified type need not actually point or refer to a cv-qualified object, but it is treated as if it does; a const-qualified access path cannot be used to modify an object even if the object referenced is a non-const object and can be modified through some other access path. [*Note:* cv-qualifiers are supported by the type system so that they cannot be subverted without casting (5.2.11).]

4   Except that any class member declared `mutable` (7.1.1) can be modified, any attempt to modify a `const` object during its lifetime (3.8) results in undefined behavior.

5   [*Example:*

```
const int ci = 3;          // cv-qualified (initialized as required)
ci = 4;                    // ill-formed: attempt to modify const
```

[80) There is no special provision for a *decl-specifier-seq* that lacks a *type-specifier* or that has a *type-specifier* that only specifies *cv-qualifiers*. The "implicit int" rule of C is no longer supported.

```
int i = 2;                              // not cv-qualified
const int* cip;                         // pointer to const int
cip = &i;                               // OK: cv-qualified access path to unqualified
*cip = 4;                               // ill-formed: attempt to modify through ptr to const

int* ip;
ip = const_cast<int*>(cip);             // cast needed to convert const int* to int*
*ip = 4;                                // defined: *ip points to i, a non-const object

const int* ciq = new const int (3);     // initialized as required
int* iq = const_cast<int*>(ciq);        // cast required
*iq = 4;                                // undefined: modifies a const object
```

6   For another example

```
class X {
    public:
        mutable int i;
        int j;
};
class Y {
    public:
        X x;
        Y();
};

const Y y;
y.x.i++;                                // well-formed: mutable member can be modified
y.x.j++;                                // ill-formed: const-qualified member modified
Y* p = const_cast<Y*>(&y);              // cast away const-ness of y
p->x.i = 99;                            // well-formed: mutable member can be modified
p->x.j = 99;                            // undefined: modifies a const member
```

     —end example]

7   If an attempt is made to refer to an object defined with a volatile-qualified type through the use of an lvalue with a non-volatile-qualified type, the program behaviour is undefined.

8   [*Note:* volatile is a hint to the implementation to avoid aggressive optimization involving the object because the value of the object might be changed by means undetectable by an implementation. See 1.9 for detailed semantics. In general, the semantics of volatile are intended to be the same in C++ as they are in C.]

7.1.5.2   Simple type specifiers   [dcl.type.simple]

1   The simple type specifiers are

simple-type-specifier:
>   ::_{opt} *nested-name-specifier*_{*opt*} *type-name*
>   ::_{opt} *nested-name-specifier* `template` *template-id*
>   `char`
>   `wchar_t`
>   `bool`
>   `short`
>   `int`
>   `long`
>   `signed`
>   `unsigned`
>   `float`
>   `double`
>   `void`

type-name:
>   *class-name*
>   *enum-name*
>   *typedef-name*

The *simple-type-specifier*s specify either a previously-declared user-defined type or one of the fundamental types (3.9.1). Table 7 summarizes the valid combinations of *simple-type-specifier*s and the types they specify.

Table 7—*simple-type-specifier*s **and the types they specify**

Specifier(s)	Type
type-name	the type named
char	"char"
unsigned char	"unsigned char"
signed char	"signed char"
bool	"bool"
unsigned	"unsigned int"
unsigned int	"unsigned int"
signed	"int"
signed int	"int"
int	"int"
unsigned short int	"unsigned short int"
unsigned short	"unsigned short int"
unsigned long int	"unsigned long int"
unsigned long	"unsigned long int"
signed long int	"long int"
signed long	"long int"
long int	"long int"
long	"long int"
signed short int	"short int"
signed short	"short int"
short int	"short int"
short	"short int"
wchar_t	"wchar_t"
float	"float"
double	"double"
long double	"long double"
void	"void"

When multiple *simple-type-specifier*s are allowed, they can be freely intermixed with other *decl-specifiers* in any order. It is implementation-defined whether bit-fields and objects of char type are represented as signed or unsigned quantities. The signed specifier forces char objects and bit-fields to be signed; it is redundant with other integral types.

7.1.5.3 Elaborated type specifiers   [dcl.type.elab]

elaborated-type-specifier:
        class-key :: $_{opt}$ *nested-name-specifier* $_{opt}$ *identifier*
        class-key :: $_{opt}$ *nested-name-specifier* $_{opt}$ *template* $_{opt}$ *template-id*
        enum :: $_{opt}$ *nested-name-specifier* $_{opt}$ *identifier*
        typename :: $_{opt}$ *nested-name-specifier identifier*
        typename :: $_{opt}$ *nested-name-specifier template* $_{opt}$ *template-id*

1   If an *elaborated-type-specifier* is the sole constituent of a declaration, the declaration is ill-formed unless it is an explicit specialization (14.7.3), an explicit instantiation (14.7.2) or it has one of the following forms:

        class-key identifier ;
        friend *class-key* :: $_{opt}$ *identifier* ;
        friend *class-key* :: $_{opt}$ *template-id* ;
        friend *class-key* :: $_{opt}$ *nested-name-specifier identifier* ;
        friend *class-key* :: $_{opt}$ *nested-name-specifier template* $_{opt}$ *template-id* ;

2 3.4.4 describes how name lookup proceeds for the *identifier* in an *elaborated-type-specifier*. If the *identifier* resolves to a *class-name* or *enum-name*, the *elaborated-type-specifier* introduces it into the declaration the same way a *simple-type-specifier* introduces its *type-name*. If the *identifier* resolves to a *typedef-name* or a template *type-parameter*, the *elaborated-type-specifier* is ill-formed. [*Note:* this implies that, within a class template with a template *type-parameter* T, the declaration

```
friend class T;
```

is ill-formed.] If name lookup does not find a declaration for the name, the *elaborated-type-specifier* is ill-formed unless it is of the simple form *class-key identifier* in which case the *identifier* is declared as described in 3.3.1.

3 The *class-key* or enum keyword present in the *elaborated-type-specifier* shall agree in kind with the declaration to which the name in the *elaborated-type-specifier* refers. This rule also applies to the form of *elaborated-type-specifier* that declares a *class-name* or friend class since it can be construed as referring to the definition of the class. Thus, in any *elaborated-type-specifier*, the enum keyword shall be used to refer to an enumeration (7.2), the union *class-key* shall be used to refer to a union (clause 9), and either the class or struct *class-key* shall be used to refer to a class (clause 9) declared using the class or struct *class-key*.

7.2 Enumeration declarations [dcl.enum]

1 An enumeration is a distinct type (3.9.1) with named constants. Its name becomes an *enum-name*, within its scope.

> *enum-name:*
> > *identifier*

> *enum-specifier:*
> > enum $identifier_{opt}$ { $enumerator\text{-}list_{opt}$ }

> *enumerator-list:*
> > *enumerator-definition*
> > *enumerator-list* , *enumerator-definition*

> *enumerator-definition:*
> > *enumerator*
> > *enumerator* = *constant-expression*

> *enumerator:*
> > *identifier*

The identifiers in an *enumerator-list* are declared as constants, and can appear wherever constants are required. An *enumerator-definition* with = gives the associated *enumerator* the value indicated by the *constant-expression*. The *constant-expression* shall be of integral or enumeration type. If the first *enumerator* has no *initializer*, the value of the corresponding constant is zero. An *enumerator-definition* without an *initializer* gives the *enumerator* the value obtained by increasing the value of the previous *enumerator* by one.

2 [*Example:*

```
enum { a, b, c=0 };
enum { d, e, f=e+2 };
```

defines a, c, and d to be zero, b and e to be 1, and f to be 3.]

3 The point of declaration for an enumerator is immediately after its *enumerator-definition*. [*Example:*

```
const int x = 12;
{ enum { x = x }; }
```

Here, the enumerator x is initialized with the value of the constant x, namely 12.]

4   Each enumeration defines a type that is different from all other types. Following the closing brace of an *enum-specifier*, each enumerator has the type of its enumeration. Prior to the closing brace, the type of each enumerator is the type of its initializing value. If an initializer is specified for an enumerator, the initializing value has the same type as the expression. If no initializer is specified for the first enumerator, the type is an unspecified integral type. Otherwise the type is the same as the type of the initializing value of the preceding enumerator unless the incremented value is not representable in that type, in which case the type is an unspecified integral type sufficient to contain the incremented value.

5   The *underlying type* of an enumeration is an integral type that can represent all the enumerator values defined in the enumeration. It is implementation-defined which integral type is used as the underlying type for an enumeration except that the underlying type shall not be larger than int unless the value of an enumerator cannot fit in an int or unsigned int. If the *enumerator-list* is empty, the underlying type is as if the enumeration had a single enumerator with value 0. The value of sizeof() applied to an enumeration type, an object of enumeration type, or an enumerator, is the value of sizeof() applied to the underlying type.

6   For an enumeration where e_{min} is the smallest enumerator and e_{max} is the largest, the values of the enumeration are the values of the underlying type in the range b_{min} to b_{max}, where b_{min} and b_{max} are, respectively, the smallest and largest values of the smallest bit-field that can store e_{min} and e_{max}.[81] It is possible to define an enumeration that has values not defined by any of its enumerators.

7   Two enumeration types are layout-compatible if they have the same *underlying type*.

8   The value of an enumerator or an object of an enumeration type is converted to an integer by integral promotion (4.5). [*Example:*

```
enum color { red, yellow, green=20, blue };
color col = red;
color* cp = &col;
if (*cp == blue)          // ...
```

makes color a type describing various colors, and then declares col as an object of that type, and cp as a pointer to an object of that type. The possible values of an object of type color are red, yellow, green, blue; these values can be converted to the integral values 0, 1, 20, and 21. Since enumerations are distinct types, objects of type color can be assigned only values of type color.

```
color c = 1;              // error: type mismatch,
                          // no conversion from int to color

int i = yellow;           // OK: yellow converted to integral value 1
                          // integral promotion
```

—*end example*]

9   An expression of arithmetic or enumeration type can be converted to an enumeration type explicitly. The value is unchanged if it is in the range of enumeration values of the enumeration type; otherwise the resulting enumeration value is unspecified.

10   The enum-name and each enumerator declared by an enum-specifier is declared in the scope that immediately contains the enum-specifier. These names obey the scope rules defined for all names in (3.3) and (3.4). An enumerator declared in class scope can be referred to using the class member access operators (::, . (dot) and -> (arrow)), see 5.2.5. [*Example:*

---

[81] On a two's-complement machine, b_{max} is the smallest value greater than or equal to $\max(abs(e_{min})-1, abs(e_{max}))$ of the form $2^M - 1$; b_{min} is zero if e_{min} is non-negative and $-(b_{max}+1)$ otherwise.

```
class X {
public:
    enum direction { left='l', right='r' };
    int f(int i)
        { return i==left ? 0 : i==right ? 1 : 2; }
};

void g(X* p)
{
    direction d;                  // error: direction not in scope
    int i;
    i = p->f(left);               // error: left not in scope
    i = p->f(X::right);           // OK
    i = p->f(p->left);            // OK
    // ...
}
```

—*end example*]

7.3 Namespaces   [basic.namespace]

1   A namespace is an optionally-named declarative region. The name of a namespace can be used to access entities declared in that namespace; that is, the members of the namespace. Unlike other declarative regions, the definition of a namespace can be split over several parts of one or more translation units.

2   The outermost declarative region of a translation unit is a namespace; see 3.3.5.

7.3.1 Namespace definition   [namespace.def]

1   The grammar for a *namespace-definition* is

> *namespace-name:*
>> *original-namespace-name*
>> *namespace-alias*
> *original-namespace-name:*
>> *identifier*
>
> *namespace-definition:*
>> *named-namespace-definition*
>> *unnamed-namespace-definition*
>
> *named-namespace-definition:*
>> *original-namespace-definition*
>> *extension-namespace-definition*
>
> *original-namespace-definition:*
>> namespace *identifier* { *namespace-body* }
>
> *extension-namespace-definition:*
>> namespace *original-namespace-name* { *namespace-body* }
>
> *unnamed-namespace-definition:*
>> namespace { *namespace-body* }
>
> *namespace-body:*
>> *declaration-seq$_{opt}$*

2   The *identifier* in an *original-namespace-definition* shall not have been previously defined in the declarative region in which the *original-namespace-definition* appears. The *identifier* in an *original-namespace-definition* is the name of the namespace. Subsequently in that declarative region, it is treated as an

original-namespace-name.

3   The *original-namespace-name* in an *extension-namespace-definition* shall have previously been defined in
     an *original-namespace-definition* in the same declarative region.

4   Every *namespace-definition* shall appear in the global scope or in a namespace scope (3.3.5).

5   Because a *namespace-definition* contains *declarations* in its *namespace-body* and a *namespace-definition* is
     itself a *declaration*, it follows that *namespace-definitions* can be nested. [*Example:*

```
namespace Outer {
        int i;
        namespace Inner {
                void f() { i++; }        // Outer::i
                int i;
                void g() { i++; }        // Inner::i
        }
}
```

—*end example*]

7.3.1.1 Unnamed namespaces   **[namespace.unnamed]**

1   An *unnamed-namespace-definition* behaves as if it were replaced by

```
namespace unique { /* empty body */ }
using namespace unique;
namespace unique { namespace-body }
```

where all occurrences of ***unique*** in a translation unit are replaced by the same identifier and this identifier
differs from all other identifiers in the entire program.[82] [*Example:*

```
namespace { int i; }             // unique::i
void f() { i++; }                // unique::i++

namespace A {
        namespace {
                int i;           // A::unique::i
                int j;           // A::unique::j
        }
        void g() { i++; }        // A::unique::i++
}

using namespace A;
void h() {
        i++;                     // error: unique::i or A::unique::i
        A::i++;                  // A::unique::i
        j++;                     // A::unique::j
}
```

—*end example*]

2   The use of the `static` keyword is deprecated when declaring objects in a namespace scope (see annex D);
     the *unnamed-namespace* provides a superior alternative.

---

[82] Although entities in an unnamed namespace might have external linkage, they are effectively qualified by a name unique to their
translation unit and therefore can never be seen from any other translation unit.

7.3.1.2 Namespace member definitions [namespace.memdef]

1 Members of a namespace can be defined within that namespace. [*Example:*

```
namespace X {
        void f() { /* ... */ }
}
```

—*end example*]

2 Members of a named namespace can also be defined outside that namespace by explicit qualification (3.4.3.2) of the name being defined, provided that the entity being defined was already declared in the namespace and the definition appears after the point of declaration in a namespace that encloses the declaration's namespace. [*Example:*

```
namespace Q {
        namespace V {
                void f();
        }
        void V::f() { /* ... */ }        // OK
        void V::g() { /* ... */ }        // error: g() is not yet a member of V
        namespace V {
                void g();
        }
}

namespace R {
        void Q::V::g() { /* ... */ }      // error: R doesn't enclose Q
}
```

—*end example*]

3 Every name first declared in a namespace is a member of that namespace. If a friend declaration in a non-local class first declares a class or function[83] the friend class or function is a member of the innermost enclosing namespace. The name of the friend is not found by simple name lookup until a matching declaration is provided in that namespace scope (either before or after the class declaration granting friendship). If a friend function is called, its name may be found by the name lookup that considers functions from namespaces and classes associated with the types of the function arguments (3.4.2). When looking for a prior declaration of a class or a function declared as a friend, and when the name of the friend class or function is neither a qualified name nor a *template-id*, scopes outside the innermost enclosing namespace scope are not considered. [*Example:*

---

[83] this implies that the name of the class or function is unqualified.

```
// Assume f and g have not yet been defined.
void h(int);
template <class T> void f2(T);
namespace A {
        class X {
                friend void f(X);           // A::f(X) is a friend
                class Y {
                        friend void g();            // A::g is a friend
                        friend void h(int);         // A::h is a friend
                                                    // ::h not considered
                        friend void f2<>(int);   // ::f2<>(int) is a friend
                };
        };

        // A::f, A::g and A::h are not visible here
        X x;
        void g() { f(x); }              // definition of A::g
        void f(X) { /* ... */}          // definition of A::f
        void h(int) { /* ... */ }       // definition of A::h
        // A::f, A::g and A::h are visible here and known to be friends
}

using A::x;

void h()
{
        A::f(x);
        A::X::f(x);                     // error: f is not a member of A::X
        A::X::Y::g();                   // error: g is not a member of A::X::Y
}
```

—end example]

7.3.2 Namespace alias [namespace.alias]

1   A *namespace-alias-definition* declares an alternate name for a namespace according to the following grammar:

> *namespace-alias:*
> > *identifier*

> *namespace-alias-definition:*
> > namespace *identifier* = *qualified-namespace-specifier* ;

> *qualified-namespace-specifier:*
> > ::$_{opt}$ *nested-name-specifier*$_{opt}$ *namespace-name*

2   The *identifier* in a *namespace-alias-definition* is a synonym for the name of the namespace denoted by the *qualified-namespace-specifier* and becomes a *namespace-alias*. [*Note:* when looking up a *namespace-name* in a *namespace-alias-definition*, only namespace names are considered, see 3.4.6.]

3   In a declarative region, a *namespace-alias-definition* can be used to redefine a *namespace-alias* declared in that declarative region to refer only to the namespace to which it already refers. [*Example:* the following declarations are well-formed:

```
namespace Company_with_very_long_name { /* ... */ }
namespace CWVLN = Company_with_very_long_name;
namespace CWVLN = Company_with_very_long_name;                 // OK: duplicate
namespace CWVLN = CWVLN;
```

—end example]

4   A *namespace-name* or *namespace-alias* shall not be declared as the name of any other entity in the same declarative region. A *namespace-name* defined at global scope shall not be declared as the name of any other entity in any global scope of the program. No diagnostic is required for a violation of this rule by declarations in different translation units.

7.3.3 The `using` declaration   [namespace.udecl]

1   A *using-declaration* introduces a name into the declarative region in which the *using-declaration* appears. That name is a synonym for the name of some entity declared elsewhere.

> *using-declaration:*
> > using typename$_{opt}$ ::$_{opt}$ *nested-name-specifier unqualified-id* ;
> > using :: *unqualified-id* ;

2   The member name specified in a *using-declaration* is declared in the declarative region in which the *using-declaration* appears. [*Note:* only the specified name is so declared; specifying an enumeration name in a *using-declaration* does not declare its enumerators in the *using-declaration*'s declarative region.]

3   Every *using-declaration* is a *declaration* and a *member-declaration* and so can be used in a class definition. [*Example:*

```
struct B {
        void f(char);
        void g(char);
        enum E { e };
        union { int x; };
};

struct D : B {
        using B::f;
        void f(int) { f('c'); }        // calls B::f(char)
        void g(int) { g('c'); }        // recursively calls D::g(int)
};
```

—*end example*]

4   A *using-declaration* used as a *member-declaration* shall refer to a member of a base class of the class being defined, shall refer to a member of an anonymous union that is a member of a base class of the class being defined, or shall refer to an enumerator for an enumeration type that is a member of a base class of the class being defined. [*Example:*

```
class C {
        int g();
};

class D2 : public B {
        using B::f;        // OK: B is a base of D2
        using B::e;        // OK: e is an enumerator of base B
        using B::x;        // OK: x is a union member of base B
        using C::g;        // error: C isn't a base of D2
};
```

—*end example*] [*Note:* since constructors and destructors do not have names, a *using-declaration* cannot refer to a constructor or a destructor for a base class. Since specializations of member templates for conversion functions are not found by name lookup, they are not considered when a *using-declaration* specifies a conversion function (14.5.2).] If an assignment operator brought from a base class into a derived class scope has the signature of a copy-assignment operator for the derived class (12.8), the *using-declaration* does not by itself suppress the implicit declaration of the derived class copy-assignment operator; the copy-assignment operator from the base class is hidden or overridden by the implicitly-declared copy-assignment operator of the derived class, as described below.

5   A *using-declaration* shall not name a *template-id*. [*Example:*

```
class A {
public:
        template <class T> void f(T);
        template <class T> struct X { };
};
class B : public A {
public:
        using A::f<double>;       // ill-formed
        using A::X<int>;          // ill-formed
};
```

—*end example*]

6   A *using-declaration* for a class member shall be a *member-declaration*. [*Example:*

```
struct X {
        int i;
        static int s;
};

void f()
{
        using X::i;               // error: X::i is a class member
                                  // and this is not a member declaration.
        using X::s;               // error: X::s is a class member
                                  // and this is not a member declaration.
}
```

—*end example*]

7   Members declared by a *using-declaration* can be referred to by explicit qualification just like other member names (3.4.3.2). In a *using-declaration*, a prefix : : refers to the global namespace. [*Example:*

```
void f();

namespace A {
        void g();
}

namespace X {
        using ::f;                // global f
        using A::g;               // A's g
}

void h()
{
        X::f();                   // calls ::f
        X::g();                   // calls A::g
}
```

—*end example*]

8   A *using-declaration* is a *declaration* and can therefore be used repeatedly where (and only where) multiple declarations are allowed. [*Example:*

```
namespace A {
        int i;
}

namespace A1 {
        using A::i;
        using A::i;                  // OK: double declaration
}

void f()
{
        using A::i;
        using A::i;                  // error: double declaration
}

class B {
public:
        int i;
};

class X : public B {
        using B::i;
        using B::i;                  // error: double member declaration
};
```

—*end example*]

9   The entity declared by a *using-declaration* shall be known in the context using it according to its definition
at the point of the *using-declaration*. Definitions added to the namespace after the *using-declaration* are
not considered when a use of the name is made. [*Example:*

```
namespace A {
        void f(int);
}

using A::f;                          // f is a synonym for A::f;
                                     // that is, for A::f(int).
namespace A {
        void f(char);
}

void foo()
{
        f('a');                      // calls f(int),
}                                    // even though f(char) exists.

void bar()
{
        using A::f;                  // f is a synonym for A::f;
                                     // that is, for A::f(int) and A::f(char).
        f('a');                      // calls f(char)
}
```

—*end example*] [*Note:* partial specializations of class templates are found by looking up the primary class
template and then considering all partial specializations of that template. If a *using-declaration* names a
class template, partial specializations introduced after the *using-declaration* are effectively visible because
the primary template is visible (14.5.4).]

10   Since a *using-declaration* is a declaration, the restrictions on declarations of the same name in the same
declarative region (3.3) also apply to *using-declarations*. [*Example:*

```
namespace A {
        int x;
}

namespace B {
        int i;
        struct g { };
        struct x { };
        void f(int);
        void f(double);
        void g(char);           // OK: hides struct g
}

void func()
{
        int i;
        using B::i;             // error: i declared twice
        void f(char);
        using B::f;             // OK: each f is a function
        f(3.5);                 // calls B::f(double)
        using B::g;
        g('a');                 // calls B::g(char)
        struct g g1;            // g1 has class type B::g
        using B::x;
        using A::x;             // OK: hides struct B::x
        x = 99;                 // assigns to A::x
        struct x x1;            // x1 has class type B::x
}
```

—end example]

11   If a function declaration in namespace scope or block scope has the same name and the same parameter
types as a function introduced by a *using-declaration*, and the declarations do not declare the same function, the program is ill-formed. [*Note:* two *using-declaration*s may introduce functions with the same name
and the same parameter types. If, for a call to an unqualified function name, function overload resolution
selects the functions introduced by such *using-declaration*s, the function call is ill-formed.
[*Example:*

```
namespace B {
        void f(int);
        void f(double);
}
namespace C {
        void f(int);
        void f(double);
        void f(char);
}

void h()
{
        using B::f;             // B::f(int) and B::f(double)
        using C::f;             // C::f(int), C::f(double), and C::f(char)
        f('h');                 // calls C::f(char)
        f(1);                   // error: ambiguous: B::f(int) or C::f(int) ?
        void f(int);            // error:
                                // f(int) conflicts with C::f(int) and B::f(int)
}
```

—end example]]

12　When a *using-declaration* brings names from a base class into a derived class scope, member functions in the derived class override and/or hide member functions with the same name and parameter types in a base class (rather than conflicting). [*Example:*

```
struct B {
        virtual void f(int);
        virtual void f(char);
        void g(int);
        void h(int);
};

struct D : B {
        using B::f;
        void f(int);            // OK: D::f(int) overrides B::f(int);

        using B::g;
        void g(char);           // OK

        using B::h;
        void h(int);            // OK: D::h(int) hides B::h(int)
};

void k(D* p)
{
        p->f(1);                // calls D::f(int)
        p->f('a');              // calls B::f(char)
        p->g(1);                // calls B::g(int)
        p->g('a');              // calls D::g(char)
}
```

—*end example*] [*Note:* two *using-declaration*s may introduce functions with the same name and the same parameter types. If, for a call to an unqualified function name, function overload resolution selects the functions introduced by such *using-declaration*s, the function call is ill-formed.]

13　For the purpose of overload resolution, the functions which are introduced by a *using-declaration* into a derived class will be treated as though they were members of the derived class. In particular, the implicit `this` parameter shall be treated as if it were a pointer to the derived class rather than to the base class. This has no effect on the type of the function, and in all other respects the function remains a member of the base class.

14　All instances of the name mentioned in a *using-declaration* shall be accessible. In particular, if a derived class uses a *using-declaration* to access a member of a base class, the member name shall be accessible. If the name is that of an overloaded member function, then all functions named shall be accessible. The base class members mentioned by a *using-declaration* shall be visible in the scope of at least one of the direct base classes of the class where the *using-declaration* is specified. [*Note:* because a *using-declaration* designates a base class member (and not a member subobject or a member function of a base class subobject), a *using-declaration* cannot be used to resolve inherited member ambiguities. For example,

```
struct A { int x(); };
struct B : A { };
struct C : A {
    using A::x;
    int x(int);
};
```

```
struct D : B, C {
    using C::x;
    int x(double);
};
int f(D* d) {
    return d->x();              // ambiguous: B::x or C::x
}
```

]

15   The alias created by the *using-declaration* has the usual accessibility for a *member-declaration*. [*Example:*

```
class A {
private:
        void f(char);
public:
        void f(int);
protected:
        void g();
};

class B : public A {
        using A::f;            // error: A::f(char) is inaccessible
public:
        using A::g;            // B::g is a public synonym for A::g
};
```

—*end example*]

16   [*Note:* use of *access-declarations* (11.3) is deprecated; member *using-declaration*s provide a better alternative.]

7.3.4 Using directive   [namespace.udir]

> *using-directive:*
>   using namespace :: *opt* *nested-name-specifier*_{opt} *namespace-name* ;

A *using-directive* shall not appear in class scope, but may appear in namespace scope or in block scope. [*Note:* when looking up a *namespace-name* in a *using-directive*, only namespace names are considered, see 3.4.6.]

1   A *using-directive* specifies that the names in the nominated namespace can be used in the scope in which the *using-directive* appears after the *using-directive*. During unqualified name lookup (3.4.1), the names appear as if they were declared in the nearest enclosing namespace which contains both the *using-directive* and the nominated namespace. [*Note:* in this context, "contains" means "contains directly or indirectly".]

A *using-directive* does not add any members to the declarative region in which it appears. [*Example:*

```
namespace A {
        int i;
        namespace B {
                namespace C {
                        int i;
                }
                using namespace A::B::C;
                void f1() {
                        i = 5;              // OK, C::i visible in B and hides A::i
                }
        }
        namespace D {
                using namespace B;
                using namespace C;
                void f2() {
                        i = 5;              // ambiguous, B::C::i or A::i?
                }
        }
        void f3() {
                i = 5;          // uses A::i
        }
}
void f4() {
        i = 5;                      // ill-formed; neither i is visible
}
```

]

2   The *using-directive* is transitive: if a scope contains a *using-directive* that nominates a second namespace that itself contains *using-directives*, the effect is as if the *using-directives* from the second namespace also appeared in the first. [*Example:*

```
namespace M {
        int i;
}

namespace N {
        int i;
        using namespace M;
}

void f()
{
        using namespace N;
        i = 7;                  // error: both M::i and N::i are visible
}
```

For another example,

```
namespace A {
        int i;
}
namespace B {
        int i;
        int j;
        namespace C {
                namespace D {
                        using namespace A;
                        int j;
                        int k;
                        int a = i;        // B::i hides A::i
                }
                using namespace D;
                int k = 89;       // no problem yet
                int l = k;        // ambiguous: C::k or D::k
                int m = i;        // B::i hides A::i
                int n = j;        // D::j hides B::j
        }
}
```

—*end example*]

3　If a namespace is extended by an *extension-namespace-definition* after a *using-directive* for that namespace is given, the additional members of the extended namespace and the members of namespaces nominated by *using-directive*s in the *extension-namespace-definition* can be used after the *extension-namespace-definition*.

4　If name lookup finds a declaration for a name in two different namespaces, and the declarations do not declare the same entity and do not declare functions, the use of the name is ill-formed. [*Note:* in particular, the name of an object, function or enumerator does not hide the name of a class or enumeration declared in a different namespace. For example,

```
namespace A {
        class X { };
        extern "C"   int g();
        extern "C++" int h();
}
namespace B {
        void X(int);
        extern "C"   int g();
        extern "C++" int h();
}
using namespace A;
using namespace B;

void f() {
        X(1);                     // error: name X found in two namespaces
        g();                      // okay: name g refers to the same entity
        h();                      // error: name h found in two namespaces
}
```

—*end note*]

5　During overload resolution, all functions from the transitive search are considered for argument matching. The set of declarations found by the transitive search is unordered. [*Note:* in particular, the order in which namespaces were considered and the relationships among the namespaces implied by the *using-directive*s do not cause preference to be given to any of the declarations found by the search.] An ambiguity exists if the best match finds two functions with the same signature, even if one is in a namespace reachable through *using-directive*s in the namespace of the other.[84]

[*Example:*

```
namespace D {
        int d1;
        void f(char);
}
using namespace D;

int d1;                              // OK: no conflict with D::d1

namespace E {
        int e;
        void f(int);
}

namespace D {                        // namespace extension
        int d2;
        using namespace E;
        void f(int);
}

void f()
{
        d1++;                        // error: ambiguous ::d1 or D::d1?
        ::d1++;                      // OK
        D::d1++;                     // OK
        d2++;                        // OK: D::d2
        e++;                         // OK: E::e
        f(1);                        // error: ambiguous: D::f(int) or E::f(int)?
        f('a');                      // OK: D::f(char)
}
```

—*end example*]

7.4 The asm declaration   [dcl.asm]

1   An asm declaration has the form

>   *asm-definition:*
>   asm (*string-literal*) ;

The meaning of an asm declaration is implementation-defined. [*Note:* Typically it is used to pass information through the implementation to an assembler.]

7.5 Linkage specifications   [dcl.link]

1   All function types, function names, and variable names have a *language linkage*. [*Note:* Some of the properties associated with an entity with language linkage are specific to each implementation and are not described here. For example, a particular language linkage may be associated with a particular form of representing names of objects and functions with external linkage, or with a particular calling convention, etc.] The default language linkage of all function types, function names, and variable names is C++ language linkage. Two function types with different language linkages are distinct types even if they are otherwise identical.

---

[84] During name lookup in a class hierarchy, some ambiguities may be resolved by considering whether one member hides the other along some paths (10.2). There is no such disambiguation when considering the set of names found as a result of following *using-directive*s.

2   Linkage (3.5) between C++ and non-C++ code fragments can be achieved using a *linkage-specification*:

> *linkage-specification:*
>   extern *string-literal* { *declaration-seq_{opt}* }
>   extern *string-literal declaration*

The *string-literal* indicates the required language linkage. The meaning of the *string-literal* is implementation-defined. A *linkage-specification* with a string that is unknown to the implementation is ill-formed. When the *string-literal* in a *linkage-specification* names a programming language, the spelling of the programming language's name is implementation-defined. [*Note:* it is recommended that the spelling be taken from the document defining that language, for example Ada (not ADA) and Fortran or FORTRAN (depending on the vintage). The semantics of a language linkage other than C++ or C are implementation-defined.]

3   Every implementation shall provide for linkage to functions written in the C programming language, "C", and linkage to C++ functions, "C++". [*Example:*

```
complex sqrt(complex);          // C++ linkage by default
extern "C" {
    double sqrt(double);        // C linkage
}
```

—*end example*]

4   Linkage specifications nest. When linkage specifications nest, the innermost one determines the language linkage. A linkage specification does not establish a scope. A *linkage-specification* shall occur only in namespace scope (3.3). In a *linkage-specification*, the specified language linkage applies to the function types of all function declarators, function names, and variable names introduced by the declaration(s). [*Example:*

```
extern "C" void f1(void(*pf)(int));
                                // the name f1 and its function type have C language
                                // linkage; pf is a pointer to a C function
extern "C" typedef void FUNC();
FUNC f2;                        // the name f2 has C++ language linkage and the
                                // function's type has C language linkage
extern "C" FUNC f3;             // the name of function f3 and the function's type
                                // have C language linkage
void (*pf2)(FUNC*);             // the name of the variable pf2 has C++ linkage and
                                // the type of pf2 is pointer to C++ function that
                                // takes one parameter of type pointer to C function
```

—*end example*] A C language linkage is ignored for the names of class members and the member function type of class member functions. [*Example:*

```
extern "C" typedef void FUNC_c();
class C {
    void mf1(FUNC_c*);          // the name of the function mf1 and the member
                                // function's type have C++ language linkage; the
                                // parameter has type pointer to C function
    FUNC_c mf2;                 // the name of the function mf2 and the member
                                // function's type have C++ language linkage
    static FUNC_c* q;           // the name of the data member q has C++ language
                                // linkage and the data member's type is pointer to
                                // C function
};
```

```
extern "C" {
    class X {
        void mf();              // the name of the function mf and the member
                                // function's type have C++ language linkage
        void mf2(void(*)());    // the name of the function mf2 has C++ language
                                // linkage; the parameter has type pointer to
                                // C function

    };
}
```

—*end example*]

5 If two declarations of the same function or object specify different *linkage-specification*s (that is, the *linkage-specification*s of these declarations specify different *string-literal*s), the program is ill-formed if the declarations appear in the same translation unit, and the one definition rule (3.2) applies if the declarations appear in different translation units. Except for functions with C++ linkage, a function declaration without a linkage specification shall not precede the first linkage specification for that function. A function can be declared without a linkage specification after an explicit linkage specification has been seen; the linkage explicitly specified in the earlier declaration is not affected by such a function declaration.

6 At most one function with a particular name can have C language linkage. Two declarations for a function with C language linkage with the same function name (ignoring the namespace names that qualify it) that appear in different namespace scopes refer to the same function. Two declarations for an object with C language linkage with the same name (ignoring the namespace names that qualify it) that appear in different namespace scopes refer to the same object. [*Note:* because of the one definition rule (3.2), only one definition for a function or object with C linkage may appear in the program; that is, such a function or object must not be defined in more than one namespace scope. For example,

```
namespace A {
    extern "C" int f();
    extern "C" int g() { return 1; }
    extern "C" int h();
}

namespace B {
    extern "C" int f();              // A::f and B::f refer
                                     // to the same function
    extern "C" int g() { return 1; } // ill-formed, the function g
                                     // with C language linkage
                                     // has two definitions
}

int A::f() { return 98; }            // definition for the function f
                                     // with C language linkage
extern "C" int h() { return 97; }
                                     // definition for the function h
                                     // with C language linkage
                                     // A::h and ::h refer to the same function
```

—*end note*]

7 Except for functions with internal linkage, a function first declared in a *linkage-specification* behaves as a function with external linkage. [*Example:*

```
extern "C" double f();
static double f();               // error
```

is ill-formed (7.1.1).] The form of *linkage-specification* that contains a brace-enclosed *declaration-seq* does not affect whether the contained declarations are definitions or not (3.1); the form of *linkage-specification* directly containing a single declaration is treated as an `extern` specifier (7.1.1) for the purpose of determining whether the contained declaration is a definition. [*Example:*

```
extern "C" int i;              // declaration
extern "C" {
        int i;                 // definition
}
```

—*end example*] A *linkage-specification* directly containing a single declaration shall not specify a storage class. [*Example:*

```
extern "C" static void f();    // error
```

—*end example*]

8   [*Note:* because the language linkage is part of a function type, when a pointer to C function (for example) is dereferenced, the function to which it refers is considered a C function.]

9   Linkage from C++ to objects defined in other languages and to objects defined in C++ from other languages is implementation-defined and language-dependent. Only where the object layout strategies of two language implementations are similar enough can such linkage be achieved.

8 Declarators [dcl.decl]

1   A declarator declares a single object, function, or type, within a declaration. The *init-declarator-list* appearing in a declaration is a comma-separated sequence of declarators, each of which can have an initializer.

> *init-declarator-list:*
> > *init-declarator*
> > *init-declarator-list , init-declarator*

> *init-declarator:*
> > *declarator initializer$_{opt}$*

2   The two components of a *declaration* are the specifiers (*decl-specifier-seq*; 7.1) and the declarators (*init-declarator-list*). The specifiers indicate the type, storage class or other properties of the objects, functions or typedefs being declared. The declarators specify the names of these objects, functions or typedefs, and (optionally) modify the type of the specifiers with operators such as * (pointer to) and () (function returning). Initial values can also be specified in a declarator; initializers are discussed in 8.5 and 12.6.

3   Each *init-declarator* in a declaration is analyzed separately as if it was in a declaration by itself.[85]

4   Declarators have the syntax

> *declarator:*
> > *direct-declarator*
> > *ptr-operator declarator*

> *direct-declarator:*
> > *declarator-id*
> > *direct-declarator (parameter-declaration-clause) cv-qualifier-seq$_{opt}$ exception-specification$_{opt}$*
> > *direct-declarator [constant-expression$_{opt}$]*
> > *(declarator)*

---

[85] A declaration with several declarators is usually equivalent to the corresponding sequence of declarations each with a single declarator. That is

```
T  D1, D2, ... Dn;
```

is usually equvalent to

```
T  D1; T D2; ... T Dn;
```

where T is a *decl-specifier-seq* and each Di is a *init-declarator*. The exception occurs when a name introduced by one of the *declarators* hides a type name used by the *dcl-specifiers*, so that when the same *dcl-specifiers* are used in a subsequent declaration, they do not have the same meaning, as in

```
struct S { ... };
S   S, T;                        // declare two instances of struct S
```

which is not equivalent to

```
struct S { ... };
S   S;
S   T;                           // error
```

ptr-operator:
>   `*` *cv-qualifier-seq*$_{opt}$
>   `&`
>   `::`$_{opt}$ *nested-name-specifier* `*` *cv-qualifier-seq*$_{opt}$

cv-qualifier-seq:
>   *cv-qualifier cv-qualifier-seq*$_{opt}$

cv-qualifier:
>   `const`
>   `volatile`

declarator-id:
>   *id-expression*
>   `::`$_{opt}$ *nested-name-specifier*$_{opt}$ *type-name*

A *class-name* has special meaning in a declaration of the class of that name and when qualified by that name using the scope resolution operator `::` (5.1, 12.1, 12.4).

8.1 Type names   [dcl.name]

1   To specify type conversions explicitly, and as an argument of `sizeof`, `new`, or `typeid`, the name of a type shall be specified. This can be done with a *type-id*, which is syntactically a declaration for an object or function of that type that omits the name of the object or function.

type-id:
>   *type-specifier-seq abstract-declarator*$_{opt}$

type-specifier-seq:
>   *type-specifier type-specifier-seq*$_{opt.}$

abstract-declarator:
>   *ptr-operator abstract-declarator*$_{opt}$
>   *direct-abstract-declarator*

direct-abstract-declarator:
>   *direct-abstract-declarator*$_{opt}$
>   `(` *parameter-declaration-clause* `)` *cv-qualifier-seq*$_{opt}$ *exception-specification*$_{opt}$
>   *direct-abstract-declarator*$_{opt}$ `[` *constant-expression*$_{opt}$ `]`
>   `(` *abstract-declarator* `)`

It is possible to identify uniquely the location in the *abstract-declarator* where the identifier would appear if the construction were a declarator in a declaration. The named type is then the same as the type of the hypothetical identifier. [*Example:*

```
int               // int i
int *             // int *pi
int *[3]          // int *p[3]
int (*)[3]        // int (*p3i)[3]
int *()           // int *f()
int (*)(double)   // int (*pf)(double)
```

name respectively the types "int," "pointer to int," "array of 3 pointers to int," "pointer to array of 3 int," "function of (no parameters) returning pointer to int," and "pointer to a function of (double) returning int."]

2   A type can also be named (often more easily) by using a *typedef* (7.1.3).

8.2 Ambiguity resolution   **[dcl.ambig.res]**

1   The ambiguity arising from the similarity between a function-style cast and a declaration mentioned in 6.8 can also occur in the context of a declaration. In that context, the choice is between a function declaration with a redundant set of parentheses around a parameter name and an object declaration with a function-style cast as the initializer. Just as for the ambiguities mentioned in 6.8, the resolution is to consider any construct that could possibly be a declaration a declaration. [*Note:* a declaration can be explicitly disambiguated by a nonfunction-style cast, by a = to indicate initialization or by removing the redundant parentheses around the parameter name.] [*Example:*

```
struct S {
    S(int);
};

void foo(double a)
{
    S w(int(a));        // function declaration
    S x(int());         // function declaration
    S y((int)a);        // object declaration
    S z = int(a);       // object declaration
}
```

—*end example*]

2   The ambiguity arising from the similarity between a function-style cast and a *type-id* can occur in different contexts. The ambiguity appears as a choice between a function-style cast expression and a declaration of a type. The resolution is that any construct that could possibly be a *type-id* in its syntactic context shall be considered a *type-id*.

3   [*Example:*

```
#include <cstddef>
char *p;
void *operator new(size_t, int);
void foo()   {
      const int x = 63;
      new (int(*p)) int;     // new-placement expression
      new (int(*[x]));       // new type-id
}
```

4   For another example,

```
template <class T>
struct S {
      T *p;
};
S<int()> x;       // type-id
S<int(1)> y;      // expression (ill-formed)
```

5   For another example,

```
void foo()
{
      sizeof(int(1));    // expression
      sizeof(int());     // type-id (ill-formed)
}
```

6   For another example,

```
void foo()
{
        (int(1));                       // expression
        (int())1;                       // type-id (ill-formed)
}
```

—*end example*]

7   Another ambiguity arises in a *parameter-declaration-clause* of a function declaration, or in a *type-id* that is
     the operand of a `sizeof` or `typeid` operator, when a *type-name* is nested in parentheses. In this case, the
     choice is between the declaration of a parameter of type pointer to function and the declaration of a parame-
     ter with redundant parentheses around the *declarator-id*. The resolution is to consider the *type-name* as a
     simple-type-specifier rather than a *declarator-id*. [*Example:*

```
class C { };
void f(int(C)) { }                      // void f (int (*fp)(C c)) { }
                                        // not: void f (int C);

int g(C);

void foo() {
        f(1);                           // error: cannot convert 1 to function pointer
        f(g);                           // OK
}
```

For another example,

```
class C { };
void h(int *(C[10]));                   // void h (int * (*_fp)(C _parm[10]));
                                        // not: void h (int *C[10]);
```

—*end example*]

8.3 Meaning of declarators   **[dcl.meaning]**

1   A list of declarators appears after an optional (clause 7) *decl-specifier-seq* (7.1). Each declarator contains
     exactly one *declarator-id*; it names the identifier that is declared. An *unqualified-id* occurring in a
     declarator-id shall be a simple *identifier* except for the declaration of some special functions (12.3, 12.4,
     13.5) and for the declaration of template specializations or partial specializations (14.7). A *declarator-id*
     shall not be qualified except for the definition of a member function (9.3) or static data member (9.4) out-
     side of its class, the definition or explicit instantiation of a function or variable member of a namespace out-
     side of its namespace, or the definition of a previously declared explicit specialization outside of its name-
     space, or the declaration of a friend function that is a member of another class or namespace (11.4). When
     the *declarator-id* is qualified, the declaration shall refer to a previously declared member of the class or
     namespace to which the qualifier refers, and the member shall not have been introduced by a *using-
     declaration* in the scope of the class or namespace nominated by the *nested-name-specifier* of the
     declarator-id. [*Note:* if the qualifier is the global `::` scope resolution operator, the *declarator-id* refers to a
     name declared in the global namespace scope.]

2   An `auto`, `static`, `extern`, `register`, `mutable`, `friend`, `inline`, `virtual`, or `typedef` spec-
     ifier applies directly to each *declarator-id* in a *init-declarator-list*; the type specified for each *declarator-id*
     depends on both the *decl-specifier-seq* and its *declarator*.

3   Thus, a declaration of a particular identifier has the form

```
    T D
```

     where T is a *decl-specifier-seq* and D is a declarator. Following is a recursive procedure for determining the
     type specified for the contained *declarator-id* by such a declaration.

4 First, the *decl-specifier-seq* determines a type. In a declaration

```
T D
```

the *decl-specifier-seq* T determines the type "T." [*Example:* in the declaration

```
int unsigned i;
```

the type specifiers int unsigned determine the type "unsigned int" (7.1.5.2).]

5 In a declaration T D where D is an unadorned identifier the type of this identifier is "T."

6 In a declaration T D where D has the form

```
( D1 )
```

the type of the contained *declarator-id* is the same as that of the contained *declarator-id* in the declaration

```
T D1
```

Parentheses do not alter the type of the embedded *declarator-id*, but they can alter the binding of complex declarators.

8.3.1 Pointers [dcl.ptr]

1 In a declaration T D where D has the form

* *cv-qualifier-seq$_{opt}$* D1

and the type of the identifier in the declaration T D1 is "*derived-declarator-type-list* T," then the type of the identifier of D is "*derived-declarator-type-list cv-qualifier-seq* pointer to T." The *cv-qualifier*s apply to the pointer and not to the object pointed to.

2 [*Example:* the declarations

```
const int ci = 10, *pc = &ci, *const cpc = pc, **ppc;
int i, *p, *const cp = &i;
```

declare ci, a constant integer; pc, a pointer to a constant integer; cpc, a constant pointer to a constant integer, ppc, a pointer to a pointer to a constant integer; i, an integer; p, a pointer to integer; and cp, a constant pointer to integer. The value of ci, cpc, and cp cannot be changed after initialization. The value of pc can be changed, and so can the object pointed to by cp. Examples of some correct operations are

```
i = ci;
*cp = ci;
pc++;
pc = cpc;
pc = p;
ppc = &pc;
```

Examples of ill-formed operations are

```
ci = 1;          // error
ci++;            // error
*pc = 2;         // error
cp = &ci;        // error
cpc++;           // error
p = pc;          // error
ppc = &p;        // error
```

Each is unacceptable because it would either change the value of an object declared const or allow it to be changed through a cv-unqualified pointer later, for example:

```
*ppc = &ci;      // OK, but would make p point to ci ...
                 // ... because of previous error
*p = 5;          // clobber ci
```

—end example]

3   See also 5.17 and 8.5.

4   [*Note:* there are no pointers to references; see 8.3.2. Since the address of a bit-field (9.6) cannot be taken, a pointer can never point to a bit-field.]

8.3.2 References   [dcl.ref]

1   In a declaration T D where D has the form

```
& D1
```

and the type of the identifier in the declaration T D1 is "*derived-declarator-type-list* T," then the type of the identifier of D is "*derived-declarator-type-list* reference to T." Cv-qualified references are ill-formed except when the cv-qualifiers are introduced through the use of a typedef (7.1.3) or of a template type argument (14.3), in which case the cv-qualifiers are ignored. [*Example:* in

```
typedef int& A;
const A aref = 3;           // ill-formed;
                            // non-const reference initialized with rvalue
```

the type of aref is "reference to int", not "const reference to int".] [*Note:* a reference can be thought of as a name of an object.] A declarator that specifies the type "reference to *cv* void" is ill-formed.

2   [*Example:*

```
void f(double& a) { a += 3.14; }
// ...
double d = 0;
f(d);
```

declares a to be a reference parameter of f so the call f(d) will add 3.14 to d.

```
int v[20];
// ...
int& g(int i) { return v[i]; }
// ...
g(3) = 7;
```

declares the function g() to return a reference to an integer so g(3)=7 will assign 7 to the fourth element of the array v. For another example,

```
struct link {
    link* next;
};

link* first;

void h(link*& p)                // p is a reference to pointer
{
    p->next = first;
    first = p;
    p = 0;
}

void k()
{
        link* q = new link;
        h(q);
}
```

declares p to be a reference to a pointer to link so h(q) will leave q with the value zero. See also 8.5.3.]

8.3.2 References

3   It is unspecified whether or not a reference requires storage (3.7).

4   There shall be no references to references, no arrays of references, and no pointers to references. The declaration of a reference shall contain an *initializer* (8.5.3) except when the declaration contains an explicit `extern` specifier (7.1.1), is a class member (9.2) declaration within a class declaration, or is the declaration of a parameter or a return type (8.3.5); see 3.1. A reference shall be initialized to refer to a valid object or function. [*Note:* in particular, a null reference cannot exist in a well-defined program, because the only way to create such a reference would be to bind it to the "object" obtained by dereferencing a null pointer, which causes undefined behavior. As described in 9.6, a reference cannot be bound directly to a bit-field.]

8.3.3 Pointers to members   [dcl.mptr]

1   In a declaration T D where D has the form

> :: *opt* *nested-name-specifier* ∗ *cv-qualifier-seq_{opt}* D1

and the *nested-name-specifier* names a class, and the type of the identifier in the declaration T D1 is "*derived-declarator-type-list* T," then the type of the identifier of D is "*derived-declarator-type-list cv-qualifier-seq* pointer to member of *class nested-name-specifier of type* T."

2   [*Example:*

```
class X {
public:
    void f(int);
    int a;
};
class Y;

int X::* pmi = &X::a;
void (X::* pmf)(int) = &X::f;
double X::* pmd;
char Y::* pmc;
```

declares pmi, pmf, pmd and pmc to be a pointer to a member of X of type int, a pointer to a member of X of type void(int), a pointer to a member of X of type double and a pointer to a member of Y of type char respectively. The declaration of pmd is well-formed even though X has no members of type double. Similarly, the declaration of pmc is well-formed even though Y is an incomplete type. pmi and pmf can be used like this:

```
X obj;
//...
obj.*pmi = 7;            // assign 7 to an integer
                         // member of obj
(obj.*pmf)(7);           // call a function member of obj
                         // with the argument 7
```

   —end example]

3   A pointer to member shall not point to a static member of a class (9.4), a member with reference type, or "*cv* void." [*Note:* see also 5.3 and 5.5. The type "pointer to member" is distinct from the type "pointer", that is, a pointer to member is declared only by the pointer to member declarator syntax, and never by the pointer declarator syntax. There is no "reference-to-member" type in C++.]

8.3.4 Arrays   [dcl.array]

1   In a declaration T D where D has the form

         D1 [*constant-expression*~*opt*~]

and the type of the identifier in the declaration T D1 is "*derived-declarator-type-list* T," then the type of the identifier of D is an array type. T is called the array *element type*; this type shall not be a reference type, the (possibly cv-qualified) type void, a function type or an abstract class type. If the *constant-expression* (5.19) is present, it shall be an integral constant expression and its value shall be greater than zero. The constant expression specifies the *bound* of (number of elements in) the array. If the value of the constant expression is N, the array has N elements numbered 0 to N-1, and the type of the identifier of D is "*derived-declarator-type-list* array of N T." An object of array type contains a contiguously allocated non-empty set of N sub-objects of type T. If the constant expression is omitted, the type of the identifier of D is "*derived-declarator-type-list* array of unknown bound of T," an incomplete object type. The type "*derived-declarator-type-list* array of N T" is a different type from the type "*derived-declarator-type-list* array of unknown bound of T," see 3.9. Any type of the form "*cv-qualifier-seq* array of N T" is adjusted to "array of N *cv-qualifier-seq* T," and similarly for "array of unknown bound of T." [*Example:*

```
typedef int A[5], AA[2][3];
typedef const A CA;              // type is ''array of 5 const int''
typedef const AA CAA;            // type is ''array of 2 array of 3 const int''
```

—*end example*] [*Note:* an "array of N *cv-qualifier-seq* T" has cv-qualified type; such an array has internal linkage unless explicitly declared extern (7.1.5.1) and must be initialized as specified in 8.5.]

2   An array can be constructed from one of the fundamental types (except void), from a pointer, from a pointer to member, from a class, from an enumeration type, or from another array.

3   When several "array of" specifications are adjacent, a multidimensional array is created; the constant expressions that specify the bounds of the arrays can be omitted only for the first member of the sequence. [*Note:* this elision is useful for function parameters of array types, and when the array is external and the definition, which allocates storage, is given elsewhere.] The first *constant-expression* can also be omitted when the declarator is followed by an *initializer* (8.5). In this case the bound is calculated from the number of initial elements (say, N) supplied (8.5.1), and the type of the identifier of D is "array of N T."

4   [*Example:*

```
float fa[17], *afp[17];
```

declares an array of float numbers and an array of pointers to float numbers. For another example,

```
static int x3d[3][5][7];
```

declares a static three-dimensional array of integers, with rank 3×5×7. In complete detail, x3d is an array of three items; each item is an array of five arrays; each of the latter arrays is an array of seven integers. Any of the expressions x3d, x3d[i], x3d[i][j], x3d[i][j][k] can reasonably appear in an expression.]

5   [*Note:* conversions affecting lvalues of array type are described in 4.2. Objects of array types cannot be modified, see 3.10.]

6   Except where it has been declared for a class (13.5.5), the subscript operator [] is interpreted in such a way that E1[E2] is identical to *((E1)+(E2)). Because of the conversion rules that apply to +, if E1 is an array and E2 an integer, then E1[E2] refers to the E2-th member of E1. Therefore, despite its asymmetric appearance, subscripting is a commutative operation.

7   A consistent rule is followed for multidimensional arrays. If E is an *n*-dimensional array of rank $i \times j \times \cdots \times k$, then E appearing in an expression is converted to a pointer to an $(n-1)$-dimensional array with rank $j \times \cdots \times k$. If the * operator, either explicitly or implicitly as a result of subscripting, is applied to this pointer, the result is the pointed-to $(n-1)$-dimensional array, which itself is immediately converted

into a pointer.

8 [*Example:* consider

```
int x[3][5];
```

Here x is a 3×5 array of integers. When x appears in an expression, it is converted to a pointer to (the first of three) five-membered arrays of integers. In the expression x[i], which is equivalent to *(x+i), x is first converted to a pointer as described; then x+i is converted to the type of x, which involves multiplying i by the length of the object to which the pointer points, namely five integer objects. The results are added and indirection applied to yield an array (of five integers), which in turn is converted to a pointer to the first of the integers. If there is another subscript the same argument applies again; this time the result is an integer.]

9 [*Note:* it follows from all this that arrays in C++ are stored row-wise (last subscript varies fastest) and that the first subscript in the declaration helps determine the amount of storage consumed by an array but plays no other part in subscript calculations.]

8.3.5 Functions [dcl.fct]

1 In a declaration T D where D has the form

> D1 (*parameter-declaration-clause*) *cv-qualifier-seq$_{opt}$ exception-specification$_{opt}$*

and the type of the contained *declarator-id* in the declaration T D1 is "*derived-declarator-type-list* T," the type of the *declarator-id* in D is "*derived-declarator-type-list* function of (*parameter-declaration-clause*) *cv-qualifier-seq$_{opt}$* returning T"; a type of this form is a *function type*[86].

> *parameter-declaration-clause:*
>> *parameter-declaration-list$_{opt}$* · · ·$_{opt}$
>> *parameter-declaration-list* , · · ·

> *parameter-declaration-list:*
>> *parameter-declaration*
>> *parameter-declaration-list* , *parameter-declaration*

> *parameter-declaration:*
>> *decl-specifier-seq declarator*
>> *decl-specifier-seq declarator* = *assignment-expression*
>> *decl-specifier-seq abstract-declarator$_{opt}$*
>> *decl-specifier-seq abstract-declarator$_{opt}$* = *assignment-expression*

2 The *parameter-declaration-clause* determines the arguments that can be specified, and their processing, when the function is called. [*Note:* the *parameter-declaration-clause* is used to convert the arguments specified on the function call; see 5.2.2.] If the *parameter-declaration-clause* is empty, the function takes no arguments. The parameter list (void) is equivalent to the empty parameter list. Except for this special case, void shall not be a parameter type (though types derived from void, such as void*, can). If the *parameter-declaration-clause* terminates with an ellipsis, the number of arguments shall be equal to or greater than the number of parameters specified. Where syntactically correct, ", ..." is synonymous with "...". [*Example:* the declaration

```
int printf(const char*, ...);
```

declares a function that can be called with varying numbers and types of arguments.

```
printf("hello world");
printf("a=%d b=%d", a, b);
```

However, the first argument must be of a type that can be converted to a const char*.] [*Note:* the

---

[86] As indicated by the syntax, cv-qualifiers are a significant component in function return types.

standard header `<cstdarg>` contains a mechanism for accessing arguments passed using the ellipsis (see 5.2.2 and 18.7).]

3   A single name can be used for several different functions in a single scope; this is function overloading (clause 13). All declarations for a function with a given parameter list shall agree exactly both in the type of the value returned and in the number and type of parameters; the presence or absence of the ellipsis is considered part of the function type. The type of a function is determined using the following rules. The type of each parameter is determined from its own *decl-specifier-seq* and *declarator*. After determining the type of each parameter, any parameter of type "array of `T`" or "function returning `T`" is adjusted to be "pointer to `T`" or "pointer to function returning `T`," respectively. After producing the list of parameter types, several transformations take place upon these types to determine the function type. Any *cv-qualifier* modifying a parameter type is deleted. [*Example:* the type `void(*)(const int)` becomes `void(*)(int)` —*end example*] Such *cv-qualifier*s affect only the definition of the parameter within the body of the function; they do not affect the function type. If a *storage-class-specifier* modifies a parameter type, the specifier is deleted. [*Example:* `register char*` becomes `char*` —*end example*] Such *storage-class-specifier*s affect only the definition of the parameter within the body of the function; they do not affect the function type. The resulting list of transformed parameter types is the function's *parameter type list*.

4   A *cv-qualifier-seq* shall only be part of the function type for a nonstatic member function, the function type to which a pointer to member refers, or the top-level function type of a function typedef declaration. The effect of a *cv-qualifier-seq* in a function declarator is not the same as adding cv-qualification on top of the function type, i.e., it does not create a cv-qualified function type. In fact, if at any time in the determination of a type a cv-qualified function type is formed, the program is ill-formed. [*Example:*

```
typedef void F();
struct S {
        const F f;                  // ill-formed:
                                    // not equivalent to: void f() const;
};
```

—*end example*] The return type, the parameter type list and the *cv-qualifier-seq*, but not the default arguments (8.3.6) or the exception specification (15.4), are part of the function type. [*Note:* function types are checked during the assignments and initializations of pointer-to-functions, reference-to-functions, and pointer-to-member-functions.]

5   [*Example:* the declaration

```
int fseek(FILE*, long, int);
```

declares a function taking three arguments of the specified types, and returning `int` (7.1.5).]

6   If the type of a parameter includes a type of the form "pointer to array of unknown bound of `T`" or "reference to array of unknown bound of `T`," the program is ill-formed.[87] Functions shall not have a return type of type array or function, although they may have a return type of type pointer or reference to such things. There shall be no arrays of functions, although there can be arrays of pointers to functions. Types shall not be defined in return or parameter types. The type of a parameter or the return type for a function definition shall not be an incomplete class type (possibly cv-qualified) unless the function definition is nested within the *member-specification* for that class (including definitions in nested classes defined within the class).

7   A typedef of function type may be used to declare a function but shall not be used to define a function (8.4). [*Example:*

---

[87] This excludes parameters of type "*ptr-arr-seq* `T2`" where T2 is "pointer to array of unknown bound of `T`" and where *ptr-arr-seq* means any sequence of "pointer to" and "array of" derived declarator types. This exclusion applies to the parameters of the function, and if a parameter is a pointer to function or pointer to member function then to its parameters also, etc.

```
typedef void F();
F   fv;                      // OK: equivalent to void fv();
F   fv { }                   // ill-formed
void fv() { }                // OK: definition of fv
```

—*end example*] A typedef of a function type whose declarator includes a *cv-qualifier-seq* shall be used only to declare the function type for a nonstatic member function, to declare the function type to which a pointer to member refers, or to declare the top-level function type of another function typedef declaration. [*Example:*

```
typedef int FIC(int) const;
FIC f;                       // ill-formed: does not declare a member function
struct S {
        FIC f;               // OK
};
FIC S::*pm = &S::f;          // OK
```

—*end example*]

8   An identifier can optionally be provided as a parameter name; if present in a function definition (8.4), it names a parameter (sometimes called "formal argument"). [*Note:* in particular, parameter names are also optional in function definitions and names used for a parameter in different declarations and the definition of a function need not be the same. If a parameter name is present in a function declaration that is not a definition, it cannot be used outside of the *parameter-declaration-clause* since it goes out of scope at the end of the function declarator (3.3).]

9   [*Example:* the declaration

```
int i,
    *pi,
    f(),
    *fpi(int),
    (*pif)(const char*, const char*),
    (*fpif(int))(int);
```

declares an integer i, a pointer pi to an integer, a function f taking no arguments and returning an integer, a function fpi taking an integer argument and returning a pointer to an integer, a pointer pif to a function which takes two pointers to constant characters and returns an integer, a function fpif taking an integer argument and returning a pointer to a function that takes an integer argument and returns an integer. It is especially useful to compare fpi and pif. The binding of *fpi(int) is *(fpi(int)), so the declaration suggests, and the same construction in an expression requires, the calling of a function fpi, and then using indirection through the (pointer) result to yield an integer. In the declarator (*pif)(const char*, const char*), the extra parentheses are necessary to indicate that indirection through a pointer to a function yields a function, which is then called.] [*Note:* typedefs are sometimes convenient when the return type of a function is complex. For example, the function fpif above could have been declared

```
typedef int  IFUNC(int);
IFUNC*  fpif(int);
```

—*end note*]

8.3.6 Default arguments [dcl.fct.default]

1   If an expression is specified in a parameter declaration this expression is used as a default argument. Default arguments will be used in calls where trailing arguments are missing.

2   [*Example:* the declaration

```
void point(int = 3, int = 4);
```

declares a function that can be called with zero, one, or two arguments of type int. It can be called in any of these ways:

```
point(1,2);  point(1);  point();
```

The last two calls are equivalent to point(1,4) and point(3,4), respectively.]

3   A default argument expression shall be specified only in the *parameter-declaration-clause* of a function declaration or in a *template-parameter* (14.1). If it is specified in a *parameter-declaration-clause*, it shall not occur within a *declarator* or *abstract-declarator* of a *parameter-declaration*.[88]

4   For non-template functions, default arguments can be added in later declarations of a function in the same scope. Declarations in different scopes have completely distinct sets of default arguments. That is, declarations in inner scopes do not acquire default arguments from declarations in outer scopes, and vice versa. In a given function declaration, all parameters subsequent to a parameter with a default argument shall have default arguments supplied in this or previous declarations. A default argument shall not be redefined by a later declaration (not even to the same value). [*Example:*

```
void f(int, int);
void f(int, int = 7);
void h()
{
    f(3);                    // OK, calls f(3, 7)
    void f(int = 1, int);    // error: does not use default
                             // from surrounding scope
}

void m()
{
    void f(int, int);        // has no defaults
    f(4);                    // error: wrong number of arguments
    void f(int, int = 5);    // OK
    f(4);                    // OK, calls f(4, 5);
    void f(int, int = 5);    // error: cannot redefine, even to
                             // same value
}
void n()
{
    f(6);                    // OK, calls f(6, 7)
}
```

—*end example*] For a given inline function defined in different translation units, the accumulated sets of default arguments at the end of the translation units shall be the same; see 3.2.

5   A default argument expression is implicitly converted (clause 4) to the parameter type. The default argument expression has the same semantic constraints as the initializer expression in a declaration of a variable of the parameter type, using the copy-initialization semantics (8.5). The names in the expression are bound, and the semantic constraints are checked, at the point where the default argument expression appears. Name lookup and checking of semantic constraints for default arguments in function templates and in

---

[88] This means that default arguments cannot appear, for example, in declarations of pointers to functions, references to functions, or typedef declarations.

member functions of class templates are performed as described in 14.7.1. [*Example:* in the following code, g will be called with the value f(2):

```
int a = 1;
int f(int);
int g(int x = f(a));            // default argument: f(::a)

void h() {
    a = 2;
    {
        int a = 3;
        g();                    // g(f(::a))
    }
}
```

—*end example*] [*Note:* in member function declarations, names in default argument expressions are looked up as described in 3.4.1. Access checking applies to names in default argument expressions as described in clause 11.]

6   Except for member functions of class templates, the default arguments in a member function definition that appears outside of the class definition are added to the set of default arguments provided by the member function declaration in the class definition. Default arguments for a member function of a class template shall be specified on the initial declaration of the member function within the class template. [*Example:*

```
class C {
        void f(int i = 3);
        void g(int i, int j = 99);
};

void C::f(int i = 3)            // error: default argument already
{ }                            // specified in class scope
void C::g(int i = 88, int j)   // in this translation unit,
{ }                            // C::g can be called with no argument
```

—*end example*]

7   Local variables shall not be used in default argument expressions. [*Example:*

```
void f()
{
    int i;
    extern void g(int x = i);   // error
    // ...
}
```

—*end example*]

8   The keyword this shall not be used in a default argument of a member function. [*Example:*

```
class A {
    void f(A* p = this) { }     // error
};
```

—*end example*]

9   Default arguments are evaluated each time the function is called. The order of evaluation of function arguments is unspecified. Consequently, parameters of a function shall not be used in default argument expressions, even if they are not evaluated. Parameters of a function declared before a default argument expression are in scope and can hide namespace and class member names. [*Example:*

```
int a;
int f(int a, int b = a);                // error: parameter a
                                        // used as default argument
typedef int I;
int g(float I, int b = I(2));           // error: parameter I found
int h(int a, int b = sizeof(a));        // error, parameter a used
                                        // in default argument
```

—*end example*] Similarly, a nonstatic member shall not be used in a default argument expression, even if it is not evaluated, unless it appears as the id-expression of a class member access expression (5.2.5) or unless it is used to form a pointer to member (5.3.1). [*Example:* the declaration of X::mem1() in the following example is ill-formed because no object is supplied for the nonstatic member X::a used as an initializer.

```
int b;
class X {
    int a;
    int mem1(int i = a);                // error: nonstatic member a
                                        // used as default argument
    int mem2(int i = b);                // OK; use X::b
    static int b;
};
```

The declaration of X::mem2() is meaningful, however, since no object is needed to access the static member X::b. Classes, objects, and members are described in clause 9.] A default argument is not part of the type of a function. [*Example:*

```
int f(int = 0);

void h()
{
    int j = f(1);
    int k = f();                        // OK, means f(0)
}

int (*p1)(int) = &f;
int (*p2)() = &f;                       // error: type mismatch
```

—*end example*] When a declaration of a function is introduced by way of a *using-declaration* (7.3.3), any default argument information associated with the declaration is made known as well. If the function is redeclared thereafter in the namespace with additional default arguments, the additional arguments are also known at any point following the redeclaration where the *using-declaration* is in scope.

10   A virtual function call (10.3) uses the default arguments in the declaration of the virtual function determined by the static type of the pointer or reference denoting the object. An overriding function in a derived class does not acquire default arguments from the function it overrides. [*Example:*

```
struct A {
    virtual void f(int a = 7);
};
struct B : public A {
    void f(int a);
};
void m()
{
    B* pb = new B;
    A* pa = pb;
    pa->f();                            // OK, calls pa->B::f(7)
    pb->f();                            // error: wrong number of arguments for B::f()
}
```

—*end example*]

8.4 Function definitions   **[dcl.fct.def]**

1   Function definitions have the form

> *function-definition:*
>> *decl-specifier-seq*$_{opt}$ *declarator ctor-initializer*$_{opt}$ *function-body*
>> *decl-specifier-seq*$_{opt}$ *declarator function-try-block*

> *function-body:*
>> *compound-statement*

The *declarator* in a *function-definition* shall have the form

> D1 (*parameter-declaration-clause*) *cv-qualifier-seq*$_{opt}$ *exception-specification*$_{opt}$

as described in 8.3.5. A function shall be defined only in namespace or class scope.

2   [*Example:* a simple example of a complete function definition is

```
int max(int a, int b, int c)
{
    int m = (a > b) ? a : b;
    return (m > c) ? m : c;
}
```

Here int is the *decl-specifier-seq*; max(int a, int b, int c) is the *declarator*; { /* ... */ } is the *function-body.*]

3   A *ctor-initializer* is used only in a constructor; see 12.1 and 12.6.

4   A *cv-qualifier-seq* can be part of a non-static member function declaration, non-static member function definition, or pointer to member function only; see 9.3.2. It is part of the function type.

5   [*Note:* unused parameters need not be named. For example,

```
void print(int a, int)
{
    printf("a = %d\n",a);
}
```

—*end note*]

8.5 Initializers   [dcl.init]

1   A declarator can specify an initial value for the identifier being declared. The identifier designates an object or reference being initialized. The process of initialization described in the remainder of 8.5 applies also to initializations specified by other syntactic contexts, such as the initialization of function parameters with argument expressions (5.2.2) or the initialization of return values (6.6.3).

> *initializer:*
>> = *initializer-clause*
>> (*expression-list*)

> *initializer-clause:*
>> *assignment-expression*
>> { *initializer-list* $_{, opt}$ }
>> { }

> *initializer-list:*
>> *initializer-clause*
>> *initializer-list* , *initializer-clause*

2   Automatic, register, static, and external variables of namespace scope can be initialized by arbitrary expressions involving literals and previously declared variables and functions. [*Example:*

```
int f(int);
int a = 2;
int b = f(a);
int c(b);
```

—*end example*]

3   [*Note:* default argument expressions are more restricted; see 8.3.6.

4   The order of initialization of static objects is described in 3.6 and 6.7.]

5   To *zero-initialize* an object of type T means:

— if T is a scalar type (3.9), the object is set to the value of 0 (zero) converted to T;

— if T is a non-union class type, each nonstatic data member and each base-class subobject is zero-initialized;

— if T is a union type, the object's first named data member[89] is zero-initialized;

— if T is an array type, each element is zero-initialized;

— if T is a reference type, no initialization is performed.

To *default-initialize* an object of type T means:

— if T is a non-POD class type (clause 9), the default constructor for T is called (and the initialization is ill-formed if T has no accessible default constructor);

— if T is an array type, each element is default-initialized;

— otherwise, the object is zero-initialized.

To *value-initialize* an object of type T means:

— if T is a class type (clause 9) with a user-declared constructor (12.1), then the default constructor for T is called (and the initialization is ill-formed if T has no accessible default constructor);

— if T is a non-union class type without a user-declared constructor, then every non-static data member and base-class component of T is value-initialized;

— if T is an array type, then each element is value-initialized;

— otherwise, the object is zero-initialized

A program that calls for default-initialization or value-initialization of an entity of reference type is ill-formed. If T is a cv-qualified type, the cv-unqualified version of T is used for these definitions of zero-initialization, default-initialization, and value-initialization.

6   Every object of static storage duration shall be zero-initialized at program startup before any other initialization takes place. [*Note:* in some cases, additional initialization is done later.]

7   An object whose initializer is an empty set of parentheses, i.e., (), shall be value-initialized.

8   [*Note:* since () is not permitted by the syntax for *initializer*,

```
X a();
```

is not the declaration of an object of class X, but the declaration of a function taking no argument and returning an X. The form () is permitted in certain other initialization contexts (5.3.4, 5.2.3, 12.6.2).]

---
[89] This member must not be static, by virtue of the requirements in 9.5.

9   If no initializer is specified for an object, and the object is of (possibly cv-qualified) non-POD class type (or array thereof), the object shall be default-initialized; if the object is of const-qualified type, the underlying class type shall have a user-declared default constructor. Otherwise, if no initializer is specified for a non-static object, the object and its subobjects, if any, have an indeterminate initial value[90]; if the object or any of its subobjects are of const-qualified type, the program is ill-formed.

10   An initializer for a static member is in the scope of the member's class. [*Example:*

```
int a;

struct X {
    static int a;
    static int b;
};

int X::a = 1;
int X::b = a;                    // X::b = X::a
```

—*end example*]

11   The form of initialization (using parentheses or =) is generally insignificant, but does matter when the entity being initialized has a class type; see below. A parenthesized initializer can be a list of expressions only when the entity being initialized has a class type.

12   The initialization that occurs in argument passing, function return, throwing an exception (15.1), handling an exception (15.3), and brace-enclosed initializer lists (8.5.1) is called *copy-initialization* and is equivalent to the form

```
T x = a;
```

The initialization that occurs in new expressions (5.3.4), static_cast expressions (5.2.9), functional notation type conversions (5.2.3), and base and member initializers (12.6.2) is called *direct-initialization* and is equivalent to the form

```
T x(a);
```

13   If T is a scalar type, then a declaration of the form

```
T x = { a };
```

is equivalent to

```
T x = a;
```

14   The semantics of initializers are as follows. The *destination type* is the type of the object or reference being initialized and the *source type* is the type of the initializer expression. The source type is not defined when the initializer is brace-enclosed or when it is a parenthesized list of expressions.

— If the destination type is a reference type, see 8.5.3.

— If the destination type is an array of characters or an array of wchar_t, and the initializer is a string literal, see 8.5.2.

— Otherwise, if the destination type is an array, see 8.5.1.

— If the destination type is a (possibly cv-qualified) class type:

  — If the class is an aggregate (8.5.1), and the initializer is a brace-enclosed list, see 8.5.1.

  — If the initialization is direct-initialization, or if it is copy-initialization where the cv-unqualified

---

[90] This does not apply to aggregate objects with automatic storage duration initialized with an incomplete brace-enclosed *initializer-list*; see 8.5.1.

version of the source type is the same class as, or a derived class of, the class of the destination, constructors are considered. The applicable constructors are enumerated (13.3.1.3), and the best one is chosen through overload resolution (13.3). The constructor so selected is called to initialize the object, with the initializer expression(s) as its argument(s). If no constructor applies, or the overload resolution is ambiguous, the initialization is ill-formed.

— Otherwise (i.e., for the remaining copy-initialization cases), user-defined conversion sequences that can convert from the source type to the destination type or (when a conversion function is used) to a derived class thereof are enumerated as described in 13.3.1.4, and the best one is chosen through overload resolution (13.3). If the conversion cannot be done or is ambiguous, the initialization is ill-formed. The function selected is called with the initializer expression as its argument; if the function is a constructor, the call initializes a temporary of the destination type. The result of the call (which is the temporary for the constructor case) is then used to direct-initialize, according to the rules above, the object that is the destination of the copy-initialization. In certain cases, an implementation is permitted to eliminate the copying inherent in this direct-initialization by constructing the intermediate result directly into the object being initialized; see 12.2, 12.8.

— Otherwise, if the source type is a (possibly cv-qualified) class type, conversion functions are considered. The applicable conversion functions are enumerated (13.3.1.5), and the best one is chosen through overload resolution (13.3). The user-defined conversion so selected is called to convert the initializer expression into the object being initialized. If the conversion cannot be done or is ambiguous, the initialization is ill-formed.

— Otherwise, the initial value of the object being initialized is the (possibly converted) value of the initializer expression. Standard conversions (clause 4) will be used, if necessary, to convert the initializer expression to the cv-unqualified version of the destination type; no user-defined conversions are considered. If the conversion cannot be done, the initialization is ill-formed. [*Note:* an expression of type "$cv1$ T" can initialize an object of type "$cv2$ T" independently of the cv-qualifiers $cv1$ and $cv2$.

```
int a;
const int b = a;
int c = b;
```

—*end note*]

8.5.1 Aggregates   [dcl.init.aggr]

1   An *aggregate* is an array or a class (clause 9) with no user-declared constructors (12.1), no private or protected non-static data members (clause 11), no base classes (clause 10), and no virtual functions (10.3).

2   When an aggregate is initialized the *initializer* can contain an *initializer-clause* consisting of a brace-enclosed, comma-separated list of *initializer-clause*s for the members of the aggregate, written in increasing subscript or member order. If the aggregate contains subaggregates, this rule applies recursively to the members of the subaggregate. [*Example:*

```
struct A {
        int x;
        struct B {
                int i;
                int j;
        } b;
} a = { 1, { 2, 3 } };
```

initializes a.x with 1, a.b.i with 2, a.b.j with 3.]

3   An aggregate that is a class can also be initialized with a single expression not enclosed in braces, as described in 8.5.

4   An array of unknown size initialized with a brace-enclosed *initializer-list* containing n *initializer*s, where n shall be greater than zero, is defined as having n elements (8.3.4). [*Example:*

```
int x[] = { 1, 3, 5 };
```

declares and initializes x as a one-dimensional array that has three elements since no size was specified and there are three initializers.] An empty initializer list { } shall not be used as the initializer for an array of unknown bound.[91)]

5   Static data members are not considered members of the class for purposes of aggregate initialization. [*Example:*

```
struct A {
        int i;
        static int s;
        int j;
} a = { 1, 2 };
```

Here, the second initializer 2 initializes a.j and not the static data member A::s.]

6   An *initializer-list* is ill-formed if the number of *initializer*s exceeds the number of members or elements to initialize. [*Example:*

```
char cv[4] = { 'a', 's', 'd', 'f', 0 };        // error
```

is ill-formed.]

7   If there are fewer *initializer*s in the list than there are members in the aggregate, then each member not explicitly initialized shall be value-initialized (8.5). [*Example:*

```
struct S { int a; char* b; int c; };
S ss = { 1, "asdf" };
```

initializes ss.a with 1, ss.b with "asdf", and ss.c with the value of an expression of the form int(), that is, 0.]

8   An *initializer* for an aggregate member that is an empty class shall have the form of an empty *initializer-list* { }. [*Example:*

```
struct S { };
struct A {
        S s;
        int i;
} a = { { } , 3 };
```

—*end example*] An empty initializer-list can be used to initialize any aggregate. If the aggregate is not an empty class, then each member of the aggregate shall be initialized with a value of the form T() (5.2.3), where T represents the type of the uninitialized member.

9   If an incomplete or empty *initializer-list* leaves a member of reference type uninitialized, the program is ill-formed.

10   When initializing a multi-dimensional array, the *initializer*s initialize the elements with the last (rightmost) index of the array varying the fastest (8.3.4). [*Example:*

```
int x[2][2] = { 3, 1, 4, 2 };
```

initializes x[0][0] to 3, x[0][1] to 1, x[1][0] to 4, and x[1][1] to 2. On the other hand,

---

[91)] The syntax provides for empty *initializer-list*s, but nonetheless C++ does not have zero length arrays.

```
float y[4][3] = {
    { 1 }, { 2 }, { 3 }, { 4 }
};
```

initializes the first column of y (regarded as a two-dimensional array) and leaves the rest zero.]

11   Braces can be elided in an *initializer-list* as follows. If the *initializer-list* begins with a left brace, then the
      succeeding comma-separated list of *initializers* initializes the members of a subaggregate; it is erroneous
      for there to be more initializers than members. If, however, the *initializer-list* for a subaggregate does not
      begin with a left brace, then only enough *initializers* from the list are taken to initialize the members of the
      subaggregate; any remaining *initializers* are left to initialize the next member of the aggregate of which the
      current subaggregate is a member. [*Example:*

```
float y[4][3] = {
    { 1, 3, 5 },
    { 2, 4, 6 },
    { 3, 5, 7 },
};
```

is a completely-braced initialization: 1, 3, and 5 initialize the first row of the array y[0], namely
y[0][0], y[0][1], and y[0][2]. Likewise the next two lines initialize y[1] and y[2]. The initializer ends early and therefore y[3]'s elements are initialized as if explicitly initialized with an expression
of the form float(), that is, are initialized with 0.0. In the following example, braces in the *initializer-
list* are elided; however the *initializer-list* has the same effect as the completely-braced *initializer-list* of the
above example,

```
float y[4][3] = {
    1, 3, 5, 2, 4, 6, 3, 5, 7
};
```

The initializer for y begins with a left brace, but the one for y[0] does not, therefore three elements from
the list are used. Likewise the next three are taken successively for y[1] and y[2]. *—end example*]

12   All implicit type conversions (clause 4) are considered when initializing the aggregate member with an ini-
      tializer from an *initializer-list*. If the *initializer* can initialize a member, the member is initialized. Other-
      wise, if the member is itself a non-empty subaggregate, brace elision is assumed and the *initializer* is con-
      sidered for the initialization of the first member of the subaggregate.
      [*Example:*

```
struct A {
    int i;
    operator int();
};
struct B {
    A a1, a2;
    int z;
};
A a;
B b = { 4, a, a };
```

Braces are elided around the *initializer* for b.a1.i. b.a1.i is initialized with 4, b.a2 is initialized with
a, b.z is initialized with whatever a.operator int() returns.]

13   [*Note:* An aggregate array or an aggregate class may contain members of a class type with a user-declared
      constructor (12.1). Initialization of these aggregate objects is described in 12.6.1.]

14   When an aggregate with static storage duration is initialized with a brace-enclosed *initializer-list*, if all the
      member initializer expressions are constant expressions, and the aggregate is a POD type, the initialization
      shall be done during the static phase of initialization (3.6.2); otherwise, it is unspecified whether the initial-
      ization of members with constant expressions takes place during the static phase or during the dynamic
      phase of initialization.

15   When a union is initialized with a brace-enclosed initializer, the braces shall only contain an initializer for
the first member of the union. [*Example:*

```
union u { int a; char* b; };

u a = { 1 };
u b = a;
u c = 1;               // error
u d = { 0, "asdf" };   // error
u e = { "asdf" };      // error
```

—*end example*] [*Note:* as described above, the braces around the initializer for a union member can be
omitted if the union is a member of another aggregate.]

8.5.2 Character arrays   [dcl.init.string]

1   A `char` array (whether plain `char`, `signed char`, or `unsigned char`) can be initialized by a *string-literal* (optionally enclosed in braces); a `wchar_t` array can be initialized by a wide *string-literal* (optionally enclosed in braces); successive characters of the *string-literal* initialize the members of the array.
[*Example:*

```
char msg[] = "Syntax error on line %s\n";
```

shows a character array whose members are initialized with a *string-literal*. Note that because `'\n'` is a
single character and because a trailing `'\0'` is appended, `sizeof(msg)` is 25.]

2   There shall not be more initializers than there are array elements. [*Example:*

```
char cv[4] = "asdf";       // error
```

is ill-formed since there is no space for the implied trailing `'\0'`.]

8.5.3 References   [dcl.init.ref]

1   A variable declared to be a `T&`, that is "reference to type `T`" (8.3.2), shall be initialized by an object, or
function, of type `T` or by an object that can be converted into a `T`. [*Example:*

```
int g(int);
void f()
{
    int i;
    int& r = i;            // r refers to i
    r = 1;                 // the value of i becomes 1
    int* p = &r;           // p points to i
    int& rr = r;           // rr refers to what r refers to, that is, to i
    int (&rg)(int) = g;    // rg refers to the function g
    rg(i);                 // calls function g
    int a[3];
    int (&ra)[3] = a;      // ra refers to the array a
    ra[1] = i;             // modifies a[1]
}
```

—*end example*]

2   A reference cannot be changed to refer to another object after initialization. Note that initialization of a reference is treated very differently from assignment to it. Argument passing (5.2.2) and function value return
(6.6.3) are initializations.

3   The initializer can be omitted for a reference only in a parameter declaration (8.3.5), in the declaration of a
function return type, in the declaration of a class member within its class declaration (9.2), and where the
`extern` specifier is explicitly used. [*Example:*

```
int& r1;                      // error: initializer missing
extern int& r2;               // OK
```

—end example]

4   Given types "*cv1* T1" and "*cv2* T2," "*cv1* T1" is *reference-related* to "*cv2* T2" if T1 is the same type as T2, or T1 is a base class of T2. "*cv1* T1" is *reference-compatible* with "*cv2* T2" if T1 is reference-related to T2 and *cv1* is the same cv-qualification as, or greater cv-qualification than, *cv2*. For purposes of overload resolution, cases for which *cv1* is greater cv-qualification than *cv2* are identified as *reference-compatible with added qualification* (see 13.3.3.2). In all cases where the reference-related or reference-compatible relationship of two types is used to establish the validity of a reference binding, and T1 is a base class of T2, a program that necessitates such a binding is ill-formed if T1 is an inaccessible (clause 11) or ambiguous (10.2) base class of T2.

5   A reference to type "*cv1* T1" is initialized by an expression of type "*cv2* T2" as follows:

— If the initializer expression

   — is an lvalue (but is not a bit-field), and "*cv1* T1" is reference-compatible with "*cv2* T2," or

   — has a class type (i.e., T2 is a class type) and can be implicitly converted to an lvalue of type "*cv3* T3," where "*cv1* T1" is reference-compatible with "*cv3* T3" [92] (this conversion is selected by enumerating the applicable conversion functions (13.3.1.6) and choosing the best one through overload resolution (13.3)),

then the reference is bound directly to the initializer expression lvalue in the first case, and the reference is bound to the lvalue result of the conversion in the second case. In these cases the reference is said to *bind directly* to the initializer expression. [*Note:* the usual lvalue-to-rvalue (4.1), array-to-pointer (4.2), and function-to-pointer (4.3) standard conversions are not needed, and therefore are suppressed, when such direct bindings to lvalues are done.]
[*Example:*

```
double d = 2.0;
double& rd = d;               // rd refers to d
const double& rcd = d;        // rcd refers to d

struct A { };
struct B : public A { } b;
A& ra = b;                    // ra refers to A sub-object in b
const A& rca = b;             // rca refers to A sub-object in b
```

   —end example]

— Otherwise, the reference shall be to a non-volatile const type (i.e., *cv1* shall be const). [*Example:*

```
double& rd2 = 2.0;            // error: not an lvalue and reference not const
int   i = 2;
double& rd3 = i;              // error: type mismatch and reference not const
```

   —end example]

   — If the initializer expression is an rvalue, with T2 a class type, and "*cv1* T1" is reference-compatible with "*cv2* T2," the reference is bound in one of the following ways (the choice is implementation-defined):

      — The reference is bound to the object represented by the rvalue (see 3.10) or to a sub-object within that object.

      — A temporary of type "*cv1* T2" [sic] is created, and a constructor is called to copy the entire

---
[92] This requires a conversion function (12.3.2) returning a reference type.

rvalue object into the temporary. The reference is bound to the temporary or to a sub-object within the temporary.[93)]

The constructor that would be used to make the copy shall be callable whether or not the copy is actually done. [*Example:*

```
struct A { };
struct B : public A { } b;
extern B f();
const A& rca = f();          // Either bound to the A sub-object of the B rvalue,
                             //   or the entire B object is copied and the reference
                             //   is bound to the A sub-object of the copy
```

—*end example*]

— Otherwise, a temporary of type "*cv1* T1" is created and initialized from the initializer expression using the rules for a non-reference copy initialization (8.5). The reference is then bound to the temporary. If T1 is reference-related to T2, *cv1* must be the same cv-qualification as, or greater cv-qualification than, *cv2*; otherwise, the program is ill-formed. [*Example:*

```
const double& rcd2 = 2;       // rcd2 refers to temporary with value 2.0
const volatile int cvi = 1;
const int& r = cvi;           // error: type qualifiers dropped
```

—*end example*]

6 [*Note:* 12.2 describes the lifetime of temporaries bound to references.]

[93)] Clearly, if the reference initialization being processed is one for the first argument of a copy constructor call, an implementation must eventually choose the first alternative (binding without copying) to avoid infinite recursion.

9 Classes

[class]

1   A class is a type. Its name becomes a *class-name* (9.1) within its scope.

> *class-name:*
>> *identifier*
>> *template-id*

*Class-specifier*s and *elaborated-type-specifier*s (7.1.5.3) are used to make *class-name*s. An object of a class consists of a (possibly empty) sequence of members and base class objects.

> *class-specifier:*
>> *class-head* { *member-specification_{opt}* }

> *class-head:*
>> *class-key identifier_{opt} base-clause_{opt}*
>> *class-key nested-name-specifier identifier base-clause_{opt}*
>> *class-key nested-name-specifier_{opt} template-id base-clause_{opt}*

> *class-key:*
>> ```
>> class
>> struct
>> union
>> ```

2   A *class-name* is inserted into the scope in which it is declared immediately after the *class-name* is seen. The *class-name* is also inserted into the scope of the class itself; this is known as the *injected-class-name*. For purposes of access checking, the injected-class-name is treated as if it were a public member name. A *class-specifier* is commonly referred to as a class definition. A class is considered defined after the closing brace of its *class-specifier* has been seen even though its member functions are in general not yet defined.

3   Complete objects and member subobjects of class type shall have nonzero size.[94] [*Note:* class objects can be assigned, passed as arguments to functions, and returned by functions (except objects of classes for which copying has been restricted; see 12.8). Other plausible operators, such as equality comparison, can be defined by the user; see 13.5.]

4   A *structure* is a class defined with the *class-key* `struct`; its members and base classes (clause 10) are public by default (clause 11). A *union* is a class defined with the *class-key* `union`; its members are public by default and it holds only one data member at a time (9.5). [*Note:* aggregates of class type are described in 8.5.1.] A *POD-struct* is an aggregate class that has no non-static data members of type non-POD-struct, non-POD-union (or array of such types) or reference, and has no user-defined copy assignment operator and no user-defined destructor. Similarly, a *POD-union* is an aggregate union that has no non-static data members of type non-POD-struct, non-POD-union (or array of such types) or reference, and has no user-defined copy assignment operator and no user-defined destructor. A *POD class* is a class that is either a POD-struct or a POD-union.

---

[94] Base class subobjects are not so constrained.

9.1 Class names   **[class.name]**

1   A class definition introduces a new type. [*Example:*

```
struct X { int a; };
struct Y { int a; };
X a1;
Y a2;
int a3;
```

declares three variables of three different types. This implies that

```
a1 = a2;                        // error: Y assigned to X
a1 = a3;                        // error: int assigned to X
```

are type mismatches, and that

```
int f(X);
int f(Y);
```

declare an overloaded (clause 13) function `f()` and not simply a single function `f()` twice. For the same reason,

```
struct S { int a; };
struct S { int a; };            // error, double definition
```

is ill-formed because it defines S twice.]

2   A class definition introduces the class name into the scope where it is defined and hides any class, object, function, or other declaration of that name in an enclosing scope (3.3). If a class name is declared in a scope where an object, function, or enumerator of the same name is also declared, then when both declarations are in scope, the class can be referred to only using an *elaborated-type-specifier* (3.4.4). [*Example:*

```
struct stat {
        // ...
};

stat gstat;                     // use plain stat to
                                // define variable

int stat(struct stat*);         // redeclare stat as function

void f()
{
    struct stat* ps;            // struct prefix needed
                                // to name struct stat
                                // ...
    stat(ps);                   // call stat()
                                // ...
}
```

—*end example*] A *declaration* consisting solely of *class-key identifier ;* is either a redeclaration of the name in the current scope or a forward declaration of the identifier as a class name. It introduces the class name into the current scope. [*Example:*

```
struct s { int a; };

void g()
{
    struct s;                                // hide global struct s
                                             //  with a local declaration
    s* p;                                    // refer to local struct s
    struct s { char* p; };                   // define local struct s
    struct s;                                // redeclaration, has no effect
}
```

—*end example*] [*Note:* Such declarations allow definition of classes that refer to each other. [*Example:*

```
class Vector;

class Matrix {
        // ...
        friend Vector operator*(Matrix&, Vector&);
};

class Vector {
        // ...
        friend Vector operator*(Matrix&, Vector&);
};
```

Declaration of friends is described in 11.4, operator functions in 13.5.]]

3   An *elaborated-type-specifier* (7.1.5.3) can also be used as a *type-specifier* as part of a declaration. It differs from a class declaration in that if a class of the elaborated name is in scope the elaborated name will refer to it. [*Example:*

```
struct s { int a; };

void g(int s)
{
        struct s* p = new struct s;     // global s
        p->a = s;                       // local s
}
```

—*end example*]

4   [*Note:* The declaration of a class name takes effect immediately after the *identifier* is seen in the class definition or *elaborated-type-specifier*. For example,

```
class A * A;
```

first specifies A to be the name of a class and then redefines it as the name of a pointer to an object of that class. This means that the elaborated form class A must be used to refer to the class. Such artistry with names can be confusing and is best avoided.]

5   A *typedef-name* (7.1.3) that names a class is a *class-name*, but shall not be used in an *elaborated-type-specifier*; see also 7.1.3.

9.2 Class members

member-specification:
    member-declaration member-specification$_{opt}$
    access-specifier : *member-specification$_{opt}$*

member-declaration:
    decl-specifier-seq$_{opt}$ member-declarator-list$_{opt}$;
    function-definition ;$_{opt}$
    : :$_{opt}$ *nested-name-specifier* template$_{opt}$ *unqualified-id* ;
    using-declaration
    template-declaration

member-declarator-list:
    member-declarator
    member-declarator-list , *member-declarator*

member-declarator:
    declarator pure-specifier$_{opt}$
    declarator constant-initializer$_{opt}$
    identifier$_{opt}$: *constant-expression*

pure-specifier:
    = 0

constant-initializer:
    = *constant-expression*

1   The *member-specification* in a class definition declares the full set of members of the class; no member can be added elsewhere. Members of a class are data members, member functions (9.3), nested types, and enumerators. Data members and member functions are static or nonstatic; see 9.4. Nested types are classes (9.1, 9.7) and enumerations (7.2) defined in the class, and arbitrary types declared as members by use of a typedef declaration (7.1.3). The enumerators of an enumeration (7.2) defined in the class are members of the class. Except when used to declare friends (11.4) or to introduce the name of a member of a base class into a derived class (7.3.3,11.3), *member-declaration*s declare members of the class, and each such *member-declaration* shall declare at least one member name of the class. A member shall not be declared twice in the *member-specification*, except that a nested class or member class template can be declared and then later defined.

2   A class is considered a completely-defined object type (3.9) (or complete type) at the closing } of the *class-specifier*. Within the class *member-specification*, the class is regarded as complete within function bodies, default arguments and constructor *ctor-initializer*s (including such things in nested classes). Otherwise it is regarded as incomplete within its own class *member-specification*.

3   [*Note:* a single name can denote several function members provided their types are sufficiently different (clause 13).]

4   A *member-declarator* can contain a *constant-initializer* only if it declares a static member (9.4) of const integral or const enumeration type, see 9.4.2.

5   A member can be initialized using a constructor; see 12.1. [*Note:* see clause 12 for a description of constructors and other special member functions.]

6   A member shall not be auto, extern, or register.

7   The *decl-specifier-seq* is omitted in constructor, destructor, and conversion function declarations only. The *member-declarator-list* can be omitted only after a *class-specifier*, an *enum-specifier*, or a *decl-specifier-seq* of the form friend *elaborated-type-specifier*. A *pure-specifier* shall be used only in the declaration of a virtual function (10.3).

8   Non-static (9.4) members that are class objects shall be objects of previously defined classes. In particular, a class cl shall not contain an object of class cl, but it can contain a pointer or reference to an object
of class cl. When an array is used as the type of a nonstatic member all dimensions shall be specified.

9   Except when used to form a pointer to member (5.3.1), when used in the body of a nonstatic member function of its class or of a class derived from its class (9.3.1), or when used in a *mem-initializer* for a constructor for its class or for a class derived from its class (12.6.2), a nonstatic data or function member of a class
shall only be referred to with the class member access syntax (5.2.5).

10   [*Note:* the type of a nonstatic member function is an ordinary function type, and the type of a nonstatic data
member is an ordinary object type. There are no special member function types or data member types.]

11   [*Example:* A simple example of a class definition is

```
struct tnode {
    char tword[20];
    int count;
    tnode *left;
    tnode *right;
};
```

which contains an array of twenty characters, an integer, and two pointers to similar structures. Once this
definition has been given, the declaration

```
tnode s, *sp;
```

declares s to be a tnode and sp to be a pointer to a tnode. With these declarations, sp->count refers
to the count member of the structure to which sp points; s.left refers to the left subtree pointer of
the structure s; and s.right->tword[0] refers to the initial character of the tword member of the
right subtree of s.]

12   Nonstatic data members of a (non-union) class declared without an intervening *access-specifier* are allocated so that later members have higher addresses within a class object. The order of allocation of nonstatic
data members separated by an *access-specifier* is unspecified (11.1). Implementation alignment requirements might cause two adjacent members not to be allocated immediately after each other; so might
requirements for space for managing virtual functions (10.3) and virtual base classes (10.1).

13   If T is the name of a class, then each of the following shall have a name different from T:

— every static data member of class T;

— every member function of class T [*Note:* this restriction does not apply to constructors, which do not
have names (12.1)] ;

— every member of class T that is itself a type;

— every enumerator of every member of class T that is an enumerated type; and

— every member of every anonymous union that is a member of class T.

13a In addition, if class T has a user-declared constructor (12.1), every nonstatic data member of class T shall
have a name different from T.

14   Two POD-struct (clause 9) types are layout-compatible if they have the same number of nonstatic data
members, and corresponding nonstatic data members (in order) have layout-compatible types (3.9).

15   Two POD-union (clause 9) types are layout-compatible if they have the same number of nonstatic data
members, and corresponding nonstatic data members (in any order) have layout-compatible types (3.9).

16   If a POD-union contains two or more POD-structs that share a common initial sequence, and if the POD-
union object currently contains one of these POD-structs, it is permitted to inspect the common initial part
of any of them. Two POD-structs share a common initial sequence if corresponding members have layout-
compatible types (and, for bit-fields, the same widths) for a sequence of one or more initial members.

17   A pointer to a POD-struct object, suitably converted using a `reinterpret_cast`, points to its initial member (or if that member is a bit-field, then to the unit in which it resides) and vice versa. [*Note:* There might therefore be unnamed padding within a POD-struct object, but not at its beginning, as necessary to achieve appropriate alignment.]

9.3 Member functions   [class.mfct]

1   Functions declared in the definition of a class, excluding those declared with a `friend` specifier (11.4), are called member functions of that class. A member function may be declared `static` in which case it is a *static* member function of its class (9.4); otherwise it is a *nonstatic* member function of its class (9.3.1, 9.3.2).

2   A member function may be defined (8.4) in its class definition, in which case it is an *inline* member function (7.1.2), or it may be defined outside of its class definition if it has already been declared but not defined in its class definition. A member function definition that appears outside of the class definition shall appear in a namespace scope enclosing the class definition. Except for member function definitions that appear outside of a class definition, and except for explicit specializations of member functions of class templates and member function templates (14.7) appearing outside of the class definition, a member function shall not be redeclared.

3   An `inline` member function (whether static or nonstatic) may also be defined outside of its class definition provided either its declaration in the class definition or its definition outside of the class definition declares the function as `inline`. [*Note:* member functions of a class in namespace scope have external linkage. Member functions of a local class (9.8) have no linkage. See 3.5.]

4   There shall be at most one definition of a non-inline member function in a program; no diagnostic is required. There may be more than one `inline` member function definition in a program. See 3.2 and 7.1.2.

5   If the definition of a member function is lexically outside its class definition, the member function name shall be qualified by its class name using the `::` operator. [*Note:* a name used in a member function definition (that is, in the *parameter-declaration-clause* including the default arguments (8.3.6), or in the member function body, or, for a constructor function (12.1), in a `mem-initializer` expression (12.6.2)) is looked up as described in 3.4.] [*Example:*

```
struct X {
        typedef int T;
        static T count;
        void f(T);
};
void X::f(T t = count) { }
```

The member function f of class X is defined in global scope; the notation X::f specifies that the function f is a member of class X and in the scope of class X. In the function definition, the parameter type T refers to the typedef member T declared in class X and the default argument count refers to the static data member count declared in class X.]

6   A `static` local variable in a member function always refers to the same object, whether or not the member function is `inline`.

7   Member functions may be mentioned in `friend` declarations after their class has been defined.

8   Member functions of a local class shall be defined inline in their class definition, if they are defined at all.

9   [*Note:* a member function can be declared (but not defined) using a typedef for a function type. The resulting member function has exactly the same type as it would have if the function declarator were provided explicitly, see 8.3.5. For example,

```
typedef void fv(void);
typedef void fvc(void) const;
struct S {
        fv memfunc1;                    // equivalent to: void memfunc1(void);
        void memfunc2();
        fvc memfunc3;                   // equivalent to: void memfunc3(void) const;
};
fv  S::* pmfv1 = &S::memfunc1;
fv  S::* pmfv2 = &S::memfunc2;
fvc S::* pmfv3 = &S::memfunc3;
```

Also see 14.3.]

9.3.1 Nonstatic member functions   [class.mfct.nonstatic]

1   A *nonstatic* member function may be called for an object of its class type, or for an object of a class derived (clause 10) from its class type, using the class member access syntax (5.2.5, 13.3.1.1). A nonstatic member function may also be called directly using the function call syntax (5.2.2, 13.3.1.1)

— from within the body of a member function of its class or of a class derived from its class, or

— from a *mem-initializer* (12.6.2) for a constructor for its class or for a class derived from its class.

If a nonstatic member function of a class X is called for an object that is not of type X, or of a type derived from X, the behavior is undefined.

2   When an *id-expression* (5.1) that is not part of a class member access syntax (5.2.5) and not used to form a pointer to member (5.3.1) is used in the body of a nonstatic member function of class X or used in the *mem-initializer* for a constructor of class X, if name lookup (3.4.1) resolves the name in the *id-expression* to a nonstatic nontype member of class X or of a base class of X, the *id-expression* is transformed into a class member access expression (5.2.5) using (*this) (9.3.2) as the *postfix-expression* to the left of the . operator. The member name then refers to the member of the object for which the function is called. Similarly during name lookup, when an *unqualified-id* (5.1) used in the definition of a member function for class X resolves to a static member, an enumerator or a nested type of class X or of a base class of X, the *unqualified-id* is transformed into a *qualified-id* (5.1) in which the *nested-name-specifier* names the class of the member function. [*Example:*

```
struct tnode {
        char tword[20];
        int count;
        tnode *left;
        tnode *right;
        void set(char*, tnode* l, tnode* r);
};

void tnode::set(char* w, tnode* l, tnode* r)
{
        count = strlen(w)+1;
        if (sizeof(tword)<=count)
                perror("tnode string too long");
        strcpy(tword,w);
        left = l;
        right = r;
}
```

```
void f(tnode n1, tnode n2)
{
        n1.set("abc",&n2,0);
        n2.set("def",0,0);
}
```

In the body of the member function tnode::set, the member names tword, count, left, and right refer to members of the object for which the function is called. Thus, in the call n1.set("abc",&n2,0), tword refers to n1.tword, and in the call n2.set("def",0,0), it refers to n2.tword. The functions strlen, perror, and strcpy are not members of the class tnode and should be declared elsewhere.[95]]

3   A nonstatic member function may be declared const, volatile, or const volatile. These *cv-qualifiers* affect the type of the this pointer (9.3.2). They also affect the function type (8.3.5) of the member function; a member function declared const is a *const* member function, a member function declared volatile is a *volatile* member function and a member function declared const volatile is a *const volatile* member function. [*Example:*

```
struct X {
        void g() const;
        void h() const volatile;
};
```

X::g is a const member function and X::h is a const volatile member function.]

4   A nonstatic member function may be declared *virtual* (10.3) or *pure virtual* (10.4).

9.3.2 The this pointer   [class.this]

1   In the body of a nonstatic (9.3) member function, the keyword this is a non-lvalue expression whose value is the address of the object for which the function is called. The type of this in a member function of a class X is X*. If the member function is declared const, the type of this is const X*, if the member function is declared volatile, the type of this is volatile X*, and if the member function is declared const volatile, the type of this is const volatile X*.

2   In a const member function, the object for which the function is called is accessed through a const access path; therefore, a const member function shall not modify the object and its non-static data members. [*Example:*

```
struct s {
    int a;
    int f() const;
    int g() { return a++; }
    int h() const { return a++; }          // error
};

int s::f() const { return a; }
```

The a++ in the body of s::h is ill-formed because it tries to modify (a part of) the object for which s::h() is called. This is not allowed in a const member function because this is a pointer to const; that is, *this has const type.]

3   Similarly, volatile semantics (7.1.5.1) apply in volatile member functions when accessing the object and its non-static data members.

4   A *cv-qualified* member function can be called on an object-expression (5.2.5) only if the object-expression is as cv-qualified or less-cv-qualified than the member function. [*Example:*

---

[95] See, for example, <cstring> (21.4).

```
void k(s& x, const s& y)
{
    x.f();
    x.g();
    y.f();
    y.g();                          // error
}
```

The call y.g() is ill-formed because y is const and s::g() is a non-const member function, that is, s::g() is less-qualified than the object-expression y.]

5   Constructors (12.1) and destructors (12.4) shall not be declared const, volatile or const volatile. [*Note:* However, these functions can be invoked to create and destroy objects with cv-qualified types, see (12.1) and (12.4).]

9.4 Static members   [class.static]

1   A data or function member of a class may be declared static in a class definition, in which case it is a *static member* of the class.

2   A static member s of class X may be referred to using the *qualified-id* expression X::s; it is not necessary to use the class member access syntax (5.2.5) to refer to a static member. A static member may be referred to using the class member access syntax, in which case the *object-expression* is evaluated. [*Example:*

```
class process {
public:
        static void reschedule();
};
process& g();

void f()
{
        process::reschedule();      // OK: no object necessary
        g().reschedule();           // g() is called
}
```

—*end example*] A static member may be referred to directly in the scope of its class or in the scope of a class derived (clause 10) from its class; in this case, the static member is referred to as if a *qualified-id* expression was used, with the *nested-name-specifier* of the *qualified-id* naming the class scope from which the static member is referenced. [*Example:*

```
int g();
struct X {
        static int g();
};
struct Y : X {
        static int i;
};
int Y::i = g();                     // equivalent to Y::g();
```

—*end example*]

3   If an *unqualified-id* (5.1) is used in the definition of a static member following the member's *declarator-id*, and name lookup (3.4.1) finds that the *unqualified-id* refers to a static member, enumerator, or nested type of the member's class (or of a base class of the member's class), the *unqualified-id* is transformed into a *qualified-id* expression in which the *nested-name-specifier* names the class scope from which the member is referenced. The definition of a static member shall not use directly the names of the nonstatic members of its class or of a base class of its class (including as operands of the sizeof operator). The definition of a static member may only refer to these members to form pointer to members

(5.3.1) or with the class member access syntax (5.2.5).

4   Static members obey the usual class member access rules (clause 11). When used in the declaration of a class member, the `static` specifier shall only be used in the member declarations that appear within the *member-specification* of the class declaration. [*Note:* it cannot be specified in member declarations that appear in namespace scope.]

9.4.1 Static member functions   [class.static.mfct]

1   [*Note:* the rules described in 9.3 apply to `static` member functions.]

2   [*Note:* a `static` member function does not have a `this` pointer (9.3.2).] A `static` member function shall not be `virtual`. There shall not be a `static` and a nonstatic member function with the same name and the same parameter types (13.1). A `static` member function shall not be declared `const`, `volatile`, or `const volatile`.

9.4.2 Static data members   [class.static.data]

1   A `static` data member is not part of the subobjects of a class. There is only one copy of a `static` data member shared by all the objects of the class.

2   The declaration of a `static` data member in its class definition is not a definition and may be of an incomplete type other than cv-qualified `void`. The definition for a `static` data member shall appear in a namespace scope enclosing the member's class definition. In the definition at namespace scope, the name of the `static` data member shall be qualified by its class name using the `::` operator. The *initializer* expression in the definition of a `static` data member is in the scope of its class (3.3.6). [*Example:*

```
class process {
        static process* run_chain;
        static process* running;
};

process* process::running = get_main();
process* process::run_chain = running;
```

The `static` data member `run_chain` of class `process` is defined in global scope; the notation `process::run_chain` specifies that the member `run_chain` is a member of class `process` and in the scope of class `process`. In the `static` data member definition, the *initializer* expression refers to the `static` data member `running` of class `process`.]

3   [*Note:* once the `static` data member has been defined, it exists even if no objects of its class have been created. [*Example:* in the example above, `run_chain` and `running` exist even if no objects of class `process` are created by the program.]]

4   If a `static` data member is of `const` integral or `const` enumeration type, its declaration in the class definition can specify a *constant-initializer* which shall be an integral constant expression (5.19). In that case, the member can appear in integral constant expressions. The member shall still be defined in a namespace scope if it is used in the program and the namespace scope definition shall not contain an *initializer*.

5   There shall be exactly one definition of a `static` data member that is used in a program; no diagnostic is required; see 3.2. Unnamed classes and classes contained directly or indirectly within unnamed classes shall not contain `static` data members. [*Note:* this is because there is no mechanism to provide the definitions for such `static` data members.]

6   `Static` data members of a class in namespace scope have external linkage (3.5). A local class shall not have `static` data members.

7   `Static` data members are initialized and destroyed exactly like non-local objects (3.6.2, 3.6.3).

8   A `static` data member shall not be `mutable` (7.1.1).

9.5 Unions [class.union]

1   In a union, at most one of the data members can be active at any time, that is, the value of at most one of
the data members can be stored in a union at any time. [*Note:* one special guarantee is made in order to
simplify the use of unions: If a POD-union contains several POD-structs that share a common initial
sequence (9.2), and if an object of this POD-union type contains one of the POD-structs, it is permitted to
inspect the common initial sequence of any of POD-struct members; see 9.2.] The size of a union is sufficient to contain the largest of its data members. Each data member is allocated as if it were the sole member of a struct. A union can have member functions (including constructors and destructors), but not virtual
(10.3) functions. A union shall not have base classes. A union shall not be used as a base class. An object
of a class with a non-trivial constructor (12.1), a non-trivial copy constructor (12.8), a non-trivial destructor
(12.4), or a non-trivial copy assignment operator (13.5.3, 12.8) cannot be a member of a union, nor can an
array of such objects. If a union contains a `static` data member, or a member of reference type, the program is ill-formed.

2   A union of the form

```
union { member-specification } ;
```

is called an anonymous union; it defines an unnamed object of unnamed type. The *member-specification* of
an anonymous union shall only define non-static data members. [*Note:* nested types and functions cannot
be declared within an anonymous union.] The names of the members of an anonymous union shall be distinct from the names of any other entity in the scope in which the anonymous union is declared. For the
purpose of name lookup, after the anonymous union definition, the members of the anonymous union are
considered to have been defined in the scope in which the anonymous union is declared. [*Example:*

```
void f()
{
    union { int a; char* p; };
    a = 1;
    // ...
    p = "Jennifer";
    // ...
}
```

Here a and p are used like ordinary (nonmember) variables, but since they are union members they have
the same address.]

3   Anonymous unions declared in a named namespace or in the global namespace shall be declared `static`.
Anonymous unions declared at block scope shall be declared with any storage class allowed for a block-
scope variable, or with no storage class. A storage class is not allowed in a declaration of an anonymous
union in a class scope. An anonymous union shall not have `private` or `protected` members (clause
11). An anonymous union shall not have function members.

4   A union for which objects or pointers are declared is not an anonymous union. [*Example:*

```
union { int aa; char* p; } obj, *ptr = &obj;
aa = 1;                              // error
ptr->aa = 1;                         // OK
```

The assignment to plain aa is ill formed since the member name is not visible outside the union, and even
if it were visible, it is not associated with any particular object.] [*Note:* Initialization of unions with no
user-declared constructors is described in (8.5.1).]

9.6 Bit-fields

1 A *member-declarator* of the form

     identifier$_{opt}$: *constant-expression*

specifies a bit-field; its length is set off from the bit-field name by a colon. The bit-field attribute is not part of the type of the class member. The *constant-expression* shall be an integral constant-expression with a value greater than or equal to zero. The constant-expression may be larger than the number of bits in the object representation (3.9) of the bit-field's type; in such cases the extra bits are used as padding bits and do not participate in the value representation (3.9) of the bit-field. Allocation of bit-fields within a class object is implementation-defined. Alignment of bit-fields is implementation-defined. Bit-fields are packed into some addressable allocation unit. [*Note:* bit-fields straddle allocation units on some machines and not on others. Bit-fields are assigned right-to-left on some machines, left-to-right on others.]

2 A declaration for a bit-field that omits the *identifier* declares an *unnamed* bit-field. Unnamed bit-fields are not members and cannot be initialized. [*Note:* an unnamed bit-field is useful for padding to conform to externally-imposed layouts.] As a special case, an unnamed bit-field with a width of zero specifies alignment of the next bit-field at an allocation unit boundary. Only when declaring an unnamed bit-field may the *constant-expression* be a value equal to zero.

3 A bit-field shall not be a static member. A bit-field shall have integral or enumeration type (3.9.1). It is implementation-defined whether a plain (neither explicitly signed nor unsigned) char, short, int or long bit-field is signed or unsigned. A bool value can successfully be stored in a bit-field of any nonzero size. The address-of operator & shall not be applied to a bit-field, so there are no pointers to bit-fields. A non-const reference shall not be bound to a bit-field (8.5.3). [*Note:* if the initializer for a reference of type const T& is an lvalue that refers to a bit-field, the reference is bound to a temporary initialized to hold the value of the bit-field; the reference is not bound to the bit-field directly. See 8.5.3.]

4 If the value true or false is stored into a bit-field of type bool of any size (including a one bit bit-field), the original bool value and the value of the bit-field shall compare equal. If the value of an enumerator is stored into a bit-field of the same enumeration type and the number of bits in the bit-field is large enough to hold all the values of that enumeration type, the original enumerator value and the value of the bit-field shall compare equal. [*Example:*

```
enum BOOL { f=0, t=1 };
struct A {
        BOOL b:1;
};
A a;
void f() {
        a.b = t;
        if (a.b == t)              // shall yield true
        { /* ... */ }
}
```

—*end example*]

9.7 Nested class declarations

1 A class can be defined within another class. A class defined within another is called a *nested* class. The name of a nested class is local to its enclosing class. The nested class is in the scope of its enclosing class. Except by using explicit pointers, references, and object names, declarations in a nested class can use only type names, static members, and enumerators from the enclosing class. [*Example:*

```
        int x;
        int y;

        class enclose {
        public:
            int x;
            static int s;

            class inner {

                void f(int i)
                { .
                    int a = sizeof(x);      // error: refers to enclose::x
                    x = i;                  // error: assign to enclose::x
                    s = i;                  // OK: assign to enclose::s
                    ::x = i;                // OK: assign to global x
                    y = i;                  // OK: assign to global y
                }

                void g(enclose* p, int i)
                {
                    p->x = i;               // OK: assign to enclose::x
                }

            };
        };

        inner* p = 0;                       // error: inner not in scope
```

—*end example*]

2   Member functions and static data members of a nested class can be defined in a namespace scope enclosing the definition of their class. [*Example:*

```
        class enclose {
        public:
            class inner {
                static int x;
                void f(int i);
            };
        };

        int enclose::inner::x = 1;

        void enclose::inner::f(int i) { /* ... */ }
```

—*end example*]

3   If class X is defined in a namespace scope, a nested class Y may be declared in class X and later defined in the definition of class X or be later defined in a namespace scope enclosing the definition of class X. [*Example:*

```
        class E {
            class I1;                       // forward declaration of nested class
            class I2;
            class I1 {};                    // definition of nested class
        };
        class E::I2 {};                     // definition of nested class
```

—*end example*]

4   Like a member function, a friend function (11.4) defined within a nested class is in the lexical scope of that class; it obeys the same rules for name binding as a static member function of that class (9.4) and has no special access rights to members of an enclosing class.

9.8 Local class declarations   [class.local]

1   A class can be defined within a function definition; such a class is called a *local* class. The name of a local class is local to its enclosing scope. The local class is in the scope of the enclosing scope, and has the same access to names outside the function as does the enclosing function. Declarations in a local class can use only type names, static variables, `extern` variables and functions, and enumerators from the enclosing scope. [*Example:*

```
int x;
void f()
{
    static int s ;
    int x;
    extern int g();

    struct local {
        int g() { return x; }    // error: x is auto
        int h() { return s; }    // OK
        int k() { return ::x; }  // OK
        int l() { return g(); }  // OK
    };
    // ...
}

local* p = 0;                    // error: local not in scope
```

—*end example*]

2   An enclosing function has no special access to members of the local class; it obeys the usual access rules (clause 11). Member functions of a local class shall be defined within their class definition, if they are defined at all.

3   If class X is a local class a nested class Y may be declared in class X and later defined in the definition of class X or be later defined in the same scope as the definition of class X. A class nested within a local class is a local class.

4   A local class shall not have static data members.

9.9 Nested type names   [class.nested.type]

1   Type names obey exactly the same scope rules as other names. In particular, type names defined within a class definition cannot be used outside their class without qualification. [*Example:*

```
class X {
public:
    typedef int I;
    class Y { /* ... */ };
    I a;
};

I b;                             // error
Y c;                             // error
X::Y d;                          // OK
X::I e;                          // OK
```

—*end example*]

10   Derived classes   [class.derived]

1   A list of base classes can be specified in a class definition using the notation:

> *base-clause:*
> >   : *base-specifier-list*
>
> *base-specifier-list:*
> >   *base-specifier*
> >   *base-specifier-list* , *base-specifier*
>
> *base-specifier:*
> >   ::$_{opt}$ *nested-name-specifier*$_{opt}$ *class-name*
> >   virtual *access-specifier*$_{opt}$ ::$_{opt}$ *nested-name-specifier*$_{opt}$ *class-name*
> >   *access-specifier* virtual$_{opt}$ ::$_{opt}$ *nested-name-specifier*$_{opt}$ *class-name*
>
> *access-specifier:*
> >   private
> >   protected
> >   public

The *class-name* in a *base-specifier* shall not be an incompletely defined class (clause 9); this class is called a *direct base class* for the class being declared. During the lookup for a base class name, non-type names are ignored (3.3.7). If the name found is not a *class-name*, the program is ill-formed. A class B is a base class of a class D if it is a direct base class of D or a direct base class of one of D's base classes. A class is an *indirect* base class of another if it is a base class but not a direct base class. A class is said to be (directly or indirectly) *derived* from its (direct or indirect) base classes. [*Note:* See clause 11 for the meaning of *access-specifier.*] Unless redefined in the derived class, members of a base class are also considered to be members of the derived class. The base class members are said to be *inherited* by the derived class. Inherited members can be referred to in expressions in the same manner as other members of the derived class, unless their names are hidden or ambiguous (10.2). [*Note:* the scope resolution operator : : (5.1) can be used to refer to a direct or indirect base member explicitly. This allows access to a name that has been redefined in the derived class. A derived class can itself serve as a base class subject to access control; see 11.2. A pointer to a derived class can be implicitly converted to a pointer to an accessible unambiguous base class (4.10). An lvalue of a derived class type can be bound to a reference to an accessible unambiguous base class (8.5.3).]

2   The *base-specifier-list* specifies the type of the *base class subobjects* contained in an object of the derived class type. [*Example:*

```
class Base {
public:
    int a, b, c;
};

class Derived : public Base {
public:
    int b;
};

class Derived2 : public Derived {
public:
    int c;
};
```

Here, an object of class Derived2 will have a sub-object of class Derived which in turn will have a sub-object of class `Base`.]

3   The order in which the base class subobjects are allocated in the most derived object (1.8) is unspecified. [*Note:* a derived class and its base class sub-objects can be represented by a directed acyclic graph (DAG) where an arrow means "directly derived from." A DAG of sub-objects is often referred to as a "sub-object lattice."

The arrows need not have a physical representation in memory.]

4   [*Note:* initialization of objects representing base classes can be specified in constructors; see 12.6.2.]

5   [*Note:* A base class subobject might have a layout (3.7) different from the layout of a most derived object of the same type. A base class subobject might have a polymorphic behavior (12.7) different from the polymorphic behavior of a most derived object of the same type. A base class subobject may be of zero size (clause 9); however, two subobjects that have the same class type and that belong to the same most derived object must not be allocated at the same address (5.10).]

10.1 Multiple base classes   [class.mi]

1   A class can be derived from any number of base classes. [*Note:* the use of more than one direct base class is often called multiple inheritance.] [*Example:*

```
class A { /* ... */ };
class B { /* ... */ };
class C { /* ... */ };
class D : public A, public B, public C { /* ... */ };
```

—*end example*]

2   [*Note:* the order of derivation is not significant except as specified by the semantics of initialization by constructor (12.6.2), cleanup (12.4), and storage layout (9.2, 11.1).]

3   A class shall not be specified as a direct base class of a derived class more than once. [*Note:* a class can be an indirect base class more than once and can be a direct and an indirect base class. There are limited things that can be done with such a class. The non-static data members and member functions of the direct base class cannot be referred to in the scope of the derived class. However, the static members, enumerations and types can be unambiguously referred to.] [*Example:*

```
class X { /* ... */ };
class Y : public X, public X { /* ... */ };        // ill-formed

class L { public: int next;  /* ... */ };
class A : public L { /* ... */ };
class B : public L { /* ... */ };
class C : public A, public B { void f(); /* ... */ };    // well-formed
class D : public A, public L { void f(); /* ... */ };    // well-formed
```

—*end example*]

4   A base class specifier that does not contain the keyword `virtual`, specifies a *nonvirtual* base class. A base class specifier that contains the keyword `virtual`, specifies a *virtual* base class. For each distinct occurrence of a nonvirtual base class in the class lattice of the most derived class, the most derived object (1.8) shall contain a corresponding distinct base class subobject of that type. For each distinct base class that is specified virtual, the most derived object shall contain a single base class subobject of that type.

[*Example:* for an object of class type C, each distinct occurrence of a (non-virtual) base class L in the class lattice of C corresponds one-to-one with a distinct L subobject within the object of type C. Given the class C defined above, an object of class C will have two sub-objects of class L as shown below.

In such lattices, explicit qualification can be used to specify which subobject is meant. The body of function C::f could refer to the member next of each L subobject:

```
void C::f() { A::next = B::next; }        // well-formed
```

Without the A:: or B:: qualifiers, the definition of C::f above would be ill-formed because of ambiguity (10.2).

5   For another example,

```
class V { /* ... */ };
class A : virtual public V { /* ... */ };
class B : virtual public V { /* ... */ };
class C : public A, public B { /* ... */ };
```

for an object c of class type C, a single subobject of type V is shared by every base subobject of c that is declared to have a virtual base class of type V. Given the class C defined above, an object of class C will have one subobject of class V, as shown below.

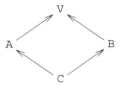

6   A class can have both virtual and nonvirtual base classes of a given type.

```
class B { /* ... */ };
class X : virtual public B { /* ... */ };
class Y : virtual public B { /* ... */ };
class Z : public B { /* ... */ };
class AA : public X, public Y, public Z { /* ... */ };
```

For an object of class AA, all virtual occurrences of base class B in the class lattice of AA correspond to a single B subobject within the object of type AA, and every other occurrence of a (non-virtual) base class B in the class lattice of AA corresponds one-to-one with a distinct B subobject within the object of type AA. Given the class AA defined above, class AA has two sub-objects of class B: Z's B and the virtual B shared by X and Y, as shown below.

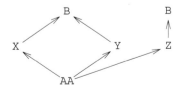

—*end example*]

10.2 Member name lookup [class.member.lookup]

1   Member name lookup determines the meaning of a name (*id-expression*) in a class scope (3.3.6). Name lookup can result in an *ambiguity*, in which case the program is ill-formed. For an *id-expression*, name lookup begins in the class scope of this; for a *qualified-id*, name lookup begins in the scope of the *nested-name-specifier*. Name lookup takes place before access control (3.4, clause 11).

2   The following steps define the result of name lookup in a class scope, C. First, every declaration for the name in the class and in each of its base class sub-objects is considered. A member name f in one sub-object B *hides* a member name f in a sub-object A if A is a base class sub-object of B. Any declarations that are so hidden are eliminated from consideration. Each of these declarations that was introduced by a *using-declaration* is considered to be from each sub-object of C that is of the type containing the declaration designated by the *using-declaration*.[96] If the resulting set of declarations are not all from sub-objects of the same type, or the set has a nonstatic member and includes members from distinct sub-objects, there is an ambiguity and the program is ill-formed. Otherwise that set is the result of the lookup.

3   [*Example:*

```
class A {
public:
    int a;
    int (*b)();
    int f();
    int f(int);
    int g();
};

class B {
    int a;
    int b();
public:
    int f();
    int g;
    int h();
    int h(int);
};

class C : public A, public B {};

void g(C* pc)
{
    pc->a = 1;           // error: ambiguous: A::a or B::a
    pc->b();             // error: ambiguous: A::b or B::b
    pc->f();             // error: ambiguous: A::f or B::f
    pc->f(1);            // error: ambiguous: A::f or B::f
    pc->g();             // error: ambiguous: A::g or B::g
    pc->g = 1;           // error: ambiguous: A::g or B::g
    pc->h();             // OK
    pc->h(1);            // OK
}
```

—*end example*] [*Example:*

---

[96] Note that *using-declaration*s cannot be used to resolve inherited member ambiguities; see 7.3.3.

```
struct U { static int i; };
struct V : U { };
struct W : U { using U::i; };
struct X : V, W { void foo(); };
void X::foo() {
        i;                      // finds U::i in two ways: as W::i and U::i in V
                                // no ambiguity because U::i is static
}
```

—*end example*]

4   If the name of an overloaded function is unambiguously found, overloading resolution (13.3) also takes place before access control. Ambiguities can often be resolved by qualifying a name with its class name. [*Example:*

```
class A {
public:
    int f();
};

class B {
public:
    int f();
};

class C : public A, public B {
    int f() { return A::f() + B::f(); }
};
```

—*end example*]

5   A static member, a nested type or an enumerator defined in a base class T can unambiguously be found even if an object has more than one base class subobject of type T. Two base class subobjects share the nonstatic member subobjects of their common virtual base classes. [*Example:*

```
class V { public: int v; };
class A {
public:
    int a;
    static int   s;
    enum { e };
};
class B : public A, public virtual V {};
class C : public A, public virtual V {};

class D : public B, public C { };

void f(D* pd)
{
    pd->v++;                 // OK: only one v (virtual)
    pd->s++;                 // OK: only one s (static)
    int i = pd->e;           // OK: only one e (enumerator)
    pd->a++;                 // error, ambiguous: two as in D
}
```

—*end example*]

6   When virtual base classes are used, a hidden declaration can be reached along a path through the sub-object lattice that does not pass through the hiding declaration. This is not an ambiguity. The identical use with nonvirtual base classes is an ambiguity; in that case there is no unique instance of the name that hides all the others. [*Example:*

```
class V { public: int f();  int x; };
class W { public: int g();  int y; };
class B : public virtual V, public W
{
public:
    int f();  int x;
    int g();  int y;
};
class C : public virtual V, public W { };

class D : public B, public C { void glorp(); };
```

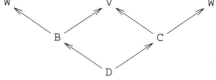

The names defined in V and the left hand instance of W are hidden by those in B, but the names defined in
the right hand instance of W are not hidden at all.

```
void D::glorp()
{
    x++;                          // OK: B::x hides V::x
    f();                          // OK: B::f() hides V::f()
    y++;                          // error: B::y and C's W::y
    g();                          // error: B::g() and C's W::g()
}
```

—*end example*]

7   An explicit or implicit conversion from a pointer to or an lvalue of a derived class to a pointer or reference
to one of its base classes shall unambiguously refer to a unique object representing the base class. [*Example:*

```
class V { };
class A { };
class B : public A, public virtual V { };
class C : public A, public virtual V { };
class D : public B, public C { };

void g()
{
    D d;
    B* pb = &d;
    A* pa = &d;                   // error, ambiguous: C's A or B's A?
    V* pv = &d;                   // OK: only one V sub-object
}
```

—*end example*]

1 Virtual functions support dynamic binding and object-oriented programming. A class that declares or inherits a virtual function is called a *polymorphic class*.

2 If a virtual member function `vf` is declared in a class `Base` and in a class `Derived`, derived directly or indirectly from `Base`, a member function `vf` with the same name and same parameter list as `Base::vf` is declared, then `Derived::vf` is also virtual (whether or not it is so declared) and it *overrides*[97] `Base::vf`. For convenience we say that any virtual function overrides itself. Then in any well-formed class, for each virtual function declared in that class or any of its direct or indirect base classes there is a unique *final overrider* that overrides that function and every other overrider of that function. The rules for member lookup (10.2) are used to determine the final overrider for a virtual function in the scope of a derived class but ignoring names introduced by *using-declarations*. [*Example:*

```
struct A {
        virtual void f();
};
struct B : virtual A {
        virtual void f();
};

struct C : B , virtual A {
        using A::f;
};
void foo() {
        C c;
        c.f();                  // calls B::f, the final overrider
        c.C::f();               // calls A::f because of the using-declaration
}
```

—*end example*]

3 [*Note:* a virtual member function does not have to be visible to be overridden, for example,

```
struct B {
        virtual void f();
};
struct D : B {
        void f(int);
};
struct D2 : D {
        void f();
};
```

the function `f(int)` in class D hides the virtual function `f()` in its base class B; `D::f(int)` is not a virtual function. However, `f()` declared in class D2 has the same name and the same parameter list as `B::f()`, and therefore is a virtual function that overrides the function `B::f()` even though `B::f()` is not visible in class D2.]

4 Even though destructors are not inherited, a destructor in a derived class overrides a base class destructor declared virtual; see 12.4 and 12.5.

5 The return type of an overriding function shall be either identical to the return type of the overridden function or *covariant* with the classes of the functions. If a function `D::f` overrides a function `B::f`, the return types of the functions are covariant if they satisfy the following criteria:

— both are pointers to classes or references to classes[98]

---

[97] A function with the same name but a different parameter list (clause 13) as a virtual function is not necessarily virtual and does not override. The use of the `virtual` specifier in the declaration of an overriding function is legal but redundant (has empty semantics). Access control (clause 11) is not considered in determining overriding.
[98] Multi-level pointers to classes or references to multi-level pointers to classes are not allowed.

— the class in the return type of B::f is the same class as the class in the return type of D::f, or is an unambiguous and accessible direct or indirect base class of the class in the return type of D::f

— both pointers or references have the same cv-qualification and the class type in the return type of D::f has the same cv-qualification as or less cv-qualification than the class type in the return type of B::f.

If the return type of D::f differs from the return type of B::f, the class type in the return type of D::f shall be complete at the point of declaration of D::f or shall be the class type D. When the overriding function is called as the final overrider of the overridden function, its result is converted to the type returned by the (statically chosen) overridden function (5.2.2). [*Example:*

```
class B {};
class D : private B { friend class Derived; };
struct Base {
    virtual void vf1();
    virtual void vf2();
    virtual void vf3();
    virtual B*   vf4();
    virtual B*   vf5();
    void f();
};

struct No_good : public Base {
    D*   vf4();                  // error: B (base class of D) inaccessible
};

class A;
struct Derived : public Base {
    void vf1();                  // virtual and overrides Base::vf1()
    void vf2(int);               // not virtual, hides Base::vf2()
    char vf3();                  // error: invalid difference in return type only
    D*   vf4();                  // OK: returns pointer to derived class
    A*   vf5();                  // error: returns pointer to incomplete class
    void f();
};

void g()
{
    Derived d;
    Base* bp = &d;               // standard conversion:
                                 // Derived* to Base*
    bp->vf1();                   // calls Derived::vf1()
    bp->vf2();                   // calls Base::vf2()
    bp->f();                     // calls Base::f() (not virtual)
    B*   p = bp->vf4();          // calls Derived::pf() and converts the
                                 //   result to B*
    Derived*  dp = &d;
    D*   q = dp->vf4();          // calls Derived::pf() and does not
                                 // convert the result to B*
    dp->vf2();                   // ill-formed: argument mismatch
}
```

—*end example*]

6   [*Note:* the interpretation of the call of a virtual function depends on the type of the object for which it is called (the dynamic type), whereas the interpretation of a call of a nonvirtual member function depends only on the type of the pointer or reference denoting that object (the static type) (5.2.2).]

7   [*Note:* the virtual specifier implies membership, so a virtual function cannot be a nonmember (7.1.2) function. Nor can a virtual function be a static member, since a virtual function call relies on a specific object for determining which function to invoke. A virtual function declared in one class can be declared a

`friend` in another class.]

8   A virtual function declared in a class shall be defined, or declared pure (10.4) in that class, or both; but no diagnostic is required (3.2).

9   [*Example:* here are some uses of virtual functions with multiple base classes:

```
struct A {
    virtual void f();
};

struct B1 : A {                       // note non-virtual derivation
    void f();
};

struct B2 : A {
    void f();
};

struct D : B1, B2 {                   // D has two separate A sub-objects
};

void foo()
{
    D    d;
//  A*   ap = &d;                      // would be ill-formed: ambiguous
    B1*  b1p = &d;
    A*   ap = b1p;
    D*   dp = &d;
    ap->f();                          // calls D::B1::f
    dp->f();                          // ill-formed: ambiguous
}
```

In class `D` above there are two occurrences of class `A` and hence two occurrences of the virtual member function `A::f`. The final overrider of `B1::A::f` is `B1::f` and the final overrider of `B2::A::f` is `B2::f`.

10   The following example shows a function that does not have a unique final overrider:

```
struct A {
    virtual void f();
};

struct VB1 : virtual A {              // note virtual derivation
    void f();
};

struct VB2 : virtual A {
    void f();
};

struct Error : VB1, VB2 {            // ill-formed
};

struct Okay : VB1, VB2 {
    void f();
};
```

Both `VB1::f` and `VB2::f` override `A::f` but there is no overrider of both of them in class `Error`. This example is therefore ill-formed. Class `Okay` is well formed, however, because `Okay::f` is a final overrider.

11   The following example uses the well-formed classes from above.

```
struct VB1a : virtual A {          // does not declare f
};

struct Da : VB1a, VB2 {
};

void foe()
{
    VB1a*  vb1ap = new Da;
    vb1ap->f();                    // calls VB2::f
}
```

—*end example*]

12   Explicit qualification with the scope operator (5.1) suppresses the virtual call mechanism. [*Example:*

```
class B { public: virtual void f(); };
class D : public B { public: void f(); };

void D::f() { /* ... */ B::f(); }
```

Here, the function call in D::f really does call B::f and not D::f.]

10.4 Abstract classes   [class.abstract]

1   The abstract class mechanism supports the notion of a general concept, such as a shape, of which only more concrete variants, such as circle and square, can actually be used. An abstract class can also be used to define an interface for which derived classes provide a variety of implementations.

2   An *abstract class* is a class that can be used only as a base class of some other class; no objects of an abstract class can be created except as sub-objects of a class derived from it. A class is abstract if it has at least one *pure virtual function*. [*Note:* such a function might be inherited: see below.] A virtual function is specified *pure* by using a *pure-specifier* (9.2) in the function declaration in the class declaration. A pure virtual function need be defined only if explicitly called with the *qualified-id* syntax (5.1). [*Example:*

```
class point { /* ... */ };
class shape {                      // abstract class
    point center;
    // ...
public:
    point where() { return center; }
    void move(point p) { center=p; draw(); }
    virtual void rotate(int) = 0;       // pure virtual
    virtual void draw() = 0;            // pure virtual
    // ...
};
```

—*end example*] [*Note:* a function declaration cannot provide both a *pure-specifier* and a definition —*end note*] [*Example:*

```
struct C {
        virtual void f() = 0 { };       // ill-formed
};
```

—*end example*]

3   An abstract class shall not be used as a parameter type, as a function return type, or as the type of an explicit conversion. Pointers and references to an abstract class can be declared. [*Example:*

```
shape x;                            // error: object of abstract class
shape* p;                           // OK
shape f();                          // error
void g(shape);                      // error
shape& h(shape&);                   // OK
```

—*end example*]

4   A class is abstract if it contains or inherits at least one pure virtual function for which the final overrider is pure virtual. [*Example:*

```
class ab_circle : public shape {
    int radius;
public:
    void rotate(int) {}
    // ab_circle::draw() is a pure virtual
};
```

Since `shape::draw()` is a pure virtual function `ab_circle::draw()` is a pure virtual by default. The alternative declaration,

```
class circle : public shape {
    int radius;
public:
    void rotate(int) {}
    void draw();                    // a definition is required somewhere
};
```

would make class `circle` nonabstract and a definition of `circle::draw()` must be provided.]

5   [*Note:* an abstract class can be derived from a class that is not abstract, and a pure virtual function may override a virtual function which is not pure.]

6   Member functions can be called from a constructor (or destructor) of an abstract class; the effect of making a virtual call (10.3) to a pure virtual function directly or indirectly for the object being created (or destroyed) from such a constructor (or destructor) is undefined.

11 Member access control   [class.access]

1   A member of a class can be

— private; that is, its name can be used only by members and friends of the class in which it is declared.

— protected; that is, its name can be used only by members and friends of the class in which it is declared, and by members and friends of classes derived from this class (see 11.5).

— public; that is, its name can be used anywhere without access restriction.

2   Members of a class defined with the keyword class are private by default. Members of a class defined with the keywords struct or union are public by default. [*Example:*

```
class X {
        int a;                  // X::a is private by default
};

struct S {
        int a;                  // S::a is public by default
};
```

—*end example*]

3   Access control is applied uniformly to all names, whether the names are referred to from declarations or expressions. [*Note:* access control applies to names nominated by friend declarations (11.4) and *using-declaration*s (7.3.3).] In the case of overloaded function names, access control is applied to the function selected by overload resolution. [*Note:* because access control applies to names, if access control is applied to a typedef name, only the accessibility of the typedef name itself is considered. The accessibility of the entity referred to by the typedef is not considered. For example,

```
class A
{
        class B { };
public:
        typedef B BB;
};

void f()
{
        A::BB x;                // OK, typedef name A::BB is public
        A::B y;                 // access error, A::B is private
}
```

—*end note*]

4   It should be noted that it is *access* to members and base classes that is controlled, not their *visibility*. Names of members are still visible, and implicit conversions to base classes are still considered, when those members and base classes are inaccessible. The interpretation of a given construct is established without regard to access control. If the interpretation established makes use of inaccessible member names or base classes, the construct is ill-formed.

5   All access controls in clause 11 affect the ability to access a class member name from a particular scope. The access control for names used in the definition of a class member that appears outside of the member's class definition is done as if the entire member definition appeared in the scope of the member's class. In particular, access controls apply as usual to member names accessed as part of a function return type, even though it is not possible to determine the access privileges of that use without first parsing the rest of the

function declarator. Similarly, access control for implicit calls to the constructors, the conversion functions, or the destructor called to create and destroy a static data member is performed as if these calls appeared in the scope of the member's class. [*Example:*

```
class A {
    typedef int I;              // private member
    I f();
    friend I g(I);
    static I x;
};

A::I A::f() { return 0; }
A::I g(A::I p = A::x);
A::I g(A::I p) { return 0; }
A::I A::x = 0;
```

Here, all the uses of A::I are well-formed because A::f and A::x are members of class A and g is a friend of class A. This implies, for example, that access checking on the first use of A::I must be deferred until it is determined that this use of A::I is as the return type of a member of class A.]

6   In the definition of a member of a nested class that appears outside of its class definition, the name of the member may be qualified by the names of enclosing classes of the member's class even if these names are private members of their enclosing classes. [*Example:*

```
class D {
    class E {
        static int m;
    };
};
int D::E::m = 1;                // OK, no access error on private E
```

—*end example*]

7   The names in a default argument expression (8.3.6) are bound at the point of declaration, and access is checked at that point rather than at any points of use of the default argument expression. Access checking for default arguments in function templates and in member functions of class templates are performed as described in 14.7.1.

11.1 Access specifiers   [class.access.spec]

1   Member declarations can be labeled by an *access-specifier* (clause 10):

    access-specifier : *member-specification*$_{opt}$

An *access-specifier* specifies the access rules for members following it until the end of the class or until another *access-specifier* is encountered. [*Example:*

```
class X {
    int a;                      // X::a is private by default: class used
public:
    int b;                      // X::b is public
    int c;                      // X::c is public
};
```

—*end example*] Any number of access specifiers is allowed and no particular order is required. [*Example:*

```
struct S {
    int a;          // S::a is public by default: struct used
protected:
    int b;          // S::b is protected
private:
    int c;          // S::c is private
public:
    int d;          // S::d is public
};
```

—*end example*]

2   The order of allocation of data members with separate *access-specifier* labels is unspecified (9.2).

3   When a member is redeclared within its class definition, the access specified at its redeclaration shall be the same as at its initial declaration. [*Example:*

```
struct S {
        class A;
private:
        class A { };     // error: cannot change access
};
```

—*end example*]

11.2 Accessibility of base classes and base class members   [class.access.base]

1   If a class is declared to be a base class (clause 10) for another class using the `public` access specifier, the `public` members of the base class are accessible as `public` members of the derived class and `protected` members of the base class are accessible as `protected` members of the derived class. If a class is declared to be a base class for another class using the `protected` access specifier, the `public` and `protected` members of the base class are accessible as `protected` members of the derived class. If a class is declared to be a base class for another class using the `private` access specifier, the `public` and `protected` members of the base class are accessible as `private` members of the derived class[99].

2   In the absence of an *access-specifier* for a base class, `public` is assumed when the derived class is declared `struct` and `private` is assumed when the class is declared `class`. [*Example:*

```
class B { /* ... */ };
class D1 : private B { /* ... */ };
class D2 : public B { /* ... */ };
class D3 : B { /* ... */ };        // B private by default
struct D4 : public B { /* ... */ };
struct D5 : private B { /* ... */ };
struct D6 : B { /* ... */ };       // B public by default
class D7 : protected B { /* ... */ };
struct D8 : protected B { /* ... */ };
```

Here B is a public base of D2, D4, and D6, a private base of D1, D3, and D5, and a protected base of D7 and D8. —*end example*]

3   [*Note:* A member of a private base class might be inaccessible as an inherited member name, but accessible directly. Because of the rules on pointer conversions (4.10) and explicit casts (5.4), a conversion from a pointer to a derived class to a pointer to an inaccessible base class might be ill-formed if an implicit conversion is used, but well-formed if an explicit cast is used. For example,

---

[99] As specified previously in clause 11, private members of a base class remain inaccessible even to derived classes unless `friend` declarations within the base class declaration are used to grant access explicitly.

```
class B {
public:
        int mi;                         // nonstatic member
        static int si;                  // static member
};
class D : private B {
};
class DD : public D {
        void f();
};

void DD::f() {
        mi = 3;                         // error: mi is private in D
        si = 3;                         // error: si is private in D
        ::B  b;
        b.mi = 3;                       // OK (b.mi is different from this->mi)
        b.si = 3;                       // OK (b.si is different from this->si)
        ::B::si = 3;                    // OK
        ::B* bp1 = this;                // error: B is a private base class
        ::B* bp2 = (::B*)this;          // OK with cast
        bp2->mi = 3;                    // OK: access through a pointer to B.
}
```

—end note]

4   A base class is said to be accessible if an invented public member of the base class is accessible. If a base class is accessible, one can implicitly convert a pointer to a derived class to a pointer to that base class (4.10, 4.11). [*Note:* it follows that members and friends of a class X can implicitly convert an X* to a pointer to a private or protected immediate base class of X.] The access to a member is affected by the class in which the member is named. This naming class is the class in which the member name was looked up and found. [*Note:* this class can be explicit, e.g., when a *qualified-id* is used, or implicit, e.g., when a class member access operator (5.2.5) is used (including cases where an implicit "this->" is added). If both a class member access operator and a *qualified-id* are used to name the member (as in p->T::m), the class naming the member is the class named by the *nested-name-specifier* of the *qualified-id* (that is, T).] A member *m* is accessible when named in class *N* if

— *m* as a member of *N* is public, or

— *m* as a member of *N* is private, and the reference occurs in a member or friend of class *N*, or

— *m* as a member of *N* is protected, and the reference occurs in a member or friend of class *N*, or in a member or friend of a class *P* derived from *N*, where *m* as a member of *P* is private or protected, or

— there exists a base class *B* of *N* that is accessible at the point of reference, and *m* is accessible when named in class *B*. [*Example:*

```
class B;
class A {
private:
  int i;
  friend void f(B*);
};
class B : public A { };
void f(B* p) {
  p->i = 1;                           // OK: B* can be implicitly cast to A*,
                                      // and f has access to i in A
}
```

—end example]

5   If a class member access operator, including an implicit "`this->`," is used to access a nonstatic data member or nonstatic member function, the reference is ill-formed if the left operand (considered as a pointer in the "`.`" operator case) cannot be implicitly converted to a pointer to the naming class of the right operand. [*Note:* this requirement is in addition to the requirement that the member be accessible as named.]

11.3 Access declarations   [class.access.dcl]

1   The access of a member of a base class can be changed in the derived class by mentioning its *qualified-id* in the derived class declaration. Such mention is called an *access declaration*. The effect of an access declaration *qualified-id* ; is defined to be equivalent to the declaration `using` *qualified-id* ;.[100)]

2   [*Example:*

```
class A {
public:
    int z;
    int z1;
};

class B : public A {
    int a;
public:
    int b, c;
    int bf();
protected:
    int x;
    int y;
};

class D : private B {
    int d;
public:
    B::c;                    // adjust access to B::c
    B::z;                    // adjust access to A::z
    A::z1;                   // adjust access to A::z1
    int e;
    int df();
protected:
    B::x;                    // adjust access to B::x
    int g;
};

class X : public D {
    int xf();
};

int ef(D&);
int ff(X&);
```

The external function `ef` can use only the names `c`, `z`, `z1`, `e`, and `df`. Being a member of `D`, the function `df` can use the names `b`, `c`, `z`, `z1`, `bf`, `x`, `y`, `d`, `e`, `df`, and `g`, but not `a`. Being a member of `B`, the function `bf` can use the members `a`, `b`, `c`, `z`, `z1`, `bf`, `x`, and `y`. The function `xf` can use the public and protected names from `D`, that is, `c`, `z`, `z1`, `e`, and `df` (public), and `x`, and `g` (protected). Thus the external function `ff` has access only to `c`, `z`, `z1`, `e`, and `df`. If `D` were a protected or private base class of `X`, `xf` would have

---

[100)] Access declarations are deprecated; member *using-declarations* (7.3.3) provide a better means of doing the same things. In earlier versions of the C++ language, access declarations were more limited; they were generalized and made equivalent to *using-declarations* in the interest of simplicity. Programmers are encouraged to use *using-declarations*, rather than the new capabilities of access declarations, in new code.

the same privileges as before, but ff would have no access at all.]

11.4 Friends [class.friend]

1   A friend of a class is a function or class that is not a member of the class but is permitted to use the private and protected member names from the class. The name of a friend is not in the scope of the class, and the friend is not called with the member access operators (5.2.5) unless it is a member of another class. [*Example:* the following example illustrates the differences between members and friends:

```
class X {
    int a;
    friend void friend_set(X*, int);
public:
    void member_set(int);
};

void friend_set(X* p, int i) { p->a = i; }
void X::member_set(int i) { a = i; }

void f()
{
    X obj;
    friend_set(&obj,10);
    obj.member_set(10);
}
```

—end example]

2   Declaring a class to be a friend implies that the names of private and protected members from the class granting friendship can be accessed in declarations of members of the befriended class. [*Note:* this means that access to private and protected names is also granted to member functions of the friend class (as if the functions were each friends) and to the static data member definitions of the friend class. This also means that private and protected type names from the class granting friendship can be used in the *base-clause* of a nested class of the friend class. However, the declarations of members of classes nested within the friend class cannot access the names of private and protected members from the class granting friendship. Also, because the *base-clause* of the friend class is not part of its member declarations, the *base-clause* of the friend class cannot access the names of the private and protected members from the class granting friendship. For example,

```
class A {
        class B { };
        friend class X;
};
class X : A::B {                 // ill-formed: A::B cannot be accessed
                                 // in the base-clause for X
        A::B mx;                 // OK: A::B used to declare member of X
        class Y : A::B {         // OK: A::B used to declare member of X
                A::B my;         // ill-formed: A::B cannot be accessed
                                 // to declare members of nested class of X
        };
};
```

] An *elaborated-type-specifier* shall be used in a friend declaration for a class.[101] A class shall not be defined in a friend declaration. [*Example:*

---

[101] The *class-key* of the *elaborated-type-specifier* is required.

```
class X {
    enum { a=100 };
    friend class Y;
};

class Y {
    int v[X::a];                          // OK, Y is a friend of X
};

class Z {
    int v[X::a];                          // error: X::a is private
};
```

—*end example*]

3   A function first declared in a friend declaration has external linkage (3.5). Otherwise, the function retains its previous linkage (7.1.1).

4   When a `friend` declaration refers to an overloaded name or operator, only the function specified by the parameter types becomes a friend. A member function of a class X can be a friend of a class Y. [*Example:*

```
class Y {
    friend char* X::foo(int);
    // ...
};
```

—*end example*]

5   A function can be defined in a friend declaration of a class if and only if the class is a non-local class (9.8), the function name is unqualified, and the function has namespace scope. [*Example:*

```
class M {
        friend void f() { }          // definition of global f, a friend of M,
                                     // not the definition of a member function
};
```

—*end example*] Such a function is implicitly `inline`. A `friend` function defined in a class is in the (lexical) scope of the class in which it is defined. A friend function defined outside the class is not (3.4.1).

6   No *storage-class-specifier* shall appear in the *decl-specifier-seq* of a friend declaration.

7   A name nominated by a friend declaration shall be accessible in the scope of the class containing the friend declaration. The meaning of the friend declaration is the same whether the friend declaration appears in the `private`, `protected` or `public` (9.2) portion of the class *member-specification*.

8   Friendship is neither inherited nor transitive. [*Example:*

```
class A {
    friend class B;
    int a;
};

class B {
    friend class C;
};
```

```
class C  {
    void f(A* p)
    {
        p->a++;                      // error: C is not a friend of A
                                     // despite being a friend of a friend
    }
};

class D : public B  {
    void f(A* p)
    {
        p->a++;                      // error: D is not a friend of A
                                     // despite being derived from a friend
    }
};
```

—end example]

9   If a friend declaration appears in a local class (9.8) and the name specified is an unqualified name, a prior declaration is looked up without considering scopes that are outside the innermost enclosing non-class scope. For a friend function declaration, if there is no prior declaration, the program is ill-formed. For a friend class declaration, if there is no prior declaration, the class that is specified belongs to the innermost enclosing non-class scope, but if it is subsequently referenced, its name is not found by name lookup until a matching declaration is provided in the innermost enclosing nonclass scope. [*Example:*

```
class X;
void a();
void f() {
    class Y;
    extern void b();
    class A {
        friend class X;          // OK, but X is a local class, not ::X
        friend class Y;          // OK
        friend class Z;          // OK, introduces local class Z
        friend void a();         // error, ::a is not considered
        friend void b();         // OK
        friend void c();         // error
    };
    X *px;                       // OK, but ::X is found
    Z *pz;                       // error, no Z is found
}
```

—end example]

11.5 Protected member access   [class.protected]

1   When a friend or a member function of a derived class references a protected nonstatic member function or protected nonstatic data member of a base class, an access check applies in addition to those described earlier in clause 11.[102] Except when forming a pointer to member (5.3.1), the access must be through a pointer to, reference to, or object of the derived class itself (or any class derived from that class) (5.2.5). If the access is to form a pointer to member, the *nested-name-specifier* shall name the derived class (or any class derived from that class). [*Example:*

---

[102] This additional check does not apply to other members, *e.g.* static data members or enumerator member constants.

```
class B {
protected:
    int i;
    static int j;
};

class D1 : public B {
};

class D2 : public B {
    friend void fr(B*,D1*,D2*);
    void mem(B*,D1*);
};

void fr(B* pb, D1* p1, D2* p2)
{
    pb->i = 1;                    // ill-formed
    p1->i = 2;                    // ill-formed
    p2->i = 3;                    // OK (access through a D2)
    p2->B::i = 4;                 // OK (access through a D2, even though
                                  //    naming class is B)
    int B::* pmi_B = &B::i;       // ill-formed
    int B::* pmi_B2 = &D2::i;     // OK (type of &D2::i is int B::*)
    B::j = 5;                     // OK (because refers to static member)
    D2::j =6;                     // OK (because refers to static member)
}

void D2::mem(B* pb, D1* p1)
{
    pb->i = 1;                    // ill-formed
    p1->i = 2;                    // ill-formed
    i = 3;                        // OK (access through this)
    B::i = 4;                     // OK (access through this, qualification ignored)
    int B::* pmi_B = &B::i;       // ill-formed
    int B::* pmi_B2 = &D2::i;     // OK
    j = 5;                        // OK (because j refers to static member)
    B::j = 6;                     // OK (because B::j refers to static member)
}

void g(B* pb, D1* p1, D2* p2)
{
    pb->i = 1;                    // ill-formed
    p1->i = 2;                    // ill-formed
    p2->i = 3;                    // ill-formed
}
```

—*end example*]

11.6 Access to virtual functions   [class.access.virt]

1   The access rules (clause 11) for a virtual function are determined by its declaration and are not affected by
the rules for a function that later overrides it. [*Example:*

```
class B {
public:
    virtual int f();
};

class D : public B {
private:
    int f();
};

void f()
{
    D d;
    B* pb = &d;
    D* pd = &d;

    pb->f();                    // OK: B::f() is public,
                                // D::f() is invoked
    pd->f();                    // error: D::f() is private
}
```

—*end example*] Access is checked at the call point using the type of the expression used to denote the object for which the member function is called (B* in the example above). The access of the member function in the class in which it was defined (D in the example above) is in general not known.

11.7 Multiple access   [class.paths]

1   If a name can be reached by several paths through a multiple inheritance graph, the access is that of the path that gives most access. [*Example:*

```
class W { public: void f(); };
class A : private virtual W { };
class B : public virtual W { };
class C : public A, public B {
    void f() { W::f(); }        // OK
};
```

Since W::f() is available to C::f() along the public path through B, access is allowed.]

11.8 Nested classes   [class.access.nest]

1   The members of a nested class have no special access to members of an enclosing class, nor to classes or functions that have granted friendship to an enclosing class; the usual access rules (clause 11) shall be obeyed. The members of an enclosing class have no special access to members of a nested class; the usual access rules (clause 11) shall be obeyed. [*Example:*

```
class E {
    int x;
    class B { };

    class I {
        B b;                    // error: E::B is private
        int y;
        void f(E* p, int i)
        {
            p->x = i;           // error: E::x is private
        }
    };
```

```
        int g(I* p)
        {
            return p->y;              // error: I::y is private
        }
    };
```

—end example]

2   [*Note:* because a *base-clause* for a nested class is part of the declaration of the nested class itself (and not part of the declarations of the members of the nested class), the *base-clause* may refer to the private members of the enclosing class. For example,

```
    class C {
            class A { };
            A *p;                   // OK
            class B : A             // OK
            {
                    A    *q;         // OK because of injection of name A in A
                    C::A *r;         // error, C::A is inaccessible
                    B    *s;         // OK because of injection of name B in B
                    C::B *t;         // error, C::B is inaccessible
            };
    };
```

—end note]

12 Special member functions [special]

1   The default constructor (12.1), copy constructor and copy assignment operator (12.8), and destructor (12.4) are *special member functions*. The implementation will implicitly declare these member functions for a class type when the program does not explicitly declare them, except as noted in 12.1. The implementation will implicitly define them if they are used, as specified in 12.1, 12.4 and 12.8. Programs shall not define implicitly-declared special member functions. Programs may explicitly refer to implicitly declared special member functions. [*Example:* a program may explicitly call, take the address of or form a pointer to member to an implicitly declared special member function.

```
struct A { };                          // implicitly-declared A::operator=
struct B : A {
        B& operator=(const B &);
};
B& B::operator=(const B& s) {
        this->A::operator=(s);   // well-formed
        return *this;
}
```

—*end example*] [*Note:* the special member functions affect the way objects of class type are created, copied, and destroyed, and how values can be converted to values of other types. Often such special member functions are called implicitly.]

2   Special member functions obey the usual access rules (clause 11). [*Example:* declaring a constructor `protected` ensures that only derived classes and friends can create objects using it.]

12.1 Constructors [class.ctor]

1   Constructors do not have names. A special declarator syntax using an optional sequence of *function-specifier*s (7.1.2) followed by the constructor's class name followed by a parameter list is used to declare or define the constructor. In such a declaration, optional parentheses around the constructor class name are ignored. [*Example:*

```
class C {
public:
        C();                       // declares the constructor
};

C::C() { }                         // defines the constructor
```

—*end example*]

2   A constructor is used to initialize objects of its class type. Because constructors do not have names, they are never found during name lookup; however an explicit type conversion using the functional notation (5.2.3) will cause a constructor to be called to initialize an object. [*Note:* for initialization of objects of class type see 12.6.]

3   A *typedef-name* that names a class is a *class-name* (7.1.3); however, a *typedef-name* that names a class shall not be used as the *identifier* in the declarator for a constructor declaration.

4   A constructor shall not be `virtual` (10.3) or `static` (9.4). A constructor can be invoked for a `const`, `volatile` or `const volatile` object. A constructor shall not be declared `const`, `volatile`, or `const volatile` (9.3.2). `const` and `volatile` semantics (7.1.5.1) are not applied on an object under construction. Such semantics only come into effect once the constructor for the most derived object (1.8) ends.

5   A *default* constructor for a class X is a constructor of class X that can be called without an argument. If there is no *user-declared* constructor for class X, a default constructor is implicitly declared. An *implicitly-declared* default constructor is an `inline public` member of its class. A constructor is *trivial* if it is an implicitly-declared default constructor and if:

   — its class has no virtual functions (10.3) and no virtual base classes (10.1), and

   — all the direct base classes of its class have trivial constructors, and

   — for all the nonstatic data members of its class that are of class type (or array thereof), each such class has a trivial constructor.

6   Otherwise, the constructor is *non-trivial*.

7   An implicitly-declared default constructor for a class is *implicitly defined* when it is used to create an object of its class type (1.8). The implicitly-defined default constructor performs the set of initializations of the class that would be performed by a user-written default constructor for that class with an empty *mem-initializer-list* (12.6.2) and an empty function body. If that user-written default constructor would be ill-formed, the program is ill-formed. Before the implicitly-declared default constructor for a class is implicitly defined, all the implicitly-declared default constructors for its base classes and its nonstatic data members shall have been implicitly defined. [*Note:* an implicitly-declared default constructor has an exception-specification (15.4).]

8   Default constructors are called implicitly to create class objects of static or automatic storage duration (3.7.1, 3.7.2) defined without an initializer (8.5), are called to create class objects of dynamic storage duration (3.7.3) created by a *new-expression* in which the *new-initializer* is omitted (5.3.4), or are called when the explicit type conversion syntax (5.2.3) is used. A program is ill-formed if the default constructor for an object is implicitly used and the constructor is not accessible (clause 11).

9   [*Note:* 12.6.2 describes the order in which constructors for base classes and non-static data members are called and describes how arguments can be specified for the calls to these constructors.]

10   A *copy constructor* for a class X is a constructor with a first parameter of type X& or of type `const X&`. [*Note:* see 12.8 for more information on copy constructors.]

11   A union member shall not be of a class type (or array thereof) that has a non-trivial constructor.

12   No return type (not even `void`) shall be specified for a constructor. A `return` statement in the body of a constructor shall not specify a return value. The address of a constructor shall not be taken.

13   A functional notation type conversion (5.2.3) can be used to create new objects of its type. [*Note:* The syntax looks like an explicit call of the constructor.] [*Example:*

```
complex zz = complex(1,2.3);
cprint( complex(7.8,1.2) );
```

   —*end example*] An object created in this way is unnamed. [*Note:* 12.2 describes the lifetime of temporary objects.] [*Note:* explicit constructor calls do not yield lvalues, see 3.10.]

14   [*Note:* some language constructs have special semantics when used during construction; see 12.6.2 and 12.7.]

15   During the construction of a `const` object, if the value of the object or any of its subobjects is accessed through an lvalue that is not obtained, directly or indirectly, from the constructor's `this` pointer, the value of the object or subobject thus obtained is unspecified. [*Example:*

```
struct C;
void no_opt(C*);

struct C {
        int c;
        C() : c(0) { no_opt(this); }
};

const C cobj;

void no_opt(C* cptr) {
        int i = cobj.c * 100;      // value of cobj.c is unspecified
        cptr->c = 1;
        cout << cobj.c * 100       // value of cobj.c is unspecified
               << '\n';
}
```

—*end example*]

12.2 Temporary objects   [class.temporary]

1   Temporaries of class type are created in various contexts: binding an rvalue to a reference (8.5.3), returning an rvalue (6.6.3), a conversion that creates an rvalue (4.1, 5.2.9, 5.2.11, 5.4), throwing an exception (15.1), entering a *handler* (15.3), and in some initializations (8.5). [*Note:* the lifetime of exception objects is described in 15.1.] Even when the creation of the temporary object is avoided (12.8), all the semantic restrictions must be respected as if the temporary object was created. [*Example:* even if the copy constructor is not called, all the semantic restrictions, such as accessibility (clause 11), shall be satisfied.]

2   [*Example:*

```
class X {
    // ...
public:
    // ...
    X(int);
    X(const X&);
    ~X();
};

X f(X);

void g()
{
    X a(1);
    X b = f(X(2));
    a = f(a);
}
```

Here, an implementation might use a temporary in which to construct X(2) before passing it to f() using X's copy-constructor; alternatively, X(2) might be constructed in the space used to hold the argument. Also, a temporary might be used to hold the result of f(X(2)) before copying it to b using X's copy-constructor; alternatively, f()'s result might be constructed in b. On the other hand, the expression a=f(a) requires a temporary for either the argument a or the result of f(a) to avoid undesired aliasing of a.]

3   When an implementation introduces a temporary object of a class that has a non-trivial constructor (12.1), it shall ensure that a constructor is called for the temporary object. Similarly, the destructor shall be called for a temporary with a non-trivial destructor (12.4). Temporary objects are destroyed as the last step in evaluating the full-expression (1.9) that (lexically) contains the point where they were created. This is true even if that evaluation ends in throwing an exception.

4   There are two contexts in which temporaries are destroyed at a different point than the end of the full-expression. The first context is when an expression appears as an initializer for a declarator defining an object. In that context, the temporary that holds the result of the expression shall persist until the object's initialization is complete. The object is initialized from a copy of the temporary; during this copying, an implementation can call the copy constructor many times; the temporary is destroyed after it has been copied, before or when the initialization completes. If many temporaries are created by the evaluation of the initializer, the temporaries are destroyed in reverse order of the completion of their construction.

5   The second context is when a reference is bound to a temporary. The temporary to which the reference is bound or the temporary that is the complete object to a subobject of which the temporary is bound persists for the lifetime of the reference except as specified below. A temporary bound to a reference member in a constructor's ctor-initializer (12.6.2) persists until the constructor exits. A temporary bound to a reference parameter in a function call (5.2.2) persists until the completion of the full expression containing the call. A temporary bound to the returned value in a function return statement (6.6.3) persists until the function exits. In all these cases, the temporaries created during the evaluation of the expression initializing the reference, except the temporary to which the reference is bound, are destroyed at the end of the full-expression in which they are created and in the reverse order of the completion of their construction. If the lifetime of two or more temporaries to which references are bound ends at the same point, these temporaries are destroyed at that point in the reverse order of the completion of their construction. In addition, the destruction of temporaries bound to references shall take into account the ordering of destruction of objects with static or automatic storage duration (3.7.1, 3.7.2); that is, if `obj1` is an object with static or automatic storage duration created before the temporary is created, the temporary shall be destroyed before `obj1` is destroyed; if `obj2` is an object with static or automatic storage duration created after the temporary is created, the temporary shall be destroyed after `obj2` is destroyed. [*Example:*

```
class C {
        // ...
public:
        C();
        C(int);
        friend C operator+(const C&, const C&);
        ~C();
};
C obj1;
const C& cr = C(16)+C(23);
C obj2;
```

the expression `C(16)+C(23)` creates three temporaries. A first temporary T1 to hold the result of the expression `C(16)`, a second temporary T2 to hold the result of the expression `C(23)`, and a third temporary T3 to hold the result of the addition of these two expressions. The temporary T3 is then bound to the reference cr. It is unspecified whether T1 or T2 is created first. On an implementation where T1 is created before T2, it is guaranteed that T2 is destroyed before T1. The temporaries T1 and T2 are bound to the reference parameters of `operator+`; these temporaries are destroyed at the end of the full expression containing the call to `operator+`. The temporary T3 bound to the reference cr is destroyed at the end of cr's lifetime, that is, at the end of the program. In addition, the order in which T3 is destroyed takes into account the destruction order of other objects with static storage duration. That is, because `obj1` is constructed before T3, and T3 is constructed before `obj2`, it is guaranteed that `obj2` is destroyed before T3, and that T3 is destroyed before `obj1`.]

12.3 Conversions [**class.conv**]

1   Type conversions of class objects can be specified by constructors and by conversion functions. These conversions are called *user-defined conversions* and are used for implicit type conversions (clause 4), for initialization (8.5), and for explicit type conversions (5.4, 5.2.9).

2   User-defined conversions are applied only where they are unambiguous (10.2, 12.3.2). Conversions obey the access control rules (clause 11). Access control is applied after ambiguity resolution (3.4).

3   [*Note:* See 13.3 for a discussion of the use of conversions in function calls as well as examples below.]

4   At most one user-defined conversion (constructor or conversion function) is implicitly applied to a single value. [*Example:*

```
class X {
    // ...
public:
    operator int();
};

class Y {
    // ...
public:
    operator X();
};

Y a;
int b = a;              // error:
                        // a.operator X().operator int() not tried
int c = X(a);           // OK: a.operator X().operator int()
```

—*end example*]

5   User-defined conversions are used implicitly only if they are unambiguous. A conversion function in a derived class does not hide a conversion function in a base class unless the two functions convert to the same type. Function overload resolution (13.3.3) selects the best conversion function to perform the conversion. [*Example:*

```
class X {
public:
    // ...
    operator int();
};

class Y : public X {
public:
    // ...
    operator char();
};

void f(Y& a)
{
    if (a) {                // ill-formed:
                            // X::operator int() or Y::operator char()
                            // ...
    }
}
```

—*end example*]

12.3.1 Conversion by constructor

1   A constructor declared without the *function-specifier* `explicit` that can be called with a single parameter specifies a conversion from the type of its first parameter to the type of its class. Such a constructor is called a converting constructor. [*Example:*

```
class X {
    // ...
public:
    X(int);
    X(const char*, int =0);
};

void f(X arg)
{
    X a = 1;                    // a = X(1)
    X b = "Jessie";             // b = X("Jessie",0)
    a = 2;                      // a = X(2)
    f(3);                       // f(X(3))
}
```

—*end example*]

2   An explicit constructor constructs objects just like non-explicit constructors, but does so only where the direct-initialization syntax (8.5) or where casts (5.2.9, 5.4) are explicitly used. A default constructor may be an explicit constructor; such a constructor will be used to perform default-initialization or value-initialization (8.5). [*Example:*

```
class Z {
public:
        explicit Z();
        explicit Z(int);
        // ...
};

Z a;                        // OK: default-initialization performed
Z a1 = 1;                   // error: no implicit conversion
Z a3 = Z(1);                // OK: direct initialization syntax used
Z a2(1);                    // OK: direct initialization syntax used
Z* p = new Z(1);            // OK: direct initialization syntax used
Z a4 = (Z)1;                // OK: explicit cast used
Z a5 = static_cast<Z>(1);   // OK: explicit cast used
```

—*end example*]

3   A non-explicit copy-constructor (12.8) is a converting constructor. An implicitly-declared copy constructor is not an explicit constructor; it may be called for implicit type conversions.

12.3.2 Conversion functions

1   A member function of a class X with a name of the form

> *conversion-function-id:*
>   `operator` *conversion-type-id*
>
> *conversion-type-id:*
>   *type-specifier-seq conversion-declarator$_{opt}$*
>
> *conversion-declarator:*
>   *ptr-operator conversion-declarator$_{opt}$*

specifies a conversion from X to the type specified by the *conversion-type-id*. Such member functions are called conversion functions. Classes, enumerations, and *typedef-name*s shall not be declared in the *type-specifier-seq*. Neither parameter types nor return type can be specified. The type of a conversion function (8.3.5) is "function taking no parameter returning *conversion-type-id*." A conversion function is never used to convert a (possibly cv-qualified) object to the (possibly cv-qualified) same object type (or a reference to it), to a (possibly cv-qualified) base class of that type (or a reference to it), or to (possibly cv-qualified) void.[103]

2   [*Example:*

```
class X {
    // ...
public:
    operator int();
};

void f(X a)
{
    int i = int(a);
    i = (int)a;
    i = a;
}
```

In all three cases the value assigned will be converted by X::operator int(). —*end example*]

3   User-defined conversions are not restricted to use in assignments and initializations. [*Example:*

```
void g(X a, X b)
{
    int i = (a) ? 1+a : 0;
    int j = (a&&b) ? a+b : i;
    if (a) {                      // ...
    }
}
```

—*end example*]

4   The *conversion-type-id* shall not represent a function type nor an array type. The *conversion-type-id* in a *conversion-function-id* is the longest possible sequence of *conversion-declarator*s. [*Note:* this prevents ambiguities between the declarator operator * and its expression counterparts. [*Example:*

```
&ac.operator int*i;              // syntax error:
                                 // parsed as: &(ac.operator int *) i
                                 // not as: &(ac.operator int) *i
```

The * is the pointer declarator and not the multiplication operator.]]

5   Conversion functions are inherited.

6   Conversion functions can be virtual.

---

[103] Even though never directly called to perform a conversion, such conversion functions can be declared and can potentially be reached through a call to a virtual conversion function in a base class

12.4 Destructors   **[class.dtor]**

1   A special declarator syntax using an optional *function-specifier* (7.1.2) followed by ˜ followed by the destructor's class name followed by an empty parameter list is used to declare the destructor in a class definition. In such a declaration, the ˜ followed by the destructor's class name can be enclosed in optional parentheses; such parentheses are ignored. A *typedef-name* that names a class is a *class-name* (7.1.3); however, a *typedef-name* that names a class shall not be used as the *identifier* in the declarator for a destructor declaration.

2   A destructor is used to destroy objects of its class type. A destructor takes no parameters, and no return type can be specified for it (not even `void`). The address of a destructor shall not be taken. A destructor shall not be `static`. A destructor can be invoked for a `const`, `volatile` or `const volatile` object. A destructor shall not be declared `const`, `volatile` or `const volatile` (9.3.2). `const` and `volatile` semantics (7.1.5.1) are not applied on an object under destruction. Such semantics stop being into effect once the destructor for the most derived object (1.8) starts.

3   If a class has no *user-declared* destructor, a destructor is declared implicitly. An *implicitly-declared* destructor is an `inline public` member of its class. A destructor is *trivial* if it is an implicitly-declared destructor and if:

— all of the direct base classes of its class have trivial destructors and

— for all of the non-static data members of its class that are of class type (or array thereof), each such class has a trivial destructor.

4   Otherwise, the destructor is *non-trivial*.

5   An implicitly-declared destructor is *implicitly defined* when it is used to destroy an object of its class type (3.7). A program is ill-formed if the class for which a destructor is implicitly defined has:

— a non-static data member of class type (or array thereof) with an inaccessible destructor, or

— a base class with an inaccessible destructor.

Before the implicitly-declared destructor for a class is implicitly defined, all the implicitly-declared destructors for its base classes and its nonstatic data members shall have been implicitly defined. [*Note:* an implicitly-declared destructor has an exception-specification (15.4).]

6   After executing the body of the destructor and destroying any automatic objects allocated within the body, a destructor for class X calls the destructors for X's direct members, the destructors for X's direct base classes and, if X is the type of the most derived class (12.6.2), its destructor calls the destructors for X's virtual base classes. All destructors are called as if they were referenced with a qualified name, that is, ignoring any possible virtual overriding destructors in more derived classes. Bases and members are destroyed in the reverse order of the completion of their constructor (see 12.6.2). A `return` statement (6.6.3) in a destructor might not directly return to the caller; before transferring control to the caller, the destructors for the members and bases are called. Destructors for elements of an array are called in reverse order of their construction (see 12.6).

7   A destructor can be declared `virtual` (10.3) or pure `virtual` (10.4); if any objects of that class or any derived class are created in the program, the destructor shall be defined. If a class has a base class with a virtual destructor, its destructor (whether user- or implicitly- declared) is virtual.

8   [*Note:* some language constructs have special semantics when used during destruction; see 12.7.]

9   A union member shall not be of a class type (or array thereof) that has a non-trivial destructor.

10   Destructors are invoked implicitly (1) for a constructed object with static storage duration (3.7.1) at program termination (3.6.3), (2) for a constructed object with automatic storage duration (3.7.2) when the block in which the object is created exits (6.7), (3) for a constructed temporary object when the lifetime of the temporary object ends (12.2), (4) for a constructed object allocated by a *new-expression* (5.3.4), through use of a *delete-expression* (5.3.5), (5) in several situations due to the handling of exceptions (15.3). A

program is ill-formed if an object of class type or array thereof is declared and the destructor for the class is not accessible at the point of the declaration. Destructors can also be invoked explicitly.

11 At the point of definition of a virtual destructor (including an implicit definition (12.8)), non-placement operator delete shall be looked up in the scope of the destructor's class (3.4.1) and if found shall be accessible and unambiguous. [*Note:* this assures that an operator delete corresponding to the dynamic type of an object is available for the *delete-expression* (12.5).]

12 In an explicit destructor call, the destructor name appears as a ˜ followed by a *type-name* that names the destructor's class type. The invocation of a destructor is subject to the usual rules for member functions (9.3), that is, if the object is not of the destructor's class type and not of a class derived from the destructor's class type, the program has undefined behavior (except that invoking `delete` on a null pointer has no effect). [*Example:*

```
struct B {
        virtual ˜B() { }
};
struct D : B {
        ˜D() { }
};

D D_object;
typedef B B_alias;
B* B_ptr = &D_object;

void f() {
        D_object.B::˜B();               // calls B's destructor
        B_ptr->˜B();                    // calls D's destructor
        B_ptr->˜B_alias();              // calls D's destructor
        B_ptr->B_alias::˜B();           // calls B's destructor
        B_ptr->B_alias::˜B_alias();     // error, no B_alias in class B
}
```

—*end example*] [*Note:* an explicit destructor call must always be written using a member access operator (5.2.5); in particular, the *unary-expression* ˜X() in a member function is not an explicit destructor call (5.3.1).]

13 [*Note:* explicit calls of destructors are rarely needed. One use of such calls is for objects placed at specific addresses using a *new-expression* with the placement option. Such use of explicit placement and destruction of objects can be necessary to cope with dedicated hardware resources and for writing memory management facilities. For example,

```
void* operator new(size_t, void* p) { return p; }
struct X {
    // ...
    X(int);
    ˜X();
};
void f(X* p);

void g()                             // rare, specialized use:
{
    char* buf = new char[sizeof(X)];
    X* p = new(buf) X(222);          // use buf[] and initialize
    f(p);
    p->X::˜X();                      // cleanup
}
```

—*end note*]

14   Once a destructor is invoked for an object, the object no longer exists; the behavior is undefined if the destructor is invoked for an object whose lifetime has ended (3.8). [*Example:* if the destructor for an automatic object is explicitly invoked, and the block is subsequently left in a manner that would ordinarily invoke implicit destruction of the object, the behavior is undefined.]

15   [*Note:* the notation for explicit call of a destructor can be used for any scalar type name (5.2.4). Allowing this makes it possible to write code without having to know if a destructor exists for a given type. For example,

```
typedef int I;
I* p;
// ...
p->I::~I();
```

—*end note*]

12.5 Free store   [class.free]

1   Any allocation function for a class `T` is a static member (even if not explicitly declared `static`).

2   [*Example:*

```
class Arena;
struct B {
    void* operator new(size_t, Arena*);
};
struct D1 : B {
};

Arena*  ap;
void foo(int i)
{
    new (ap) D1;            // calls B::operator new(size_t, Arena*)
    new D1[i];              // calls ::operator new[](size_t)
    new D1;                 // ill-formed: ::operator new(size_t) hidden
}
```

—*end example*]

3   When an object is deleted with a *delete-expression* (5.3.5), a *deallocation function* (`operator delete()` for non-array objects or `operator delete[]()` for arrays) is (implicitly) called to reclaim the storage occupied by the object (3.7.3.2).

4   If a *delete-expression* begins with a unary `::` operator, the deallocation function's name is looked up in global scope. Otherwise, if the *delete-expression* is used to deallocate a class object whose static type has a virtual destructor, the deallocation function is the one found by the lookup in the definition of the dynamic type's virtual destructor (12.4).[104] Otherwise, if the *delete-expression* is used to deallocate an object of class `T` or array thereof, the static and dynamic types of the object shall be identical and the deallocation function's name is looked up in the scope of `T`. If this lookup fails to find the name, the name is looked up in the global scope. If the result of the lookup is ambiguous or inaccessible, or if the lookup selects a placement deallocation function, the program is ill-formed.

5   When a *delete-expression* is executed, the selected deallocation function shall be called with the address of the block of storage to be reclaimed as its first argument and (if the two-parameter style is used) the size of the block as its second argument.[105]

---

[104] A similar lookup is not needed for the array version of `operator delete` because 5.3.5 requires that in this situation, the static type of the *delete-expression*'s operand be the same as its dynamic type.

[105] If the static type in the *delete-expression* is different from the dynamic type and the destructor is not virtual the size might be incorrect, but that case is already undefined; see 5.3.5.

6   Any deallocation function for a class X is a static member (even if not explicitly declared `static`). [*Example:*

```
class X {
    // ...
    void operator delete(void*);
    void operator delete[](void*, size_t);
};

class Y {
    // ...
    void operator delete(void*, size_t);
    void operator delete[](void*);
};
```

—*end example*]

7   Since member allocation and deallocation functions are `static` they cannot be virtual. [*Note:* however, when the *cast-expression* of a *delete-expression* refers to an object of class type, because the deallocation function actually called is looked up in the scope of the class that is the dynamic type of the object, if the destructor is virtual, the effect is the same. For example,

```
struct B {
    virtual ~B();
    void operator delete(void*, size_t);
};

struct D : B {
    void operator delete(void*);
};

void f()
{
    B* bp = new D;
    delete bp;                    //1: uses D::operator delete(void*)
}
```

Here, storage for the non-array object of class D is deallocated by `D::operator delete()`, due to the virtual destructor.] [*Note:* virtual destructors have no effect on the deallocation function actually called when the *cast-expression* of a *delete-expression* refers to an array of objects of class type. For example,

```
struct B {
    virtual ~B();
    void operator delete[](void*, size_t);
};

struct D : B {
    void operator delete[](void*, size_t);
};

void f(int i)
{
    D* dp = new D[i];
    delete [] dp;                 // uses D::operator delete[](void*, size_t)
    B* bp = new D[i];
    delete[] bp;                  // undefined behavior
}
```

—*end note*]

8   Access to the deallocation function is checked statically. Hence, even though a different one might actually be executed, the statically visible deallocation function is required to be accessible. [*Example:* for the call on line //1 above, if `B::operator delete()` had been `private`, the delete expression would have been ill-formed.]

12.6 Initialization   [class.init]

1   When no initializer is specified for an object of (possibly cv-qualified) class type (or array thereof), or the initializer has the form `()`, the object is initialized as specified in 8.5. The object is default-initialized if there is no initializer, or value-initialized if the initializer is `()`.

2   An object of class type (or array thereof) can be explicitly initialized; see 12.6.1 and 12.6.2.

3   When an array of class objects is initialized (either explicitly or implicitly), the constructor shall be called for each element of the array, following the subscript order; see 8.3.4. [*Note:* destructors for the array elements are called in reverse order of their construction.]

12.6.1 Explicit initialization   [class.expl.init]

1   An object of class type can be initialized with a parenthesized *expression-list*, where the *expression-list* is construed as an argument list for a constructor that is called to initialize the object. Alternatively, a single *assignment-expression* can be specified as an *initializer* using the = form of initialization. Either direct-initialization semantics or copy-initialization semantics apply; see 8.5. [*Example:*

```
class complex {
    // ...
public:
    complex();
    complex(double);
    complex(double,double);
    // ...
};

complex sqrt(complex,complex);

        complex a(1);                    // initialize by a call of
                                         // complex(double)
        complex b = a;                   // initialize by a copy of a
        complex c = complex(1,2);        // construct complex(1,2)
                                         // using complex(double,double)
                                         // copy it into c
        complex d = sqrt(b,c);           // call sqrt(complex,complex)
                                         // and copy the result into d
        complex e;                       // initialize by a call of
                                         // complex()
        complex f = 3;                   // construct complex(3) using
                                         // complex(double)
                                         // copy it into f
        complex g = { 1, 2 };            // error; constructor is required
```

—*end example*] [*Note:* overloading of the assignment operator (13.5.3) has no effect on initialization.]

2   When an aggregate (whether class or array) contains members of class type and is initialized by a brace-enclosed *initializer-list* (8.5.1), each such member is copy-initialized (see 8.5) by the corresponding *assignment-expression*. If there are fewer *initializers* in the *initializer-list* than members of the aggregate, each member not explicitly initialized shall be value-initialized (8.5). [*Note:* 8.5.1 describes how *assignment-expression*s in an *initializer-list* are paired with the aggregate members they initialize.] [*Example:*

```
complex v[6] = { 1,complex(1,2),complex(),2 };
```

Here, `complex::complex(double)` is called for the initialization of `v[0]` and `v[3]`, `complex::complex(double,double)` is called for the initialization of `v[1]`, `complex::complex()` is called for the initialization `v[2]`, `v[4]`, and `v[5]`. For another example,

```
class X {
public:
        int i;
        float f;
        complex c;
} x = { 99, 88.8, 77.7 };
```

Here, `x.i` is initialized with 99, `x.f` is initialized with 88.8, and `complex::complex(double)` is called for the initialization of `x.c`.] [*Note:* braces can be elided in the *initializer-list* for any aggregate, even if the aggregate has members of a class type with user-defined type conversions; see 8.5.1.]

3   [*Note:* if `T` is a class type with no default constructor, any declaration of an object of type `T` (or array thereof) is ill-formed if no *initializer* is explicitly specified (see 12.6 and 8.5).]

4   [*Note:* the order in which objects with static storage duration are initialized is described in 3.6.2 and 6.7.]

12.6.2 Initializing bases and members   [class.base.init]

1   In the definition of a constructor for a class, initializers for direct and virtual base subobjects and nonstatic data members can be specified by a *ctor-initializer*, which has the form

> *ctor-initializer:*
> > : *mem-initializer-list*
>
> *mem-initializer-list:*
> > *mem-initializer*
> > *mem-initializer* , *mem-initializer-list*
>
> *mem-initializer:*
> > *mem-initializer-id* (*expression-list_{opt}*)
>
> *mem-initializer-id:*
> > : :_{opt} *nested-name-specifier_{opt} class-name*
> > *identifier*

2   Names in a *mem-initializer-id* are looked up in the scope of the constructor's class and, if not found in that scope, are looked up in the scope containing the constructor's definition. [*Note:* if the constructor's class contains a member with the same name as a direct or virtual base class of the class, a *mem-initializer-id* naming the member or base class and composed of a single identifier refers to the class member. A *mem-initializer-id* for the hidden base class may be specified using a qualified name.] Unless the *mem-initializer-id* names a nonstatic data member of the constructor's class or a direct or virtual base of that class, the *mem-initializer* is ill-formed. A *mem-initializer-list* can initialize a base class using any name that denotes that base class type. [*Example:*

```
struct A { A(); };
typedef A global_A;
struct B { };
struct C: public A, public B { C(); };
C::C(): global_A() { }          // mem-initializer for base A
```

—*end example*] If a *mem-initializer-id* is ambiguous because it designates both a direct non-virtual base class and an inherited virtual base class, the *mem-initializer* is ill-formed. [*Example:*

```
struct A { A(); };
struct B: public virtual A { };
struct C: public A, public B { C(); };
C::C(): A() { }                           // ill-formed: which A?
```

—*end example*] A *ctor-initializer* may initialize the member of an anonymous union that is a member of the constructor's class. If a *ctor-initializer* specifies more than one *mem-initializer* for the same member, for the same base class or for multiple members of the same union (including members of anonymous unions), the *ctor-initializer* is ill-formed.

3   The *expression-list* in a *mem-initializer* is used to initialize the base class or nonstatic data member subobject denoted by the *mem-initializer-id*. The semantics of a *mem-initializer* are as follows:

— if the *expression-list* of the *mem-initializer* is omitted, the base class or member subobject is value-initialized (see 8.5);

— otherwise, the subobject indicated by *mem-initializer-id* is direct-initialized using *expression-list* as the *initializer* (see 8.5).

[*Example:*

```
struct B1 { B1(int); /* ... */ };
struct B2 { B2(int); /* ... */ };
struct D : B1, B2 {
    D(int);
    B1 b;
    const int c;
};

D::D(int a) : B2(a+1), B1(a+2), c(a+3), b(a+4)
{ /* ... */ }
D d(10);
```

—*end example*] There is a sequence point (1.9) after the initialization of each base and member. The *expression-list* of a *mem-initializer* is evaluated as part of the initialization of the corresponding base or member.

4   If a given nonstatic data member or base class is not named by a *mem-initializer-id* (including the case where there is no *mem-initializer-list* because the constructor has no *ctor-initializer*), then

— If the entity is a nonstatic data member of (possibly cv-qualified) class type (or array thereof) or a base class, and the entity class is a non-POD class, the entity is default-initialized (8.5). If the entity is a nonstatic data member of a const-qualified type, the entity class shall have a user-declared default constructor.

— Otherwise, the entity is not initialized. If the entity is of const-qualified type or reference type, or of a (possibly cv-qualified) POD class type (or array thereof) containing (directly or indirectly) a member of a const-qualified type, the program is ill-formed.

After the call to a constructor for class X has completed, if a member of X is neither specified in the constructor's *mem-initializers*, nor default-initialized, nor value-initialized, nor given a value during execution of the body of the constructor, the member has indeterminate value.

5   Initialization shall proceed in the following order:

— First, and only for the constructor of the most derived class as described below, virtual base classes shall be initialized in the order they appear on a depth-first left-to-right traversal of the directed acyclic graph of base classes, where "left-to-right" is the order of appearance of the base class names in the derived class *base-specifier-list*.

— Then, direct base classes shall be initialized in declaration order as they appear in the *base-specifier-list* (regardless of the order of the *mem-initializers*).

— Then, nonstatic data members shall be initialized in the order they were declared in the class definition (again regardless of the order of the *mem-initializers*).

— Finally, the body of the constructor is executed.

[*Note:* the declaration order is mandated to ensure that base and member subobjects are destroyed in the reverse order of initialization.]

6   All sub-objects representing virtual base classes are initialized by the constructor of the most derived class (1.8). If the constructor of the most derived class does not specify a *mem-initializer* for a virtual base class V, then V's default constructor is called to initialize the virtual base class subobject. If V does not have an accessible default constructor, the initialization is ill-formed. A *mem-initializer* naming a virtual base class shall be ignored during execution of the constructor of any class that is not the most derived class. [*Example:*

```
class V {
public:
    V();
    V(int);
    // ...
};

class A : public virtual V {
public:
    A();
    A(int);
    // ...
};

class B : public virtual V {
public:
    B();
    B(int);
    // ...
};

class C : public A, public B, private virtual V {
public:
    C();
    C(int);
    // ...
};

A::A(int i) : V(i) { /* ... */ }
B::B(int i) { /* ... */ }
C::C(int i) { /* ... */ }

V v(1);                          // use V(int)
A a(2);                          // use V(int)
B b(3);                          // use V()
C c(4);                          // use V()
```

—*end example*]

7   Names in the *expression-list* of a *mem-initializer* are evaluated in the scope of the constructor for which the *mem-initializer* is specified. [*Example:*

```
class X {
    int a;
    int b;
    int i;
    int j;
public:
    const int& r;
    X(int i): r(a), b(i), i(i), j(this->i) {}
};
```

initializes `X::r` to refer to `X::a`, initializes `X::b` with the value of the constructor parameter `i`, initializes `X::i` with the value of the constructor parameter `i`, and initializes `X::j` with the value of `X::i`; this takes place each time an object of class `X` is created.] [*Note:* because the *mem-initializer* are evaluated in the scope of the constructor, the `this` pointer can be used in the *expression-list* of a *mem-initializer* to refer to the object being initialized.]

8   Member functions (including virtual member functions, 10.3) can be called for an object under construction. Similarly, an object under construction can be the operand of the `typeid` operator (5.2.8) or of a `dynamic_cast` (5.2.7). However, if these operations are performed in a *ctor-initializer* (or in a function called directly or indirectly from a *ctor-initializer*) before all the *mem-initializer*s for base classes have completed, the result of the operation is undefined. [*Example:*

```
class A {
public:
        A(int);
};

class B : public A {
        int j;
public:
        int f();
        B() : A(f()),          // undefined: calls member function
                               // but base A not yet initialized
            j(f()) { }         // well-defined: bases are all initialized
};

class C {
public:
        C(int);
};

class D : public B, C {
        int i;
public:
        D() : C(f()),          // undefined: calls member function
                               // but base C not yet initialized
            i(f()) {}          // well-defined: bases are all initialized
};
```

—*end example*]

9   [*Note:* 12.7 describes the result of virtual function calls, `typeid` and `dynamic_cast`s during construction for the well-defined cases; that is, describes the *polymorphic behavior* of an object under construction.]

12.7 Construction and destruction [**class.cdtor**]

1   For an object of non-POD class type (clause 9), before the constructor begins execution and after the destructor finishes execution, referring to any nonstatic member or base class of the object results in undefined behavior. [*Example:*

```
struct X { int i; };
struct Y : X { };
struct A { int a; };
struct B : public A { int j; Y y; };

extern B bobj;
B* pb = &bobj;                 // OK
int* p1 = &bobj.a;             // undefined, refers to base class member
int* p2 = &bobj.y.i;           // undefined, refers to member's member

A* pa = &bobj;                 // undefined, upcast to a base class type
B bobj;                        // definition of bobj

extern X xobj;
int* p3 = &xobj.i;             // OK, X is a POD class
X xobj;
```

For another example,

```
struct W { int j; };
struct X : public virtual W { };
struct Y {
        int *p;
        X x;
        Y() : p(&x.j)          // undefined, x is not yet constructed
        { }
};
```

—*end example*]

2   To explicitly or implicitly convert a pointer (an lvalue) referring to an object of class X to a pointer (reference) to a direct or indirect base class B of X, the construction of X and the construction of all of its direct or indirect bases that directly or indirectly derive from B shall have started and the destruction of these classes shall not have completed, otherwise the conversion results in undefined behavior. To form a pointer to (or access the value of) a direct nonstatic member of an object obj, the construction of obj shall have started and its destruction shall not have completed, otherwise the computation of the pointer value (or accessing the member value) results in undefined behavior. [*Example:*

```
struct A { };
struct B : virtual A { };
struct C : B { };
struct D : virtual A { D(A*); };
struct X { X(A*); };
```

```
struct E : C, D, X {
        E() : D(this),          // undefined: upcast from E* to A*
                                 // might use path E* → D* → A*
                                 // but D is not constructed
                                 // D((C*)this), // defined:
                                 // E* → C* defined because E() has started
                                 // and C* → A* defined because
                                 // C fully constructed
                X(this)          // defined: upon construction of X,
                                 // C/B/D/A sublattice is fully constructed

                { }
};
```

—end example]

3   Member functions, including virtual functions (10.3), can be called during construction or destruction
     (12.6.2). When a virtual function is called directly or indirectly from a constructor (including from the
     mem-initializer for a data member) or from a destructor, and the object to which the call applies is the
     object under construction or destruction, the function called is the one defined in the constructor or
     destructor's own class or in one of its bases, but not a function overriding it in a class derived from the con-
     structor or destructor's class, or overriding it in one of the other base classes of the most derived object
     (1.8). If the virtual function call uses an explicit class member access (5.2.5) and the object-expression
     refers to the object under construction or destruction but its type is neither the constructor or destructor's
     own class or one of its bases, the result of the call is undefined. [*Example:*

```
class V {
public:
        virtual void f();
        virtual void g();
};

class A : public virtual V {
public:
        virtual void f();
};

class B : public virtual V {
public:
        virtual void g();
        B(V*, A*);
};

class D : public A, B {
public:
        virtual void f();
        virtual void g();
        D() : B((A*)this, this) { }
};

B::B(V* v, A* a) {
        f();            // calls V::f, not A::f
        g();            // calls B::g, not D::g
        v->g();         // v is base of B, the call is well-defined, calls B::g
        a->f();         // undefined behavior, a's type not a base of B
}
```

—end example]

4   The typeid operator (5.2.8) can be used during construction or destruction (12.6.2). When typeid is used in a constructor (including from the *mem-initializer* for a data member) or in a destructor, or used in a function called (directly or indirectly) from a constructor or destructor, if the operand of typeid refers to the object under construction or destruction, typeid yields the type_info representing the constructor or destructor's class. If the operand of typeid refers to the object under construction or destruction and the static type of the operand is neither the constructor or destructor's class nor one of its bases, the result of typeid is undefined.

5   Dynamic_casts (5.2.7) can be used during construction or destruction (12.6.2). When a dynamic_cast is used in a constructor (including from the *mem-initializer* for a data member) or in a destructor, or used in a function called (directly or indirectly) from a constructor or destructor, if the operand of the dynamic_cast refers to the object under construction or destruction, this object is considered to be a most derived object that has the type of the constructor or destructor's class. If the operand of the dynamic_cast refers to the object under construction or destruction and the static type of the operand is not a pointer to or object of the constructor or destructor's own class or one of its bases, the dynamic_cast results in undefined behavior.

6   [*Example:*

```
class V {
public:
        virtual void f();
};

class A : public virtual V { };

class B : public virtual V {
public:
        B(V*, A*);
};

class D : public A, B {
public:
        D() : B((A*)this, this) { }
};

B::B(V* v, A* a) {
        typeid(*this);              // type_info for B
        typeid(*v);                 // well-defined: *v has type V, a base of B
                                    // yields type_info for B
        typeid(*a);                 // undefined behavior: type A not a base of B
        dynamic_cast<B*>(v);        // well-defined: v of type V*, V base of B
                                    // results in B*
        dynamic_cast<B*>(a);        // undefined behavior,
                                    // a has type A*, A not a base of B
}
```

—*end example*]

12.8 Copying class objects   [class.copy]

1   A class object can be copied in two ways, by initialization (12.1, 8.5), including for function argument passing (5.2.2) and for function value return (6.6.3), and by assignment (5.17). Conceptually, these two operations are implemented by a copy constructor (12.1) and copy assignment operator (13.5.3).

2   A non-template constructor for class X is a *copy* constructor if its first parameter is of type X&, const X&, volatile X& or const volatile X&, and either there are no other parameters or else all other parameters have default arguments (8.3.6).[106] [*Example:* X::X(const X&) and X::X(X&, int=1)

---

[106] Because a template constructor is never a copy constructor, the presence of such a template does not suppress the implicit declaration of a copy constructor. Template constructors participate in overload resolution with other constructors, including copy construc-

are copy constructors.

```
class X {
    // ...
public:
    X(int);
    X(const X&, int = 1);
};
X a(1);                              // calls X(int);
X b(a, 0);                           // calls X(const X&, int);
X c = b;                             // calls X(const X&, int);
```

—*end example*] [*Note:* all forms of copy constructor may be declared for a class. [*Example:*

```
class X {
    // ...
public:
        X(const X&);
        X(X&);                       // OK
};
```

—*end example*] —*end note*] [*Note:* if a class X only has a copy constructor with a parameter of type X&, an initializer of type const X or volatile X cannot initialize an object of type (possibly cv-qualified) X. [*Example:*

```
struct X {
        X();                         // default constructor
        X(X&);                       // copy constructor with a nonconst parameter
};
const X cx;
X x = cx;                            // error – X::X(X&) cannot copy cx into x
```

—*end example*] —*end note*]

3   A declaration of a constructor for a class X is ill-formed if its first parameter is of type (optionally cv-qualified) X and either there are no other parameters or else all other parameters have default arguments. A member function template is never instantiated to perform the copy of a class object to an object of its class type. [*Example:*

```
struct S {
        template<typename T> S(T);
};

S f();

void g() {
        S a( f() );  // does not instantiate member template
}
```

—*end example*]

4   If the class definition does not explicitly declare a copy constructor, one is declared *implicitly*. Thus, for the class definition

```
struct X {
        X(const X&, int);
};
```

a copy constructor is implicitly-declared. If the user-declared constructor is later defined as

---

tors, and a template constructor may be used to copy an object if it provides a better match than other constructors.

```
X::X(const X& x, int i =0) { /* ... */ }
```

then any use of X's copy constructor is ill-formed because of the ambiguity; no diagnostic is required.

5   The implicitly-declared copy constructor for a class X will have the form

```
X::X(const X&)
```

if

— each direct or virtual base class B of X has a copy constructor whose first parameter is of type const B& or const volatile B&, and

— for all the nonstatic data members of X that are of a class type M (or array thereof), each such class type has a copy constructor whose first parameter is of type const M& or const volatile M&.[107]

Otherwise, the implicitly declared copy constructor will have the form

```
X::X(X&)
```

An implicitly-declared copy constructor is an inline public member of its class.

6   A copy constructor for class X is *trivial* if it is implicitly declared and if

— class X has no virtual functions (10.3) and no virtual base classes (10.1), and

— each direct base class of X has a trivial copy constructor, and

— for all the nonstatic data members of X that are of class type (or array thereof), each such class type has a trivial copy constructor;

otherwise the copy constructor is *non-trivial*.

7   An implicitly-declared copy constructor is *implicitly defined* if it is used to initialize an object of its class type from a copy of an object of its class type or of a class type derived from its class type[108]. [*Note:* the copy constructor is implicitly defined even if the implementation elided its use (12.2).] A program is ill-formed if the class for which a copy constructor is implicitly defined has:

— a nonstatic data member of class type (or array thereof) with an inaccessible or ambiguous copy constructor, or

— a base class with an inaccessible or ambiguous copy constructor.

Before the implicitly-declared copy constructor for a class is implicitly defined, all implicitly-declared copy constructors for its direct and virtual base classes and its nonstatic data members shall have been implicitly defined. [*Note:* an implicitly-declared copy constructor has an exception-specification (15.4).]

8   The implicitly-defined copy constructor for class X performs a memberwise copy of its subobjects. The order of copying is the same as the order of initialization of bases and members in a user-defined constructor (see 12.6.2). Each subobject is copied in the manner appropriate to its type:

— if the subobject is of class type, the copy constructor for the class is used;

— if the subobject is an array, each element is copied, in the manner appropriate to the element type;

— if the subobject is of scalar type, the built-in assignment operator is used.

Virtual base class subobjects shall be copied only once by the implicitly-defined copy constructor (see 12.6.2).

---

[107] This implies that the reference parameter of the implicitly-declared copy constructor cannot bind to a volatile lvalue; see C.1.8.

[108] See 8.5 for more details on direct and copy initialization.

9   A user-declared *copy* assignment operator `X::operator=` is a non-static non-template member function of class X with exactly one parameter of type `X`, `X&`, `const X&`, `volatile X&` or `const volatile X&`.[109] [*Note:* an overloaded assignment operator must be declared to have only one parameter; see 13.5.3.] [*Note:* more than one form of copy assignment operator may be declared for a class.] [*Note:* if a class X only has a copy assignment operator with a parameter of type X&, an expression of type const X cannot be assigned to an object of type X. [*Example:*

```
struct X {
        X();
        X& operator=(X&);
};
const X cx;
X x;
void f() {
        x = cx;                      // error:
                                     // X::operator=(X&) cannot assign cx into x

}
```

—end example] —end note]

10   If the class definition does not explicitly declare a copy assignment operator, one is declared *implicitly*. The implicitly-declared copy assignment operator for a class X will have the form

```
X& X::operator=(const X&)
```

if

— each direct base class B of X has a copy assignment operator whose parameter is of type `const B&`, `const volatile B&` or B, and

— for all the nonstatic data members of X that are of a class type M (or array thereof), each such class type has a copy assignment operator whose parameter is of type `const M&`, `const volatile M&` or M.[110]

Otherwise, the implicitly declared copy assignment operator will have the form

```
X& X::operator=(X&)
```

The implicitly-declared copy assignment operator for class X has the return type `X&`; it returns the object for which the assignment operator is invoked, that is, the object assigned to. An implicitly-declared copy assignment operator is an `inline public` member of its class. Because a copy assignment operator is implicitly declared for a class if not declared by the user, a base class copy assignment operator is always hidden by the copy assignment operator of a derived class (13.5.3). A *using-declaration* (7.3.3) that brings in from a base class an assignment operator with a parameter type that could be that of a copy-assignment operator for the derived class is not considered an explicit declaration of a copy-assignment operator and does not suppress the implicit declaration of the derived class copy-assignment operator; the operator introduced by the *using-declaration* is hidden by the implicitly-declared copy-assignment operator in the derived class.

11   A copy assignment operator for class X is *trivial* if it is implicitly declared and if

— class X has no virtual functions (10.3) and no virtual base classes (10.1), and

— each direct base class of X has a trivial copy assignment operator, and

---

[109] Because a template assignment operator is never a copy assignment operator, the presence of such a template does not suppress the implicit declaration of a copy assignment operator. Template assignment operators participate in overload resolution with other assignment operators, including copy assignment operators, and a template assignment operator may be used to assign an object if it provides a better match than other assignment operators.

[110] This implies that the reference parameter of the implicitly-declared copy assignment operator cannot bind to a `volatile` lvalue; see C.1.8.

— for all the nonstatic data members of X that are of class type (or array thereof), each such class type has a trivial copy assignment operator;

otherwise the copy assignment operator is *non-trivial*.

12   An implicitly-declared copy assignment operator is *implicitly defined* when an object of its class type is assigned a value of its class type or a value of a class type derived from its class type. A program is ill-formed if the class for which a copy assignment operator is implicitly defined has:

— a nonstatic data member of const type, or

— a nonstatic data member of reference type, or

— a nonstatic data member of class type (or array thereof) with an inaccessible copy assignment operator, or

— a base class with an inaccessible copy assignment operator.

Before the implicitly-declared copy assignment operator for a class is implicitly defined, all implicitly-declared copy assignment operators for its direct base classes and its nonstatic data members shall have been implicitly defined. [*Note:* an implicitly-declared copy assignment operator has an exception-specification (15.4).]

13   The implicitly-defined copy assignment operator for class X performs memberwise assignment of its subobjects. The direct base classes of X are assigned first, in the order of their declaration in the *base-specifier-list*, and then the immediate nonstatic data members of X are assigned, in the order in which they were declared in the class definition. Each subobject is assigned in the manner appropriate to its type:

— if the subobject is of class type, the copy assignment operator for the class is used (as if by explicit qualification; that is, ignoring any possible virtual overriding functions in more derived classes);

— if the subobject is an array, each element is assigned, in the manner appropriate to the element type;

— if the subobject is of scalar type, the built-in assignment operator is used.

It is unspecified whether subobjects representing virtual base classes are assigned more than once by the implicitly-defined copy assignment operator. [*Example:*

```
struct V { };
struct A : virtual V { };
struct B : virtual V { };
struct C : B, A { };
```

it is unspecified whether the virtual base class subobject V is assigned twice by the implicitly-defined copy assignment operator for C. —*end example*]

14   A program is ill-formed if the copy constructor or the copy assignment operator for an object is implicitly used and the special member function is not accessible (clause 11). [*Note:* Copying one object into another using the copy constructor or the copy assignment operator does not change the layout or size of either object.]

15   When certain criteria are met, an implementation is allowed to omit the copy construction of a class object, even if the copy constructor and/or destructor for the object have side effects. In such cases, the implementation treats the source and target of the omitted copy operation as simply two different ways of referring to the same object, and the destruction of that object occurs at the later of the times when the two objects would have been destroyed without the optimization.[111] This elision of copy operations is permitted in the following circumstances (which may be combined to eliminate multiple copies):

— in a return statement in a function with a class return type, when the expression is the name of a

---

[111] Because only one object is destroyed instead of two, and one copy constructor is not executed, there is still one object destroyed for each one constructed.

non-volatile automatic object with the same cv-unqualified type as the function return type, the copy operation can be omitted by constructing the automatic object directly into the function's return value

— when a temporary class object that has not been bound to a reference (12.2) would be copied to a class object with the same cv-unqualified type, the copy operation can be omitted by constructing the temporary object directly into the target of the omitted copy

[*Example:*

```
class Thing {
public:
    Thing();
    ~Thing();
    Thing(const Thing&);
};

Thing f() {
    Thing t;
    return t;
}

Thing t2 = f();
```

Here the criteria for elision can be combined to eliminate two calls to the copy constructor of class Thing: the copying of the local automatic object t into the temporary object for the return value of function f() and the copying of that temporary object into object t2. Effectively, the construction of the local object t can be viewed as directly initializing the global object t2, and that object's destruction will occur at program exit. —*end example*]

13 Overloading [over]

1   When two or more different declarations are specified for a single name in the same scope, that name is said to be *overloaded*. By extension, two declarations in the same scope that declare the same name but with different types are called *overloaded declarations*. Only function declarations can be overloaded; object and type declarations cannot be overloaded.

2   When an overloaded function name is used in a call, which overloaded function declaration is being referenced is determined by comparing the types of the arguments at the point of use with the types of the parameters in the overloaded declarations that are visible at the point of use. This function selection process is called *overload resolution* and is defined in 13.3. [*Example:*

```
double abs(double);
int abs(int);

abs(1);                         // call abs(int);
abs(1.0);                       // call abs(double);
```

—*end example*]

13.1 Overloadable declarations [over.load]

1   Not all function declarations can be overloaded. Those that cannot be overloaded are specified here. A program is ill-formed if it contains two such non-overloadable declarations in the same scope. [*Note:* this restriction applies to explicit declarations in a scope, and between such declarations and declarations made through a *using-declaration* (7.3.3). It does not apply to sets of functions fabricated as a result of name lookup (e.g., because of *using-directive*s) or overload resolution (e.g., for operator functions).]

2   Certain function declarations cannot be overloaded:

— Function declarations that differ only in the return type cannot be overloaded.

— Member function declarations with the same name and the same parameter types cannot be overloaded if any of them is a `static` member function declaration (9.4). Likewise, member function template declarations with the same name, the same parameter types, and the same template parameter lists cannot be overloaded if any of them is a `static` member function template declaration. The types of the implicit object parameters constructed for the member functions for the purpose of overload resolution (13.3.1) are not considered when comparing parameter types for enforcement of this rule. In contrast, if there is no `static` member function declaration among a set of member function declarations with the same name and the same parameter types, then these member function declarations can be overloaded if they differ in the type of their implicit object parameter. [*Example:* the following illustrates this distinction:

```
class X {
    static void f();
    void f();                       // ill-formed
    void f() const;                 // ill-formed
    void f() const volatile;        // ill-formed
    void g();
    void g() const;                 // OK: no static g
    void g() const volatile;        // OK: no static g
};
```

—*end example*]

3   [*Note:* as specified in 8.3.5, function declarations that have equivalent parameter declarations declare the same function and therefore cannot be overloaded:

— Parameter declarations that differ only in the use of equivalent typedef "types" are equivalent. A `typedef` is not a separate type, but only a synonym for another type (7.1.3). [*Example:*

```
typedef int Int;

void f(int i);
void f(Int i);                    // OK: redeclaration of f(int)
void f(int i) { /* ... */ }
void f(Int i) { /* ... */ }       // error: redefinition of f(int)
```

—*end example*]

Enumerations, on the other hand, are distinct types and can be used to distinguish overloaded function declarations. [*Example:*

```
enum E { a };

void f(int i) { /* ... */ }
void f(E i)   { /* ... */ }
```

—*end example*]

— Parameter declarations that differ only in a pointer * versus an array [] are equivalent. That is, the array declaration is adjusted to become a pointer declaration (8.3.5). Only the second and subsequent array dimensions are significant in parameter types (8.3.4). [*Example:*

```
int f(char*);
int f(char[]);                    // same as f(char*);
int f(char[7]);                   // same as f(char*);
int f(char[9]);                   // same as f(char*);

int g(char(*)[10]);
int g(char[5][10]);               // same as g(char(*)[10]);
int g(char[7][10]);               // same as g(char(*)[10]);
int g(char(*)[20]);               // different from g(char(*)[10]);
```

—*end example*]

— Parameter declarations that differ only in that one is a function type and the other is a pointer to the same function type are equivalent. That is, the function type is adjusted to become a pointer to function type (8.3.5). [*Example:*

```
void h(int());
void h(int (*)());                // redeclaration of h(int())
void h(int x()) { }               // definition of h(int())
void h(int (*x)()) { }            // ill-formed: redefinition of h(int())
```

]

— Parameter declarations that differ only in the presence or absence of `const` and/or `volatile` are equivalent. That is, the `const` and `volatile` type-specifiers for each parameter type are ignored when determining which function is being declared, defined, or called. [*Example:*

```
typedef const int cInt;

int f (int);
int f (const int);                // redeclaration of f(int)
int f (int) { ... }               // definition of f(int)
int f (cInt) { ... }              // error: redefinition of f(int)
```

—*end example*]

Only the `const` and `volatile` type-specifiers at the outermost level of the parameter type specification are ignored in this fashion; `const` and `volatile` type-specifiers buried within a parameter type specification are significant and can be used to distinguish overloaded function declarations.[112] In particular, for any type T, "pointer to T," "pointer to `const` T," and "pointer to `volatile` T" are considered distinct parameter types, as are "reference to T," "reference to `const` T," and "reference to `volatile` T."

— Two parameter declarations that differ only in their default arguments are equivalent. [*Example:* consider the following:

```
void f (int i, int j);
void f (int i, int j = 99);       // OK: redeclaration of f(int, int)
void f (int i = 88, int j);       // OK: redeclaration of f(int, int)
void f ();                        // OK: overloaded declaration of f

void prog ()
{
    f (1, 2);                     // OK: call f(int, int)
    f (1);                        // OK: call f(int, int)
    f ();                         // Error: f(int, int) or f()?
}
```

—*end example*] —*end note*]

13.2 Declaration matching   [over.dcl]

1   Two function declarations of the same name refer to the same function if they are in the same scope and have equivalent parameter declarations (13.1). A function member of a derived class is *not* in the same scope as a function member of the same name in a base class. [*Example:*

```
class B {
public:
    int f(int);
};

class D : public B {
public:
    int f(char*);
};
```

Here `D::f(char*)` hides `B::f(int)` rather than overloading it.

```
void h(D* pd)
{
    pd->f(1);            // error:
                         // D::f(char*) hides B::f(int)
    pd->B::f(1);         // OK
    pd->f("Ben");        // OK, calls D::f
}
```

—*end example*]

2   A locally declared function is not in the same scope as a function in a containing scope. [*Example:*

---

[112] When a parameter type includes a function type, such as in the case of a parameter type that is a pointer to function, the `const` and `volatile` type-specifiers at the outermost level of the parameter type specifications for the inner function type are also ignored.

```
int f(char*);
void g()
{
    extern f(int);
    f("asdf");                          // error: f(int) hides f(char*)
                                        // so there is no f(char*) in this scope
}

void caller ()
{
    extern void callee(int, int);
    {
        extern void callee(int);        // hides callee(int, int)
        callee(88, 99);                 // error: only callee(int) in scope
    }
}
```

—*end example*]

3   Different versions of an overloaded member function can be given different access rules. [*Example:*

```
class buffer {
private:
    char* p;
    int size;

protected:
    buffer(int s, char* store) { size = s; p = store; }
    // ...

public:
    buffer(int s) { p = new char[size = s]; }
    // ...
};
```

—*end example*]

13.3 Overload resolution   **[over.match]**

1   Overload resolution is a mechanism for selecting the best function to call given a list of expressions that are to be the arguments of the call and a set of *candidate functions* that can be called based on the context of the call. The selection criteria for the best function are the number of arguments, how well the arguments match the types of the parameters of the candidate function, how well (for nonstatic member functions) the object matches the implied object parameter, and certain other properties of the candidate function. [*Note:* the function selected by overload resolution is not guaranteed to be appropriate for the context. Other restrictions, such as the accessibility of the function, can make its use in the calling context ill-formed.]

2   Overload resolution selects the function to call in seven distinct contexts within the language:

— invocation of a function named in the function call syntax (13.3.1.1.1);

— invocation of a function call operator, a pointer-to-function conversion function, a reference-to-pointer-to-function conversion function, or a reference-to-function conversion function on a class object named in the function call syntax (13.3.1.1.2);

— invocation of the operator referenced in an expression (13.3.1.2);

— invocation of a constructor for direct-initialization (8.5) of a class object (13.3.1.3);

— invocation of a user-defined conversion for copy-initialization (8.5) of a class object (13.3.1.4);

— invocation of a conversion function for initialization of an object of a nonclass type from an expression of class type (13.3.1.5); and

— invocation of a conversion function for conversion to an lvalue to which a reference (8.5.3) will be directly bound (13.3.1.6).

3   Each of these contexts defines the set of candidate functions and the list of arguments in its own unique way. But, once the candidate functions and argument lists have been identified, the selection of the best function is the same in all cases:

— First, a subset of the candidate functions—those that have the proper number of arguments and meet certain other conditions—is selected to form a set of viable functions (13.3.2).

— Then the best viable function is selected based on the implicit conversion sequences (13.3.3.1) needed to match each argument to the corresponding parameter of each viable function.

4   If a best viable function exists and is unique, overload resolution succeeds and produces it as the result. Otherwise overload resolution fails and the invocation is ill-formed. When overload resolution succeeds, and the best viable function is not accessible (clause 11) in the context in which it is used, the program is ill-formed.

13.3.1 Candidate functions and argument lists   [over.match.funcs]

1   The subclauses of 13.3.1 describe the set of candidate functions and the argument list submitted to overload resolution in each of the seven contexts in which overload resolution is used. The source transformations and constructions defined in these subclauses are only for the purpose of describing the overload resolution process. An implementation is not required to use such transformations and constructions.

2   The set of candidate functions can contain both member and non-member functions to be resolved against the same argument list. So that argument and parameter lists are comparable within this heterogeneous set, a member function is considered to have an extra parameter, called the *implicit object parameter*, which represents the object for which the member function has been called. For the purposes of overload resolution, both static and non-static member functions have an implicit object parameter, but constructors do not.

3   Similarly, when appropriate, the context can construct an argument list that contains an *implied object argument* to denote the object to be operated on. Since arguments and parameters are associated by position within their respective lists, the convention is that the implicit object parameter, if present, is always the first parameter and the implied object argument, if present, is always the first argument.

4   For non-static member functions, the type of the implicit object parameter is "reference to cv X" where X is the class of which the function is a member and *cv* is the cv-qualification on the member function declaration. [*Example:* for a `const` member function of class X, the extra parameter is assumed to have type "reference to `const` X".] For conversion functions, the function is considered to be a member of the class of the implicit object argument for the purpose of defining the type of the implicit object parameter. For non-conversion functions introduced by a *using-declaration* into a derived class, the function is considered to be a member of the derived class for the purpose of defining the type of the implicit object parameter. For static member functions, the implicit object parameter is considered to match any object (since if the function is selected, the object is discarded). [*Note:* no actual type is established for the implicit object parameter of a static member function, and no attempt will be made to determine a conversion sequence for that parameter (13.3.3).]

5   During overload resolution, the implied object argument is indistinguishable from other arguments. The implicit object parameter, however, retains its identity since conversions on the corresponding argument shall obey these additional rules:

— no temporary object can be introduced to hold the argument for the implicit object parameter;

— no user-defined conversions can be applied to achieve a type match with it; and

— even if the implicit object parameter is not `const`-qualified, an rvalue temporary can be bound to the parameter as long as in all other respects the temporary can be converted to the type of the implicit object parameter.

6   Because only one user-defined conversion is allowed in an implicit conversion sequence, special rules apply when selecting the best user-defined conversion (13.3.3, 13.3.3.1). [*Example:*

```
class T {
public:
        T();
        // ...
};

class C : T {
public:
        C(int);
        // ...
};
T a = 1;                        // ill-formed: T(C(1)) not tried
```

—*end example*]

7   In each case where a candidate is a function template, candidate function template specializations are generated using template argument deduction (14.8.3, 14.8.2). Those candidates are then handled as candidate functions in the usual way.[113] A given name can refer to one or more function templates and also to a set of overloaded non-template functions. In such a case, the candidate functions generated from each function template are combined with the set of non-template candidate functions.

13.3.1.1 Function call syntax   [over.match.call]

1   Recall from 5.2.2, that a *function call* is a *postfix-expression*, possibly nested arbitrarily deep in parentheses, followed by an optional *expression-list* enclosed in parentheses:

      (... ($_{opt}$ *postfix-expression*) ...) $_{opt}$ (*expression-list*$_{opt}$)

Overload resolution is required if the *postfix-expression* is the name of a function, a function template (14.5.5), an object of class type, or a set of pointers-to-function.

2   13.3.1.1.1 describes how overload resolution is used in the first two of the above cases to determine the function to call. 13.3.1.1.2 describes how overload resolution is used in the third of the above cases to determine the function to call.

3   The fourth case arises from a *postfix-expression* of the form &F, where F names a set of overloaded functions. In the context of a function call, the set of functions named by F shall contain only non-member functions and static member functions[114]. And in this context using &F behaves the same as using the name F by itself. Thus, (&F) (*expression-list*$_{opt}$) is simply (F) (*expression-list*$_{opt}$), which is discussed in 13.3.1.1.1. (The resolution of &F in other contexts is described in 13.4.)

---

[113] The process of argument deduction fully determines the parameter types of the function template specializations, i.e., the parameters of function template specializations contain no template parameter types. Therefore the function template specializations can be treated as normal (non-template) functions for the remainder of overload resolution.

[114] If F names a non-static member function, &F is a pointer-to-member, which cannot be used with the function call syntax.

13.3.1.1.1 Call to named function [over.call.func]

1   Of interest in 13.3.1.1.1 are only those function calls in which the *postfix-expression* ultimately contains a name that denotes one or more functions that might be called. Such a *postfix-expression*, perhaps nested arbitrarily deep in parentheses, has one of the following forms:

> *postfix-expression:*
>> *postfix-expression* . *id-expression*
>> *postfix-expression* -> *id-expression*
>> *primary-expression*

These represent two syntactic subcategories of function calls: qualified function calls and unqualified function calls.

2   In qualified function calls, the name to be resolved is an *id-expression* and is preceded by an -> or . operator. Since the construct A->B is generally equivalent to (*A).B, the rest of clause 13 assumes, without loss of generality, that all member function calls have been normalized to the form that uses an object and the . operator. Furthermore, clause 13 assumes that the *postfix-expression* that is the left operand of the . operator has type "*cv* T" where T denotes a class[115]. Under this assumption, the *id-expression* in the call is looked up as a member function of T following the rules for looking up names in classes (10.2). If a member function is found, that function and its overloaded declarations constitute the set of candidate functions. The argument list is the *expression-list* in the call augmented by the addition of the left operand of the . operator in the normalized member function call as the implied object argument (13.3.1).

3   In unqualified function calls, the name is not qualified by an -> or . operator and has the more general form of a *primary-expression*. The name is looked up in the context of the function call following the normal rules for name lookup in function calls (3.4.2). If the name resolves to a non-member function declaration, that function and its overloaded declarations constitute the set of candidate functions[116]. The argument list is the same as the *expression-list* in the call. If the name resolves to a nonstatic member function, then the function call is actually a member function call. If the keyword this (9.3.2) is in scope and refers to the class of that member function, or a derived class thereof, then the function call is transformed into a normalized qualified function call using (*this) as the *postfix-expression* to the left of the . operator. The candidate functions and argument list are as described for qualified function calls above. If the keyword this is not in scope or refers to another class, then name resolution found a static member of some class T. In this case, all overloaded declarations of the function name in T become candidate functions and a contrived object of type T becomes the implied object argument[117]. The call is ill-formed, however, if overload resolution selects one of the non-static member functions of T in this case.

13.3.1.1.2 Call to object of class type [over.call.object]

1   If the *primary-expression* E in the function call syntax evaluates to a class object of type "*cv* T", then the set of candidate functions includes at least the function call operators of T. The function call operators of T are obtained by ordinary lookup of the name operator() in the context of (E).operator().

2   In addition, for each conversion function declared in T of the form

> operator *conversion-type-id* () *cv-qualifier*;

where *cv-qualifier* is the same cv-qualification as, or a greater cv-qualification than, *cv*, and where *conversion-type-id* denotes the type "pointer to function of (P1,...,Pn) returning R", or the type "reference to pointer to function of (P1,...,Pn) returning R", or the type "reference to function of (P1,...,Pn) returning R", a *surrogate call function* with the unique name *call-function* and having the form

---

[115] Note that cv-qualifiers on the type of objects are significant in overload resolution for both lvalue and class rvalue objects.
[116] Because of the usual name hiding rules, these will be introduced by declarations or by *using-directive*s all found in the same block or all found at namespace scope.
[117] An implied object argument must be contrived to correspond to the implicit object parameter attributed to member functions during overload resolution. It is not used in the call to the selected function. Since the member functions all have the same implicit object parameter, the contrived object will not be the cause to select or reject a function.

```
R call-function (conversion-type-id F, P1 a1,...,Pn an) { return F (a1,...,an); }
```

is also considered as a candidate function. Similarly, surrogate call functions are added to the set of candidate functions for each conversion function declared in an accessible base class provided the function is not hidden within T by another intervening declaration[118].

3   If such a surrogate call function is selected by overload resolution, its body, as defined above, will be executed to convert E to the appropriate function and then to invoke that function with the arguments of the call.

4   The argument list submitted to overload resolution consists of the argument expressions present in the function call syntax preceded by the implied object argument (E). [*Note:* when comparing the call against the function call operators, the implied object argument is compared against the implicit object parameter of the function call operator. When comparing the call against a surrogate call function, the implied object argument is compared against the first parameter of the surrogate call function. The conversion function from which the surrogate call function was derived will be used in the conversion sequence for that parameter since it converts the implied object argument to the appropriate function pointer or reference required by that first parameter.] [*Example:*

```
int f1(int);
int f2(float);
typedef int (*fp1)(int);
typedef int (*fp2)(float);
struct A {
    operator fp1() { return f1; }
    operator fp2() { return f2; }
} a;
int i = a(1);                      // Calls f1 via pointer returned from
                                   // conversion function
```

—*end example*]

13.3.1.2 Operators in expressions   [over.match.oper]

1   If no operand of an operator in an expression has a type that is a class or an enumeration, the operator is assumed to be a built-in operator and interpreted according to clause 5. [*Note:* because ., .*, and :: cannot be overloaded, these operators are always built-in operators interpreted according to clause 5. ?: cannot be overloaded, but the rules in this subclause are used to determine the conversions to be applied to the second and third operands when they have class or enumeration type (5.16).] [*Example:*

---

[118] Note that this construction can yield candidate call functions that cannot be differentiated one from the other by overload resolution because they have identical declarations or differ only in their return type. The call will be ambiguous if overload resolution cannot select a match to the call that is uniquely better than such undifferentiable functions.

```
class String {
public:
    String (const String&);
    String (char*);
        operator char* ();
};
String operator + (const String&, const String&);

void f(void)
{
    char* p= "one" + "two";        // ill-formed because neither
                                   // operand has user defined type
    int I = 1 + 1;                 // Always evaluates to 2 even if
                                   // user defined types exist which
                                   // would perform the operation.

}
```

—*end example*]

2   If either operand has a type that is a class or an enumeration, a user-defined operator function might be declared that implements this operator or a user-defined conversion can be necessary to convert the operand to a type that is appropriate for a built-in operator. In this case, overload resolution is used to determine which operator function or built-in operator is to be invoked to implement the operator. Therefore, the operator notation is first transformed to the equivalent function-call notation as summarized in Table 8 (where @ denotes one of the operators covered in the specified subclause).

Table 8—relationship between operator and function call notation

Subclause	Expression	As member function	As non-member function
13.5.1	@a	(a).operator@ ()	operator@ (a)
13.5.2	a@b	(a).operator@ (b)	operator@ (a, b)
13.5.3	a=b	(a).operator= (b)	
13.5.5	a[b]	(a).operator[](b)	
13.5.6	a->	(a).operator-> ()	
13.5.7	a@	(a).operator@ (0)	operator@ (a, 0)

3   For a unary operator @ with an operand of a type whose cv-unqualified version is T1, and for a binary operator @ with a left operand of a type whose cv-unqualified version is T1 and a right operand of a type whose cv-unqualified version is T2, three sets of candidate functions, designated *member candidates*, *non-member candidates* and *built-in candidates*, are constructed as follows:

— If T1 is a class type, the set of member candidates is the result of the qualified lookup of T1::operator@ (13.3.1.1.1); otherwise, the set of member candidates is empty.

— The set of non-member candidates is the result of the unqualified lookup of operator@ in the context of the expression according to the usual rules for name lookup in unqualified function calls (3.4.2) except that all member functions are ignored. However, if no operand has a class type, only those non-member functions in the lookup set that have a first parameter of type T1 or "reference to (possibly cv-qualified) T1", when T1 is an enumeration type, or (if there is a right operand) a second parameter of type T2 or "reference to (possibly cv-qualified) T2", when T2 is an enumeration type, are candidate functions.

— For the operator , , the unary operator &, or the operator ->, the built-in candidates set is empty. For all other operators, the built-in candidates include all of the candidate operator functions defined in 13.6 that, compared to the given operator,

— have the same operator name, and

— accept the same number of operands, and

— accept operand types to which the given operand or operands can be converted according to 13.3.3.1, and

— do not have the same parameter type list as any non-template non-member candidate.

4   For the built-in assignment operators, conversions of the left operand are restricted as follows:

— no temporaries are introduced to hold the left operand, and

— no user-defined conversions are applied to the left operand to achieve a type match with the left-most parameter of a built-in candidate.

5   For all other operators, no such restrictions apply.

6   The set of candidate functions for overload resolution is the union of the member candidates, the non-member candidates, and the built-in candidates. The argument list contains all of the operands of the operator. The best function from the set of candidate functions is selected according to 13.3.2 and 13.3.3.[119)]
[*Example:*

```
struct A {
    operator int();
};
A operator+(const A&, const A&);
void m() {
    A a, b;
    a + b;                       // operator+(a,b) chosen over int(a) + int(b)
}
```

—*end example*]

7   If a built-in candidate is selected by overload resolution, the operands are converted to the types of the corresponding parameters of the selected operation function. Then the operator is treated as the corresponding built-in operator and interpreted according to clause 5.

8   The second operand of operator -> is ignored in selecting an operator-> function, and is not an argument when the operator-> function is called. When operator-> returns, the operator -> is applied to the value returned, with the original second operand.[120)]

9   If the operator is the operator , , the unary operator &, or the operator ->, and there are no viable functions, then the operator is assumed to be the built-in operator and interpreted according to clause 5.

10   [*Note:* the lookup rules for operators in expressions are different than the lookup rules for operator function names in a function call, as shown in the following example:

[119)] If the set of candidate functions is empty, overload resolution is unsuccessful.
[120)] If the value returned by the operator-> function has class type, this may result in selecting and calling another operator-> function. The process repeats until an operator-> function returns a value of non-class type.

```
struct A { };
void operator + (A, A);

struct B {
  void operator + (B);
  void f ();
};

A a;

void B::f() {
  operator+ (a,a);          // ERROR – global operator hidden by member
  a + a;                    // OK – calls global operator+
}
```

—end note]

13.3.1.3 Initialization by constructor   [over.match.ctor]

1   When objects of class type are direct-initialized (8.5), or copy-initialized from an expression of the same or a derived class type (8.5), overload resolution selects the constructor. For direct-initialization, the candidate functions are all the constructors of the class of the object being initialized. For copy-initialization, the candidate functions are all the converting constructors (12.3.1) of that class. The argument list is the *expression-list* within the parentheses of the initializer.

13.3.1.4 Copy-initialization of class by user-defined conversion   [over.match.copy]

1   Under the conditions specified in 8.5, as part of a copy-initialization of an object of class type, a user-defined conversion can be invoked to convert an initializer expression to the type of the object being initialized. Overload resolution is used to select the user-defined conversion to be invoked. Assuming that "*cv1* T" is the type of the object being initialized, with T a class type, the candidate functions are selected as follows:

— The converting constructors (12.3.1) of T are candidate functions.

— When the type of the initializer expression is a class type "*cv* S", the conversion functions of S and its base classes are considered. Those that are not hidden within S and yield a type whose cv-unqualified version is the same type as T or is a derived class thereof are candidate functions. Conversion functions that return "reference to X" return lvalues of type X and are therefore considered to yield X for this process of selecting candidate functions.

2   In both cases, the argument list has one argument, which is the initializer expression. [*Note:* this argument will be compared against the first parameter of the constructors and against the implicit object parameter of the conversion functions.]

13.3.1.5 Initialization by conversion function   [over.match.conv]

1   Under the conditions specified in 8.5, as part of an initialization of an object of nonclass type, a conversion function can be invoked to convert an initializer expression of class type to the type of the object being initialized. Overload resolution is used to select the conversion function to be invoked. Assuming that "*cv1* T" is the type of the object being initialized, and "*cv* S" is the type of the initializer expression, with S a class type, the candidate functions are selected as follows:

— The conversion functions of S and its base classes are considered. Those that are not hidden within S and yield type T or a type that can be converted to type T via a standard conversion sequence (13.3.3.1.1) are candidate functions. Conversion functions that return a cv-qualified type are considered to yield the cv-unqualified version of that type for this process of selecting candidate functions. Conversion functions that return "reference to *cv2* X" return lvalues of type "*cv2* X" and are therefore considered to yield X for this process of selecting candidate functions.

2   The argument list has one argument, which is the initializer expression. [*Note:* this argument will be compared against the implicit object parameter of the conversion functions.]

13.3.1.6 Initialization by conversion function for direct reference binding   [over.match.ref]

1   Under the conditions specified in 8.5.3, a reference can be bound directly to an lvalue that is the result of applying a conversion function to an initializer expression. Overload resolution is used to select the conversion function to be invoked. Assuming that "*cv1* T" is the underlying type of the reference being initialized, and "*cv* S" is the type of the initializer expression, with S a class type, the candidate functions are selected as follows:

— The conversion functions of S and its base classes are considered. Those that are not hidden within S and yield type "reference to *cv2* T2", where "*cv1* T" is reference-compatible (8.5.3) with "*cv2* T2", are candidate functions.

2   The argument list has one argument, which is the initializer expression. [*Note:* this argument will be compared against the implicit object parameter of the conversion functions.]

13.3.2 Viable functions   [over.match.viable]

1   From the set of candidate functions constructed for a given context (13.3.1), a set of viable functions is chosen, from which the best function will be selected by comparing argument conversion sequences for the best fit (13.3.3). The selection of viable functions considers relationships between arguments and function parameters other than the ranking of conversion sequences.

2   First, to be a viable function, a candidate function shall have enough parameters to agree in number with the arguments in the list.

— If there are m arguments in the list, all candidate functions having exactly m parameters are viable.

— A candidate function having fewer than m parameters is viable only if it has an ellipsis in its parameter list (8.3.5). For the purposes of overload resolution, any argument for which there is no corresponding parameter is considered to ''match the ellipsis'' (13.3.3.1.3) .

— A candidate function having more than m parameters is viable only if the *(m+1)*–st parameter has a default argument (8.3.6).[121] For the purposes of overload resolution, the parameter list is truncated on the right, so that there are exactly m parameters.

3   Second, for F to be a viable function, there shall exist for each argument an *implicit conversion sequence* (13.3.3.1) that converts that argument to the corresponding parameter of F. If the parameter has reference type, the implicit conversion sequence includes the operation of binding the reference, and the fact that a reference to non-const cannot be bound to an rvalue can affect the viability of the function (see 13.3.3.1.4).

13.3.3 Best Viable Function   [over.match.best]

1   Define ICS*i*(F) as follows:

— if F is a static member function, ICS*1*(F) is defined such that ICS*1*(F) is neither better nor worse than ICS*1*(G) for any function G, and, symmetrically, ICS*1*(G) is neither better nor worse than ICS*1*(F)[122]; otherwise,

— let ICS*i*(F) denote the implicit conversion sequence that converts the *i*-th argument in the list to the type

---

[121] According to 8.3.6, parameters following the *(m+1)*–st parameter must also have default arguments.

[122] If a function is a static member function, this definition means that the first argument, the implied object parameter, has no effect in the determination of whether the function is better or worse than any other function.

of the *i*-th parameter of viable function F. 13.3.3.1 defines the implicit conversion sequences and 13.3.3.2 defines what it means for one implicit conversion sequence to be a better conversion sequence or worse conversion sequence than another.

Given these definitions, a viable function F1 is defined to be a *better* function than another viable function F2 if for all arguments *i*, ICS*i*(F1) is not a worse conversion sequence than ICS*i*(F2), and then

— for some argument *j*, ICS*j*(F1) is a better conversion sequence than ICS*j*(F2), or, if not that,

— F1 is a non-template function and F2 is a function template specialization, or, if not that,

— F1 and F2 are function template specializations, and the function template for F1 is more specialized than the template for F2 according to the partial ordering rules described in 14.5.5.2, or, if not that,

— the context is an initialization by user-defined conversion (see 8.5, 13.3.1.5, and 13.3.1.6) and the standard conversion sequence from the return type of F1 to the destination type (i.e., the type of the entity being initialized) is a better conversion sequence than the standard conversion sequence from the return type of F2 to the destination type. [*Example:*

```
struct A {
    A();
    operator int();
    operator double();
} a;
int i = a;          // a.operator int() followed by no conversion
                    // is better than a.operator double() followed by
                    // a conversion to int
float x = a;        // ambiguous: both possibilities require conversions,
                    // and neither is better than the other
```

—*end example*]

2   If there is exactly one viable function that is a better function than all other viable functions, then it is the one selected by overload resolution; otherwise the call is ill-formed[123].

---

[123] The algorithm for selecting the best viable function is linear in the number of viable functions. Run a simple tournament to find a function W that is not worse than any opponent it faced. Although another function F that W did not face might be at least as good as W, F cannot be the best function because at some point in the tournament F encountered another function G such that F was not better than G. Hence, W is either the best function or there is no best function. So, make a second pass over the viable functions to verify that W is better than all other functions.

3   [*Example:*

```
void Fcn(const int*,  short);
void Fcn(int*, int);

int i;
short s = 0;

void f() {
  Fcn(&i, s);                    // is ambiguous because
                                 // &i → int* is better than &i → const int*
                                 // but s → short is also better than s → int

    Fcn(&i, 1L);                 // calls Fcn(int*, int), because
                                 // &i → int* is better than &i → const int*
                                 // and 1L → short and 1L → int are indistinguishable

    Fcn(&i,'c');                 // calls Fcn(int*, int), because
                                 // &i → int* is better than &i → const int*
                                 // and c → int is better than c → short

}
```

—*end example*]

4   If the best viable function resolves to a function for which multiple declarations were found, and if at least
two of these declarations – or the declarations they refer to in the case of *using-declaration*s – specify a
default argument that made the function viable, the program is ill-formed. [*Example:*

```
namespace A {
    extern "C" void f(int = 5);
}
namespace B {
    extern "C" void f(int = 5);
}

using A::f;
using B::f;

void use() {
    f(3);                        // OK, default argument was not used for viability
    f();                         // Error: found default argument twice
}
```

—*end example*]

13.3.3.1 Implicit conversion sequences   [over.best.ics]

1   An *implicit conversion sequence* is a sequence of conversions used to convert an argument in a function
call to the type of the corresponding parameter of the function being called. The sequence of conversions is
an implicit conversion as defined in clause 4, which means it is governed by the rules for initialization of an
object or reference by a single expression (8.5, 8.5.3).

2   Implicit conversion sequences are concerned only with the type, cv-qualification, and lvalue-ness of the
argument and how these are converted to match the corresponding properties of the parameter. Other properties, such as the lifetime, storage class, alignment, or accessibility of the argument and whether or not the
argument is a bit-field are ignored. So, although an implicit conversion sequence can be defined for a given
argument-parameter pair, the conversion from the argument to the parameter might still be ill-formed in the
final analysis.

3   A well-formed implicit conversion sequence is one of the following forms:

— a *standard conversion sequence* (13.3.3.1.1),

— a *user-defined conversion sequence* (13.3.3.1.2), or

— an *ellipsis conversion sequence* (13.3.3.1.3).

4 However, when considering the argument of a user-defined conversion function that is a candidate by 13.3.1.3 when invoked for the copying of the temporary in the second step of a class copy-initialization, or by 13.3.1.4, 13.3.1.5, or 13.3.1.6 in all cases, only standard conversion sequences and ellipsis conversion sequences are allowed.

5 For the case where the parameter type is a reference, see 13.3.3.1.4.

6 When the parameter type is not a reference, the implicit conversion sequence models a copy-initialization of the parameter from the argument expression. The implicit conversion sequence is the one required to convert the argument expression to an rvalue of the type of the parameter. [*Note:* when the parameter has a class type, this is a conceptual conversion defined for the purposes of clause 13; the actual initialization is defined in terms of constructors and is not a conversion.] Any difference in top-level cv-qualification is subsumed by the initialization itself and does not constitute a conversion. [*Example:* a parameter of type A can be initialized from an argument of type const A. The implicit conversion sequence for that case is the identity sequence; it contains no "conversion" from const A to A.] When the parameter has a class type and the argument expression has the same type, the implicit conversion sequence is an identity conversion. When the parameter has a class type and the argument expression has a derived class type, the implicit conversion sequence is a derived-to-base Conversion from the derived class to the base class. [*Note:* there is no such standard conversion; this derived-to-base Conversion exists only in the description of implicit conversion sequences.] A derived-to-base Conversion has Conversion rank (13.3.3.1.1).

7 In all contexts, when converting to the implicit object parameter or when converting to the left operand of an assignment operation only standard conversion sequences that create no temporary object for the result are allowed.

8 If no conversions are required to match an argument to a parameter type, the implicit conversion sequence is the standard conversion sequence consisting of the identity conversion (13.3.3.1.1).

9 If no sequence of conversions can be found to convert an argument to a parameter type or the conversion is otherwise ill-formed, an implicit conversion sequence cannot be formed.

10 If several different sequences of conversions exist that each convert the argument to the parameter type, the implicit conversion sequence associated with the parameter is defined to be the unique conversion sequence designated the *ambiguous conversion sequence*. For the purpose of ranking implicit conversion sequences as described in 13.3.3.2, the ambiguous conversion sequence is treated as a user-defined sequence that is indistinguishable from any other user-defined conversion sequence[124]. If a function that uses the

---

[124] The ambiguous conversion sequence is ranked with user-defined conversion sequences because multiple conversion sequences for an argument can exist only if they involve different user-defined conversions. The ambiguous conversion sequence is indistinguishable from any other user-defined conversion sequence because it represents at least two user-defined conversion sequences, each with a different user-defined conversion, and any other user-defined conversion sequence must be indistinguishable from at least one of them.

This rule prevents a function from becoming non-viable because of an ambiguous conversion sequence for one of its parameters. Consider this example,

```
class B;
class A { A (B&); };
class B { operator A (); };
class C { C (B&); };
void f(A) { }
void f(C) { }
B b;
f(b);                           // ambiguous because b -> C via constructor and
                                // b → A via constructor or conversion function.
```

If it were not for this rule, f (A) would be eliminated as a viable function for the call f (b) causing overload resolution to select f (C) as the function to call even though it is not clearly the best choice. On the other hand, if an f (B) were to be declared then f (b) would resolve to that f (B) because the exact match with f (B) is better than any of the sequences required to match f (A).

ambiguous conversion sequence is selected as the best viable function, the call will be ill-formed because the conversion of one of the arguments in the call is ambiguous.

11   The three forms of implicit conversion sequences mentioned above are defined in the following subclauses.

13.3.3.1.1 Standard conversion sequences   [over.ics.scs]

1   Table 9 summarizes the conversions defined in clause 4 and partitions them into four disjoint categories: Lvalue Transformation, Qualification Adjustment, Promotion, and Conversion. [*Note:* these categories are orthogonal with respect to lvalue-ness, cv-qualification, and data representation: the Lvalue Transformations do not change the cv-qualification or data representation of the type; the Qualification Adjustments do not change the lvalue-ness or data representation of the type; and the Promotions and Conversions do not change the lvalue-ness or cv-qualification of the type.]

2   [*Note:* As described in clause 4, a standard conversion sequence is either the Identity conversion by itself (that is, no conversion) or consists of one to three conversions from the other four categories. At most one conversion from each category is allowed in a single standard conversion sequence. If there are two or more conversions in the sequence, the conversions are applied in the canonical order: **Lvalue Transformation**, **Promotion** or **Conversion**, **Qualification Adjustment**. —*end note*]

3   Each conversion in Table 9 also has an associated rank (Exact Match, Promotion, or Conversion). These are used to rank standard conversion sequences (13.3.3.2). The rank of a conversion sequence is determined by considering the rank of each conversion in the sequence and the rank of any reference binding (13.3.3.1.4). If any of those has Conversion rank, the sequence has Conversion rank; otherwise, if any of those has Promotion rank, the sequence has Promotion rank; otherwise, the sequence has Exact Match rank.

Table 9—conversions

Conversion	Category	Rank	Subclause
No conversions required	Identity		
Lvalue-to-rvalue conversion			4.1
Array-to-pointer conversion	Lvalue Transformation	Exact Match	4.2
Function-to-pointer conversion			4.3
Qualification conversions	Qualification Adjustment		4.4
Integral promotions	Promotion	Promotion	4.5
Floating point promotion			4.6
Integral conversions			4.7
Floating point conversions			4.8
Floating-integral conversions	Conversion	Conversion	4.9
Pointer conversions			4.10
Pointer to member conversions			4.11
Boolean conversions			4.12

13.3.3.1.2 User-defined conversion sequences [over.ics.user]

1   A user-defined conversion sequence consists of an initial standard conversion sequence followed by a user-defined conversion (12.3) followed by a second standard conversion sequence. If the user-defined conversion is specified by a constructor (12.3.1), the initial standard conversion sequence converts the source type to the type required by the argument of the constructor. If the user-defined conversion is specified by a conversion function (12.3.2), the initial standard conversion sequence converts the source type to the implicit object parameter of the conversion function.

2   The second standard conversion sequence converts the result of the user-defined conversion to the target type for the sequence. Since an implicit conversion sequence is an initialization, the special rules for initialization by user-defined conversion apply when selecting the best user-defined conversion for a user-defined conversion sequence (see 13.3.3 and 13.3.3.1).

3   If the user-defined conversion is specified by a template conversion function, the second standard conversion sequence must have exact match rank.

4   A conversion of an expression of class type to the same class type is given Exact Match rank, and a conversion of an expression of class type to a base class of that type is given Conversion rank, in spite of the fact that a copy constructor (i.e., a user-defined conversion function) is called for those cases.

13.3.3.1.3 Ellipsis conversion sequences [over.ics.ellipsis]

1   An ellipsis conversion sequence occurs when an argument in a function call is matched with the ellipsis parameter specification of the function called.

13.3.3.1.4 Reference binding [over.ics.ref]

1   When a parameter of reference type binds directly (8.5.3) to an argument expression, the implicit conversion sequence is the identity conversion, unless the argument expression has a type that is a derived class of the parameter type, in which case the implicit conversion sequence is a derived-to-base Conversion (13.3.3.1). [*Example:*

```
struct A {};
struct B : public A {} b;
int f(A&);
int f(B&);
int i = f(b);              // Calls f(B&), an exact match, rather than
                           // f(A&), a conversion
```

—*end example*] If the parameter binds directly to the result of applying a conversion function to the argument expression, the implicit conversion sequence is a user-defined conversion sequence (13.3.3.1.2), with the second standard conversion sequence either an identity conversion or, if the conversion function returns an entity of a type that is a derived class of the parameter type, a derived-to-base Conversion.

2   When a parameter of reference type is not bound directly to an argument expression, the conversion sequence is the one required to convert the argument expression to the underlying type of the reference according to 13.3.3.1. Conceptually, this conversion sequence corresponds to copy-initializing a temporary of the underlying type with the argument expression. Any difference in top-level cv-qualification is subsumed by the initialization itself and does not constitute a conversion.

3   A standard conversion sequence cannot be formed if it requires binding a reference to non-const to an rvalue (except when binding an implicit object parameter; see the special rules for that case in 13.3.1). [*Note:* this means, for example, that a candidate function cannot be a viable function if it has a non-const reference parameter (other than the implicit object parameter) and the corresponding argument is a temporary or would require one to be created to initialize the reference (see 8.5.3).]

4   Other restrictions on binding a reference to a particular argument do not affect the formation of a standard conversion sequence, however. [*Example:* a function with a "reference to int" parameter can be a viable

candidate even if the corresponding argument is an `int` bit-field. The formation of implicit conversion sequences treats the `int` bit-field as an `int` lvalue and finds an exact match with the parameter. If the function is selected by overload resolution, the call will nonetheless be ill-formed because of the prohibition on binding a non-`const` reference to a bit-field (8.5.3).]

5   The binding of a reference to an expression that is *reference-compatible with added qualification* influences the rank of a standard conversion; see 13.3.3.2 and 8.5.3.

13.3.3.2 Ranking implicit conversion sequences   [over.ics.rank]

1   13.3.3.2 defines a partial ordering of implicit conversion sequences based on the relationships *better conversion sequence* and *better conversion*. If an implicit conversion sequence S1 is defined by these rules to be a better conversion sequence than S2, then it is also the case that S2 is a *worse conversion sequence* than S1. If conversion sequence S1 is neither better than nor worse than conversion sequence S2, S1 and S2 are said to be *indistinguishable conversion sequences*.

2   When comparing the basic forms of implicit conversion sequences (as defined in 13.3.3.1)

— a standard conversion sequence (13.3.3.1.1) is a better conversion sequence than a user-defined conversion sequence or an ellipsis conversion sequence, and

— a user-defined conversion sequence (13.3.3.1.2) is a better conversion sequence than an ellipsis conversion sequence (13.3.3.1.3).

3   Two implicit conversion sequences of the same form are indistinguishable conversion sequences unless one of the following rules apply:

— Standard conversion sequence S1 is a better conversion sequence than standard conversion sequence S2 if

— S1 is a proper subsequence of S2 (comparing the conversion sequences in the canonical form defined by 13.3.3.1.1, excluding any Lvalue Transformation; the identity conversion sequence is considered to be a subsequence of any non-identity conversion sequence) or, if not that,

— the rank of S1 is better than the rank of S2, or S1 and S2 have the same rank and are distinguishable by the rules in the paragraph below, or, if not that,

— S1 and S2 differ only in their qualification conversion and yield similar types T1 and T2 (4.4), respectively, and the cv-qualification signature of type T1 is a proper subset of the cv-qualification signature of type T2, and S1 is not the deprecated string literal array-to-pointer conversion (4.2). [*Example:*

```
int f(const int *);
int f(int *);
int i;
int j = f(&i);                     // Calls f(int *)
```

—*end example*] or, if not that,

— S1 and S2 are reference bindings (8.5.3), and the types to which the references refer are the same type except for top-level cv-qualifiers, and the type to which the reference initialized by S2 refers is more cv-qualified than the type to which the reference initialized by S1 refers. [*Example:*

```
int f(const int &);
int f(int &);
int g(const int &);
int g(int);

int i;
int j = f(i);                      // Calls f(int &)
int k = g(i);                      // ambiguous
```

```
class X {
public:
    void f() const;
    void f();
};
void g(const X& a, X b)
{
    a.f();                          // Calls X::f() const
    b.f();                          // Calls X::f()
}
```

—*end example*]

— User-defined conversion sequence U1 is a better conversion sequence than another user-defined conversion sequence U2 if they contain the same user-defined conversion function or constructor and if the second standard conversion sequence of U1 is better than the second standard conversion sequence of U2. [*Example:*

```
struct A {
    operator short();
} a;
int f(int);
int f(float);
int i = f(a);                   // Calls f(int), because short → int is
                                // better than short → float.
```

—*end example*]

4   Standard conversion sequences are ordered by their ranks: an Exact Match is a better conversion than a Promotion, which is a better conversion than a Conversion. Two conversion sequences with the same rank are indistinguishable unless one of the following rules applies:

— A conversion that is not a conversion of a pointer, or pointer to member, to bool is better than another conversion that is such a conversion.

— If class B is derived directly or indirectly from class A, conversion of B* to A* is better than conversion of B* to void*, and conversion of A* to void* is better than conversion of B* to void*.

— If class B is derived directly or indirectly from class A and class C is derived directly or indirectly from B,

— conversion of C* to B* is better than conversion of C* to A*, [*Example:*

```
struct A {};
struct B : public A {};
struct C : public B {};
C *pc;
int f(A *);
int f(B *);
int i = f(pc);                  // Calls f(B *)
```

—*end example*]

— binding of an expression of type C to a reference of type B& is better than binding an expression of type C to a reference of type A&,

— conversion of A::* to B::* is better than conversion of A::* to C::*,

— conversion of C to B is better than conversion of C to A,

— conversion of B* to A* is better than conversion of C* to A*,

— binding of an expression of type B to a reference of type A& is better than binding an expression of type C to a reference of type A&,

— conversion of B::* to C::* is better than conversion of A::* to C::*, and

— conversion of B to A is better than conversion of C to A.

[*Note:* compared conversion sequences will have different source types only in the context of comparing the second standard conversion sequence of an initialization by user-defined conversion (see 13.3.3); in all other contexts, the source types will be the same and the target types will be different.]

13.4 Address of overloaded function   [over.over]

1   A use of an overloaded function name without arguments is resolved in certain contexts to a function, a pointer to function or a pointer to member function for a specific function from the overload set. A function template name is considered to name a set of overloaded functions in such contexts. The function selected is the one whose type matches the target type required in the context. The target can be

— an object or reference being initialized (8.5, 8.5.3),

— the left side of an assignment (5.17),

— a parameter of a function (5.2.2),

— a parameter of a user-defined operator (13.5),

— the return value of a function, operator function, or conversion (6.6.3),

— an explicit type conversion (5.2.3, 5.2.9, 5.4), or

— a non-type *template-parameter* (14.3.2).

The overloaded function name can be preceded by the & operator. An overloaded function name shall not be used without arguments in contexts other than those listed. [*Note:* any redundant set of parentheses surrounding the overloaded function name is ignored (5.1).]

2   If the name is a function template, template argument deduction is done (14.8.2.2), and if the argument deduction succeeds, the resulting template argument list is used to generate a single function template specialization, which is added to the set of overloaded functions considered.

3   Non-member functions and static member functions match targets of type "pointer-to-function" or "reference-to-function." Nonstatic member functions match targets of type "pointer-to-member-function;" the function type of the pointer to member is used to select the member function from the set of overloaded member functions. If a nonstatic member function is selected, the reference to the overloaded function name is required to have the form of a pointer to member as described in 5.3.1.

4   If more than one function is selected, any function template specializations in the set are eliminated if the set also contains a non-template function, and any given function template specialization F1 is eliminated if the set contains a second function template specialization whose function template is more specialized than the function template of F1 according to the partial ordering rules of 14.5.5.2. After such eliminations, if any, there shall remain exactly one selected function.

5   [*Example:*

```
int f(double);
int f(int);
int (*pfd)(double) = &f;        // selects f(double)
int (*pfi)(int) = &f;           // selects f(int)
int (*pfe)(...) = &f;           // error: type mismatch
int (&rfi)(int) = f;            // selects f(int)
int (&rfd)(double) = f;         // selects f(double)
void g() {
   (int (*)(int))&f;            // cast expression as selector
}
```

The initialization of pfe is ill-formed because no f() with type int(...) has been defined, and not because of any ambiguity. For another example,

```
struct X {
    int f(int);
    static int f(long);
};

int (X::*p1)(int)  = &X::f;      // OK
int    (*p2)(int)  = &X::f;      // error: mismatch
int    (*p3)(long) = &X::f;      // OK
int (X::*p4)(long) = &X::f;      // error: mismatch
int (X::*p5)(int)  = &(X::f);    // error: wrong syntax for
                                 // pointer to member
int    (*p6)(long) = &(X::f);    // OK
```

—end example]

6   [*Note:* if f() and g() are both overloaded functions, the cross product of possibilities must be considered to resolve f(&g), or the equivalent expression f(g).]

7   [*Note:* there are no standard conversions (clause 4) of one pointer-to-function type into another. In particular, even if B is a public base of D, we have

```
D* f();
B* (*p1)() = &f;                 // error

void g(D*);
void (*p2)(B*) = &g;             // error
```

—end note]

13.5 Overloaded operators   [over.oper]

1   A function declaration having one of the following *operator-function-id*s as its name declares an *operator function*. An operator function is said to *implement* the operator named in its *operator-function-id*.

operator-function-id:
        operator *operator*
        operator *operator* < *template-argument-list*$_{opt}$ >

operator: one of
        new   delete   new[]   delete[]
        +   -   *   /   %   ^   & | ~
        !   =   <   >   +=   -=   *=   /=   %=
        ^=   &= |=   <<   >>   >>= <<= ==   !=
        <=   >=   && || ++   --   ,   ->* ->
        ()   []

[*Note:* the last two operators are function call (5.2.2) and subscripting (5.2.1). The operators new[], delete[], (), and [] are formed from more than one token.]

2   Both the unary and binary forms of

        +   -   *   &

can be overloaded.

3   The following operators cannot be overloaded:

        .   .*   ::   ?:

nor can the preprocessing symbols # and ## (clause 16).

4   Operator functions are usually not called directly; instead they are invoked to evaluate the operators they implement (13.5.1 - 13.5.7). They can be explicitly called, however, using the *operator-function-id* as the name of the function in the function call syntax (5.2.2). [*Example:*

```
complex z = a.operator+(b);      // complex z = a+b;
void* p = operator new(sizeof(int)*n);
```

—end example]

5   The allocation and deallocation functions, `operator new`, `operator new[]`, `operator delete` and `operator delete[]`, are described completely in 3.7.3. The attributes and restrictions found in the rest of this subclause do not apply to them unless explicitly stated in 3.7.3.

6   An operator function shall either be a non-static member function or be a non-member function and have at least one parameter whose type is a class, a reference to a class, an enumeration, or a reference to an enumeration. It is not possible to change the precedence, grouping, or number of operands of operators. The meaning of the operators =, (unary) &, and , (comma), predefined for each type, can be changed for specific class and enumeration types by defining operator functions that implement these operators. Operator functions are inherited in the same manner as other base class functions.

7   The identities among certain predefined operators applied to basic types (for example, ++a ≡ a+=1) need not hold for operator functions. Some predefined operators, such as +=, require an operand to be an lvalue when applied to basic types; this is not required by operator functions.

8   An operator function cannot have default arguments (8.3.6), except where explicitly stated below. Operator functions cannot have more or fewer parameters than the number required for the corresponding operator, as described in the rest of this subclause.

9   Operators not mentioned explicitly in subclauses 13.5.3 through 13.5.7 act as ordinary unary and binary operators obeying the rules of 13.5.1 or 13.5.2.

13.5.1 Unary operators   [over.unary]

1   A prefix unary operator shall be implemented by a non-static member function (9.3) with no parameters or a non-member function with one parameter. Thus, for any prefix unary operator @, @x can be interpreted as either `x.operator@()` or `operator@(x)`. If both forms of the operator function have been declared, the rules in 13.3.1.2 determine which, if any, interpretation is used. See 13.5.7 for an explanation of the postfix unary operators ++ and --.

2   The unary and binary forms of the same operator are considered to have the same name. [*Note:* consequently, a unary operator can hide a binary operator from an enclosing scope, and vice versa.]

13.5.2 Binary operators   [over.binary]

1   A binary operator shall be implemented either by a non-static member function (9.3) with one parameter or by a non-member function with two parameters. Thus, for any binary operator @, x@y can be interpreted as either `x.operator@(y)` or `operator@(x,y)`. If both forms of the operator function have been declared, the rules in 13.3.1.2 determines which, if any, interpretation is used.

13.5.3 Assignment   [over.ass]

1   An assignment operator shall be implemented by a non-static member function with exactly one parameter. Because a copy assignment operator `operator=` is implicitly declared for a class if not declared by the user (12.8), a base class assignment operator is always hidden by the copy assignment operator of the derived class.

2   Any assignment operator, even the copy assignment operator, can be virtual. [*Note:* for a derived class D with a base class B for which a virtual copy assignment has been declared, the copy assignment operator in D does not override B's virtual copy assignment operator. [*Example:*

```
struct B {
        virtual int operator= (int);
        virtual B& operator= (const B&);
};
struct D : B {
        virtual int operator= (int);
        virtual D& operator= (const B&);
};

D dobj1;
D dobj2;
B* bptr = &dobj1;
void f() {
        bptr->operator=(99);      // calls D::operator=(int)
        *bptr = 99;               // ditto
        bptr->operator=(dobj2);   // calls D::operator=(const B&)
        *bptr = dobj2;            // ditto
        dobj1 = dobj2;            // calls implicitly-declared
                                  // D::operator=(const D&)

}
```

—*end example*] —*end note*]

13.5.4 Function call   [over.call]

1   operator() shall be a non-static member function with an arbitrary number of parameters. It can have default arguments. It implements the function call syntax

　　　postfix-expression (*expression-list$_{opt}$*)

where the *postfix-expression* evaluates to a class object and the possibly empty *expression-list* matches the parameter list of an operator() member function of the class. Thus, a call x(arg1,...) is interpreted as x.operator()(arg1,...) for a class object x of type T if T::operator()(T1, T2, T3) exists and if the operator is selected as the best match function by the overload resolution mechanism (13.3.3).

13.5.5 Subscripting   [over.sub]

1   operator[] shall be a non-static member function with exactly one parameter. It implements the subscripting syntax

　　　postfix-expression [*expression*]

Thus, a subscripting expression x[y] is interpreted as x.operator[](y) for a class object x of type T if T::operator[](T1) exists and if the operator is selected as the best match function by the overload resolution mechanism (13.3.3).

13.5.6 Class member access   [over.ref]

1   operator-> shall be a non-static member function taking no parameters. It implements class member access using ->

　　　postfix-expression -> *id-expression*

An expression x->m is interpreted as (x.operator->())->m for a class object x of type T if T::operator->() exists and if the operator is selected as the best match function by the overload resolution mechanism (13.3).

13.5.7 Increment and decrement   [over.inc]

1   The user-defined function called `operator++` implements the prefix and postfix `++` operator. If this
function is a member function with no parameters, or a non-member function with one parameter of class or
enumeration type, it defines the prefix increment operator `++` for objects of that type. If the function is a
member function with one parameter (which shall be of type `int`) or a non-member function with two
parameters (the second of which shall be of type `int`), it defines the postfix increment operator `++` for
objects of that type. When the postfix increment is called as a result of using the `++` operator, the `int`
argument will have value zero.[125] [*Example:*

```
class X {
public:
    X&      operator++();            // prefix ++a
    X       operator++(int);         // postfix a++
};

class Y { };
Y&    operator++(Y&);                // prefix ++b
Y     operator++(Y&, int);           // postfix b++

void f(X a, Y b) {
    ++a;                             // a.operator++();
    a++;                             // a.operator++(0);
    ++b;                             // operator++(b);
    b++;                             // operator++(b, 0);

    a.operator++();                  // explicit call: like ++a;
    a.operator++(0);                 // explicit call: like a++;
    operator++(b);                   // explicit call: like ++b;
    operator++(b, 0);                // explicit call: like b++;
}
```

—*end example*]

2   The prefix and postfix decrement operators `- -` are handled analogously.

13.6 Built-in operators   [over.built]

1   The candidate operator functions that represent the built-in operators defined in clause 5 are specified in
this subclause. These candidate functions participate in the operator overload resolution process as
described in 13.3.1.2 and are used for no other purpose. [*Note:* because built-in operators take only
operands with non-class type, and operator overload resolution occurs only when an operand expression
originally has class or enumeration type, operator overload resolution can resolve to a built-in operator only
when an operand has a class type that has a user-defined conversion to a non-class type appropriate for the
operator, or when an operand has an enumeration type that can be converted to a type appropriate for the
operator. Also note that some of the candidate operator functions given in this subclause are more permis-
sive than the built-in operators themselves. As described in 13.3.1.2, after a built-in operator is selected by
overload resolution the expression is subject to the requirements for the built-in operator given in clause 5,
and therefore to any additional semantic constraints given there. If there is a user-written candidate with
the same name and parameter types as a built-in candidate operator function, the built-in operator function
is hidden and is not included in the set of candidate functions.]

2   In this subclause, the term *promoted integral type* is used to refer to those integral types which are preserved by integral promotion (including e.g. `int` and `long` but excluding e.g. `char`). Similarly, the term
promoted arithmetic type refers to promoted integral types plus floating types. [*Note:* in all cases where a

---

[125] Calling `operator++` explicitly, as in expressions like `a.operator++(2)`, has no special properties: The argument to
`operator++` is 2.

promoted integral type or promoted arithmetic type is required, an operand of enumeration type will be acceptable by way of the integral promotions.]

3   For every pair (*T*, *VQ*), where *T* is an arithmetic type, and *VQ* is either `volatile` or empty, there exist candidate operator functions of the form

```
VQ T&    operator++(VQ T&);
T        operator++(VQ T&, int);
```

4   For every pair (*T*, *VQ*), where *T* is an arithmetic type other than *bool*, and *VQ* is either `volatile` or empty, there exist candidate operator functions of the form

```
VQ T&    operator--(VQ T&);
T        operator--(VQ T&, int);
```

5   For every pair (*T*, *VQ*), where *T* is a cv-qualified or cv-unqualified object type, and *VQ* is either `volatile` or empty, there exist candidate operator functions of the form

```
T*VQ&    operator++(T*VQ&);
T*VQ&    operator--(T*VQ&);
T*       operator++(T*VQ&, int);
T*       operator--(T*VQ&, int);
```

6   For every cv-qualified or cv-unqualified object type *T*, there exist candidate operator functions of the form

```
T&       operator*(T*);
```

7   For every function type *T*, there exist candidate operator functions of the form

```
T&       operator*(T*);
```

8   For every type *T*, there exist candidate operator functions of the form

```
T*       operator+(T*);
```

9   For every promoted arithmetic type *T*, there exist candidate operator functions of the form

```
T        operator+(T);
T        operator-(T);
```

10   For every promoted integral type *T*, there exist candidate operator functions of the form

```
T        operator~(T);
```

11   For every quintuple (*C1*, *C2*, *T*, *CV1*, *CV2*), where *C2* is a class type, *C1* is the same type as C2 or is a derived class of C2, *T* is an object type or a function type, and *CV1* and *CV2* are *cv-qualifier-seq*s, there exist candidate operator functions of the form

```
CV12 T&  operator->*(CV1 C1*, CV2 T C2::*);
```

where *CV12* is the union of *CV1* and *CV2*.

12   For every pair of promoted arithmetic types *L* and *R*, there exist candidate operator functions of the form

```
LR        operator*(L, R);
LR        operator/(L, R);
LR        operator+(L, R);
LR        operator-(L, R);
bool      operator<(L, R);
bool      operator>(L, R);
bool      operator<=(L, R);
bool      operator>=(L, R);
bool      operator==(L, R);
bool      operator!=(L, R);
```

where *LR* is the result of the usual arithmetic conversions between types *L* and *R*.

13   For every cv-qualified or cv-unqualified object type *T* there exist candidate operator functions of the form

```
T*        operator+(T*, ptrdiff_t);
T&        operator[](T*, ptrdiff_t);
T*        operator-(T*, ptrdiff_t);
T*        operator+(ptrdiff_t, T*);
T&        operator[](ptrdiff_t, T*);
```

14   For every *T*, where *T* is a pointer to object type, there exist candidate operator functions of the form

```
ptrdiff_t        operator-(T, T);
```

15   For every pointer or enumeration type *T*, there exist candidate operator functions of the form

```
bool      operator<(T, T);
bool      operator>(T, T);
bool      operator<=(T, T);
bool      operator>=(T, T);
bool      operator==(T, T);
bool      operator!=(T, T);
```

16   For every pointer to member type *T*, there exist candidate operator functions of the form

```
bool      operator==(T, T);
bool      operator!=(T, T);
```

17   For every pair of promoted integral types *L* and *R*, there exist candidate operator functions of the form

```
LR        operator%(L, R);
LR        operator&(L, R);
LR        operator^(L, R);
LR        operator|(L, R);
L         operator<<(L, R);
L         operator>>(L, R);
```

where *LR* is the result of the usual arithmetic conversions between types *L* and *R*.

18   For every triple (*L*, *VQ*, *R*), where *L* is an arithmetic type, *VQ* is either volatile or empty, and *R* is a promoted arithmetic type, there exist candidate operator functions of the form

```
VQ L&     operator=(VQ L&, R);
VQ L&     operator*=(VQ L&, R);
VQ L&     operator/=(VQ L&, R);
VQ L&     operator+=(VQ L&, R);
VQ L&     operator-=(VQ L&, R);
```

19   For every pair (*T*, *VQ*), where *T* is any type and *VQ* is either volatile or empty, there exist candidate operator functions of the form

```
T*VQ&    operator=(T*VQ&, T*);
```

20   For every pair (*T*, *VQ*), where *T* is an enumeration or pointer to member type and *VQ* is either `volatile` or empty, there exist candidate operator functions of the form

```
VQ T&    operator=(VQ T&, T);
```

21   For every pair (*T*, *VQ*), where *T* is a cv-qualified or cv-unqualified object type and *VQ* is either `volatile` or empty, there exist candidate operator functions of the form

```
T*VQ&    operator+=(T*VQ&, ptrdiff_t);
T*VQ&    operator-=(T*VQ&, ptrdiff_t);
```

22   For every triple (*L*, *VQ*, *R*), where *L* is an integral type, *VQ* is either `volatile` or empty, and *R* is a promoted integral type, there exist candidate operator functions of the form

```
VQ L&    operator%=(VQ L&, R);
VQ L&    operator<<=(VQ L&, R);
VQ L&    operator>>=(VQ L&, R);
VQ L&    operator&=(VQ L&, R);
VQ L&    operator^=(VQ L&, R);
VQ L&    operator|=(VQ L&, R);
```

23   There also exist candidate operator functions of the form

```
bool     operator!(bool);
bool     operator&&(bool, bool);
bool     operator||(bool, bool);
```

24   For every pair of promoted arithmetic types *L* and *R*, there exist candidate operator functions of the form

```
LR       operator?(bool, L, R);
```

where *LR* is the result of the usual arithmetic conversions between types *L* and *R*. [*Note:* as with all these descriptions of candidate functions, this declaration serves only to describe the built-in operator for purposes of overload resolution. The operator "?" cannot be overloaded.]

25   For every type *T*, where *T* is a pointer or pointer-to-member type, there exist candidate operator functions of the form

```
T        operator?(bool, T, T);
```

14 Templates [temp]

1   A *template* defines a family of classes or functions.

> *template-declaration*:
>   export*_{opt}* template < *template-parameter-list* > *declaration*
>
> *template-parameter-list*:
>   *template-parameter*
>   *template-parameter-list* , *template-parameter*

The *declaration* in a *template-declaration* shall

— declare or define a function or a class, or

— define a member function, a member class or a static data member of a class template or of a class nested within a class template, or

— define a member template of a class or class template.

A *template-declaration* is a *declaration*. A *template-declaration* is also a definition if its *declaration* defines a function, a class, or a static data member.

2   A *template-declaration* can appear only as a namespace scope or class scope declaration. In a function template declaration, the *declarator-id* shall be a *template-name* (i.e., not a *template-id*). [*Note:* in a class template declaration, if the class name is a *template-id*, the declaration declares a class template partial specialization (14.5.4).]

3   In a *template-declaration*, explicit specialization, or explicit instantiation the *init-declarator-list* in the declaration shall contain at most one declarator. When such a declaration is used to declare a class template, no declarator is permitted.

4   A template name has linkage (3.5). A non-member function template can have internal linkage; any other template name shall have external linkage. Entities generated from a template with internal linkage are distinct from all entities generated in other translation units. A template, a template explicit specialization (14.7.3), or a class template partial specialization shall not have C linkage. If the linkage of one of these is something other than C or C++, the behavior is implementation-defined. Template definitions shall obey the one definition rule (3.2). [*Note:* default arguments for function templates and for member functions of class templates are considered definitions for the purpose of template instantiation (14.5) and must also obey the one definition rule.]

5   A class template shall not have the same name as any other template, class, function, object, enumeration, enumerator, namespace, or type in the same scope (3.3), except as specified in (14.5.4). Except that a function template can be overloaded either by (non-template) functions with the same name or by other function templates with the same name (14.8.3), a template name declared in namespace scope or in class scope shall be unique in that scope.

6   A namespace-scope declaration or definition of a non-inline function template, a non-inline member function template, a non-inline member function of a class template or a static data member of a class template may be preceded by the export keyword. If such a template is defined in the same translation unit in which it is declared as exported, the definition is considered to be *exported*. The first declaration of the template containing the export keyword must not follow the definition.

7   Declaring a class template exported is equivalent to declaring all of its non-inline function members, static data members, member classes, member class templates and non-inline function member templates which are defined in that translation unit exported.

8   Templates defined in an unnamed namespace shall not be exported. A template shall be exported only once
     in a program. An implementation is not required to diagnose a violation of this rule. A non-exported tem-
     plate must be defined in every translation unit in which it is implicitly instantiated (14.7.1), unless the cor-
     responding specialization is explicitly instantiated (14.7.2) in some translation unit; no diagnostic is
     required. [*Note:* See also 14.7.2.] An exported template need only be declared (and not necessarily
     defined) in a translation unit in which it is instantiated. A function template declared both exported and
     inline is just inline and not exported.

9   [*Note:* an implementation may require that a translation unit containing the definition of an exported tem-
     plate be compiled before any translation unit containing an instantiation of that template.]

14.1 Template parameters   [temp.param]

1   The syntax for *template-parameter*s is:

> *template-parameter:*
>> *type-parameter*
>> *parameter-declaration*

> *type-parameter:*
>> class *identifier$_{opt}$*
>> class *identifier$_{opt}$* = *type-id*
>> typename *identifier$_{opt}$*
>> typename *identifier$_{opt}$* = *type-id*
>> template < *template-parameter-list* > class *identifier$_{opt}$*
>> template < *template-parameter-list* > class *identifier$_{opt}$* = *id-expression*

2   There is no semantic difference between class and typename in a *template-parameter*. typename
     followed by an *unqualified-id* names a template type parameter. typename followed by a *qualified-id*
     denotes the type in a non-type [126] *parameter-declaration*. A storage class shall not be specified in a
     template-parameter declaration. [*Note:* a template parameter may be a class template. For example,

```
template<class T> class myarray { /* ... */ };

template<class K, class V, template<class T> class C = myarray>
class Map {
        C<K> key;
        C<V> value;
        // ...
};
```

     —*end note*]

3   A *type-parameter* defines its *identifier* to be a *type-name* (if declared with class or typename) or
     template-name (if declared with template) in the scope of the template declaration. [*Note:* because of
     the name lookup rules, a *template-parameter* that could be interpreted as either a non-type *template-
     parameter* or a *type-parameter* (because its *identifier* is the name of an already existing class) is taken as a
     type-parameter. For example,

---

[126] Since template *template-parameter*s and template *template-argument*s are treated as types for descriptive purposes, the terms
non-type parameter and *non-type argument* are used to refer to non-type, non-template parameters and arguments.

```
class T { /* ... */ };
int i;

template<class T, T i> void f(T t)
{
        T t1 = i;                    // template-parameters T and i
        ::T t2 = ::i;                // global namespace members T and i
}
```

Here, the template f has a *type-parameter* called T, rather than an unnamed non-type *template-parameter* of class T.]

4   A non-type *template-parameter* shall have one of the following (optionally *cv-qualified*) types:

— integral or enumeration type,

— pointer to object or pointer to function,

— reference to object or reference to function,

— pointer to member.

5   [*Note:* other types are disallowed either explicitly below or implicitly by the rules governing the form of *template-argument*s (14.3).] The top-level *cv-qualifiers* on the *template-parameter* are ignored when determining its type.

6   A non-type non-reference *template-parameter* is not an lvalue. It shall not be assigned to or in any other way have its value changed. A non-type non-reference *template-parameter* cannot have its address taken. When a non-type non-reference *template-parameter* is used as an initializer for a reference, a temporary is always used. [*Example:*

```
template<const X& x, int i> void f()
{
        i++;                         // error: change of template-parameter value

        &x;                          // OK
        &i;                          // error: address of non-reference template-parameter

        int& ri = i;                 // error: non-const reference bound to temporary
        const int& cri = i;          // OK: const reference bound to temporary
}
```

—*end example*]

7   A non-type *template-parameter* shall not be declared to have floating point, class, or void type. [*Example:*

```
template<double d> class X;      // error
template<double* pd> class Y;    // OK
template<double& rd> class Z;    // OK
```

—*end example*]

8   A non-type *template-parameter* of type "array of T" or "function returning T" is adjusted to be of type "pointer to T" or "pointer to function returning T", respectively. [*Example:*

```
template<int *a>   struct R { /* ... */ };
template<int b[5]> struct S { /* ... */ };
int p;
R<&p> w;                         // OK
S<&p> x;                         // OK due to parameter adjustment
int v[5];
R<v> y;                          // OK due to implicit argument conversion
S<v> z;                          // OK due to both adjustment and conversion
```

—end example]

9   A *default template-argument* is a *template-argument* (14.3) specified after = in a *template-parameter*. A default *template-argument* may be specified for any kind of *template-parameter* (type, non-type, template). A default *template-argument* may be specified in a class template declaration or a class template definition. A default *template-argument* shall not be specified in a function template declaration or a function template definition, nor in the *template-parameter-list* of the definition of a member of a class template. A default *template-argument* shall not be specified in a friend template declaration.

10   The set of default *template-argument*s available for use with a template declaration or definition is obtained by merging the default arguments from the definition (if in scope) and all declarations in scope in the same way default function arguments are (8.3.6). [*Example:*

```
template<class T1, class T2 = int> class A;
template<class T1 = int, class T2> class A;
```

is equivalent to

```
template<class T1 = int, class T2 = int> class A;
```

—end example]

11   If a *template-parameter* has a default *template-argument,* all subsequent *template-parameter*s shall have a default *template-argument* supplied. [*Example:*

```
template<class T1 = int, class T2> class B;      // error
```

—end example]

12   A *template-parameter* shall not be given default arguments by two different declarations in the same scope. [*Example:*

```
template<class T = int> class X;
template<class T = int> class X { /*... */ }; // error
```

—end example]

13   The scope of a *template-parameter* extends from its point of declaration until the end of its template. In particular, a *template-parameter* can be used in the declaration of subsequent *template-parameter*s and their default arguments. [*Example:*

```
template<class T, T* p, class U = T> class X { /* ... */ };
template<class T> void f(T* p = new T);
```

—end example]

14   A *template-parameter* shall not be used in its own default argument.

15   When parsing a default *template-argument* for a non-type *template-parameter*, the first non-nested > is taken as the end of the *template-parameter-list* rather than a greater-than operator. [*Example:*

```
template<int i = 3 > 4 >           // syntax error
    class X { /* ... */ };

template<int i = (3 > 4) >         // OK
    class Y { /* ... */ };
```

—end example]

14.2 Names of template specializations **[temp.names]**

1   A template specialization (14.7) can be referred to by a *template-id*:

> *template-id* :
>> *template-name* < *template-argument-list*_{opt} >

> *template-name* :
>> *identifier*

> *template-argument-list* :
>> *template-argument*
>> *template-argument-list* , *template-argument*

> *template-argument* :
>> *assignment-expression*
>> *type-id*
>> *id-expression*

[*Note:* the name lookup rules (3.4) are used to associate the use of a name with a template declaration; that is, to identify a name as a *template-name.*]

2   For a *template-name* to be explicitly qualified by the template arguments, the name must be known to refer to a template.

3   After name lookup (3.4) finds that a name is a *template-name*, if this name is followed by a <, the < is always taken as the beginning of a *template-argument-list* and never as a name followed by the less-than operator. When parsing a *template-id*, the first non-nested >[127] is taken as the end of the *template-argument-list* rather than a greater-than operator. [*Example:*

```
template<int i> class X { /* ... */ };

X< 1>2 >        x1;        // syntax error
X<(1>2)>        x2;        // OK

template<class T> class Y { /* ... */ };
Y< X<1> >       x3;        // OK
Y<X<6>> 1> >    x4;        // OK: Y< X< (6>>1) > >
```

—*end example*]

4   When the name of a member template specialization appears after . or -> in a *postfix-expression*, or after *nested-name-specifier* in a *qualified-id*, and the postfix-expression or qualified-id explicitly depends on a template-parameter (14.6.2), the member template name must be prefixed by the keyword `template`. Otherwise the name is assumed to name a non-template. [*Example:*

---

[127] A > that encloses the *type-id* of a `dynamic_cast`, `static_cast`, `reinterpret_cast` or `const_cast`, or which encloses the *template-arguments* of a subsequent *template-id*, is considered nested for the purpose of this description.

```
class X {
public:
        template<size_t> X* alloc();
        template<size_t> static X* adjust();
};
template<class T> void f(T* p)
{
        T* p1 = p->alloc<200>();
                // ill-formed: < means less than

        T* p2 = p->template alloc<200>();
                // OK: < starts template argument list

        T::adjust<100>();
                // ill-formed: < means less than

        T::template adjust<100>();
                // OK: < starts template argument list
}
```

—end example]

5   If a name prefixed by the keyword `template` is not the name of a member template, the program is ill-formed. [*Note:* the keyword `template` may not be applied to non-template members of class templates.] Furthermore, names of member templates shall not be prefixed by the keyword `template` if the *postfix-expression* or *qualified-id* does not appear in the scope of a template. [*Note:* just as is the case with the `typename` prefix, the `template` prefix is allowed in cases where it is not strictly necessary; i.e., when the expression on the left of the `->` or `.`, or the *nested-name-specifier* is not dependent on a *template-parameter.*]

6   A *template-id* that names a class template specialization is a *class-name* (clause 9).

14.3 Template arguments   [temp.arg]

1   There are three forms of *template-argument*, corresponding to the three forms of *template-parameter*: type, non-type and template. The type and form of each *template-argument* specified in a *template-id* shall match the type and form specified for the corresponding parameter declared by the template in its *template-parameter-list*. [*Example:*

```
template<class T> class Array {
        T* v;
        int sz;
public:
        explicit Array(int);
        T& operator[](int);
        T& elem(int i) { return v[i]; }
        // ...
};

Array<int> v1(20);
typedef complex<double> dcomplex;      // complex is a standard
                                       // library template
Array<dcomplex> v2(30);
Array<dcomplex> v3(40);

void bar() {
        v1[3] = 7;
        v2[3] = v3.elem(4) = dcomplex(7,8);
}
```

—end example]

2 In a *template-argument*, an ambiguity between a *type-id* and an expression is resolved to a *type-id*, regardless of the form of the corresponding *template-parameter*.[128] [*Example:*

```
template<class T> void f();
template<int I> void f();

void g()
{
        f<int()>();                     // int() is a type-id: call the first f()
}
```

—end example]

3 The name of a *template-argument* shall be accessible at the point where it is used as a *template-argument*. [*Note:* if the name of the *template-argument* is accessible at the point where it is used as a *template-argument*, there is no further access restriction in the resulting instantiation where the corresponding *template-parameter* name is used.] [*Example:*

```
template<class T> class X {
        static T t;
};

class Y {
private:
        struct S { /* ... */ };
        X<S> x;                         // OK: S is accessible
                                        // X<Y::S> has a static member of type Y::S
                                        // OK: even though Y::S is private
};

X<Y::S> y;                              // error: S not accessible
```

—end example] For a *template-argument* of class type, the template definition has no special access rights to the inaccessible members of the template argument type.

4 When default *template-argument*s are used, a *template-argument* list can be empty. In that case the empty `<>` brackets shall still be used as the *template-argument-list*. [*Example:*

```
template<class T = char> class String;
String<>* p;                            // OK: String<char>
String* q;                              // syntax error
```

—end example]

5 An explicit destructor call (12.4) for an object that has a type that is a class template specialization may explicitly specify the *template-argument*s. [*Example:*

```
template<class T> struct A {
        ~A();
};
void f(A<int>* p, A<int>* q) {
        p->A<int>::~A();                // OK: destructor call
        q->A<int>::~A<int>();           // OK: destructor call
}
```

—end example]

---

[128] There is no such ambiguity in a default *template-argument* because the form of the *template-parameter* determines the allowable forms of the *template-argument*.

6   If the use of a *template-argument* gives rise to an ill-formed construct in the instantiation of a template specialization, the program is ill-formed.

7   When the template in a *template-id* is an overloaded function template, both non-template functions in the overload set and function templates in the overload set for which the *template-argument*s do not match the *template-parameter*s are ignored. If none of the function templates have matching *template-parameter*s, the program is ill-formed.

14.3.1 Template type arguments   [temp.arg.type]

1   A *template-argument* for a *template-parameter* which is a type shall be a *type-id*.

2   A local type, a type with no linkage, an unnamed type or a type compounded from any of these types shall not be used as a *template-argument* for a template *type-parameter*. [*Example:*

```
template <class T> class X { /* ... */ };
void f()
{
    struct S { /* ... */ };

    X<S> x3;                         // error: local type used as template-argument
    X<S*> x4;                        // error: pointer to local type used as template-argument
}
```

—*end example*] [*Note:* a template type argument may be an incomplete type (3.9).]

3   If a declaration acquires a function type through a type dependent on a *template-parameter* and this causes a declaration that does not use the syntactic form of a function declarator to have function type, the program is ill-formed. [*Example:*

```
template<class T> struct A {
        static T t;
};
typedef int function();
A<function> a;                       // ill-formed: would declare A<function>::t
                                     // as a static member function
```

—*end example*]

14.3.2 Template non-type arguments   [temp.arg.nontype]

1   A *template-argument* for a non-type, non-template *template-parameter* shall be one of:

— an integral *constant-expression* of integral or enumeration type; or

— the name of a non-type *template-parameter*; or

— the address of an object or function with external linkage, including function templates and function *template-id*s but excluding non-static class members, expressed as & *id-expression* where the & is optional if the name refers to a function or array, or if the corresponding *template-parameter* is a reference; or

— a pointer to member expressed as described in 5.3.1 .

2   [*Note:* A string literal (2.13.4) does not satisfy the requirements of any of these categories and thus is not an acceptable *template-argument*. [*Example:*

```
template<class T, char* p> class X {
        // ...
        X();
        X(const char* q) { /* ... */ }
};

X<int,"Studebaker"> x1;          // error: string literal as template-argument

char p[] = "Vivisectionist";
X<int,p> x2;                     // OK
```

—*end example*] —*end note*]

3   [*Note:* Addresses of array elements and names or addresses of non-static class members are not acceptable *template-argument*s. [*Example:*

```
template<int* p> class X { };

int a[10];
struct S { int m; static int s; } s;

X<&a[2]> x3;                     // error: address of array element
X<&s.m> x4;                      // error: address of non-static member
X<&s.s> x5;                      // error: &S::s must be used
X<&S::s> x6;                     // OK: address of static member
```

—*end example*] —*end note*]

4   [*Note:* Temporaries, unnamed lvalues, and named lvalues that do not have external linkage are not acceptable *template-argument*s when the corresponding *template-parameter* has reference type. [*Example:*

```
template<const int& CRI> struct B { /* ... */ };

B<1> b2;                         // error: temporary would be required for template argument

int c = 1;
B<c> b1;                         // OK
```

—*end example*] —*end note*]

5   The following conversions are performed on each expression used as a non-type *template-argument*. If a non-type *template-argument* cannot be converted to the type of the corresponding *template-parameter* then the program is ill-formed.

— for a non-type *template-parameter* of integral or enumeration type, integral promotions (4.5) and integral conversions (4.7) are applied.

— for a non-type *template-parameter* of type pointer to object, qualification conversions (4.4) and the array-to-pointer conversion (4.2) are applied. [*Note:* In particular, neither the null pointer conversion (4.10) nor the derived-to-base conversion (4.10) are applied. Although 0 is a valid *template-argument* for a non-type *template-parameter* of integral type, it is not a valid *template-argument* for a non-type *template-parameter* of pointer type.]

— For a non-type *template-parameter* of type reference to object, no conversions apply. The type referred to by the reference may be more cv-qualified than the (otherwise identical) type of the *template-argument*. The *template-parameter* is bound directly to the *template-argument*, which must be an lvalue.

— For a non-type *template-parameter* of type pointer to function, only the function-to-pointer conversion (4.3) is applied. If the *template-argument* represents a set of overloaded functions (or a pointer to such), the matching function is selected from the set (13.4).

— For a non-type *template-parameter* of type reference to function, no conversions apply. If the *template-argument* represents a set of overloaded functions, the matching function is selected from the set (13.4).

— For a non-type *template-parameter* of type pointer to member function, no conversions apply. If the *template-argument* represents a set of overloaded member functions, the matching member function is selected from the set (13.4).

— For a non-type *template-parameter* of type pointer to data member, qualification conversions (4.4) are applied.

[*Example:*

```
template<const int* pci> struct X { /* ... */ };
int ai[10];
X<ai> xi;                       // array to pointer and qualification conversions

struct Y { /* ... */ };
template<const Y& b> struct Z { /* ... */ };
Y y;
Z<y> z;                         // no conversion, but note extra cv-qualification

template<int (&pa)[5]> struct W { /* ... */ };
int b[5];
W<b> w;                         // no conversion

void f(char);
void f(int);

template<void (*pf)(int)> struct A { /* ... */ };

A<&f> a;                        // selects f(int)
```

—*end example*]

14.3.3 Template template arguments   **[temp.arg.template]**

1   A *template-argument* for a template *template-parameter* shall be the name of a class template, expressed as *id-expression*. Only primary class templates are considered when matching the template template argument with the corresponding parameter; partial specializations are not considered even if their parameter lists match that of the template template parameter.

2   Any partial specializations (14.5.4) associated with the primary class template are considered when a specialization based on the template *template-parameter* is instantiated. If a specialization is not visible at the point of instantiation, and it would have been selected had it been visible, the program is ill-formed; no diagnostic is required. [*Example:*

```
template<class T> class A {          // primary template
        int x;
};
template<class T> class A<T*> {  // partial specialization
        long x;
};
template<template<class U> class V> class C {
        V<int>  y;
        V<int*> z;
};
C<A> c;                              // V<int> within C<A> uses the primary template,
                                     // so c.y.x has type int
                                     // V<int*> within C<A> uses the partial specialization,
                                     // so c.z.x has type long
```

—*end example*]

14.4 Type equivalence   [temp.type]

1   Two *template-id*s refer to the same class or function if their template names are identical, they refer to the same template, their type *template-argument*s are the same type, their non-type *template-argument*s of integral or enumeration type have identical values, their non-type *template-argument*s of pointer or reference type refer to the same external object or function, and their template *template-argument*s refer to the same template. [*Example:*

```
template<class E, int size> class buffer { /* ... */ };
buffer<char,2*512> x;
buffer<char,1024> y;
```

declares x and y to be of the same type, and

```
template<class T, void(*err_fct)()> class list { /* ... */ };
list<int,&error_handler1> x1;
list<int,&error_handler2> x2;
list<int,&error_handler2> x3;
list<char,&error_handler2> x4;
```

declares x2 and x3 to be of the same type. Their type differs from the types of x1 and x4.]

14.5 Template declarations   [temp.decls]

1   A *template-id*, that is, the *template-name* followed by a *template-argument-list* shall not be specified in the declaration of a primary template declaration. [*Example:*

```
template<class T1, class T2, int I> class A<T1, T2, I> { };  // error
template<class T1, int I> void sort<T1, I>(T1 data[I]);      // error
```

—*end example*] [*Note:* however, this syntax is allowed in class template partial specializations (14.5.4).]

2   For purposes of name lookup and instantiation, default arguments of function templates and default arguments of member functions of class templates are considered definitions; each default argument is a separate definition which is unrelated to the function template definition or to any other default arguments.

14.5.1 Class templates [temp.class]

1   A class *template* defines the layout and operations for an unbounded set of related types. [*Example:* a single class template List might provide a common definition for list of int, list of float, and list of pointers to Shapes.]

2   [*Example:* An array class template might be declared like this:

```
template<class T> class Array {
    T* v;
    int sz;
public:
    explicit Array(int);
    T& operator[](int);
    T& elem(int i) { return v[i]; }
    // ...
};
```

The prefix template <class T> specifies that a template is being declared and that a *type-name* T will be used in the declaration. In other words, Array is a parameterized type with T as its parameter.]

3   When a member function, a member class, a static data member or a member template of a class template is defined outside of the class template definition, the member definition is defined as a template definition in which the *template-parameters* are those of the class template. The names of the template parameters used in the definition of the member may be different from the template parameter names used in the class template definition. The template argument list following the class template name in the member definition shall name the parameters in the same order as the one used in the template parameter list of the member. [*Example:*

```
template<class T1, class T2> struct A {
    void f1();
    void f2();
};

template<class T2, class T1> void A<T2,T1>::f1() { }    // OK
template<class T2, class T1> void A<T1,T2>::f2() { }    // error
```

—*end example*]

4   In a redeclaration, partial specialization, explicit specialization or explicit instantiation of a class template, the *class-key* shall agree in kind with the original class template declaration (7.1.5.3).

14.5.1.1 Member functions of class templates [temp.mem.func]

1   A member function of a class template may be defined outside of the class template definition in which it is declared. [*Example:*

```
template<class T> class Array {
    T* v;
    int sz;
public:
    explicit Array(int);
    T& operator[](int);
    T& elem(int i) { return v[i]; }
    // ...
};
```

declares three function templates. The subscript function might be defined like this:

```
template<class T> T& Array<T>::operator[](int i)
{
    if (i<0 || sz<=i) error("Array: range error");
    return v[i];
}
```

—end example]

2   The *template-argument*s for a member function of a class template are determined by the *template-argument*s of the type of the object for which the member function is called. [*Example:* the *template-argument* for `Array<T>::operator[]()` will be determined by the `Array` to which the subscripting operation is applied.

```
Array<int> v1(20);
Array<dcomplex> v2(30);

v1[3] = 7;                     // Array<int>::operator[]()
v2[3] = dcomplex(7,8);         // Array<dcomplex>::operator[]()
```

—end example]

14.5.1.2 Member classes of class templates   **[temp.mem.class]**

1   A class member of a class template may be defined outside the class template definition in which it is declared. [*Note:* the class member must be defined before its first use that requires an instantiation (14.7.1). For example,

```
template<class T> struct A {
        class B;
};
A<int>::B* b1;                 // OK: requires A to be defined but not A::B
template<class T> class A<T>::B { };
A<int>::B b2;                  // OK: requires A::B to be defined
```

—end note]

14.5.1.3 Static data members of class templates   **[temp.static]**

1   A definition for a static data member may be provided in a namespace scope enclosing the definition of the static member's class template. [*Example:*

```
template<class T> class X {
        static T s;
};
template<class T> T X<T>::s = 0;
```

—end example]

14.5.2 Member templates   **[temp.mem]**

1   A template can be declared within a class or class template; such a template is called a member template. A member template can be defined within or outside its class definition or class template definition. A member template of a class template that is defined outside of its class template definition shall be specified with the *template-parameter*s of the class template followed by the *template-parameter*s of the member template. [*Example:*

```
template<class T> class string {
public:
        template<class T2> int compare(const T2&);
        template<class T2> string(const string<T2>& s) { /* ... */ }
        // ...
};

template<class T> template<class T2> int string<T>::compare(const T2& s)
{
        // ...
}
```

—*end example*]

2   A local class shall not have member templates. Access control rules (clause 11) apply to member template names. A destructor shall not be a member template. A normal (non-template) member function with a given name and type and a member function template of the same name, which could be used to generate a specialization of the same type, can both be declared in a class. When both exist, a use of that name and type refers to the non-template member unless an explicit template argument list is supplied. [*Example:*

```
template <class T> struct A {
        void f(int);
        template <class T2> void f(T2);
};

template <> void A<int>::f(int) { }                      // non-template member
template <> template <> void A<int>::f<>(int) { }        // template member

int main()
{
        A<char> ac;
        ac.f(1);                 // non-template
        ac.f('c');               // template
        ac.f<>(1);               // template
}
```

—*end example*]

3   A member function template shall not be virtual. [*Example:*

```
template <class T> struct AA {
        template <class C> virtual void g(C);    // error
        virtual void f();                        // OK
};
```

—*end example*]

4   A specialization of a member function template does not override a virtual function from a base class. [*Example:*

```
class B {
        virtual void f(int);
};

class D : public B {
        template <class T> void f(T);    // does not override B::f(int)
        void f(int i) { f<>(i); }        // overriding function that calls
                                         // the template instantiation
};
```

—*end example*]

5   A specialization of a template conversion function is referenced in the same way as a non-template conversion function that converts to the same type. [*Example:*

```
struct A {
        template <class T> operator T*();
};
template <class T> A::operator T*(){ return 0; }
template <> A::operator char*(){ return 0; }      // specialization
template A::operator void*();                      // explicit instantiation

int main()
{
        A       a;
        int*    ip;

        ip = a.operator int*();          // explicit call to template operator
                                         // A::operator int*()
}
```

—*end example*] [*Note:* because the explicit template argument list follows the function template name, and because conversion member function templates and constructor member function templates are called without using a function name, there is no way to provide an explicit template argument list for these function templates.]

6   A specialization of a template conversion function is not found by name lookup. Instead, any template conversion functions visible in the context of the use are considered. For each such operator, if argument deduction succeeds (14.8.2.3), the resulting specialization is used as if found by name lookup.

7   A using-declaration in a derived class cannot refer to a specialization of a template conversion function in a base class.

8   Overload resolution (13.3.3.2) and partial ordering (14.5.5.2) are used to select the best conversion function among multiple template conversion functions and/or non-template conversion functions.

14.5.3 Friends   [temp.friend]

1   A friend of a class or class template can be a function template or class template, a specialization of a function template or class template, or an ordinary (nontemplate) function or class. For a friend function declaration that is not a template declaration:

— if the name of the friend is a qualified or unqualified *template-id*, the friend declaration refers to a specialization of a function template, otherwise

— if the name of the friend is a *qualified-id* and a matching nontemplate function is found in the specified class or namespace, the friend declaration refers to that function, otherwise,

— if the name of the friend is a *qualified-id* and a matching specialization of a function template is found in the specified class or namespace, the friend declaration refers to that function template specialization, otherwise,

— the name shall be an *unqualified-id* that declares (or redeclares) an ordinary (nontemplate) function.

[*Example:*

```
template<class T> class task;
template<class T> task<T>* preempt(task<T>*);
```

```
template<class T> class task {
        // ...
        friend void next_time();
        friend void process(task<T>*);
        friend task<T>* preempt<T>(task<T>*);
        template<class C> friend int func(C);

        friend class task<int>;
        template<class P> friend class frd;
        // ...
};
```

Here, each specialization of the task class template has the function next_time as a friend; because process does not have explicit *template-argument*s, each specialization of the task class template has an appropriately typed function process as a friend, and this friend is not a function template specialization; because the friend preempt has an explicit *template-argument* <T>, each specialization of the task class template has the appropriate specialization of the function template preempt as a friend; and each specialization of the task class template has all specializations of the function template func as friends. Similarly, each specialization of the task class template has the class template specialization task<int> as a friend, and has all specializations of the class template frd as friends. —*end example*]

2   A friend function declaration that is not a template declaration and in which the name of the friend is an unqualified *template-id* shall refer to a specialization of a function template declared in the nearest enclosing namespace scope. [*Example:*

```
namespace N {
        template <class T> void f(T);
        void g(int);
        namespace M {
                template <class T> void h(T);
                template <class T> void i(T);
                struct A {
                        friend void f<>(int);      // ill-formed – N::f
                        friend void h<>(int);      // OK – M::h
                        friend void g(int);        // OK – new decl of M::g
                        template <class T> void i(T);
                        friend void i<>(int);      // ill-formed – A::i
                };
        }
}
```

—*end example*]

3   A friend template may be declared within a class or class template. A friend function template may be defined within a class or class template, but a friend class template may not be defined in a class or class template. In these cases, all specializations of the friend class or friend function template are friends of the class or class template granting friendship. [*Example:*

```
class A {
        template<class T> friend class B;          // OK
        template<class T> friend void f(T){ /* ... */ }          // OK
};
```

—*end example*]

4   A template friend declaration specifies that all specializations of that template, whether they are implicitly instantiated (14.7.1), partially specialized (14.5.4) or explicitly specialized (14.7.3), are friends of the class containing the template friend declaration. [*Example:*

```
class X {
        template<class T> friend struct A;
        class Y { };
};

template<class T> struct A { X::Y ab; };        // OK
template<class T> struct A<T*> { X::Y ab; };     // OK
```

—end example]

5   When a function is defined in a friend function declaration in a class template, the function is defined at each instantiation of the class template. The function is defined even if it is never used. The same restrictions on multiple declarations and definitions which apply to non-template function declarations and definitions also apply to these implicit definitions. [*Note:* if the function definition is ill-formed for a given specialization of the enclosing class template, the program is ill-formed even if the function is never used.]

6   A member of a class template may be declared to be a friend of a non-template class. In this case, the corresponding member of every specialization of the class template is a friend of the class granting friendship. [*Example:*

```
template<class T> struct A {
        struct B { };
        void f();
};

class C {
        template<class T> friend struct A<T>::B;
        template<class T> friend void A<T>::f();
};
```

—end example]

7   [*Note:* a friend declaration may first declare a member of an enclosing namespace scope (14.6.5).]

8   A friend template shall not be declared in a local class.

9   Friend declarations shall not declare partial specializations. [*Example:*

```
template<class T> class A { };
class X {
        template<class T> friend class A<T*>;     // error
};
```

—end example]

10   When a friend declaration refers to a specialization of a function template, the function parameter declarations shall not include default arguments, nor shall the inline specifier be used in such a declaration.

14.5.4 Class template partial specializations   **[temp.class.spec]**

1   A *primary* class template declaration is one in which the class template name is an identifier. A template declaration in which the class template name is a *template-id*, is a *partial specialization* of the class template named in the *template-id*. A partial specialization of a class template provides an alternative definition of the template that is used instead of the primary definition when the arguments in a specialization match those given in the partial specialization (14.5.4.1). The primary template shall be declared before any specializations of that template. If a template is partially specialized then that partial specialization shall be declared before the first use of that partial specialization that would cause an implicit instantiation to take place, in every translation unit in which such a use occurs; no diagnostic is required.

2   When a partial specialization is used within the instantiation of an exported template, and the unspecialized template name is non-dependent in the exported template, a declaration of the partial specialization must be declared before the definition of the exported template, in the translation unit containing that definition. A

similar restriction applies to explicit specialization; see 14.7.

3   Each class template partial specialization is a distinct template and definitions shall be provided for the members of a template partial specialization (14.5.4.3).

4   [*Example:*

```
template<class T1, class T2, int I> class A            { };    // #1
template<class T, int I>             class A<T, T*, I>  { };    // #2
template<class T1, class T2, int I> class A<T1*, T2, I> { };   // #3
template<class T>                    class A<int, T*, 5> { };   // #4
template<class T1, class T2, int I> class A<T1, T2*, I> { };   // #5
```

The first declaration declares the primary (unspecialized) class template. The second and subsequent declarations declare partial specializations of the primary template.]

5   The template parameters are specified in the angle bracket enclosed list that immediately follows the keyword `template`. For partial specializations, the template argument list is explicitly written immediately following the class template name. For primary templates, this list is implicitly described by the template parameter list. Specifically, the order of the template arguments is the sequence in which they appear in the template parameter list. [*Example:* the template argument list for the primary template in the example above is `<T1, T2, I>`.] [*Note:* the template argument list shall not be specified in the primary template declaration. For example,

```
template<class T1, class T2, int I> class A<T1, T2, I>  { };    // error
```

—*end note*]

6   A class template partial specialization may be declared or redeclared in any namespace scope in which its definition may be defined (14.5.1 and 14.5.2). [*Example:*

```
template<class T> struct A {
        class C {
                template<class T2> struct B { };
        };
};

// partial specialization of A<T>::C::B<T2>
template<class T> template<class T2>
        struct A<T>::C::B<T2*> { };

A<short>::C::B<int*> absip;     // uses partial specialization
```

—*end example*]

7   Partial specialization declarations themselves are not found by name lookup. Rather, when the primary template name is used, any previously declared partial specializations of the primary template are also considered. One consequence is that a *using-declaration* which refers to a class template does not restrict the set of partial specializations which may be found through the *using-declaration*. [*Example:*

```
namespace N {
        template<class T1, class T2> class A { };      // primary template
}

using N::A;                      // refers to the primary template

namespace N {
        template<class T> class A<T, T*> { };   // partial specialization
}

A<int,int*> a;                   // uses the partial specialization, which is found through
                                 // the using declaration which refers to the primary template
```

—end example]

8   A non-type argument is non-specialized if it is the name of a non-type parameter. All other non-type arguments are specialized.

9   Within the argument list of a class template partial specialization, the following restrictions apply:

— A partially specialized non-type argument expression shall not involve a template parameter of the partial specialization except when the argument expression is a simple *identifier*. [*Example:*

```
template <int I, int J> struct A {};
template <int I> struct A<I+5, I*2> {}; // error

template <int I, int J> struct B {};
template <int I> struct B<I, I> {};      // OK
```

—end example]

— The type of a template parameter corresponding to a specialized non-type argument shall not be dependent on a parameter of the specialization. [*Example:*

```
template <class T, T t> struct C {};
template <class T> struct C<T, 1>;                // error

template< int X, int (*array_ptr)[X] > class A {};
int array[5];
template< int X > class A<X,&array> { };          // error
```

—end example]

— The argument list of the specialization shall not be identical to the implicit argument list of the primary template.

10   The template parameter list of a specialization shall not contain default template argument values.[129]

14.5.4.1 Matching of class template partial specializations   [temp.class.spec.match]

1   When a class template is used in a context that requires an instantiation of the class, it is necessary to determine whether the instantiation is to be generated using the primary template or one of the partial specializations. This is done by matching the template arguments of the class template specialization with the template argument lists of the partial specializations.

— If exactly one matching specialization is found, the instantiation is generated from that specialization.

— If more than one matching specialization is found, the partial order rules (14.5.4.2) are used to determine whether one of the specializations is more specialized than the others. If none of the specializations is more specialized than all of the other matching specializations, then the use of the class template is ambiguous and the program is ill-formed.

— If no matches are found, the instantiation is generated from the primary template.

2   A partial specialization matches a given actual template argument list if the template arguments of the partial specialization can be deduced from the actual template argument list (14.8.2). [*Example:*

```
A<int, int, 1>   a1;       // uses #1
A<int, int*, 1>  a2;       // uses #2, T is int, I is 1
A<int, char*, 5> a3;       // uses #4, T is char
A<int, char*, 1> a4;       // uses #5, T1 is int, T2 is char, I is 1
A<int*, int*, 2> a5;       // ambiguous: matches #3 and #5
```

—end example]

---

[129] There is no way in which they could be used.

3   A non-type template argument can also be deduced from the value of an actual template argument of a non-type parameter of the primary template. [*Example:* the declaration of `a2` above.]

4   In a type name that refers to a class template specialization, (e.g., `A<int, int, 1>`) the argument list must match the template parameter list of the primary template. The template arguments of a specialization are deduced from the arguments of the primary template.

14.5.4.2 Partial ordering of class template specializations   [temp.class.order]

1   For two class template partial specializations, the first is at least as specialized as the second if, given the following rewrite to two function templates, the first function template is at least as specialized as the second according to the ordering rules for function templates (14.5.5.2):

— the first function template has the same template parameters as the first partial specialization and has a single function parameter whose type is a class template specialization with the template arguments of the first partial specialization, and

— the second function template has the same template parameters as the second partial specialization and has a single function parameter whose type is a class template specialization with the template arguments of the second partial specialization.

2   [*Example:*

```
template<int I, int J, class T> class X { };
template<int I, int J>          class X<I, J, int> { };      // #1
template<int I>                 class X<I, I, int> { };      // #2

template<int I, int J> void f(X<I, J, int>);    // #A
template<int I>        void f(X<I, I, int>);     // #B
```

The partial specialization #2 is more specialized than the partial specialization #1 because the function template #B is more specialized than the function template #A according to the ordering rules for function templates.]

14.5.4.3 Members of class template specializations   [temp.class.spec.mfunc]

1   The template parameter list of a member of a class template partial specialization shall match the template parameter list of the class template partial specialization. The template argument list of a member of a class template partial specialization shall match the template argument list of the class template partial specialization. A class template specialization is a distinct template. The members of the class template partial specialization are unrelated to the members of the primary template. Class template partial specialization members that are used in a way that requires a definition shall be defined; the definitions of members of the primary template are never used as definitions for members of a class template partial specialization. An explicit specialization of a member of a class template partial specialization is declared in the same way as an explicit specialization of the primary template. [*Example:*

```
// primary template
template<class T, int I> struct A {
        void f();
};

template<class T, int I> void A<T,I>::f() { }
```

```
// class template partial specialization
template<class T> struct A<T,2> {
        void f();
        void g();
        void h();
};

// member of class template partial specialization
template<class T> void A<T,2>::g() { }

// explicit specialization
template<> void A<char,2>::h() { }

int main()
{
        A<char,0> a0;
        A<char,2> a2;
        a0.f();                  // OK, uses definition of primary template's member
        a2.g();                  // OK, uses definition of
                                 // partial specialization's member
        a2.h();                  // OK, uses definition of
                                 // explicit specialization's member
        a2.f();                  // ill-formed, no definition of f for A<T,2>
                                 // the primary template is not used here
}
```

—*end example*]

2   If a member template of a class template is partially specialized, the member template partial specializations are member templates of the enclosing class template; if the enclosing class template is instantiated (14.7.1, 14.7.2), a declaration for every member template partial specialization is also instantiated as part of creating the members of the class template specialization. If the primary member template is explicitly specialized for a given (implicit) specialization of the enclosing class template, the partial specializations of the member template are ignored for this specialization of the enclosing class template. If a partial specialization of the member template is explicitly specialized for a given (implicit) specialization of the enclosing class template, the primary member template and its other partial specializations are still considered for this specialization of the enclosing class template. [*Example:*

```
template<class T> struct A {
        template<class T2> struct B {};          // #1
        template<class T2> struct B<T2*> {};     // #2
};

template<> template<class T2> struct A<short>::B {};     // #3

A<char>::B<int*>  abcip;          // uses #2
A<short>::B<int*> absip;          // uses #3
A<char>::B<int>   abci;           // uses #1
```

—*end example*]

14.5.5 Function templates [temp.fct]

1 A function template defines an unbounded set of related functions. [*Example:* a family of sort functions might be declared like this:

```
template<class T> class Array { };
template<class T> void sort(Array<T>&);
```

—*end example*]

2 A function template can be overloaded with other function templates and with normal (non-template) functions. A normal function is not related to a function template (i.e., it is never considered to be a specialization), even if it has the same name and type as a potentially generated function template specialization.[130]

14.5.5.1 Function template overloading [temp.over.link]

1 It is possible to overload function templates so that two different function template specializations have the same type. [*Example:*

```
// file1.c                      // file2.c
template<class T>               template<class T>
    void f(T*);                     void f(T);
void g(int* p) {                void h(int* p) {
    f(p); // call                   f(p); // call
          // f<int>(int*)                 // f<int*>(int*)
}                               }
```

—*end example*]

2 Such specializations are distinct functions and do not violate the one definition rule (3.2).

3 The signature of a function template specialization consists of the signature of the function template and of the actual template arguments (whether explicitly specified or deduced).

4 The signature of a function template consists of its function signature, its return type and its template parameter list. The names of the template parameters are significant only for establishing the relationship between the template parameters and the rest of the signature. [*Note:* two distinct function templates may have identical function return types and function parameter lists, even if overload resolution alone cannot distinguish them.

```
template<class T> void f();
template<int I> void f();       // OK: overloads the first template
                                // distinguishable with an explicit template argument list
```

—*end note*]

5 When an expression that references a template parameter is used in the function parameter list or the return type in the declaration of a function template, the expression that references the template parameter is part of the signature of the function template. This is necessary to permit a declaration of a function template in one translation unit to be linked with another declaration of the function template in another translation unit and, conversely, to ensure that function templates that are intended to be distinct are not linked with one another. [*Example:*

```
template <int I, int J> A<I+J> f(A<I>, A<J>);   // #1
template <int K, int L> A<K+L> f(A<K>, A<L>);   // same as #1
template <int I, int J> A<I-J> f(A<I>, A<J>);   // different from #1
```

—*end example*] [*Note:* Most expressions that use template parameters use non-type template parameters,

---

[130] That is, declarations of non-template functions do not merely guide overload resolution of function template specializations with the same name. If such a non-template function is used in a program, it must be defined; it will not be implicitly instantiated using the function template definition.

but it is possible for an expression to reference a type parameter. For example, a template type parameter can be used in the `sizeof` operator.]

6   Two expressions involving template parameters are considered *equivalent* if two function definitions containing the expressions would satisfy the one definition rule (3.2), except that the tokens used to name the template parameters may differ as long as a token used to name a template parameter in one expression is replaced by another token that names the same template parameter in the other expression. [*Example:*

```
template <int I, int J> void f(A<I+J>);      // #1
template <int K, int L> void f(A<K+L>);      // same as #1
```

—*end example*] Two expressions involving template parameters that are not equivalent are *functionally equivalent* if, for any given set of template arguments, the evaluation of the expression results in the same value.

7   Two function templates are *equivalent* if they are declared in the same scope, have the same name, have identical template parameter lists, and have return types and parameter lists that are equivalent using the rules described above to compare expressions involving template parameters. Two function templates are *functionally equivalent* if they are equivalent except that one or more expressions that involve template parameters in the return types and parameter lists are functionally equivalent using the rules described above to compare expressions involving template parameters. If a program contains declarations of function templates that are functionally equivalent but not equivalent, the program is ill-formed; no diagnostic is required.

8   [*Note:* This rule guarantees that equivalent declarations will be linked with one another, while not requiring implementations to use heroic efforts to guarantee that functionally equivalent declarations will be treated as distinct. For example, the last two declarations are functionally equivalent and would cause a program to be ill-formed:

```
// Guaranteed to be the same
template <int I> void f(A<I>, A<I+10>);
template <int I> void f(A<I>, A<I+10>);

// Guaranteed to be different
template <int I> void f(A<I>, A<I+10>);
template <int I> void f(A<I>, A<I+11>);

// Ill-formed, no diagnostic required
template <int I> void f(A<I>, A<I+10>);
template <int I> void f(A<I>, A<I+1+2+3+4>);
```

—*end note*]

14.5.5.2 Partial ordering of function templates   [temp.func.order]

1   If a function template is overloaded, the use of a function template specialization might be ambiguous because template argument deduction (14.8.2) may associate the function template specialization with more than one function template declaration. *Partial ordering* of overloaded function template declarations is used in the following contexts to select the function template to which a function template specialization refers:

— during overload resolution for a call to a function template specialization (13.3.3);

— when the address of a function template specialization is taken;

— when a placement operator delete that is a function template specialization is selected to match a placement operator new (3.7.3.2, 5.3.4);

— when a friend function declaration (14.5.3), an explicit instantiation (14.7.2) or an explicit specialization (14.7.3) refers to a function template specialization.

2   Given two overloaded function templates, whether one is more specialized than another can be determined
by transforming each template in turn and using argument deduction (14.8.2) to compare it to the other.

3   The transformation used is:

— For each type template parameter, synthesize a unique type and substitute that for each occurrence of
that parameter in the function parameter list, or for a template conversion function, in the return type.

— For each non-type template parameter, synthesize a unique value of the appropriate type and substitute
that for each occurrence of that parameter in the function parameter list, or for a template conversion
function, in the return type.

— For each template template parameter, synthesize a unique class template and substitute that for each
occurrence of that parameter in the function parameter list, or for a template conversion function, in the
return type.

4   Using the transformed function parameter list, perform argument deduction against the other function template. The transformed template is at least as specialized as the other if, and only if, the deduction succeeds
and the deduced parameter types are an exact match (so the deduction does not rely on implicit conversions).

5   A template is more specialized than another if, and only if, it is at least as specialized as the other template
and that template is not at least as specialized as the first. [*Example:*

```
template<class T> struct A { A(); };

template<class T> void f(T);
template<class T> void f(T*);
template<class T> void f(const T*);

template<class T> void g(T);
template<class T> void g(T&);

template<class T> void h(const T&);
template<class T> void h(A<T>&);

void m() {
        const int *p;
        f(p);                       // f(const T*) is more specialized than f(T) or f(T*)
        float x;
        g(x);                       // Ambiguous: g(T) or g(T&)
        A<int> z;
        h(z);                       // overload resolution selects h(A<T>&)
        const A<int> z2;
        h(z2);                      // h(const T&) is called because h(A<T>&) is not callable
}
```

—*end example*]

6   The presence of unused ellipsis and default arguments has no effect on the partial ordering of function templates. [*Example:*

```
template<class T> void f(T);            // #1
template<class T> void f(T*, int=1);    // #2
template<class T> void g(T);            // #3
template<class T> void g(T*, ...);      // #4
```

```
int main() {
        int* ip;
        f(ip);                  // calls #2
        g(ip);                  // calls #4
}
```

—*end example*]

14.6 Name resolution [temp.res]

1   Three kinds of names can be used within a template definition:

— The name of the template itself, and names declared within the template itself.

— Names dependent on a *template-parameter* (14.6.2).

— Names from scopes which are visible within the template definition.

2   A name used in a template declaration or definition and that is dependent on a *template-parameter* is assumed not to name a type unless the applicable name lookup finds a type name or the name is qualified by the keyword typename. [*Example:*

```
// no B declared here

class X;

template<class T> class Y {
        class Z;                // forward declaration of member class

        void f() {
                X* a1;          // declare pointer to X
                T* a2;          // declare pointer to T
                Y* a3;          // declare pointer to Y<T>
                Z* a4;          // declare pointer to Z
                typedef typename T::A TA;
                TA* a5;                 // declare pointer to T's A
                typename T::A* a6;      // declare pointer to T's A
                T::A* a7;               // T::A is not a type name:
                                        // multiply T::A by a7; ill-formed,
                                        // no visible declaration of a7
                B* a8;                  // B is not a type name:
                                        // multiply B by a8; ill-formed,
                                        // no visible declarations of B and a8

        }
};
```

—*end example*]

3   A *qualified-id* that refers to a type and in which the *nested-name-specifier* depends on a *template-parameter* (14.6.2) shall be prefixed by the keyword typename to indicate that the *qualified-id* denotes a type, forming an *elaborated-type-specifier* (7.1.5.3).

> *elaborated-type-specifier:*
>   . . .
>   typename ::$_{opt}$ *nested-name-specifier identifier*
>   typename ::$_{opt}$ *nested-name-specifier* template$_{opt}$ *template-id*
>   . . .

4   If a specialization of a template is instantiated for a set of *template-argument*s such that the *qualified-id* prefixed by typename does not denote a type, the specialization is ill-formed. The usual qualified name lookup (3.4.3) is used to find the *qualified-id* even in the presence of typename. [*Example:*

```
struct A {
        struct X { };
        int X;
};
template<class T> void f(T t) {
        typename T::X x;          // ill-formed: finds the data member X
                                  // not the member type X
}
```

—*end example*]

5   The keyword `typename` shall only be used in template declarations and definitions, including in the return type of a function template or member function template, in the return type for the definition of a member function of a class template or of a class nested within a class template, and in the *type-specifier* for the definition of a static member of a class template or of a class nested within a class template. The keyword `typename` shall be applied only to qualified names, but those names need not be dependent. The keyword `typename` shall be used only in contexts in which dependent names can be used. This includes template declarations and definitions but excludes explicit specialization declarations and explicit instantiation declarations. The keyword `typename` is not permitted in a *base-specifier* or in a *mem-initializer*; in these contexts a *qualified-id* that depends on a *template-parameter* (14.6.2) is implicitly assumed to be a type name.

6   Within the definition of a class template or within the definition of a member of a class template, the keyword `typename` is not required when referring to the unqualified name of a previously declared member of the class template that declares a type. The keyword `typename` shall always be specified when the member is referred to using a qualified name, even if the qualifier is simply the class template name. [*Example:*

```
template<class T> struct A {
    typedef int B;
    A::B b;                  // ill-formed: typename required before A::B
    void f(A<T>::B);         // ill-formed: typename required before A<T>::B
    typename A::B g();       // OK
};
```

The keyword `typename` is required whether the qualified name is A or A<T> because A or A<T> are synonyms within a class template with the parameter list <T>.]

7   Knowing which names are type names allows the syntax of every template definition to be checked. No diagnostic shall be issued for a template definition for which a valid specialization can be generated. If no valid specialization can be generated for a template definition, and that template is not instantiated, the template definition is ill-formed, no diagnostic required. If a type used in a non-dependent name is incomplete at the point at which a template is defined but is complete at the point at which an instantiation is done, and if the completeness of that type affects whether or not the program is well-formed or affects the semantics of the program, the program is ill-formed; no diagnostic is required. [*Note:* if a template is instantiated, errors will be diagnosed according to the other rules in this Standard. Exactly when these errors are diagnosed is a quality of implementation issue.] [*Example:*

```
int j;
template<class T> class X {
        // ...
        void f(T t, int i, char* p)
        {
                t = i;                  // diagnosed if X::f is instantiated
                                        // and the assignment to t is an error
                p = i;                  // may be diagnosed even if X::f is
                                        // not instantiated
                p = j;                  // may be diagnosed even if X::f is
                                        // not instantiated

        }
        void g(T t) {
                +;                      // may be diagnosed even if X::g is
                                        // not instantiated

        }
};
```

—end example]

8   When looking for the declaration of a name used in a template definition, the usual lookup rules (3.4.1, 3.4.2) are used for nondependent names. The lookup of names dependent on the template parameters is postponed until the actual template argument is known (14.6.2). [*Example:*

```
#include <iostream>
using namespace std;

template<class T> class Set {
        T* p;
        int cnt;
public:
        Set();
        Set<T>(const Set<T>&);
        void printall()
        {
                for (int i = 0; i<cnt; i++)
                        cout << p[i] << '\n';
        }
        // ...
};
```

in the example, i is the local variable i declared in printall, cnt is the member cnt declared in Set, and cout is the standard output stream declared in iostream. However, not every declaration can be found this way; the resolution of some names must be postponed until the actual *template-arguments* are known. For example, even though the name operator<< is known within the definition of printall() and a declaration of it can be found in <iostream>, the actual declaration of operator<< needed to print p[i] cannot be known until it is known what type T is (14.6.2).]

9   If a name does not depend on a *template-parameter* (as defined in 14.6.2), a declaration (or set of declarations) for that name shall be in scope at the point where the name appears in the template definition; the name is bound to the declaration (or declarations) found at that point and this binding is not affected by declarations that are visible at the point of instantiation. [*Example:*

```
void f(char);

template<class T> void g(T t)
{
        f(1);                    // f(char)
        f(T(1));                 // dependent
        f(t);                    // dependent
        dd++;                    // not dependent
                                 // error: declaration for dd not found

}

void f(int);

double dd;
void h()
{
        g(2);                    // will cause one call of f(char) followed
                                 // by two calls of f(int)
        g('a');                  // will cause three calls of f(char)
}
```

—*end example*]

10   [*Note:* for purposes of name lookup, default arguments of function templates and default arguments of member functions of class templates are considered definitions (14.5). —*end note*]

14.6.1 Locally declared names   [temp.local]

1   Like normal (non-template) classes, class templates have an injected-class-name (clause 9). The injected-class-name can be used with or without a *template-argument-list*. When it is used without a *template-argument-list*, it is equivalent to the injected-class-name followed by the *template-parameter*s of the class template enclosed in < >. When it is used with a *template-argument-list*, it refers to the specified class template specialization, which could be the current specialization or another specialization.

2   Within the scope of a class template specialization or partial specialization, when the injected-class-name is not followed by a <, it is equivalent to the injected-class-name followed by the *template-argument*s of the class template specialization or partial specialization enclosed in < >. [*Example:*

```
template<class T> class Y;
template<> class Y<int> {
    Y* p;                       // meaning Y<int>
    Y<char>* q;                 // meaning Y<char>
};
```

—*end example*]

2a   The injected-class-name of a class template or class template specialization can be used either with or without a *template-argument-list* wherever it is in scope. [*Example:*

```
template <class T> struct Base {
    Base* p;
};

template <class T> struct Derived: public Base<T> {
    typename Derived::Base* p;  // meaning Derived::Base<T>
};
```

—*end example*]

2b   A lookup that finds an injected-class-name (10.2) can result in an ambiguity in certain cases (for example, if it is found in more than one base class). If all of the injected-class-names that are found refer to specializations of the same class template, and if the name is followed by a *template-argument-list*, the reference refers to the class template itself and not a specialization thereof, and is not ambiguous. [*Example:*

```
template <class T> struct Base { };
template <class T> struct Derived: Base<int>, Base<char> {
    typename Derived::Base b;            // error: ambiguous
    typename Derived::Base<double> d;    // OK
};
```

—*end example*]

2c   When the normal name of the template (i.e., the name from the enclosing scope, not the injected-class-name) is used without a *template-argument-list*, it refers to the class template itself and not a specialization of the template. [*Example:*

```
template <class T> class X {
    X* p;                    // meaning X<T>
    X<T>* p2;
    X<int>* p3;
    ::X* p4;                 // error: missing template argument list
                             // ::X does not refer to the injected-class-name
};
```

—*end example*]

2d   Within the scope of a class template, when the unqualified name of a nested class of the class template is referred to, it is equivalent to the name of the nested class qualified by the name of the enclosing class template. [*Example:*

```
template <class T> struct A {
    class B { };             // B is equivalent to A::B, which is equivalent to A<T>::B,

                             // which is dependent.
    class C : B { };
};
```

—*end example*]

3   The scope of a *template-parameter* extends from its point of declaration until the end of its template. A *template-parameter* hides any entity with the same name in the enclosing scope. [*Note:* this implies that a *template-parameter* can be used in the declaration of subsequent *template-parameter*s and their default arguments but cannot be used in preceding *template-parameter*s or their default arguments. For example,

```
template<class T, T* p, class U = T> class X { /* ... */ };
template<class T> void f(T* p = new T);
```

This also implies that a *template-parameter* can be used in the specification of base classes. For example,

```
template<class T> class X : public Array<T> { /* ... */ };
template<class T> class Y : public T { /* ... */ };
```

The use of a *template-parameter* as a base class implies that a class used as a *template-argument* must be defined and not just declared when the class template is instantiated.]

4   A *template-parameter* shall not be redeclared within its scope (including nested scopes). A *template-parameter* shall not have the same name as the template name. [*Example:*

```
template<class T, int i> class Y {
        int T;                          // error: template-parameter redeclared
        void f() {
                char T;                 // error: template-parameter redeclared
        }
};

template<class X> class X;              // error: template-parameter redeclared
```

—end example]

5   In the definition of a member of a class template that appears outside of the class template definition, the
    name of a member of this template hides the name of a *template-parameter*. [*Example:*

```
template<class T> struct A {
        struct B { /* ... */ };
        void f();
};

template<class B> void A<B>::f() {
        B b;                            // A's B, not the template parameter
}
```

—end example]

6   In the definition of a member of a class template that appears outside of the namespace containing the class
    template definition, the name of a *template-parameter* hides the name of a member of this namespace.
    [*Example:*

```
namespace N {
        class C { };
        template<class T> class B {
                void f(T);
        };
}
template<class C> void N::B<C>::f(C) {
        C b;                            // C is the template parameter, not N::C
}
```

—end example]

7   In the definition of a class template or in the definition of a member of such a template that appears outside
    of the template definition, for each base class which does not depend on a *template-parameter* (14.6.2), if
    the name of the base class or the name of a member of the base class is the same as the name of a *template-
    parameter*, the base class name or member name hides the *template-parameter* name (3.3.7). [*Example:*

```
struct A {
        struct B { /* ... */ };
        int a;
        int Y;
};

template<class B, class a> struct X : A {
        B b;                    // A's B
        a b;                    // error: A's a isn't a type name
};
```

—end example]

14.6.2 Dependent names [temp.dep]

1   Inside a template, some constructs have semantics which may differ from one instantiation to another. Such a construct *depends* on the template parameters. In particular, types and expressions may depend on the type and/or value of template parameters (as determined by the template arguments) and this determines the context for name lookup for certain names. Expressions may be *type-dependent* (on the type of a template parameter) or *value-dependent* (on the value of a non-type template parameter). In an expression of the form:

$$\textit{postfix-expression} \quad (\quad \textit{expression-list}_{\text{opt}} \quad)$$

where the *postfix-expression* is an *identifier*, the *identifier* denotes a *dependent name* if and only if any of the expressions in the *expression-list* is a type-dependent expression (14.6.2.2). If an operand of an operator is a type-dependent expression, the operator also denotes a dependent name. Such names are unbound and are looked up at the point of the template instantiation (14.6.4.1) in both the context of the template definition and the context of the point of instantiation.

2   [*Example:*

```
template<class T> struct X : B<T> {
        typename T::A* pa;
        void f(B<T>* pb) {
                static int i = B<T>::i;
                pb->j++;
        }
};
```

the base class name B<T>, the type name T::A, the names B<T>::i and pb->j explicitly depend on the *template-parameter*. —*end example*]

3   In the definition of a class template or a member of a class template, if a base class of the class template depends on a *template-parameter*, the base class scope is not examined during unqualified name lookup either at the point of definition of the class template or member or during an instantiation of the class template or member. [*Example:*

```
typedef double A;
template<class T> class B {
        typedef int A;
};
template<class T> struct X : B<T> {
        A a;                       // a has type double
};
```

The type name A in the definition of X<T> binds to the typedef name defined in the global namespace scope, not to the typedef name defined in the base class B<T>.] [*Example:*

```
struct A {
        struct B { /* ... */ };
        int a;
        int Y;
};

int a;
```

```
template<class T> struct Y : T {
        struct B { /* ... */ };
        B b;                                    // The B defined in Y
        void f(int i) { a = i; }                // ::a
        Y* p;                                   // Y<T>
};

Y<A> ya;
```

The members `A::B`, `A::a`, and `A::Y` of the template argument `A` do not affect the binding of names in `Y<A>.`]

14.6.2.1 Dependent types   [temp.dep.type]

1   A type is dependent if it is

— a template parameter,

— a *qualified-id* with a *nested-name-specifier* which contains a *class-name* that names a dependent type or whose *unqualified-id* names a dependent type,

— a cv-qualified type where the cv-unqualified type is dependent,

— a compound type constructed from any dependent type,

— an array type constructed from any dependent type or whose size is specified by a constant expression that is value-dependent,

— a *template-id* in which either the template name is a template parameter or any of the template arguments is a dependent type or an expression that is type-dependent or value-dependent.

14.6.2.2 Type-dependent expressions   [temp.dep.expr]

1   Except as described below, an expression is type-dependent if any subexpression is type-dependent.

2   `this` is type-dependent if the class type of the enclosing member function is dependent (14.6.2.1).

3   An *id-expression* is type-dependent if it contains:

— an *identifier* that was declared with a dependent type,

— a *template-id* that is dependent,

— a *conversion-function-id* that specifies a dependent type,

— a *nested-name-specifier* that contains a *class-name* that names a dependent type.

Expressions of the following forms are type-dependent only if the type specified by the *type-id*, *simple-type-specifier* or *new-type-id* is dependent, even if any subexpression is type-dependent:

simple-type-specifier (*expression-list*$_{opt}$)
`::`$_{opt}$ `new` *new-placement*$_{opt}$ *new-type-id* *new-initializer*$_{opt}$
`::`$_{opt}$ `new` *new-placement*$_{opt}$ (*type-id*) *new-initializer*$_{opt}$
`dynamic_cast` < *type-id* > (*expression*)
`static_cast` < *type-id* > (*expression*)
`const_cast` < *type-id* > (*expression*)
`reinterpret_cast` < *type-id* > (*expression*)
(*type-id*) *cast-expression*

4   Expressions of the following forms are never type-dependent (because the type of the expression cannot be dependent):

> *literal*
> *postfix-expression* . *pseudo-destructor-name*
> *postfix-expression* -> *pseudo-destructor-name*
> sizeof *unary-expression*
> sizeof (*type-id*)
> typeid (*expression*)
> typeid (*type-id*)
> ::$_{opt}$ delete *cast-expression*
> ::$_{opt}$ delete [ ] *cast-expression*
> throw *assignment-expression*$_{opt}$

14.6.2.3 Value-dependent expressions [temp.dep.constexpr]

1 Except as described below, a constant expression is value-dependent if any subexpression is value-dependent.

2 An *identifier* is value-dependent if it is:

— a name declared with a dependent type,

— the name of a non-type template parameter,

— a constant with integral or enumeration type and is initialized with an expression that is value-dependent.

Expressions of the following form are value-dependent if the *unary-expression* is type-dependent or the *type-id* is dependent (even if sizeof *unary-expression* and sizeof (*type-id*) are not type-dependent):

> sizeof *unary-expression*
> sizeof (*type-id*)

3 Expressions of the following form are value-dependent if either the *type-id* or *simple-type-specifier* is dependent or the *expression* or *cast-expression* is value-dependent:

> *simple-type-specifier* (*expression-list*$_{opt}$)
> static_cast < *type-id* > (*expression*)
> const_cast < *type-id* > (*expression*)
> reinterpret_cast < *type-id* > (*expression*)
> (*type-id*) *cast-expression*

14.6.2.4 Dependent template arguments [temp.dep.temp]

1 A type *template-argument* is dependent if the type it specifies is dependent.

2 An integral non-type *template-argument* is dependent if the constant expression it specifies is value-dependent.

3 A non-integral non-type *template-argument* is dependent if its type is dependent or it has either of the following forms

> *qualified-id*
> & *qualified-id*

and contains a *nested-name-specifier* which specifies a *class-name* that names a dependent type.

4 A template *template-argument* is dependent if it names a *template-parameter* or is a *qualified-id* with a *nested-name-specifier* which contains a *class-name* that names a dependent type.

14.6.3 Non-dependent names   [temp.nondep]

1   Non-dependent names used in a template definition are found using the usual name lookup and bound at the
     point they are used. [*Example:*

```
void g(double);
void h();

template<class T> class Z {
public:
        void f() {
                g(1);           // calls g(double)
                h++;            // ill-formed: cannot increment function;
                                // this could be diagnosed either here or
                                // at the point of instantiation

        }
};

void g(int);                    // not in scope at the point of the template
                                // definition, not considered for the call g(1)
```

—*end example*]

14.6.4 Dependent name resolution   [temp.dep.res]

1   In resolving dependent names, names from the following sources are considered:

     — Declarations that are visible at the point of definition of the template.

     — Declarations from namespaces associated with the types of the function arguments both from the instan-
     tiation context (14.6.4.1) and from the definition context.

14.6.4.1 Point of instantiation   [temp.point]

1   For a function template specialization, a member function template specialization, or a specialization for a
     member function or static data member of a class template, if the specialization is implicitly instantiated
     because it is referenced from within another template specialization and the context from which it is refer-
     enced depends on a template parameter, the point of instantiation of the specialization is the point of instan-
     tiation of the enclosing specialization. Otherwise, the point of instantiation for such a specialization imme-
     diately follows the namespace scope declaration or definition that refers to the specialization.

2   If a function template or member function of a class template is called in a way which uses the definition of
     a default argument of that function template or member function, the point of instantiation of the default
     argument is the point of instantiation of the function template or member function specialization.

3   For a class template specialization, a class member template specialization, or a specialization for a class
     member of a class template, if the specialization is implicitly instantiated because it is referenced from
     within another template specialization, if the context from which the specialization is referenced depends
     on a template parameter, and if the specialization is not instantiated previous to the instantiation of the
     enclosing template, the point of instantiation is immediately before the point of instantiation of the enclos-
     ing template. Otherwise, the point of instantiation for such a specialization immediately precedes the
     namespace scope declaration or definition that refers to the specialization.

4   If a virtual function is implicitly instantiated, its point of instantiation is immediately following the point of
     instantiation of its enclosing class template specialization.

5   An explicit instantiation directive is an instantiation point for the specialization or specializations specified
     by the explicit instantiation directive.

6   The instantiation context of an expression that depends on the template arguments is the set of declarations
     with external linkage declared prior to the point of instantiation of the template specialization in the same

translation unit.

7   A specialization for a function template, a member function template, or of a member function or static data member of a class template may have multiple points of instantiations within a translation unit. A specialization for a class template has at most one point of instantiation within a translation unit. A specialization for any template may have points of instantiation in multiple translation units. If two different points of instantiation give a template specialization different meanings according to the one definition rule (3.2), the program is ill-formed, no diagnostic required.

14.6.4.2 Candidate functions   [temp.dep.candidate]

1   For a function call that depends on a template parameter, if the function name is an *unqualified-id* but not a *template-id*, the candidate functions are found using the usual lookup rules (3.4.1, 3.4.2) except that:

— For the part of the lookup using unqualified name lookup (3.4.1), only function declarations with external linkage from the template definition context are found.

— For the part of the lookup using associated namespaces (3.4.2), only function declarations with external linkage found in either the template definition context or the template instantiation context are found.

If the call would be ill-formed or would find a better match had the lookup within the associated namespaces considered all the function declarations with external linkage introduced in those namespaces in all translation units, not just considering those declarations found in the template definition and template instantiation contexts, then the program has undefined behavior.

14.6.5 Friend names declared within a class template   [temp.inject]

1   Friend classes or functions can be declared within a class template. When a template is instantiated, the names of its friends are treated as if the specialization had been explicitly declared at its point of instantiation.

2   As with non-template classes, the names of namespace-scope friend functions of a class template specialization are not visible during an ordinary lookup unless explicitly declared at namespace scope (11.4). Such names may be found under the rules for associated classes (3.4.2).[131] [*Example:*

```
template<typename T> class number {
public:
        number(int);
        //...
        friend number gcd(number& x, number& y);
        //...
};

void g()
{
        number<double> a(3), b(4);
        //...
        a = gcd(a,b);                   // finds gcd because number<double> is an
                                        // associated class, making gcd visible
                                        // in its namespace (global scope)
        b = gcd(3,4);                   // ill-formed; gcd is not visible
}
```
—*end example*]

---

[131] Friend declarations do not introduce new names into any scope, either when the template is declared or when it is instantiated.

14.7 Template instantiation and specialization   **[temp.spec]**

1   The act of instantiating a function, a class, a member of a class template or a member template is referred to
     as *template instantiation*.

2   A function instantiated from a function template is called an instantiated function. A class instantiated from
     a class template is called an instantiated class. A member function, a member class, or a static data member
     of a class template instantiated from the member definition of the class template is called, respectively, an
     instantiated member function, member class or static data member. A member function instantiated from a
     member function template is called an instantiated member function. A member class instantiated from a
     member class template is called an instantiated member class.

3   An explicit specialization may be declared for a function template, a class template, a member of a class
     template or a member template. An explicit specialization declaration is introduced by `template<>`. In
     an explicit specialization declaration for a class template, a member of a class template or a class member
     template, the name of the class that is explicitly specialized shall be a *template-id*. In the explicit special-
     ization declaration for a function template or a member function template, the name of the function or
     member function explicitly specialized may be a *template-id*. [*Example:*

```
template<class T = int> struct A {
        static int x;
};
template<class U> void g(U) { }

template<> struct A<double> { };        // specialize for T == double
template<> struct A<> { };              // specialize for T == int
template<> void g(char) { }             // specialize for U == char
                                        // U is deduced from the parameter type
template<> void g<int>(int) { }         // specialize for U == int
template<> int A<char>::x = 0;          // specialize for T == char

template<class T = int> struct B {
        static int x;
};
template<> int B<>::x = 1;       // specialize for T == int
```

     —*end example*]

4   An instantiated template specialization can be either implicitly instantiated (14.7.1) for a given argument
     list or be explicitly instantiated (14.7.2). A specialization is a class, function, or class member that is either
     instantiated or explicitly specialized (14.7.3).

5   No program shall explicitly instantiate any template more than once, both explicitly instantiate and explic-
     itly specialize a template, or specialize a template more than once for a given set of *template-argument*s.
     An implementation is not required to diagnose a violation of this rule.

6   Each class template specialization instantiated from a template has its own copy of any static members.
     [*Example:*

```
template<class T> class X {
        static T s;
        // ...
};
template<class T> T X<T>::s = 0;
X<int> aa;
X<char*> bb;
```

     `X<int>` has a static member s of type `int` and `X<char*>` has a static member s of type `char*`.]

14.7.1 Implicit instantiation **[temp.inst]**

1   Unless a class template specialization has been explicitly instantiated (14.7.2) or explicitly specialized (14.7.3), the class template specialization is implicitly instantiated when the specialization is referenced in a context that requires a completely-defined object type or when the completeness of the class type affects the semantics of the program. The implicit instantiation of a class template specialization causes the implicit instantiation of the declarations, but not of the definitions or default arguments, of the class member functions, member classes, static data members and member templates; and it causes the implicit instantiation of the definitions of member anonymous unions. Unless a member of a class template or a member template has been explicitly instantiated or explicitly specialized, the specialization of the member is implicitly instantiated when the specialization is referenced in a context that requires the member definition to exist; in particular, the initialization (and any associated side-effects) of a static data member does not occur unless the static data member is itself used in a way that requires the definition of the static data member to exist.

2   Unless a function template specialization has been explicitly instantiated or explicitly specialized, the function template specialization is implicitly instantiated when the specialization is referenced in a context that requires a function definition to exist. Unless a call is to a function template explicit specialization or to a member function of an explicitly specialized class template, a default argument for a function template or a member function of a class template is implicitly instantiated when the function is called in a context that requires the value of the default argument.

3   [*Example:*

```
template<class T> class Z {
public:
        void f();
        void g();
};

void h()
{
        Z<int> a;              // instantiation of class Z<int> required
        Z<char>* p;            // instantiation of class Z<char> not
                               // required
        Z<double>* q;          // instantiation of class Z<double>
                               // not required

        a.f();                 // instantiation of Z<int>::f() required
        p->g();                // instantiation of class Z<char> required, and
                               // instantiation of Z<char>::g() required
}
```

Nothing in this example requires class Z<double>, Z<int>::g(), or Z<char>::f() to be implicitly instantiated.]

4   A class template specialization is implicitly instantiated if the class type is used in a context that requires a completely-defined object type or if the completeness of the class type affects the semantics of the program; in particular, if an expression whose type is a class template specialization is involved in overload resolution, pointer conversion, pointer to member conversion, the class template specialization is implicitly instantiated (3.2); in addition, a class template specialization is implicitly instantiated if the operand of a delete expression is of class type or is of pointer to class type and the class type is a template specialization. [*Example:*

```
template<class T> class B { /* ... */ };
template<class T> class D : public B<T> { /* ... */ };

void f(void*);
void f(B<int>*);

void g(D<int>* p, D<char>* pp, D<double> ppp)
{
        f(p);                     // instantiation of D<int> required: call f(B<int>*)

        B<char>* q = pp;          // instantiation of D<char> required:
                                  // convert D<char>* to B<char>*

        delete ppp;               // instantiation of D<double> required
}
```

—end example]

5   If the overload resolution process can determine the correct function to call without instantiating a class
     template definition, it is unspecified whether that instantiation actually takes place. [*Example:*

```
template <class T> struct S {
        operator int();
};

void f(int);
void f(S<int>&);
void f(S<float>);

void g(S<int>& sr) {
        f(sr);                    // instantiation of S<int> allowed but not required
                                  // instantiation of S<float> allowed but not required
};
```

—end example]

6   If an implicit instantiation of a class template specialization is required and the template is declared but not
     defined, the program is ill-formed. [*Example:*

```
template<class T> class X;

X<char> ch;                       // error: definition of X required
```

—end example]

7   The implicit instantiation of a class template does not cause any static data members of that class to be
     implicitly instantiated.

8   If a function template or a member function template specialization is used in a way that involves overload
     resolution, a declaration of the specialization is implicitly instantiated (14.8.3).

9   An implementation shall not implicitly instantiate a function template, a member template, a non-virtual
     member function, a member class or a static data member of a class template that does not require instantia-
     tion. It is unspecified whether or not an implementation implicitly instantiates a virtual member function of
     a class template if the virtual member function would not otherwise be instantiated. The use of a template
     specialization in a default argument shall not cause the template to be implicitly instantiated except that a
     class template may be instantiated where its complete type is needed to determine the correctness of the
     default argument. The use of a default argument in a function call causes specializations in the default
     argument to be implicitly instantiated.

10   Implicitly instantiated class and function template specializations are placed in the namespace where the template is defined. Implicitly instantiated specializations for members of a class template are placed in the namespace where the enclosing class template is defined. Implicitly instantiated member templates are placed in the namespace where the enclosing class or class template is defined. [*Example:*

```
namespace N {
        template<class T> class List {
        public:
                T* get();
        // ...
        };
}

template<class K, class V> class Map {
        N::List<V> lt;
        V get(K);
        // ...
};

void g(Map<char*,int>& m)
{
        int i = m.get("Nicholas");
        // ...
}
```

a call of `lt.get()` from `Map<char*,int>::get()` would place `List<int>::get()` in the namespace N rather than in the global namespace.]

11   If a function template f is called in a way that requires a default argument expression to be used, the dependent names are looked up, the semantics constraints are checked, and the instantiation of any template used in the default argument expression is done as if the default argument expression had been an expression used in a function template specialization with the same scope, the same template parameters and the same access as that of the function template f used at that point. This analysis is called *default argument instantiation.* The instantiated default argument is then used as the argument of f.

12   Each default argument is instantiated independently. [*Example:*

```
template<class T> void f(T x, T y = ydef(T()), T z = zdef(T()));

class A { };

A zdef(A);

void g(A a, A b, A c) {
        f(a, b, c);                  // no default argument instantiation
        f(a, b);                     // default argument z = zdef(T()) instantiated
        f(a);                        // ill-formed; ydef is not declared
}
```

—*end example*]

13   [*Note:* 14.6.4.1 defines the point of instantiation of a template specialization.]

14   There is an implementation-defined quantity that specifies the limit on the total depth of recursive instantiations, which could involve more than one template. The result of an infinite recursion in instantiation is undefined. [*Example:*

```
template<class T> class X {
        X<T>* p;                        // OK
        X<T*> a;                        // implicit generation of X<T> requires
                                        // the implicit instantiation of X<T*> which requires
                                        // the implicit instantiation of X<T**> which ...
};
```

—*end example*]

14.7.2 Explicit instantiation   [temp.explicit]

1   A class, a function or member template specialization can be explicitly instantiated from its template. A member function, member class or static data member of a class template can be explicitly instantiated from the member definition associated with its class template.

2   The syntax for explicit instantiation is:

> *explicit-instantiation*:
>   template *declaration*

If the explicit instantiation is for a class, a function or a member template specialization, the *unqualified-id* in the *declaration* shall be either a *template-id* or, where all template arguments can be deduced, a *template-name*. [*Note:* the declaration may declare a *qualified-id*, in which case the *unqualified-id* of the *qualified-id* must be a *template-id*.] If the explicit instantiation is for a member function, a member class or a static data member of a class template specialization, the name of the class template specialization in the *qualified-id* for the member *declarator* shall be a *template-id*. [*Example:*

```
template<class T> class Array { void mf(); };
template class Array<char>;
template void Array<int>::mf();

template<class T> void sort(Array<T>& v) { /* ... */ }
template void sort(Array<char>&);            // argument is deduced here

namespace N {
        template<class T> void f(T&) { }
}
template void N::f<int>(int&);
```

—*end example*]

3   A declaration of a function template shall be in scope at the point of the explicit instantiation of the function template. A definition of the class or class template containing a member function template shall be in scope at the point of the explicit instantiation of the member function template. A definition of a class template or class member template shall be in scope at the point of the explicit instantiation of the class template or class member template. A definition of a class template shall be in scope at the point of an explicit instantiation of a member function or a static data member of the class template. A definition of a member class of a class template shall be in scope at the point of an explicit instantiation of the member class. If the *declaration* of the explicit instantiation names an implicitly-declared special member function (clause 12), the program is ill-formed.

4   The definition of a non-exported function template, a non-exported member function template, or a non-exported member function or static data member of a class template shall be present in every translation unit in which it is explicitly instantiated.

5   An explicit instantiation of a class or function template specialization is placed in the namespace in which the template is defined. An explicit instantiation for a member of a class template is placed in the namespace where the enclosing class template is defined. An explicit instantiation for a member template is placed in the namespace where the enclosing class or class template is defined. [*Example:*

```
namespace N {
        template<class T> class Y { void mf() { } };
}

template class Y<int>;                  // error: class template Y not visible
                                        // in the global namespace

using N::Y;
template class Y<int>;                  // OK: explicit instantiation in namespace N

template class N::Y<char*>;                      // OK: explicit instantiation in namespace N
template void N::Y<double>::mf();                // OK: explicit instantiation
                                                 //    in namespace N
```

—*end example*]

6   A trailing *template-argument* can be left unspecified in an explicit instantiation of a function template specialization or of a member function template specialization provided it can be deduced from the type of a function parameter (14.8.2). [*Example:*

```
template<class T> class Array { /* ... */ };
template<class T> void sort(Array<T>& v);

// instantiate sort(Array<int>&) – template-argument deduced
template void sort<>(Array<int>&);
```

—*end example*]

7   The explicit instantiation of a class template specialization implies the instantiation of all of its members not previously explicitly specialized in the translation unit containing the explicit instantiation.

8   The usual access checking rules do not apply to names used to specify explicit instantiations. [*Note:* In particular, the template arguments and names used in the function declarator (including parameter types, return types and exception specifications) may be private types or objects which would normally not be accessible and the template may be a member template or member function which would not normally be accessible.]

9   An explicit instantiation does not constitute a use of a default argument, so default argument instantiation is not done. [*Example:*

```
char* p = 0;
template<class T> T g(T = &p);
template int g<int>(int);            // OK even though &p isn't an int.
```

—*end example*]

14.7.3 Explicit specialization   [temp.expl.spec]

1   An explicit specialization of any of the following:

— function template

— class template

— member function of a class template

— static data member of a class template

— member class of a class template

— member class template of a class template

— member function template of a class template

can be declared by a declaration introduced by `template<>`; that is:

> *explicit-specialization*:
>   `template < >` *declaration*

[*Example:*

```
template<class T> class stream;

template<> class stream<char> { /* ... */ };

template<class T> class Array { /* ... */ };
template<class T> void sort(Array<T>& v) { /* ... */ }

template<> void sort<char*>(Array<char*>&) ;
```

Given these declarations, `stream<char>` will be used as the definition of streams of `char`s; other streams will be handled by class template specializations instantiated from the class template. Similarly, `sort<char*>` will be used as the sort function for arguments of type `Array<char*>`; other `Array` types will be sorted by functions generated from the template.]

2   An explicit specialization shall be declared in the namespace of which the template is a member, or, for member templates, in the namespace of which the enclosing class or enclosing class template is a member. An explicit specialization of a member function, member class or static data member of a class template shall be declared in the namespace of which the class template is a member. Such a declaration may also be a definition. If the declaration is not a definition, the specialization may be defined later in the name-space in which the explicit specialization was declared, or in a namespace that encloses the one in which the explicit specialization was declared.

3   A declaration of a function template or class template being explicitly specialized shall be in scope at the point of declaration of an explicit specialization. [*Note:* a declaration, but not a definition of the template is required.] The definition of a class or class template shall be in scope at the point of declaration of an explicit specialization for a member template of the class or class template. [*Example:*

```
template<> class X<int> { /* ... */ };          // error: X not a template

template<class T> class X;

template<> class X<char*> { /* ... */ };         // OK: X is a template
```

—*end example*]

4   A member function, a member class or a static data member of a class template may be explicitly special-ized for a class specialization that is implicitly instantiated; in this case, the definition of the class template shall be in scope at the point of declaration of the explicit specialization for the member of the class tem-plate. If such an explicit specialization for the member of a class template names an implicitly-declared special member function (clause 12), the program is ill-formed.

5   A member of an explicitly specialized class is not implicitly instantiated from the member declaration of the class template; instead, the member of the class template specialization shall itself be explicitly defined. In this case, the definition of the class template explicit specialization shall be in scope at the point of decla-ration of the explicit specialization of the member. The definition of an explicitly specialized class is unre-lated to the definition of a generated specialization. That is, its members need not have the same names, types, etc. as the members of the a generated specialization. Definitions of members of an explicitly spe-cialized class are defined in the same manner as members of normal classes, and not using the explicit spe-cialization syntax. [*Example:*

```
template<class T> struct A {
        void f(T) { /* ... */ }
};

template<> struct A<int> {
        void f(int);
};

void h()
{
        A<int> a;
        a.f(16);                        // A<int>::f must be defined somewhere
}

// explicit specialization syntax not used for a member of
// explicitly specialized class template specialization
void A<int>::f() { /* ... */ }
```

—end example]

6   If a template, a member template or the member of a class template is explicitly specialized then that specialization shall be declared before the first use of that specialization that would cause an implicit instantiation to take place, in every translation unit in which such a use occurs; no diagnostic is required. If the program does not provide a definition for an explicit specialization and either the specialization is used in a
way that would cause an implicit instantiation to take place or the member is a virtual member function, the
program is ill-formed, no diagnostic required. An implicit instantiation is never generated for an explicit
specialization that is declared but not defined. [*Example:*

```
template<class T> class Array { /* ... */ };
template<class T> void sort(Array<T>& v) { /* ... */ }

void f(Array<String>& v)
{
        sort(v);                        // use primary template
                                        // sort(Array<T>&), T is String
}

template<> void sort<String>(Array<String>& v);  // error: specialization
                                                 // after use of primary template
template<> void sort<>(Array<char*>& v);         // OK: sort<char*> not yet used
```

—end example]

7   The placement of explicit specialization declarations for function templates, class templates, member functions of class templates, static data members of class templates, member classes of class templates, member
class templates of class templates, member function templates of class templates, member functions of
member templates of class templates, member functions of member templates of non-template classes,
member function templates of member classes of class templates, etc., and the placement of partial specialization declarations of class templates, member class templates of non-template classes, member class templates of class templates, etc., can affect whether a program is well-formed according to the relative positioning of the explicit specialization declarations and their points of instantiation in the translation unit as
specified above and below. When writing a specialization, be careful about its location; or to make it compile will be such a trial as to kindle its self-immolation.

8   When a specialization for which an explicit specialization exists is used within the instantiation of an
exported template, and the unspecialized template name is non-dependent in the exported template, a declaration of the explicit specialization shall be declared before the definition of the exported template, in the
translation unit containing that definition. [*Example:*

```
// file #1
#include <vector>
// Primary class template vector
export template<class T> void f(t) {
        std::vector<T>; vec;      // should match the specialization
        /* ... */
}

// file #2
#include <vector>
class B { };
// Explicit specialization of vector for vector<B>
namespace std {
        template<> class vector<B> { /* ... */ };
}
template<class T> void f(T);
void g(B b) {
        f(b);                     // ill-formed:
                                  // f<B> should refer to vector<B>, but the
                                  // specialization was not declared with the
                                  // definition of f in file #1

}
```

—end example]

9   A template explicit specialization is in the scope of the namespace in which the template was defined.
[*Example:*

```
namespace N {
        template<class T> class X { /* ... */ };
        template<class T> class Y { /* ... */ };

        template<> class X<int> { /* ... */ };    // OK: specialization
                                                  //   in same namespace
        template<> class Y<double>;               // forward declare intent to
                                                  // specialize for double
}

template<> class N::Y<double> { /* ... */ };      // OK: specialization
                                                  //   in same namespace
```

—end example]

10 A *template-id* that names a class template explicit specialization that has been declared but not defined can
be used exactly like the names of other incompletely-defined classes (3.9). [*Example:*

```
template<class T> class X;      // X is a class template
template<> class X<int>;

X<int>* p;                      // OK: pointer to declared class X<int>
X<int> x;                       // error: object of incomplete class X<int>
```

—end example]

11 A trailing *template-argument* can be left unspecified in the *template-id* naming an explicit function template specialization provided it can be deduced from the function argument type. [*Example:*

```
template<class T> class Array { /* ... */ };
template<class T> void sort(Array<T>& v);

// explicit specialization for sort(Array<int>&)
// with deduces template-argument of type int
template<> void sort(Array<int>&);
```

—end example]

12   [*Note:* This paragraph is intentionally empty.]

13   A function with the same name as a template and a type that exactly matches that of a template specialization is not an explicit specialization (14.5.5).

14   An explicit specialization of a function template is inline only if it is explicitly declared to be, and independently of whether its function template is. [*Example:*

```
template<class T> void f(T) { /* ... */ }
template<class T> inline T g(T) { /* ... */ }

template<> inline void f<>(int) { /* ... */ }    // OK: inline
template<> int g<>(int) { /* ... */ }            // OK: not inline
```

—end example]

15   An explicit specialization of a static data member of a template is a definition if the declaration includes an initializer; otherwise, it is a declaration. [*Note:* there is no syntax for the definition of a static data member of a template that requires default initialization.

```
template<> X Q<int>::x;
```

This is a declaration regardless of whether X can be default initialized (8.5).]

16   A member or a member template of a class template may be explicitly specialized for a given implicit instantiation of the class template, even if the member or member template is defined in the class template definition. An explicit specialization of a member or member template is specified using the template specialization syntax. [*Example:*

```
template<class T> struct A {
        void f(T);
        template<class X1> void g1(T, X1);
        template<class X2> void g2(T, X2);
        void h(T) { }
};

// specialization
template<> void A<int>::f(int);

// out of class member template definition
template<class T> template<class X1> void A<T>::g1(T, X1) { }

// member template specialization
template<> template<class X1> void A<int>::g1(int, X1);

// member template specialization
template<> template<>
        void A<int>::g1(int, char);      // X1 deduced as char
template<> template<>
        void A<int>::g2<char>(int, char); // X2 specified as char

// member specialization even if defined in class definition
template<> void A<int>::h(int) { }
```

—end example]

17 A member or a member template may be nested within many enclosing class templates. If the declaration of an explicit specialization for such a member appears in namespace scope, the member declaration shall be preceded by a `template<>` for each enclosing class template that is explicitly specialized. [*Example:*

```
template<class T1> class A {
        template<class T2> class B {
                void mf();
        };
};
template<> template<> class A<int>::B<double>;
template<> template<> void A<char>::B<char>::mf();
```

—end example]

18 In an explicit specialization declaration for a member of a class template or a member template that appears in namespace scope, the member template and some of its enclosing class templates may remain unspecialized, except that the declaration shall not explicitly specialize a class member template if its enclosing class templates are not explicitly specialized as well. In such explicit specialization declaration, the keyword `template` followed by a *template-parameter-list* shall be provided instead of the `template<>` preceding the explicit specialization declaration of the member. The types of the *template-parameters* in the *template-parameter-list* shall be the same as those specified in the primary template definition. [*Example:*

```
template<class T1> class A {
        template<class T2> class B {
                template<class T3> void mf1(T3);
                void mf2();
        };
};
template<> template<class X>
  class A<int>::B { };
template<> template<> template<class T>
  void A<int>::B<double>::mf1(T t) { }
template<class Y> template<>
  void A<Y>::B<double>::mf2() { }     // ill-formed; B<double> is specialized but
                                       // its enclosing class template A is not
```

—end example]

19 A specialization of a member function template or member class template of a non-specialized class template is itself a template.

20 An explicit specialization declaration shall not be a friend declaration.

21 Default function arguments shall not be specified in a declaration or a definition for one of the following explicit specializations:

— the explicit specialization of a function template;

— the explicit specialization of a member function template;

— the explicit specialization of a member function of a class template where the class template specialization to which the member function specialization belongs is implicitly instantiated. [*Note:* default function arguments may be specified in the declaration or definition of a member function of a class template specialization that is explicitly specialized.]

1   A function instantiated from a function template is called a function template specialization; so is an explicit specialization of a function template. Template arguments can either be explicitly specified when naming the function template specialization or be deduced (14.8.2) from the context, e.g. from the function arguments in a call to the function template specialization.

2   Each function template specialization instantiated from a template has its own copy of any static variable. [*Example:*

```
template<class T> void f(T* p)
{
        static T s;
        // ...
};

void g(int a, char* b)
{
        f(&a);                  // call f<int>(int*)
        f(&b);                  // call f<char*>(char**)
}
```

Here f<int>(int*) has a static variable s of type int and f<char*>(char**) has a static variable s of type char*.]

14.8.1 Explicit template argument specification [temp.arg.explicit]

1   Template arguments can be specified when referring to a function template specialization by qualifying the function template name with the list of *template-argument*s in the same way as *template-argument*s are specified in uses of a class template specialization. [*Example:*

```
template<class T> void sort(Array<T>& v);
void f(Array<dcomplex>& cv, Array<int>& ci)
{
        sort<dcomplex>(cv);     // sort(Array<dcomplex>&)
        sort<int>(ci);          // sort(Array<int>&)
}
```

and

```
template<class U, class V> U convert(V v);

void g(double d)
{
        int i = convert<int,double>(d);     // int convert(double)
        char c = convert<char,double>(d);   // char convert(double)
}
```

—*end example*]

2   A template argument list may be specified when referring to a specialization of a function template

— when a function is called,

— when the address of a function is taken, when a function initializes a reference to function, or when a pointer to member function is formed,

— in an explicit specialization,

— in an explicit instantiation, or

— in a friend declaration.

Trailing template arguments that can be deduced (14.8.2) may be omitted from the list of explicit *template-*

arguments. If all of the template arguments can be deduced, they may all be omitted; in this case, the empty template argument list `<>` itself may also be omitted. [*Example:*

```
template<class X, class Y> X f(Y);
void g()
{
        int i = f<int>(5.6);    // Y is deduced to be double
        int j = f(5.6);         // ill-formed: X cannot be deduced
}
```

—*end example*] [*Note:* An empty template argument list can be used to indicate that a given use refers to a specialization of a function template even when a normal (i.e., nontemplate) function is visible that would otherwise be used. For example:

```
template <class T> int f(T);    // #1
int f(int);                     // #2
int k = f(1);                   // uses #2
int l = f<>(1);                 // uses #1
```

—*end note*]

3   Template arguments that are present shall be specified in the declaration order of their corresponding *template-parameters*. The template argument list shall not specify more *template-arguments* than there are corresponding *template-parameters*. [*Example:*

```
template<class X, class Y, class Z> X f(Y,Z);
void g()
{
        f<int,char*,double>("aa",3.0);
        f<int,char*>("aa",3.0); // Z is deduced to be double
        f<int>("aa",3.0);       // Y is deduced to be char*, and
                                // Z is deduced to be double
        f("aa",3.0);            // error: X cannot be deduced
}
```

—*end example*]

4   Implicit conversions (clause 4) will be performed on a function argument to convert it to the type of the corresponding function parameter if the parameter type contains no *template-parameters* that participate in template argument deduction. [*Note:* template parameters do not participate in template argument deduction if they are explicitly specified. For example,

```
template<class T> void f(T);

class Complex {
        // ...
        Complex(double);
};

void g()
{
        f<Complex>(1);          // OK, means f<Complex>(Complex(1))
}
```

—*end note*]

5   [*Note:* because the explicit template argument list follows the function template name, and because conversion member function templates and constructor member function templates are called without using a function name, there is no way to provide an explicit template argument list for these function templates.]

6   [*Note:* For simple function names, argument dependent lookup (3.4.2) applies even when the function name is not visible within the scope of the call. This is because the call still has the syntactic form of a function call (3.4.1). But when a function template with explicit template arguments is used, the call does not have

the correct syntactic form unless there is a function template with that name visible at the point of the call. If no such name is visible, the call is not syntactically well-formed and argument-dependent lookup does not apply. If some such name is visible, argument dependent lookup applies and additional function templates may be found in other namespaces. [*Example:*

```
namespace A {
        struct B { };
        template<int X> void f(B);
}
namespace C {
        template<class T> void f(T t);
}
void g(A::B b) {
        f<3>(b);                // ill-formed: not a function call
        A::f<3>(b);             // well-formed
        C::f<3>(b);             // ill-formed; argument dependent lookup
                                // applies only to unqualified names

        using C::f;
        f<3>(b);                // well-formed because C::f is visible; then
                                // A::f is found by argument dependent lookup

}
```

—*end example*] —*end note*]

14.8.2 Template argument deduction   [temp.deduct]

1   When a function template specialization is referenced, all of the template arguments must have values. The values can be either explicitly specified or, in some cases, deduced from the use. [*Example:*

```
void f(Array<dcomplex>& cv, Array<int>& ci)
{
        sort(cv);               // call sort(Array<dcomplex>&)
        sort(ci);               // call sort(Array<int>&)
}
```

and

```
void g(double d)
{
        int i = convert<int>(d);        // call convert<int,double>(double)
        int c = convert<char>(d);       // call convert<char,double>(double)
}
```

—*end example*]

2   When an explicit template argument list is specified, the template arguments must be compatible with the template parameter list and must result in a valid function type as described below; otherwise type deduction fails. Specifically, the following steps are performed when evaluating an explicitly specified template argument list with respect to a given function template:

— The specified template arguments must match the template parameters in kind (i.e., type, nontype, template), and there must not be more arguments than there are parameters; otherwise type deduction fails.

— Nontype arguments must match the types of the corresponding nontype template parameters, or must be convertible to the types of the corresponding nontype parameters as specified in 14.3.2, otherwise type deduction fails.

— All references in the function type of the function template to the corresponding template parameters are replaced by the specified template argument values. If a substitution in a template parameter or in the function type of the function template results in an invalid type, type deduction fails. [Note: The equivalent substitution in exception specifications is done only when the function is instantiated, at which point a program is ill-formed if the substitution results in an invalid type.] Type deduction may fail for the following reasons:

— Attempting to create an array with an element type that is void, a function type, or a reference type, or attempting to create an array with a size that is zero or negative. [*Example:*

```
template <class T> int f(T[5]);
int I = f<int>(0);
int j = f<void>(0);                    // invalid array
```

]

— Attempting to use a type that is not a class type in a qualified name. [*Example:*

```
template <class T> int f(typename T::B*);
int i = f<int>(0);
```

]

— Attempting to use a type in the qualifier portion of a qualified name that names a type when that type does not contain the specified member, or if the specified member is not a type where a type is required. [*Example:*

```
template <class T> int f(typename T::B*);
struct A {};
struct C { int B; };
int i = f<A>(0);
int j = f<C>(0);
```

]

— Attempting to create a pointer to reference type.

— Attempting to create a reference to a reference type or a reference to void.

— Attempting to create "pointer to member of T" when T is not a class type. [*Example:*

```
template <class T> int f(int T::*);
int i = f<int>(0);
```

]

— Attempting to perform an invalid conversion in either a template argument expression, or an expression used in the function declaration. [*Example:*

```
template <class T, T*> int f(int);
int i2 = f<int,1>(0);                  // can't conv 1 to int*
```

]

— Attempting to create a function type in which a parameter has a type of void.

— Attempting to create a *cv-qualified* function type.

3   After this substitution is performed, the function parameter type adjustments described in 8.3.5 are performed. [*Example:* A parameter type of "void ()(const int, int[5])" becomes "void(*)(int,int*)".] [*Note:* A top-level qualifier in a function parameter declaration does not affect the function type but still affects the type of the function parameter variable within the function. —*end note*] [*Example:*

```
template <class T> void f(T t);
template <class X> void g(const X x);
template <class Z> void h(Z, Z*);

int main()
{
        // #1: function type is f(int), t is nonconst
        f<int>(1);

        // #2: function type is f(int), t is const
        f<const int>(1);

        // #3: function type is g(int), x is const
        g<int>(1);

        // #4: function type is g(int), x is const
        g<const int>(1);

        // #5: function type is h(int, const int*)
        h<const int>(1,0);
}
```

—*end example*] [*Note:* f<int>(1) and f<const int>(1) call distinct functions even though both of the functions called have the same function type. —*end note*]

4   The resulting substituted and adjusted function type is used as the type of the function template for template argument deduction. When all template arguments have been deduced, all uses of template parameters in nondeduced contexts are replaced with the corresponding deduced argument values. If the substitution results in an invalid type, as described above, type deduction fails.

5   Except as described above, the use of an invalid value shall not cause type deduction to fail. [*Example:* In the following example 1000 is converted to signed char and results in an implementation-defined value as specified in (4.7). In other words, both templates are considered even though 1000, when converted to signed char, results in an implementation-defined value.

```
template <int> int f(int);
template <signed char> int f(int);
int i1 = f<1>(0);                    // ambiguous
int i2 = f<1000>(0);                 // ambiguous
```

—*end example*]

14.8.2.1 Deducing template arguments from a function call   [temp.deduct.call]

1   Template argument deduction is done by comparing each function template parameter type (call it P) with the type of the corresponding argument of the call (call it A) as described below.

2   If P is not a reference type:

— If A is an array type, the pointer type produced by the array-to-pointer standard conversion (4.2) is used in place of A for type deduction; otherwise,

— If A is a function type, the pointer type produced by the function-to-pointer standard conversion (4.3) is used in place of A for type deduction; otherwise,

— If A is a cv-qualified type, the top level cv-qualifiers of A's type are ignored for type deduction.

If P is a cv-qualified type, the top level cv-qualifiers of P's type are ignored for type deduction. If P is a reference type, the type referred to by P is used for type deduction.

3　　In general, the deduction process attempts to find template argument values that will make the deduced A identical to A (after the type A is transformed as described above). However, there are three cases that allow a difference:

— If the original P is a reference type, the deduced A (i.e., the type referred to by the reference) can be more cv-qualified than A.

— A can be another pointer or pointer to member type that can be converted to the deduced A via a qualification conversion (4.4).

— If P is a class, and P has the form *template-id*, then A can be a derived class of the deduced A. Likewise, if P is a pointer to a class of the form *template-id*, A can be a pointer to a derived class pointed to by the deduced A.

These alternatives are considered only if type deduction would otherwise fail. If they yield more than one possible deduced A, the type deduction fails. [*Note:* if a *template-parameter* is not used in any of the function parameters of a function template, or is used only in a non-deduced context, its corresponding *template-argument* cannot be deduced from a function call and the *template-argument* must be explicitly specified.]

14.8.2.2　Deducing template arguments taking the address of a function template　　　　　　[temp.deduct.funcaddr]

1　　Template arguments can be deduced from the type specified when taking the address of an overloaded function (13.4). The function template's function type and the specified type are used as the types of P and A, and the deduction is done as described in 14.8.2.4.

14.8.2.3　Deducing conversion function template arguments　　　　　　[temp.deduct.conv]

1　　Template argument deduction is done by comparing the return type of the template conversion function (call it P) with the type that is required as the result of the conversion (call it A) as described in 14.8.2.4.

2　　If A is not a reference type:

— If P is an array type, the pointer type produced by the array-to-pointer standard conversion (4.2) is used in place of P for type deduction; otherwise,

— If P is a function type, the pointer type produced by the function-to-pointer standard conversion (4.3) is used in place of P for type deduction; otherwise,

— If P is a cv-qualified type, the top level cv-qualifiers of P's type are ignored for type deduction.

If A is a cv-qualified type, the top level cv-qualifiers of A's type are ignored for type deduction. If A is a reference type, the type referred to by A is used for type deduction.

3　　In general, the deduction process attempts to find template argument values that will make the deduced A identical to A. However, there are two cases that allow a difference:

— If the original A is a reference type, A can be more cv-qualified than the deduced A (i.e., the type referred to by the reference)

— The deduced A can be another pointer or pointer to member type that can be converted to A via a qualification conversion.

These alternatives are considered only if type deduction would otherwise fail. If they yield more than one possible deduced A, the type deduction fails.

14.8.2.4 Deducing template arguments from a type   [temp.deduct.type]

1   Template arguments can be deduced in several different contexts, but in each case a type that is specified in terms of template parameters (call it P) is compared with an actual type (call it A), and an attempt is made to find template argument values (a type for a type parameter, a value for a non-type parameter, or a template for a template parameter) that will make P, after substitution of the deduced values (call it the deduced A), compatible with A.

2   In some cases, the deduction is done using a single set of types P and A, in other cases, there will be a set of corresponding types P and A. Type deduction is done independently for each P/A pair, and the deduced template argument values are then combined. If type deduction cannot be done for any P/A pair, or if for any pair the deduction leads to more than one possible set of deduced values, or if different pairs yield different deduced values, or if any template argument remains neither deduced nor explicitly specified, template argument deduction fails.

3   A given type P can be composed from a number of other types, templates, and non-type values:

— A function type includes the types of each of the function parameters and the return type.

— A pointer to member type includes the type of the class object pointed to and the type of the member pointed to.

— A type that is a specialization of a class template (e.g., A<int>) includes the types, templates, and non-type values referenced by the template argument list of the specialization.

— An array type includes the array element type and the value of the array bound.

In most cases, the types, templates, and non-type values that are used to compose P participate in template argument deduction. That is, they may be used to determine the value of a template argument, and the value so determined must be consistent with the values determined elsewhere. In certain contexts, however, the value does not participate in type deduction, but instead uses the values of template arguments that were either deduced elsewhere or explicitly specified. If a template parameter is used only in nondeduced contexts and is not explicitly specified, template argument deduction fails.

4   The nondeduced contexts are:

— The *nested-name-specifier* of a type that was specified using a *qualified-id*.

— A type that is a *template-id* in which one or more of the *template-arguments* is an expression that references a *template-parameter*.

When a type name is specified in a way that includes a nondeduced context, all of the types that comprise that type name are also nondeduced. However, a compound type can include both deduced and nondeduced types. [*Example:* If a type is specified as A<T>::B<T2>, both T and T2 are nondeduced. Likewise, if a type is specified as A<I+J>::X<T>, I, J, and T are nondeduced. If a type is specified as void f(typename A<T>::B, A<T>), the T in A<T>::B is nondeduced but the T in A<T> is deduced.]

5   [*Example:* Here is an example in which different parameter/argument pairs produce inconsistent template argument deductions:

```
template<class T> void f(T x, T y) { /* ... */ }
struct A { /* ... */ };
struct B : A { /* ... */ };
int g(A a, B b)
{
        f(a,b);                 // error: T could be A or B
        f(b,a);                 // error: T could be A or B
        f(a,a);                 // OK: T is A
        f(b,b);                 // OK: T is B
}
```

6   Here is an example where two template arguments are deduced from a single function parameter/argument pair. This can lead to conflicts that cause type deduction to fail:

```
template <class T, class U> void f(  T (*)( T, U, U )  );

int g1( int, float, float);
char g2( int, float, float);
int g3( int, char, float);

void r()
{
        f(g1);                   // OK: T is int and U is float
        f(g2);                   // error: T could be char or int
        f(g3);                   // error: U could be char or float
}
```

7   Here is an example where a qualification conversion applies between the argument type on the function call and the deduced template argument type:

```
template<class T> void f(const T*) {}
int *p;
void s()
{
        f(p);                    // f(const int *)
}
```

8   Here is an example where the template argument is used to instantiate a derived class type of the corresponding function parameter type:

```
template <class T> struct B { };
template <class T> struct D : public B<T> {};
struct D2 : public B<int> {};
template <class T> void f(B<T>&){}
void t()
{
        D<int> d;
        D2      d2;
        f(d);                    // calls f(B<int>&)
        f(d2);                   // calls f(B<int>&)
}
```

      —end example]

9   A template type argument T, a template template argument TT or a template non-type argument i can be deduced if P and A have one of the following forms:

```
T
cv-list T
T*
T&
T [integer-constant]
template-name<T>    (where template-name refers to a class template)
type (*) (T)
T (*) ()
T (*) (T)
T type::*
type T::*
T T::*
T (type::*) ()
type (T::*) ()
type (type::*) (T)
type (T::*) (T)
T (type::*) (T)
T (T::*) ()
T (T::*) (T)
type [i]
template-name<i>    (where template-name refers to a class template)
TT<T>
TT<i>
TT<>
```

where (T) represents argument lists where at least one argument type contains a T, and () represents argument lists where no parameter contains a T. Similarly, <T> represents template argument lists where at least one argument contains a T, <i> represents template argument lists where at least one argument contains an i and <> represents template argument lists where no argument contains a T or an i.

10   These forms can be used in the same way as T is for further composition of types. [*Example:*

```
X<int> (*) (char[6])
```

is of the form

template-name<T> (*) (*type* [i])

which is a variant of

type (*) (T)

where type is X<int> and T is char[6].]

11   Template arguments cannot be deduced from function arguments involving constructs other than the ones specified above.

12   A template type argument cannot be deduced from the type of a non-type *template-argument*. [*Example:*

```
template<class T, T i> void f(double a[10][i]);
int v[10][20];
f(v);                              // error: argument for template-parameter T cannot be deduced
```

—*end example*]

13   [*Note:* except for reference and pointer types, a major array bound is not part of a function parameter type and cannot be deduced from an argument:

```
template<int i> void f1(int a[10][i]);
template<int i> void f2(int a[i][20]);
template<int i> void f3(int (&a)[i][20]);
```

```
void g()
{
        int v[10][20];
        f1(v);                          // OK: i deduced to be 20
        f1<20>(v);                      // OK
        f2(v);                          // error: cannot deduce template-argument i
        f2<10>(v);                      // OK
        f3(v);                          // OK: i deduced to be 10
}
```

14   If, in the declaration of a function template with a non-type *template-parameter*, the non-type *template-parameter* is used in an expression in the function parameter-list, the corresponding *template-argument* must always be explicitly specified or deduced elsewhere because type deduction would otherwise always fail for such a *template-argument*.

```
template<int i> class A { /* ... */ };
template<short s> void g(A<s+1>);
void k() {
    A<1> a;
    g(a);                               // error: deduction fails for expression s+1
    g<0>(a);                            // OK
}
```

—*end note*] [*Note:* template parameters do not participate in template argument deduction if they are used only in nondeduced contexts. For example,

```
template<int i, typename T>
T deduce(typename A<T>::X x,       // T is not deduced here
                  T         t,      // but T is deduced here
         typename B<i>::Y y);      // i is not deduced here
A<int> a;
B<77>  b;

int    x = deduce<77>(a.xm, 62, y.ym);
// T is deduced to be int, a.xm must be convertible to
// A<int>::X
// i is explicitly specified to be 77, y.ym must be convertible
// to B<77>::Y
```

—*end note*]

15   If, in the declaration of a function template with a non-type *template-parameter,* the non-type *template-parameter* is used in an expression in the function parameter-list and, if the corresponding *template-argument* is deduced, the *template-argument* type shall match the type of the *template-parameter* exactly, except that a *template-argument* deduced from an array bound may be of any integral type.[132] [*Example:*

```
template<int i> class A { /* ... */ };
template<short s> void f(A<s>);
void k1() {
    A<1> a;
    f(a);                               // error: deduction fails for conversion from int to short
    f<1>(a);                            // OK
}
```

---

[132] Although the *template-argument* corresponding to a *template-parameter* of type bool may be deduced from an array bound, the resulting value will always be true because the array bound will be non-zero.

```
template<const short cs> class B { };
template<short s> void h(B<s>);
void k2() {
    B<1> b;
    g(b);                          // OK: cv-qualifiers are ignored on template parameter types
}
```

—*end example*]

16   A *template-argument* can be deduced from a pointer to function or pointer to member function argument if the set of overloaded functions does not contain function templates and at most one of a set of overloaded functions provides a unique match. [*Example:*

```
template<class T> void f(void(*)(T,int));
template<class T> void foo(T,int);
void g(int,int);
void g(char,int);

void h(int,int,int);
void h(char,int);
int m()
{
        f(&g);                     // error: ambiguous
        f(&h);                     // OK: void h(char,int) is a unique match
        f(&foo);                   // error: type deduction fails because foo is a template
}
```

—*end example*]

17   A template *type-parameter* cannot be deduced from the type of a function default argument. [*Example:*

```
template <class T> void f(T = 5, T = 7);
void g()
{
        f(1);                      // OK: call f<int>(1,7)
        f();                       // error: cannot deduce T
        f<int>();                  // OK: call f<int>(5,7)
}
```

—*end example*]

18   The *template-argument* corresponding to a template *template-parameter* is deduced from the type of the *template-argument* of a class template specialization used in the argument list of a function call. [*Example:*

```
template <template <class T> class X> struct A { };
template <template <class T> class X> void f(A<X>) { }
template<class T> struct B { };
A<B> ab;
f(ab);                             // calls f(A<B>)
```

—*end example*] [*Note:* a default *template-argument* cannot be specified in a function template declaration or definition; therefore default *template-argument*s cannot be used to influence template argument deduction.]

14.8.3   Overload resolution

1   A function template can be overloaded either by (non-template) functions of its name or by (other) function templates of the same name. When a call to that name is written (explicitly, or implicitly using the operator notation), template argument deduction (14.8.2) and checking of any explicit template arguments (14.3) are performed for each function template to find the template argument values (if any) that can be used with that function template to instantiate a function template specialization that can be invoked with the call arguments. For each function template, if the argument deduction and checking succeeds, the *template-argument*s (deduced and/or explicit) are used to instantiate a single function template specialization which is added to the candidate functions set to be used in overload resolution. If, for a given function template, argument deduction fails, no such function is added to the set of candidate functions for that template. The complete set of candidate functions includes all the function templates instantiated in this way and all of the non-template overloaded functions of the same name. The function template specializations are treated like any other functions in the remainder of overload resolution, except as explicitly noted in 13.3.3.[133)]

2   [*Example:*

```
template<class T> T max(T a, T b) { return a>b?a:b; }

void f(int a, int b, char c, char d)
{
        int m1 = max(a,b);        // max(int a, int b)
        char m2 = max(c,d);       // max(char a, char b)
        int m3 = max(a,c);        // error: cannot generate max(int,char)
}
```

3   Adding the non-template function

```
int max(int,int);
```

to the example above would resolve the third call, by providing a function that could be called for `max(a,c)` after using the standard conversion of `char` to `int` for `c`.

4   Here is an example involving conversions on a function argument involved in *template-argument* deduction:

```
template<class T> struct B { /* ... */ };
template<class T> struct D : public B<T> { /* ... */ };
template<class T> void f(B<T>&);

void g(B<int>& bi, D<int>& di)
{
        f(bi);                    // f(bi)
        f(di);                    // f( (B<int>&)di )
}
```

5   Here is an example involving conversions on a function argument not involved in *template-parameter* deduction:

```
template<class T> void f(T*,int);       // #1
template<class T> void f(T,char);       // #2
```

[133)] The parameters of function template specializations contain no template parameter types. The set of conversions allowed on deduced arguments is limited, because the argument deduction process produces function templates with parameters that either match the call arguments exactly or differ only in ways that can be bridged by the allowed limited conversions. Non-deduced arguments allow the full range of conversions. Note also that 13.3.3 specifies that a non-template function will be given preference over a template specialization if the two functions are otherwise equally good candidates for an overload match.

```
void h(int* pi, int i, char c)
{
        f(pi,i);                        // #1: f<int>(pi,i)
        f(pi,c);                        // #2: f<int*>(pi,c)

        f(i,c);                         // #2: f<int>(i,c);
        f(i,i);                         // #2: f<int>(i,char(i))
}
```

—*end example*]

6   Only the signature of a function template specialization is needed to enter the specialization in a set of can-
     didate functions. Therefore only the function template declaration is needed to resolve a call for which a
     template specialization is a candidate. [*Example:*

```
template<class T> void f(T);      // declaration

void g()
{
        f("Annemarie");           // call of f<const char*>
}
```

The call of f is well-formed even if the template f is only declared and not defined at the point of the call.
The program will be ill-formed unless a specialization for f<const char*>, either implicitly or explicitly generated, is present in some translation unit.]

15 Exception handling [except]

1 Exception handling provides a way of transferring control and information from a point in the execution of a program to an exception handler associated with a point previously passed by the execution. A handler will be invoked only by a *throw-expression* invoked in code executed in the handler's try block or in functions called from the handler's try block .

> *try-block:*
>> try *compound-statement handler-seq*
>
> *function-try-block:*
>> try *ctor-initializer_{opt} function-body handler-seq*
>
> *handler-seq:*
>> *handler handler-seq_{opt}*
>
> *handler:*
>> catch (*exception-declaration*) *compound-statement*
>
> *exception-declaration:*
>> *type-specifier-seq declarator*
>> *type-specifier-seq abstract-declarator*
>> *type-specifier-seq*
>> . . .
>
> *throw-expression:*
>> throw *assignment-expression_{opt}*

A *try-block* is a *statement* (clause 6). A *throw-expression* is of type void. Code that executes a *throw-expression* is said to "throw an exception;" code that subsequently gets control is called a "handler." [*Note:* within this clause "try block" is taken to mean both *try-block* and *function-try-block.*]

2 A goto or switch statement shall not be used to transfer control into a try block or into a handler. [*Example:*

```
void f() {
    goto l1;            // Ill-formed
    goto l2;            // Ill-formed
    try {
        goto l1;        // OK
        goto l2;        // Ill-formed
        l1: ;
    } catch (...) {
        l2: ;
        goto l1;        // Ill-formed
        goto l2;        // OK
    }
}
```

—*end example*] A goto, break, return, or continue statement can be used to transfer control out of a try block or handler. When this happens, each variable declared in the try block will be destroyed in the context that directly contains its declaration. [*Example:*

```
lab:  try {
            T1 t1;
            try {
                    T2 t2;
                    if (condition)
                            goto lab;
            } catch(...) { /* handler 2 */ }
      } catch(...) { /* handler 1 */ }
```

Here, executing `goto lab;` will destroy first `t2`, then `t1`, assuming the *condition* does not declare a variable. Any exception raised while destroying `t2` will result in executing *handler 2*; any exception raised while destroying `t1` will result in executing *handler 1*.]

3   A *function-try-block* associates a *handler-seq* with the *ctor-initializer*, if present, and the *function-body*. An exception thrown during the execution of the initializer expressions in the *ctor-initializer* or during the execution of the *function-body* transfers control to a handler in a *function-try-block* in the same way as an exception thrown during the execution of a *try-block* transfers control to other handlers. [*Example:*

```
int f(int);
class C {
        int i;
        double d;
public:
        C(int, double);
};

C::C(int ii, double id)
try
        : i(f(ii)), d(id)
{
        // constructor function body
}
catch (...)
{
        // handles exceptions thrown from the ctor-initializer
        // and from the constructor function body
}
```

—*end example*]

15.1 Throwing an exception   [except.throw]

1   Throwing an exception transfers control to a handler. An object is passed and the type of that object determines which handlers can catch it. [*Example:*

```
throw "Help!";
```

can be caught by a *handler* of `const char*` type:

```
try {
        // ...
}
catch(const char* p) {
        // handle character string exceptions here
}
```

and

```
class Overflow {
        // ...
public:
    Overflow(char,double,double);
};

void f(double x)
{
        // ...
        throw Overflow('+',x,3.45e107);
}
```

can be caught by a handler for exceptions of type `Overflow`

```
try {
        // ...
        f(1.2);
        // ...
}
catch(Overflow& oo) {
        // handle exceptions of type Overflow here
}
```

—*end example*]

2   When an exception is thrown, control is transferred to the nearest handler with a matching type (15.3); "nearest" means the handler for which the *compound-statement*, *ctor-initializer*, or *function-body* following the `try` keyword was most recently entered by the thread of control and not yet exited.

3   A *throw-expression* initializes a temporary object, called the *exception object*, the type of which is determined by removing any top-level *cv-qualifiers* from the static type of the operand of `throw` and adjusting the type from "array of `T`" or "function returning `T`" to "pointer to `T`" or "pointer to function returning `T`", respectively. [*Note:* the temporary object created for a *throw-expression* that is a string literal is never of type `char*` or `wchar_t*`; that is, the special conversions for string literals from the types "array of `const char`" and "array of `const wchar_t`" to the types "pointer to `char`" and "pointer to `wchar_t`", respectively (4.2), are never applied to a *throw-expression*.] The temporary is used to initialize the variable named in the matching *handler* (15.3). The type of the *throw-expression* shall not be an incomplete type, or a pointer or reference to an incomplete type, other than `void*`, `const void*`, `volatile void*`, or `const volatile void*`. Except for these restrictions and the restrictions on type matching mentioned in 15.3, the operand of `throw` is treated exactly as a function argument in a call (5.2.2) or the operand of a return statement.

4   The memory for the temporary copy of the exception being thrown is allocated in an unspecified way, except as noted in 3.7.3.1. The temporary persists as long as there is a handler being executed for that exception. In particular, if a handler exits by executing a `throw;` statement, that passes control to another handler for the same exception, so the temporary remains. When the last handler being executed for the exception exits by any means other than `throw;` the temporary object is destroyed and the implementation may deallocate the memory for the temporary object; any such deallocation is done in an unspecified way. The destruction occurs immediately after the destruction of the object declared in the *exception-declaration* in the handler.

5   If the use of the temporary object can be eliminated without changing the meaning of the program except for the execution of constructors and destructors associated with the use of the temporary object (12.2), then the exception in the handler can be initialized directly with the argument of the throw expression. When the thrown object is a class object, and the copy constructor used to initialize the temporary copy is not accessible, the program is ill-formed (even when the temporary object could otherwise be eliminated). Similarly, if the destructor for that object is not accessible, the program is ill-formed (even when the temporary object could otherwise be eliminated).

6   A *throw-expression* with no operand rethrows the exception being handled. The exception is reactivated with the existing temporary; no new temporary exception object is created. The exception is no longer considered to be caught; therefore, the value of uncaught_exception() will again be true. [*Example:* code that must be executed because of an exception yet cannot completely handle the exception can be written like this:

```
try {
        // ...
}
catch (...) {                            // catch all exceptions

        // respond (partially) to exception

        throw;                           // pass the exception to some
                                         // other handler
}
```

—*end example*]

7   The exception thrown is the one most recently caught and not finished. An exception is considered caught when initialization is complete for the formal parameter of the corresponding catch clause, or when terminate() or unexpected() is entered due to a throw. An exception is considered finished when the corresponding catch clause exits or when unexpected() exits after being entered due to a throw.

8   If no exception is presently being handled, executing a *throw-expression* with no operand calls terminate() (15.5.1).

15.2 Constructors and destructors [except.ctor]

1   As control passes from a *throw-expression* to a handler, destructors are invoked for all automatic objects constructed since the try block was entered. The automatic objects are destroyed in the reverse order of the completion of their construction.

2   An object that is partially constructed or partially destroyed will have destructors executed for all of its fully constructed subobjects, that is, for subobjects for which the constructor has completed execution and the destructor has not yet begun execution. Should a constructor for an element of an automatic array throw an exception, only the constructed elements of that array will be destroyed. If the object or array was allocated in a *new-expression*, the matching deallocation function (3.7.3.2, 5.3.4, 12.5), if any, is called to free the storage occupied by the object.

3   The process of calling destructors for automatic objects constructed on the path from a try block to a *throw-expression* is called "*stack unwinding.*" [*Note:* If a destructor called during stack unwinding exits with an exception, terminate is called (15.5.1). So destructors should generally catch exceptions and not let them propagate out of the destructor. —*end note*]

15.3 Handling an exception [except.handle]

1   The *exception-declaration* in a *handler* describes the type(s) of exceptions that can cause that *handler* to be entered. The *exception-declaration* shall not denote an incomplete type. The *exception-declaration* shall not denote a pointer or reference to an incomplete type, other than void*, const void*, volatile void*, or const volatile void*. Types shall not be defined in an *exception-declaration*.

2   A handler of type "array of T" or "function returning T" is adjusted to be of type "pointer to T" or "pointer to function returning T", respectively.

3   A *handler* is a match for an exception object of type E if

     — The *handler* is of type cv T or cv T& and E and T are the same type (ignoring the top-level *cv-qualifiers*), or

— the *handler* is of type *cv* T or *cv* T& and T is an unambiguous public base class of E, or

— the *handler* is of type *cv1* T* *cv2* and E is a pointer type that can be converted to the type of the *handler* by either or both of

— a standard pointer conversion (4.10) not involving conversions to pointers to private or protected or ambiguous classes

— a qualification conversion

[*Note:* a *throw-expression* which is an integral constant expression of integer type that evaluates to zero does not match a handler of pointer type; that is, the null pointer constant conversions (4.10, 4.11) do not apply.]

4   [*Example:*

```
class Matherr { /* ... */ virtual vf(); };
class Overflow: public Matherr { /* ... */ };
class Underflow: public Matherr { /* ... */ };
class Zerodivide: public Matherr { /* ... */ };

void f()
{
    try {
        g();
    }

    catch (Overflow oo) {
        // ...
    }
    catch (Matherr mm) {
        // ...
    }
}
```

Here, the Overflow handler will catch exceptions of type Overflow and the Matherr handler will catch exceptions of type Matherr and of all types publicly derived from Matherr including exceptions of type Underflow and Zerodivide.]

5   The handlers for a try block are tried in order of appearance. That makes it possible to write handlers that can never be executed, for example by placing a handler for a derived class after a handler for a corresponding base class.

6   A . . . in a handler's *exception-declaration* functions similarly to . . . in a function parameter declaration; it specifies a match for any exception. If present, a . . . handler shall be the last handler for its try block.

7   If no match is found among the handlers for a try block, the search for a matching handler continues in a dynamically surrounding try block.

8   An exception is considered handled upon entry to a handler. [*Note:* the stack will have been unwound at that point.]

9   If no matching handler is found in a program, the function terminate() is called; whether or not the stack is unwound before this call to terminate() is implementation-defined (15.5.1).

10   Referring to any non-static member or base class of an object in the handler for a *function-try-block* of a constructor or destructor for that object results in undefined behavior.

11   The fully constructed base classes and members of an object shall be destroyed before entering the handler of a *function-try-block* of a constructor or destructor for that object.

12   The scope and lifetime of the parameters of a function or constructor extend into the handlers of a *function-try-block*.

13   Exceptions thrown in destructors of objects with static storage duration or in constructors of namespace-scope objects are not caught by a *function-try-block* on `main()`.

14   If the handlers of a *function-try-block* contain a jump into the body of a constructor or destructor, the program is ill-formed.

15   If a return statement appears in a handler of the *function-try-block* of a constructor, the program is ill-formed.

16   The exception being handled is rethrown if control reaches the end of a handler of the *function-try-block* of a constructor or destructor. Otherwise, a function returns when control reaches the end of a handler for the *function-try-block* (6.6.3). Flowing off the end of a *function-try-block* is equivalent to a `return` with no value; this results in undefined behavior in a value-returning function (6.6.3).

17   When the *exception-declaration* specifies a class type, a copy constructor is used to initialize either the object declared in the *exception-declaration* or, if the *exception-declaration* does not specify a name, a temporary object of that type. The object shall not have an abstract class type. The object is destroyed when the handler exits, after the destruction of any automatic objects initialized within the handler. The copy constructor and destructor shall be accessible in the context of the handler. If the copy constructor and destructor are implicitly declared (12.8), such a use in the handler causes these functions to be implicitly defined; otherwise, the program shall provide a definition for these functions.

18   If the use of a temporary object can be eliminated without changing the meaning of the program except for execution of constructors and destructors associated with the use of the temporary object, then the optional name can be bound directly to the temporary object specified in a *throw-expression* causing the handler to be executed. The copy constructor and destructor associated with the object shall be accessible even when the temporary object is eliminated.

19   When the handler declares a non-constant object, any changes to that object will not affect the temporary object that was initialized by execution of the *throw-expression*. When the handler declares a reference to a non-constant object, any changes to the referenced object are changes to the temporary object initialized when the *throw-expression* was executed and will have effect should that object be rethrown.

15.4 Exception specifications   [except.spec]

1   A function declaration lists exceptions that its function might directly or indirectly throw by using an *exception-specification* as a suffix of its declarator.

> *exception-specification:*
>   throw (*type-id-list*$_{opt}$)
>
> *type-id-list:*
>   *type-id*
>   *type-id-list* , *type-id*

An *exception-specification* shall appear only on a function declarator in a function, pointer, reference or pointer to member declaration or definition. An *exception-specification* shall not appear in a typedef declaration. [*Example:*

```
void f() throw(int);                // OK
void (*fp)() throw (int);           // OK
void g(void pfa() throw(int));      // OK
typedef int (*pf)() throw(int);     // ill-formed
```

—*end example*] A type denoted in an *exception-specification* shall not denote an incomplete type. A type denoted in an *exception-specification* shall not denote a pointer or reference to an incomplete type, other than `void*`, `const void*`, `volatile void*`, or `const volatile void*`.

2   If any declaration of a function has an *exception-specification*, all declarations, including the definition and an explicit specialization, of that function shall have an *exception-specification* with the same set of *type-ids*. If any declaration of a pointer to function, reference to function, or pointer to member function has an *exception-specification*, all occurrences of that declaration shall have an *exception-specification* with the same set of *type-ids*. In an explicit instantiation directive an *exception-specification* may be specified, but is not required. If an *exception-specification* is specified in an explicit instantiation directive, it shall have the same set of *type-ids* as other declarations of that function. A diagnostic is required only if the sets of *type-ids* are different within a single translation unit.

3   If a virtual function has an *exception-specification*, all declarations, including the definition, of any function that overrides that virtual function in any derived class shall only allow exceptions that are allowed by the *exception-specification* of the base class virtual function. [*Example:*

```
struct B {
    virtual void f() throw (int, double);
    virtual void g();
};

struct D: B {
    void f();                     // ill-formed
    void g() throw (int);         // OK
};
```

The declaration of `D::f` is ill-formed because it allows all exceptions, whereas `B::f` allows only `int` and `double`.] A similar restriction applies to assignment to and initialization of pointers to functions, pointers to member functions, and references to functions: the target entity shall allow at least the exceptions allowed by the source value in the assignment or initialization. [*Example:*

```
class A { /* ... */ };
void (*pf1)();                   // no exception specification
void (*pf2)() throw(A);

void f()
{
        pf1 = pf2;               // OK: pf1 is less restrictive
        pf2 = pf1;               // error: pf2 is more restrictive
}
```

—*end example*]

4   In such an assignment or initialization, *exception-specifications* on return types and parameter types shall match exactly. In other assignments or initializations, *exception-specifications* shall match exactly.

5   Types shall not be defined in *exception-specifications*.

6   An *exception-specification* can include the same type more than once and can include classes that are related by inheritance, even though doing so is redundant. An *exception-specification* can also include the class `std::bad_exception` (18.6.2.1).

7   A function is said to *allow* an exception of type E if its *exception-specification* contains a type T for which a handler of type T would be a match (15.3) for an exception of type E.

8   Whenever an exception is thrown and the search for a handler (15.3) encounters the outermost block of a function with an *exception-specification*, the function `unexpected()` is called (15.5.2) if the *exception-specification* does not allow the exception. [*Example:*

```
class X { };
class Y { };
class Z: public X { };
class W { };

void f() throw (X, Y)
{
    int n = 0;
    if (n) throw X();          // OK
    if (n) throw Z();          // also OK
    throw W();                 // will call unexpected()
}
```

—*end example*]

9   The function `unexpected()` may throw an exception that will satisfy the *exception-specification* for which it was invoked, and in this case the search for another handler will continue at the call of the function with this *exception-specification* (see 15.5.2), or it may call `terminate()`.

10 An implementation shall not reject an expression merely because when executed it throws or might throw an exception that the containing function does not allow. [*Example:*

```
extern void f() throw(X, Y);

void g() throw(X)
{
        f();                   // OK
}
```

the call to `f` is well-formed even though when called, `f` might throw exception `Y` that `g` does not allow.]

11 A function with no *exception-specification* allows all exceptions. A function with an empty *exception-specification*, `throw()`, does not allow any exceptions.

12 An *exception-specification* is not considered part of a function's type.

13 An implicitly declared special member function (clause 12) shall have an exception-specification. If `f` is an implicitly declared default constructor, copy constructor, destructor, or copy assignment operator, its implicit exception-specification specifies the *type-id* `T` if and only if `T` is allowed by the exception-specification of a function directly invoked by `f`'s implicit definition; `f` shall allow all exceptions if any function it directly invokes allows all exceptions, and `f` shall allow no exceptions if every function it directly invokes allows no exceptions. [*Example:*

```
struct A {
    A();
    A(const A&) throw();
    ~A() throw(X);
};
struct B {
    B() throw();
    B(const B&) throw();
    ~B() throw(Y);
};
struct D : public A, public B {
        // Implicit declaration of D::D();
        // Implicit declaration of D::D(const D&) throw();
        // Implicit declaration of D::~D() throw (X,Y);
};
```

Furthermore, if `A::~A()` or `B::~B()` were virtual, `D::~D()` would not be as restrictive as that of `A::~A`, and the program would be ill-formed since a function that overrides a virtual function from a base class shall have an exception-specification at least as restrictive as that in the base class.]

15.5 Special functions   [except.special]

1   The exception handling mechanism relies on two functions, `terminate()` and `unexpected()`, for coping with errors related to the exception handling mechanism itself (18.6).

15.5.1 The `terminate()` function   [except.terminate]

1   In the following situations exception handling must be abandoned for less subtle error handling techniques:

— when the exception handling mechanism, after completing evaluation of the expression to be thrown but before the exception is caught (15.1), calls a user function that exits via an uncaught exception,[134]

— when the exception handling mechanism cannot find a handler for a thrown exception (15.3), or

— when the destruction of an object during stack unwinding (15.2) exits using an exception, or

— when construction or destruction of a non-local object with static storage duration exits using an exception (3.6.2), or

— when execution of a function registered with `atexit` exits using an exception (18.3), or

— when a *throw-expression* with no operand attempts to rethrow an exception and no exception is being handled (15.1), or

— when `unexpected` throws an exception which is not allowed by the previously violated *exception-specification*, and `std::bad_exception` is not included in that *exception-specification* (15.5.2), or

— when the implementation's default `unexpected_handler` is called (18.6.2.2)

2   In such cases,

```
void terminate();
```

is called (18.6.3). In the situation where no matching handler is found, it is implementation-defined whether or not the stack is unwound before `terminate()` is called. In all other situations, the stack shall not be unwound before `terminate()` is called. An implementation is not permitted to finish stack unwinding prematurely based on a determination that the unwind process will eventually cause a call to `terminate()`.

15.5.2 The `unexpected()` function   [except.unexpected]

1   If a function with an *exception-specification* throws an exception that is not listed in the *exception-specification*, the function

```
void unexpected();
```

is called (18.6.2) immediately after completing the stack unwinding for the former function

2   The `unexpected()` function shall not return, but it can throw (or re-throw) an exception. If it throws a new exception which is allowed by the exception specification which previously was violated, then the search for another handler will continue at the call of the function whose exception specification was violated. If it throws or rethrows an exception that the *exception-specification* does not allow then the following happens: If the *exception-specification* does not include the class `std::bad_exception` (18.6.2.1) then the function `terminate()` is called, otherwise the thrown exception is replaced by an implementation-defined object of the type `std::bad_exception` and the search for another handler will continue at the call of the function whose *exception-specification* was violated.

---

[134] For example, if the object being thrown is of a class with a copy constructor, `terminate()` will be called if that copy constructor exits with an exception during a `throw`.

3   Thus, an *exception-specification* guarantees that only the listed exceptions will be thrown. If the *exception-specification* includes the type `std::bad_exception` then any exception not on the list may be replaced by `std::bad_exception` within the function `unexpected()`.

15.5.3 The `uncaught_exception()` function [except.uncaught]

1   The function

```
bool uncaught_exception() throw()
```

returns `true` after completing evaluation of the object to be thrown until completing the initialization of the *exception-declaration* in the matching handler (18.6.4). This includes stack unwinding. If the exception is rethrown (15.1), `uncaught_exception()` returns `true` from the point of rethrow until the rethrown exception is caught again.

15.6 Exceptions and access [except.access]

1   If the *exception-declaration* in a catch clause has class type, and the function in which the catch clause occurs does not have access to the destructor of that class, the program is ill-formed.

2   An object can be thrown if it can be copied and destroyed in the context of the function in which the *throw-expression* occurs.

16   Preprocessing directives [cpp]

1   A preprocessing directive consists of a sequence of preprocessing tokens. The first token in the sequence is a # preprocessing token that is either the first character in the source file (optionally after white space containing no new-line characters) or that follows white space containing at least one new-line character. The last token in the sequence is the first new-line character that follows the first token in the sequence.[135]

> *preprocessing-file:*
>> *group*$_{opt}$

> *group:*
>> *group-part*
>> *group group-part*

> *group-part:*
>> *pp-tokens*$_{opt}$ *new-line*
>> *if-section*
>> *control-line*

> *if-section:*
>> *if-group elif-groups*$_{opt}$ *else-group*$_{opt}$ *endif-line*

> *if-group:*
>> `# if`   *constant-expression new-line group*$_{opt}$
>> `# ifdef` *identifier new-line group*$_{opt}$
>> `# ifndef` *identifier new-line group*$_{opt}$

> *elif-groups:*
>> *elif-group*
>> *elif-groups elif-group*

> *elif-group:*
>> `# elif`   *constant-expression new-line group*$_{opt}$

> *else-group:*
>> `# else`   *new-line group*$_{opt}$

> *endif-line:*
>> `# endif` *new-line*

> *control-line:*
>> `# include` *pp-tokens new-line*
>> `# define` *identifier replacement-list new-line*
>> `# define` *identifier lparen identifier-list*$_{opt}$) *replacement-list new-line*
>> `# undef`   *identifier new-line*
>> `# line`   *pp-tokens new-line*
>> `# error`   *pp-tokens*$_{opt}$ *new-line*
>> `# pragma` *pp-tokens*$_{opt}$ *new-line*
>> `#`   *new-line*

---

[135] Thus, preprocessing directives are commonly called "lines." These "lines" have no other syntactic significance, as all white space is equivalent except in certain situations during preprocessing (see the # character string literal creation operator in 16.3.2, for example).

lparen:

>   the left-parenthesis character without preceding white-space

replacement-list:
>   *pp-tokens*_{opt}

pp-tokens:

>   *preprocessing-token*
>   *pp-tokens   preprocessing-token*

new-line:
>   the new-line character

2   The only white-space characters that shall appear between preprocessing tokens within a preprocessing directive (from just after the introducing # preprocessing token through just before the terminating new-line character) are space and horizontal-tab (including spaces that have replaced comments or possibly other white-space characters in translation phase 3).

3   The implementation can process and skip sections of source files conditionally, include other source files, and replace macros. These capabilities are called *preprocessing*, because conceptually they occur before translation of the resulting translation unit.

4   The preprocessing tokens within a preprocessing directive are not subject to macro expansion unless otherwise stated.

16.1 Conditional inclusion   [cpp.cond]

1   The expression that controls conditional inclusion shall be an integral constant expression except that: it shall not contain a cast; identifiers (including those lexically identical to keywords) are interpreted as described below;[136] and it may contain unary operator expressions of the form

>   defined *identifier*

   or

>   defined (*identifier*)

which evaluate to 1 if the identifier is currently defined as a macro name (that is, if it is predefined or if it has been the subject of a #define preprocessing directive without an intervening #undef directive with the same subject identifier), zero if it is not.

2   Each preprocessing token that remains after all macro replacements have occurred shall be in the lexical form of a token (2.6).

3   Preprocessing directives of the forms

>   # if   *constant-expression new-line group*_{opt}
>   # elif *constant-expression new-line group*_{opt}

check whether the controlling constant expression evaluates to nonzero.

4   Prior to evaluation, macro invocations in the list of preprocessing tokens that will become the controlling constant expression are replaced (except for those macro names modified by the defined unary operator), just as in normal text. If the token defined is generated as a result of this replacement process or use of the defined unary operator does not match one of the two specified forms prior to macro replacement, the behavior is undefined. After all replacements due to macro expansion and the defined unary operator have been performed, all remaining identifiers and keywords[137], except for true and false, are

---

[136] Because the controlling constant expression is evaluated during translation phase 4, all identifiers either are or are not macro names — there simply are no keywords, enumeration constants, and so on.
[137] An alternative token (2.5) is not an identifier, even when its spelling consists entirely of letters and underscores. Therefore it is not subject to this replacement.

replaced with the pp-number 0, and then each preprocessing token is converted into a token. The resulting tokens comprise the controlling constant expression which is evaluated according to the rules of 5.19 using arithmetic that has at least the ranges specified in 18.2, except that `int` and `unsigned int` act as if they have the same representation as, respectively, `long` and `unsigned long`. This includes interpreting character literals, which may involve converting escape sequences into execution character set members. Whether the numeric value for these character literals matches the value obtained when an identical character literal occurs in an expression (other than within a `#if` or `#elif` directive) is implementation-defined.[138] Also, whether a single-character character literal may have a negative value is implementation-defined. Each subexpression with type `bool` is subjected to integral promotion before processing continues.

5   Preprocessing directives of the forms

> # ifdef *identifier new-line group*$_{opt}$
> # ifndef *identifier new-line group*$_{opt}$

check whether the identifier is or is not currently defined as a macro name. Their conditions are equivalent to `#if defined` *identifier* and `#if !defined` *identifier* respectively.

6   Each directive's condition is checked in order. If it evaluates to false (zero), the group that it controls is skipped: directives are processed only through the name that determines the directive in order to keep track of the level of nested conditionals; the rest of the directives' preprocessing tokens are ignored, as are the other preprocessing tokens in the group. Only the first group whose control condition evaluates to true (nonzero) is processed. If none of the conditions evaluates to true, and there is a `#else` directive, the group controlled by the `#else` is processed; lacking a `#else` directive, all the groups until the `#endif` are skipped.[139]

16.2 Source file inclusion [cpp.include]

1   A `#include` directive shall identify a header or source file that can be processed by the implementation.

2   A preprocessing directive of the form

> # include *<h-char-sequence> new-line*

searches a sequence of implementation-defined places for a header identified uniquely by the specified sequence between the < and > delimiters, and causes the replacement of that directive by the entire contents of the header. How the places are specified or the header identified is implementation-defined.

3   A preprocessing directive of the form

> # include *"q-char-sequence" new-line*

causes the replacement of that directive by the entire contents of the source file identified by the specified sequence between the " delimiters. The named source file is searched for in an implementation-defined manner. If this search is not supported, or if the search fails, the directive is reprocessed as if it read

> # include *<h-char-sequence> new-line*

with the identical contained sequence (including > characters, if any) from the original directive.

---

[138] Thus, the constant expression in the following `#if` directive and `if` statement is not guaranteed to evaluate to the same value in these two contexts.

> `#if 'z' - 'a' == 25`
> `if ('z' - 'a' == 25)`

[139] As indicated by the syntax, a preprocessing token shall not follow a `#else` or `#endif` directive before the terminating new-line character. However, comments may appear anywhere in a source file, including within a preprocessing directive.

4   A preprocessing directive of the form

    # include *pp-tokens new-line*

(that does not match one of the two previous forms) is permitted. The preprocessing tokens after `include` in the directive are processed just as in normal text (each identifier currently defined as a macro name is replaced by its replacement list of preprocessing tokens). If the directive resulting after all replacements does not match one of the two previous forms, the behavior is undefined.[140] The method by which a sequence of preprocessing tokens between a < and a > preprocessing token pair or a pair of " characters is combined into a single header name preprocessing token is implementation-defined.

5   The mapping between the delimited sequence and the external source file name is implementation-defined. The implementation provides unique mappings for sequences consisting of one or more *nondigits* (2.10) followed by a period (`.`) and a single *nondigit*. The implementation may ignore the distinctions of alphabetical case.

6   A `#include` preprocessing directive may appear in a source file that has been read because of a `#include` directive in another file, up to an implementation-defined nesting limit.

7   [*Example:* The most common uses of `#include` preprocessing directives are as in the following:

```
#include <stdio.h>
#include "myprog.h"
```

—*end example*]

8   [*Example:* Here is a macro-replaced `#include` directive:

```
#if VERSION == 1
        #define INCFILE   "vers1.h"
#elif VERSION == 2
        #define INCFILE   "vers2.h"    /* and so on */
#else
        #define INCFILE   "versN.h"
#endif
#include INCFILE
```

—*end example*]

16.3 Macro replacement   [cpp.replace]

1   Two replacement lists are identical if and only if the preprocessing tokens in both have the same number, ordering, spelling, and white-space separation, where all white-space separations are considered identical.

2   An identifier currently defined as a macro without use of lparen (an *object-like* macro) may be redefined by another `#define` preprocessing directive provided that the second definition is an object-like macro definition and the two replacement lists are identical, otherwise the program is ill-formed.

3   An identifier currently defined as a macro using lparen (a *function-like* macro) may be redefined by another `#define` preprocessing directive provided that the second definition is a function-like macro definition that has the same number and spelling of parameters, and the two replacement lists are identical, otherwise the program is ill-formed.

4   The number of arguments in an invocation of a function-like macro shall agree with the number of parameters in the macro definition, and there shall exist a) preprocessing token that terminates the invocation.

5   A parameter identifier in a function-like macro shall be uniquely declared within its scope.

---

[140] Note that adjacent string literals are not concatenated into a single string literal (see the translation phases in 2.1); thus, an expansion that results in two string literals is an invalid directive.

6 The identifier immediately following the `define` is called the *macro name*. There is one name space for macro names. Any white-space characters preceding or following the replacement list of preprocessing tokens are not considered part of the replacement list for either form of macro.

7 If a # preprocessing token, followed by an identifier, occurs lexically at the point at which a preprocessing directive could begin, the identifier is not subject to macro replacement.

8 A preprocessing directive of the form

> # `define` *identifier replacement-list new-line*

defines an object-like macro that causes each subsequent instance of the macro name[141] to be replaced by the replacement list of preprocessing tokens that constitute the remainder of the directive.[142] The replacement list is then rescanned for more macro names as specified below.

9 A preprocessing directive of the form

> # `define` *identifier lparen identifier-list$_{opt}$) replacement-list new-line*

defines a function-like macro with parameters, similar syntactically to a function call. The parameters are specified by the optional list of identifiers, whose scope extends from their declaration in the identifier list until the new-line character that terminates the `#define` preprocessing directive. Each subsequent instance of the function-like macro name followed by a (as the next preprocessing token introduces the sequence of preprocessing tokens that is replaced by the replacement list in the definition (an invocation of the macro). The replaced sequence of preprocessing tokens is terminated by the matching) preprocessing token, skipping intervening matched pairs of left and right parenthesis preprocessing tokens. Within the sequence of preprocessing tokens making up an invocation of a function-like macro, new-line is considered a normal white-space character.

10 The sequence of preprocessing tokens bounded by the outside-most matching parentheses forms the list of arguments for the function-like macro. The individual arguments within the list are separated by comma preprocessing tokens, but comma preprocessing tokens between matching inner parentheses do not separate arguments. If (before argument substitution) any argument consists of no preprocessing tokens, the behavior is undefined. If there are sequences of preprocessing tokens within the list of arguments that would otherwise act as preprocessing directives, the behavior is undefined.

16.3.1 Argument substitution [cpp.subst]

1 After the arguments for the invocation of a function-like macro have been identified, argument substitution takes place. A parameter in the replacement list, unless preceded by a # or ## preprocessing token or followed by a ## preprocessing token (see below), is replaced by the corresponding argument after all macros contained therein have been expanded. Before being substituted, each argument's preprocessing tokens are completely macro replaced as if they formed the rest of the translation unit; no other preprocessing tokens are available.

---

[141] Since, by macro-replacement time, all character literals and string literals are preprocessing tokens, not sequences possibly containing identifier-like subsequences (see 2.1.1.2, translation phases), they are never scanned for macro names or parameters.

[142] An alternative token (2.5) is not an identifier, even when its spelling consists entirely of letters and underscores. Therefore it is not possible to define a macro whose name is the same as that of an alternative token.

16.3.2   The # operator   **[cpp.stringize]**

1   Each # preprocessing token in the replacement list for a function-like macro shall be followed by a parameter as the next preprocessing token in the replacement list.

2   If, in the replacement list, a parameter is immediately preceded by a # preprocessing token, both are replaced by a single character string literal preprocessing token that contains the spelling of the preprocessing token sequence for the corresponding argument. Each occurrence of white space between the argument's preprocessing tokens becomes a single space character in the character string literal. White space before the first preprocessing token and after the last preprocessing token comprising the argument is deleted. Otherwise, the original spelling of each preprocessing token in the argument is retained in the character string literal, except for special handling for producing the spelling of string literals and character literals: a \ character is inserted before each " and \ character of a character literal or string literal (including the delimiting " characters). If the replacement that results is not a valid character string literal, the behavior is undefined. The order of evaluation of # and ## operators is unspecified.

16.3.3   The ## operator   **[cpp.concat]**

1   A ## preprocessing token shall not occur at the beginning or at the end of a replacement list for either form of macro definition.

2   If, in the replacement list, a parameter is immediately preceded or followed by a ## preprocessing token, the parameter is replaced by the corresponding argument's preprocessing token sequence.

3   For both object-like and function-like macro invocations, before the replacement list is reexamined for more macro names to replace, each instance of a ## preprocessing token in the replacement list (not from an argument) is deleted and the preceding preprocessing token is concatenated with the following preprocessing token. If the result is not a valid preprocessing token, the behavior is undefined. The resulting token is available for further macro replacement. The order of evaluation of ## operators is unspecified.

16.3.4   Rescanning and further replacement   **[cpp.rescan]**

1   After all parameters in the replacement list have been substituted, the resulting preprocessing token sequence is rescanned with all subsequent preprocessing tokens of the source file for more macro names to replace.

2   If the name of the macro being replaced is found during this scan of the replacement list (not including the rest of the source file's preprocessing tokens), it is not replaced. Further, if any nested replacements encounter the name of the macro being replaced, it is not replaced. These nonreplaced macro name preprocessing tokens are no longer available for further replacement even if they are later (re)examined in contexts in which that macro name preprocessing token would otherwise have been replaced.

3   The resulting completely macro-replaced preprocessing token sequence is not processed as a preprocessing directive even if it resembles one.

16.3.5   Scope of macro definitions   **[cpp.scope]**

1   A macro definition lasts (independent of block structure) until a corresponding #undef directive is encountered or (if none is encountered) until the end of the translation unit.

2   A preprocessing directive of the form

> # undef *identifier new-line*

causes the specified identifier no longer to be defined as a macro name. It is ignored if the specified identifier is not currently defined as a macro name.

3   [*Note:* The simplest use of this facility is to define a "manifest constant," as in

```
#define TABSIZE 100

int table[TABSIZE];
```

4   The following defines a function-like macro whose value is the maximum of its arguments. It has the advantages of working for any compatible types of the arguments and of generating in-line code without the overhead of function calling. It has the disadvantages of evaluating one or the other of its arguments a second time (including side effects) and generating more code than a function if invoked several times. It also cannot have its address taken, as it has none.

```
#define max(a, b)  ((a) > (b) ? (a) : (b))
```

The parentheses ensure that the arguments and the resulting expression are bound properly.

5   To illustrate the rules for redefinition and reexamination, the sequence

```
#define x     3
#define f(a)  f(x * (a))
#undef  x
#define x     2
#define g     f
#define z     z[0]
#define h     g(~
#define m(a)  a(w)
#define w     0,1
#define t(a)  a

f(y+1) + f(f(z)) % t(t(g)(0) + t)(1);
g(x+(3,4)-w) | h 5) & m
          (f)^m(m);
```

results in

```
f(2 * (y+1)) + f(2 * (f(2 * (z[0])))) % f(2 * (0)) + t(1);
f(2 * (2+(3,4)-0,1)) | f(2 * (~5)) & f(2 * (0,1))^m(0,1);
```

6   To illustrate the rules for creating character string literals and concatenating tokens, the sequence

```
#define str(s)       # s
#define xstr(s)      str(s)
#define debug(s, t)  printf("x" # s "= %d, x" # t "= %s", \
                             x ## s, x ## t)
#define INCFILE(n)   vers ## n   /* from previous #include example */
#define glue(a, b)   a ## b
#define xglue(a, b)  glue(a, b)
#define HIGHLOW      "hello"
#define LOW          LOW ", world"

debug(1, 2);
fputs(str(strncmp("abc\0d", "abc", '\4')  /* this goes away */
         == 0) str(: @\n), s);
#include xstr(INCFILE(2).h)
glue(HIGH, LOW);
xglue(HIGH, LOW)
```

results in

```
printf("x" "1" "= %d, x" "2" "= %s", x1, x2);
fputs("strncmp(\"abc\\0d\", \"abc\", '\\4') == 0" ": @\n", s);
#include "vers2.h"     (after macro replacement, before file access)
"hello";
"hello" ", world"
```

or, after concatenation of the character string literals,

```
printf("x1= %d, x2= %s", x1, x2);
fputs("strncmp(\"abc\\0d\", \"abc\", '\\4') == 0: @\n", s);
#include "vers2.h"      (after macro replacement, before file access)
"hello";
"hello, world"
```

Space around the # and ## tokens in the macro definition is optional.

7   And finally, to demonstrate the redefinition rules, the following sequence is valid.

```
#define OBJ_LIKE      (1-1)
#define OBJ_LIKE      /* white space */ (1-1) /* other */
#define FTN_LIKE(a)   ( a )
#define FTN_LIKE( a )(            /* note the white space */ \
                         a /* other stuff on this line
                            */ )
```

But the following redefinitions are invalid:

```
#define OBJ_LIKE     (0)      /* different token sequence */
#define OBJ_LIKE     (1 - 1)  /* different white space */
#define FTN_LIKE(b)  ( a )    /* different parameter usage */
#define FTN_LIKE(b)  ( b )    /* different parameter spelling */
```

—*end note*]

16.4 Line control   [cpp.line]

1   The string literal of a #line directive, if present, shall be a character string literal.

2   The *line number* of the current source line is one greater than the number of new-line characters read or introduced in translation phase 1 (2.1) while processing the source file to the current token.

3   A preprocessing directive of the form

> # line *digit-sequence new-line*

causes the implementation to behave as if the following sequence of source lines begins with a source line that has a line number as specified by the digit sequence (interpreted as a decimal integer). If the digit sequence specifies zero or a number greater than 32767, the behavior is undefined.

4   A preprocessing directive of the form

> # line *digit-sequence* "*s-char-sequence$_{opt}$*" *new-line*

sets the line number similarly and changes the presumed name of the source file to be the contents of the character string literal.

5   A preprocessing directive of the form

> # line *pp-tokens new-line*

(that does not match one of the two previous forms) is permitted. The preprocessing tokens after line on the directive are processed just as in normal text (each identifier currently defined as a macro name is replaced by its replacement list of preprocessing tokens). If the directive resulting after all replacements does not match one of the two previous forms, the behavior is undefined; otherwise, the result is processed as appropriate.

16.5 Error directive [cpp.error]

1 A preprocessing directive of the form

> # error *pp-tokens*_{opt} *new-line*

causes the implementation to produce a diagnostic message that includes the specified sequence of preprocessing tokens, and renders the program ill-formed.

16.6 Pragma directive [cpp.pragma]

1 A preprocessing directive of the form

> # pragma *pp-tokens*_{opt} *new-line*

causes the implementation to behave in an implementation-defined manner. Any pragma that is not recognized by the implementation is ignored.

16.7 Null directive [cpp.null]

1 A preprocessing directive of the form

> # *new-line*

has no effect.

16.8 Predefined macro names [cpp.predefined]

1 The following macro names shall be defined by the implementation:

__LINE__ The line number of the current source line (a decimal constant).

__FILE__ The presumed name of the source file (a character string literal).

__DATE__ The date of translation of the source file (a character string literal of the form "Mmm dd yyyy", where the names of the months are the same as those generated by the asctime function, and the first character of dd is a space character if the value is less than 10). If the date of translation is not available, an implementation-defined valid date is supplied.

__TIME__ The time of translation of the source file (a character string literal of the form "hh:mm:ss" as in the time generated by the asctime function). If the time of translation is not available, an implementation-defined valid time is supplied.

__STDC__ Whether __STDC__ is predefined and if so, what its value is, are implementation-defined.

__cplusplus The name __cplusplus is defined to the value 199711L when compiling a C++ translation unit. [143]

2 The values of the predefined macros (except for __LINE__ and __FILE__) remain constant throughout the translation unit.

3 If any of the pre-defined macro names in this subclause, or the identifier defined, is the subject of a #define or a #undef preprocessing directive, the behavior is undefined.

---

[143] It is intended that future versions of this standard will replace the value of this macro with a greater value. Non-conforming compilers should use a value with at most five decimal digits.

17   Library introduction   [lib.library]

1   This clause describes the contents of the *C++ Standard Library*, how a well-formed C++ program makes use of the library, and how a conforming implementation may provide the entities in the library.

2   The C++ Standard Library provides an extensible framework, and contains components for: language support, diagnostics, general utilities, strings, locales, containers, iterators, algorithms, numerics, and input/output. The language support components are required by certain parts of the C++ language, such as memory allocation (5.3.4, 5.3.5) and exception processing (clause 15).

3   The general utilities include components used by other library elements, such as a predefined storage allocator for dynamic storage management (3.7.3). The diagnostics components provide a consistent framework for reporting errors in a C++ program, including predefined exception classes.

4   The strings components provide support for manipulating text represented as sequences of type `char`, sequences of type `wchar_t`, or sequences of any other ''character-like'' type. The localization components extend internationalization support for such text processing.

5   The containers, iterators, and algorithms provide a C++ program with access to a subset of the most widely used algorithms and data structures.

6   Numeric algorithms and the complex number components extend support for numeric processing. The `valarray` components provide support for *n*-at-a-time processing, potentially implemented as parallel operations on platforms that support such processing.

7   The `iostreams` components are the primary mechanism for C++ program input/output. They can be used with other elements of the library, particularly strings, locales, and iterators.

8   This library also makes available the facilities of the Standard C library, suitably adjusted to ensure static type safety.

9   The following subclauses describe the definitions (17.1), and method of description (17.3) for the library. Clause 17.4 and clauses 18 through 27 specify the contents of the library, and library requirements and constraints on both well-formed C++ programs and conforming implementations.

17.1 Definitions   [lib.definitions]

17.1.1 arbitrary-positional stream   [defns.arbitrary.stream]
a stream (described in clause 27) that can seek to any integral position within the length of the stream. Every arbitrary-positional stream is also a repositional stream (17.1.16).

17.1.2 character   [defns.character]
in clauses 21, 22, and 27, means any object which, when treated sequentially, can represent text. The term does not only mean `char` and `wchar_t` objects, but any value that can be represented by a type that provides the definitions specified in these clauses.

17.1.3 character container type   [defns.character.container]

a class or a type used to represent a *character* (17.1.2). It is used for one of the template parameters of the string and iostream class templates. A character container class shall be a POD (3.9) type.

17.1.4 comparison function   [defns.comparison]

an operator function (13.5) for any of the equality (5.10) or relational (5.9) operators.

17.1.5 component   [defns.component]

a group of library entities directly related as members, parameters, or return types. For example, the class template basic_string and the non-member function templates that operate on strings are referred to as the *string component*.

17.1.6 default behavior   [defns.default.behavior]

a description of *replacement function* and *handler function* semantics. Any specific behavior provided by the implementation, within the scope of the *required behavior*.

17.1.7 handler function   [defns.handler]

a non-*reserved function* whose definition may be provided by a C++ program. A C++ program may designate a handler function at various points in its execution, by supplying a pointer to the function when calling any of the library functions that install handler functions (clause 18).

17.1.8 iostream class templates   [defns.iostream.templates]

templates, defined in clause 27, that take two template arguments: charT and traits. The argument charT is a character container class, and the argument traits is a structure which defines additional characteristics and functions of the character type represented by charT necessary to implement the iostream class templates.

17.1.9 modifier function   [defns.modifier]

a class member function (9.3), other than constructors, assignment, or destructor, that alters the state of an object of the class.

17.1.10 object state   [defns.obj.state]

the current value of all nonstatic class members of an object (9.2). The state of an object can be obtained by using one or more *observer functions*.

17.1.11 narrow-oriented iostream classes

the instantiations of the iostream class templates on the character container class char and the default value of the traits parameter. The traditional iostream classes are regarded as the narrow-oriented iostream classes (27.3.1).

17.1.12 NTCTS   [defns.ntcts]

a sequence of values that have *character type*, that precede the terminating null character type value charT().

17.1.13 observer function   [defns.observer]

a class member function (9.3) that accesses the state of an object of the class, but does not alter that state. Observer functions are specified as const member functions (9.3.2).

17.1.14 replacement function [defns.replacement]

a non-*reserved function* whose definition is provided by a C++ program. Only one definition for such a function is in effect for the duration of the program's execution, as the result of creating the program (2.1) and resolving the definitions of all translation units (3.5).

17.1.15 required behavior [defns.required.behavior]

a description of *replacement function* and *handler function* semantics, applicable to both the behavior provided by the implementation and the behavior that shall be provided by any function definition in the program. If a function defined in a C++ program fails to meet the required behavior when it executes, the behavior is undefined.

17.1.16 repositional stream [defns.repositional.stream]

a stream (described in clause 27) that can seek only to a position that was previously encountered.

17.1.17 reserved function [defns.reserved.function]

a function, specified as part of the C++ Standard Library, that must be defined by the implementation. If a C++ program provides a definition for any reserved function, the results are undefined.

17.1.18 traits class [defns.traits]

a class that encapsulates a set of types and functions necessary for class templates and function templates to manipulate objects of types for which they are instantiated. Traits classes defined in clauses 21, 22 and 27 are *chararacter traits*, which provide the character handling support needed by the string and iostream classes.

17.1.19 wide-oriented iostream classes

the instantiations of the iostream class templates on the character container class wchar_t and the default value of the traits parameter (27.3.2).

17.2 Additional definitions [defns.additional]

1   1.3 defines additional terms used elsewhere in this International Standard.

17.3 Method of description (Informative) [lib.description]

1   17.3 describes the conventions used to describe the C++ Standard Library. It describes the structures of the normative clauses 18 through 27 (17.3.1), and other editorial conventions (17.3.2).

17.3.1 Structure of each subclause [lib.structure]

1   17.4.1 provides a summary of the C++ Standard library's contents. Other Library clauses provide detailed specifications for each of the components in the library, as shown in Table 10:

Table 10—Library Categories

Clause	Category
18	Language support
19	Diagnostics
20	General utilities
21	Strings
22	Localization
23	Containers
24	Iterators
25	Algorithms
26	Numerics
27	Input/output

2   Each Library clause contains the following elements, as applicable:[144)]

— Summary

— Requirements

— Detailed specifications

— References to the Standard C library

17.3.1.1 Summary   [lib.structure.summary]

1   The Summary provides a synopsis of the category, and introduces the first-level subclauses. Each sub-clause also provides a summary, listing the headers specified in the subclause and the library entities provided in each header.

2   Paragraphs labelled ''Note(s):'' or ''Example(s):'' are informative, other paragraphs are normative.

3   The summary and the detailed specifications are presented in the order:

— Macros

— Values

— Types

— Classes

— Functions

— Objects

[144)] To save space, items that do not apply to a clause are omitted. For example, if a clause does not specify any requirements, there will be no ''Requirements'' subclause.

17.3.1.2 Requirements [lib.structure.requirements]

1 The library can be extended by a C++ program. Each clause, as applicable, describes the requirements that such extensions must meet. Such extensions are generally one of the following:

— Template arguments

— Derived classes

— Containers, iterators, and/or algorithms that meet an interface convention

2 The string and iostreams components use an explicit representation of operations required of template arguments. They use a class template `char_traits` to define these constraints.

3 Interface convention requirements are stated as generally as possible. Instead of stating "class X has to define a member function `operator++()`," the interface requires "for any object x of class X, `++x` is defined." That is, whether the operator is a member is unspecified.

4 Requirements are stated in terms of well-defined expressions, which define valid terms of the types that satisfy the requirements. For every set of requirements there is a table that specifies an initial set of the valid expressions and their semantics (20.1.5, 23.1, 24.1). Any generic algorithm (clause 25) that uses the requirements is described in terms of the valid expressions for its formal type parameters.

5 Template argument requirements are sometimes referenced by name. See 17.3.2.1.

6 In some cases the semantic requirements are presented as C++ code. Such code is intended as a specification of equivalence of a construct to another construct, not necessarily as the way the construct must be implemented.[145]

17.3.1.3 Specifications [lib.structure.specifications]

1 The detailed specifications each contain the following elements:[146]

— Name and brief description

— Synopsis (class definition or function prototype, as appropriate)

— Restrictions on template arguments, if any

— Description of class invariants

— Description of function semantics

2 Descriptions of class member functions follow the order (as appropriate):[147]

— Constructor(s) and destructor

— Copying & assignment functions

— Comparison functions

— Modifier functions

— Observer functions

— Operators and other non-member functions

3 Descriptions of function semantics contain the following elements (as appropriate):[148]

---

[145] Although in some cases the code given is unambiguously the optimum implementation.

[146] The form of these specifications was designed to follow the conventions established by existing C++ library vendors.

[147] To save space, items that do not apply to a class are omitted. For example, if a class does not specify any comparison functions, there will be no "Comparison functions" subclause.

[148] To save space, items that do not apply to a function are omitted. For example, if a function does not specify any further preconditions, there will be no "Requires" paragraph.

— **Requires:** the preconditions for calling the function

— **Effects:** the actions performed by the function

— **Postconditions:** the observable results established by the function

— **Returns:** a description of the value(s) returned by the function

— **Throws:** any exceptions thrown by the function, and the conditions that would cause the exception

— **Complexity:** the time and/or space complexity of the function

4   For non-reserved replacement and handler functions, Clause 18 specifies two behaviors for the functions in question: their required and default behavior. The *default behavior* describes a function definition provided by the implementation. The *required behavior* describes the semantics of a function definition provided by either the implementation or a C++ program. Where no distinction is explicitly made in the description, the behavior described is the required behavior.

5   Complexity requirements specified in the library clauses are upper bounds, and implementations that provide better complexity guarantees satisfy the requirements.

17.3.1.4 C Library   [lib.structure.see.also]

1   Paragraphs labelled ''SEE ALSO:'' contain cross-references to the relevant portions of this Standard and the ISO C standard, which is incorporated into this Standard by reference.

17.3.2 Other conventions   [lib.conventions]

1   This subclause describes several editorial conventions used to describe the contents of the C++ Standard Library. These conventions are for describing implementation-defined types (17.3.2.1), and member functions (17.3.2.2).

17.3.2.1 Type descriptions   [lib.type.descriptions]

1   The Requirements subclauses may describe names that are used to specify constraints on template arguments.[149] These names are used in clauses 20, 23, 25, and 26 to describe the types that may be supplied as arguments by a C++ program when instantiating template components from the library.

2   Certain types defined in clause 27 are used to describe implementation-defined types. They are based on other types, but with added constraints.

17.3.2.1.1 Enumerated types   [lib.enumerated.types]

1   Several types defined in clause 27 are *enumerated types*. Each enumerated type may be implemented as an enumeration or as a synonym for an enumeration.[150]

2   The enumerated type *enumerated* can be written:

```
enum enumerated { V0, V1, V2, V3, .....};

static const enumerated C0(V0);
static const enumerated C1(V1);
static const enumerated C2(V2);
static const enumerated C3(V3);
    .....
```

---

[149] Examples from 20.1 include: `EqualityComparable`, `LessThanComparable`, `CopyConstructable`, etc. Examples from 24.1 include: `InputIterator`, `ForwardIterator`, `Function`, `Predicate`, etc.
[150] Such as an integer type, with constant integer values (3.9.1).

3   Here, the names *C0*, *C1*, etc. represent *enumerated elements* for this particular enumerated type. All such elements have distinct values.

17.3.2.1.2 Bitmask types [lib.bitmask.types]

1   Several types defined in clause 27 are *bitmask types*. Each bitmask type can be implemented as an enumerated type that overloads certain operators, as an integer type, or as a `bitset` (23.3.5).

2   The bitmask type *bitmask* can be written:

```
enum bitmask {
  V0 = 1 << 0, V1 = 1 << 1, V2 = 1 << 2, V3 = 1 << 3, .....
};

static const bitmask C0(V0);
static const bitmask C1(V1);
static const bitmask C2(V2);
static const bitmask C3(V3);
  .....

bitmask  operator& (bitmask  X, bitmask Y)
        // For exposition only.
        // int_type is an integral type capable of
        // representing all values of bitmask
        { return static_cast<bitmask>(
                    static_cast<int_type>(X) &
                    static_cast<int_type>(Y)); }

bitmask  operator| (bitmask  X, bitmask Y)
        { return static_cast<bitmask>(
                    static_cast<int_type>(X) |
                    static_cast<int_type>(Y)); }
bitmask  operator^ (bitmask  X, bitmask Y)
        { return static_cast<bitmask>(
                    static_cast<int_type>(X) ^
                    static_cast<int_type>(Y)); }
bitmask  operator~ (bitmask  X)
        { return static_cast<bitmask>(static_cast<int_type>(~X)); }

bitmask& operator&=(bitmask& X, bitmask Y)
        { X = X & Y; return X; }
bitmask& operator|=(bitmask& X, bitmask Y)
        { X = X | Y; return X; }
bitmask& operator^=(bitmask& X, bitmask Y)
        { X = X ^ Y; return X; }
```

3   Here, the names *C0*, *C1*, etc. represent *bitmask elements* for this particular bitmask type. All such elements have distinct values such that, for any pair Ci and Cj, Ci & Ci is nonzero and Ci & Cj is zero.

4   The following terms apply to objects and values of bitmask types:

— To *set* a value Y in an object X is to evaluate the expression X |= Y.

— To *clear* a value Y in an object X is to evaluate the expression X &= ~Y.

— The value Y *is set* in the object X if the expression X & Y is nonzero.

17.3.2.1.3 Character sequences [lib.character.seq]

1   The Standard C library makes widespread use of characters and character sequences that follow a few uniform conventions:

— A *letter* is any of the 26 lowercase or 26 uppercase letters in the basic execution character set.[151]

— The *decimal-point character* is the (single-byte) character used by functions that convert between a (single-byte) character sequence and a value of one of the floating-point types. It is used in the character sequence to denote the beginning of a fractional part. It is represented in clauses 18 through 27 by a period, '.', which is also its value in the "C" locale, but may change during program execution by a call to `setlocale(int, const char*)`,[152] or by a change to a `locale` object, as described in clauses 22.1 and 27.

— A *character sequence* is an array object (8.3.4) A that can be declared as $T\ A[N]$, where T is any of the types `char`, `unsigned char`, or `signed char` (3.9.1), optionally qualified by any combination of `const` or `volatile`. The initial elements of the array have defined contents up to and including an element determined by some predicate. A character sequence can be designated by a pointer value S that points to its first element.

17.3.2.1.3.1 Byte strings [lib.byte.strings]

1   A *null-terminated byte string*, or *NTBS*, is a character sequence whose highest-addressed element with defined content has the value zero (the *terminating null* character).[153]

2   The *length of an NTBS* is the number of elements that precede the terminating null character. An *empty NTBS* has a length of zero.

3   The *value of an NTBS* is the sequence of values of the elements up to and including the terminating null character.

4   A *static NTBS* is an NTBS with static storage duration.[154]

17.3.2.1.3.2 Multibyte strings [lib.multibyte.strings]

1   A *null-terminated multibyte string*, or *NTMBS*, is an NTBS that constitutes a sequence of valid multibyte characters, beginning and ending in the initial shift state.[155]

2   A *static NTMBS* is an NTMBS with static storage duration.

17.3.2.1.3.3 Wide-character sequences [lib.wide.characters]

1   A *wide-character sequence* is an array object (8.3.4) A that can be declared as $T\ A[N]$, where T is type `wchar_t` (3.9.1), optionally qualified by any combination of `const` or `volatile`. The initial elements of the array have defined contents up to and including an element determined by some predicate. A character sequence can be designated by a pointer value S that designates its first element.

2   A *null-terminated wide-character string*, or *NTWCS*, is a wide-character sequence whose highest-addressed element with defined content has the value zero.[156]

---

[151] Note that this definition differs from the definition in ISO C subclause 7.1.1.
[152] declared in `<clocale>` (22.3).
[153] Many of the objects manipulated by function signatures declared in `<cstring>` (21.4) are character sequences or NTBSs. The size of some of these character sequences is limited by a length value, maintained separately from the character sequence.
[154] A string literal, such as "abc", is a static NTBS.
[155] An NTBS that contains characters only from the basic execution character set is also an NTMBS. Each multibyte character then consists of a single byte.
[156] Many of the objects manipulated by function signatures declared in `<cwchar>` are wide-character sequences or NTWCSs.

3   The *length of an NTWCS* is the number of elements that precede the terminating null wide character. An *empty NTWCS* has a length of zero.

4   The *value of an NTWCS* is the sequence of values of the elements up to and including the terminating null character.

5   A *static NTWCS* is an NTWCS with static storage duration.[157]

17.3.2.2 Functions within classes   [lib.functions.within.classes]

1   For the sake of exposition, clauses 18 through 27 do not describe copy constructors, assignment operators, or (non-virtual) destructors with the same apparent semantics as those that can be generated by default (12.1, 12.4, 12.8).

2   It is unspecified whether the implementation provides explicit definitions for such member function signatures, or for virtual destructors that can be generated by default.

17.3.2.3 Private members   [lib.objects.within.classes]

1   Clauses 18 through 27 do not specify the representation of classes, and intentionally omit specification of class members (9.2). An implementation may define static or non-static class members, or both, as needed to implement the semantics of the member functions specified in clauses 18 through 27.

2   Objects of certain classes are sometimes required by the external specifications of their classes to store data, apparently in member objects. For the sake of exposition, some subclauses provide representative declarations, and semantic requirements, for private member objects of classes that meet the external specifications of the classes. The declarations for such member objects and the definitions of related member types are enclosed in a comment that ends with ***exposition only***, as in:

```
//     streambuf* sb;   exposition only
```

3   Any alternate implementation that provides equivalent external behavior is equally acceptable.

17.4 Library-wide requirements   [lib.requirements]

1   This subclause specifies requirements that apply to the entire C++ Standard library. Clauses 18 through 27 specify the requirements of individual entities within the library.

2   The following subclauses describe the library's contents and organization (17.4.1), how well-formed C++ programs gain access to library entities (17.4.2), constraints on such programs (17.4.3), and constraints on conforming implementations (17.4.4).

17.4.1 Library contents and organization   [lib.organization]

1   This subclause provides a summary of the entities defined in the C++ Standard Library. In general, these entites are defined in library headers, which subclause 17.4.1.2 lists alphabetically.

---

[157] A wide string literal, such as L"abc", is a static NTWCS.

17.4.1.1 Library contents   [lib.contents]

1 The C++ Standard Library provides definitions for the following types of entities: Macros, Values, Types, Templates, Classes, Functions, Objects.

2 All library entities except macros, `operator new` and `operator delete` are defined within the namespace `std` or namespaces nested within namespace `std`.

17.4.1.2 Headers   [lib.headers]

1 The elements of the C++ Standard Library are declared or defined (as appropriate) in a *header*.[158]

2 The C++ Standard Library provides 33 C++ *headers*, as shown in Table 11:

Table 11—C++ Library Headers

`<algorithm>`	`<iomanip>`	`<list>`	`<queue>`	`<streambuf>`
`<bitset>`	`<ios>`	`<locale>`	`<set>`	`<string>`
`<complex>`	`<iosfwd>`	`<map>`	`<sstream>`	`<typeinfo>`
`<deque>`	`<iostream>`	`<memory>`	`<stack>`	`<utility>`
`<exception>`	`<istream>`	`<new>`	`<stdexcept>`	`<valarray>`
`<fstream>`	`<iterator>`	`<numeric>`	`<strstream>`	`<vector>`
`<functional>`	`<limits>`	`<ostream>`		

3 The facilities of the Standard C Library are provided in 18 additional headers, as shown in Table 12:

Table 12—C++ Headers for C Library Facilities

`<cassert>`	`<ciso646>`	`<csetjmp>`	`<cstdio>`	`<ctime>`
`<cctype>`	`<climits>`	`<csignal>`	`<cstdlib>`	`<cwchar>`
`<cerrno>`	`<clocale>`	`<cstdarg>`	`<cstring>`	`<cwctype>`
`<cfloat>`	`<cmath>`	`<cstddef>`		

4 Except as noted in clauses 18 through 27, the contents of each header c*name* shall be the same as that of the corresponding header *name*.h, as specified in ISO/IEC 9899:1990 Programming Languages C (Clause 7), or ISO/IEC:1990 Programming Languages—C AMENDMENT 1: C Integrity, (Clause 7), as appropriate, as if by inclusion. In the C++ Standard Library, however, the declarations and definitions (except for names which are defined as macros in C) are within namespace scope (3.3.5) of the namespace `std`.

5 Names which are defined as macros in C shall be defined as macros in the C++ Standard Library, even if C grants license for implementation as functions. [*Note:* the names defined as macros in C include the following: `assert`, `errno`, `offsetof`, `setjmp`, `va_arg`, `va_end`, and `va_start`. —*end note*]

6 Names that are defined as functions in C shall be defined as functions in the C++ Standard Library.[159]

7 D.5, Standard C library headers, describes the effects of using the *name*.h (C header) form in a C++ program.[160]

---

[158] A header is not necessarily a source file, nor are the sequences delimited by `<` and `>` in header names necessarily valid source file names (16.2).

[159] This disallows the practice, allowed in C, of providing a "masking macro" in addition to the function prototype. The only way to achieve equivalent "inline" behavior in C++ is to provide a definition as an extern inline function.

[160] The ".h" headers dump all their names into the global namespace, whereas the newer forms keep their names in namespace `std`. Therefore, the newer forms are the preferred forms for all uses except for C++ programs which are intended to be strictly compatible with C.

17.4.1.3 Freestanding implementations **[lib.compliance]**

1   Two kinds of implementations are defined: *hosted* and *freestanding* (1.4). For a hosted implementation, this International Standard describes the set of available headers.

2   A freestanding implementation has an implementation-defined set of headers. This set shall include at least the following headers, as shown in Table 13:

Table 13—C++ Headers for Freestanding Implementations

Subclause	Header(s)
18.1 Types	`<cstddef>`
18.2 Implementation properties	`<limits>`
18.3 Start and termination	`<cstdlib>`
18.4 Dynamic memory management	`<new>`
18.5 Type identification	`<typeinfo>`
18.6 Exception handling	`<exception>`
18.7 Other runtime support	`<cstdarg>`

3   The supplied version of the header `<cstdlib>` shall declare at least the functions `abort()`, `atexit()`, and `exit()` (18.3).

17.4.2 Using the library   [lib.using]

1   This subclause describes how a C++ program gains access to the facilities of the C++ Standard Library. 17.4.2.1 describes effects during translation phase 4, while 17.4.2.2 describes effects during phase 8 (2.1).

17.4.2.1 Headers   [lib.using.headers]

1   The entities in the C++ Standard Library are defined in headers, whose contents are made available to a translation unit when it contains the appropriate `#include` preprocessing directive (16.2).

2   A translation unit may include library headers in any order (clause 2). Each may be included more than once, with no effect different from being included exactly once, except that the effect of including either `<cassert>` or `<assert.h>` depends each time on the lexically current definition of NDEBUG.[161]

3   A translation unit shall include a header only outside of any external declaration or definition, and shall include the header lexically before the first reference to any of the entities it declares or first defines in that translation unit.

17.4.2.2 Linkage   [lib.using.linkage]

1   Entities in the C++ Standard Library have external linkage (3.5). Unless otherwise specified, objects and functions have the default `extern "C++"` linkage (7.5).

2   It is implementation-defined whether a name from the Standard C library declared with external linkage has `extern "C"` or `extern "C++"` linkage.[162] It is recommended that an implementation use `extern "C++"` linkage for this purpose.

3   Objects and functions defined in the library and required by a C++ program are included in the program prior to program startup.

---

[161] This is the same as the Standard C library.

[162] The only reliable way to declare an object or function signature from the Standard C library is by including the header that declares it, notwithstanding the latitude granted in subclause 7.1.7 of the C Standard.

SEE ALSO: replacement functions (17.4.3.4), run-time changes (17.4.3.5).

17.4.3 Constraints on programs [lib.constraints]

1 This subclause describes restrictions on C++ programs that use the facilities of the C++ Standard Library. The following subclauses specify constraints on the program's namespace (17.4.3.1), its use of headers (17.4.3.2), classes derived from standard library classes (17.4.3.3), definitions of replacement functions (17.4.3.4), and installation of handler functions during execution (17.4.3.5).

17.4.3.1 Reserved names [lib.reserved.names]

1 It is undefined for a C++ program to add declarations or definitions to namespace std or namespaces within namespace std unless otherwise specified. A program may add template specializations for any standard library template to namespace std. Such a specialization (complete or partial) of a standard library template results in undefined behavior unless the declaration depends on a user-defined name of external linkage and unless the specialization meets the standard library requirements for the original template.[163]

2 The C++ Standard Library reserves the following kinds of names:

— Macros

— Global names

— Names with external linkage

3 If the program declares or defines a name in a context where it is reserved, other than as explicitly allowed by this clause, the behavior is undefined.

17.4.3.1.1 Macro names [lib.macro.names]

1 Each name defined as a macro in a header is reserved to the implementation for any use if the translation unit includes the header.[164]

2 A translation unit that includes a header shall not contain any macros that define names declared or defined in that header. Nor shall such a translation unit define macros for names lexically identical to keywords.

17.4.3.1.2 Global names [lib.global.names]

1 Certain sets of names and function signatures are always reserved to the implementation:

— Each name that contains a double underscore (_ _) or begins with an underscore followed by an upper-case letter (2.11) is reserved to the implementation for any use.

— Each name that begins with an underscore is reserved to the implementation for use as a name in the global namespace.[165]

---

[163] Any library code that instantiates other library templates must be prepared to work adequately with any user-supplied specialization that meets the minimum requirements of the Standard.

[164] It is not permissible to remove a library macro definition by using the #undef directive.

[165] Such names are also reserved in namespace ::std (17.4.3.1).

17.4.3.1.3 External linkage [lib.extern.names]

1   Each name declared as an object with external linkage in a header is reserved to the implementation to designate that library object with external linkage,[166] both in namespace `std` and in the global namespace.

2   Each global function signature declared with external linkage in a header is reserved to the implementation to designate that function signature with external linkage.[167]

3   Each name having two consecutive underscores (2.11) is reserved to the implementation for use as a name with both `extern "C"` and `extern "C++"` linkage.

4   Each name from the Standard C library declared with external linkage is reserved to the implementation for use as a name with `extern "C"` linkage, both in namespace std and in the global namespace.

5   Each function signature from the Standard C library declared with external linkage is reserved to the implementation for use as a function signature with both `extern "C"` and `extern "C++"` linkage,[168] or as a name of namespace scope in the global namespace.

17.4.3.1.4 Types [lib.extern.types]

1   For each type T from the Standard C library,[169] the types `::T` and `std::T` are reserved to the implementation and, when defined, `::T` shall be identical to `std::T`.

17.4.3.2 Headers [lib.alt.headers]

1   If a file with a name equivalent to the derived file name for one of the C++ Standard Library headers is not provided as part of the implementation, and a file with that name is placed in any of the standard places for a source file to be included (16.2), the behavior is undefined.

17.4.3.3 Derived classes [lib.derived.classes]

1   Virtual member function signatures defined for a base class in the C++ Standard library may be overridden in a derived class defined in the program (10.3).

17.4.3.4 Replacement functions [lib.replacement.functions]

1   Clauses 18 through 27 describe the behavior of numerous functions defined by the C++ Standard Library. Under some circumstances, however, certain of these function descriptions also apply to replacement functions defined in the program (17.1).

2   A C++ program may provide the definition for any of eight dynamic memory allocation function signatures declared in header `<new>` (3.7.3, clause 18):

— `operator new(size_t)`

— `operator new(size_t, const std::nothrow_t&)`

— `operator new[](size_t)`

— `operator new[](size_t, const std::nothrow_t&)`

— `operator delete(void*)`

— `operator delete(void*, const std::nothrow_t&)`

---

[166] The list of such reserved names includes `errno`, declared or defined in `<cerrno>`.

[167] The list of such reserved function signatures with external linkage includes `setjmp(jmp_buf)`, declared or defined in `<csetjmp>`, and `va_end(va_list)`, declared or defined in `<cstdarg>`.

[168] The function signatures declared in `<cwchar>` and `<cwctype>` are always reserved, notwithstanding the restrictions imposed in subclause 4.5.1 of Amendment 1 to the C Standard for these headers.

[169] These types are `clock_t`, `div_t`, `FILE`, `fpos_t`, `lconv`, `ldiv_t`, `mbstate_t`, `ptrdiff_t`, `sig_atomic_t`, `size_t`, `time_t`, `tm`, `va_list`, `wctrans_t`, `wctype_t`, and `wint_t`.

— `operator delete[](void*)`

— `operator delete[](void*, const std::nothrow_t&)`

3   The program's definitions are used instead of the default versions supplied by the implementation (18.4). Such replacement occurs prior to program startup (3.2, 3.6).

17.4.3.5 Handler functions   [lib.handler.functions]

1   The C++ Standard Library provides default versions of the following handler functions (clause 18):

— `unexpected_handler`

— `terminate_handler`

2   A C++ program may install different handler functions during execution, by supplying a pointer to a function defined in the program or the library as an argument to (respectively):

— `set_new_handler`

— `set_unexpected`

— `set_terminate`

SEE ALSO: subclauses 18.4.2, Storage allocation errors, and 18.6, Exception handling.

17.4.3.6 Other functions   [lib.res.on.functions]

1   In certain cases (replacement functions, handler functions, operations on types used to instantiate standard library template components), the C++ Standard Library depends on components supplied by a C++ program. If these components do not meet their requirements, the Standard places no requirements on the implementation.

2   In particular, the effects are undefined in the following cases:

— for replacement functions (18.4.1), if the installed replacement function does not implement the semantics of the applicable **Required behavior** paragraph.

— for handler functions (18.4.2.2, 18.6.3.1, 18.6.2.2), if the installed handler function does not implement the semantics of the applicable **Required behavior** paragraph

— for types used as template arguments when instantiating a template component, if the operations on the type do not implement the semantics of the applicable **Requirements** subclause (20.1.5, 23.1, 24.1, 26.1). Operations on such types can report a failure by throwing an exception unless otherwise specified.

— if any replacement function or handler function or destructor operation throws an exception, unless specifically allowed in the applicable **Required behavior** paragraph.

— if an incomplete type (3.9) is used as a template argument when instantiating a template component.

17.4.3.7 Function arguments   [lib.res.on.arguments]

1   Each of the following statements applies to all arguments to functions defined in the C++ Standard Library, unless explicitly stated otherwise.

— If an argument to a function has an invalid value (such as a value outside the domain of the function, or a pointer invalid for its intended use), the behavior is undefined.

— If a function argument is described as being an array, the pointer actually passed to the function shall have a value such that all address computations and accesses to objects (that would be valid if the pointer did point to the first element of such an array) are in fact valid.

17.4.3.8 Required paragraph [lib.res.on.required]

1 Violation of the preconditions specified in a function's **Required behavior** paragraph results in undefined behavior unless the function's **Throws** paragraph specifies throwing an exception when the precondition is violated.

17.4.4 Conforming implementations [lib.conforming]

1 This subclause describes the constraints upon, and latitude of, implementations of the C++ Standard library. The following subclauses describe an implementation's use of headers (17.4.4.1), macros (17.4.4.2), global functions (17.4.4.3), member functions (17.4.4.4), reentrancy (17.4.4.5), access specifiers (17.4.4.6), class derivation (17.4.4.7), and exceptions (17.4.4.8).

17.4.4.1 Headers [lib.res.on.headers]

1 A C++ header may include other C++ headers.[170]

2 Certain types and macros are defined in more than one header. For such an entity, a second or subsequent header that also defines it may be included after the header that provides its initial definition (3.2).

3 Header inclusion is limited as follows:

— The C headers (.h form, described in Annex D, D.5) shall include only their corresponding C++ header, as described above (17.4.1.2).

17.4.4.2 Restrictions on macro definitions [lib.res.on.macro.definitions]

1 The names or global function signatures described in 17.4.1.1 are reserved to the implementation.

2 All object-like macros defined by the Standard C library and described in this clause as expanding to integral constant expressions are also suitable for use in `#if` preprocessing directives, unless explicitly stated otherwise.

17.4.4.3 Global or non-member functions [lib.global.functions]

1 It is unspecified whether any global or non-member functions in the C++ Standard Library are defined as `inline` (7.1.2).

2 A call to a global or non-member function signature described in Clauses 18 through 27 behaves the same as if the implementation declares no additional global or non-member function signatures.[171]

3 A global or non-member function cannot be declared by the implementation as taking additional default arguments.

17.4.4.4 Member functions [lib.member.functions]

1 It is unspecified whether any member functions in the C++ Standard Library are defined as `inline` (7.1.2).

2 An implementation can declare additional non-virtual member function signatures within a class:

— by adding arguments with default values to a member function signature;[172] The same latitude does *not* extend to the implementation of virtual or global or non-member functions, however.

— by replacing a member function signature with default values by two or more member function signatures with equivalent behavior;

---

[170] C++ headers must include a C++ header that contains any needed definition (3.2).

[171] A valid C++ program always calls the expected library global or non-member function. An implementation may also define additional global or non-member functions that would otherwise not be called by a valid C++ program.

[172] Hence, taking the address of a member function has an unspecified type.

— by adding a member function signature for a member function name.

3   A call to a member function signature described in the C++ Standard library behaves the same as if the implementation declares no additional member function signatures.[173]

17.4.4.5 Reentrancy   [lib.reentrancy]

1   Which of the functions in the C++ Standard Library are not *reentrant subroutines* is implementation-defined.

17.4.4.6 Protection within classes   [lib.protection.within.classes]

1   It is unspecified whether a function signature or class described in clauses 18 through 27 is a `friend` of another class in the C++ Standard Library.

17.4.4.7 Derived classes   [lib.derivation]

1   It is unspecified whether a class in the C++ Standard Library is itself derived from other classes (with names reserved to the implementation).

2   Certain classes defined in the C++ Standard Library are derived from other classes in the C++ Standard Library:

     — It is unspecified whether a class described in the C++ Standard Library as derived from another class is derived from that class directly, or through other classes (with names reserved to the implementation) that are derived from the specified base class.

3   In any case:

     — A base class described as `virtual` is always virtual;

     — A base class described as non-`virtual` is never virtual;

     — Unless explicitly stated otherwise, types with distinct names are distinct types.[174]

---

[173] A valid C++ program always calls the expected library member function, or one with equivalent behavior. An implementation may also define additional member functions that would otherwise not be called by a valid C++ program.
[174] An implicit exception to this rule are types described as synonyms for basic integral types, such as `size_t` (18.1) and `streamoff` (27.4.1).

17.4.4.8 Restrictions on exception handling **[lib.res.on.exception.handling]**

1   Any of the functions defined in the C++ Standard Library can report a failure by throwing an exception of the type(s) described in their **Throws:** paragraph and/or their *exception-specification* (15.4). An implementation may strengthen the *exception-specification* for a non-virtual function by removing listed exceptions.[175)]

2   None of the functions from the Standard C library shall report an error by throwing an exception,[176)] unless it calls a program-supplied function that throws an exception.[177)]

3   No destructor operation defined in the C++ Standard Library will throw an exception. Any other functions defined in the C++ Standard Library that do not have an *exception-specification* may throw implementation-defined exceptions unless otherwise specified.[178)] An implementation may strengthen this implicit *exception-specification* by adding an explicit one.[179)]

[175)] That is, an implementation of the function will have an explicit *exception-specification* that lists fewer exceptions than those specified in this International Standard. It may not, however, change the types of exceptions listed in the *exception-specification* from those specified, nor add others.

[176)] That is, the C library functions all have a throw() *exception-specification*. This allows implementations to make performance optimizations based on the absence of exceptions at runtime.

[177)] The functions qsort() and bsearch() (25.4) meet this condition.

[178)] In particular, they can report a failure to allocate storage by throwing an exception of type bad_alloc, or a class derived from bad_alloc (18.4.2.1). Library implementations are encouraged (but not required) to report errors by throwing exceptions from (or derived from) the standard exception classes (18.4.2.1, 18.6, 19.1).

[179)] That is, an implementation may provide an explicit *exception-specification* that defines the subset of "any" exceptions thrown by that function. This implies that the implementation may list implementation-defined types in such an *exception-specification*.

18 Language support library [lib.language.support]

1 This clause describes the function signatures that are called implicitly, and the types of objects generated implicitly, during the execution of some C++ programs. It also describes the headers that declare these function signatures and define any related types.

2 The following subclauses describe common type definitions used throughout the library, characteristics of the predefined types, functions supporting start and termination of a C++ program, support for dynamic memory management, support for dynamic type identification, support for exception processing, and other runtime support, as summarized in Table 14:

Table 14—Language support library summary

Subclause	Header(s)
18.1 Types	`<cstddef>`

18.2 Implementation properties	`<limits>`
	 `<climits>`
	 `<cfloat>`

18.3 Start and termination	`<cstdlib>`
18.4 Dynamic memory management	`<new>`
18.5 Type identification	`<typeinfo>`
18.6 Exception handling	`<exception>`

18.7 Other runtime support	`<cstdarg>`
	 `<csetjmp>`
	 `<ctime>`
	 `<csignal>`
	 `<cstdlib>`

18.1 Types [lib.support.types]

1 Common definitions.

2 Header `<cstddef>` (Table 15):

Table 15—Header `<cstddef>` synopsis

Kind	Name(s)	
Macros:	NULL	offsetof
Types:	ptrdiff_t	size_t

3 The contents are the same as the Standard C library header `<stddef.h>`, with the following changes:

4 The macro NULL is an implementation-defined C++ null pointer constant in this International Standard (4.10).[180]

[180) Possible definitions include 0 and 0L, but not (void*)0.

5   The macro `offsetof` accepts a restricted set of *type* arguments in this International Standard. *type* shall be a POD structure or a POD union (clause 9). The result of applying the offsetof macro to a field that is a static data member or a function member is undefined.

SEE ALSO: subclause 5.3.3, Sizeof, subclause 5.7, Additive operators, subclause 12.5, Free store, and ISO C subclause 7.1.6.

18.2 Implementation properties   [lib.support.limits]

1   The headers `<limits>`, `<climits>`, and `<cfloat>` supply characteristics of implementation-dependent fundamental types (3.9.1).

18.2.1 Numeric limits   [lib.limits]

1   The `numeric_limits` component provides a C++ program with information about various properties of the implementation's representation of the fundamental types.

2   Specializations shall be provided for each fundamental type, both floating point and integer, including `bool`. The member `is_specialized` shall be `true` for all such specializations of `numeric_limits`.

3   For all members declared `static const` in the `numeric_limits` template, specializations shall define these values in such a way that they are usable as integral constant expressions.

4   Non-fundamental standard types, such as `complex<T>` (26.2.2), shall not have specializations.

Header `<limits>` synopsis

```
namespace std {
  template<class T> class numeric_limits;
  enum float_round_style;
  enum float_denorm_style;

  template<> class numeric_limits<bool>;

  template<> class numeric_limits<char>;
  template<> class numeric_limits<signed char>;
  template<> class numeric_limits<unsigned char>;
  template<> class numeric_limits<wchar_t>;

  template<> class numeric_limits<short>;
  template<> class numeric_limits<int>;
  template<> class numeric_limits<long>;
  template<> class numeric_limits<unsigned short>;
  template<> class numeric_limits<unsigned int>;
  template<> class numeric_limits<unsigned long>;

  template<> class numeric_limits<float>;
  template<> class numeric_limits<double>;
  template<> class numeric_limits<long double>;
}
```

18.2.1.1 Class template `numeric_limits`   **[lib.numeric.limits]**

```
namespace std {
  template<class T> class numeric_limits {
  public:
    static const bool is_specialized = false;
    static T min() throw();
    static T max() throw();

    static const int  digits = 0;
    static const int  digits10 = 0;
    static const bool is_signed = false;
    static const bool is_integer = false;
    static const bool is_exact = false;
    static const int  radix = 0;
    static T epsilon() throw();
    static T round_error() throw();

    static const int  min_exponent = 0;
    static const int  min_exponent10 = 0;
    static const int  max_exponent = 0;
    static const int  max_exponent10 = 0;

    static const bool has_infinity = false;
    static const bool has_quiet_NaN = false;
    static const bool has_signaling_NaN = false;
    static const float_denorm_style has_denorm = denorm_absent;
    static const bool has_denorm_loss = false;
    static T infinity() throw();
    static T quiet_NaN() throw();
    static T signaling_NaN() throw();
    static T denorm_min() throw();

    static const bool is_iec559 = false;
    static const bool is_bounded = false;
    static const bool is_modulo = false;

    static const bool traps = false;
    static const bool tinyness_before = false;
    static const float_round_style round_style = round_toward_zero;
  };
}
```

1 The member `is_specialized` makes it possible to distinguish between fundamental types, which have specializations, and non-scalar types, which do not.

2 The default `numeric_limits<T>` template shall have all members, but with 0 or `false` values.

18.2.1.2 `numeric_limits` members   **[lib.numeric.limits.members]**

```
static T min() throw();
```

1 Minimum finite value.[181]

2 For floating types with denormalization, returns the minimum positive normalized value.

---

[181] Equivalent to CHAR_MIN, SHRT_MIN, FLT_MIN, DBL_MIN, etc.

3   Meaningful for all specializations in which `is_bounded != false`, or `is_bounded == false && is_signed == false`.

```
static T max() throw();
```

4   Maximum finite value.[182]

5   Meaningful for all specializations in which `is_bounded != false`.

```
static const int  digits;
```

6   Number of `radix` digits that can be represented without change.

7   For built-in integer types, the number of non-sign bits in the representation.

8   For floating point types, the number of `radix` digits in the mantissa.[183]

```
static const int  digits10;
```

9   Number of base 10 digits that can be represented without change.[184]

10   Meaningful for all specializations in which `is_bounded != false`.

```
static const bool is_signed;
```

11   True if the type is signed.

12   Meaningful for all specializations.

```
static const bool is_integer;
```

13   True if the type is integer.

14   Meaningful for all specializations.

```
static const bool is_exact;
```

15   True if the type uses an exact representation. All integer types are exact, but not all exact types are integer. For example, rational and fixed-exponent representations are exact but not integer.

16   Meaningful for all specializations.

```
static const int  radix;
```

17   For floating types, specifies the base or radix of the exponent representation (often 2).[185]

18   For integer types, specifies the base of the representation.[186]

19   Meaningful for all specializations.

---

[182] Equivalent to CHAR_MAX, SHRT_MAX, FLT_MAX, DBL_MAX, etc.
[183] Equivalent to FLT_MANT_DIG, DBL_MANT_DIG, LDBL_MANT_DIG.
[184] Equivalent to FLT_DIG, DBL_DIG, LDBL_DIG.
[185] Equivalent to FLT_RADIX.
[186] Distinguishes types with bases other than 2 (e.g. BCD).

```
static T epsilon() throw();
```

20   Machine epsilon: the difference between 1 and the least value greater than 1 that is representable.[187]

21   Meaningful for all floating point types.

```
static T round_error() throw();
```

22   Measure of the maximum rounding error.[188]

```
static const int  min_exponent;
```

23   Minimum negative integer such that `radix` raised to the power of one less than that integer is a normalized floating point number.[189]

24   Meaningful for all floating point types.

```
static const int  min_exponent10;
```

25   Minimum negative integer such that 10 raised to that power is in the range of normalized floating point numbers.[190]

26   Meaningful for all floating point types.

```
static const int  max_exponent;
```

27   Maximum positive integer such that `radix` raised to the power one less than that integer is a representable finite floating point number.[191]

28   Meaningful for all floating point types.

```
static const int  max_exponent10;
```

29   Maximum positive integer such that 10 raised to that power is in the range of representable finite floating point numbers.[192]

30   Meaningful for all floating point types.

```
static const bool has_infinity;
```

31   True if the type has a representation for positive infinity.

32   Meaningful for all floating point types.

33   Shall be `true` for all specializations in which `is_iec559 != false`.

---

[187] Equivalent to FLT_EPSILON, DBL_EPSILON, LDBL_EPSILON.

[188] Rounding error is described in ISO/IEC 10967-1 Language independent arithmetic – Part 1 Section 5.2.8 and Annex A Rationale Section A.5.2.8 – Rounding constants.

[189] Equivalent to FLT_MIN_EXP, DBL_MIN_EXP, LDBL_MIN_EXP.

[190] Equivalent to FLT_MIN_10_EXP, DBL_MIN_10_EXP, LDBL_MIN_10_EXP.

[191] Equivalent to FLT_MAX_EXP, DBL_MAX_EXP, LDBL_MAX_EXP.

[192] Equivalent to FLT_MAX_10_EXP, DBL_MAX_10_EXP, LDBL_MAX_10_EXP.

```
static const bool has_quiet_NaN;
```

34 True if the type has a representation for a quiet (non-signaling) "Not a Number."[193]

35 Meaningful for all floating point types.

36 Shall be `true` for all specializations in which `is_iec559 != false`.

```
static const bool has_signaling_NaN;
```

37 True if the type has a representation for a signaling "Not a Number."[194]

38 Meaningful for all floating point types.

39 Shall be `true` for all specializations in which `is_iec559 != false`.

```
static const float_denorm_style has_denorm;
```

40 `denorm_present` if the type allows denormalized values (variable number of exponent bits)[195], `denorm_absent` if the type does not allow denormalized values, and `denorm_indeterminate` if it is indeterminate at compile time whether the type allows denormalized values.

41 Meaningful for all floating point types.

```
static const bool has_denorm_loss;
```

42 True if loss of accuracy is detected as a denormalization loss, rather than as an inexact result.[196]

```
static T infinity() throw();
```

43 Representation of positive infinity, if available.[197]

44 Meaningful for all specializations for which `has_infinity != false`. Required in specializations for which `is_iec559 != false`.

```
static T quiet_NaN() throw();
```

45 Representation of a quiet "Not a Number," if available.[198]

46 Meaningful for all specializations for which `has_quiet_NaN != false`. Required in specializations for which `is_iec559 != false`.

```
static T signaling_NaN() throw();
```

47 Representation of a signaling "Not a Number," if available.[199]

48 Meaningful for all specializations for which `has_signaling_NaN != false`. Required in specializations for which `is_iec559 != false`.

---

[193] Required by LIA-1.
[194] Required by LIA-1.
[195] Required by LIA-1.
[196] See IEC 559.
[197] Required by LIA-1.
[198] Required by LIA-1.
[199] Required by LIA-1.

```
static T denorm_min() throw();
```

49   Minimum positive denormalized value.[200]

50   Meaningful for all floating point types.

51   In specializations for which `has_denorm == false`, returns the minimum positive normalized value.

```
static const bool is_iec559;
```

52   True if and only if the type adheres to IEC 559 standard.[201]

53   Meaningful for all floating point types.

```
static const bool is_bounded;
```

54   True if the set of values representable by the type is finite.[202] All built-in types are bounded, this member would be false for arbitrary precision types.

55   Meaningful for all specializations.

```
static const bool is_modulo;
```

56   True if the type is modulo.[203] A type is modulo if it is possible to add two positive numbers and have a result that wraps around to a third number that is less.

57   Generally, this is `false` for floating types, `true` for unsigned integers, and `true` for signed integers on most machines.

58   Meaningful for all specializations.

```
static const bool traps;
```

59   `true` if trapping is implemented for the type.[204]

60   Meaningful for all specializations.

```
static const bool tinyness_before;
```

61   `true` if tinyness is detected before rounding.[205]

62   Meaningful for all floating point types.

```
static const float_round_style round_style;
```

63   The rounding style for the type.[206]

64   Meaningful for all floating point types. Specializations for integer types shall return `round_toward_zero`.

---

[200] Required by LIA-1.
[201] International Electrotechnical Commission standard 559 is the same as IEEE 754.
[202] Required by LIA-1.
[203] Required by LIA-1.
[204] Required by LIA-1.
[205] Refer to IEC 559. Required by LIA-1.
[206] Equivalent to FLT_ROUNDS. Required by LIA-1.

18.2.1.3 Type `float_round_style`   [lib.round.style]

```
namespace std {
  enum float_round_style {
    round_indeterminate      = -1,
    round_toward_zero        =  0,
    round_to_nearest         =  1,
    round_toward_infinity    =  2,
    round_toward_neg_infinity =  3
  };
}
```

1   The rounding mode for floating point arithmetic is characterized by the values:

— `round_indeterminate` if the rounding style is indeterminable

— `round_toward_zero` if the rounding style is toward zero

— `round_to_nearest` if the rounding style is to the nearest representable value

— `round_toward_infinity` if the rounding style is toward infinity

— `round_toward_neg_infinity` if the rounding style is toward negative infinity

18.2.1.4 Type `float_denorm_style`   [lib.denorm.style]

```
namespace std {
  enum float_denorm_style {
    denorm_indeterminate = -1;
    denorm_absent = 0;
    denorm_present = 1;
  };
}
```

1   The presence or absence of denormalization (variable number of exponent bits) is characterized by the values:

— `denorm_indeterminate` if it cannot be determined whether or not the type allows denormalized values

— `denorm_absent` if the type does not allow denormalized values

— `denorm_present` if the type does allow denormalized values

18.2.1.5 `numeric_limits` specializations   [lib.numeric.special]

1   All members shall be provided for all specializations. However, many values are only required to be meaningful under certain conditions (for example, `epsilon()` is only meaningful if `is_integer` is `false`). Any value that is not ''meaningful'' shall be set to 0 or `false`.

2   [*Example:*

```
namespace std {
  template<> class numeric_limits<float> {
  public:
    static const bool is_specialized = true;

    inline static float min() throw() { return 1.17549435E-38F; }
    inline static float max() throw() { return 3.40282347E+38F; }
```

```
        static const int digits    = 24;
        static const int digits10 =  6;

        static const bool is_signed  = true;
        static const bool is_integer = false;
        static const bool is_exact   = false;

        static const int radix = 2;
        inline static float epsilon() throw()     { return 1.19209290E-07F; }
        inline static float round_error() throw() { return 0.5F; }

        static const int min_exponent   = -125;
        static const int min_exponent10 = - 37;
        static const int max_exponent   = +128;
        static const int max_exponent10 = + 38;

        static const bool has_infinity               = true;
        static const bool has_quiet_NaN              = true;
        static const bool has_signaling_NaN          = true;
        static const float_denorm_style has_denorm = denorm_absent;
        static const bool has_denorm_loss            = false;

        inline static float infinity()      throw() { return ...; }
        inline static float quiet_NaN()     throw() { return ...; }
        inline static float signaling_NaN() throw() { return ...; }
        inline static float denorm_min()    throw() { return min(); }

        static const bool is_iec559  = true;
        static const bool is_bounded = true;
        static const bool is_modulo  = false;
        static const bool traps      = true;
        static const bool tinyness_before = true;

        static const float_round_style round_style = round_to_nearest;
    };
  }
```

—*end example*]

18.2.2 C Library   [lib.c.limits]

1   Header <climits> (Table 16):

Table 16—Header `<climits>` synopsis

Type	Name(s)				
Values:					
CHAR_BIT	INT_MAX	LONG_MIN	SCHAR_MIN	UCHAR_MAX	USHRT_MAX
CHAR_MAX	INT_MIN	MB_LEN_MAX	SHRT_MAX	UINT_MAX	
CHAR_MIN	LONG_MAX	SCHAR_MAX	SHRT_MIN	ULONG_MAX	

2   The contents are the same as the Standard C library header <limits.h>.

3   Header <cfloat> (Table 17):

Table 17—Header `<cfloat>` synopsis

Type			Name(s)
Values:			
DBL_DIG	DBL_MIN_EXP	FLT_MIN_10_EXP	LDBL_MAX_10_EXP
DBL_EPSILON	FLT_DIG	FLT_MIN_EXP	LDBL_MAX_EXP
DBL_MANT_DIG	FLT_EPSILON	FLT_RADIX	LDBL_MIN
DBL_MAX	FLT_MANT_DIG	FLT_ROUNDS	LDBL_MIN_10_EXP
DBL_MAX_10_EXP	FLT_MAX	LDBL_DIG	LDBL_MIN_EXP
DBL_MAX_EXP	FLT_MAX_10_EXP	LDBL_EPSILON	
DBL_MIN	FLT_MAX_EXP	LDBL_MANT_DIG	
DBL_MIN_10_EXP	FLT_MIN	LDBL_MAX	

4   The contents are the same as the Standard C library header `<float.h>`.

SEE ALSO: ISO C subclause 7.1.5, 5.2.4.2.2, 5.2.4.2.1.

18.3 Start and termination   [lib.support.start.term]

1   Header `<cstdlib>` (partial), Table 18:

Table 18—Header `<cstdlib>` synopsis

Type	Name(s)	
Macros:	EXIT_FAILURE	EXIT_SUCCESS
Functions:	abort atexit	exit

2   The contents are the same as the Standard C library header `<stdlib.h>`, with the following changes:

```
abort(void)
```

3   The function `abort()` has additional behavior in this International Standard:

— The program is terminated without executing destructors for objects of automatic or static storage duration and without calling the functions passed to `atexit()` (3.6.3).

```
extern "C" int atexit(void (*f)(void))
extern "C++" int atexit(void (*f)(void))
```

4   **Effects:** The `atexit()` functions register the function pointed to by f, to be called without arguments at normal program termination.

5   For the execution of a function registered with `atexit()`, if control leaves the function because it provides no handler for a thrown exception, `terminate()` is called (18.6.3.3).

6   **Implementation Limits:** The implementation shall support the registration of at least 32 functions.

7   **Returns:** The `atexit()` function returns zero if the registration succeeds, nozero if it fails.

```
exit(int status)
```

8   The function exit() has additional behavior in this International Standard:

— First, objects with static storage duration are destroyed and functions registered by calling atexit are called. Non-local objects with static storage duration are destroyed in the reverse order of the completion of their constructor. (Automatic objects are not destroyed as a result of calling exit().)[207] Functions registered with atexit are called in the reverse order of their registration, except that a function is called after any previously registered functions that had already been called at the time it was registered.[208] A function registered with atexit before a non-local object obj1 of static storage duration is initialized will not be called until obj1's destruction has completed. A function registered with atexit after a non-local object obj2 of static storage duration is initialized will be called before obj2's destruction starts. A local static object obj3 is destroyed at the same time it would be if a function calling the obj3 destructor were registered with atexit at the completion of the obj3 constructor.

— Next, all open C streams (as mediated by the function signatures declared in <cstdio>) with unwritten buffered data are flushed, all open C streams are closed, and all files created by calling tmpfile() are removed.[209]

— Finally, control is returned to the host environment. If *status* is zero or EXIT_SUCCESS, an implementation-defined form of the status *successful termination* is returned. If *status* is EXIT_FAILURE, an implementation-defined form of the status *unsuccessful termination* is returned. Otherwise the status returned is implementation-defined.[210]

9   The function exit() never returns to its caller.

SEE ALSO: subclauses 3.6, 3.6.3, ISO C subclause 7.10.4.

18.4 Dynamic memory management   [lib.support.dynamic]

1   The header <new> defines several functions that manage the allocation of dynamic storage in a program. It also defines components for reporting storage management errors.

Header <new> synopsis

```
namespace std {
  class bad_alloc;
  struct nothrow_t {};
  extern const nothrow_t nothrow;
  typedef void (*new_handler)();
  new_handler set_new_handler(new_handler new_p) throw();
}
```

---

[207] Objects with automatic storage duration are all destroyed in a program whose function main() contains no automatic objects and executes the call to exit(). Control can be transferred directly to such a main() by throwing an exception that is caught in main().

[208] A function is called for every time it is registered.

[209] Any C streams associated with cin, cout, etc (27.3) are flushed and closed when static objects are destroyed in the previous phase. The function tmpfile() is declared in <cstdio>.

[210] The macros EXIT_FAILURE and EXIT_SUCCESS are defined in <cstdlib>.

```
void* operator new(std::size_t size) throw(std::bad_alloc);
void* operator new(std::size_t size, const std::nothrow_t&) throw();
void  operator delete(void* ptr) throw();
void  operator delete(void* ptr, const std::nothrow_t&) throw();
void* operator new[](std::size_t size) throw(std::bad_alloc);
void* operator new[](std::size_t size, const std::nothrow_t&) throw();
void  operator delete[](void* ptr) throw();
void  operator delete[](void* ptr, const std::nothrow_t&) throw();

void* operator new   (std::size_t size, void* ptr) throw();
void* operator new[](std::size_t size, void* ptr) throw();
void  operator delete  (void* ptr, void*) throw();
void  operator delete[](void* ptr, void*) throw();
```

SEE ALSO: 1.7, 3.7.3, 5.3.4, 5.3.5, 12.5, 20.4.

18.4.1 Storage allocation and deallocation   [lib.new.delete]

1   Except where otherwise specified, the provisions of (3.7.3) apply to the library versions of operator new and operator delete.

18.4.1.1 Single-object forms   [lib.new.delete.single]

```
void* operator new(std::size_t size) throw(std::bad_alloc);
```

1   **Effects:** The *allocation function* (3.7.3.1) called by a *new-expression* (5.3.4) to allocate size bytes of storage suitably aligned to represent any object of that size.

2   **Replaceable:** a C++ program may define a function with this function signature that displaces the default version defined by the C++ Standard library.

3   **Required behavior:** Return a non-null pointer to suitably aligned storage (3.7.3), or else throw a bad_alloc exception. This requirement is binding on a replacement version of this function.

4   **Default behavior:**

— Executes a loop: Within the loop, the function first attempts to allocate the requested storage. Whether the attempt involves a call to the Standard C library function malloc is unspecified.

— Returns a pointer to the allocated storage if the attempt is successful. Otherwise, if the last argument to set_new_handler() was a null pointer, throw bad_alloc.

— Otherwise, the function calls the current *new_handler* (18.4.2.2). If the called function returns, the loop repeats.

— The loop terminates when an attempt to allocate the requested storage is successful or when a called *new_handler* function does not return.

```
void* operator new(std::size_t size, const std::nothrow_t&) throw();
```

5   **Effects:** Same as above, except that it is called by a placement version of a *new-expression* when a C++ program prefers a null pointer result as an error indication, instead of a bad_alloc exception.

6   **Replaceable:** a C++ program may define a function with this function signature that displaces the default version defined by the C++ Standard library.

7   **Required behavior:** Return a non-null pointer to suitably aligned storage (3.7.3), or else return a null pointer. This nothrow version of operator new returns a pointer obtained as if acquired from the ordinary version. This requirement is binding on a replacement version of this function.

8   **Default behavior:**

— Executes a loop: Within the loop, the function first attempts to allocate the requested storage. Whether the attempt involves a call to the Standard C library function malloc is unspecified.

— Returns a pointer to the allocated storage if the attempt is successful. Otherwise, if the last argument to `set_new_handler()` was a null pointer, return a null pointer.

— Otherwise, the function calls the current *new_handler* (18.4.2.2). If the called function returns, the loop repeats.

— The loop terminates when an attempt to allocate the requested storage is successful or when a called *new_handler* function does not return. If the called *new_handler* function terminates by throwing a `bad_alloc` exception, the function returns a null pointer.

9   [*Example:*

```
T* p1 = new T;              // throws bad_alloc if it fails
T* p2 = new(nothrow) T;     // returns 0 if it fails
```

—*end example*]

```
void operator delete(void* ptr) throw();
void operator delete(void* ptr, const std::nothrow_t&) throw();
```

10   **Effects:** The *deallocation function* (3.7.3.2) called by a *delete-expression* to render the value of `ptr` invalid.

11   **Replaceable:** a C++ program may define a function with this function signature that displaces the default version defined by the C++ Standard library.

12   **Required behavior:** accept a value of `ptr` that is null or that was returned by an earlier call to the default `operator new(std::size_t)` or `operator new(std::size_t,const std::nothrow_t&)`.

13   **Default behavior:**

— For a null value of `ptr`, do nothing.

— Any other value of `ptr` shall be a value returned earlier by a call to the default `operator new`, which was not invalidated by an intervening call to `operator delete(void*)` (17.4.3.7). For such a non-null value of `ptr`, reclaims storage allocated by the earlier call to the default `operator new`.

14   **Notes:** It is unspecified under what conditions part or all of such reclaimed storage is allocated by a subsequent call to `operator new` or any of `calloc`, `malloc`, or `realloc`, declared in `<cstdlib>`.

18.4.1.2 Array forms   [lib.new.delete.array]

```
void* operator new[](std::size_t size) throw(std::bad_alloc);
```

1   **Effects:** The *allocation function* (3.7.3.1) called by the array form of a *new-expression* (5.3.4) to allocate `size` bytes of storage suitably aligned to represent any array object of that size or smaller.[211]

2   **Replaceable:** a C++ program can define a function with this function signature that displaces the default version defined by the C++ Standard library.

3   **Required behavior:** Same as for `operator new(std::size_t)`. This requirement is binding on a replacement version of this function.

4   **Default behavior:** Returns `operator new(size)`.

---

[211] It is not the direct responsibility of `operator new[](std::size_t)` or `operator delete[](void*)` to note the repetition count or element size of the array. Those operations are performed elsewhere in the array `new` and `delete` expressions. The array `new` expression, may, however, increase the `size` argument to `operator new[](std::size_t)` to obtain space to store supplemental information.

```
void* operator new[](std::size_t size, const std::nothrow_t&) throw();
```

5   **Effects:** Same as above, except that it is called by a placement version of a *new-expression* when a C++ program prefers a null pointer result as an error indication, instead of a `bad_alloc` exception.

6   **Replaceable:** a C++ program can define a function with this function signature that displaces the default version defined by the C++ Standard library.

7   **Required behavior:** Same as for `operator new(std::size_t,const std::nothrow_t&)`. This nothrow version of `operator new[]` returns a pointer obtained as if acquired from the ordinary version.

8   **Default behavior:** Returns `operator new(size,nothrow)`.

```
void operator delete[](void* ptr) throw();
void operator delete[](void* ptr, const std::nothrow_t&) throw();
```

9   **Effects:** The *deallocation function* (3.7.3.2) called by the array form of a *delete-expression* to render the value of `ptr` invalid.

10 **Replaceable:** a C++ program can define a function with this function signature that displaces the default version defined by the C++ Standard library.

11 **Required behavior:** accept a value of `ptr` that is null or that was returned by an earlier call to `operator new[](std::size_t)` or `operator new[](std::size_t,const std::nothrow_t&)`.

12 **Default behavior:**

— For a null value of `ptr`, does nothing.

— Any other value of `ptr` shall be a value returned earlier by a call to the default `operator new[](std::size_t)`.[212] For such a non-null value of `ptr`, reclaims storage allocated by the earlier call to the default `operator new[]`.

13 It is unspecified under what conditions part or all of such reclaimed storage is allocated by a subsequent call to `operator new` or any of `calloc`, `malloc`, or `realloc`, declared in `<cstdlib>`.

18.4.1.3 Placement forms   **[lib.new.delete.placement]**

1   These functions are reserved, a C++ program may not define functions that displace the versions in the Standard C++ library (17.4.3). The provisions of (3.7.3) do not apply to these reserved placement forms of `operator new` and `operator delete`.

```
void* operator new(std::size_t size, void* ptr) throw();
```

2   **Returns:** `ptr`.

3   **Notes:** Intentionally performs no other action.

4   [*Example:* This can be useful for constructing an object at a known address:

```
void* place = operator new(sizeof(Something));
Something* p = new (place) Something();
```

—*end example*]

---

[212] The value must not have been invalidated by an intervening call to `operator delete[](void*)` (17.4.3.7).

```
void* operator new[](std::size_t size, void* ptr) throw();
```

5   **Returns:** *ptr*.

6   **Notes:** Intentionally performs no other action.

```
void operator delete(void* ptr, void*) throw();
```

7   **Effects:** Intentionally performs no action.

8   **Notes:** Default function called when any part of the initialization in a placement new expression that invokes the library's non-array placement operator new terminates by throwing an exception (5.3.4).

```
void operator delete[](void* ptr, void*) throw();
```

9   **Effects:** Intentionally performs no action.

10 **Notes:** Default function called when any part of the initialization in a placement new expression that invokes the library's array placement operator new terminates by throwing an exception (5.3.4).

18.4.2 Storage allocation errors   **[lib.alloc.errors]**

18.4.2.1 Class `bad_alloc`   **[lib.bad.alloc]**

```
namespace std {
  class bad_alloc : public exception {
  public:
    bad_alloc() throw();
    bad_alloc(const bad_alloc&) throw();
    bad_alloc& operator=(const bad_alloc&) throw();
    virtual ~bad_alloc() throw();
    virtual const char* what() const throw();
  };
}
```

1   The class `bad_alloc` defines the type of objects thrown as exceptions by the implementation to report a failure to allocate storage.

```
bad_alloc() throw();
```

2   **Effects:** Constructs an object of class `bad_alloc`.

3   **Notes:** The result of calling `what()` on the newly constructed object is implementation-defined.

```
bad_alloc(const bad_alloc&) throw();
bad_alloc& operator=(const bad_alloc&) throw();
```

4   **Effects:** Copies an object of class `bad_alloc`.

```
virtual const char* what() const throw();
```

5   **Returns:** An implementation-defined NTBS.

18.4.2.2 Type `new_handler`   **[lib.new.handler]**

```
typedef void (*new_handler)();
```

1   The type of a *handler function* to be called by `operator new()` or `operator new[]()` (18.4.1) when they cannot satisfy a request for additional storage.

2   **Required behavior:** A *new_handler* shall perform one of the following:

— make more storage available for allocation and then return;

— throw an exception of type `bad_alloc` or a class derived from `bad_alloc`;

— call either `abort()` or `exit()`;

18.4.2.3 `set_new_handler`   [lib.set.new.handler]

```
new_handler set_new_handler(new_handler new_p) throw();
```

1   **Effects:** Establishes the function designated by *new_p* as the current *new_handler*.

2   **Returns:** 0 on the first call, the previous *new_handler* on subsequent calls.

18.5 Type identification   [lib.support.rtti]

1   The header `<typeinfo>` defines a type associated with type information generated by the implementation. It also defines two types for reporting dynamic type identification errors.

Header `<typeinfo>` synopsis

```
namespace std {
  class type_info;
  class bad_cast;
  class bad_typeid;
}
```

SEE ALSO: 5.2.7, 5.2.8.

18.5.1 Class `type_info`   [lib.type.info]

```
namespace std {
  class type_info {
  public:
    virtual ~type_info();
    bool operator==(const type_info& rhs) const;
    bool operator!=(const type_info& rhs) const;
    bool before(const type_info& rhs) const;
    const char* name() const;
  private:
    type_info(const type_info& rhs);
    type_info& operator=(const type_info& rhs);
  };
}
```

1   The class `type_info` describes type information generated by the implementation. Objects of this class
effectively store a pointer to a name for the type, and an encoded value suitable for comparing two types for
equality or collating order. The names, encoding rule, and collating sequence for types are all unspecified
and may differ between programs.

```
bool operator==(const type_info& rhs) const;
```

2   **Effects:** Compares the current object with *rhs*.

3   **Returns:** `true` if the two values describe the same type.

```
bool operator!=(const type_info& rhs) const;
```

4   **Returns:** `!(*this == rhs)`.

```
bool before(const type_info& rhs) const;
```

5   **Effects:** Compares the current object with *rhs*.

6   **Returns:** `true` if `*this` precedes *rhs* in the implementation's collation order.

```
const char* name() const;
```

7   **Returns:** an implementation-defined NTBS.

8   **Notes:** The message may be a null-terminated multibyte string (17.3.2.1.3.2), suitable for conversion and display as a `wstring` (21.2, 22.2.1.5)

```
type_info(const type_info& rhs);
type_info& operator=(const type_info& rhs);
```

9   **Effects:** Copies a `type_info` object.

10   **Notes:** Since the copy constructor and assignment operator for `type_info` are private to the class, objects of this type cannot be copied.

18.5.2 Class `bad_cast`   [lib.bad.cast]

```
namespace std {
  class bad_cast : public exception {
  public:
    bad_cast() throw();
    bad_cast(const bad_cast&) throw();
    bad_cast& operator=(const bad_cast&) throw();
    virtual ~bad_cast() throw();
    virtual const char* what() const throw();
  };
}
```

1   The class `bad_cast` defines the type of objects thrown as exceptions by the implementation to report the execution of an invalid *dynamic-cast* expression (5.2.7).

```
bad_cast() throw();
```

2   **Effects:** Constructs an object of class `bad_cast`.

3   **Notes:** The result of calling `what()` on the newly constructed object is implementation-defined.

```
bad_cast(const bad_cast&) throw();
bad_cast& operator=(const bad_cast&) throw();
```

4   **Effects:** Copies an object of class `bad_cast`.

```
virtual const char* what() const throw();
```

5   **Returns:** An implementation-defined NTBS.

6   **Notes:** The message may be a null-terminated multibyte string (17.3.2.1.3.2), suitable for conversion and display as a `wstring` (21.2, 22.2.1.5)

18.5.3   Class `bad_typeid`   [lib.bad.typeid]

```
namespace std {
  class bad_typeid : public exception {
  public:
    bad_typeid() throw();
    bad_typeid(const bad_typeid&) throw();
    bad_typeid& operator=(const bad_typeid&) throw();
    virtual ~bad_typeid() throw();
    virtual const char* what() const throw();
  };
}
```

1   The class `bad_typeid` defines the type of objects thrown as exceptions by the implementation to report a null pointer in a *typeid* expression (5.2.8).

```
bad_typeid() throw();
```

2   **Effects:** Constructs an object of class `bad_typeid`.

3   **Notes:** The result of calling `what()` on the newly constructed object is implementation-defined.

```
bad_typeid(const bad_typeid&) throw();
bad_typeid& operator=(const bad_typeid&) throw();
```

4   **Effects:** Copies an object of class `bad_typeid`.

```
virtual const char* what() const throw();
```

5   **Returns:** An implementation-defined NTBS.

6   **Notes:** The message may be a null-terminated multibyte string (17.3.2.1.3.2), suitable for conversion and display as a `wstring` (21.2, 22.2.1.5)

18.6   Exception handling   [lib.support.exception]

1   The header `<exception>` defines several types and functions related to the handling of exceptions in a C++ program.

Header `<exception>` synopsis

```
namespace std {
  class exception;
  class bad_exception;

  typedef void (*unexpected_handler)();
  unexpected_handler set_unexpected(unexpected_handler f) throw();
  void unexpected();

  typedef void (*terminate_handler)();
  terminate_handler set_terminate(terminate_handler f) throw();
  void terminate();

  bool uncaught_exception() throw();
}
```

SEE ALSO: 15.5.

18.6.1 Class exception   [lib.exception]

```
namespace std {
  class exception {
  public:
    exception() throw();
    exception(const exception&) throw();
    exception& operator=(const exception&) throw();
    virtual ~exception() throw();
    virtual const char* what() const throw();
  };
}
```

1   The class exception defines the base class for the types of objects thrown as exceptions by C++ Standard library components, and certain expressions, to report errors detected during program execution.

```
exception() throw();
```

2   **Effects:** Constructs an object of class exception.

3   **Notes:** Does not throw any exceptions.

```
exception(const exception&) throw();
exception& operator=(const exception&) throw();
```

4   **Effects:** Copies an exception object.

5   **Notes:** The effects of calling what() after assignment are implementation-defined.

```
virtual ~exception() throw();
```

6   **Effects:** Destroys an object of class exception.

7   **Notes:** Does not throw any exceptions.

```
virtual const char* what() const throw();
```

8   **Returns:** An implementation-defined NTBS.

9   **Notes:** The message may be a null-terminated multibyte string (17.3.2.1.3.2), suitable for conversion and display as a wstring (21.2, 22.2.1.5). The return value remains valid until the exception object from which it is obtained is destroyed or a non-const member function of the exception object is called.

18.6.2 Violating *exception-specifications*   [lib.exception.unexpected]

18.6.2.1 Class bad_exception   [lib.bad.exception]

```
namespace std {
  class bad_exception : public exception {
  public:
    bad_exception() throw();
    bad_exception(const bad_exception&) throw();
    bad_exception& operator=(const bad_exception&) throw();
    virtual ~bad_exception() throw();
    virtual const char* what() const throw();
  };
}
```

1   The class bad_exception defines the type of objects thrown as described in (15.5.2).

```
bad_exception() throw();
```

2   **Effects:** Constructs an object of class `bad_exception`.

3   **Notes:** The result of calling `what()` on the newly constructed object is implementation-defined.

```
bad_exception(const bad_exception&) throw();
bad_exception& operator=(const bad_exception&) throw();
```

4   **Effects:** Copies an object of class `bad_exception`.

```
virtual const char* what() const throw();
```

5   **Returns:** An implementation-defined NTBS.

6   **Notes:** The message may be a null-terminated multibyte string (17.3.2.1.3.2), suitable for conversion and display as a `wstring` (21.2, 22.2.1.5).

18.6.2.2 Type `unexpected_handler`   [lib.unexpected.handler]

```
typedef void (*unexpected_handler)();
```

1   The type of a *handler function* to be called by `unexpected()` when a function attempts to throw an exception not listed in its *exception-specification.*

2   **Required behavior:** An `unexpected_handler` shall not return. See also 15.5.2.

3   **Default behavior:** The implementation's default *unexpected_handler* calls `terminate()`.

18.6.2.3 `set_unexpected`   [lib.set.unexpected]

```
unexpected_handler set_unexpected(unexpected_handler f) throw();
```

1   **Effects:** Establishes the function designated by `f` as the current *unexpected_handler.*

2   **Requires:** `f` shall not be a null pointer.

3   **Returns:** The previous *unexpected_handler.*

18.6.2.4 `unexpected`   [lib.unexpected]

```
void unexpected();
```

1   Called by the implementation when a function exits via an exception not allowed by its *exception-specification* (15.5.2). May also be called directly by the program.

2   **Effects:** Calls the `unexpected_handler` function in effect immediately after evaluating the *throw-expression* (18.6.2.2), if called by the implementation, or calls the current `unexpected_handler`, if called by the program.

18.6.3 Abnormal termination   [lib.exception.terminate]

18.6.3.1 Type `terminate_handler`   [lib.terminate.handler]

```
typedef void (*terminate_handler)();
```

1   The type of a *handler function* to be called by `terminate()` when terminating exception processing.

2   **Required behavior:** A *terminate_handler* shall terminate execution of the program without returning to the caller.

3   **Default behavior:** The implementation's default *terminate_handler* calls `abort()`.

18.6.3.2 set_terminate   **[lib.set.terminate]**

```
terminate_handler set_terminate(terminate_handler f) throw();
```

1   **Effects:** Establishes the function designated by *f* as the current handler function for terminating exception processing.

2   **Requires:** *f* shall not be a null pointer.

3   **Returns:** The previous *terminate_handler*.

18.6.3.3 terminate   **[lib.terminate]**

```
void terminate();
```

1   Called by the implementation when exception handling must be abandoned for any of several reasons (15.5.1). May also be called directly by the program.

2   **Effects:** Calls the terminate_handler function in effect immediately after evaluating the *throw-expression* (18.6.3.1), if called by the implementation, or calls the current terminate_handler function, if called by the program.

18.6.4 uncaught_exception   **[lib.uncaught]**

```
bool uncaught_exception() throw();
```

1   **Returns:** true after completing evaluation of a *throw-expression* until either completing initialization of the *exception-declaration* in the matching handler or entering unexpected() due to the throw; or after entering terminate() for any reason other than an explicit call to terminate(). [*Note:* This includes stack unwinding (15.2). —*end note*]

2   **Notes:** When uncaught_exception() is true, throwing an exception can result in a call of terminate() (15.5.1).

18.7 Other runtime support   **[lib.support.runtime]**

1   Headers <cstdarg> (variable arguments), <csetjmp> (nonlocal jumps), <ctime> (system clock clock(), time()), <csignal> (signal handling), and <cstdlib> (runtime environment getenv(), system()).

Table 19—Header <cstdarg> synopsis

Type	Name(s)		
Macros:	va_arg	va_end	va_start
Type:	va_list		

Table 20—Header <csetjmp> synopsis

Type	Name(s)
Macro:	setjmp
Type:	jmp_buf
Function:	longjmp

Table 21—Header `<ctime>` synopsis

Type	Name(s)
Macros:	CLOCKS_PER_SEC
Types:	clock_t
Functions:	clock

Table 22—Header `<csignal>` synopsis

Type	Name(s)			
Macros:	SIGABRT	SIGILL	SIGSEGV	SIG_DFL
SIG_IGN	SIGFPE	SIGINT	SIGTERM	SIG_ERR
Type:	sig_atomic_t			
Functions:	raise	signal		

Table 23—Header `<cstdlib>` synopsis

Type	Name(s)	
Functions:	getenv	system

2 The contents of these headers are the same as the Standard C library headers `<stdarg.h>`, `<setjmp.h>`, `<time.h>`, `<signal.h>`, and `<stdlib.h>` respectively, with the following changes:

3 The restrictions that ISO C places on the second parameter to the `va_start()` macro in header `<stdarg.h>` are different in this International Standard. The parameter `parmN` is the identifier of the rightmost parameter in the variable parameter list of the function definition (the one just before the . . .). If the parameter `parmN` is declared with a function, array, or reference type, or with a type that is not compatible with the type that results when passing an argument for which there is no parameter, the behavior is undefined.

SEE ALSO: ISO C subclause 4.8.1.1.

4 The function signature `longjmp(jmp_buf jbuf, int val)` has more restricted behavior in this International Standard. If any automatic objects would be destroyed by a thrown exception transferring control to another (destination) point in the program, then a call to `longjmp(jbuf, val)` at the throw point that transfers control to the same (destination) point has undefined behavior.

SEE ALSO: ISO C subclause 7.10.4, 7.8, 7.6, 7.12.

5 The common subset of the C and C++ languages consists of all declarations, definitions, and expressions that may appear in a well formed C++ program and also in a conforming C program. A POF (''plain old function'') is a function that uses only features from this common subset, and that does not directly or indirectly use any function that is not a POF. All signal handlers shall have C linkage. A POF that could be used as a signal handler in a conforming C program does not produce undefined behavior when used as a signal handler in a C++ program. The behavior of any other function used as a signal handler in a C++ program is implementation defined.[213]

---
[213] In particular, a signal handler using exception handling is very likely to have problems

19   Diagnostics library   [lib.diagnostics]

1   This clause describes components that C++ programs may use to detect and report error conditions.

2   The following subclauses describe components for reporting several kinds of exceptional conditions, documenting program assertions, and a global variable for error number codes, as summarized in Table 24:

Table 24—Diagnostics library summary

Subclause	Header(s)
19.1 Exception classes	`<stdexcept>`
19.2 Assertions	`<cassert>`
19.3 Error numbers	`<cerrno>`

19.1 Exception classes   [lib.std.exceptions]

1   The Standard C++ library provides classes to be used to report certain errors (17.4.4.8) in C++ programs. In the error model reflected in these classes, errors are divided into two broad categories: *logic* errors and *runtime* errors.

2   The distinguishing characteristic of logic errors is that they are due to errors in the internal logic of the program. In theory, they are preventable.

3   By contrast, runtime errors are due to events beyond the scope of the program. They cannot be easily predicted in advance. The header `<stdexcept>` defines several types of predefined exceptions for reporting errors in a C++ program. These exceptions are related by inheritance.

Header `<stdexcept>` synopsis

```
namespace std {
  class logic_error;
    class domain_error;
    class invalid_argument;
    class length_error;
    class out_of_range;
  class runtime_error;
    class range_error;
    class overflow_error;
    class underflow_error;
}
```

19.1.1 Class `logic_error`   [lib.logic.error]

```
namespace std {
  class logic_error : public exception {
  public:
    explicit logic_error(const string& what_arg);
  };
}
```

1   The class `logic_error` defines the type of objects thrown as exceptions to report errors presumably detectable before the program executes, such as violations of logical preconditions or class invariants.

```
logic_error(const string& what_arg);
```

2   **Effects:** Constructs an object of class `logic_error`.
3   **Postcondition:** `strcmp(what(), what_arg.c_str()) == 0`.

19.1.2 Class `domain_error`   [lib.domain.error]

```
namespace std {
  class domain_error : public logic_error {
  public:
    explicit domain_error(const string& what_arg);
  };
}
```

1   The class `domain_error` defines the type of objects thrown as exceptions by the implementation to report domain errors.

```
domain_error(const string& what_arg);
```

2   **Effects:** Constructs an object of class `domain_error`.
3   **Postcondition:** `strcmp(what(), what_arg.c_str()) == 0`.

19.1.3 Class `invalid_argument`   [lib.invalid.argument]

```
namespace std {
  class invalid_argument : public logic_error {
  public:
    explicit invalid_argument(const string& what_arg);
  };
}
```

1   The class `invalid_argument` defines the type of objects thrown as exceptions to report an invalid argument.

```
invalid_argument(const string& what_arg);
```

2   **Effects:** Constructs an object of class `invalid_argument`.
3   **Postcondition:** `strcmp(what(), what_arg.c_str()) == 0`.

19.1.4 Class `length_error`   [lib.length.error]

```
namespace std {
  class length_error : public logic_error {
  public:
    explicit length_error(const string& what_arg);
  };
}
```

1   The class `length_error` defines the type of objects thrown as exceptions to report an attempt to produce an object whose length exceeds its maximum allowable size.

```
length_error(const string& what_arg);
```

2   **Effects:** Constructs an object of class `length_error`.
3   **Postcondition:** `strcmp(what(), what_arg.c_str()) == 0`.

19.1.5 Class `out_of_range` [lib.out.of.range]

```
namespace std {
  class out_of_range : public logic_error {
  public:
    explicit out_of_range(const string& what_arg);
  };
}
```

1   The class `out_of_range` defines the type of objects thrown as exceptions to report an argument value not in its expected range.

```
out_of_range(const string& what_arg);
```

2   **Effects:** Constructs an object of class `out_of_range`.

3   **Postcondition:** `strcmp(what(), what_arg.c_str()) == 0`.

19.1.6 Class `runtime_error` [lib.runtime.error]

```
namespace std {
  class runtime_error : public exception {
  public:
    explicit runtime_error(const string& what_arg);
  };
}
```

1   The class `runtime_error` defines the type of objects thrown as exceptions to report errors presumably detectable only when the program executes.

```
runtime_error(const string& what_arg);
```

2   **Effects:** Constructs an object of class `runtime_error`.

3   **Postcondition:** `strcmp(what(), what_arg.c_str()) == 0`.

19.1.7 Class `range_error` [lib.range.error]

```
namespace std {
  class range_error : public runtime_error {
  public:
    explicit range_error(const string& what_arg);
  };
}
```

1   The class `range_error` defines the type of objects thrown as exceptions to report range errors in internal computations.

```
range_error(const string& what_arg);
```

2   **Effects:** Constructs an object of class `range_error`.

3   **Postcondition:** `strcmp(what(), what_arg.c_str()) == 0`.

19.1.8 Class `overflow_error` [lib.overflow.error]

```
namespace std {
  class overflow_error : public runtime_error {
  public:
    explicit overflow_error(const string& what_arg);
  };
}
```

1 The class `overflow_error` defines the type of objects thrown as exceptions to report an arithmetic overflow error.

```
overflow_error(const string& what_arg);
```

2 **Effects:** Constructs an object of class `overflow_error`.

3 **Postcondition:** `strcmp(what(), what_arg.c_str()) == 0`.

19.1.9 Class `underflow_error` [lib.underflow.error]

```
namespace std {
  class underflow_error : public runtime_error {
  public:
    explicit underflow_error(const string& what_arg);
  };
}
```

1 The class `underflow_error` defines the type of objects thrown as exceptions to report an arithmetic underflow error.

```
underflow_error(const string& what_arg);
```

2 **Effects:** Constructs an object of class `underflow_error`.

3 **Postcondition:** `strcmp(what(), what_arg.c_str()) == 0`.

19.2 Assertions [lib.assertions]

1 Provides macros for documenting C++ program assertions, and for disabling the assertion checks.

2 Header `<cassert>` (Table 25):

Table 25—Header `<cassert>` synopsis

Type	Name(s)
Macro:	assert

3 The contents are the same as the Standard C library header `<assert.h>`.

SEE ALSO: ISO C subclause 7.2.

19.3 Error numbers [lib.errno]

1   Header <cerrno> (Table 26):

Table 26—Header <cerrno> synopsis

Type	Name(s)		
Macros:	EDOM	ERANGE	errno

2   The contents are the same as the Standard C library header <errno.h>.

SEE ALSO: ISO C subclause 7.1.4, 7.2, Amendment 1 subclause 4.3.

20 General utilities library [lib.utilities]

1 This clause describes components used by other elements of the Standard C++ library. These components may also be used by C++ programs.

2 The following clauses describe utility and allocator requirements, utility components, function objects, dynamic memory management utilities, and date/time utilities, as summarized in Table 27:

Table 27—General utilities library summary

Clause	Header(s)
20.1 Requirements	
20.2 Utility components	`<utility>`
20.3 Function objects	`<functional>`
20.4 Memory	`<memory>`
20.5 Date and time	`<ctime>`

20.1 Requirements [lib.utility.requirements]

1 20.1 describes requirements on template arguments. 20.1.1 through 20.1.3 describe requirements on types used to instantiate templates. 20.1.5 describes the requirements on storage allocators.

20.1.1 Equality comparison [lib.equalitycomparable]

1 In Table 28, T is a type to be supplied by a C++ program instantiating a template, a, b and c are values of type T.

Table 28—EqualityComparable requirements

expression	return type	requirement
a == b	convertible to `bool`	== is an equivalence relation, that is, it satisfies the following properties:
		— For all a, a == a.
		— If a == b, then b == a.
		— If a == b and b == c, then a == c.

20.1.2 Less than comparison [lib.lessthancomparable]

1 In the following Table 29, T is a type to be supplied by a C++ program instantiating a template, a and b are values of type T.

Table 29—LessThanComparable requirements

expression	return type	requirement
a < b	convertible to bool	< is a strict weak ordering relation (25.3)

20.1.3 Copy construction   [lib.copyconstructible]

1   In the following Table 30, T is a type to be supplied by a C++ program instantiating a template, t is a value
of type T, and u is a value of type const T.

Table 30—CopyConstructible requirements

expression	return type	requirement
T(t)		t is equivalent to T(t)
T(u)		u is equivalent to T(u)
t.~T()		
&t	T*	denotes the address of t
&u	const T*	denotes the address of u

20.1.4 Default construction   [lib.default.con.req]

1   The default constructor is not required. Certain container class member function signatures specify the
default constructor as a default argument. T() shall be a well-defined expression (8.5) if one of those signatures is called using the default argument (8.3.6).

20.1.5 Allocator requirements   [lib.allocator.requirements]

1   The library describes a standard set of requirements for *allocators*, which are objects that encapsulate the
information about an allocation model. This information includes the knowledge of pointer types, the type
of their difference, the type of the size of objects in this allocation model, as well as the memory allocation
and deallocation primitives for it. All of the containers (clause 23) are parameterized in terms of allocators.

2   Table 31 describes the requirements on types manipulated through allocators. All the operations on the
allocators are expected to be amortized constant time. Table 32 describes the requirements on allocator
types.

Table 31—Descriptive variable definitions

Variable	Definition
`T, U`	any type
`X`	an Allocator class for type `T`
`Y`	the corresponding Allocator class for type `U`
`t`	a value of type `const  T&`
`a, a1, a2`	values of type `X&`
`b`	a value of type `Y`
`p`	a value of type `X::pointer`, obtained by calling `a1.allocate`, where `a1 == a`.
`q`	a value of type `X::const_pointer` obtained by conversion from a value `p`.
`r`	a value of type `X::reference` obtained by the expression `*p`.
`s`	a value of type `X::const_reference` obtained by the expression `*q` or by conversion from a value `r`.
`u`	a value of type `Y::const_pointer` obtained by calling `Y::allocate`, or else 0.
`n`	a value of type `X::size_type`.

Table 32—Allocator requirements

expression	return type	assertion/note pre/post-condition
`X::pointer`	Pointer to T.	
`X::const_pointer`	Pointer to `const T`.	
`X::reference`	`T&`	
`X::const_reference`	`T const&`	
`X::value_type`	Identical to T	
`X::size_type`	unsigned integral type	a type that can represent the size of the largest object in the allocation model.
`X::difference_type`	signed integral type	a type that can represent the difference between any two pointers in the allocation model.
`typename X::template rebind<U>::other`	Y	For all U (including T), `Y::template rebind<T>::other` is X.
`a.address(r)`	`X::pointer`	
`a.address(s)`	`X::const_pointer`	
`a.allocate(n)` `a.allocate(n,u)`	`X::pointer`	Memory is allocated for n objects of type T but objects are not constructed. allocate may raise an appropriate exception. The result is a random access iterator.[214] [*Note:* If n == 0, the return value is unspecified.]
`a.deallocate(p, n)`	(not used)	All n T objects in the area pointed by p shall be destroyed prior to this call. n shall match the value passed to `allocate` to obtain this memory. Does not throw exceptions. [*Note:* p shall not be null.]
`a.max_size()`	`X::size_type`	the largest value that can meaningfully be passed to `X::allocate()`.
`a1 == a2`	`bool`	returns true iff storage allocated from each can be deallocated via the other.
`a1 != a2`	`bool`	same as `!(a1 == a2)`
`X()`		creates a default instance. Note: a destructor is assumed.
`X a(b);`		post: `Y(a) == b`
`a.construct(p,t)`	(not used)	Effect: `new((void*)p) T(t)`
`a.destroy(p)`	(not used)	Effect: `((T*)p)->~T()`

---

[214] It is intended that `a.allocate` be an efficient means of allocating a single object of type T, even when `sizeof(T)` is small. That is, there is no need for a container to maintain its own "free list".

3   The member class template `rebind` in the table above is effectively a typedef template: if the name Allocator is bound to `SomeAllocator<T>`, then `Allocator::rebind<U>::other` is the same type as `SomeAllocator<U>`.

4   Implementations of containers described in this International Standard are permitted to assume that their Allocator template parameter meets the following two additional requirements beyond those in Table 32.

     — All instances of a given allocator type are required to be interchangeable and always compare equal to each other.

     — The typedef members `pointer`, `const_pointer`, `size_type`, and `difference_type` are required to be `T*`, `T const*`, `size_t`, and `ptrdiff_t`, respectively.

5   Implementors are encouraged to supply libraries that can accept allocators that encapsulate more general memory models and that support non-equal instances. In such implementations, any requirements imposed on allocators by containers beyond those requirements that appear in Table 32, and the semantics of containers and algorithms when allocator instances compare non-equal, are implementation-defined.

20.2 Utility components   **[lib.utility]**

1   This subclause contains some basic function and class templates that are used throughout the rest of the library.

Header `<utility>` synopsis

```
namespace std {
  // 20.2.1, operators:
  namespace rel_ops {
    template<class T> bool operator!=(const T&, const T&);
    template<class T> bool operator> (const T&, const T&);
    template<class T> bool operator<=(const T&, const T&);
    template<class T> bool operator>=(const T&, const T&);
  }

  // 20.2.2, pairs:
  template <class T1, class T2> struct pair;
  template <class T1, class T2>
    bool operator==(const pair<T1,T2>&, const pair<T1,T2>&);
  template <class T1, class T2>
    bool operator< (const pair<T1,T2>&, const pair<T1,T2>&);
  template <class T1, class T2>
    bool operator!=(const pair<T1,T2>&, const pair<T1,T2>&);
  template <class T1, class T2>
    bool operator> (const pair<T1,T2>&, const pair<T1,T2>&);
  template <class T1, class T2>
    bool operator>=(const pair<T1,T2>&, const pair<T1,T2>&);
  template <class T1, class T2>
    bool operator<=(const pair<T1,T2>&, const pair<T1,T2>&);
  template <class T1, class T2> pair<T1,T2> make_pair(T1, T2);
}
```

20.2.1 Operators [lib.operators]

1 To avoid redundant definitions of operator!= out of operator== and operators >, <=, and >= out of operator<, the library provides the following:

```
template <class T> bool operator!=(const T& x, const T& y);
```

2 **Requires:** Type T is EqualityComparable (20.1.1).
3 **Returns:** !(x == y).

```
template <class T> bool operator>(const T& x, const T& y);
```

4 **Requires:** Type T is LessThanComparable (20.1.2).
5 **Returns:** y < x.

```
template <class T> bool operator<=(const T& x, const T& y);
```

6 **Requires:** Type T is LessThanComparable (20.1.2).
7 **Returns:** !(y < x).

```
template <class T> bool operator>=(const T& x, const T& y);
```

8 **Requires:** Type T is LessThanComparable (20.1.2).
9 **Returns:** !(x < y).

10 In this library, whenever a declaration is provided for an operator!=, operator>, operator>=, or operator<=, and requirements and semantics are not explicitly provided, the requirements and semantics are as specified in this clause.

20.2.2 Pairs [lib.pairs]

1 The library provides a template for heterogeneous pairs of values. The library also provides a matching function template to simplify their construction.

```
template <class T1, class T2>
struct pair {
  typedef T1 first_type;
  typedef T2 second_type;

  T1 first;
  T2 second;
  pair();
  pair(const T1& x, const T2& y);
  template<class U, class V> pair(const pair<U, V> &p);
};
```

```
pair();
```

2 **Effects:** Initializes its members as if implemented: pair() : first(T1()), second(T2()) {}

```
pair(const T1& x, const T2& y);
```

3 **Effects:** The constructor initializes first with x and second with y.

```
template<class U, class V> pair(const pair<U, V> &p);
```

4   **Effects:** Initializes members from the corresponding members of the argument, performing implicit conversions as needed.

```
template <class T1, class T2>
  bool operator==(const pair<T1, T2>& x, const pair<T1, T2>& y);
```

5   **Returns:** `x.first == y.first && x.second == y.second`.

```
template <class T1, class T2>
  bool operator<(const pair<T1, T2>& x, const pair<T1, T2>& y);
```

6   **Returns:** `x.first < y.first || (!(y.first < x.first) && x.second < y.second)`.

```
template <class T1, class T2>
  pair<T1, T2> make_pair(T1 x, T2 y);
```

7   **Returns:** `pair<T1, T2>(x, y)`.[214a]

8   [*Example:* In place of:

```
return pair<int, double>(5, 3.1415926);    // explicit types
```

a C++ program may contain:

```
return make_pair(5, 3.1415926);            // types are deduced
```

—*end example*]

20.3 Function objects   [lib.function.objects]

1   Function objects are objects with an `operator()` defined. They are important for the effective use of the library. In the places where one would expect to pass a pointer to a function to an algorithmic template (clause 25), the interface is specified to accept an object with an `operator()` defined. This not only makes algorithmic templates work with pointers to functions, but also enables them to work with arbitrary function objects.

Header <functional> synopsis

```
namespace std {
  // 20.3.1, base:
  template <class Arg, class Result> struct unary_function;
  template <class Arg1, class Arg2, class Result> struct binary_function;

  // 20.3.2, arithmetic operations:
  template <class T> struct plus;
  template <class T> struct minus;
  template <class T> struct multiplies;
  template <class T> struct divides;
  template <class T> struct modulus;
  template <class T> struct negate;
```

[214a)] According to (12.8), an implementation is permitted to not perform a copy of an argument, thus avoiding unnecessary copies.

```
// 20.3.3, comparisons:
template <class T> struct equal_to;
template <class T> struct not_equal_to;
template <class T> struct greater;
template <class T> struct less;
template <class T> struct greater_equal;
template <class T> struct less_equal;

// 20.3.4, logical operations:
template <class T> struct logical_and;
template <class T> struct logical_or;
template <class T> struct logical_not;

// 20.3.5, negators:
template <class Predicate> struct unary_negate;
template <class Predicate>
  unary_negate<Predicate>  not1(const Predicate&);
template <class Predicate> struct binary_negate;
template <class Predicate>
  binary_negate<Predicate> not2(const Predicate&);

// 20.3.6, binders:
template <class Operation>  class binder1st;
template <class Operation, class T>
  binder1st<Operation> bind1st(const Operation&, const T&);
template <class Operation> class binder2nd;
template <class Operation, class T>
  binder2nd<Operation> bind2nd(const Operation&, const T&);

// 20.3.7, adaptors:
template <class Arg, class Result> class pointer_to_unary_function;
template <class Arg, class Result>
  pointer_to_unary_function<Arg,Result> ptr_fun(Result (*)(Arg));
template <class Arg1, class Arg2, class Result>
  class pointer_to_binary_function;
template <class Arg1, class Arg2, class Result>
  pointer_to_binary_function<Arg1,Arg2,Result>
    ptr_fun(Result (*)(Arg1,Arg2));
```

```
// 20.3.8, adaptors:
template<class S, class T> class mem_fun_t;
template<class S, class T, class A> class mem_fun1_t;
template<class S, class T>
    mem_fun_t<S,T> mem_fun(S (T::*f)());
template<class S, class T, class A>
    mem_fun1_t<S,T,A> mem_fun(S (T::*f)(A));
template<class S, class T> class mem_fun_ref_t;
template<class S, class T, class A> class mem_fun1_ref_t;
template<class S, class T>
    mem_fun_ref_t<S,T> mem_fun_ref(S (T::*f)());
template<class S, class T, class A>
    mem_fun1_ref_t<S,T,A> mem_fun_ref(S (T::*f)(A));

template <class S, class T> class const_mem_fun_t;
template <class S, class T, class A> class const_mem_fun1_t;
template <class S, class T>
  const_mem_fun_t<S,T> mem_fun(S (T::*f)() const);
template <class S, class T, class A>
  const_mem_fun1_t<S,T,A> mem_fun(S (T::*f)(A) const);
template <class S, class T> class const_mem_fun_ref_t;
template <class S, class T, class A> class const_mem_fun1_ref_t;
template <class S, class T>
  const_mem_fun_ref_t<S,T> mem_fun_ref(S (T::*f)() const);
template <class S, class T, class A>
  const_mem_fun1_ref_t<S,T,A> mem_fun_ref(S (T::*f)(A) const);
}
```

2   Using function objects together with function templates increases the expressive power of the library as well as making the resulting code much more efficient.

3   [*Example:* If a C++ program wants to have a by-element addition of two vectors a and b containing double and put the result into a, it can do:

```
transform(a.begin(), a.end(), b.begin(), a.begin(), plus<double>());
```

—*end example*]

4   [*Example:* To negate every element of a:

```
transform(a.begin(), a.end(), a.begin(), negate<double>());
```

The corresponding functions will inline the addition and the negation.   —*end example*]

5   To enable adaptors and other components to manipulate function objects that take one or two arguments it is required that the function objects correspondingly provide typedefs argument_type and result_type for function objects that take one argument and first_argument_type, second_argument_type, and result_type for function objects that take two arguments.

20.3.1 Base   [lib.base]

1   The following classes are provided to simplify the typedefs of the argument and result types:

```
template <class Arg, class Result>
struct unary_function {
  typedef Arg    argument_type;
  typedef Result result_type;
};
```

```
template <class Arg1, class Arg2, class Result>
struct binary_function {
  typedef Arg1   first_argument_type;
  typedef Arg2   second_argument_type;
  typedef Result result_type;
};
```

20.3.2 Arithmetic operations   [lib.arithmetic.operations]

1   The library provides basic function object classes for all of the arithmetic operators in the language (5.6, 5.7).

```
template <class T> struct plus : binary_function<T,T,T> {
  T operator()(const T& x, const T& y) const;
};
```

2   `operator()` returns $x + y$.

```
template <class T> struct minus : binary_function<T,T,T> {
  T operator()(const T& x, const T& y) const;
};
```

3   `operator()` returns $x - y$.

```
template <class T> struct multiplies : binary_function<T,T,T> {
  T operator()(const T& x, const T& y) const;
};
```

4   `operator()` returns $x * y$.

```
template <class T> struct divides : binary_function<T,T,T> {
  T operator()(const T& x, const T& y) const;
};
```

5   `operator()` returns x / y.

```
template <class T> struct modulus : binary_function<T,T,T> {
  T operator()(const T& x, const T& y) const;
};
```

6   `operator()` returns $x \% y$.

```
template <class T> struct negate : unary_function<T,T> {
  T operator()(const T& x) const;
};
```

7   `operator()` returns $-x$.

20.3.3 Comparisons [lib.comparisons]

1   The library provides basic function object classes for all of the comparison operators in the language (5.9, 5.10).

```
template <class T> struct equal_to : binary_function<T,T,bool> {
  bool operator()(const T& x, const T& y) const;
};
```

2   operator() returns $x == y$.

```
template <class T> struct not_equal_to : binary_function<T,T,bool> {
  bool operator()(const T& x, const T& y) const;
};
```

3   operator() returns $x \mathrel{!=} y$.

```
template <class T> struct greater : binary_function<T,T,bool> {
  bool operator()(const T& x, const T& y) const;
};
```

4   operator() returns $x > y$.

```
template <class T> struct less : binary_function<T,T,bool> {
  bool operator()(const T& x, const T& y) const;
};
```

5   operator() returns $x < y$.

```
template <class T> struct greater_equal : binary_function<T,T,bool> {
  bool operator()(const T& x, const T& y) const;
};
```

6   operator() returns $x >= y$.

```
template <class T> struct less_equal : binary_function<T,T,bool> {
  bool operator()(const T& x, const T& y) const;
};
```

7   operator() returns $x <= y$.

8   For templates `greater`, `less`, `greater_equal`, and `less_equal`, the specializations for any pointer type yield a total order, even if the built-in operators <, >, <=, >= do not.

20.3.4 Logical operations [lib.logical.operations]

1   The library provides basic function object classes for all of the logical operators in the language (5.14, 5.15, 5.3.1).

```
template <class T> struct logical_and : binary_function<T,T,bool> {
  bool operator()(const T& x, const T& y) const;
};
```

2   operator() returns $x \mathrel{\&\&} y$.

```
template <class T> struct logical_or : binary_function<T,T,bool> {
  bool operator()(const T& x, const T& y) const;
};
```

3   operator() returns $x \mid\mid y$.

```
template <class T> struct logical_not : unary_function<T,bool> {
  bool operator()(const T& x) const;
};
```

4   operator() returns $!x$.

20.3.5 Negators   [lib.negators]

1   Negators not1 and not2 take a unary and a binary predicate, respectively, and return their complements (5.3.1).

```
template <class Predicate>
  class unary_negate
    : public unary_function<typename Predicate::argument_type,bool> {
public:
  explicit unary_negate(const Predicate& pred);
  bool operator()(const typename Predicate::argument_type& x) const;
};
```

2   operator() returns $!pred(x)$.

```
template <class Predicate>
  unary_negate<Predicate> not1(const Predicate& pred);
```

3   **Returns:** unary_negate<Predicate>(*pred*).

```
template <class Predicate>
  class binary_negate
    : public binary_function<typename Predicate::first_argument_type,
        typename Predicate::second_argument_type, bool> {
public:
  explicit binary_negate(const Predicate& pred);
  bool operator()(const typename Predicate::first_argument_type&  x,
      const typename Predicate::second_argument_type& y) const;
};
```

4   operator() returns $!pred(x, y)$.

```
template <class Predicate>
  binary_negate<Predicate> not2(const Predicate& pred);
```

5   **Returns:** binary_negate<Predicate>(*pred*).

20.3.6 Binders [lib.binders]

1   Binders `bind1st` and `bind2nd` take a function object `f` of two arguments and a value `x` and return a function object of one argument constructed out of `f` with the first or second argument correspondingly bound to `x`.

20.3.6.1 Class template `binder1st` [lib.binder.1st]

```
template <class Operation>
class binder1st
  : public unary_function<typename Operation::second_argument_type,
                          typename Operation::result_type> {
protected:
  Operation                        op;
  typename Operation::first_argument_type value;

public:
  binder1st(const Operation& x,
            const typename Operation::first_argument_type& y);
  typename Operation::result_type
    operator()(const typename Operation::second_argument_type& x) const;
};
```

1   The constructor initializes op with x and value with y.

2   `operator()` returns op(value, x).

20.3.6.2 `bind1st` [lib.bind.1st]

```
template <class Operation, class T>
  binder1st<Operation> bind1st(const Operation& op, const T& x);
```

1   **Returns:** `binder1st<Operation>`(op, `typename Operation::first_argument_type`(x)).

20.3.6.3 Class template `binder2nd` [lib.binder.2nd]

```
template <class Operation>
class binder2nd
  : public unary_function<typename Operation::first_argument_type,
                          typename Operation::result_type> {
protected:
  Operation                        op;
  typename Operation::second_argument_type value;

public:
  binder2nd(const Operation& x,
            const typename Operation::second_argument_type& y);
  typename Operation::result_type
    operator()(const typename Operation::first_argument_type& x) const;
};
```

1   The constructor initializes op with x and value with y.

2   `operator()` returns op(x, value).

```
template <class Operation, class T>
  binder2nd<Operation> bind2nd(const Operation& op, const T& x);
```

1   **Returns:** `binder2nd<Operation>(op, typename Operation::second_argument_type(x))`.

2   [*Example:*

```
find_if(v.begin(), v.end(), bind2nd(greater<int>(), 5));
```

finds the first integer in vector v greater than 5;

```
find_if(v.begin(), v.end(), bind1st(greater<int>(), 5));
```

finds the first integer in v less than 5. *—end example*]

20.3.7 Adaptors for pointers to functions   **[lib.function.pointer.adaptors]**

1   To allow pointers to (unary and binary) functions to work with function adaptors the library provides:

```
template <class Arg, class Result>
class pointer_to_unary_function : public unary_function<Arg, Result> {
public:
  explicit pointer_to_unary_function(Result (*f)(Arg));
  Result operator()(Arg x) const;
};
```

2   `operator()` returns $f(x)$.

```
template <class Arg, class Result>
  pointer_to_unary_function<Arg, Result> ptr_fun(Result (*f)(Arg));
```

3   **Returns:** `pointer_to_unary_function<Arg, Result>(f)`.

```
template <class Arg1, class Arg2, class Result>
class pointer_to_binary_function :
  public binary_function<Arg1,Arg2,Result> {
public:
  explicit pointer_to_binary_function(Result (*f)(Arg1, Arg2));
  Result operator()(Arg1 x, Arg2 y) const;
};
```

4   `operator()` returns $f(x,y)$.

```
template <class Arg1, class Arg2, class Result>
  pointer_to_binary_function<Arg1,Arg2,Result>
    ptr_fun(Result (*f)(Arg1, Arg2));
```

5   **Returns:** `pointer_to_binary_function<Arg1,Arg2,Result>(f)`.

6   [*Example:*

```
replace_if(v.begin(), v.end(), not1(bind2nd(ptr_fun(strcmp), "C")), "C++");
```

replaces each C with C++ in sequence v.[215] *—end example*]

---

[215] Implementations that have multiple pointer to function types provide additional `ptr_fun` function templates.

20.3.8 Adaptors for pointers to members **[lib.member.pointer.adaptors]**

1   The purpose of the following is to provide the same facilities for pointer to members as those provided for pointers to functions in 20.3.7.

```
template <class S, class T> class mem_fun_t
         : public unary_function<T*, S> {
public:
  explicit mem_fun_t(S (T::*p)());
  S operator()(T* p) const;
};
```

2   mem_fun_t calls the member function it is initialized with given a pointer argument.

```
template <class S, class T, class A> class mem_fun1_t
         : public binary_function<T*, A, S> {
public:
  explicit mem_fun1_t(S (T::*p)(A));
  S operator()(T* p, A x) const;
};
```

3   mem_fun1_t calls the member function it is initialized with given a pointer argument and an additional argument of the appropriate type.

```
template<class S, class T> mem_fun_t<S,T>
  mem_fun(S (T::*f)());

template<class S, class T, class A> mem_fun1_t<S,T,A>
  mem_fun(S (T::*f)(A));
```

4   mem_fun(&X::f) returns an object through which X::f can be called given a pointer to an X followed by the argument required for f (if any).

```
template <class S, class T> class mem_fun_ref_t
         : public unary_function<T, S> {
public:
  explicit mem_fun_ref_t(S (T::*p)());
  S operator()(T& p) const;
};
```

5   mem_fun_ref_t calls the member function it is initialized with given a reference argument.

```
template <class S, class T, class A> class mem_fun1_ref_t
         : public binary_function<T, A, S> {
public:
  explicit mem_fun1_ref_t(S (T::*p)(A));
  S operator()(T& p, A x) const;
};
```

6   mem_fun1_ref_t calls the member function it is initialized with given a reference argument and an additional argument of the appropriate type.

```
template<class S, class T> mem_fun_ref_t<S,T>
  mem_fun_ref(S (T::*f)());

template<class S, class T, class A> mem_fun1_ref_t<S,T,A>
  mem_fun_ref(S (T::*f)(A));
```

7   mem_fun_ref(&X::f) returns an object through which X::f can be called given a reference to an X followed by the argument required for f (if any).

```
template <class S, class T> class const_mem_fun_t
     : public unary_function<T*, S> {
public:
  explicit const_mem_fun_t(S (T::*p)() const);
  S operator()(const T* p) const;
};
```

8   `const_mem_fun_t` calls the member function it is initialized with given a pointer argument.

```
template <class S, class T, class A> class const_mem_fun1_t
     : public binary_function<T*, A, S> {
public:
  explicit const_mem_fun1_t(S (T::*p)(A) const);
  S operator()(const T* p, A x) const;
};
```

9   `const_mem_fun1_t` calls the member function it is initialized with given a pointer argument and an additional argument of the appropriate type.

```
template<class S, class T> const_mem_fun_t<S,T>
  mem_fun(S (T::*f)() const);

template<class S, class T, class A> const_mem_fun1_t<S,T,A>
  mem_fun(S (T::*f)(A) const);
```

10   `mem_fun(&X::f)` returns an object through which `X::f` can be called given a pointer to an X followed by the argument required for `f` (if any).

```
template <class S, class T> class const_mem_fun_ref_t
     : public unary_function<T, S> {
public:
  explicit const_mem_fun_ref_t(S (T::*p)() const);
  S operator()(const T& p) const;
};
```

11   `const_mem_fun_ref_t` calls the member function it is initialized with given a reference argument.

```
template <class S, class T, class A> class const_mem_fun1_ref_t
     : public binary_function<T, A, S> {
public:
  explicit const_mem_fun1_ref_t(S (T::*p)(A) const);
  S operator()(const T& p, A x) const;
};
```

12   `const_mem_fun1_ref_t` calls the member function it is initialized with given a reference argument and an additional argument of the appropriate type.

```
template<class S, class T> const_mem_fun_ref_t<S,T>
  mem_fun_ref(S (T::*f)() const);

template<class S, class T, class A> const_mem_fun1_ref_t<S,T,A>
  mem_fun_ref(S (T::*f)(A) const);
```

13   `mem_fun_ref(&X::f)` returns an object through which `X::f` can be called given a reference to an X followed by the argument required for `f` (if any).

20.4 Memory [lib.memory]

Header `<memory>` synopsis

```
namespace std {
  // 20.4.1, the default allocator:
  template <class T> class allocator;
  template <> class allocator<void>;
  template <class T, class U>
    bool operator==(const allocator<T>&, const allocator<U>&) throw();
  template <class T, class U>
    bool operator!=(const allocator<T>&, const allocator<U>&) throw();

  // 20.4.2, raw storage iterator:
  template <class OutputIterator, class T> class raw_storage_iterator;

  // 20.4.3, temporary buffers:
  template <class T>
    pair<T*,ptrdiff_t> get_temporary_buffer(ptrdiff_t n);
  template <class T>
    void return_temporary_buffer(T* p);

  // 20.4.4, specialized algorithms:
  template <class InputIterator, class ForwardIterator>
    ForwardIterator
      uninitialized_copy(InputIterator first, InputIterator last,
                         ForwardIterator result);
  template <class ForwardIterator, class T>
    void uninitialized_fill(ForwardIterator first, ForwardIterator last,
                            const T& x);
  template <class ForwardIterator, class Size, class T>
    void uninitialized_fill_n(ForwardIterator first, Size n, const T& x);
  // 20.4.5, pointers:
  template<class X> class auto_ptr;
}
```

20.4.1 The default allocator [lib.default.allocator]

```
namespace std {
  template <class T> class allocator;

  // specialize for void:
  template <> class allocator<void> {
  public:
    typedef void*       pointer;
    typedef const void* const_pointer;
    // reference-to-void members are impossible.
    typedef void  value_type;
    template <class U> struct rebind { typedef allocator<U> other; };
  };
```

```
template <class T> class allocator {
public:
  typedef size_t      size_type;
  typedef ptrdiff_t   difference_type;
  typedef T*          pointer;
  typedef const T*    const_pointer;
  typedef T&          reference;
  typedef const T&    const_reference;
  typedef T           value_type;
  template <class U> struct rebind { typedef allocator<U> other; };

  allocator() throw();
  allocator(const allocator&) throw();
  template <class U> allocator(const allocator<U>&) throw();
  ~allocator() throw();

  pointer address(reference x) const;
  const_pointer address(const_reference x) const;

  pointer allocate(
    size_type, allocator<void>::const_pointer hint = 0);
  void deallocate(pointer p, size_type n);
  size_type max_size() const throw();

  void construct(pointer p, const T& val);
  void destroy(pointer p);
};
}
```

20.4.1.1 allocator members   [lib.allocator.members]

```
pointer address(reference x) const;
```

1   **Returns:** &*x*.

```
const_pointer address(const_reference x) const;
```

2   **Returns:** &*x*.

```
pointer allocate(size_type n, allocator<void>::const_pointer hint=0);
```

3   **Notes:** Uses `::operator new(size_t)` (18.4.1).

4   **Requires:** *hint* either 0 or previously obtained from member `allocate` and not yet passed to member `deallocate`. The value *hint* may be used by an implementation to help improve performance[216].

5   **Returns:** a pointer to the initial element of an array of storage of size *n* `* sizeof(T)`, aligned appropriately for objects of type T.

6   **Note:** the storage is obtained by calling `::operator new(size_t)`, but it is unspecified when or how often this function is called. The use of *hint* is unspecified, but intended as an aid to locality if an implementation so desires.

7   **Throws:** `bad_alloc` if the storage cannot be obtained.

---

216) In a container member function, the address of an adjacent element is often a good choice to pass for this argument.

```
    void deallocate(pointer p, size_type n);
```

8   **Requires:** p shall be a pointer value obtained from `allocate()`. n shall equal the value passed as the first argument to the invocation of allocate which returned p.

9   **Effects:** Deallocates the storage referenced by p.

10 **Notes:** Uses `::operator delete(void*)` (18.4.1), but it is unspecified when this function is called.

```
    size_type max_size() const throw();
```

11 **Returns:** the largest value N for which the call `allocate`$(N, 0)$ might succeed.

```
    void construct(pointer p, const_reference val);
```

12 **Returns:** `new((void *)p) T(`*val*`)`

```
    void destroy(pointer p);
```

13 **Returns:** `((T*)p)->~T()`

20.4.1.2 allocator globals   [lib.allocator.globals]

```
    template <class T1, class T2>
      bool operator==(const allocator<T1>&, const allocator<T2>&) throw();
```

1   **Returns:** `true`.

```
    template <class T1, class T2>
      bool operator!=(const allocator<T1>&, const allocator<T2>&) throw();
```

2   **Returns:** `false`.

20.4.2 Raw storage iterator   [lib.storage.iterator]

1   `raw_storage_iterator` is provided to enable algorithms to store their results into uninitialized memory. The formal template parameter `OutputIterator` is required to have its `operator*` return an object for which `operator&` is defined and returns a pointer to `T`, and is also required to satisfy the requirements of an output iterator (24.1.2).

```
    namespace std {
      template <class OutputIterator, class T>
      class raw_storage_iterator
        : public iterator<output_iterator_tag,void,void,void,void> {
      public:
        explicit raw_storage_iterator(OutputIterator x);

        raw_storage_iterator<OutputIterator,T>& operator*();
        raw_storage_iterator<OutputIterator,T>& operator=(const T& element);
        raw_storage_iterator<OutputIterator,T>& operator++();
        raw_storage_iterator<OutputIterator,T>  operator++(int);
      };
    }
```

```
    raw_storage_iterator(OutputIterator x);
```

2   **Effects:** Initializes the iterator to point to the same value to which x points.

```
raw_storage_iterator<OutputIterator,T>& operator*();
```

3   **Returns:** *this

```
raw_storage_iterator<OutputIterator,T>& operator=(const T& element);
```

4   **Effects:** Constructs a value from *element* at the location to which the iterator points.
5   **Returns:** A reference to the iterator.

```
raw_storage_iterator<OutputIterator,T>& operator++();
```

6   **Effects:** Pre-increment: advances the iterator and returns a reference to the updated iterator.

```
raw_storage_iterator<OutputIterator,T> operator++(int);
```

7   **Effects:** Post-increment: advances the iterator and returns the old value of the iterator.

20.4.3 Temporary buffers   [lib.temporary.buffer]

```
template <class T>
  pair<T*, ptrdiff_t> get_temporary_buffer(ptrdiff_t n);
```

1   **Effects:** Obtains a pointer to storage sufficient to store up to *n* adjacent *T* objects.
2   **Returns:** A `pair` containing the buffer's address and capacity (in the units of `sizeof(T)`), or a pair of
      0 values if no storage can be obtained.

```
template <class T> void return_temporary_buffer(T* p);
```

3   **Effects:** Deallocates the buffer to which *p* points.
4   **Requires:** The buffer shall have been previously allocated by `get_temporary_buffer`.

20.4.4 Specialized algorithms   [lib.specialized.algorithms]

1   All the iterators that are used as formal template parameters in the following algorithms are required to
      have their `operator*` return an object for which `operator&` is defined and returns a pointer to `T`. In
      the algorithm `uninitialized_copy`, the formal template parameter `InputIterator` is required to
      satisfy the requirements of an input iterator (24.1.1). In all of the following algorithms, the formal template
      parameter `ForwardIterator` is required to satisfy the requirements of a forward iterator (24.1.3) and
      also to satisfy the requirements of a mutable iterator (24.1), and is required to have the property that no
      exceptions are thrown from increment, assignment, comparison, or dereference of valid iterators. In the fol-
      lowing algorithms, if an exception is thrown there are no effects.

20.4.4.1 `uninitialized_copy`   [lib.uninitialized.copy]

```
template <class InputIterator, class ForwardIterator>
  ForwardIterator
    uninitialized_copy(InputIterator first, InputIterator last,
                       ForwardIterator result);
```

1   **Effects:**

```
for (; first != last; ++result, ++first)
    new (static_cast<void*>(&*result))
            typename iterator_traits<ForwardIterator>::value_type(*first);
```

2   **Returns:** *result*

20.4.4.2 uninitialized_fill [lib.uninitialized.fill]

```
template <class ForwardIterator, class T>
  void uninitialized_fill(ForwardIterator first, ForwardIterator last,
                          const T& x);
```

1 **Effects:**

```
for (; first != last; ++first)
   new (static_cast<void*>(&*first))
           typename iterator_traits<ForwardIterator>::value_type(x);
```

20.4.4.3 uninitialized_fill_n [lib.uninitialized.fill.n]

```
template <class ForwardIterator, class Size, class T>
  void uninitialized_fill_n(ForwardIterator first, Size n, const T& x);
```

1 **Effects:**

```
for (; n--; ++first)
   new (static_cast<void*>(&*first))
           typename iterator_traits<ForwardIterator>::value_type(x);
```

20.4.5 Class template auto_ptr [lib.auto.ptr]

1 Template auto_ptr stores a pointer to an object obtained via new and deletes that object when it itself is destroyed (such as when leaving block scope 6.7).

2 Template auto_ptr_ref holds a reference to an auto_ptr. It is used by the auto_ptr conversions to allow auto_ptr objects to be passed to and returned from functions.

```
namespace std {
  template <class Y> struct auto_ptr_ref {};

  template<class X> class auto_ptr {
  public:
    typedef X element_type;

    // 20.4.5.1 construct/copy/destroy:
    explicit auto_ptr(X* p =0) throw();
    auto_ptr(auto_ptr&) throw();
    template<class Y> auto_ptr(auto_ptr<Y>&) throw();
    auto_ptr& operator=(auto_ptr&) throw();
    template<class Y> auto_ptr& operator=(auto_ptr<Y>&) throw();
    auto_ptr& operator=(auto_ptr_ref<X> r) throw();
    ~auto_ptr() throw();
```

```
// 20.4.5.2 members:
X& operator*() const throw();
X* operator->() const throw();
X* get() const throw();
X* release() throw();
void reset(X* p =0) throw();

// 20.4.5.3 conversions:
auto_ptr(auto_ptr_ref<X>) throw();
template<class Y> operator auto_ptr_ref<Y>() throw();
template<class Y> operator auto_ptr<Y>() throw();
};
}
```

3   The `auto_ptr` provides a semantics of strict ownership. An `auto_ptr` owns the object it holds a pointer to. Copying an `auto_ptr` copies the pointer and transfers ownership to the destination. If more than one `auto_ptr` owns the same object at the same time the behavior of the program is undefined. [*Note:* The uses of `auto_ptr` include providing temporary exception-safety for dynamically allocated memory, passing ownership of dynamically allocated memory to a function, and returning dynamically allocated memory from a function. `auto_ptr` does not meet the `CopyConstructible` and `Assignable` requirements for Standard Library container elements and thus instantiating a Standard Library container with an `auto_ptr` results in undefined behavior. *—end note*]

20.4.5.1 `auto_ptr` constructors   [lib.auto.ptr.cons]

```
explicit auto_ptr(X* p =0) throw();
```

1   **Postconditions:** `*this` holds the pointer p.

```
auto_ptr(auto_ptr& a) throw();
```

2   **Effects:** Calls `a.release()`.
3   **Postconditions:** `*this` holds the pointer returned from `a.release()`.

```
template<class Y> auto_ptr(auto_ptr<Y>& a) throw();
```

4   **Requires:** $Y*$ can be implicitly converted to $X*$.
5   **Effects:** Calls `a.release()`.
6   **Postconditions:** `*this` holds the pointer returned from `a.release()`.

```
auto_ptr& operator=(auto_ptr& a) throw();
```

7   **Requires:** The expression `delete get()` is well formed.
8   **Effects:** `reset(a.release())`.
9   **Returns:** `*this`.

```
template<class Y> auto_ptr& operator=(auto_ptr<Y>& a) throw();
```

10 **Requires:** $Y*$ can be implicitly converted to $X*$. The expression `delete get()` is well formed.
11 **Effects:** `reset(a.release())`.
12 **Returns:** `*this`.

```
~auto_ptr() throw();
```

13   **Requires:** The expression `delete get()` is well formed.
14   **Effects:** `delete get()`.

20.4.5.2 auto_ptr members   [lib.auto.ptr.members]

```
X& operator*() const throw();
```

1   **Requires:** `get() != 0`
2   **Returns:** `*get()`

```
X* operator->() const throw();
```

3   **Returns:** `get()`

```
X* get() const throw();
```

4   **Returns:** The pointer `*this` holds.

```
X* release() throw();
```

5   **Returns:** `get()`
6   **Postcondition:** `*this` holds the null pointer.

```
void reset(X* p=0) throw();
```

7   **Effects:** If `get() != p` then `delete get()`.
8   **Postconditions:** `*this` holds the pointer `p`.

20.4.5.3 auto_ptr conversions   [lib.auto.ptr.conv]

```
auto_ptr(auto_ptr_ref<X> r) throw();
```

1   **Effects:** Calls `p.release()` for the `auto_ptr p` that `r` holds.
2   **Postconditions:** `*this` hold the pointer returned from `release()`.

```
template<class Y> operator auto_ptr_ref<Y>() throw();
```

3   **Returns:** An `auto_ptr_ref<Y>` that holds `*this`.

```
template<class Y> operator auto_ptr<Y>() throw();
```

4   **Effects:** Calls `release()`.
5   **Returns:** An `auto_ptr<Y>` that holds the pointer returned from `release()`.

```
auto_ptr& operator=(auto_ptr_ref<X> r) throw()
```

6   **Effects:** Calls `reset(p.release())` for the `auto_ptr p` that `r` holds a reference to.
7   **Returns:** `*this`

1   Header <cstdlib> (Table 33):

Table 33—Header <cstdlib> synopsis

Type	Name(s)	
Functions:	calloc	malloc
	free	realloc

2   The contents are the same as the Standard C library header <stdlib.h>, with the following changes:

3   The functions calloc(), malloc(), and realloc() do not attempt to allocate storage by calling ::operator new() (18.4).

4   The function free() does not attempt to deallocate storage by calling ::operator delete().

   SEE ALSO: ISO C clause 7.11.2.

5   Header <cstring> (Table 34):

Table 34—Header <cstring> synopsis

Type	Name(s)	
Macro:	NULL	
Type:	size_t	
Functions:	memchr	memcmp
memcpy	memmove	memset

6   The contents are the same as the Standard C library header <string.h>, with the change to memchr() specified in 21.4.

   SEE ALSO: ISO C clause 7.11.2.

20.5 Date and time **[lib.date.time]**

1   Header <ctime> (Table 35):

Table 35—Header <ctime> synopsis

Type	Name(s)			
Macros:	NULL			
Types:	size_t	clock_t	time_t	
Struct:	tm			
Functions:				
asctime	clock	difftime	localtime	strftime
ctime	gmtime	mktime	time	

2   The contents are the same as the Standard C library header <time.h>.

   SEE ALSO: ISO C clause 7.12, Amendment 1 clause 4.6.4.

21   Strings library   [lib.strings]

1   This clause describes components for manipulating sequences of "characters," where characters may be of any POD (3.9) type. In this clause such types are called char-like types, and objects of char-like types are called char-like objects or simply "characters."

2   The following subclauses describe a character traits class, a string class, and null-terminated sequence utilities, as summarized in Table 36:

Table 36—Strings library summary

Subclause	Header(s)
21.1 Character traits	`<string>`
21.2 String classes	`<string>`
21.4 Null-terminated sequence utilities	`<cctype>` `<cwctype>` `<cstring>` `<cwchar>` `<cstdlib>`

21.1 Character traits   [lib.char.traits]

1   This subclause defines requirements on classes representing *character traits*, and defines a class template `char_traits<charT>`, along with two specializations, `char_traits<char>` and `char_traits<wchar_t>`, that satisfy those requirements.

2   Most classes specified in clauses 21.2 and 27 need a set of related types and functions to complete the definition of their semantics. These types and functions are provided as a set of member typedefs and functions in the template parameter 'traits' used by each such template. This subclause defines the semantics guaranteed by these members.

3   To specialize those templates to generate a string or iostream class to handle a particular character container type `CharT`, that and its related character traits class `Traits` are passed as a pair of parameters to the string or iostream template as formal parameters `charT` and `traits`. `Traits::char_type` shall be the same as `CharT`.

4   This subclause specifies a struct template, `char_traits<charT>`, and two explicit specializations of it, `char_traits<char>` and `char_traits<wchar_t>`, all of which appear in the header `<string>` and satisfy the requirements below.

21.1.1 Character traits requirements   [lib.char.traits.require]

1   In Table 37, X denotes a Traits class defining types and functions for the character container type `CharT`; c and d denote values of type `CharT`; p and q denote values of type `const CharT*`; s denotes a value of type `CharT*`; n, i and j denote values of type `size_t`; e and f denote values of type `X::int_type`; pos denotes a value of type `X::pos_type`; and `state` denotes a value of type `X::state_type`. Operations on Traits shall not throw exceptions.

Table 37—Traits requirements

expression	return type	assertion/note pre/post-condition	complexity
`X::char_type`	`charT`	(described in 21.1.2)	compile-time
`X::int_type`		(described in 21.1.2)	compile-time
`X::off_type`		(described in 21.1.2)	compile-time
`X::pos_type`		(described in 21.1.2)	compile-time
`X::state_type`		(described in 21.1.2)	compile-time
`X::assign(c,d)`	(not used)	assigns c=d.	constant
`X::eq(c,d)`	`bool`	yields: whether c is to be treated as equal to d.	constant
`X::lt(c,d)`	`bool`	yields: whether c is to be treated as less than d.	constant
`X::compare (p,q,n)`	`int`	yields: 0 if for each i in [0,n), `X::eq(p[i],q[i])` is true; else, a negative value if, for some j in [0,n), `X::lt(p[j],q[j])` is true and for each i in [0,j) `X::eq(p[i],q[i])` is true; else a positive value.	linear
`X::length(p)`	`size_t`	yields: the smallest i such that `X::eq(p[i],charT())` is true.	linear
`X::find(p,n,c)`	`const X:: char_type*`	yields: the smallest q in [p,p+n) such that `X::eq(*q,c)` is true, zero otherwise.	linear
`X::move(s,p,n)`	`X:: char_type*`	for each i in [0,n), performs `X::assign(s[i],p[i])`. Copies correctly even where the ranges [p, p+n) and [s, s+n) overlap. yields: s.	linear
`X::copy(s,p,n)`	`X:: char_type*`	pre: p not in [s,s+n). yields: s. for each i in [0,n), performs `X::assign(s[i],p[i])`.	linear
`X::assign (s,n,c)`	`X:: char_type*`	for each i in [0,n), performs `X::assign(s[i],c)`. yields: s.	linear
`X::not_eof(e)`	`int_type`	yields: e if `X::eq_int_type(e,X::eof())` is false, otherwise a value f such that `X::eq_int_type(f,X::eof())` is false.	constant
`X::to_char_type (e)`	`X:: char_type`	yields: if for some c, `X::eq_int_type(e,X::to_int_type(c))` is true, c; else some unspecified value.	constant
`X::to_int_type (c)`	`X:: int_type`	yields: some value e, constrained by the definitions of `to_char_type` and `eq_int_type`.	constant
`X::eq_int_type (e,f)`	`bool`	yields: for all c and d, `X::eq(c,d)` is equal to `X::eq_int_type(X::to_int_type(c), X::to_int_type(d))`; otherwise, yields true if e and f are both copies of `X::eof()`; otherwise, yields false if one of e and f are copies of `X::eof()` and the other is not; otherwise the value is unspecified.	constant
`X::eof()`	`X:: int_type`	yields: a value e such that `X::eq_int_type(e,X::to_int_type(c))` is false for all values c.	constant

2   The struct template

```
template<class charT> struct char_traits;
```

shall be provided in the header `<string>` as a basis for explicit specializations.

3   In the following subclauses, the token `charT` represents the parameter of the traits template.

21.1.2 traits typedefs   [lib.char.traits.typedefs]

```
typedef CHAR_T char_type;
```

1   The type `char_type` is used to refer to the character container type in the implementation of the library classes defined in 21.2 and clause 27.

```
typedef INT_T int_type;
```

2   **Requires:** For a certain character container type `char_type`, a related container type `INT_T` shall be a type or class which can represent all of the valid characters converted from the corresponding `char_type` values, as well as an end-of-file value, `eof()`. The type `int_type` represents a character container type which can hold end-of-file to be used as a return type of the iostream class member functions.[217]

```
typedef OFF_T off_type;
typedef POS_T pos_type;
```

3   **Requires:** Requirements for `off_type` and `pos_type` are described in 27.1.2.

```
typedef STATE_T state_type;
```

4   **Requires:** `state_type` shall meet the requirements of `CopyConstructible` types (20.1.3).

21.1.3 `char_traits` specializations   [lib.char.traits.specializations]

```
namespace std {
  template<> struct char_traits<char>;
  template<> struct char_traits<wchar_t>;
}
```

1   The header `<string>` declares two structs that are specializations of the template struct `char_traits`.

2   The struct `char_traits<char>` is the `char` type specialization of the template struct `char_traits`, which contains all of the types and functions necessary to ensure the behavior of the classes in 21.2 and clause 27.

3   The types and static member functions are described in detail in 21.1.1.

---

[217] If `eof()` can be held in `char_type` then some iostreams operations may give surprising results.

21.1.3.1 struct char_traits<char>   **[lib.char.traits.specializations.char]**

```
namespace std {
  template<>
  struct char_traits<char> {
    typedef char          char_type;
    typedef int           int_type;
    typedef streamoff     off_type;
    typedef streampos     pos_type;
    typedef mbstate_t     state_type;

    static void assign(char_type& c1, const char_type& c2);
    static bool eq(const char_type& c1, const char_type& c2);
    static bool lt(const char_type& c1, const char_type& c2);

    static int compare(const char_type* s1, const char_type* s2, size_t n);
    static size_t length(const char_type* s);
    static const char_type* find(const char_type* s, size_t n,
                                 const char_type& a);
    static char_type* move(char_type* s1, const char_type* s2, size_t n);
    static char_type* copy(char_type* s1, const char_type* s2, size_t n);
    static char_type* assign(char_type* s, size_t n, char_type a);

    static int_type not_eof(const int_type& c);
    static char_type to_char_type(const int_type& c);
    static int_type to_int_type(const char_type& c);
    static bool eq_int_type(const int_type& c1, const int_type& c2);
    static int_type eof();
  };
}
```

1   The header <string> (21.2) declares a specialization of the template struct char_traits for char. It is for narrow-oriented iostream classes.

2   The defined types for int_type, pos_type, off_type, and state_type are int, streampos, streamoff, and mbstate_t respectively.

3   The type streampos is an implementation-defined type that satisfies the requirements for POS_T in 21.1.2.

4   The type streamoff is an implementation-defined type that satisfies the requirements for OFF_T in 21.1.2.

5   The type mbstate_t is defined in <cwchar> and can represent any of the conversion states possible to occur in an implementation-defined set of supported multibyte character encoding rules.

6   The two-argument members assign, eq, and lt are defined identically to the built-in operators =, ==, and < respectively.

7   The member eof() returns EOF.

21.1.3.2 struct char_traits<wchar_t> **[lib.char.traits.specializations.wchar.t]**

```
namespace std {
  template<>
  struct char_traits<wchar_t> {
    typedef wchar_t      char_type;
    typedef wint_t       int_type;
    typedef streamoff    off_type;
    typedef wstreampos   pos_type;
    typedef mbstate_t    state_type;

    static void assign(char_type& c1, const char_type& c2);
    static bool eq(const char_type& c1, const char_type& c2);
    static bool lt(const char_type& c1, const char_type& c2);

    static int compare(const char_type* s1, const char_type* s2, size_t n);
    static size_t length(const char_type* s);
    static const char_type* find(const char_type* s, size_t n,
                                 const char_type& a);
    static char_type* move(char_type* s1, const char_type* s2, size_t n);
    static char_type* copy(char_type* s1, const char_type* s2, size_t n);
    static char_type* assign(char_type* s, size_t n, char_type a);

    static int_type not_eof(const int_type& c);
    static char_type to_char_type(const int_type& c);
    static int_type to_int_type(const char_type& c);
    static bool eq_int_type(const int_type& c1, const int_type& c2);
    static int_type eof();
  };
}
```

The header <string> (21.2) declares a specialization of the template struct char_traits for wchar_t. It is for wide-oriented iostream classes.

1   The defined types for int_type, pos_type, and state_type are wint_t, wstreampos, and mbstate_t respectively.

2   The type wstreampos is an implementation-defined type that satisfies the requirements for POS_T in 21.1.2.

3   [*Note:* This paragraph is intentionally empty. *—end note*]

4   The type mbstate_t is defined in <cwchar> and can represent any of the conversion states possible to occur in an implementation-defined set of supported multibyte character encoding rules.

5   The two-argument members assign, eq, and lt are defined identically to the built-in operators =, ==, and < respectively.

6   The member eof() returns WEOF.

21.2 String classes [lib.string.classes]

1   The header <string> defines a basic string class template and its traits that can handle all char-like (clause 21) template arguments with several function signatures for manipulating varying-length sequences of char-like objects.

2   The header <string> also defines two specific template classes string and wstring and their special traits.

Header <string> synopsis

```
namespace std {
  // 21.1, character traits:
  template<class charT>
    struct char_traits;
  template <> struct char_traits<char>;
  template <> struct char_traits<wchar_t>;

  // 21.3, basic_string:
  template<class charT, class traits = char_traits<charT>,
           class Allocator = allocator<charT> >
    class basic_string;

  template<class charT, class traits, class Allocator>
    basic_string<charT,traits,Allocator>
      operator+(const basic_string<charT,traits,Allocator>& lhs,
                const basic_string<charT,traits,Allocator>& rhs);
  template<class charT, class traits, class Allocator>
    basic_string<charT,traits,Allocator>
      operator+(const charT* lhs,
                const basic_string<charT,traits,Allocator>& rhs);
  template<class charT, class traits, class Allocator>
    basic_string<charT,traits,Allocator>
      operator+(charT lhs, const basic_string<charT,traits,Allocator>& rhs);
  template<class charT, class traits, class Allocator>
    basic_string<charT,traits,Allocator>
      operator+(const basic_string<charT,traits,Allocator>& lhs,
                const charT* rhs);
  template<class charT, class traits, class Allocator>
    basic_string<charT,traits,Allocator>
      operator+(const basic_string<charT,traits,Allocator>& lhs, charT rhs);

  template<class charT, class traits, class Allocator>
    bool operator==(const basic_string<charT,traits,Allocator>& lhs,
                    const basic_string<charT,traits,Allocator>& rhs);
  template<class charT, class traits, class Allocator>
    bool operator==(const charT* lhs,
                    const basic_string<charT,traits,Allocator>& rhs);
  template<class charT, class traits, class Allocator>
    bool operator==(const basic_string<charT,traits,Allocator>& lhs,
                    const charT* rhs);
  template<class charT, class traits, class Allocator>
    bool operator!=(const basic_string<charT,traits,Allocator>& lhs,
                    const basic_string<charT,traits,Allocator>& rhs);
  template<class charT, class traits, class Allocator>
    bool operator!=(const charT* lhs,
                    const basic_string<charT,traits,Allocator>& rhs);
  template<class charT, class traits, class Allocator>
    bool operator!=(const basic_string<charT,traits,Allocator>& lhs,
                    const charT* rhs);
```

```
template<class charT, class traits, class Allocator>
  bool operator< (const basic_string<charT,traits,Allocator>& lhs,
                  const basic_string<charT,traits,Allocator>& rhs);
template<class charT, class traits, class Allocator>
  bool operator< (const basic_string<charT,traits,Allocator>& lhs,
                  const charT* rhs);
template<class charT, class traits, class Allocator>
  bool operator< (const charT* lhs,
                  const basic_string<charT,traits,Allocator>& rhs);
template<class charT, class traits, class Allocator>
  bool operator> (const basic_string<charT,traits,Allocator>& lhs,
                  const basic_string<charT,traits,Allocator>& rhs);
template<class charT, class traits, class Allocator>
  bool operator> (const basic_string<charT,traits,Allocator>& lhs,
                  const charT* rhs);
template<class charT, class traits, class Allocator>
  bool operator> (const charT* lhs,
                  const basic_string<charT,traits,Allocator>& rhs);

template<class charT, class traits, class Allocator>
  bool operator<=(const basic_string<charT,traits,Allocator>& lhs,
                  const basic_string<charT,traits,Allocator>& rhs);
template<class charT, class traits, class Allocator>
  bool operator<=(const basic_string<charT,traits,Allocator>& lhs,
                  const charT* rhs);
template<class charT, class traits, class Allocator>
  bool operator<=(const charT* lhs,
                  const basic_string<charT,traits,Allocator>& rhs);
template<class charT, class traits, class Allocator>
  bool operator>=(const basic_string<charT,traits,Allocator>& lhs,
                  const basic_string<charT,traits,Allocator>& rhs);
template<class charT, class traits, class Allocator>
  bool operator>=(const basic_string<charT,traits,Allocator>& lhs,
                  const charT* rhs);
template<class charT, class traits, class Allocator>
  bool operator>=(const charT* lhs,
                  const basic_string<charT,traits,Allocator>& rhs);

// 21.3.7.8:
template<class charT, class traits, class Allocator>
  void swap(basic_string<charT,traits,Allocator>& lhs,
            basic_string<charT,traits,Allocator>& rhs);
```

```
template<class charT, class traits, class Allocator>
  basic_istream<charT,traits>&
    operator>>(basic_istream<charT,traits>& is,
               basic_string<charT,traits,Allocator>& str);
template<class charT, class traits, class Allocator>
  basic_ostream<charT, traits>&
    operator<<(basic_ostream<charT, traits>& os,
               const basic_string<charT,traits,Allocator>& str);
template<class charT, class traits, class Allocator>
  basic_istream<charT,traits>&
    getline(basic_istream<charT,traits>& is,
            basic_string<charT,traits,Allocator>& str,
            charT delim);
template<class charT, class traits, class Allocator>
  basic_istream<charT,traits>&
    getline(basic_istream<charT,traits>& is,
            basic_string<charT,traits,Allocator>& str);

typedef basic_string<char> string;
typedef basic_string<wchar_t> wstring;
}
```

21.3 Class template `basic_string`   [lib.basic.string]

1   For a char-like type `charT`, the class template `basic_string` describes objects that can store a
sequence consisting of a varying number of arbitrary char-like objects (clause 21). The first element of the
sequence is at position zero. Such a sequence is also called a "string" if the given char-like type is clear
from context. In the rest of this clause, `charT` denotes such a given char-like type. Storage for the string
is allocated and freed as necessary by the member functions of class `basic_string`, via the
`Allocator` class passed as template parameter. `Allocator::value_type` shall be the same as
`charT`.

2   The class template `basic_string` conforms to the requirements of a Sequence, as specified in (23.1.1).
Additionally, because the iterators supported by `basic_string` are random access iterators (24.1.5),
`basic_string` conforms to the the requirements of a Reversible Container, as specified in (23.1).

3   In all cases, `size() <= capacity()`.

4   The functions described in this clause can report two kinds of errors, each associated with a distinct exception:

     — a *length* error is associated with exceptions of type `length_error` (19.1.4);

     — an *out-of-range* error is associated with exceptions of type `out_of_range` (19.1.5).

4a   For any string operation, if as a result of the operation, `size()` would exceed `max_size()` then the
operation throws `length_error`.

5   References, pointers, and iterators referring to the elements of a basic_string sequence may be invalidated
by the following uses of that basic_string object:

     — As an argument to non-member functions `swap()` (21.3.7.8), `operator>>()` (21.3.7.9), and
     `getline()` (21.3.7.9).

     — As an argument to `basic_string::swap()`.

     — Calling `data()` and `c_str()` member functions.

     — Calling non-const member functions, except `operator[]()`, `at()`, `begin()`, `rbegin()`,
     `end()`, and `rend()`.

— Subsequent to any of the above uses except the forms of `insert()` and `erase()` which return iterators, the first call to non-const member functions `operator[]()`, `at()`, `begin()`, `rbegin()`, `end()`, or `rend()`.

6   [*Note:* These rules are formulated to allow, but not require, a reference counted implementation. A reference counted implementation must have the same semantics as a non-reference counted implementation. [*Example:*

```
string s1("abc");

string::iterator i = s1.begin();
string s2 = s1;

*i = 'a';                       // Must modify only s1
```

—*end example*] —*end note*]

```
namespace std {
  template<class charT, class traits = char_traits<charT>,
          class Allocator = allocator<charT> >
  class basic_string {
  public:
    // types:
    typedef             traits                    traits_type;
    typedef typename traits::char_type            value_type;
    typedef             Allocator                 allocator_type;
    typedef typename Allocator::size_type         size_type;
    typedef typename Allocator::difference_type   difference_type;

    typedef typename Allocator::reference         reference;
    typedef typename Allocator::const_reference   const_reference;
    typedef typename Allocator::pointer           pointer;
    typedef typename Allocator::const_pointer     const_pointer;

    typedef implementation defined                iterator;          // See 23.1
    typedef implementation defined                const_iterator;    // See 23.1
    typedef std::reverse_iterator<iterator> reverse_iterator;
    typedef std::reverse_iterator<const_iterator> const_reverse_iterator;
    static const size_type npos = -1;

    // 21.3.1 construct/copy/destroy:
    explicit basic_string(const Allocator& a = Allocator());
    basic_string(const basic_string& str);
    basic_string(const basic_string& str, size_type pos, size_type n = npos,
                const Allocator& a = Allocator());
    basic_string(const charT* s,
                size_type n, const Allocator& a = Allocator());
    basic_string(const charT* s, const Allocator& a = Allocator());
    basic_string(size_type n, charT c, const Allocator& a = Allocator());
    template<class InputIterator>
      basic_string(InputIterator begin, InputIterator end,
                  const Allocator& a = Allocator());
    ~basic_string();
    basic_string& operator=(const basic_string& str);
    basic_string& operator=(const charT* s);
    basic_string& operator=(charT c);
```

```
// 21.3.2 iterators:
iterator        begin();
const_iterator  begin() const;
iterator        end();
const_iterator  end() const;

reverse_iterator        rbegin();
const_reverse_iterator  rbegin() const;
reverse_iterator        rend();
const_reverse_iterator  rend() const;

// 21.3.3 capacity:
size_type size() const;
size_type length() const;
size_type max_size() const;
void resize(size_type n, charT c);
void resize(size_type n);
size_type capacity() const;
void reserve(size_type res_arg = 0);
void clear();
bool empty() const;

// 21.3.4 element access:
const_reference operator[](size_type pos) const;
reference        operator[](size_type pos);
const_reference at(size_type n) const;
reference        at(size_type n);

// 21.3.5 modifiers:
basic_string& operator+=(const basic_string& str);
basic_string& operator+=(const charT* s);
basic_string& operator+=(charT c);
basic_string& append(const basic_string& str);
basic_string& append(const basic_string& str, size_type pos,
                     size_type n);
basic_string& append(const charT* s, size_type n);
basic_string& append(const charT* s);
basic_string& append(size_type n, charT c);
template<class InputIterator>
  basic_string& append(InputIterator first, InputIterator last);
void push_back(charT c);

basic_string& assign(const basic_string& str);
basic_string& assign(const basic_string& str, size_type pos,
                     size_type n);
basic_string& assign(const charT* s, size_type n);
basic_string& assign(const charT* s);
basic_string& assign(size_type n, charT c);
template<class InputIterator>
  basic_string& assign(InputIterator first, InputIterator last);
```

```
basic_string& insert(size_type pos1, const basic_string& str);
basic_string& insert(size_type pos1, const basic_string& str,
                     size_type pos2, size_type n);
basic_string& insert(size_type pos, const charT* s, size_type n);
basic_string& insert(size_type pos, const charT* s);
basic_string& insert(size_type pos, size_type n, charT c);
iterator insert(iterator p, charT c);
void     insert(iterator p, size_type n, charT c);
template<class InputIterator>
  void insert(iterator p, InputIterator first, InputIterator last);

basic_string& erase(size_type pos = 0, size_type n = npos);
iterator erase(iterator position);
iterator erase(iterator first, iterator last);

basic_string& replace(size_type pos1, size_type n1,
                      const basic_string& str);
basic_string& replace(size_type pos1, size_type n1,
                      const basic_string& str,
                      size_type pos2, size_type n2);
basic_string& replace(size_type pos, size_type n1, const charT* s,
                      size_type n2);
basic_string& replace(size_type pos, size_type n1, const charT* s);
basic_string& replace(size_type pos, size_type n1, size_type n2,
                      charT c);

basic_string& replace(iterator i1, iterator i2,
                      const basic_string& str);
basic_string& replace(iterator i1, iterator i2, const charT* s,
                      size_type n);
basic_string& replace(iterator i1, iterator i2, const charT* s);
basic_string& replace(iterator i1, iterator i2,
                      size_type n, charT c);
template<class InputIterator>
  basic_string& replace(iterator i1, iterator i2,
                        InputIterator j1, InputIterator j2);

size_type copy(charT* s, size_type n, size_type pos = 0) const;
void swap(basic_string& str);

// 21.3.6 string operations:
const charT* c_str() const;              // explicit
const charT* data() const;
allocator_type get_allocator() const;

size_type find (const basic_string& str, size_type pos = 0) const;
size_type find (const charT* s, size_type pos, size_type n) const;
size_type find (const charT* s, size_type pos = 0) const;
size_type find (charT c, size_type pos = 0) const;
size_type rfind(const basic_string& str, size_type pos = npos) const;
size_type rfind(const charT* s, size_type pos, size_type n) const;
size_type rfind(const charT* s, size_type pos = npos) const;
size_type rfind(charT c, size_type pos = npos) const;
```

```
        size_type find_first_of(const basic_string& str,
                                size_type pos = 0) const;
        size_type find_first_of(const charT* s,
                                size_type pos, size_type n) const;
        size_type find_first_of(const charT* s, size_type pos = 0) const;
        size_type find_first_of(charT c, size_type pos = 0) const;
        size_type find_last_of (const basic_string& str,
                                size_type pos = npos) const;
        size_type find_last_of (const charT* s,
                                size_type pos, size_type n) const;
        size_type find_last_of (const charT* s, size_type pos = npos) const;
        size_type find_last_of (charT c, size_type pos = npos) const;

        size_type find_first_not_of(const basic_string& str,
                                    size_type pos = 0) const;
        size_type find_first_not_of(const charT* s, size_type pos,
                                    size_type n) const;
        size_type find_first_not_of(const charT* s, size_type pos = 0) const;
        size_type find_first_not_of(charT c, size_type pos = 0) const;
        size_type find_last_not_of (const basic_string& str,
                                    size_type pos = npos) const;
        size_type find_last_not_of (const charT* s, size_type pos,
                                    size_type n) const;
        size_type find_last_not_of (const charT* s,
                                    size_type pos = npos) const;
        size_type find_last_not_of (charT c, size_type pos = npos) const;

        basic_string substr(size_type pos = 0, size_type n = npos) const;
        int compare(const basic_string& str) const;
        int compare(size_type pos1, size_type n1,
                    const basic_string& str) const;
        int compare(size_type pos1, size_type n1,
                    const basic_string& str,
                    size_type pos2, size_type n2) const;
        int compare(const charT* s) const;
        int compare(size_type pos1, size_type n1,
                    const charT* s) const;
        int compare(size_type pos1, size_type n1,
                    const charT* s, size_type n2) const;
    };
}
```

21.3.1 `basic_string` constructors   **[lib.string.cons]**

1   In all `basic_string` constructors, a copy of the `Allocator` argument is used for any memory allocation performed by the constructor or member functions during the lifetime of the object.

```
        explicit basic_string(const Allocator& a = Allocator());
```

2   **Effects:** Constructs an object of class `basic_string`. The postconditions of this function are indicated in Table 38:

Table 38—basic_string(const Allocator&) effects

Element	Value
data()	a non-null pointer that is copyable and can have 0 added to it
size()	0
capacity()	an unspecified value

```
basic_string(const basic_string<charT,traits,Allocator>& str);

basic_string(const basic_string<charT,traits,Allocator>& str,
             size_type pos, size_type n = npos,
             const Allocator& a = Allocator());
```

3   **Requires:** *pos* <= *str*.size()

4   **Throws:** out_of_range if *pos* > *str*.size().

5   **Effects:** Constructs an object of class basic_string and determines the effective length *rlen* of the initial string value as the smaller of *n* and *str*.size() - *pos*, as indicated in Table 39. In the first form, the Allocator value used is copied from *str*.get_allocator().

**Table 39—basic_string(basic_string, size_type,
size_type, const Allocator&) effects**

Element	Value
data()	points at the first element of an allocated copy of *rlen* consecutive elements of the string controlled by *str* beginning at position *pos*
size()	*rlen*
capacity()	a value at least as large as size()

```
basic_string(const charT* s, size_type n,
             const Allocator& a = Allocator());
```

6   **Requires:** *s* shall not be a null pointer and *n* < npos.

7   [*Note:* This paragraph is intentionally empty. —*end note*]

8   **Effects:** Constructs an object of class basic_string and determines its initial string value from the array of charT of length *n* whose first element is designated by *s*, as indicated in Table 40:

**Table 40—basic_string(const charT*, size_type,
const Allocator&) effects**

Element	Value
data()	points at the first element of an allocated copy of the array whose first element is pointed at by *s*
size()	*n*
capacity()	a value at least as large as size()

```
basic_string(const charT* s, const Allocator& a = Allocator());
```

9   **Requires:** *s* shall not be a null pointer.

10   **Effects:** Constructs an object of class `basic_string` and determines its initial string value from the array of `charT` of length `traits::length(s)` whose first element is designated by *s*, as indicated in Table 41:

Table 41—`basic_string(const charT*, const Allocator&)` effects

Element	Value
`data()`	points at the first element of an allocated copy of the array whose first element is pointed at by *s*
`size()`	`traits::length(s)`
`capacity()`	a value at least as large as `size()`

11   **Notes:** Uses `traits::length()`.

```
basic_string(size_type n, charT c, const Allocator& a = Allocator());
```

12   **Requires:** *n* < npos

13   [*Note:* This paragraph is intentionally empty.   —*end note*]

14   **Effects:** Constructs an object of class `basic_string` and determines its initial string value by repeating the char-like object *c* for all *n* elements, as indicated in Table 42:

Table 42—`basic_string(size_type, charT, const Allocator&)` effects

Element	Value
`data()`	points at the first element of an allocated array of *n* elements, each storing the initial value *c*
`size()`	*n*
`capacity()`	a value at least as large as `size()`

```
template<class InputIterator>
    basic_string(InputIterator begin, InputIterator end,
                 const Allocator& a = Allocator());
```

15   **Effects:** If *InputIterator* is an integral type, equivalent to

```
basic_string(static_cast<size_type>(begin), static_cast<value_type>(end))
```

Otherwise constructs a string from the values in the range [*begin*, *end*), as indicated in the Sequence Requirements table (see 23.1.1).

```
basic_string<charT,traits,Allocator>&
    operator=(const basic_string<charT,traits,Allocator>& str);
```

16   **Effects:** If `*this` and *str* are not the same object, modifies `*this` as shown in Table 43:

**Table 43—operator=(const basic_string<charT, traits, Allocator>&)
effects**

Element	Value
data()	points at the first element of an allocated copy of the array whose first element is pointed at by *str*.data()
size()	*str*.size()
capacity()	a value at least as large as size()

If *this and *str* are the same object, the member has no effect.

17 **Returns:** *this

```
basic_string<charT,traits,Allocator>&
  operator=(const charT* s);
```

18 **Returns:** *this = basic_string<charT,traits,Allocator>(*s*).
19 **Notes:** Uses traits::length().

```
basic_string<charT,traits,Allocator>& operator=(charT c);
```

20 **Returns:** *this = basic_string<charT,traits,Allocator>(1,*c*).

21.3.2 basic_string iterator support [lib.string.iterators]

```
iterator       begin();
const_iterator begin() const;
```

1 **Returns:** an iterator referring to the first character in the string.

```
iterator       end();
const_iterator end() const;
```

2 **Returns:** an iterator which is the past-the-end value.

```
reverse_iterator       rbegin();
const_reverse_iterator rbegin() const;
```

3 **Returns:** an iterator which is semantically equivalent to reverse_iterator(end()).

```
reverse_iterator       rend();
const_reverse_iterator rend() const;
```

4 **Returns:** an iterator which is semantically equivalent to reverse_iterator(begin()).

21.3.3 basic_string capacity [lib.string.capacity]

```
size_type size() const;
```

1 **Returns:** a count of the number of char-like objects currently in the string.

```
size_type length() const;
```

2   **Returns:** size().

```
size_type max_size() const;
```

3   **Returns:** The maximum size of the string.
4   **Note:** See Container requirements table (23.1).

```
void resize(size_type n, charT c);
```

5   **Requires:** n <= max_size()
6   **Throws:** length_error if n > max_size().
7   **Effects:** Alters the length of the string designated by *this as follows:

— If n <= size(), the function replaces the string designated by *this with a string of length n whose elements are a copy of the initial elements of the original string designated by *this.

— If n > size(), the function replaces the string designated by *this with a string of length n whose first size() elements are a copy of the original string designated by *this, and whose remaining elements are all initialized to c.

```
void resize(size_type n);
```

8   **Effects:** resize(n, charT()).

```
size_type capacity() const;
```

9   **Returns:** the size of the allocated storage in the string.

```
void reserve(size_type res_arg=0);
```

10   The member function reserve() is a directive that informs a basic_string object of a planned change in size, so that it can manage the storage allocation accordingly.
11   **Effects:** After reserve(), capacity() is greater or equal to the argument of reserve. [*Note:* Calling reserve() with a *res_arg* argument less than capacity() is in effect a non-binding shrink request. A call with *res_arg* <= size() is in effect a non-binding shrink-to-fit request. —*end note*]
12   **Throws:** length_error if *res_arg* > max_size().[218]

```
void clear();
```

13   **Effects:** Behaves as if the function calls:

```
erase(begin(), end());
```

```
bool empty() const;
```

14   **Returns:** size() == 0.

---

[218] reserve() uses Allocator::allocate() which may throw an appropriate exception.

21.3.4 basic_string element access [lib.string.access]

```
const_reference operator[](size_type pos) const;
reference       operator[](size_type pos);
```

1   **Returns:** If *pos* < size(), returns data()[*pos*]. Otherwise, if *pos* == size(), the const version returns charT(). Otherwise, the behavior is undefined.

```
const_reference at(size_type pos) const;
reference       at(size_type pos);
```

2   **Requires:** *pos* < size()
3   **Throws:** out_of_range if *pos* >= size().
4   **Returns:** operator[](*pos*).

21.3.5 basic_string modifiers [lib.string.modifiers]

21.3.5.1 basic_string::operator+= [lib.string::op+=]

```
basic_string<charT,traits,Allocator>&
  operator+=(const basic_string<charT,traits,Allocator>& str);
```

1   **Returns:** append(*str*).

```
basic_string<charT,traits,Allocator>& operator+=(const charT* s);
```

2   **Returns:** *this += basic_string<charT,traits,Allocator>(*s*).
3   **Notes:** Uses traits::length().

```
basic_string<charT,traits,Allocator>& operator+=(charT c);
```

4   **Returns:** *this += basic_string<charT,traits,Allocator>(1,*c*).

21.3.5.2 basic_string::append [lib.string::append]

```
basic_string<charT,traits,Allocator>&
  append(const basic_string<charT,traits>& str);
```

1   **Returns:** append(*str*, 0, npos).

```
basic_string<charT,traits,Allocator>&
  append(const basic_string<charT,traits>& str, size_type pos, size_type n);
```

2   **Requires:** *pos* <= *str*.size()
3   **Throws:** out_of_range if *pos* > *str*.size().
4   **Effects:** Determines the effective length *rlen* of the string to append as the smaller of *n* and *str*.size() - *pos*. The function then throws length_error if size() >= npos - *rlen*.
    Otherwise, the function replaces the string controlled by *this with a string of length size() + *rlen* whose first size() elements are a copy of the original string controlled by *this and whose remaining elements are a copy of the initial elements of the string controlled by *str* beginning at position *pos*.
5   **Returns:** *this.

```
basic_string<charT,traits,Allocator>&
    append(const charT* s, size_type n);
```

6   **Returns:** append(basic_string<charT,traits,Allocator>(*s*,*n*)).

```
basic_string<charT,traits,Allocator>& append(const charT* s);
```

7   **Returns:** append(basic_string<charT,traits,Allocator>(*s*)).
8   **Notes:** Uses traits::length().

```
basic_string<charT,traits,Allocator>&
    append(size_type n, charT c);
```

9   **Returns:** append(basic_string<charT,traits,Allocator>(*n*,*c*)).

```
template<class InputIterator>
    basic_string& append(InputIterator first, InputIterator last);
```

10   **Returns:** append(basic_string<charT,traits,Allocator>(*first*,*last*)).

```
void push_back(charT c)
```

11   **Effects:** Equivalent to append(static_cast<size_type>(1), c).

21.3.5.3 basic_string::assign   [lib.string::assign]

```
basic_string<charT,traits,Allocator>&
    assign(const basic_string<charT,traits>& str);
```

1   **Returns:** assign(*str*, 0, npos).

```
basic_string<charT,traits,Allocator>&
    assign(const basic_string<charT,traits>& str, size_type pos,
        size_type n);
```

2   **Requires:** *pos* <= *str*.size()
3   **Throws:** out_of_range if *pos* > *str*.size().
4   **Effects:** Determines the effective length *rlen* of the string to assign as the smaller of *n* and
     str.size() - *pos*.
     The function then replaces the string controlled by *this with a string of length *rlen* whose elements
     are a copy of the string controlled by *str* beginning at position *pos*.
5   **Returns:** *this.

```
basic_string<charT,traits,Allocator>&
    assign(const charT* s, size_type n);
```

6   **Returns:** assign(basic_string<charT,traits,Allocator>(*s*,*n*)).

```
basic_string<charT,traits,Allocator>& assign(const charT* s);
```

7   **Returns:** assign(basic_string<charT, traits, Allocator>(*s*)).
8   **Notes:** Uses traits::length().

```
basic_string<charT,traits,Allocator>&
    assign(size_type n, charT c);
```

9   **Returns:** assign(basic_string<charT,traits,Allocator>(*n*,*c*)).

```
template<class InputIterator>
  basic_string& assign(InputIterator first, InputIterator last);
```

10   **Returns:** `assign(basic_string<charT,traits,Allocator>(first,last))`.

21.3.5.4 `basic_string::insert` [lib.string::insert]

```
basic_string<charT,traits,Allocator>&
  insert(size_type pos1,
         const basic_string<charT,traits,Allocator>& str);
```

1   **Returns:** `insert(pos1,str,0,npos)`.

```
basic_string<charT,traits,Allocator>&
  insert(size_type pos1,
         const basic_string<charT,traits,Allocator>& str,
         size_type pos2, size_type n);
```

2   **Requires** $pos1$ `<= size()` and $pos2$ `<=` str`.size()`

3   **Throws:** `out_of_range` if $pos1$ `> size()` or $pos2$ `>` str`.size()`.

4   **Effects:** Determines the effective length $rlen$ of the string to insert as the smaller of n and str`.size()`
     `-` $pos2$. Then throws `length_error` if `size() >= npos -` $rlen$.
     Otherwise, the function replaces the string controlled by `*this` with a string of length `size() +`
     $rlen$ whose first $pos1$ elements are a copy of the initial elements of the original string controlled by
     `*this`, whose next $rlen$ elements are a copy of the elements of the string controlled by str begin-
     ning at position $pos2$, and whose remaining elements are a copy of the remaining elements of the origi-
     nal string controlled by `*this`.

5   **Returns:** `*this`.

```
basic_string<charT,traits,Allocator>&
  insert(size_type pos, const charT* s, size_type n);
```

6   **Returns:** `insert(pos,basic_string<charT,traits,Allocator>(s,n))`.

```
basic_string<charT,traits,Allocator>&
  insert(size_type pos, const charT* s);
```

7   **Returns:** `insert(pos,basic_string<charT,traits,Allocator>(s))`.

8   **Notes:** Uses `traits::length()`.

```
basic_string<charT,traits,Allocator>&
  insert(size_type pos, size_type n, charT c);
```

9   **Returns:** `insert(pos,basic_string<charT,traits,Allocator>(n,c))`.

```
iterator insert(iterator p, charT c);
```

10   **Requires:** p is a valid iterator on `*this`.

11   **Effects:** inserts a copy of c before the character referred to by p.

12   **Returns:** an iterator which refers to the copy of the inserted character.

```
void insert(iterator p, size_type n, charT c);
```

13   **Requires:** p is a valid iterator on `*this`.

14   **Effects:** inserts n copies of c before the character referred to by p.

```
template<class InputIterator>
    void insert(iterator p, InputIterator first, InputIterator last);
```

15   **Requires:** *p* is a valid iterator on *this. [*first,last*) is a valid range.
16   **Effects:** Equivalent to insert(p - begin(), basic_string(first, last)).

21.3.5.5 basic_string::erase   [lib.string::erase]

```
basic_string<charT,traits,Allocator>&
    erase(size_type pos = 0, size_type n = npos);
```

1   **Requires:** *pos* <= size()
2   **Throws:** out_of_range if *pos* > size().
3   **Effects:** Determines the effective length *xlen* of the string to be removed as the smaller of *n* and
      size() - *pos*.
      The function then replaces the string controlled by *this with a string of length size() - *xlen*
      whose first *pos* elements are a copy of the initial elements of the original string controlled by *this,
      and whose remaining elements are a copy of the elements of the original string controlled by *this
      beginning at position *pos* + *xlen*.
4   **Returns:** *this.

```
iterator erase(iterator p);
```

5   **Requires:** *p* is a valid iterator on *this.
6   **Effects:** removes the character referred to by *p*.
7   **Returns:** an iterator which points to the element immediately following *p* prior to the element being
      erased. If no such element exists, end() is returned.

```
iterator erase(iterator first, iterator last);
```

8   **Requires:** *first* and *last* are valid iterators on *this, defining a range [*first,last*).
9   **Effects:** removes the characters in the range [*first,last*).
10   **Returns:** an iterator which points to the element pointed to by *last* prior to the other elements being
      erased. If no such element exists, end() is returned.

21.3.5.6 basic_string::replace   [lib.string::replace]

```
basic_string<charT,traits,Allocator>&
    replace(size_type pos1, size_type n1,
            const basic_string<charT,traits,Allocator>& str);
```

1   **Returns:** replace(*pos1*, *n1*, *str*, 0, *npos*).

```
basic_string<charT,traits,Allocator>&
    replace(size_type pos1, size_type n1,
            const basic_string<charT,traits,Allocator>& str,
            size_type pos2, size_type n2);
```

2   **Requires:** *pos1* <= size() && *pos2* <= str.size().
3   **Throws:** out_of_range if *pos1* > size() or *pos2* > str.size().
4   **Effects:** Determines the effective length *xlen* of the string to be removed as the smaller of *n1* and
      size() - *pos1*. It also determines the effective length *rlen* of the string to be inserted as the
      smaller of *n2* and str.size() - *pos2*.
5   **Throws:** length_error if size() - *xlen* >= npos - *rlen*.
      Otherwise, the function replaces the string controlled by *this with a string of length size() -
      xlen + *rlen* whose first *pos1* elements are a copy of the initial elements of the original string con-
      trolled by *this, whose next *rlen* elements are a copy of the initial elements of the string controlled
```
```

by *str* beginning at position *pos2*, and whose remaining elements are a copy of the elements of the original string controlled by *this beginning at position *pos1* + *xlen*.

6 **Returns:** *this.

```
basic_string<charT,traits,Allocator>&
    replace(size_type pos, size_type n1, const charT* s, size_type n2);
```

7 **Returns:** replace(*pos*,*n1*,basic_string<charT,traits,Allocator>(*s*,*n2*)).

```
basic_string<charT,traits,Allocator>&
    replace(size_type pos, size_type n1, const charT* s);
```

8 **Returns:** replace(*pos*,*n1*,basic_string<charT,traits,Allocator>(*s*)).
9 **Notes:** Uses traits::length().

```
basic_string<charT,traits,Allocator>&
    replace(size_type pos, size_type n1,
            size_type n2, charT c);
```

10 **Returns:** replace(*pos*,*n1*,basic_string<charT,traits,Allocator>(*n2*,*c*)).

```
basic_string& replace(iterator i1, iterator i2, const basic_string& str);
```

11 **Requires:** The iterators *i1* and *i2* are valid iterators on *this, defining a range [*i1*,*i2*).
12 **Effects:** Replaces the string controlled by *this with a string of length size() - (*i2* - *i1*) + *str*.size() whose first begin() - *i1* elements are a copy of the initial elements of the original string controlled by *this, whose next *str*.size() elements are a copy of the string controlled by *str*, and whose remaining elements are a copy of the elements of the original string controlled by *this beginning at position *i2*.
13 **Returns:** *this.
14 **Notes:** After the call, the length of the string will be changed by: *str*.size() - (*i2* - *i1*).

```
basic_string&
    replace(iterator i1, iterator i2, const charT* s, size_type n);
```

15 **Returns:** replace(*i1*,*i2*,basic_string(*s*,*n*)).
16 **Notes:** Length change: *n* - (*i2* - *i1*).

```
basic_string& replace(iterator i1, iterator i2, const charT* s);
```

17 **Returns:** replace(*i1*,*i2*,basic_string(*s*)).
18 **Notes:** Length change: traits::length(*s*) - (*i2* - *i1*).
   Uses traits::length().

```
basic_string& replace(iterator i1, iterator i2, size_type n,
                      charT c);
```

19 **Returns:** replace(*i1*,*i2*,basic_string(*n*,*c*)).
20 **Notes:** Length change: *n* - (*i2* - *i1*).

```
template<class InputIterator>
    basic_string& replace(iterator i1, iterator i2,
                          InputIterator j1, InputIterator j2);
```

21 **Returns:** replace(*i1*,*i2*,basic_string(*j1*,*j2*)).
22 **Notes:** Length change: *j2* - *j1* - (*i2* - *i1*).

21.3.5.7 basic_string::copy [lib.string::copy]

```
size_type copy(charT* s, size_type n, size_type pos = 0) const;
```

1 **Requires:** *pos* <= size()

2 **Throws:** out_of_range if *pos* > size().

3 **Effects:** Determines the effective length *rlen* of the string to copy as the smaller of *n* and size() - *pos*. *s* shall designate an array of at least *rlen* elements.
The function then replaces the string designated by *s* with a string of length *rlen* whose elements are a copy of the string controlled by *this beginning at position *pos*.
The function does not append a null object to the string designated by *s*.

4 **Returns:** *rlen*.

21.3.5.8 basic_string::swap [lib.string::swap]

```
void swap(basic_string<charT,traits,Allocator>& s);
```

1 **Effects:** Swaps the contents of the two strings.

2 **Postcondition:** *this contains the characters that were in *s*, *s* contains the characters that were in *this.

3 **Complexity:** constant time.

21.3.6 basic_string string operations [lib.string.ops]

```
const charT* c_str() const;
```

1 **Returns:** A pointer to the initial element of an array of length size() + 1 whose first size() elements equal the corresponding elements of the string controlled by *this and whose last element is a null character specified by charT().

2 **Requires:** The program shall not alter any of the values stored in the array. Nor shall the program treat the returned value as a valid pointer value after any subsequent call to a non-const member function of the class basic_string that designates the same object as this.

```
const charT* data() const;
```

3 **Returns:** If size() is nonzero, the member returns a pointer to the initial element of an array whose first size() elements equal the corresponding elements of the string controlled by *this. If size() is zero, the member returns a non-null pointer that is copyable and can have zero added to it.

4 **Requires:** The program shall not alter any of the values stored in the character array. Nor shall the program treat the returned value as a valid pointer value after any subsequent call to a non- const member function of basic_string that designates the same object as this.

```
allocator_type get_allocator() const;
```

5 **Returns:** a copy of the Allocator object used to construct the string.

21.3.6.1 basic_string::find [lib.string::find]

```
size_type find(const basic_string<charT,traits,Allocator>& str,
               size_type pos = 0) const;
```

1 **Effects:** Determines the lowest position *xpos*, if possible, such that both of the following conditions obtain:

— *pos* <= *xpos* and *xpos* + *str*.size() <= size();

— at(*xpos*+*I*) == *str*.at(*I*) for all elements *I* of the string controlled by *str*.

2 **Returns:** *xpos* if the function can determine such a value for *xpos*. Otherwise, returns npos.

3 **Notes:** Uses `traits::eq()`.

```
size_type find(const charT* s, size_type pos, size_type n) const;
```

4 **Returns:** `find(basic_string<charT,traits,Allocator>(s,n),pos)`.

```
size_type find(const charT* s, size_type pos = 0) const;
```

5 **Returns:** `find(basic_string<charT,traits,Allocator>(s),pos)`.

6 **Notes:** Uses `traits::length()`.

```
size_type find(charT c, size_type pos = 0) const;
```

7 **Returns:** `find(basic_string<charT,traits,Allocator>(1,c),pos)`.

21.3.6.2 `basic_string::rfind` [lib.string::rfind]

```
size_type rfind(const basic_string<charT,traits,Allocator>& str,
                size_type pos = npos) const;
```

1 **Effects:** Determines the highest position *xpos*, if possible, such that both of the following conditions obtain:

— *xpos* `<=` *pos* and *xpos* `+` `str.size()` `<=` `size()`;

— `at(`*xpos+I*`)` `==` `str.at(`*I*`)` for all elements *I* of the string controlled by *str*.

2 **Returns:** *xpos* if the function can determine such a value for *xpos*. Otherwise, returns npos.

3 **Notes:** Uses `traits::eq()`.

```
size_type rfind(const charT* s, size_type pos, size_type n) const;
```

4 **Returns:** `rfind(basic_string<charT,traits,Allocator>(s,n),pos)`.

```
size_type rfind(const charT* s, size_type pos = npos) const;
```

5 **Returns:** `rfind(basic_string<charT,traits,Allocator>(s),pos)`.

6 **Notes:** Uses `traits::length()`.

```
size_type rfind(charT c, size_type pos = npos) const;
```

7 **Returns:** `rfind(basic_string<charT,traits,Allocator>(1,c),pos)`.

21.3.6.3 `basic_string::find_first_of` [lib.string::find.first.of]

```
size_type
    find_first_of(const basic_string<charT,traits,Allocator>& str,
                  size_type pos = 0) const;
```

1 **Effects:** Determines the lowest position *xpos*, if possible, such that both of the following conditions obtain:

— *pos* `<=` *xpos* and *xpos* `<` `size()`;

— `at(`*xpos*`)` `==` `str.at(`*I*`)` for some element *I* of the string controlled by *str*.

2 **Returns:** *xpos* if the function can determine such a value for *xpos*. Otherwise, returns npos.

3 **Notes:** Uses `traits::eq()`.

```
      size_type
        find_first_of(const charT* s, size_type pos, size_type n) const;
```

4   **Returns:** `find_first_of(basic_string<charT,traits,Allocator>(s,n),pos)`.

```
      size_type find_first_of(const charT* s, size_type pos = 0) const;
```

5   **Returns:** `find_first_of(basic_string<charT,traits,Allocator>(s),pos)`.
6   **Notes:** Uses `traits::length()`.

```
      size_type find_first_of(charT c, size_type pos = 0) const;
```

7   **Returns:** `find_first_of(basic_string<charT,traits,Allocator>(1,c),pos)`.

21.3.6.4 basic_string::find_last_of   [lib.string::find.last.of]

```
      size_type
        find_last_of(const basic_string<charT,traits,Allocator>& str,
                     size_type pos = npos) const;
```

1   **Effects:** Determines the highest position *xpos*, if possible, such that both of the following conditions obtain:

— *xpos* `<=` *pos* and *xpos* `<` `size()`;

— `at(`*xpos*`) == `*str*`.at(`*I*`)` for some element *I* of the string controlled by *str*.

2   **Returns:** *xpos* if the function can determine such a value for *xpos*. Otherwise, returns npos.
3   **Notes:** Uses `traits::eq()`.

```
      size_type find_last_of(const charT* s, size_type pos, size_type n) const;
```

4   **Returns:** `find_last_of(basic_string<charT,traits,Allocator>(s,n),pos)`.

```
      size_type find_last_of(const charT* s, size_type pos = npos) const;
```

5   **Returns:** `find_last_of(basic_string<charT,traits,Allocator>(s),pos)`.
6   **Notes:** Uses `traits::length()`.

```
      size_type find_last_of(charT c, size_type pos = npos) const;
```

7   **Returns:** `find_last_of(basic_string<charT,traits,Allocator>(1,c),pos)`.

21.3.6.5 basic_string::find_first_not_of   [lib.string::find.first.not.of]

```
      size_type
        find_first_not_of(const basic_string<charT,traits,Allocator>& str,
                          size_type pos = 0) const;
```

1   **Effects:** Determines the lowest position *xpos*, if possible, such that both of the following conditions obtain:

— *pos* `<=` *xpos* and *xpos* `<` `size()`;

— `at(`*xpos*`) == `*str*`.at(`*I*`)` for no element *I* of the string controlled by *str*.

2   **Returns:** *xpos* if the function can determine such a value for *xpos*. Otherwise, returns npos.
3   **Notes:** Uses `traits::eq()`.

```
        size_type
          find_first_not_of(const charT* s, size_type pos, size_type n) const;
```

4   **Returns:** `find_first_not_of(basic_string<charT,traits,Allocator>(s,n),pos)`.

```
        size_type find_first_not_of(const charT* s, size_type pos = 0) const;
```

5   **Returns:** `find_first_not_of(basic_string<charT,traits,Allocator>(s),pos)`.
6   **Notes:** Uses `traits::length()`.

```
        size_type find_first_not_of(charT c, size_type pos = 0) const;
```

7   **Returns:** `find_first_not_of(basic_string<charT,traits,Allocator>(1,c),pos)`.

21.3.6.6 basic_string::find_last_not_of [lib.string::find.last.not.of]

```
        size_type
          find_last_not_of(const basic_string<charT,traits,Allocator>& str,
                           size_type pos = npos) const;
```

1   **Effects:** Determines the highest position *xpos*, if possible, such that both of the following conditions obtain:

— *xpos* `<=` *pos* and *xpos* `<` `size()`;

— `at(`*xpos*`)` `==` *str*`.at(`*I*`))` for no element *I* of the string controlled by *str*.

2   **Returns:** *xpos* if the function can determine such a value for *xpos*. Otherwise, returns npos.
3   **Notes:** Uses `traits::eq()`.

```
        size_type find_last_not_of(const charT* s, size_type pos,
                                   size_type n) const;
```

4   **Returns:** `find_last_not_of(basic_string<charT,traits,Allocator>(s,n),pos)`.

```
        size_type find_last_not_of(const charT* s, size_type pos = npos) const;
```

5   **Returns:** `find_last_not_of(basic_string<charT,traits,Allocator>(s),pos)`.
6   **Notes:** Uses `traits::length()`.

```
        size_type find_last_not_of(charT c, size_type pos = npos) const;
```

7   **Returns:** `find_last_not_of(basic_string<charT,traits,Allocator>(1,c),pos)`.

21.3.6.7 basic_string::substr [lib.string::substr]

```
        basic_string<charT,traits,Allocator>
          substr(size_type pos = 0, size_type n = npos) const;
```

1   **Requires:** *pos* `<=` `size()`
2   **Throws:** `out_of_range` if *pos* `>` `size()`.
3   **Effects:** Determines the effective length `rlen` of the string to copy as the smaller of *n* and `size()` - *pos*.
4   **Returns:** `basic_string<charT,traits,Allocator>(data()+`*pos*`,`*rlen*`)`.

```
int compare(const basic_string<charT,traits,Allocator>& str) const
```

1   **Effects:** Determines the effective length *rlen* of the strings to compare as the smallest of `size()` and `str.size()`. The function then compares the two strings by calling `traits::compare(data(), str.data(), rlen)`.

2   **Returns:** the nonzero result if the result of the comparison is nonzero. Otherwise, returns a value as indicated in Table 44:

Table 44—<code>compare()</code> results

Condition	Return Value
`size() < str.size()`	`< 0`
`size() == str.size()`	`0`
`size() > str.size()`	`> 0`

```
int compare(size_type pos1, size_type n1,
            const basic_string<charT,traits,Allocator>& str) const;
```

3   **Returns:**

```
basic_string<charT,traits,Allocator>(*this,pos1,n1).compare(
        str) .
```

```
int compare(size_type pos1, size_type n1,
            const basic_string<charT,traits,Allocator>& str,
            size_type pos2, size_type n2) const;
```

4   **Returns:**

```
basic_string<charT,traits,Allocator>(*this,pos1,n1).compare(
        basic_string<charT,traits,Allocator>(str,pos2,n2)) .
```

```
int compare(const charT *s) const;
```

5   **Returns:** `this->compare(basic_string<charT,traits,Allocator>(s))`.

```
int compare(size_type pos, size_type n1,
            const charT *s) const;
```

6   **Returns:**

```
basic_string<charT,traits,Allocator>(*this,pos,n1).compare(
        basic_string<charT,traits,Allocator>(s))
```

```
int compare(size_type pos, size_type n1,
            const charT *s, size_type n2) const;
```

7   **Returns:**

```
basic_string<charT,traits,Allocator>(*this,pos,n1).compare(
          basic_string<charT,traits,Allocator>(s,n2))
```

21.3.7 `basic_string` non-member functions [lib.string.nonmembers]

21.3.7.1 `operator+` [lib.string::op+]

```
template<class charT, class traits, class Allocator>
  basic_string<charT,traits,Allocator>
    operator+(const basic_string<charT,traits,Allocator>& lhs,
             const basic_string<charT,traits,Allocator>& rhs);
```

1   **Returns:** `basic_string<charT,traits,Allocator>(lhs).append(rhs)`

```
template<class charT, class traits, class Allocator>
  basic_string<charT,traits,Allocator>
    operator+(const charT* lhs,
             const basic_string<charT,traits,Allocator>& rhs);
```

2   **Returns:** `basic_string<charT,traits,Allocator>(lhs) + rhs.`
3   **Notes:** Uses `traits::length()`.

```
template<class charT, class traits, class Allocator>
  basic_string<charT,traits,Allocator>
    operator+(charT lhs,
             const basic_string<charT,traits,Allocator>& rhs);
```

4   **Returns:** `basic_string<charT,traits,Allocator>(1,lhs) + rhs.`

```
template<class charT, class traits, class Allocator>
  basic_string<charT,traits,Allocator>
    operator+(const basic_string<charT,traits,Allocator>& lhs,
             const charT* rhs);
```

5   **Returns:** `lhs + basic_string<charT,traits,Allocator>(rhs).`
6   **Notes:** Uses `traits::length()`.

```
template<class charT, class traits, class Allocator>
  basic_string<charT,traits,Allocator>
    operator+(const basic_string<charT,traits,Allocator>& lhs,
             charT rhs);
```

7   **Returns:** `lhs + basic_string<charT,traits,Allocator>(1,rhs).`

21.3.7.2 `operator==` [lib.string::operator==]

```
template<class charT, class traits, class Allocator>
  bool operator==(const basic_string<charT,traits,Allocator>& lhs,
               const basic_string<charT,traits,Allocator>& rhs);
```

1   **Returns:** `lhs.compare(rhs) == 0.`

```
template<class charT, class traits, class Allocator>
  bool operator==(const charT* lhs,
               const basic_string<charT,traits,Allocator>& rhs);
```

2   **Returns:** `basic_string<charT,traits,Allocator>(lhs) == rhs.`

```
template<class charT, class traits, class Allocator>
  bool operator==(const basic_string<charT,traits,Allocator>& lhs,
                  const charT* rhs);
```

3   **Returns:** *lhs* == basic_string<charT,traits,Allocator>(*rhs*).

4   **Notes:** Uses traits::length().

21.3.7.3 operator!=   [lib.string::op!=]

```
template<class charT, class traits, class Allocator>
  bool operator!=(const basic_string<charT,traits,Allocator>& lhs,
                  const basic_string<charT,traits,Allocator>& rhs);
```

1   **Returns:** !(*lhs* == *rhs*).

```
template<class charT, class traits, class Allocator>
  bool operator!=(const charT* lhs,
                  const basic_string<charT,traits,Allocator>& rhs);
```

2   **Returns:** basic_string<charT,traits,Allocator>(*lhs*) != *rhs*.

```
template<class charT, class traits, class Allocator>
  bool operator!=(const basic_string<charT,traits,Allocator>& lhs,
                  const charT* rhs);
```

3   **Returns:** *lhs* != basic_string<charT,traits,Allocator>(*rhs*).

4   **Notes:** Uses traits::length().

21.3.7.4 operator<   [lib.string::op<]

```
template<class charT, class traits, class Allocator>
  bool operator< (const basic_string<charT,traits,Allocator>& lhs,
                  const basic_string<charT,traits,Allocator>& rhs);
```

1   **Returns:** *lhs*.compare(*rhs*) < 0.

```
template<class charT, class traits, class Allocator>
  bool operator< (const charT* lhs,
                  const basic_string<charT,traits,Allocator>& rhs);
```

2   **Returns:** basic_string<charT,traits,Allocator>(*lhs*) < *rhs*.

```
template<class charT, class traits, class Allocator>
  bool operator< (const basic_string<charT,traits,Allocator>& lhs,
                  const charT* rhs);
```

3   **Returns:** *lhs* < basic_string<charT,traits,Allocator>(*rhs*).

21.3.7.5 operator>   [lib.string::op>]

```
template<class charT, class traits, class Allocator>
  bool operator> (const basic_string<charT,traits,Allocator>& lhs,
                  const basic_string<charT,traits,Allocator>& rhs);
```

1   **Returns:** *lhs*.compare(*rhs*) > 0.

```
template<class charT, class traits, class Allocator>
  bool operator> (const charT* lhs,
                  const basic_string<charT,traits,Allocator>& rhs);
```

2   **Returns:** `basic_string<charT,traits,Allocator>(`*lhs*`) >` *rhs*.

```
template<class charT, class traits, class Allocator>
  bool operator> (const basic_string<charT,traits,Allocator>& lhs,
                  const charT* rhs);
```

3   **Returns:** *lhs* `> basic_string<charT,traits,Allocator>(`*rhs*`)`.

21.3.7.6 operator<=   [lib.string::op<=]

```
template<class charT, class traits, class Allocator>
  bool operator<=(const basic_string<charT,traits,Allocator>& lhs,
                  const basic_string<charT,traits,Allocator>& rhs);
```

1   **Returns:** *lhs*`.compare(`*rhs*`) <= 0`.

```
template<class charT, class traits, class Allocator>
  bool operator<=(const charT* lhs,
                  const basic_string<charT,traits,Allocator>& rhs);
```

2   **Returns:** `basic_string<charT,traits,Allocator>(`*lhs*`) <=` *rhs*.

```
template<class charT, class traits, class Allocator>
  bool operator<=(const basic_string<charT,traits,Allocator>& lhs,
                  const charT* rhs);
```

3   **Returns:** *lhs* `<= basic_string<charT,traits,Allocator>(`*rhs*`)`.

21.3.7.7 operator>=   [lib.string::op>=]

```
template<class charT, class traits, class Allocator>
  bool operator>=(const basic_string<charT,traits,Allocator>& lhs,
                  const basic_string<charT,traits,Allocator>& rhs);
```

1   **Returns:** *lhs*`.compare(`*rhs*`) >= 0`.

```
template<class charT, class traits, class Allocator>
  bool operator>=(const charT* lhs,
                  const basic_string<charT,traits,Allocator>& rhs);
```

2   **Returns:** `basic_string<charT,traits,Allocator>(`*lhs*`) >=` *rhs*.

```
template<class charT, class traits, class Allocator>
  bool operator>=(const basic_string<charT,traits,Allocator>& lhs,
                  const charT* rhs);
```

3   **Returns:** *lhs* `>= basic_string<charT,traits,Allocator>(`*rhs*`)`.

```
template<class charT, class traits, class Allocator>
    void swap(basic_string<charT,traits,Allocator>& lhs,
            basic_string<charT,traits,Allocator>& rhs);
```

1　**Effects:** *lhs*.swap(*rhs*);

21.3.7.9 Inserters and extractors　　　　　　　　　　　　　　　　**[lib.string.io]**

```
template<class charT, class traits, class Allocator>
  basic_istream<charT,traits>&
    operator>>(basic_istream<charT,traits>& is,
            basic_string<charT,traits,Allocator>& str);
```

1　**Effects:** Begins by constructing a sentry object k as if k were constructed by typename basic_istream<charT,traits>::sentry k(*is*). If bool(k) is true, it calls *str*.erase() and then extracts characters from *is* and appends them to *str* as if by calling *str*.append(1,c). If *is*.width() is greater than zero, the maximum number n of characters appended is *is*.width(); otherwise n is *str*.max_size(). Characters are extracted and appended until any of the following occurs:

— n characters are stored;

— end-of-file occurs on the input sequence;

— isspace(c,*is*.getloc()) is true for the next available input character c.

2　After the last character (if any) is extracted, *is*.width(0) is called and the sentry object k is destroyed.

2a　If the function extracts no characters, it calls *is*.setstate(ios::failbit), which may throw ios_base::failure (27.4.4.3).

3　**Returns:** *is*

```
template<class charT, class traits, class Allocator>
  basic_ostream<charT, traits>&
    operator<<(basic_ostream<charT, traits>& os,
            const basic_string<charT,traits,Allocator>& str);
```

4　**Effects:** Begins by constructing a sentry object k as if k were constructed by typename basic_ostream<charT,traits>::sentry k(*os*). If bool(k) is true, inserts characters as if by calling *os*.rdbuf()->sputn(*str*.data(), n), padding as described in stage 3 of 22.2.2.2.2, where n is the larger of *os*.width() and *str*.size(); then calls *os*.width(0). If the call to sputn fails, calls *os*.setstate(ios_base::failbit).

5　**Returns:** *os*

```
template<class charT, class traits, class Allocator>
  basic_istream<charT,traits>&
    getline(basic_istream<charT,traits>& is,
            basic_string<charT,traits,Allocator>& str,
            charT delim);
```

6　**Effects:** Begins by constructing a sentry object k as if by typename basic_istream<charT,traits>::sentry k(*is*, true). If bool(k) is true, it calls *str*.erase() and then extracts characters from *is* and appends them to *str* as if by calling *str*.append(1,c) until any of the following occurs:

— end-of-file occurs on the input sequence (in which case, the getline function calls *is*.setstate(ios_base::eofbit)).

— c == $delim$ for the next available input character c (in which case, c is extracted but not appended) (27.4.4.3)

— str.max_size() characters are stored (in which case, the function calls is.setstate(ios_base::failbit) (27.4.4.3)

7 The conditions are tested in the order shown. In any case, after the last character is extracted, the sentry object k is destroyed.

8 If the function extracts no characters, it calls is.setstate(ios_base::failbit) which may throw ios_base::failure (27.4.4.3).

9 **Returns:** is.

```
template<class charT, class traits, class Allocator>
  basic_istream<charT,traits>&
    getline(basic_istream<charT,traits>& is,
            basic_string<charT,traits,Allocator>& str)
```

10 **Returns:** getline(is,str,is.widen('\n'))

21.4 Null-terminated sequence utilities [lib.c.strings]

1 Tables 45, 46, 47, 48, and 49 describe headers <cctype>, <cwctype>, <cstring>, <cwchar>, and <cstdlib> (multibyte conversions), respectively.

Table 45—Header <cctype> synopsis

Type	Name(s)			
Functions:				
isalnum	isdigit	isprint	isupper	tolower
isalpha	isgraph	ispunct	isxdigit	toupper
iscntrl	islower	isspace		

Table 46—Header <cwctype> synopsis

Type	Name(s)				
Macro:	WEOF <cwctype>				
Types:	wctrans_t	wctype_t	wint_t <cwctype>		
Functions:					
iswalnum	iswctype	iswlower	iswspace	towctrans	wctrans
iswalpha	iswdigit	iswprint	iswupper	towlower	wctype
iswcntrl	iswgraph	iswpunct	iswxdigit	towupper	

Table 47—Header `<cstring>` synopsis

Type	Name(s)			
Macro:	NULL `<cstring>`			
Type:	size_t `<cstring>`			
Functions:				
memchr	strcat	strcspn	strncpy	strtok
memcmp	strchr	strerror	strpbrk	strxfrm
memcpy	strcmp	strlen	strrchr	
memmove	strcoll	strncat	strspn	
memset	strcpy	strncmp	strstr	

Table 48—Header `<cwchar>` synopsis

Type	Name(s)				
Macros:	NULL `<cwchar>`	WCHAR_MAX		WCHAR_MIN	WEOF `<cwchar>`
Types:	mbstate_t	wint_t `<cwchar>`		size_t	
Functions:					
btowc	getwchar	ungetwc	wcscpy	wcsrtombs	wmemchr
fgetwc	mbrlen	vfwprintf	wcscspn	wcsspn	wmemcmp
fgetws	mbrtowc	vswprintf	wcsftime	wcsstr	wmemcpy
fputwc	mbsinit	vwprintf	wcslen	wcstod	wmemmove
fputws	mbsrtowcs	wcrtomb	wcsncat	wcstok	wmemset
fwide	putwc	wcscat	wcsncmp	wcstol	wprintf
fwprintf	putwchar	wcschr	wcsncpy	wcstoul	wscanf
fwscanf	swprintf	wcscmp	wcspbrk	wcsxfrm	
getwc	swscanf	wcscoll	wcsrchr	wctob	

Table 49—Header `<cstdlib>` synopsis

Type	Name(s)		
Macros:	MB_CUR_MAX		
Functions:			
atol	mblen	strtod	wctomb
atof	mbstowcs	strtol	wcstombs
atoi	mbtowc	strtoul	

2   The contents of these headers are the same as the Standard C library headers `<ctype.h>`, `<wctype.h>`, `<string.h>`, `<wchar.h>` and `<stdlib.h>` respectively, with the following modifications:

3   None of the headers shall define the type wchar_t (2.11).

4   The function signature strchr(const char*, int) is replaced by the two declarations:

```
const char* strchr(const char* s, int c);
      char* strchr(      char* s, int c);
```

5   both of which have the same behavior as the original declaration.

6   The function signature strpbrk(const char*, const char*) is replaced by the two declara-
     tions:

```
const char* strpbrk(const char* s1, const char* s2);
      char* strpbrk(      char* s1, const char* s2);
```

7   both of which have the same behavior as the original declaration.

8   The function signature strrchr(const char*, int) is replaced by the two declarations:

```
const char* strrchr(const char* s, int c);
      char* strrchr(      char* s, int c);
```

9   both of which have the same behavior as the original declaration.

10   The function signature strstr(const char*, const char*) is replaced by the two declarations:

```
const char* strstr(const char* s1, const char* s2);
      char* strstr(      char* s1, const char* s2);
```

11   both of which have the same behavior as the original declaration.

12   The function signature memchr(const void*, int, size_t) is replaced by the two declarations:

```
const void* memchr(const void* s, int c, size_t n);
      void* memchr(      void* s, int c, size_t n);
```

13   both of which have the same behavior as the original declaration.

14   The function signature wcschr(const wchar_t*, wchar_t) is replaced by the two declarations:

```
const wchar_t* wcschr(const wchar_t* s, wchar_t c);
      wchar_t* wcschr(      wchar_t* s, wchar_t c);
```

15   both of which have the same behavior as the original declaration.

16   The function signature wcspbrk(const wchar_t*, const wchar_t*) is replaced by the two
     declarations:

```
const wchar_t* wcspbrk(const wchar_t* s1, const wchar_t* s2);
      wchar_t* wcspbrk(      wchar_t* s1, const wchar_t* s2);
```

17   both of which have the same behavior as the original declaration.

18   The function signature wcsrchr(const wchar_t*, wchar_t) is replaced by the two declarations:

```
const wchar_t* wcsrchr(const wchar_t* s, wchar_t c);
      wchar_t* wcsrchr(      wchar_t* s, wchar_t c);
```

19   both of which have the same behavior as the original declaration.

20   The function signature wcsstr(const wchar_t*, const wchar_t*) is replaced by the two dec-
     larations:

```
const wchar_t* wcsstr(const wchar_t* s1, const wchar_t* s2);
      wchar_t* wcsstr(      wchar_t* s1, const wchar_t* s2);
```

21   both of which have the same behavior as the original declaration.

22   The function signature wmemchr(const wwchar_t*, int, size_t) is replaced by the two decla-
      rations:

```
const wchar_t* wmemchr(const wchar_t* s, wchar_t c, size_t n);
      wchar_t* wmemchr(      wchar_t* s, wchar_t c, size_t n);
```

23   both of which have the same behavior as the original declaration.

      SEE ALSO: ISO C subclauses 7.3, 7.10.7, 7.10.8, and 7.11. Amendment 1 subclauses 4.4, 4.5, and 4.6.

22 Localization library [lib.localization]

1 This clause describes components that C++ programs may use to encapsulate (and therefore be more portable when confronting) cultural differences. The locale facility includes internationalization support for character classification and string collation, numeric, monetary, and date/time formatting and parsing, and message retrieval.

2 The following subclauses describe components for locales themselves, the standard facets, and facilities from the ISO C library, as summarized in Table 50:

Table 50—Localization library summary

Subclause	Header(s)
22.1 Locales 22.2 Standard `locale` Categories	`<locale>`
22.3 C library locales	`<clocale>`

22.1 Locales [lib.locales]

Header `<locale>` synopsis

```
namespace std {
  // 22.1.1, locale:
  class locale;
  template <class Facet> const Facet& use_facet(const locale&);
  template <class Facet> bool        has_facet(const locale&) throw();

  // 22.1.3, convenience interfaces:
  template <class charT> bool isspace (charT c, const locale& loc);
  template <class charT> bool isprint (charT c, const locale& loc);
  template <class charT> bool iscntrl (charT c, const locale& loc);
  template <class charT> bool isupper (charT c, const locale& loc);
  template <class charT> bool islower (charT c, const locale& loc);
  template <class charT> bool isalpha (charT c, const locale& loc);
  template <class charT> bool isdigit (charT c, const locale& loc);
  template <class charT> bool ispunct (charT c, const locale& loc);
  template <class charT> bool isxdigit(charT c, const locale& loc);
  template <class charT> bool isalnum (charT c, const locale& loc);
  template <class charT> bool isgraph (charT c, const locale& loc);
  template <class charT> charT toupper(charT c, const locale& loc);
  template <class charT> charT tolower(charT c, const locale& loc);
```

```
// 22.2.1 and 22.2.1.3, ctype:
class ctype_base;
template <class charT> class ctype;
template <>             class ctype<char>;              // specialization
template <class charT> class ctype_byname;
template <>             class ctype_byname<char>;        // specialization
class codecvt_base;
template <class internT, class externT, class stateT>
  class codecvt;
template <class internT, class externT, class stateT>
  class codecvt_byname;

// 22.2.2 and 22.2.3, numeric:
template <class charT, class InputIterator>  class num_get;
template <class charT, class OutputIterator> class num_put;
template <class charT> class numpunct;
template <class charT> class numpunct_byname;

// 22.2.4, collation:
template <class charT> class collate;
template <class charT> class collate_byname;

// 22.2.5, date and time:
class time_base;
template <class charT, class InputIterator>  class time_get;
template <class charT, class InputIterator>  class time_get_byname;
template <class charT, class OutputIterator> class time_put;
template <class charT, class OutputIterator> class time_put_byname;

// 22.2.6, money:
class money_base;
template <class charT, class InputIterator>  class money_get;
template <class charT, class OutputIterator> class money_put;
template <class charT, bool Intl> class moneypunct;
template <class charT, bool Intl> class moneypunct_byname;

// 22.2.7, message retrieval:
class messages_base;
template <class charT> class messages;
template <class charT> class messages_byname;
}
```

1   The header `<locale>` defines classes and declares functions that encapsulate and manipulate the information peculiar to a locale.[219]

22.1.1 Class `locale`   [lib.locale]

---

[219] In this subclause, the type name `struct tm` is an incomplete type that is defined in `<ctime>`.

```
namespace std {
  class locale {
  public:
    // types:
    class facet;
    class id;
    typedef int category;
    static const category    // values assigned here are for exposition only
      none     = 0,
      collate  = 0x010, ctype    = 0x020,
      monetary = 0x040, numeric  = 0x080,
      time     = 0x100, messages = 0x200,
      all = collate | ctype | monetary | numeric | time   | messages;

    // construct/copy/destroy:
    locale() throw();
    locale(const locale& other) throw();
    explicit locale(const char* std_name);
    locale(const locale& other, const char* std_name, category);
    template <class Facet> locale(const locale& other, Facet* f);
    locale(const locale& other, const locale& one, category);
    ~locale() throw();                    // non-virtual
    const locale& operator=(const locale& other) throw();
    template <class Facet> locale combine(const locale& other) const;

    // locale operations:
    basic_string<char>                      name() const;

    bool operator==(const locale& other) const;
    bool operator!=(const locale& other) const;

    template <class charT, class Traits, class Allocator>
      bool operator()(const basic_string<charT,Traits,Allocator>& s1,
                      const basic_string<charT,Traits,Allocator>& s2) const;

    // global locale objects:
    static        locale  global(const locale&);
    static const locale& classic();
  };
}
```

1   Class `locale` implements a type-safe polymorphic set of facets, indexed by facet *type*. In other words, a facet has a dual role: in one sense, it's just a class interface; at the same time, it's an index into a locale's set of facets.

2   Access to the facets of a `locale` is via two function templates, `use_facet<>` and `has_facet<>`.

3   [*Example:* An iostream `operator<<` might be implemented as:[220)

[220) Notice that, in the call to `put`, the stream is implicitly converted to an `ostreambuf_iterator<charT,traits>`.

```
template <class charT, class traits>
  basic_ostream<charT,traits>&
  operator<< (basic_ostream<charT,traits>& s, Date d)
{
  typename basic_ostream<charT,traits>::sentry cerberos(s);
  if (cerberos) {
    ios_base::iostate err = 0;
    tm tmbuf; d.extract(tmbuf);
    use_facet< time_put<charT,ostreambuf_iterator<charT,traits> > >(
      s.getloc()).put(s, s, s.fill(), err, &tmbuf, 'x');
    s.setstate(err);              // might throw
  }
  return s;
}
```

—end example]

4   In the call to use_facet<Facet>(loc), the type argument chooses a facet, making available all members of the named type. If Facet is not present in a locale, it throws the standard exception bad_cast. A C++ program can check if a locale implements a particular facet with the function template has_facet<Facet>(). User-defined facets may be installed in a locale, and used identically as may standard facets (22.2.8).

5   [*Note:* All locale semantics are accessed via use_facet<> and has_facet<>, except that:

  — A   member   operator   template   operator()(basic_string<C,T,A>&, basic_string<C,T,A>&) is provided so that a locale may be used as a predicate argument to the standard collections, to collate strings.

  — Convenient global interfaces are provided for traditional ctype functions such as isdigit() and isspace(), so that given a locale object *loc* a C++ program can call isspace(c, loc). (This eases upgrading existing extractors (27.6.1.2).) *—end note*]

6   Once a facet reference is obtained from a locale object by calling use_facet<>, that reference remains usable, and the results from member functions of it may be cached and re-used, as long as some locale object refers to that facet.

7   In successive calls to a locale facet member function during a call to an iostream inserter or extractor or a streambuf member function, the returned result shall be identical. [*Note:* This implies that such results may safely be reused without calling the locale facet member function again, and that member functions of iostream classes cannot safely call imbue() themselves, except as specified elsewhere. *—end note*]

8   A locale constructed from a name string (such as "POSIX"), or from parts of two named locales, has a name; all others do not. Named locales may be compared for equality; an unnamed locale is equal only to (copies of) itself. For an unnamed locale, locale::name() returns the string "*".

22.1.1.1 locale types   **[lib.locale.types]**

22.1.1.1.1 Type locale::category   **[lib.locale.category]**

```
typedef int category;
```

1   *Valid* category values include the locale member bitmask elements none, collate, ctype, monetary, numeric, time, and messages. In addition, locale member all is defined such that the expression

```
(collate | ctype | monetary | numeric | time | messages | all) == all
```

is true. Further, the result of applying operators | and & to any two valid values is valid, and results in the setwise union and intersection, respectively, of the argument categories.

2   `locale` member functions expecting a `category` argument require either a valid `category` value or one of the constants `LC_CTYPE` etc., defined in `<clocale>`. Such a `category` value identifies a set of locale categories. Each locale category, in turn, identifies a set of locale facets, including at least those shown in Table 51:

Table 51—Locale Category Facets

Category	Includes Facets
`collate`	`collate<char>`, `collate<wchar_t>`

`ctype`	`ctype<char>`, `ctype<wchar_t>`
	`codecvt<char,char,mbstate_t>`,
	`codecvt<wchar_t,char,mbstate_t>`

`monetary`	`moneypunct<char>`, `moneypunct<wchar_t>`
	`moneypunct<char,true>`, `moneypunct<wchar_t,true>`,
	`money_get<char>`, `money_get<wchar_t>`
	`money_put<char>`, `money_put<wchar_t>`

`numeric`	`numpunct<char>`, `numpunct<wchar_t>`,
	`num_get<char>`, `num_get<wchar_t>`
	`num_put<char>`, `num_put<wchar_t>`

`time`	`time_get<char>`, `time_get<wchar_t>`, `time_put<char>`, `time_put<wchar_t>`
`messages`	`messages<char>`, `messages<wchar_t>`

3   For any locale *loc* either constructed, or returned by `locale::classic()`, and any facet *Facet* that is a member of a standard category, `has_facet<Facet>(loc)` is true. Each `locale` member function which takes a `locale::category` argument operates on the corresponding set of facets.

4   An implementation is required to provide those instantiations for facet templates identified as members of a category, and for those shown in Table 52:

Table 52—Required Instantiations

Category	Includes Facets
collate	`collate_byname<char>`, `collate_byname<wchar_t>`
ctype	`ctype_byname<char>`, `ctype_byname<wchar_t>`, `codecvt_byname<char,char,mbstate_t>`, `codecvt_byname<wchar_t,char,mbstate_t>`
monetary	`moneypunct_byname<char,International>`, `moneypunct_byname<wchar_t,International>`, `money_get<C,InputIterator>`, `money_put<C,OutputIterator>`
numeric	`numpunct_byname<char>`, `numpunct_byname<wchar_t>` `num_get<C,InputIterator>`, `num_put<C,OutputIterator>`

time	`time_get<char,InputIterator>`,
	`time_get_byname<char,InputIterator>`,
	`time_get<wchar_t,OutputIterator>`,
	`time_get_byname<wchar_t,OutputIterator>`,
	`time_put<char,OutputIterator>`,
	`time_put_byname<char,OutputIterator>`,
	`time_put<wchar_t,OutputIterator>`
	`time_put_byname<wchar_t,OutputIterator>`

messages	`messages_byname<char>`, `messages_byname<wchar_t>`

5   The provided implementation of members of facets `num_get<charT>` and `num_put<charT>` calls `use_facet<F>(l)` only for facet `F` of types `numpunct<charT>` and `ctype<charT>`, and for locale `l` the value obtained by calling member `getloc()` on the `ios_base&` argument to these functions.

6   In declarations of facets, a template formal parameter with name `InputIterator` or `OutputIterator` indicates the set of all possible instantiations on parameters that satisfy the requirements of an Input Iterator or an Output Iterator, respectively (24.1). A template formal parameter with name `C` represents the set of all possible instantiations on a parameter that satisfies the requirements for a character on which any of the iostream components can be instantiated. A template formal parameter with name `International` represents the set of all possible instantiations on a bool parameter.

22.1.1.1.2 Class `locale::facet`   [lib.locale.facet]

```
namespace std {
  class locale::facet {
  protected:
    explicit facet(size_t refs = 0);
    virtual ~facet();
  private:
    facet(const facet&);            // not defined
    void operator=(const facet&);   // not defined
  };
}
```

1   Class `facet` is the base class for locale feature sets. A class is a *facet* if it is publicly derived from another facet, or if it is a class derived from `locale::facet` and containing a publicly-accessible declaration as follows:[221]

---

[221] This is a complete list of requirements; there are no other requirements. Thus, a facet class need not have a public copy construc-

```
      static ::std::locale::id id;
```

Template parameters in this clause which are required to be facets are those named `Facet` in declarations. A program that passes a type that is *not* a facet, as an (explicit or deduced) template parameter to a locale function expecting a facet, is ill-formed.

2   The *refs* argument to the constructor is used for lifetime management.

— For *refs* == 0, the implementation performs `delete static_cast<locale::facet*>(f)` (where `f` is a pointer to the facet) when the last `locale` object containing the facet is destroyed; for *refs* == 1, the implementation never destroys the facet.

3   Constructors of all facets defined in this clause take such an argument and pass it along to their `facet` base class constructor. All one-argument constructors defined in this clause are *explicit*, preventing their participation in automatic conversions.

4   For some standard facets a standard "..._byname" class, derived from it, implements the virtual function semantics equivalent to that facet of the locale constructed by `locale(const char*)` with the same name. Each such facet provides a constructor that takes a `const char*` argument, which names the locale, and a *refs* argument, which is passed to the base class constructor. If there is no "..._byname" version of a facet, the base class implements named locale semantics itself by reference to other facets.

22.1.1.1.3 Class `locale::id`   [lib.locale.id]

```
namespace std {
  class locale::id {
  public:
    id();
  private:
    void operator=(const id&);   // not defined
    id(const id&);               // not defined
  };
}
```

1   The class locale::id provides identification of a locale facet interfaces, used as an index for lookup and to encapsulate initialization.

2   [*Note:* Because facets are used by iostreams, potentially while static constructors are running, their initialization cannot depend on programmed static initialization. One initialization strategy is for `locale` to initialize each facet's `id` member the first time an instance of the facet is installed into a locale. This depends only on static storage being zero before constructors run (3.6.2). —*end note*]

22.1.1.2 `locale` constructors and destructor   [lib.locale.cons]

```
      locale() throw();
```

1   Default constructor: a snapshot of the current global locale.

2   **Effects:** Constructs a copy of the argument last passed to `locale::global(locale&)`, if it has been called; else, the resulting facets have virtual function semantics identical to those of `locale::classic()`. [*Note:* This constructor is commonly used as the default value for arguments of functions that take a `const locale&` argument. —*end note*]

---

tor, assignment, default constructor, destructor, etc.

```
locale(const locale& other) throw();
```

3   **Effects:** Constructs a locale which is a copy of *other*.

```
const locale& operator=(const locale& other) throw();
```

4   **Effects:** Creates a copy of *other*, replacing the current value.

5   **Returns:** *this

```
explicit locale(const char* std_name);
```

6   **Effects:** Constructs a locale using standard C locale names, e.g. "POSIX". The resulting locale imple-
       ments semantics defined to be associated with that name.

7   **Throws:** runtime_error if the argument is not valid, or is null.

8   **Notes:** The set of valid string argument values is "C", "", and any implementation-defined values.

```
locale(const locale& other, const char* std_name, category);
```

9   **Effects:** Constructs a locale as a copy of other except for the facets identified by the category argu-
       ment, which instead implement the same semantics as locale(*std_name*).

10   **Throws:** runtime_error if the argument is not valid, or is null.

11   **Notes:** The locale has a name if and only if other has a name.

```
template <class Facet> locale(const locale& other, Facet* f);
```

12   **Effects:** Constructs a locale incorporating all facets from the first argument except that of type Facet, and
       installs the second argument as the remaining facet. If *f* is null, the resulting object is a copy of
       other.

13   **Notes:** The resulting locale has no name.

```
locale(const locale& other, const locale& one, category cats);
```

14   **Effects:** Constructs a locale incorporating all facets from the first argument except those that implement
       cats, which are instead incorporated from the second argument.

15   **Notes:** The resulting locale has a name if and only if the first two arguments have names.

```
~locale() throw();
```

16   A non-virtual destructor that throws no exceptions.

22.1.1.3 locale members   [lib.locale.members]

```
template <class Facet> locale combine(const locale& other) const;
```

1   **Effects:** Constructs a locale incorporating all facets from *this except for that one facet of other that is
       identified by Facet.

2   **Returns:** The newly created locale.

3   **Throws:** runtime_error if has_facet<Facet>(other) is false.

4   **Notes:** The resulting locale has no name.

```
basic_string<char> name() const;
```

5   **Returns:** The name of *this, if it has one; otherwise, the string "*". If *this has a name, then
       locale(name().c_str()) is equivalent to *this. Details of the contents of the resulting string
       are otherwise implementation-defined.

22.1.1.4 **locale operators** [lib.locale.operators]

```
bool operator==(const locale& other) const;
```

1   **Returns:** `true` if both arguments are the same locale, or one is a copy of the other, or each has a name and the names are identical; `false` otherwise.

```
bool operator!=(const locale& other) const;
```

2   **Returns:** The result of the expression: `!(*this == other)`

```
template <class charT, class Traits, class Allocator>
  bool operator()(const basic_string<charT,Traits,Allocator>& s1,
                  const basic_string<charT,Traits,Allocator>& s2) const;
```

3   **Effects:** Compares two strings according to the `collate<charT>` facet.

4   **Notes:** This member operator template (and therefore `locale` itself) satisfies requirements for a comparator predicate template argument (clause 25) applied to strings.

5   **Returns:** The result of the following expression:

```
use_facet< collate<charT> >(*this).compare
    (s1.data(), s1.data()+s1.size(), s2.data(), s2.data()+s2.size()) < 0;
```

6   [*Example:* A vector of strings v can be collated according to collation rules in locale `loc` simply by (25.3.1, 23.2.4):

```
std::sort(v.begin(), v.end(), loc);
```

—*end example*]

22.1.1.5 `locale` static members   [lib.locale.statics]

```
static locale global(const locale& loc);
```

1   Sets the global locale to its argument.

2   **Effects:** Causes future calls to the constructor `locale()` to return a copy of the argument. If the argument has a name, does

```
std::setlocale(LC_ALL, loc.name().c_str());
```

otherwise, the effect on the C locale, if any, is implementation-defined. No library function other than `locale::global()` shall affect the value returned by `locale()`.

3   **Returns:** The previous value of `locale()`.

```
static const locale& classic();
```

4   The `"C"` locale.

5   **Returns:** A locale that implements the classic `"C"` locale semantics, equivalent to the value `locale("C")`.

6   **Notes:** This locale, its facets, and their member functions, do not change with time.

22.1.2 `locale` globals   [lib.locale.global.templates]

```
template <class Facet> const Facet& use_facet(const locale& loc);
```

1   **Requires:** `Facet` is a facet class whose definition contains the public static member `id` as defined in 22.1.1.1.2.

2   **Returns:** a reference to the corresponding facet of *loc*, if present.

3   **Throws:** `bad_cast` if `has_facet<Facet>(loc)` is `false`.

4   **Notes:** The reference returned remains valid at least as long as any copy of *loc* exists.

```
template <class Facet> bool has_facet(const locale& loc) throw();
```

5   **Returns:** true if the facet requested is present in *loc*; otherwise false

22.1.3 Convenience interfaces   [lib.locale.convenience]

22.1.3.1 Character classification   [lib.classification]

```
template <class charT> bool isspace (charT c, const locale& loc);
template <class charT> bool isprint (charT c, const locale& loc);
template <class charT> bool iscntrl (charT c, const locale& loc);
template <class charT> bool isupper (charT c, const locale& loc);
template <class charT> bool islower (charT c, const locale& loc);
template <class charT> bool isalpha (charT c, const locale& loc);
template <class charT> bool isdigit (charT c, const locale& loc);
template <class charT> bool ispunct (charT c, const locale& loc);
template <class charT> bool isxdigit(charT c, const locale& loc);
template <class charT> bool isalnum (charT c, const locale& loc);
template <class charT> bool isgraph (charT c, const locale& loc);
```

1   Each of these functions `is`*F* returns the result of the expression:

```
use_facet< ctype<charT> >(loc).is(ctype_base::F, c)
```

where *F* is the `ctype_base::mask` value corresponding to that function (22.2.1).[222]

22.1.3.2 Character conversions   [lib.conversions]

```
template <class charT> charT toupper(charT c, const locale& loc);
```

1   **Returns:** `use_facet<ctype<charT> >(loc).toupper(c)`.

```
template <class charT> charT tolower(charT c, const locale& loc);
```

2   **Returns:** `use_facet<ctype<charT> >(loc).tolower(c)`.

22.2 Standard `locale` categories   [lib.locale.categories]

1   Each of the standard categories includes a family of facets. Some of these implement formatting or parsing of a datum, for use by standard or users' iostream operators `<<` and `>>`, as members `put()` and `get()`, respectively. Each such member function takes an `ios_base&` argument whose members `flags()`, `precision()`, and `width()`, specify the format of the corresponding datum. (27.4.2). Those functions which need to use other facets call its member `getloc()` to retrieve the locale imbued there. Formatting facets use the character argument *fill* to fill out the specified width where necessary.

---

[222] When used in a loop, it is faster to cache the `ctype<>` facet and use it directly, or use the vector form of `ctype<>::is`.

2   The put () members make no provision for error reporting. (Any failures of the OutputIterator argument must be extracted from the returned iterator.) The get () members take an ios_base::iostate& argument whose value they ignore, but set to ios_base::failbit in case of a parse error.

22.2.1 The `ctype` category [lib.category.ctype]

```
namespace std {
  class ctype_base {
  public:
    enum mask {              // numeric values are for exposition only.
      space=1<<0, print=1<<1, cntrl=1<<2, upper=1<<3, lower=1<<4,
      alpha=1<<5, digit=1<<6, punct=1<<7, xdigit=1<<8,
      alnum=alpha|digit, graph=alnum|punct
    };
  };
}
```

1   The type mask is a bitmask type.

22.2.1.1 Class template `ctype` [lib.locale.ctype]

```
template <class charT>
class ctype : public locale::facet, public ctype_base {
public:
  typedef charT char_type;
  explicit ctype(size_t refs = 0);

  bool          is(mask m, charT c) const;
  const charT*  is(const charT* low, const charT* high, mask* vec) const;
  const charT*  scan_is(mask m,
                        const charT* low, const charT* high) const;
  const charT*  scan_not(mask m,
                        const charT* low, const charT* high) const;
  charT         toupper(charT c) const;
  const charT*  toupper(charT* low, const charT* high) const;
  charT         tolower(charT c) const;
  const charT*  tolower(charT* low, const charT* high) const;

  charT         widen(char c) const;
  const char*   widen(const char* low, const char* high, charT* to) const;
  char          narrow(charT c, char dfault) const;
  const charT*  narrow(const charT* low, const charT*, char dfault,
                        char* to) const;

  static locale::id id;
```

```
    protected:
     ~ctype();                          // virtual
      virtual bool          do_is(mask m, charT c) const;
      virtual const charT*  do_is(const charT* low, const charT* high,
                                  mask* vec) const;
      virtual const charT*  do_scan_is(mask m,
                                  const charT* low, const charT* high) const;
      virtual const charT*  do_scan_not(mask m,
                                  const charT* low, const charT* high) const;
      virtual charT         do_toupper(charT) const;
      virtual const charT*  do_toupper(charT* low, const charT* high) const;
      virtual charT         do_tolower(charT) const;
      virtual const charT*  do_tolower(charT* low, const charT* high) const;
      virtual charT         do_widen(char) const;
      virtual const char*   do_widen(const char* low, const char* high,
                                  charT* dest) const;
      virtual char          do_narrow(charT, char dfault) const;
      virtual const charT*  do_narrow(const charT* low, const charT* high,
                                  char dfault, char* dest) const;
    };
```

1   Class `ctype` encapsulates the C library `<cctype>` features. `istream` members are required to use `ctype<>` for character classing during input parsing.

2   The instantiations required in Table 51 (22.1.1.1.1), namely `ctype<char>` and `ctype<wchar_t>`, implement character classing appropriate to the implementation's native character set.

22.2.1.1.1 ctype members   [lib.locale.ctype.members]

```
    bool          is(mask m, charT c) const;
    const charT*  is(const charT* low, const charT* high,
                      mask* vec) const;
```

1   **Returns:** `do_is(m, c)` or `do_is(low, high, vec)`

```
    const charT*  scan_is(mask m,
                      const charT* low, const charT* high) const;
```

2   **Returns:** `do_scan_is(m, low, high)`

```
    const charT*  scan_not(mask m,
                      const charT* low, const charT* high) const;
```

3   **Returns:** `do_scan_not(m, low, high)`

```
    charT         toupper(charT) const;
    const charT*  toupper(charT* low, const charT* high) const;
```

4   **Returns:** `do_toupper(c)` or `do_toupper(low, high)`

```
    charT         tolower(charT c) const;
    const charT*  tolower(charT* low, const charT* high) const;
```

5   **Returns:** `do_tolower(c)` or `do_tolower(low, high)`

```
charT       widen(char c) const;
const char* widen(const char* low, const char* high, charT* to) const;
```

6   **Returns:** do_widen(*c*) or do_widen(*low,high,to*)

```
char        narrow(charT c, char dfault) const;
const charT* narrow(const charT* low, const charT*, char dfault,
                    char* to) const;
```

7   **Returns:** do_narrow(*c,dfault*) or do_narrow(*low,high,dfault,to*)

22.2.1.1.2 ctype virtual functions   [lib.locale.ctype.virtuals]

```
bool        do_is(mask m, charT c) const;
const charT* do_is(const charT* low, const charT* high,
                    mask* vec) const;
```

1   **Effects:** Classifies a character or sequence of characters. For each argument character, identifies a value *M* of type ctype_base::mask. The second form identifies a value *M* of type ctype_base::mask for each **p* where (*low<=p* && *p<high*), and places it into *vec[p-low]*.

2   **Returns:** The first form returns the result of the expression (*M* & *m*) != 0; i.e., true if the character has the characteristics specified. The second form returns *high*.

```
const charT* do_scan_is(mask m,
                    const charT* low, const charT* high) const;
```

3   **Effects:** Locates a character in a buffer that conforms to a classification *m*.

4   **Returns:** The smallest pointer *p* in the range [*low*, *high*) such that is(*m*, **p*) would return true; otherwise, returns *high*.

```
const charT* do_scan_not(mask m,
                    const charT* low, const charT* high) const;
```

5   **Effects:** Locates a character in a buffer that fails to conform to a classification m.

6   **Returns:** The smallest pointer *p*, if any, in the range [*low*, *high*) such that is(*m*, **p*) would return false; otherwise, returns *high*.

```
charT       do_toupper(charT c) const;
const charT* do_toupper(charT* low, const charT* high) const;
```

7   **Effects:** Converts a character or characters to upper case. The second form replaces each character **p* in the range [*low*, *high*) for which a corresponding upper-case character exists, with that character.

8   **Returns:** The first form returns the corresponding upper-case character if it is known to exist, or its argument if not. The second form returns *high*.

```
charT       do_tolower(charT c) const;
const charT* do_tolower(charT* low, const charT* high) const;
```

9   **Effects:** Converts a character or characters to lower case. The second form replaces each character **p* in the range [*low*, *high*) and for which a corresponding lower-case character exists, with that character.

10   **Returns:** The first form returns the corresponding lower-case character if it is known to exist, or its argument if not. The second form returns *high*.

```
charT       do_widen(char c) const;
const char* do_widen(const char* low, const char* high,
                     charT* dest) const;
```

11   **Effects:** Applies the simplest reasonable transformation from a char value or sequence of char values to
the corresponding charT value or values.[223] The only characters for which unique transformations are
required are those in the basic source character set (2.2).
For any named ctype category with a ctype<charT> facet *ctw* and valid ctype_base::mask
value M (is(M, *c*) || !*ctw*.is(M, do_widen(*c*))) is true.[224]
The second form transforms each character *p in the range [*low*, *high*), placing the result in
dest[*p-low*].

12   **Returns:** The first form returns the transformed value. The second form returns *high*.

```
char       do_narrow(charT c, char dfault) const;
const charT* do_narrow(const charT* low, const charT* high,
                       char dfault, char* dest) const;
```

13   **Effects:** Applies the simplest reasonable transformation from a charT value or sequence of charT values to the corresponding char value or values.
For any character *c* in the basic source character set(2.2) the transformation is such that

```
    do_widen(do_narrow(c,0)) == c
```

For any named ctype category with a ctype<char> facet *ctc* however, and
ctype_base::mask value M,

```
    (is(M,c) || !ctc.is(M, do_narrow(c,dfault)) )
```

is true (unless do_narrow returns *dfault*). In addition, for any digit character *c*, the expression
(do_narrow(*c*,*dfault*)-'0') evaluates to the digit value of the character. The second form
transforms each character *p in the range [*low*, *high*), placing the result (or *dfault* if no simple
transformation is readly available) in *dest*[*p-low*].

14   **Returns:** The first form returns the transformed value; or *dfault* if no mapping is readily available. The
second form returns *high*.

22.2.1.2 Class template ctype_byname   [lib.locale.ctype.byname]

```
namespace std {
  template <class charT>
  class ctype_byname : public ctype<charT> {
  public:
    typedef ctype<charT>::mask mask;
    explicit ctype_byname(const char*, size_t refs = 0);
  protected:
   ~ctype_byname();                   // virtual
```

---

[223] The char argument of do_widen is intended to accept values derived from character literals for conversion the locale's encoding.
[224] In other words, the transformed character is not a member of any character classification that *c* is not also a member of.

```
      virtual bool        do_is(mask m, charT c) const;
      virtual const charT* do_is(const charT* low, const charT* high,
                             mask* vec) const;
      virtual const charT* do_scan_is(mask m,
                         const charT* low, const charT* high) const;
      virtual const charT* do_scan_not(mask m,
                         const charT* low, const charT* high) const;
      virtual charT        do_toupper(charT) const;
      virtual const charT* do_toupper(charT* low, const charT* high) const;
      virtual charT        do_tolower(charT) const;
      virtual const charT* do_tolower(charT* low, const charT* high) const;
      virtual charT        do_widen(char) const;
      virtual const char*  do_widen(const char* low, const char* high,
                             charT* dest) const;
      virtual char         do_narrow(charT, char dfault) const;
      virtual const charT* do_narrow(const charT* low, const charT* high,
                             char dfault, char* dest) const;
    };
}
```

22.2.1.3 `ctype` specializations   [lib.facet.ctype.special]

```
namespace std {
  template <> class ctype<char>
    : public locale::facet, public ctype_base {
  public:
    typedef char char_type;

    explicit ctype(const mask* tab = 0, bool del = false,
                 size_t refs = 0);

    bool is(mask m, char c) const;
    const char* is(const char* low, const char* high, mask* vec) const;
    const char* scan_is (mask m,
                     const char* low, const char* high) const;
    const char* scan_not(mask m,
                     const char* low, const char* high) const;

    char        toupper(char c) const;
    const char* toupper(char* low, const char* high) const;
    char        tolower(char c) const;
    const char* tolower(char* low, const char* high) const;

    char  widen(char c) const;
    const char* widen(const char* low, const char* high, char* to) const;
    char  narrow(char c, char dfault) const;
    const char* narrow(const char* low, const char* high, char dfault,
                     char* to) const;

    static locale::id id;
    static const size_t table_size = IMPLEMENTATION_DEFINED;

  protected:
    const mask* table() const throw();
    static const mask* classic_table() throw();
```

```
    ~ctype();                         // virtual
    virtual char         do_toupper(char c) const;
    virtual const char*  do_toupper(char* low, const char* high) const;
    virtual char         do_tolower(char c) const;
    virtual const char*  do_tolower(char* low, const char* high) const;

    virtual char         do_widen(char c) const;
    virtual const char*  do_widen(const char* low,
                                  const char* high,
                                  char* to) const;
    virtual char         do_narrow(char c, char dfault) const;
    virtual const char*  do_narrow(const char* low,
                                   const char* high,
                                   char dfault, char* to) const;
  };
}
```

1   A specialization ctype<char> is provided so that the member functions on type char can be imple-
     mented inline.[225] The implementation-defined value of member table_size is at least 256.

22.2.1.3.1 ctype<char> destructor   [lib.facet.ctype.char.dtor]

```
    ~ctype();
```

1   **Effects:** If the constructor's first argument was nonzero, and its second argument was true, does delete
     [] table().

22.2.1.3.2 ctype<char> members   [lib.facet.ctype.char.members]

1   In the following member descriptions, for unsigned char values v where (v >= table_size),
     table()[v] is assumed to have an implementation-defined value (possibly different for each such value
     v) without performing the array lookup.

```
    explicit ctype(const mask* tbl = 0, bool del = false,
                   size_t refs = 0);
```

2   **Precondition:** tbl either 0 or an array of at least table_size elements.
3   **Effects:** Passes its refs argument to its base class constructor.

```
    bool         is(mask m, char c) const;
    const char*  is(const char* low, const char* high,
                    mask* vec) const;
```

4   **Effects:** The second form, for all *p in the range [low, high), assigns into vec[p-low] the value
     table()[(unsigned char)*p].
5   **Returns:** The first form returns table()[(unsigned char)c] & m; the second form returns
     high.

---

[225] Only the char (not unsigned char and signed char) form is provided. The specialization is specified in the standard,
and not left as an implementation detail, because it affects the derivation interface for ctype<char>.

```
const char* scan_is(mask m,
                    const char* low, const char* high) const;
```

6   **Returns:** The smallest p in the range [low, $high$) such that

```
table()[(unsigned char) *p] & m
```

is true.

```
const char* scan_not(mask m,
                     const char* low, const char* high) const;
```

7   **Returns:** The smallest p in the range [low, $high$) such that

```
table()[(unsigned char) *p] & m
```

is false.

```
char        toupper(char c) const;
const char* toupper(char* low, const char* high) const;
```

8   **Returns:** do_toupper(c) or do_toupper(low, $high$), respectively.

```
char        tolower(char c) const;
const char* tolower(char* low, const char* high) const;
```

9   **Returns:** do_tolower(c) or do_tolower(low, $high$), respectively.

```
char  widen(char c) const;
const char* widen(const char* low, const char* high,
    char* to) const;
```

10   **Returns:** do_widen(c) or do_widen(low, $high$, to), respectively.

```
char        narrow(char c, char /*dfault*/) const;
const char* narrow(const char* low, const char* high,
                   char /*dfault*/, char* to) const;
```

11   **Returns:** do_narrow(c) or do_narrow(low, $high$, to), respectively.

```
const mask* table() const throw();
```

12   **Returns:** The first constructor argument, if it was non-zero, otherwise classic_table().

22.2.1.3.3 ctype<char> static members   **[lib.facet.ctype.char.statics]**

```
static const mask* classic_table() throw();
```

1   **Returns:** A pointer to the initial element of an array of size table_size which represents the classifications of characters in the "C" locale.

22.2.1.3.4 ctype<char> virtual functions   **[lib.facet.ctype.char.virtuals]**

```
char        do_toupper(char) const;
const char* do_toupper(char* low, const char* high) const;
char        do_tolower(char) const;
const char* do_tolower(char* low, const char* high) const;
```

```
virtual char       do_widen(char c) const;
virtual const char* do_widen(const char* low,
                             const char* high,
                             char* to) const;
virtual char       do_narrow(char c, char dfault) const;
virtual const char* do_narrow(const char* low,
                              const char* high,
                              char dfault, char* to) const;
```

These functions are described identically as those members of the same name in the ctype class template
(22.2.1.1.1).

22.2.1.4 Class ctype_byname<char>   [lib.locale.ctype.byname.special]

```
namespace std {
  template <> class ctype_byname<char> : public ctype<char> {
  public:
    explicit ctype_byname(const char*, size_t refs = 0);
  protected:
    ~ctype_byname();                // virtual
    virtual char       do_toupper(char c) const;
    virtual const char* do_toupper(char* low, const char* high) const;
    virtual char       do_tolower(char c) const;
    virtual const char* do_tolower(char* low, const char* high) const;

    virtual char       do_widen(char c) const;
    virtual const char* do_widen(const char* low,
                                 const char* high,
                                 char* to) const;
    virtual char       do_narrow(char c, char dfault) const;
    virtual const char* do_narrow(const char* low,
                                  const char* high,
                                  char dfault, char* to) const;
  };
}
```

1

22.2.1.5 Class template codecvt   [lib.locale.codecvt]

```
namespace std {
 class codecvt_base {
 public:
  enum result { ok, partial, error, noconv };
 };
 template <class internT, class externT, class stateT>
 class codecvt : public locale::facet, public codecvt_base {
 public:
  typedef internT  intern_type;
  typedef externT  extern_type;
  typedef stateT state_type;

  explicit codecvt(size_t refs = 0);
```

```
        result out(stateT& state,
          const internT* from, const internT* from_end, const internT*& from_next,
                externT*   to,         externT* to_limit, externT*& to_next) const;
        result unshift(stateT& state,
                externT*   to,         externT* to_limit, externT*& to_next) const;
        result in(stateT& state,
          const externT* from, const externT* from_end, const externT*& from_next,
                internT*   to,         internT* to_limit, internT*& to_next) const;
        int encoding() const throw();
        bool always_noconv() const throw();
        int length(stateT&, const externT* from, const externT* end,
                size_t max) const;
        int max_length() const throw();

        static locale::id id;

      protected:
        ~codecvt();                        // virtual
        virtual result do_out(stateT& state,
          const internT* from, const internT* from_end, const internT*& from_next,
                externT* to,           externT* to_limit, externT*& to_next) const;
        virtual result do_in(stateT& state,
          const externT* from, const externT* from_end, const externT*& from_next,
                internT* to,           internT* to_limit, internT*& to_next) const;
        virtual result do_unshift(stateT& state,
                externT* to,           externT* to_limit, externT*& to_next) const;
        virtual int do_encoding() const throw();
        virtual bool do_always_noconv() const throw();
        virtual int do_length(stateT&, const externT* from,
                          const externT* end, size_t max) const;
        virtual int do_max_length() const throw();
      };
    }
```

1   The class `codecvt<internT,externT,stateT>` is for use when converting from one codeset to another, such as from wide characters to multibyte characters, between wide character encodings such as Unicode and EUC.

2   The `stateT` argument selects the pair of codesets being mapped between.

3   The instantiations required in the Table 51 (22.1.1.1.1), namely `codecvt<wchar_t,char,mbstate_t>` and `codecvt<char,char,mbstate_t>`, convert the implementation-defined native character set. `codecvt<char,char,mbstate_t>` implements a degenerate conversion; it does not convert at all. `codecvt<wchar_t,char,mbstate_t>` converts between the native character sets for tiny and wide characters. Instantiations on `mbstate_t` perform conversion between encodings known to the library implementor. Other encodings can be converted by specializing on a user-defined `stateT` type. The `stateT` object can contain any state that is useful to communicate to or from the specialized `do_in` or `do_out` members.

```
result out(stateT& state,
    const internT* from, const internT* from_end, const internT*& from_next,
        externT* to, externT* to_limit, externT*& to_next) const;
```

1   **Returns:** do_out(*state*, *from*, *from_end*, *from_next*, *to*, *to_limit*, *to_next*)

```
result unshift(stateT& state,
        externT* to, externT* to_limit, externT*& to_next) const;
```

2   **Returns:** do_unshift(*state*, *to*, *to_limit*, *to_next*)

```
result in(stateT& state,
    const externT* from, const externT* from_end, const externT*& from_next,
        internT* to, internT* to_limit, internT*& to_next) const;
```

3   **Returns:** do_in(*state*, *from*, *from_end*, *from_next*, *to*, *to_limit*, *to_next*)

```
int encoding() const throw();
```

4   **Returns:** do_encoding()

```
bool always_noconv() const throw();
```

5   **Returns:** do_always_noconv()

```
int length(stateT& state, const externT* from, const externT* from_end,
        size_t max) const;
```

6   **Returns:** do_length(*state*, *from*, *from_end*, *max*)

```
int max_length() const throw();
```

7   **Returns:** do_max_length()

```
result do_out(stateT& state,
    const internT* from, const internT* from_end, const internT*& from_next,
    externT* to, externT* to_limit, externT*& to_next) const;
```

```
result do_in(stateT& state,
    const externT* from, const externT* from_end, const externT*& from_next,
        internT* to, internT* to_limit, internT*& to_next) const;
```

1   **Preconditions:** (*from*<=*from_end* && *to*<=*to_end*) well-defined and true; *state* initialized, if at the beginning of a sequence, or else equal to the result of converting the preceding characters in the sequence.

2   **Effects:** Translates characters in the source range [*from*, *from_end*), placing the results in sequential positions starting at destination *to*. Converts no more than (*from_end*-*from*) source elements, and stores no more than (*to_limit*-*to*) destination elements.
      Stops if it encounters a character it cannot convert. It always leaves the *from_next* and *to_next* pointers pointing one beyond the last element successfully converted. If returns noconv, internT and externT are the same type and the converted sequence is identical to the input sequence [*from*, *from_next*). *to_next* is set equal to *to*, the value of *state* is unchanged, and there are no changes to the values in [*to*, *to_limit*).

3   **Notes:** Its operations on *state* are unspecified.
      [*Note:* This argument can be used, for example, to maintain shift state, to specify conversion options (such as count only), or to identify a cache of seek offsets. —*end note*]

4   **Returns:** An enumeration value, as summarized in Table 53:

Table 53—convert result values

Value	Meaning
ok	completed the conversion
partial	not all source characters converted
error	encountered a character in [*from*, *from_end*) that it could not convert
noconv	internT and externT are the same type, and input sequence is identical to converted sequence

A return value of partial, if (*from_next*==*from_end*), indicates that either the destination sequence has not absorbed all the available destination elements, or that additional source elements are needed before another destination element can be produced.

```
result do_unshift(stateT& state,
    externT* to, externT* to_limit, externT*& to_next) const;
```

5   **Effects** Places characters starting at *to* that should be appended to terminate a sequence when the current stateT is given by *state*.[226] The instantiations required in Table 51 (22.1.1.1.1), namely codecvt<wchar_t,char,mbstate_t> and codecvt<char,char,mbstate_t>, store no characters. Stores no more than (*to_limit-to*) destination elements. It always leaves the *to_next* pointer pointing one beyond the last element successfully stored.

6   **Returns** An enumeration value, as summarized in Table 54:

Table 54—convert result values

Value	Meaning
ok	completed the sequence
partial	more characters need to be supplied to complete termination
error	*state* has invalid value.
noconv	no termination is needed for this state_type

codecvt<char,char,mbstate_t>, returns noconv.

```
int do_encoding() const throw();
```

7   **Returns:** -1 if the encoding of the externT sequence is state-dependent; else the constant number of externT characters needed to produce an internal character; or 0 if this number is not a constant[227].

```
bool do_always_noconv() const throw();
```

8   **Returns:** true if do_in() and do_out() return noconv for all valid argument values. codecvt<char,char,mbstate_t> returns true.

---

[226] Typically these will be characters to return the state to stateT().

[227] If encoding() yields -1, then more than max_length() externT elements may be consumed when producing a single internT character, and additional externT elements may appear at the end of a sequence after those that yield the final internT character.

```
int do_length(stateT& state, const externT* from, const externT* from_end,
         size_t max) const;
```

9 **Preconditions:** (from<=from_end) well-defined and true; state initialized, if at the beginning of a sequence, or else equal to the result of converting the preceding characters in the sequence.

9a **Effects:** The effect on the state argument is "as if" it called do_in(state, from, from_end, from, to, to+max, to) for to pointing to a buffer of at least max elements.

10 **Returns:** (from_next-from) where from_next is the largest value in the range [from, from_end] such that the sequence of values in the range [from, from_next) represents max or fewer valid complete characters of type internT. The instantiations required in Table 51 (22.1.1.1.1), namely codecvt<wchar_t, char, mbstate_t> and codecvt<char, char, mbstate_t>, return the lesser of max and (from_end-from).

```
int do_max_length() const throw();
```

11 **Returns:** The maximum value that do_length(state, from, from_end, 1) can return for any valid range [from, from_end) and stateT value state. The specialization codecvt<char, char, mbstate_t>::do_max_length() returns 1.

22.2.1.6 Class template codecvt_byname   [lib.locale.codecvt.byname]

```
namespace std {
 template <class internT, class externT, class stateT>
 class codecvt_byname : public codecvt<internT, externT, stateT> {
 public:
  explicit codecvt_byname(const char*, size_t refs = 0);
 protected:
 ~codecvt_byname();                // virtual
  virtual result do_out(stateT& state,
    const internT* from, const internT* from_end, const internT*& from_next,
        externT* to,          externT* to_limit, externT*& to_next) const;
  virtual result do_in(stateT& state,
    const externT* from, const externT* from_end, const externT*& from_next,
        internT* to,          internT* to_limit, internT*& to_next) const;
  virtual result do_unshift(stateT& state,
        externT* to,          externT* to_limit, externT*& to_next) const;
  virtual int do_encoding() const throw();
  virtual bool do_always_noconv() const throw();
  virtual int do_length(stateT&, const externT* from,
                   const externT* end, size_t max) const;
  virtual result do_unshift(stateT& state,
       externT* to, externT* to_limit, externT*& to_next) const;
  virtual int do_max_length() const throw();
  };
}
```

22.2.2 The numeric category   [lib.category.numeric]

1 The classes num_get<> and num_put<> handle numeric formatting and parsing. Virtual functions are provided for several numeric types. Implementations may (but are not required to) delegate extraction of smaller types to extractors for larger types.[228]

2 All specifications of member functions for num_put and num_get in the subclauses of 22.2.2 only apply to the instantiations required in Tables 51 and 52 (22.1.1.1.1), namely num_get<char>, num_get<wchar_t>, num_get<C, InputIterator>, num_put<char>, num_put<wchar_t>,

---

[228] Parsing "-1" correctly into (e.g.) an unsigned short requires that the corresponding member get() at least extract the sign before delegating.

and num_put<C,OutputIterator>. These instantiations refer to the ios_base& argument for formatting specifications (22.2), and to its imbued locale for the numpunct<> facet to identify all numeric punctuation preferences, and also for the ctype<> facet to perform character classification.

3   Extractor and inserter members of the standard iostreams use num_get<> and num_put<> member functions for formatting and parsing numeric values (27.6.1.2.1, 27.6.2.5.1).

22.2.2.1 Class template num_get   [lib.locale.num.get]

```
namespace std {
  template <class charT, class InputIterator = istreambuf_iterator<charT> >
  class num_get : public locale::facet {
  public:
    typedef charT           char_type;
    typedef InputIterator   iter_type;

    explicit num_get(size_t refs = 0);

    iter_type get(iter_type in, iter_type end, ios_base&,
                  ios_base::iostate& err, bool& v)          const;
    iter_type get(iter_type in, iter_type end, ios_base& ,
                  ios_base::iostate& err, long& v)          const;
    iter_type get(iter_type in, iter_type end, ios_base&,
                  ios_base::iostate& err, unsigned short& v) const;
    iter_type get(iter_type in, iter_type end, ios_base&,
                  ios_base::iostate& err, unsigned int& v)  const;
    iter_type get(iter_type in, iter_type end, ios_base&,
                  ios_base::iostate& err, unsigned long& v) const;
    iter_type get(iter_type in, iter_type end, ios_base&,
                  ios_base::iostate& err, float& v)         const;
    iter_type get(iter_type in, iter_type end, ios_base&,
                  ios_base::iostate& err, double& v)        const;
    iter_type get(iter_type in, iter_type end, ios_base&,
                  ios_base::iostate& err, long double& v)   const;
    iter_type get(iter_type in, iter_type end, ios_base&,
                  ios_base::iostate& err, void*& v)         const;

    static locale::id id;
```

```
      protected:
        ~num_get();                          // virtual
        virtual iter_type do_get(iter_type, iter_type, ios_base&,
            ios_base::iostate& err, bool& v) const;
        virtual iter_type do_get(iter_type, iter_type, ios_base&,
            ios_base::iostate& err, long& v) const;
        virtual iter_type do_get(iter_type, iter_type, ios_base&,
            ios_base::iostate& err, unsigned short& v) const;
        virtual iter_type do_get(iter_type, iter_type, ios_base&,
            ios_base::iostate& err, unsigned int& v) const;
        virtual iter_type do_get(iter_type, iter_type, ios_base&,
            ios_base::iostate& err, unsigned long& v) const;
        virtual iter_type do_get(iter_type, iter_type, ios_base&,
            ios_base::iostate& err, float& v) const;
        virtual iter_type do_get(iter_type, iter_type, ios_base&,
            ios_base::iostate& err, double& v) const;
        virtual iter_type do_get(iter_type, iter_type, ios_base&,
            ios_base::iostate& err, long double& v) const;
        virtual iter_type do_get(iter_type, iter_type, ios_base&,
            ios_base::iostate& err, void*& v) const;
      };
  }
```

1   The facet num_get is used to parse numeric values from an input sequence such as an istream.

22.2.2.1.1 num_get members   [lib.facet.num.get.members]

```
      iter_type get(iter_type in, iter_type end, ios_base& str,
                ios_base::iostate& err, bool& val) const;
      iter_type get(iter_type in, iter_type end, ios_base& str,
                ios_base::iostate& err, long& val) const;
      iter_type get(iter_type in, iter_type end, ios_base& str,
                ios_base::iostate& err, unsigned short& val) const;
      iter_type get(iter_type in, iter_type end, ios_base& str,
                ios_base::iostate& err, unsigned int& val) const;
      iter_type get(iter_type in, iter_type end, ios_base& str,
                ios_base::iostate& err, unsigned long& val) const;
      iter_type get(iter_type in, iter_type end, ios_base& str,
                ios_base::iostate& err, short& val) const;
      iter_type get(iter_type in, iter_type end, ios_base& str,
                ios_base::iostate& err, double& val) const;
      iter_type get(iter_type in, iter_type end, ios_base& str,
                ios_base::iostate& err, long double& val) const;
      iter_type get(iter_type in, iter_type end, ios_base& str,
                ios_base::iostate& err, void*& val) const;
```

1   **Returns:** do_get(*in*, *end*, *str*, *err*, *val*).

22.2.2.1.2 num_get virtual functions   [lib.facet.num.get.virtuals]

```
iter_type do_get(iter_type in, iter_type end, ios_base& str,
                 ios_base::iostate& err, long& val) const;
iter_type do_get(iter_type in, iter_type end, ios_base& str,
                 ios_base::iostate& err, unsigned short& val) const;
iter_type do_get(iter_type in, iter_type end, ios_base& str,
                 ios_base::iostate& err, unsigned int& val) const;
iter_type do_get(iter_type in, iter_type end, ios_base& str,
                 ios_base::iostate& err, unsigned long& val) const;
iter_type do_get(iter_type in, iter_type end, ios_base& str,
                 ios_base::iostate& err, float& val) const;
iter_type do_get(iter_type in, iter_type end, ios_base& str,
                 ios_base::iostate& err, double& val) const;
iter_type do_get(iter_type in, iter_type end, ios_base& str,
                 ios_base::iostate& err, long double& val) const;
iter_type do_get(iter_type in, iter_type end, ios_base& str,
                 ios_base::iostate& err, void*& val) const;
```

1   **Effects:** Reads characters from *in*, interpreting them according to *str*.flags(), use_facet< ctype<charT> >(*loc*), and use_facet< numpunct<charT> >(*loc*), where *loc* is *str*.getloc(). If an error occurs, *val* is unchanged; otherwise it is set to the resulting value.

2   The details of this operation occur in three stages

— Stage 1: Determine a conversion specifier

— Stage 2: Extract characters from *in* and determine a corresponding char value for the format expected by the conversion specification determined in stage 1.

— Stage 3: Store results
The details of the stages are presented below.

3   **Stage 1:** The function initializes local variables via

```
fmtflags flags = str.flags();
fmtflags basefield = (flags & ios_base::basefield);
fmtflags uppercase = (flags & ios_base::uppercase);
fmtflags boolalpha = (flags & ios_base::boolalpha);
```

4   For conversion to an integral type, the function determines the integral conversion specifier as indicated in Table 55. The table is ordered. That is, the first line whose condition is true applies.

Table 55—Integer conversions

State	stdio equivalent
basefield == oct	%o
basefield == hex	%X
basefield == 0	%i
signed integral type	%d
unsigned integral type	%u

5   For conversions to a floating type the specifier is %g.
6   For conversions to void* the specifier is %p.
7   A length specifier is added to the conversion specification, if needed, as indicated in Table 56.

Table 56—Length Modifier

type	length modifier
short	h
unsigned short	h
long	l
unsigned long	l
double	l
long double	L

8   **Stage 2:** If *in==end* then stage 2 terminates. Otherwise a charT is taken from *in* and local variables are initialized as if by

```
char_type ct = *in ;
char c = src[find(atoms, atoms + sizeof(src) - 1, ct) - atoms];
if ( ct ==  use_facet<numpunct<charT> >(loc).decimal_point() )
    c = '.';
bool discard =
    ( ct == use_facet<numpunct<charT> >(loc).thousands_sep()
        &&
    use_facet<numpunct<charT> >(loc).grouping().length() != 0 );
```

where the values src and atoms are defined as if by:

```
static const char src[] = "0123456789abcdefABCDEF+-";
char_type atoms[sizeof(src)];
use_facet<ctype<charT> >(loc).widen(src, src + sizeof(src), atoms);
```

for this value of loc.

9   If *discard* is true then the position of the character is remembered, but the character is otherwise ignored. If it is not discarded, then a check is made to determine if c is allowed as the next character of an input field of the conversion specifier returned by stage 1. If so it is accumulated.

10   If the character is either discarded or accumulated then *in* is advanced by ++in and processing returns to the beginning of stage 2.

11   **Stage 3:** The result of stage 2 processing can be one of

— A sequence of chars has been accumulated in stage 2 that is converted (according to the rules of scanf) to a value of the type of *val*. This value is stored in *val* and ios_base::goodbit is stored in *err*.

— The sequence of chars accumulated in stage 2 would have caused scanf to report an input failure. ios_base::failbit is assigned to *err*.

12   Digit grouping is checked. That is, the positions of discarded separators is examined for consistency with use_facet<numpunct<charT> >(loc).grouping(). If they are not consistent then ios_base::failbit is assigned to *err*.

13   In any case, if stage 2 processing was terminated by the test for *in==end* then *err*|=ios_base::eofbit is performed.

```
iter_type do_get(iter_type in, iter_type end, ios_base& str,
                 ios_base::iostate& err, bool& val) const;
```

14   **Effects:** If (*str*.**flags()&ios_base::boolalpha**)==0 then input proceeds as it would for a long except that if a value is being stored into *val*, the value is determined according to the following: If the value to be stored is 0 then false is stored. If the value is 1 then true is stored. Otherwise *err*|=ios_base::failbit is performed and no value is stored.

15   Otherwise target sequences are determined "as if" by calling the members `falsename()` and `truename()` of the facet obtained by `use_facet<numpunct<charT> >(str.getloc())`. Successive characters in the range `[in,end)` (see 23.1.1) are obtained and matched against corresponding positions in the target sequences only as necessary to identify a unique match. The input iterator `in` is compared to `end` only when necessary to obtain a character. If and only if a target sequence is uniquely matched, `val` is set to the corresponding value.

16   The `in` iterator is always left pointing one position beyond the last character successfully matched. If `val` is set, then `err` is set to `str.goodbit`; or to `str.eofbit` if, when seeking another character to match, it is found that (`in == end`). If `val` is not set, then `err` is set to `str.failbit`; or to (`str.failbit|str.eofbit`) if the reason for the failure was that (`in == end`). [*Example:* For targets `true`: `"a"` and `false`: `"abb"`, the input sequence `"a"` yields `val == true` and `err == str.eofbit`; the input sequence `"abc"` yields `err = str.failbit`, with `in` ending at the `'c'` element. For targets `true`: `"1"` and `false`: `"0"`, the input sequence `"1"` yields `val == true` and `err == str.goodbit`. For empty targets (`""`), any input sequence yields `err == str.failbit`. —*end example*]

17   **Returns:** `in`.

22.2.2.2 Class template `num_put` [lib.locale.nm.put]

```
namespace std {
  template <class charT, class OutputIterator = ostreambuf_iterator<charT> >
  class num_put : public locale::facet {
  public:
    typedef charT          char_type;
    typedef OutputIterator iter_type;

    explicit num_put(size_t refs = 0);

    iter_type put(iter_type s, ios_base& f, char_type fill, bool v) const;
    iter_type put(iter_type s, ios_base& f, char_type fill, long v) const;
    iter_type put(iter_type s, ios_base& f, char_type fill,
                  unsigned long v) const;
    iter_type put(iter_type s, ios_base& f, char_type fill,
                  double v) const;
    iter_type put(iter_type s, ios_base& f, char_type fill,
                  long double v) const;
    iter_type put(iter_type s, ios_base& f, char_type fill,
                  const void* v) const;

    static locale::id id;
```

```
    protected:
      ~num_put();                              // virtual
      virtual iter_type do_put(iter_type, ios_base&, char_type fill,
                             bool v) const;
      virtual iter_type do_put(iter_type, ios_base&, char_type fill,
                             long v) const;
      virtual iter_type do_put(iter_type, ios_base&, char_type fill,
                             unsigned long) const;
      virtual iter_type do_put(iter_type, ios_base&, char_type fill,
                             double v) const;
      virtual iter_type do_put(iter_type, ios_base&, char_type fill,
                             long double v) const;
      virtual iter_type do_put(iter_type, ios_base&, char_type fill,
                             const void* v) const;
    };
  }
```

1   The facet num_put is used to format numeric values to a character sequence such as an ostream.

22.2.2.2.1 num_put members   [lib.facet.num.put.members]

```
      iter_type put(iter_type out, ios_base& str, char_type fill,
                  bool val) const;
      iter_type put(iter_type out, ios_base& str, char_type fill,
                  long val) const;
      iter_type put(iter_type out, ios_base& str, char_type fill,
                  unsigned long val) const;
      iter_type put(iter_type out, ios_base& str, char_type fill,
                  double val) const;
      iter_type put(iter_type out, ios_base& str, char_type fill,
                  long double val) const;
      iter_type put(iter_type out, ios_base& str, char_type fill,
                  const void* val) const;
```

1   **Returns:** do_put(*out*, *str*, *fill*, *val*).

22.2.2.2.2 num_put virtual functions   [lib.facet.num.put.virtuals]

```
      iter_type do_put(iter_type out, ios_base& str, char_type fill,
                     bool val) const;
      iter_type do_put(iter_type out, ios_base& str, char_type fill,
                     long val) const;
      iter_type do_put(iter_type out, ios_base& str, char_type fill,
                     unsigned long val) const;
      iter_type do_put(iter_type out, ios_base& str, char_type fill,
                     double val) const;
      iter_type do_put(iter_type out, ios_base& str, char_type fill,
                     long double val) const;
      iter_type do_put(iter_type out, ios_base& str, char_type fill,
                     const void* val) const;
```

1   **Effects:** Writes characters to the sequence *out*, formatting *val* as desired. In the following description, a local variable initialized with

```
          locale loc = str.getloc();
```

2   The details of this operation occur in several stages:

— Stage 1: Determine a printf conversion specifier *spec* and determining the characters that would be printed by printf(27.8.2) given this conversion specifier for

```
printf(spec, val)
```

assuming that the current locale is the "C" locale.

— Stage 2: Adjust the representation by converting each char determined by stage 1 to a charT using a conversion and values returned by members of use_facet< numpunct<charT> >(str.getloc())

— Stage 3: Determine where padding is required.

— Stage 4: Insert the sequence into the *out*.

3   Detailed descriptions of each stage follow.

4   **Returns:** *out*.

5   **Stage 1:** The first action of stage 1 is to determine a conversion specifier. The tables that describe this determination use the following local variables

```
fmtflags flags = str.flags() ;
fmtflags basefield =  (flags & (ios_base::basefield));
fmtflags uppercase =  (flags & (ios_base::uppercase));
fmtflags floatfield = (flags & (ios_base::floatfield));
fmtflags showpos =    (flags & (ios_base::showpos));
fmtflags showbase =   (flags & (ios_base::showbase));
```

6   All tables used in describing stage 1 are ordered. That is, the first line whose condition is true applies. A line without a condition is the default behavior when none of the earlier lines apply.

7   For conversion from an integral type other than a character type, the function determines the integral conversion specifier as indicated in Table 57.

Table 57—Integer conversions

State	stdio equivalent
basefield == ios_base::oct	%o
(basefield == ios_base::hex) && !uppercase	%x
(basefield == ios_base::hex)	%X
for a signed integral type	%d
for an unsigned integral type	%u

8   For conversion from a floating-point type, the function determines the floating-point conversion specifier as indicated in Table 58:

Table 58—Floating-point conversions

State	stdio equivalent
floatfield == ios_base::fixed	%f
floatfield == ios_base::scientific && !uppercase	%e
floatfield == ios_base::scientific	%E
!uppercase	%g
otherwise	%G

9   For conversions from an integral or floating type a length modifier is added to the conversion specifier as indicated in Table 59.

Table 59—Length modifier

type	length modifier
long	l
unsigned long	l
long double	L
otherwise	*none*

10   The conversion specifier has the following optional additional qualifiers prepended as indicated in Table 60:

Table 60—Numeric conversions

Type(s)	State	`stdio` equivalent
an integral type	flags & showpos	+
	flags & showbase	#
a floating-point type	flags & showpos	+
	flags & showpoint	#

11   For conversion from a floating-point type, if `(flags & fixed) != 0` or if *str.*precision() > 0, then *str.*precision() is specified in the conversion specification.

12   For conversion from `void*` the specifier is `%p`.

13   The representations at the end of stage 1 consists of the `char`'s that would be printed by a call of `printf(s, val)` where *s* is the conversion specifier determined above.

14   **Stage 2:** Any character *c* other than a decimal point(.) is converted to a `charT` via `use_facet<ctype<charT> >(loc).widen(c)`

15   A local variable *punct* is initialized via

        numpunct<charT> punct = use_facet< numpunct<charT> >(str.getloc())

16   For integral types, *punct.*thousands_sep() characters are inserted into the sequence as determined by the value returned by *punct.*do_grouping() using the method described in 22.2.3.1.2

17   Decimal point characters(.) are replaced by *punct.*decimal_point()

18   **Stage 3:** A local variable is initialized as

            fmtflags adjustfield=   (flags & (ios_base::adjustfield));

19   The location of any padding[229] is determined according to Table 61:

---

[229] The conversion specification #o generates a leading 0 which is *not* a padding character.

Table 61—Fill padding

State	Location
`adjustfield == ios_base::left`	pad after
`adjustfield == ios_base::right`	pad before
`adjustfield == internal` and a sign occurs in the representation	pad after the sign
`adjustfield == internal` and representation after stage 1 began with 0x or 0X	pad after x or X
otherwise	pad before

20 If *str*.width() is nonzero and the number of charT's in the sequence after stage 2 is less than *str*.width(), then enough *fill* characters are added to the sequence at the position indicated for padding to bring the length of the sequence to *str*.width().

21 *str*.width(0) is called.

22 **Stage 4:** The sequence of charT's at the end of stage 3 are output via

```
*out++ = c
```

```
iter_type put(iter_type out, ios_base& str, char_type fill,
              bool val) const;
```

23 **Effects:** If (*str*.flags()&ios_base::boolalpha)==0 then do

```
out = do_put(out, str, fill, (int)val)
```

Otherwise do

```
const numpunct<charT>& np = use_facet<numpunct<charT> >(loc);
string_type s = val ? np.truename() : np.falsename();
```

and then insert the characters of *s* into *out*. *out*.

22.2.3 The numeric punctuation facet   [lib.facet.numpunct]

22.2.3.1 Class template `numpunct`   [lib.locale.numpunct]

```
namespace std {
  template <class charT>
  class numpunct : public locale::facet {
  public:
    typedef charT            char_type;
    typedef basic_string<charT> string_type;

    explicit numpunct(size_t refs = 0);

    char_type    decimal_point()   const;
    char_type    thousands_sep()   const;
    string       grouping()        const;
    string_type  truename()        const;
    string_type  falsename()       const;

    static locale::id id;
```

```
       protected:
        ~numpunct();                            // virtual
          virtual char_type      do_decimal_point() const;
          virtual char_type      do_thousands_sep() const;
          virtual string         do_grouping()     const;
          virtual string_type    do_truename()     const;    // for bool
          virtual string_type    do_falsename()    const;    // for bool
        };
     }
```

1   numpunct<> specifies numeric punctuation. The instantiations required in Table 51 (22.1.1.1.1), namely
     numpunct<wchar_t> and numpunct<char>, provide classic "C" numeric formats, i.e. they contain
     information equivalent to that contained in the "C" locale or their wide character counterparts as if obtained
     by a call to widen.

2   The syntax for number formats is as follows, where digit represents the radix set specified by the
     fmtflags argument value, whitespace is as determined by the facet ctype<charT> (22.2.1.1), and
     thousands-sep and decimal-point are the results of corresponding numpunct<charT> mem-
     bers. Integer values have the format:

```
          integer     ::= [sign] units
          sign        ::= plusminus [whitespace]
          plusminus   ::= '+' | '-'
          units       ::= digits [thousands-sep units]
          digits      ::= digit [digits]
```

     and floating-point values have:

```
          floatval ::= [sign] units [decimal-point [digits]] [e [sign] digits] |
                       [sign]          decimal-point  digits  [e [sign] digits]
          e        ::= 'e' | 'E'
```

     where the number of digits between thousands-seps is as specified by do_grouping(). For pars-
     ing, if the digits portion contains no thousands-separators, no grouping constraint is applied.

22.2.3.1.1 numpunct members   [lib.facet.numpunct.members]

```
       char_type decimal_point() const;
```

1   **Returns:** do_decimal_point()

```
       char_type thousands_sep() const;
```

2   **Returns:** do_thousands_sep()

```
       string grouping()  const;
```

3   **Returns:** do_grouping()

```
       string_type truename()  const;
       string_type falsename() const;
```

4   **Returns:** do_truename() or do_falsename(), respectively.

22.2.3.1.2 **numpunct virtual functions** [lib.facet.numpunct.virtuals]

```
char_type do_decimal_point() const;
```

1 **Returns:** A character for use as the decimal radix separator. The required instantiations return `' . '` or `L' . '`.

```
char_type do_thousands_sep() const;
```

2 **Returns:** A character for use as the digit group separator. The required instantiations return `' , '` or `L' , '`.

```
string do_grouping() const;
```

3 **Returns:** A basic_string<char> *vec* used as a vector of integer values, in which each element *vec*[i] represents the number of digits[230] in the group at position *i*, starting with position 0 as the rightmost group. If *vec*.size() <= *i*, the number is the same as group (*i*-1); if (*i*<0 || *vec*[i]<=0 || *vec*[i]==CHAR_MAX), the size of the digit group is unlimited.
The required instantiations return the empty string, indicating no grouping.

```
string_type do_truename()  const;
string_type do_falsename() const;
```

4 **Returns:** A string representing the name of the boolean value `true` or `false`, respectively.
In the base class implementation these names are `"true"` and `"false"`, or `L"true"` and `L"false"`.

22.2.3.2 **Class template numpunct_byname** [lib.locale.numpunct.byname]

```
namespace std {
  template <class charT>
  class numpunct_byname : public numpunct<charT> {
// this class is specialized for char and wchar_t.
  public:
    typedef charT              char_type;
    typedef basic_string<charT> string_type;
    explicit numpunct_byname(const char*, size_t refs = 0);
  protected:
   ~numpunct_byname();              // virtual
    virtual char_type    do_decimal_point() const;
    virtual char_type    do_thousands_sep() const;
    virtual string       do_grouping()      const;
    virtual string_type  do_truename()      const;    // for bool
    virtual string_type  do_falsename()     const;    // for bool
  };
}
```

---

[230] Thus, the string `"\003"` specifies groups of 3 digits each, and `"3"` probably indicates groups of 51 (!) digits each, because 51 is the ASCII value of `"3"`.

22.2.4 The collate category   [lib.category.collate]

22.2.4.1 Class template `collate`   [lib.locale.collate]

```
namespace std {
  template <class charT>
  class collate : public locale::facet {
  public:
    typedef charT               char_type;
    typedef basic_string<charT> string_type;

    explicit collate(size_t refs = 0);

    int compare(const charT* low1, const charT* high1,
                const charT* low2, const charT* high2) const;
    string_type transform(const charT* low, const charT* high) const;
    long hash(const charT* low, const charT* high) const;

    static locale::id id;

  protected:
    ~collate();                           // virtual
    virtual int     do_compare(const charT* low1, const charT* high1,
                               const charT* low2, const charT* high2) const;
    virtual string_type do_transform
                              (const charT* low, const charT* high) const;
    virtual long    do_hash   (const charT* low, const charT* high) const;
  };
}
```

1   The class `collate<charT>` provides features for use in the collation (comparison) and hashing of strings. A locale member function template, `operator()`, uses the collate facet to allow a locale to act directly as the predicate argument for standard algorithms (clause 25) and containers operating on strings. The instantiations required in Table 51 (22.1.1.1.1), namely `collate<char>` and `collate<wchar_t>`, apply lexicographic ordering (25.3.8).

2   Each function compares a string of characters `*p` in the range `[low, high)`.

22.2.4.1.1 `collate` members   [lib.locale.collate.members]

```
int compare(const charT* low1, const charT* high1,
            const charT* low2, const charT* high2) const;
```

1   **Returns:** `do_compare(low1, high1, low2, high2)`

```
string_type transform(const charT* low, const charT* high) const;
```

2   **Returns:** `do_transform(low, high)`

```
long hash(const charT* low, const charT* high) const;
```

3   **Returns:** `do_hash(low, high)`

22.2.4.1.2 collate virtual functions **[lib.locale.collate.virtuals]**

```
int do_compare(const charT* low1, const charT* high1,
               const charT* low2, const charT* high2) const;
```

1 **Returns:** 1 if the first string is greater than the second, -1 if less, zero otherwise. The instantiations required in the Table 51 (22.1.1.1.1), namely collate<char> and collate<wchar_t>, implement a lexicographical comparison (25.3.8).

```
string_type do_transform(const charT* low, const charT* high) const;
```

2 **Returns:** A basic_string<charT> value that, compared lexicographically with the result of calling transform() on another string, yields the same result as calling do_compare() on the same two strings.[231]

```
long do_hash(const charT* low, const charT* high) const;
```

3 **Returns:** An integer value equal to the result of calling hash() on any other string for which do_compare() returns 0 (equal) when passed the two strings. [*Note:* The probability that the result equals that for another string which does not compare equal should be very small, approaching (1.0/numeric_limits<unsigned long>::max()). —*end note*]

22.2.4.2 Class template collate_byname [lib.locale.collate.byname]

```
namespace std {
  template <class charT>
  class collate_byname : public collate<charT> {
  public:
    typedef basic_string<charT> string_type;
    explicit collate_byname(const char*, size_t refs = 0);
  protected:
    ~collate_byname();              // virtual
    virtual int    do_compare(const charT* low1, const charT* high1,
                              const charT* low2, const charT* high2) const;
    virtual string_type do_transform
                              (const charT* low, const charT* high) const;
    virtual long   do_hash  (const charT* low, const charT* high) const;
  };
}
```

22.2.5 The time category [lib.category.time]

1 Templates time_get<charT,InputIterator> and time_put<charT,OutputIterator> provide date and time formatting and parsing. All specifications of member functions for time_put and time_get in the subclauses of 22.2.5 only apply to the instantiations required in Tables 51 and 52 (22.1.1.1.1). Their members use their ios_base&, ios_base::iostate&, and *fill* arguments as described in (22.2), and the ctype<> facet, to determine formatting details.

---
[231] This function is useful when one string is being compared to many other strings.

22.2.5.1 Class template `time_get`   **[lib.locale.time.get]**

```
namespace std {
  class time_base {
  public:
    enum dateorder { no_order, dmy, mdy, ymd, ydm };
  };

  template <class charT, class InputIterator = istreambuf_iterator<charT> >
  class time_get : public locale::facet, public time_base {
  public:
    typedef charT           char_type;
    typedef InputIterator   iter_type;

    explicit time_get(size_t refs = 0);

    dateorder date_order()  const { return do_date_order(); }
    iter_type get_time(iter_type s, iter_type end, ios_base& f,
                       ios_base::iostate& err, tm* t)  const;
    iter_type get_date(iter_type s, iter_type end, ios_base& f,
                       ios_base::iostate& err, tm* t)  const;
    iter_type get_weekday(iter_type s, iter_type end, ios_base& f,
                          ios_base::iostate& err, tm* t) const;
    iter_type get_monthname(iter_type s, iter_type end, ios_base& f,
                            ios_base::iostate& err, tm* t) const;
    iter_type get_year(iter_type s, iter_type end, ios_base& f,
                       ios_base::iostate& err, tm* t) const;

    static locale::id id;

  protected:
    ~time_get();                         // virtual
    virtual dateorder do_date_order()  const;
    virtual iter_type do_get_time(iter_type s, iter_type end, ios_base&,
                                  ios_base::iostate& err, tm* t) const;
    virtual iter_type do_get_date(iter_type s, iter_type end, ios_base&,
                                  ios_base::iostate& err, tm* t) const;
    virtual iter_type do_get_weekday(iter_type s, iter_type end, ios_base&,
                                     ios_base::iostate& err, tm* t) const;
    virtual iter_type do_get_monthname(iter_type s, iter_type end, ios_base&,
                                       ios_base::iostate& err, tm* t) const;
    virtual iter_type do_get_year(iter_type s, iter_type end, ios_base&,
                                  ios_base::iostate& err, tm* t) const;
  };
}
```

1   `time_get` is used to parse a character sequence, extracting components of a time or date into a `struct tm` record. Each `get` member parses a format as produced by a corresponding format specifier to `time_put<>::put`. If the sequence being parsed matches the correct format, the corresponding members of the `struct tm` argument are set to the values used to produce the sequence; otherwise either an error is reported or unspecified values are assigned.[232]

---

[232] In other words, user confirmation is required for reliable parsing of user-entered dates and times, but machine-generated formats can be parsed reliably. This allows parsers to be aggressive about interpreting user variations on standard formats.

22.2.5.1.1 `time_get` members **[lib.locale.time.get.members]**

```
dateorder date_order() const;
```

1 **Returns:** `do_date_order()`

```
iter_type get_time(iter_type s, iter_type end, ios_base& str,
                   ios_base::iostate& err, tm* t) const;
```

2 **Returns:** `do_get_time(s, end, str, err, t)`

```
iter_type get_date(iter_type s, iter_type end, ios_base& str,
                   ios_base::iostate& err, tm* t) const;
```

3 **Returns:** `do_get_date(s, end, str, err, t)`

```
iter_type get_weekday(iter_type s, iter_type end, ios_base& str,
                      ios_base::iostate& err, tm* t) const;
iter_type get_monthname(iter_type s, iter_type end, ios_base& str,
                        ios_base::iostate& err, tm* t) const;
```

4 **Returns:** `do_get_weekday(s, end, str, err, t)` or `do_get_monthname(s, end, str, err, t)`

```
iter_type get_year(iter_type s, iter_type end, ios_base& str,
                   ios_base::iostate& err, tm* t) const;
```

5 **Returns:** `do_get_year(s, end, str, err, t)`

22.2.5.1.2 `time_get` virtual functions **[lib.locale.time.get.virtuals]**

```
dateorder do_date_order() const;
```

1 **Returns:** An enumeration value indicating the preferred order of components for those date formats that are composed of day, month, and year.[233] Returns `no_order` if the date format specified by `'x'` contains other variable components (e.g. Julian day, week number, week day).

```
iter_type do_get_time(iter_type s, iter_type end, ios_base& str,
                      ios_base::iostate& err, tm* t) const;
```

2 **Effects:** Reads characters starting at `s` until it has extracted those `struct tm` members, and remaining format characters, used by `time_put<>::put` to produce the format specified by `'X'`, or until it encounters an error or end of sequence.

3 **Returns:** An iterator pointing immediately beyond the last character recognized as possibly part of a valid time.

```
iter_type do_get_date(iter_type s, iter_type end, ios_base& str,
                      ios_base::iostate& err, tm* t) const;
```

4 **Effects:** Reads characters starting at `s` until it has extracted those `struct tm` members, and remaining format characters, used by `time_put<>::put` to produce the format specified by `'x'`, or until it encounters an error.

5 **Returns:** An iterator pointing immediately beyond the last character recognized as possibly part of a valid date.

---

[233] This function is intended as a convenience only, for common formats, and may return `no_order` in valid locales.

```
iter_type do_get_weekday(iter_type s, iter_type end, ios_base& str,
                         ios_base::iostate& err, tm* t) const;
iter_type do_get_monthname(iter_type s, iter_type end, ios_base& str,
                           ios_base::iostate& err, tm* t) const;
```

6   **Effects:** Reads characters starting at *s* until it has extracted the (perhaps abbreviated) name of a weekday or month. If it finds an abbreviation that is followed by characters that could match a full name, it continues reading until it matches the full name or fails. It sets the appropriate struct tm member accordingly.

7   **Returns:** An iterator pointing immediately beyond the last character recognized as part of a valid name.

```
iter_type do_get_year(iter_type s, iter_type end, ios_base& str,
                      ios_base::iostate& err, tm* t) const;
```

8   **Effects:** Reads characters starting at *s* until it has extracted an unambiguous year identifier. It is implementation-defined whether two-digit year numbers are accepted, and (if so) what century they are assumed to lie in. Sets the t->tm_year member accordingly.

9   **Returns:** An iterator pointing immediately beyond the last character recognized as part of a valid year identifier.

22.2.5.2 Class template time_get_byname   [lib.locale.time.get.byname]

```
namespace std {
  template <class charT, class InputIterator = istreambuf_iterator<charT> >
  class time_get_byname : public time_get<charT, InputIterator> {
  public:
    typedef time_base::dateorder dateorder;
    typedef InputIterator        iter_type;

    explicit time_get_byname(const char*, size_t refs = 0);
  protected:
   ~time_get_byname();              // virtual
    virtual dateorder do_date_order()  const;
    virtual iter_type do_get_time(iter_type s, iter_type end, ios_base&,
                                  ios_base::iostate& err, tm* t) const;

    virtual iter_type do_get_date(iter_type s, iter_type end, ios_base&,
                                  ios_base::iostate& err, tm* t) const;
    virtual iter_type do_get_weekday(iter_type s, iter_type end, ios_base&,
                                     ios_base::iostate& err, tm* t) const;
    virtual iter_type do_get_monthname(iter_type s, iter_type end, ios_base&,
                                       ios_base::iostate& err, tm* t) const;
    virtual iter_type do_get_year(iter_type s, iter_type end, ios_base&,
                                  ios_base::iostate& err, tm* t) const;
  };
}
```

22.2.5.3 Class template time_put   [lib.locale.time.put]

```
namespace std {
  template <class charT, class OutputIterator = ostreambuf_iterator<charT> >
  class time_put : public locale::facet {
  public:
    typedef charT          char_type;
    typedef OutputIterator iter_type;

    explicit time_put(size_t refs = 0);
```

```
                   // the following is implemented in terms of other member functions.
      iter_type put(iter_type s, ios_base& f, char_type fill, const tm* tmb,
                    const charT* pattern, const charT* pat_end) const;
      iter_type put(iter_type s, ios_base& f, char_type fill,
                    const tm* tmb, char format, char modifier = 0) const;

      static locale::id id;

    protected:
      ~time_put();                      // virtual
        virtual iter_type do_put(iter_type s, ios_base&, char_type, const tm* t,
                                 char format, char modifier) const;
      };
    }
```

22.2.5.3.1 `time_put` members   [lib.locale.time.put.members]

```
      iter_type put(iter_type s, ios_base& str, char_type fill, const tm* t,
              const charT* pattern, const charT* pat_end) const;
      iter_type put(iter_type s, ios_base& str, char_type fill, const tm* t,
              char format, char modifier = 0) const;
```

1   **Effects:** The first form steps through the sequence from `pattern` to `pat_end`, identifying characters that are part of a format sequence. Each character that is not part of a format sequence is written to `s` immediately, and each format sequence, as it is identified, results in a call to `do_put`; thus, format elements and other characters are interleaved in the output in the order in which they appear in the pattern. Format sequences are identified by converting each character `c` to a `char` value as if by `ct.narrow(c, 0)`, where `ct` is a reference to `ctype<charT>` obtained from `str.getloc()`. The first character of each sequence is equal to `'%'`, followed by an optional modifier character `mod`[234] and a format specifier character `spec` as defined for the function `strftime`. If no modifier character is present, `mod` is zero. For each valid format sequence identified, calls `do_put(s, str, fill, t, spec, mod)`.

2   The second form calls `do_put(s, str, fill, t, format, modifier)`.

2a [*Note:* The `fill` argument may be used in the implementation-defined formats, or by derivations. A space character is a reasonable default for this argument.   —*end note*]

3   **Returns:** An iterator pointing immediately after the last character produced.

22.2.5.3.2 `time_put` virtual functions   [lib.locale.time.put.virtuals]

```
      iter_type do_put(iter_type s, ios_base&, char_type fill, const tm* t,
              char format, char modifier) const;
```

1   **Effects:** Formats the contents of the parameter `t` into characters placed on the output sequence `s`. Formatting is controlled by the parameters `format` and `modifier`, interpreted identically as the format specifiers in the string argument to the standard library function `strftime()`.[235] except that the sequence of characters produced for those specifiers that are described as depending on the C locale are instead implementation-defined.[236]

2   **Returns:** An iterator pointing immediately after the last character produced.

---

[234] Although the C programming language defines no modifiers, most vendors do.

[235] Interpretation of the `modifier` argument is implementation-defined, but should follow POSIX conventions.

[236] Implementations are encouraged to refer to other standards (such as POSIX) for these definitions.

22.2.5.4 Class template `time_put_byname`   [lib.locale.time.put.byname]

```
namespace std {
  template <class charT, class OutputIterator = ostreambuf_iterator<charT> >
  class time_put_byname : public time_put<charT, OutputIterator>
  {
  public:
    typedef charT          char_type;
    typedef OutputIterator iter_type;

    explicit time_put_byname(const char*, size_t refs = 0);
  protected:
    ~time_put_byname();            // virtual
    virtual iter_type do_put(iter_type s, ios_base&, char_type, const tm* t,
                             char format, char modifier) const;
  };
}
```

22.2.6 The monetary category   [lib.category.monetary]

1   These templates handle monetary formats. A template parameter indicates whether local or international monetary formats are to be used.

2   All specifications of member functions for `money_put` and `money_get` in the subclauses of 22.2.6 only apply to the instantiations required in Tables 51 and 52 (22.1.1.1.1). Their members use their `ios_base&`, `ios_base::iostate&`, and *fill* arguments as described in (22.2), and the `moneypunct<>` and `ctype<>` facets, to determine formatting details.

22.2.6.1 Class template `money_get`   [lib.locale.money.get]

```
namespace std {
  template <class charT,
            class InputIterator = istreambuf_iterator<charT> >
  class money_get : public locale::facet {
  public:
    typedef charT             char_type;
    typedef InputIterator     iter_type;
    typedef basic_string<charT> string_type;

    explicit money_get(size_t refs = 0);

    iter_type get(iter_type s, iter_type end, bool intl,
                  ios_base& f, ios_base::iostate& err,
                  long double& units) const;
    iter_type get(iter_type s, iter_type end, bool intl,
                  ios_base& f, ios_base::iostate& err,
                  string_type& digits) const;

    static locale::id id;

  protected:
    ~money_get();                  // virtual
    virtual iter_type do_get(iter_type, iter_type, bool, ios_base&,
                    ios_base::iostate& err, long double& units) const;
    virtual iter_type do_get(iter_type, iter_type, bool, ios_base&,
                    ios_base::iostate& err, string_type& digits) const;
  };
}
```

22.2.6.1.1 money_get members   **[lib.locale.money.get.members]**

```
iter_type get(iter_type s, iter_type end, bool intl,
              ios_base& f, ios_base::iostate& err,
              long double& quant) const;
iter_type get(s, iter_type end, bool intl, ios_base&f,
              ios_base::iostate& err, string_type& quant) const;
```

1   **Returns:** do_get(*s, end, intl, f, err, quant*)

22.2.6.1.2 money_get virtual functions   **[lib.locale.money.get.virtuals]**

```
iter_type do_get(iter_type s, iter_type end, bool intl,
                 ios_base& str, ios_base::iostate& err,
                 long double& units) const;
iter_type do_get(iter_type s, iter_type end, bool intl,
                 ios_base& str, ios_base::iostate& err,
                 string_type& digits) const;
```

1   **Effects:** Reads characters from s to parse and construct a monetary value according to the format specified by a moneypunct<charT, Intl> facet reference mp and the character mapping specified by a ctype<charT> facet reference ct obtained from the locale returned by str.getloc(), and str.flags(). If a valid sequence is recognized, does not change *err*; otherwise, sets *err* to (*err*|*str*.failbit), or (*err*|*str*.failbit|*str*.eofbit) if no more characters are available, and does not change *units* or *digits*. Uses the pattern returned by mp.neg_format() to parse all values. The result is returned as an integral value stored in units or as a sequence of digits possibly preceded by a minus sign (as produced by ct.widen(c) where c is '-' or in the range from '0' through '9', inclusive) stored in digits. [*Example:* The sequence $1,056.23 in a common United States locale would yield, for units, 105623, or, for digits, "105623". —*end example*] If mp.grouping() indicates that no thousands separators are permitted, any such characters are not read, and parsing is terminated at the point where they first appear. Otherwise, thousands separators are optional; if present, they are checked for correct placement only after all format components have been read.

2   Where space or none appears in the format pattern, except at the end, optional white space (as recognized by ct.is) is consumed after any required space. If (str.flags() & str.showbase) is false, the currency symbol is optional and is consumed only if other characters are needed to complete the format; otherwise, the currency symbol is required.

3   If the first character (if any) in the string pos returned by mp.positive_sign() or the string neg returned by mp.negative_sign() is recognized in the position indicated by sign in the format pattern, it is consumed and any remaining characters in the string are required after all the other format components. [*Example:* If showbase is off, then for a neg value of "()" and a currency symbol of "L", in "(100 L)" the "L" is consumed; but if neg is "-", the "L" in "-100 L" is not consumed.] If pos or neg is empty, the sign component is optional, and if no sign is detected, the result is given the sign that corresponds to the source of the empty string. Otherwise, the character in the indicated position must match the first character of pos or neg, and the result is given the corresponding sign. If the first character of pos is equal to the first character of neg, or if both strings are empty, the result is given a positive sign.

4   Digits in the numeric monetary component are extracted and placed in digits, or into a character buffer buf1 for conversion to produce a value for units, in the order in which they appear, preceded by a minus sign if and only if the result is negative. The value units is produced as if by[237]

---

[237] The semantics here are different from ct.narrow.

```
for (int i = 0; i < n; ++i)
        buf2[i] = src[find(atoms, atoms+sizeof(src), buf1[i]) - atoms];
buf2[n] = 0;
sscanf(buf2, "%Lf", &units);
```

where n is the number of characters placed in buf1, buf2 is a character buffer, and the values src and atoms are defined as if by

```
static const char src[] = "0123456789-";
charT atoms[sizeof(src)];
ct.widen(src, src + sizeof(src) - 1, atoms);
```

5   **Returns:** An iterator pointing immediately beyond the last character recognized as part of a valid monetary quantity.

22.2.6.2 Class template `money_put`   [lib.locale.money.put]

```
namespace std {
  template <class charT,
            class OutputIterator = ostreambuf_iterator<charT> >
  class money_put : public locale::facet {
  public:
    typedef charT              char_type;
    typedef OutputIterator     iter_type;
    typedef basic_string<charT> string_type;

    explicit money_put(size_t refs = 0);

    iter_type put(iter_type s, bool intl, ios_base& f,
                  char_type fill, long double units) const;
    iter_type put(iter_type s, bool intl, ios_base& f,
                  char_type fill, const string_type& digits) const;

    static locale::id id;

  protected:
    ~money_put();                       // virtual
    virtual iter_type
      do_put(iter_type, bool, ios_base&, char_type fill,
             long double units) const;
    virtual iter_type
      do_put(iter_type, bool, ios_base&, char_type fill,
             const string_type& digits) const;
  };
}
```

22.2.6.2.1 `money_put` members   [lib.locale.money.put.members]

```
iter_type put(iter_type s, bool intl, ios_base& f, char_type fill,
              long double quant) const;
iter_type put(iter_type s, bool intl, ios_base& f, char_type fill,
              const string_type& quant) const;
```

1   **Returns:** do_put(s, intl, f, loc, quant)

22.2.6.2.2 money_put virtual functions   **[lib.locale.money.put.virtuals]**

```
iter_type do_put(iter_type s, bool intl, ios_base& str,
                 char_type fill, long double units) const;
iter_type do_put(iter_type s, bool intl, ios_base& str,
                 char_type fill, const string_type& digits) const;
```

1   **Effects:** Writes characters to s according to the format specified by a moneypunct<charT, Intl> facet reference mp and the character mapping specified by a ctype<charT> facet reference ct obtained from the locale returned by str.getloc(), and str.flags(). The argument units is transformed into a sequence of wide characters as if by

```
ct.widen(buf1, buf1 + sprintf(buf1, "%.01f", units), buf2)
```

for character buffers buf1 and buf2. If the first character in digits or buf2 is equal to ct.widen('-'), then the pattern used for formatting is the result of mp.neg_format(); otherwise the pattern is the result of mp.pos_format(). Digit characters are written, interspersed with any thousands separators and decimal point specified by the format, in the order they appear (after the optional leading minus sign) in digits or buf2. In digits, only the optional leading minus sign and the immediately subsequent digit characters (as classified according to ct) are used; any trailing characters (including digits appearing after a non-digit character) are ignored. Calls str.width(0).

2   **Notes:** The currency symbol is generated if and only if (str.flags() & str.showbase) is nonzero. If the number of characters generated for the specified format is less than the value returned by str.width() on entry to the function, then copies of fill are inserted as necessary to pad to the specified width. For the value af equal to (str.flags() & str.adjustfield), if (af == str.internal) is true, the fill characters are placed where none or space appears in the formatting pattern; otherwise if (af == str.left) is true, they are placed after the other characters; otherwise, they are placed before the other characters. [*Note:* It is possible, with some combinations of format patterns and flag values, to produce output that cannot be parsed using num_get<>::get. —*end note*]

3   **Returns:** An iterator pointing immediately after the last character produced.

22.2.6.3 Class template moneypunct   [lib.locale.moneypunct]

```
namespace std {
  class money_base {
  public:
    enum part { none, space, symbol, sign, value };
    struct pattern { char field[4]; };
  };

  template <class charT, bool International = false>
  class moneypunct : public locale::facet, public money_base {
  public:
    typedef charT char_type;
    typedef basic_string<charT> string_type;

    explicit moneypunct(size_t refs = 0);

    charT        decimal_point() const;
    charT        thousands_sep() const;
    string       grouping()      const;
    string_type  curr_symbol()   const;
    string_type  positive_sign() const;
    string_type  negative_sign() const;
    int          frac_digits()   const;
    pattern      pos_format()    const;
    pattern      neg_format()    const;
```

```
        static locale::id id;
        static const bool intl = International;

    protected:
      ~moneypunct();                          // virtual
        virtual charT          do_decimal_point()  const;
        virtual charT          do_thousands_sep()  const;
        virtual string         do_grouping()       const;
        virtual string_type    do_curr_symbol()    const;
        virtual string_type    do_positive_sign()  const;
        virtual string_type    do_negative_sign()  const;
        virtual int            do_frac_digits()    const;
        virtual pattern        do_pos_format()     const;
        virtual pattern        do_neg_format()     const;
    };
}
```

1   The moneypunct<> facet defines monetary formatting parameters used by money_get<> and
      money_put<>. A monetary format is a sequence of four components, specified by a pattern value p,
      such that the part value static_cast<part>(p.field[i]) determines the ith component of the
      format[238] In the field member of a pattern object, each value symbol, sign, value, and either
      space or none appears exactly once. The value none, if present, is not first; the value space, if pre-
      sent, is neither first nor last.

2   Where none or space appears, white space is permitted in the format, except where none appears at the
      end, in which case no white space is permitted. The value space indicates that at least one space is
      required at that position. Where symbol appears, the sequence of characters returned by
      curr_symbol() is permitted, and can be required. Where sign appears, the first (if any) of the
      sequence of characters returned by positive_sign() or negative_sign() (respectively as the
      monetary value is non-negative or negative) is required. Any remaining characters of the sign sequence are
      required after all other format components. Where value appears, the absolute numeric monetary value is
      required.

3   The format of the numeric monetary value is a decimal number:

```
        value ::= units [ decimal-point [ digits ]] |
          decimal-point digits
```

      if frac_digits() returns a positive value, or

```
        value ::= units
```

      otherwise. The symbol decimal-point indicates the character returned by decimal_point(). The
      other symbols are defined as follows:

```
        units ::= digits [ thousands-sep units ]
        digits ::= adigit [ digits ]
```

      In the syntax specification, the symbol adigit is any of the values ct.widen(c) for c in the range
      '0' through '9', inclusive, and ct is a reference of type const ctype<charT>& obtained as
      described in the definitions of money_get<> and money_put<>. The symbol thousands-sep is
      the character returned by thousands_sep(). The space character used is the value ct.widen(' ').
      White space characters are those characters c for which ci.is(space, c) returns true. The number
      of digits required after the decimal point (if any) is exactly the value returned by frac_digits().

4   The placement of thousands-separator characters (if any) is determined by the value returned by
      grouping(), defined identically as the member numpunct<>::do_grouping().

---

[238] An array of char, rather than an array of part, is specified for pattern::field purely for efficiency.

22.2.6.3.1 moneypunct members   [lib.locale.moneypunct.members]

```
charT        decimal_point()  const;
charT        thousands_sep()  const;
string       grouping()       const;
string_type  curr_symbol()    const;
string_type  positive_sign()  const;
string_type  negative_sign()  const;
int          frac_digits()    const;
pattern      pos_format()     const;
pattern      neg_format()     const;
```

1   Each of these functions F returns the result of calling the corresponding virtual member function do_*F*().

22.2.6.3.2 moneypunct virtual functions   [lib.locale.moneypunct.virtuals]

```
charT do_decimal_point() const;
```

1   **Returns:** The radix separator to use in case do_frac_digits() is greater than zero.[239]

```
charT do_thousands_sep() const;
```

2   **Returns:** The digit group separator to use in case do_grouping() specifies a digit grouping pattern.[240]

```
string      do_grouping() const;
```

3   **Returns:** A pattern defined identically as the result of numpunct<charT>::do_grouping().[241]

```
string_type do_curr_symbol() const;
```

4   **Returns:** A string to use as the currency identifier symbol.[242]

```
string_type do_positive_sign() const;
string_type do_negative_sign() const;
```

5   **Returns:** do_positive_sign() returns the string to use to indicate a positive monetary value;[243] do_negative_sign() returns the string to use to indicate a negative value.

```
int do_frac_digits() const;
```

6   **Returns:** The number of digits after the decimal radix separator, if any.[244]

```
pattern do_pos_format() const;
pattern do_neg_format() const;
```

7   **Returns:** The instantiations required in Table 51 (22.1.1.1.1), namely moneypunct<char>, moneypunct<wchar_t>, moneypunct<char,true>, and moneypunct<wchar_t,true>, return an object of type pattern initialized to { symbol, sign, none, value }.[245]

---

[239] In common U.S. locales this is '.'.
[240] In common U.S. locales this is ','.
[241] This is most commonly the value "\003" (*not* "3").
[242] For international instantiations (second template parameter true) this is always four characters long, usually three letters and a space.
[243] This is usually the empty string.
[244] In common U.S. locales, this is 2.
[245] Note that the international symbol returned by do_curr_sym() usually contains a space, itself; for example, "USD ".

22.2.6.4 Class template `moneypunct_byname`　　　　　　**[lib.locale.moneypunct.byname]**

```
namespace std {
  template <class charT, bool Intl = false>
  class moneypunct_byname : public moneypunct<charT, Intl> {
  public:
    typedef money_base::pattern pattern;
    typedef basic_string<charT> string_type;

    explicit moneypunct_byname(const char*, size_t refs = 0);
  protected:
    ~moneypunct_byname();            // virtual
    virtual charT        do_decimal_point()  const;
    virtual charT        do_thousands_sep()  const;
    virtual string       do_grouping()       const;
    virtual string_type  do_curr_symbol()    const;
    virtual string_type  do_positive_sign()  const;
    virtual string_type  do_negative_sign()  const;
    virtual int          do_frac_digits()    const;
    virtual pattern      do_pos_format()     const;
    virtual pattern      do_neg_format()     const;
  };
}
```

22.2.7 The message retrieval category　　　　　　　　　　　　**[lib.category.messages]**

1　　Class `messages<charT>` implements retrieval of strings from message catalogs.

22.2.7.1 Class template `messages`　　　　　　　　　　　　　**[lib.locale.messages]**

```
namespace std {
  class messages_base {
  public:
    typedef int catalog;
  };

  template <class charT>
  class messages : public locale::facet, public messages_base {
  public:
    typedef charT char_type;
    typedef basic_string<charT> string_type;

    explicit messages(size_t refs = 0);

    catalog open(const basic_string<char>& fn, const locale&) const;
    string_type  get(catalog c, int set, int msgid,
                   const string_type& dfault) const;
    void     close(catalog c) const;

    static locale::id id;

  protected:
    ~messages();                    // virtual
    virtual catalog do_open(const basic_string<char>&, const locale&) const;
    virtual string_type  do_get(catalog, int set, int msgid,
                         const string_type& dfault) const;
    virtual void    do_close(catalog) const;
  };
}
```

1   Values of type messages_base::catalog usable as arguments to members get and close can be obtained only by calling member open.

22.2.7.1.1 messages members   [lib.locale.messages.members]

```
catalog open(const basic_string<char>& name, const locale& loc) const;
```

1   **Returns:** do_open(name, loc).

```
string_type get(catalog cat, int set, int msgid,
                const string_type& dfault) const;
```

2   **Returns:** do_get(cat, set, msgid, dfault).

```
void  close(catalog cat) const;
```

3   **Effects:** Calls do_close(cat).

22.2.7.1.2 messages virtual functions   [lib.locale.messages.virtuals]

```
catalog do_open(const basic_string<char>& name,
                const locale& loc) const;
```

1   **Returns:** A value that may be passed to get() to retrieve a message, from the message catalog identified by the string name according to an implementation-defined mapping. The result can be used until it is passed to close().
Returns a value less than 0 if no such catalog can be opened.

2   **Notes:** The locale argument loc is used for character set code conversion when retrieving messages, if needed.

```
string_type do_get(catalog cat, int set, int msgid,
                   const string_type& dfault) const;
```

3   **Requires:** A catalog cat obtained from open() and not yet closed.
4   **Returns:** A message identified by arguments set, msgid, and dfault, according to an implementation-defined mapping. If no such message can be found, returns dfault.

```
void do_close(catalog cat) const;
```

5   **Requires:** A catalog cat obtained from open() and not yet closed.
6   **Effects:** Releases unspecified resources associated with cat.
7   **Notes:** The limit on such resources, if any, is implementation-defined.

22.2.7.2 Class template messages_byname   [lib.locale.messages.byname]

```
namespace std {
  template <class charT>
  class messages_byname : public messages<charT> {
  public:
    typedef messages_base::catalog catalog;
    typedef basic_string<charT>    string_type;

    explicit messages_byname(const char*, size_t refs = 0);
  protected:
    ~messages_byname();                  // virtual
    virtual catalog do_open(const basic_string<char>&, const locale&) const;
    virtual string_type  do_get(catalog, int set, int msgid,
                                const string_type& dfault) const;
    virtual void    do_close(catalog) const;
  };
}
```

22.2.8 Program-defined facets   [lib.facets.examples]

1   A C++ program may define facets to be added to a locale and used identically as the built-in facets. To create a new facet interface, C++ programs simply derive from `locale::facet` a class containing a static
member: `static locale::id id`.

2   [*Note:* The locale member function templates verify its type and storage class. —*end note*]

3   [*Note:* This paragraph is intentionally empty. —*end note*]

4   [*Example:* Traditional global localization is still easy:

```
#include <iostream>
#include <locale>
int main(int argc, char** argv)
{
  using namespace std;
  locale::global(locale(""));          // set the global locale
                                       // imbue it on all the std streams

  cin.imbue(locale());
  cout.imbue(locale());
  cerr.imbue(locale());
  wcin.imbue(locale());
  wcout.imbue(locale());
  wcerr.imbue(locale());

  return MyObject(argc, argv).doit();
}
```
—*end example*]

5   [*Example:* Greater flexibility is possible:

```
#include <iostream>
#include <locale>
int main()
{
  using namespace std;
  cin.imbue(locale(""));         // the user's preferred locale
  cout.imbue(locale::classic());
  double f;
  while (cin >> f) cout << f << endl;
  return (cin.fail() != 0);
}
```

In a European locale, with input 3.456,78, output is 3456.78. —*end example*]

6   This can be important even for simple programs, which may need to write a data file in a fixed format, regardless of a user's preference.

7   [*Example:* Here is an example of the use of locales in a library interface.

```
// file: Date.h
#include <iosfwd>
#include <string>
#include <locale>
    ...
class Date {
  ...
 public:
   Date(unsigned day, unsigned month, unsigned year);
   std::string asString(const std::locale& = std::locale());
};
istream& operator>>(istream& s, Date& d);
ostream& operator<<(ostream& s, Date d);
  ...
```

This example illustrates two architectural uses of class `locale`.

8   The first is as a default argument in `Date::asString()`, where the default is the global (presumably user-preferred) locale.

9   The second is in the operators `<<` and `>>`, where a locale "hitchhikes" on another object, in this case a stream, to the point where it is needed.

```
// file: Date.C
#include "Date"                    // includes <ctime>
#include <sstream>
std::string Date::asString(const std::locale& l)
{
  using namespace std;
  ostringstream s; s.imbue(l);
  s << *this; return s.str();
}

std::istream& operator>>(std::istream& s, Date& d)
{
  using namespace std;
  istream::sentry cerberos(s);
  if (cerberos) {
    ios_base::iostate err = goodbit;
    struct tm t;
    use_facet< time_get<char> >(s.getloc()).get_date(s, 0, s, err, &t);
    if (!err) d = Date(t.tm_day, t.tm_mon + 1, t.tm_year + 1900);
    s.setstate(err);
  }
  return s;
}
```

—*end example*]

10   A locale object may be extended with a new facet simply by constructing it with an instance of a class derived from `locale::facet`. The only member a C++ program must define is the static member `id`, which identifies your class interface as a new facet.

11   [*Example:* Classifying Japanese characters:

```
// file: <jctype>
#include <locale>
namespace My {
  using namespace std;
  class JCtype : public locale::facet {
  public:
    static locale::id id;                // required for use as a new locale facet
    bool is_kanji (wchar_t c) const;
    JCtype() {}
  protected:
    ~JCtype() {}
  };
}
```

```
// file: filt.C
#include <iostream>
#include <locale>
#include "jctype"                        // above
std::locale::id My::JCtype::id;          // the static JCtype member declared above.

int main()
{
  using namespace std;
  typedef ctype<wchar_t> wctype;
  locale loc(locale(""),                 // the user's preferred locale ...
             new My::JCtype);            // and a new feature ...
  wchar_t c = use_facet<wctype>(loc).widen('!');
  if (!use_facet<My::JCtype>(loc).is_kanji(c))
      cout << "no it isn't!" << endl;
  return 0;
}
```

12   The new facet is used exactly like the built-in facets. *—end example*]

13   [*Example:* Replacing an existing facet is even easier. Here we do not define a member id because we are reusing the numpunct<charT> facet interface:

```
// file: my_bool.C
#include <iostream>
#include <locale>
#include <string>
namespace My {
  using namespace std;
  typedef numpunct_byname<char> cnumpunct;
  class BoolNames : public cnumpunct {
   protected:
    string do_truename()  const { return "Oui Oui!"; }
    string do_falsename() const { return "Mais Non!"; }
    ~BoolNames() {}
   public:
    BoolNames(const char* name) : cnumpunct(name) {}
  };
}
```

```
int main(int argc, char** argv)
{
  using namespace std;
  // make the user's preferred locale, except for...
  locale loc(locale(""), new My::BoolNames(""));
  cout.imbue(loc);
  cout << boolalpha << "Any arguments today? " << (argc > 1) << endl;
  return 0;
}
```

—*end example*]

22.3 C Library Locales   [lib.c.locales]

1   Header `<clocale>` (Table 62):

Table 62—Header `<clocale>` synopsis

Type	Name(s)		
Macros:			
	`LC_ALL`	`LC_COLLATE`	`LC_CTYPE`
	`LC_MONETARY`	`LC_NUMERIC`	`LC_TIME`
	`NULL`		
Struct:	`lconv`		
Functions:	`localeconv`	`setlocale`	

2   The contents are the same as the Standard C library header `<locale.h>`.

SEE ALSO: ISO C clause 7.4.

1   This clause describes components that C++ programs may use to organize collections of information.

2   The following subclauses describe container requirements, and components for sequences and associative containers, as summarized in Table 63:

Table 63—Containers library summary

Subclause	Header(s)
23.1 Requirements	
23.2 Sequences	`<deque>` `<list>` `<queue>` `<stack>` `<vector>`
23.3 Associative containers	`<map>` `<set>`
23.3.5 `bitset`	`<bitset>`

23.1 Container requirements   [lib.container.requirements]

1   Containers are objects that store other objects. They control allocation and deallocation of these objects through constructors, destructors, insert and erase operations.

2   All of the complexity requirements in this clause are stated solely in terms of the number of operations on the contained objects. [*Example:* the copy constructor of type `vector <vector<int> >` has linear complexity, even though the complexity of copying each contained `vector<int>` is itself linear.]

3   The type of objects stored in these components must meet the requirements of `CopyConstructible` types (20.1.3), and the additional requirements of `Assignable` types.

4   In Table 64, `T` is the type used to instantiate the container, `t` is a value of `T`, and `u` is a value of (possibly `const`) `T`.

Table 64—`Assignable` requirements

expression	return type	post-condition
`t = u`	`T&`	`t` is equivalent to `u`

5   In Tables 65 and 66, `X` denotes a container class containing objects of type `T`, `a` and `b` denote values of type `X`, `u` denotes an identifier and `r` denotes a value of `X&`.

Table 65—Container requirements

expression	return type	assertion/note pre/post-condition	complexity
`X::value_type`	`T`	`T` is `Assignable`	compile time
`X::reference`	lvalue of `T`		compile time
`X::const_reference`	const lvalue of `T`		compile time
`X::iterator`	iterator type pointing to `T`	any iterator category except output iterator. convertible to `X::const_iterator`.	compile time
`X::const_iterator`	iterator type pointing to const `T`	any iterator category except output iterator.	compile time
`X::difference_type`	signed integral type	is identical to the difference type of `X::iterator` and `X::const_iterator`	compile time
`X::size_type`	unsigned integral type	`size_type` can represent any non-negative value of `difference_type`	compile time
`X u;`		post: `u.size() == 0.`	constant
`X();`		`X().size() == 0.`	constant
`X(a);`		`a == X(a).`	linear
`X u(a);` `X u = a;`		post: `u == a.` Equivalent to: `X u; u = a;`	linear
`(&a)->~X();`	`void`	note: the destructor is applied to every element of a; all the memory is deallocated.	linear

`a.begin();`	`iterator;`
	`const_iterator`
	for constant a
			constant

`a.end();`	`iterator;`
	`const_iterator`
	for constant a
			constant

`a == b`	convertible to `bool`	`==` is an equivalence relation.
		`a.size()==b.size()`
		`&& equal(a.begin(),`
		`a.end(), b.begin())`
			linear

`a != b`	convertible to `bool`	Equivalent to: `!(a == b)`	linear
`a.swap(b);`	`void`	`swap(a,b)`	(Note A)

Table 65—Container requirements (continued)

expression	return type	operational semantics	assertion/note pre/post-condition	complexity
`r = a`	`X&`		post: `r == a.`	linear
`a.size()`	`size_type`	`a.end()-a.begin()`		(Note A)
`a.max_size()`	`size_type`	`size()` of the largest possible container.		(Note A)
`a.empty()`	convertible to `bool`	`a.size() == 0`		constant
`a < b`	convertible to `bool`	`lexicographical_compare (a.begin(), a.end(), b.begin(), b.end())`	pre: < is defined for values of T. < is a total ordering relation.	linear
`a > b`	convertible to `bool`	`b < a`		linear
`a <= b`	convertible to `bool`	`!(a > b)`		linear
`a >= b`	convertible to `bool`	`!(a < b)`		linear

Notes: the algorithms `swap()`, `equal()` and `lexicographical_compare()` are defined in clause 25. Those entries marked ''(Note A)'' should have constant complexity.

6   The member function `size()` returns the number of elements in the container. Its semantics is defined by the rules of constructors, inserts, and erases.

7   `begin()` returns an iterator referring to the first element in the container. `end()` returns an iterator which is the past-the-end value for the container. If the container is empty, then `begin() == end()`;

8   Copy constructors for all container types defined in this clause copy an allocator argument from their respective first parameters. All other constructors for these container types take an `Allocator&` argument (20.1.5), an allocator whose value type is the same as the container's value type. A copy of this argument is used for any memory allocation performed, by these constructors and by all member functions, during the lifetime of each container object. In all container types defined in this clause, the member `get_allocator()` returns a copy of the Allocator object used to construct the container.

9   If the iterator type of a container belongs to the bidirectional or random access iterator categories (24.1), the container is called *reversible* and satisfies the additional requirements in Table 66:

Table 66—Reversible container requirements

expression	return type	assertion/note pre/post-condition	complexity
`X::reverse_` `iterator`	iterator type pointing to T	`reverse_iterator <itera-` `tor>`	compile time

`X::const_`
`reverse_`
`iterator`
	iterator type pointing to const
	T
		`reverse_iterator`
		`<const_iterator>`
			compile time

`a.rbegin()`	`reverse_iterator;`
	`const_reverse_iterator`
	for constant a
		`reverse_iterator(end())`	constant

`a.rend()`	`reverse_iterator;`
	`const_reverse_iterator`
	for constant a
		`reverse_iterator(begin())`	constant

10   Unless otherwise specified (see 23.2.1.3 and 23.2.4.3) all container types defined in this clause meet the
following additional requirements:

— if an exception is thrown by an `insert()` function while inserting a single element, that function has
no effects.

— if an exception is thrown by a `push_back()` or `push_front()` function, that function has no
effects.

— no `erase()`, `pop_back()` or `pop_front()` function throws an exception.

— no copy constructor or assignment operator of a returned iterator throws an exception.

— no `swap()` function throws an exception unless that exception is thrown by the copy constructor or
assignment operator of the container's Compare object (if any; see 23.1.2).

— no `swap()` function invalidates any references, pointers, or iterators referring to the elements of the
containers being swapped.

11   Unless otherwise specified (either explicitly or by defining a function in terms of other functions), invoking
a container member function or passing a container as an argument to a library function shall not invalidate
iterators to, or change the values of, objects within that container.

23.1.1 Sequences   [lib.sequence.reqmts]

1   A sequence is a kind of container that organizes a finite set of objects, all of the same type, into a strictly
linear arrangement. The library provides three basic kinds of sequence containers: `vector`, `list`, and
`deque`. It also provides container adaptors that make it easy to construct abstract data types, such as
`stacks` or `queues`, out of the basic sequence kinds (or out of other kinds of sequences that the user might
define).

2   `vector`, `list`, and `deque` offer the programmer different complexity trade-offs and should be used
accordingly. `vector` is the type of sequence that should be used by default. `list` should be used when
there are frequent insertions and deletions from the middle of the sequence. `deque` is the data structure of
choice when most insertions and deletions take place at the beginning or at the end of the sequence.

3   In Tables 67 and 68, X denotes a sequence class, a denotes a value of X, i and j denote iterators satisfying
input iterator requirements, [i, j) denotes a valid range, n denotes a value of `X::size_type`, p
denotes a valid iterator to a, q denotes a valid dereferenceable iterator to a, [q1, q2) denotes a valid
range in a, and t denotes a value of `X::value_type`.

4   The complexities of the expressions are sequence dependent.

Table 67—Sequence requirements (in addition to container)

expression	return type	assertion/note pre/post-condition
`X(n, t)` `X a(n, t);`		post: `size() == n`. constructs a sequence with n copies of t.
`X(i, j)` `X a(i, j);`		post: `size() == distance` between i and j. constructs a sequence equal to the range `[i,j)`.
`a.insert(p,t)`	`iterator`	inserts a copy of t before p.
`a.insert(p,n,t)`	`void`	inserts n copies of t before p.
`a.insert(p,i,j)`	`void`	pre: i,j are not iterators into a. inserts copies of elements in `[i,j)` before p.
`a.erase(q)`	`iterator`	erases the element pointed to by q.
`a.erase(q1,q2)`	`iterator`	erases the elements in the range `[q1,q2)`.
`a.clear()`	`void`	`erase(begin(), end())` post: `size() == 0`.

5   `iterator` and `const_iterator` types for sequences must be at least of the forward iterator category.

6   The iterator returned from `a.insert(p,t)` points to the copy of t inserted into a.

7   The iterator returned from `a.erase(q)` points to the element immediately following q prior to the element being erased. If no such element exists, `a.end()` is returned.

8   The iterator returned by `a.erase(q1,q2)` points to the element pointed to by q2 prior to any elements being erased. If no such element exists, `a.end()` is returned.

9   For every sequence defined in this clause and in clause 21:

— the constructor

```
template <class InputIterator>
X(InputIterator f, InputIterator l, const Allocator& a = Allocator())
```

shall have the same effect as:

```
X(static_cast<typename X::size_type>(f),
  static_cast<typename X::value_type>(l),
  a)
```

if `InputIterator` is an integral type.

— the member functions in the forms:

```
template <class InputIterator>          // such as insert()
rt fx1(iterator p, InputIterator f, InputIterator l);

template <class InputIterator>          // such as append(), assign()
rt fx2(InputIterator f, InputIterator l);

template <class InputIterator>          // such as replace()
rt fx3(iterator i1, iterator i2, InputIterator f, InputIterator l);
```

shall have the same effect, respectively, as:

```
fx1(p,
    static_cast<typename X::size_type>(f),
    static_cast<typename X::value_type>(1));

fx2(static_cast<typename X::size_type>(f),
    static_cast<typename X::value_type>(1));

fx3(i1, i2,
    static_cast<typename X::size_type>(f),
    static_cast<typename X::value_type>(1));
```

if `InputIterator` is an integral type.

10   [*Note:* This follows directly from the requirements in the Iterator Requirements Table. Integral types cannot be iterators, so, if n1 and n2 are values of an integral type *N*, the expression X(n1, n2) cannot possibly be interpreted as construction from a range of iterators. It must be taken to mean the first constructor in the Iterator Requirements Table, not the second one. If there is no conversion from *N* to X::value_type, then this is not a valid expression at all.

11   One way that sequence implementors can satisfy this requirement is to specialize the member template for every integral type. Less cumbersome implementation techniques also exist. —*end note*] [*Example:*

```
list<int> x;
...
vector<int> y(x.begin(), x.end());      // Construct a vector
                                        // from a range of iterators.
vector<int> z(100, 1);                  // Construct a vector of 100
                                        // elements, all initialized
                                        // to 1. The arguments are
                                        // not interpreted as iterators.
z.insert(z.begin(), x.begin(), x.end());// Insert a range of
                                        // iterators.
z.insert(z.begin(), 20, 0);             // Insert 20 copies of the
                                        // number 0.
```

—*end example*]

12   Table 68 lists sequence operations that are provided for some types of sequential containers but not others. An implementation shall provide these operations for all container types shown in the ''container'' column, and shall implement them so as to take amortized constant time.

Table 68—Optional sequence operations

expression	return type	operational semantics	container
a.front()	reference; const_reference for constant a	*a.begin()	vector, list, deque
a.back()	reference; const_reference for constant a	*--a.end()	vector, list, deque
a.push_front(x)	void	a.insert(a.begin(),x)	list, deque
a.push_back(x)	void	a.insert(a.end(),x)	vector, list, deque
a.pop_front()	void	a.erase(a.begin())	list, deque
a.pop_back()	void	a.erase(--a.end())	vector, list, deque
a[n]	reference; const_reference for constant a	*(a.begin() + n)	vector, deque
a.at(n)	reference; const_reference for constant a	*(a.begin() + n)	vector, deque

13 The member function at() provides bounds-checked access to container elements. at() throws out_of_range if n >= a.size().

23.1.2 Associative containers [lib.associative.reqmts]

1 Associative containers provide an ability for fast retrieval of data based on keys. The library provides four basic kinds of associative containers: set, multiset, map and multimap.

2 Each associative container is parameterized on Key and an ordering relation Compare that induces a strict weak ordering (25.3) on elements of Key. In addition, map and multimap associate an arbitrary type T with the Key. The object of type Compare is called the *comparison object* of a container. This comparison object may be a pointer to function or an object of a type with an appropriate function call operator.

3 The phrase ''equivalence of keys'' means the equivalence relation imposed by the comparison and *not* the operator== on keys. That is, two keys k1 and k2 are considered to be equivalent if for the comparison object comp, comp(k1, k2) == false && comp(k2, k1) == false.

4 An associative container supports *unique keys* if it may contain at most one element for each key. Otherwise, it supports *equivalent keys*. The set and map classes support unique keys; the multiset and multimap classes support equivalent keys.

5 For set and multiset the value type is the same as the key type. For map and multimap it is equal to pair<const Key, T>.

6 iterator of an associative container is of the bidirectional iterator category.

7 In Table 69, X is an associative container class, a is a value of X, a_uniq is a value of X when X supports unique keys, and a_eq is a value of X when X supports multiple keys, i and j satisfy input iterator requirements and refer to elements of value_type, [i, j) is a valid range, p is a valid iterator to a, q is a valid dereferenceable iterator to a, [q1, q2) is a valid range in a, t is a value of X::value_type, k is a value of X::key_type and c is a value of type X::key_compare.

Table 69—Associative container requirements (in addition to container)

expression	return type	assertion/note pre/post-condition	complexity
`X::key_type`	`Key`	`Key` is `Assignable`	compile time
`X::key_compare`	`Compare`	defaults to `less<key_type>`	compile time
`X::` `value_compare`	a binary predicate type	is the same as `key_compare` for `set` and `multiset`; is an ordering relation on pairs induced by the first component (i.e. `Key`) for `map` and `multimap`.	compile time
`X(c)` `X a(c);`		constructs an empty container; uses `c` as a comparison object	constant
`X()` `X a;`		constructs an empty container; uses `Compare()` as a comparison object	constant
`X(i,j,c);` `X a(i,j,c);`		constructs an empty container and inserts elements from the range `[i, j)` into it; uses `c` as a comparison object	`NlogN` in general (`N` is the distance from `i` to `j`); linear if `[i, j)` is sorted with `value_comp()`

`X(i, j)`
 	
`X a(i, j);`
		same as above, but uses `Compare()` as a comparison object.	same as above

`a.key_comp()`	`X::key_compare`	returns the comparison object out of which `a` was constructed.	constant
`a.value_comp()`	`X::` `value_compare`	returns an object of `value_compare` constructed out of the comparison object	constant
`a_uniq.` `insert(t)`	`pair<iterator,` `bool>`	inserts `t` if and only if there is no element in the container with key equivalent to the key of `t`. The `bool` component of the returned pair indicates whether the insertion takes place and the `iterator` component of the pair points to the element with key equivalent to the key of `t`.	logarithmic
`a_eq.insert(t)`	`iterator`	inserts `t` and returns the iterator pointing to the newly inserted element.	logarithmic

Table 69—Associative container requirements

expression	return type	assertion/note pre/post-condition	complexity
`a.insert(p,t)`	`iterator`	inserts `t` if and only if there is no element with key equivalent to the key of `t` in containers with unique keys; always inserts `t` in containers with equivalent keys. always returns the iterator pointing to the element with key equivalent to the key of `t`. iterator `p` is a hint pointing to where the insert should start to search.	logarithmic in general, but amortized constant if `t` is inserted right after `p`.
`a.insert(i,j)`	`void`	pre: `i,j` are not iterators into `a`. inserts each element from the range `[i, j)` if and only if there is no element with key equivalent to the key of that element in containers with unique keys; always inserts that element in containers with equivalent keys.	`Nlog(size()+N)` (`N` is the distance from `i` to `j`) in general; linear if `[i, j)` is sorted according to `value_comp()`
`a.erase(k)`	`size_type`	erases all the elements in the container with key equivalent to `k`. returns the number of erased elements.	`log(size())` + `count(k)`
`a.erase(q)`	`void`	erases the element pointed to by `q`.	amortized constant
`a.erase(q1,q2)`	`void`	erases all the elements in the range `[q1, q2)`.	`log(size())+ N` where `N` is the distance from `q1` to `q2`.
`a.clear()`	`void`	`erase(a.begin(), a.end())` post: `size == 0`	Linear in `size()`.
`a.find(k)`	`iterator;` `const_iterator` for constant `a`	returns an iterator pointing to an element with the key equivalent to `k`, or `a.end()` if such an element is not found.	logarithmic
`a.count(k)`	`size_type`	returns the number of elements with key equivalent to `k`	`log(size())` + `count(k)`
`a.lower_bound(k)`	`iterator;` `const_iterator` for constant `a`	returns an iterator pointing to the first element with key not less than `k`.	logarithmic
`a.upper_bound(k)`	`iterator;` `const_iterator` for constant `a`	returns an iterator pointing to the first element with key greater than `k`.	logarithmic
`a.equal_range(k)`	`pair<iterator, iterator>;pair< const_iterator, const_iterator>` for constant `a`	equivalent to `make_pair( a.lower_bound(k), a.upper_bound(k))`.	logarithmic

8   The insert members shall not affect the validity of iterators and references to the container, and the erase members shall invalidate only iterators and references to the erased elements.

9   The fundamental property of iterators of associative containers is that they iterate through the containers in the non-descending order of keys where non-descending is defined by the comparison that was used to construct them. For any two dereferenceable iterators `i` and `j` such that distance from `i` to `j` is positive,

```
value_comp(*j, *i) == false
```

10   For associative containers with unique keys the stronger condition holds,

```
value_comp(*i, *j) != false.
```

11   When an associative container is constructed by passing a comparison object the container shall not store a pointer or reference to the passed object, even if that object is passed by reference. When an associative container is copied, either through a copy constructor or an assignment operator, the target container shall then use the comparison object from the container being copied, as if that comparison object had been passed to the target container in its constructor.

23.2 Sequences   [lib.sequences]

1   Headers `<deque>`, `<list>`, `<queue>`, `<stack>`, and `<vector>`.

Header `<deque>` synopsis

```
namespace std {
  template <class T, class Allocator = allocator<T> > class deque;
  template <class T, class Allocator>
    bool operator==
      (const deque<T,Allocator>& x, const deque<T,Allocator>& y);
  template <class T, class Allocator>
    bool operator<
      (const deque<T,Allocator>& x, const deque<T,Allocator>& y);
  template <class T, class Allocator>
    bool operator!=
      (const deque<T,Allocator>& x, const deque<T,Allocator>& y);
  template <class T, class Allocator>
    bool operator>
      (const deque<T,Allocator>& x, const deque<T,Allocator>& y);
  template <class T, class Allocator>
    bool operator>=
      (const deque<T,Allocator>& x, const deque<T,Allocator>& y);
  template <class T, class Allocator>
    bool operator<=
      (const deque<T,Allocator>& x, const deque<T,Allocator>& y);
  template <class T, class Allocator>
    void swap(deque<T,Allocator>& x, deque<T,Allocator>& y);
}
```

Header <list> synopsis

```
namespace std {
  template <class T, class Allocator = allocator<T> > class list;
  template <class T, class Allocator>
    bool operator==(const list<T,Allocator>& x, const list<T,Allocator>& y);
  template <class T, class Allocator>
    bool operator< (const list<T,Allocator>& x, const list<T,Allocator>& y);
  template <class T, class Allocator>
    bool operator!=(const list<T,Allocator>& x, const list<T,Allocator>& y);
  template <class T, class Allocator>
    bool operator> (const list<T,Allocator>& x, const list<T,Allocator>& y);
  template <class T, class Allocator>
    bool operator>=(const list<T,Allocator>& x, const list<T,Allocator>& y);
  template <class T, class Allocator>
    bool operator<=(const list<T,Allocator>& x, const list<T,Allocator>& y);
  template <class T, class Allocator>
    void swap(list<T,Allocator>& x, list<T,Allocator>& y);
}
```

Header <queue> synopsis

```
namespace std {
  template <class T, class Container = deque<T> > class queue;
  template <class T, class Container>
    bool operator==(const queue<T, Container>& x,
                    const queue<T, Container>& y);
  template <class T, class Container>
    bool operator< (const queue<T, Container>& x,
                    const queue<T, Container>& y);
  template <class T, class Container>
    bool operator!=(const queue<T, Container>& x,
                    const queue<T, Container>& y);
  template <class T, class Container>
    bool operator> (const queue<T, Container>& x,
                    const queue<T, Container>& y);
  template <class T, class Container>
    bool operator>=(const queue<T, Container>& x,
                    const queue<T, Container>& y);
  template <class T, class Container>
    bool operator<=(const queue<T, Container>& x,
                    const queue<T, Container>& y);

  template <class T, class Container = vector<T>,
            class Compare = less<typename Container::value_type> >
  class priority_queue;
}
```

Header `<stack>` synopsis

```
namespace std {
  template <class T, class Container = deque<T> > class stack;
  template <class T, class Container>
    bool operator==(const stack<T, Container>& x,
                    const stack<T, Container>& y);
  template <class T, class Container>
    bool operator< (const stack<T, Container>& x,
                    const stack<T, Container>& y);
  template <class T, class Container>
    bool operator!=(const stack<T, Container>& x,
                    const stack<T, Container>& y);
  template <class T, class Container>
    bool operator> (const stack<T, Container>& x,
                    const stack<T, Container>& y);
  template <class T, class Container>
    bool operator>=(const stack<T, Container>& x,
                    const stack<T, Container>& y);
  template <class T, class Container>
    bool operator<=(const stack<T, Container>& x,
                    const stack<T, Container>& y);
}
```

Header `<vector>` synopsis

```
namespace std {
  template <class T, class Allocator = allocator<T> > class vector;
  template <class T, class Allocator>
    bool operator==(const vector<T,Allocator>& x,
                    const vector<T,Allocator>& y);
  template <class T, class Allocator>
    bool operator< (const vector<T,Allocator>& x,
                    const vector<T,Allocator>& y);
  template <class T, class Allocator>
    bool operator!=(const vector<T,Allocator>& x,
                    const vector<T,Allocator>& y);
  template <class T, class Allocator>
    bool operator> (const vector<T,Allocator>& x,
                    const vector<T,Allocator>& y);
  template <class T, class Allocator>
    bool operator>=(const vector<T,Allocator>& x,
                    const vector<T,Allocator>& y);
  template <class T, class Allocator>
    bool operator<=(const vector<T,Allocator>& x,
                    const vector<T,Allocator>& y);
  template <class T, class Allocator>
    void swap(vector<T,Allocator>& x, vector<T,Allocator>& y);
```

```
template <class Allocator> class vector<bool,Allocator>;
template <class Allocator>
  bool operator==(const vector<bool,Allocator>& x,
                  const vector<bool,Allocator>& y);
template <class Allocator>
  bool operator< (const vector<bool,Allocator>& x,
                  const vector<bool,Allocator>& y);
template <class Allocator>
  bool operator!=(const vector<bool,Allocator>& x,
                  const vector<bool,Allocator>& y);
template <class Allocator>
  bool operator> (const vector<bool,Allocator>& x,
                  const vector<bool,Allocator>& y);
template <class Allocator>
  bool operator>=(const vector<bool,Allocator>& x,
                  const vector<bool,Allocator>& y);
template <class Allocator>
  bool operator<=(const vector<bool,Allocator>& x,
                  const vector<bool,Allocator>& y);
template <class Allocator>
  void swap(vector<bool,Allocator>& x, vector<bool,Allocator>& y);
}
```

23.2.1 Class template `deque` [lib.deque]

1 A deque is a kind of sequence that, like a vector (23.2.4), supports random access iterators. In addition,
it supports constant time insert and erase operations at the beginning or the end; insert and erase in the middle take linear time. That is, a deque is especially optimized for pushing and popping elements at the
beginning and end. As with vectors, storage management is handled automatically.

2 A deque satisfies all of the requirements of a container and of a reversible container (given in tables in
23.1) and of a sequence, including the optional sequence requirements (23.1.1). Descriptions are provided
here only for operations on deque that are not described in one of these tables or for operations where
there is additional semantic information.

```
namespace std {
  template <class T, class Allocator = allocator<T> >
  class deque {
  public:
    // types:
    typedef typename Allocator::reference        reference;
    typedef typename Allocator::const_reference  const_reference;
    typedef implementation defined               iterator;        // See 23.1
    typedef implementation defined               const_iterator;  // See 23.1
    typedef implementation defined               size_type;       // See 23.1
    typedef implementation defined               difference_type; // See 23.1
    typedef T                                    value_type;
    typedef Allocator                            allocator_type;
    typedef typename Allocator::pointer          pointer;
    typedef typename Allocator::const_pointer    const_pointer;
    typedef std::reverse_iterator<iterator>      reverse_iterator;
    typedef std::reverse_iterator<const_iterator> const_reverse_iterator;
```

```
// 23.2.1.1 construct/copy/destroy:
explicit deque(const Allocator& = Allocator());
explicit deque(size_type n, const T& value = T(),
    const Allocator& = Allocator());
template <class InputIterator>
  deque(InputIterator first, InputIterator last,
        const Allocator& = Allocator());
deque(const deque<T,Allocator>& x);
~deque();
deque<T,Allocator>& operator=(const deque<T,Allocator>& x);
template <class InputIterator>
  void assign(InputIterator first, InputIterator last);
void assign(size_type n, const T& t);
allocator_type get_allocator() const;

// iterators:
iterator               begin();
const_iterator         begin() const;
iterator               end();
const_iterator         end() const;
reverse_iterator       rbegin();
const_reverse_iterator rbegin() const;
reverse_iterator       rend();
const_reverse_iterator rend() const;

// 23.2.1.2 capacity:
size_type size() const;
size_type max_size() const;
void      resize(size_type sz, T c = T());
bool      empty() const;

// element access:
reference       operator[](size_type n);
const_reference operator[](size_type n) const;
reference       at(size_type n);
const_reference at(size_type n) const;
reference       front();
const_reference front() const;
reference       back();
const_reference back() const;

// 23.2.1.3 modifiers:
void push_front(const T& x);
void push_back(const T& x);

iterator insert(iterator position, const T& x);
void     insert(iterator position, size_type n, const T& x);
template <class InputIterator>
  void insert (iterator position,
               InputIterator first, InputIterator last);

void pop_front();
void pop_back();
```

```
          iterator erase(iterator position);
          iterator erase(iterator first, iterator last);
          void      swap(deque<T,Allocator>&);
          void      clear();
        };

        template <class T, class Allocator>
          bool operator==(const deque<T,Allocator>& x,
                          const deque<T,Allocator>& y);
        template <class T, class Allocator>
          bool operator< (const deque<T,Allocator>& x,
                          const deque<T,Allocator>& y);
        template <class T, class Allocator>
          bool operator!=(const deque<T,Allocator>& x,
                          const deque<T,Allocator>& y);
        template <class T, class Allocator>
          bool operator> (const deque<T,Allocator>& x,
                          const deque<T,Allocator>& y);
        template <class T, class Allocator>
          bool operator>=(const deque<T,Allocator>& x,
                          const deque<T,Allocator>& y);
        template <class T, class Allocator>
          bool operator<=(const deque<T,Allocator>& x,
                          const deque<T,Allocator>& y);


        // specialized algorithms:
        template <class T, class Allocator>
          void swap(deque<T,Allocator>& x, deque<T,Allocator>& y);
      }
```

23.2.1.1 deque constructors, copy, and assignment   [lib.deque.cons]

```
        explicit deque(const Allocator& = Allocator());
```

1 **Effects:** Constructs an empty deque, using the specified allocator.
2 **Complexity:** Constant.

```
        explicit deque(size_type n, const T& value = T(),
                       const Allocator& = Allocator());
```

3 **Effects:** Constructs a deque with n copies of *value*, using the specified allocator.
4 **Complexity:** Linear in n.

```
        template <class InputIterator>
          deque(InputIterator first, InputIterator last,
                const Allocator& = Allocator());
```

5 **Effects:** Constructs a deque equal to the the range [*first*, *last*), using the specified allocator.
6 **Complexity:** Makes distance(*first*, *last*) calls to the copy constructor of T.

---
246) This footnote is intentionally empty.

```
template <class InputIterator>
  void assign(InputIterator first, InputIterator last);
```

7   **Effects:**

```
        erase(begin(), end());
        insert(begin(), first, last);
```

```
void assign(size_type n, const T& t);
```

8   **Effects:**

```
        erase(begin(), end());
        insert(begin(), n, t);
```

23.2.1.2 deque capacity   [lib.deque.capacity]

```
void resize(size_type sz, T c = T());
```

1   **Effects:**

```
        if (sz > size())
          insert(end(), sz-size(), c);
        else if (sz < size())
          erase(begin()+sz, end());
        else
          ;                                       // do nothing
```

23.2.1.3 deque modifiers   [lib.deque.modifiers]

```
iterator insert(iterator position, const T& x);
void     insert(iterator position, size_type n, const T& x);
template <class InputIterator>
  void insert(iterator position,
              InputIterator first, InputIterator last);
```

1   **Effects:** An insert in the middle of the deque invalidates all the iterators and references to elements of the deque. An insert at either end of the deque invalidates all the iterators to the deque, but has no effect on the validity of references to elements of the deque.

2   **Notes:** If an exception is thrown other than by the copy constructor or assignment operator of T there are no effects.

3   **Complexity:** In the worst case, inserting a single element into a deque takes time linear in the minimum of the distance from the insertion point to the beginning of the deque and the distance from the insertion point to the end of the deque. Inserting a single element either at the beginning or end of a deque always takes constant time and causes a single call to the copy constructor of T.

```
iterator erase(iterator position);
iterator erase(iterator first, iterator last);
```

4   **Effects:** An erase in the middle of the deque invalidates all the iterators and references to elements of the deque. An erase at either end of the deque invalidates only the iterators and the references to the erased elements.

5   **Complexity:** The number of calls to the destructor is the same as the number of elements erased, but the number of the calls to the assignment operator is at most equal to the minimum of the number of elements before the erased elements and the number of elements after the erased elements.

6   **Throws:** Nothing unless an exception is thrown by the copy constructor or assignment operator of T.

23.2.1.4 `deque` specialized algorithms [lib.deque.special]

```
template <class T, class Allocator>
  void swap(deque<T,Allocator>& x, deque<T,Allocator>& y);
```

1   **Effects:**

```
x.swap(y);
```

23.2.2 Class template `list` [lib.list]

1   A `list` is a kind of sequence that supports bidirectional iterators and allows constant time insert and erase operations anywhere within the sequence, with storage management handled automatically. Unlike vectors (23.2.4) and deques (23.2.1), fast random access to list elements is not supported, but many algorithms only need sequential access anyway.

2   A `list` satisfies all of the requirements of a container and of a reversible container (given in two tables in 23.1) and of a sequence, including most of the the optional sequence requirements (23.1.1). The exceptions are the `operator[]` and at member functions, which are not provided.[247] Descriptions are provided here only for operations on `list` that are not described in one of these tables or for operations where there is additional semantic information.

```
namespace std {
  template <class T, class Allocator = allocator<T> >
  class list {
  public:
    // types:
    typedef typename Allocator::reference         reference;
    typedef typename Allocator::const_reference   const_reference;
    typedef implementation defined                iterator;      // See 23.1
    typedef implementation defined                const_iterator; // See 23.1
    typedef implementation defined                size_type;     // See 23.1
    typedef implementation defined                difference_type;// See 23.1
    typedef T                                     value_type;
    typedef Allocator                             allocator_type;
    typedef typename Allocator::pointer           pointer;
    typedef typename Allocator::const_pointer     const_pointer;
    typedef std::reverse_iterator<iterator>       reverse_iterator;
    typedef std::reverse_iterator<const_iterator> const_reverse_iterator;

    // 23.2.2.1 construct/copy/destroy:
    explicit list(const Allocator& = Allocator());
    explicit list(size_type n, const T& value = T(),
                  const Allocator& = Allocator());
    template <class InputIterator>
      list(InputIterator first, InputIterator last,
           const Allocator& = Allocator());
    list(const list<T,Allocator>& x);
    ~list();
    list<T,Allocator>& operator=(const list<T,Allocator>& x);
    template <class InputIterator>
      void assign(InputIterator first, InputIterator last);
    void assign(size_type n, const T& t);
    allocator_type get_allocator() const;
```

---

[247] These member functions are only provided by containers whose iterators are random access iterators.

```
// iterators:
iterator                begin();
const_iterator          begin() const;
iterator                end();
const_iterator          end() const;
reverse_iterator        rbegin();
const_reverse_iterator  rbegin() const;
reverse_iterator        rend();
const_reverse_iterator  rend() const;

// 23.2.2.2 capacity:
bool        empty() const;
size_type size() const;
size_type max_size() const;
void        resize(size_type sz, T c = T());

// element access:
reference        front();
const_reference front() const;
reference        back();
const_reference back() const;

// 23.2.2.3 modifiers:
void push_front(const T& x);
void pop_front();
void push_back(const T& x);
void pop_back();

iterator insert(iterator position, const T& x);
void        insert(iterator position, size_type n, const T& x);
template <class InputIterator>
  void insert(iterator position, InputIterator first,
              InputIterator last);

iterator erase(iterator position);
iterator erase(iterator position, iterator last);
void        swap(list<T,Allocator>&);
void        clear();

// 23.2.2.4 list operations:
void splice(iterator position, list<T,Allocator>& x);
void splice(iterator position, list<T,Allocator>& x, iterator i);
void splice(iterator position, list<T,Allocator>& x, iterator first,
            iterator last);

void remove(const T& value);
template <class Predicate> void remove_if(Predicate pred);

void unique();
template <class BinaryPredicate>
  void unique(BinaryPredicate binary_pred);

void merge(list<T,Allocator>& x);
template <class Compare> void merge(list<T,Allocator>& x, Compare comp);

void sort();
template <class Compare> void sort(Compare comp);
```

```
  void reverse();
};

template <class T, class Allocator>
  bool operator==(const list<T,Allocator>& x, const list<T,Allocator>& y);
template <class T, class Allocator>
  bool operator< (const list<T,Allocator>& x, const list<T,Allocator>& y);
template <class T, class Allocator>
  bool operator!=(const list<T,Allocator>& x, const list<T,Allocator>& y);
template <class T, class Allocator>
  bool operator> (const list<T,Allocator>& x, const list<T,Allocator>& y);
template <class T, class Allocator>
  bool operator>=(const list<T,Allocator>& x, const list<T,Allocator>& y);
template <class T, class Allocator>
  bool operator<=(const list<T,Allocator>& x, const list<T,Allocator>& y);

// specialized algorithms:
template <class T, class Allocator>
  void swap(list<T,Allocator>& x, list<T,Allocator>& y);
}
```

23.2.2.1 `list` constructors, copy, and assignment [lib.list.cons]

```
explicit list(const Allocator& = Allocator());
```

1   **Effects:** Constructs an empty list, using the specified allocator.

2   **Complexity:** Constant.

```
explicit list(size_type n, const T& value = T(),
              const Allocator& = Allocator());
```

3   **Effects:** Constructs a `list` with n copies of `value`, using the specified allocator.

4   **Complexity:** Linear in n.

```
template <class InputIterator>
list(InputIterator first, InputIterator last,
     const Allocator& = Allocator());
```

5   **Effects:** Constructs a `list` equal to the range [*first*, *last*).

6   **Complexity:** Linear in *first* - *last*.

```
template <class InputIterator>
  void assign(InputIterator first, InputIterator last);
```

7   **Effects:**

```
        erase(begin(), end());
        insert(begin(), first, last);
```

```
void assign(size_type n, const T& t);
```

8   **Effects:**

```
        erase(begin(), end());
        insert(begin(), n, t);
```

```
void resize(size_type sz, T c = T());
```

1   **Effects:**

```
if (sz > size())
  insert(end(), sz-size(), c);
else if (sz < size()) {
  iterator i = begin();
  advance(i, sz);
  erase(i, end());
}
else
  ;                            // do nothing
```

23.2.2.3 list modifiers [lib.list.modifiers]

```
iterator insert(iterator position, const T& x);
void     insert(iterator position, size_type n, const T& x);
template <class InputIterator>
  void insert(iterator position, InputIterator first,
              InputIterator last);
```

```
void push_front(const T& x);
void push_back(const T& x);
```

1   **Notes:** Does not affect the validity of iterators and references. If an exception is thrown there are no effects.

2   **Complexity:** Insertion of a single element into a list takes constant time and exactly one call to the copy constructor of T. Insertion of multiple elements into a list is linear in the number of elements inserted, and the number of calls to the copy constructor of T is exactly equal to the number of elements inserted.

```
iterator erase(iterator position);
iterator erase(iterator first, iterator last);
```

```
void pop_front();
void pop_back();
void clear();
```

3   **Effects:** Invalidates only the iterators and references to the erased elements.

4   **Throws:** Nothing.

5   **Complexity:** Erasing a single element is a constant time operation with a single call to the destructor of T. Erasing a range in a list is linear time in the size of the range and the number of calls to the destructor of type T is exactly equal to the size of the range.

23.2.2.4 list operations [lib.list.ops]

1   Since lists allow fast insertion and erasing from the middle of a list, certain operations are provided specifically for them.

2   list provides three splice operations that destructively move elements from one list to another.

```
void splice(iterator position, list<T,Allocator>& x);
```

3   **Requires:** &x != this.

4   **Effects:** Inserts the contents of x before position and x becomes empty. Invalidates all iterators and references to the list x.

5   **Throws:** Nothing

6   **Complexity:** Constant time.

```
void splice(iterator position, list<T,Allocator>& x, iterator i);
```

7   **Effects:** Inserts an element pointed to by i from list x before position and removes the element from x. The result is unchanged if position == i or position == ++i. Invalidates only the iterators and references to the spliced element.

8   **Throws:** Nothing

9   **Requires:** i is a valid dereferenceable iterator of x.

10   **Complexity:** Constant time.

```
void splice(iterator position, list<T,Allocator>& x, iterator first,
            iterator last);
```

11   **Effects:** Inserts elements in the range [first, last) before position and removes the elements from x.

12   **Requires:** [first, last) is a valid range in x. The result is undefined if position is an iterator in the range [first, last). Invalidates only the iterators and references to the spliced elements.

13   **Throws:** Nothing

14   **Complexity:** Constant time if &x == this; otherwise, linear time.

```
void remove(const T& value);
template <class Predicate> void remove_if(Predicate pred);
```

15   **Effects:** Erases all the elements in the list referred by a list iterator i for which the following conditions hold: *i == value, pred(*i) != false.

16   **Throws:** Nothing unless an exception is thrown by *i == value or pred(*i) != false.

17   **Notes:** Stable: the relative order of the elements that are not removed is the same as their relative order in the original list.

18   **Complexity:** Exactly size() applications of the corresponding predicate.

```
void unique();
template <class BinaryPredicate> void unique(BinaryPredicate binary_pred);
```

19   **Effects:** Eliminates all but the first element from every consecutive group of equal elements referred to by the iterator i in the range [first + 1, last) for which *i == *(i-1) (for the version of unique with no arguments) or pred(*i, *(i - 1)) (for the version of unique with a predicate argument) holds.

20   **Throws:** Nothing unless an exception in thrown by *i == *(i-1) or pred(*i, *(i - 1))

21   **Complexity:** If the range (last - first) is not empty, exactly (last - first) - 1 applications of the corresponding predicate, otherwise no applications of the predicate.

```
void   merge(list<T,Allocator>& x);
template <class Compare> void merge(list<T,Allocator>& x, Compare comp);
```

22   **Requires:** comp defines a strict weak ordering (25.3), and the list and the argument list are both sorted according to this ordering.

23   **Effects:** Merges the argument list into the list.

24   **Notes:** Stable: for equivalent elements in the two lists, the elements from the list always precede the elements from the argument list. x is empty after the merge.

25   **Complexity:** At most `size()` + `x.size()` - 1 comparisons. If an exception is thrown other than
     by a comparison there are no effects.

```
void reverse();
```

26   **Effects:** Reverses the order of the elements in the list.
27   **Throws:** Nothing.
28   **Complexity:** Linear time.

```
                    void sort();
template <class Compare> void sort(Compare comp);
```

29   **Requires:** `operator<` (for the first version) or *comp* (for the second version) defines a strict weak
     ordering (25.3).
30   **Effects:** Sorts the list according to the `operator<` or a `Compare` function object.
31   **Notes:** Stable: the relative order of the equivalent elements is preserved. If an exception is thrown the
     order of the elements in the list is indeterminate.
32   **Complexity:** Approximately `NlogN` comparisons, where `N == size()`.

23.2.2.5 `list` specialized algorithms   **[lib.list.special]**

```
template <class T, class Allocator>
    void swap(list<T,Allocator>& x, list<T,Allocator>& y);
```

1   **Effects:**

```
x.swap(y);
```

23.2.3 Container adaptors   **[lib.container.adaptors]**

1   The container adaptors each take a Container template parameter, and each constructor takes a Container
    reference argument. This container is copied into the Container member of each adaptor.

23.2.3.1 Class template `queue`   **[lib.queue]**

1   Any sequence supporting operations `front()`, `back()`, `push_back()` and `pop_front()` can be
    used to instantiate `queue`. In particular, `list` (23.2.2) and `deque` (23.2.1) can be used.

```
namespace std {
  template <class T, class Container = deque<T> >
  class queue {
  public:
    typedef typename Container::value_type     value_type;
    typedef typename Container::size_type      size_type;
    typedef          Container                 container_type;
  protected:
    Container c;
```

```
public:
  explicit queue(const Container& = Container());

  bool      empty() const          { return c.empty(); }
  size_type size()  const          { return c.size(); }
  value_type&       front()        { return c.front(); }
  const value_type& front() const  { return c.front(); }
  value_type&       back()         { return c.back(); }
  const value_type& back() const   { return c.back(); }
  void push(const value_type& x)   { c.push_back(x); }
  void pop()                       { c.pop_front(); }
};

template <class T, class Container>
  bool operator==(const queue<T, Container>& x,
                  const queue<T, Container>& y);
template <class T, class Container>
  bool operator< (const queue<T, Container>& x,
                  const queue<T, Container>& y);
template <class T, class Container>
  bool operator!=(const queue<T, Container>& x,
                  const queue<T, Container>& y);
template <class T, class Container>
  bool operator> (const queue<T, Container>& x,
                  const queue<T, Container>& y);
template <class T, class Container>
  bool operator>=(const queue<T, Container>& x,
                  const queue<T, Container>& y);
template <class T, class Container>
  bool operator<=(const queue<T, Container>& x,
                  const queue<T, Container>& y);
}
```

```
operator==
```

2 **Returns:** `x.c == y.c`.

```
operator<
```

3 **Returns:** `x.c < y.c`.

23.2.3.2 Class template `priority_queue` [lib.priority.queue]

1 Any sequence with random access iterator and supporting operations `front()`, `push_back()` and `pop_back()` can be used to instantiate `priority_queue`. In particular, `vector` (23.2.4) and `deque` (23.2.1) can be used. Instantiating `priority_queue` also involves supplying a function or function object for making priority comparisons; the library assumes that the function or function object defines a strict weak ordering (25.3).

```
namespace std {
  template <class T, class Container = vector<T>,
            class Compare = less<typename Container::value_type> >
  class priority_queue {
  public:
    typedef typename Container::value_type          value_type;
    typedef typename Container::size_type           size_type;
    typedef           Container                     container_type;
  protected:
    Container c;
    Compare comp;

  public:
    explicit priority_queue(const Compare& x = Compare(),
                            const Container& = Container());
    template <class InputIterator>
      priority_queue(InputIterator first, InputIterator last,
                     const Compare& x = Compare(),
                     const Container& = Container());

    bool      empty() const     { return c.empty(); }
    size_type size()  const     { return c.size(); }
    const value_type& top() const { return c.front(); }
    void push(const value_type& x);
    void pop();
  };
                              // no equality is provided
}
```

23.2.3.2.1 priority_queue constructors   [lib.priqueue.cons]

```
priority_queue(const Compare& x = Compare(),
               const Container& y = Container());
```

1   **Requires:** *x* defines a strict weak ordering (25.3).
2   **Effects:** Initializes comp with x and c with y; calls make_heap(c.begin(), c.end(), comp).

```
template <class InputIterator>
  priority_queue(InputIterator first, InputIterator last,
                 const Compare& x = Compare(),
                 const Container& y = Container());
```

3   **Requires:** *x* defines a strict weak ordering (25.3).
4   **Effects:** Initializes c with y and comp with x; calls c.insert(c.end(), first, last); and
    finally calls make_heap(c.begin(), c.end(), comp).

23.2.3.2.2 priority_queue members   [lib.priqueue.members]

```
void push(const value_type& x);
```

1   **Effects:**

```
            c.push_back(x);
            push_heap(c.begin(), c.end(), comp);
```

```
        void pop();
```

2   **Effects:**

```
            pop_heap(c.begin(), c.end(), comp);
            c.pop_back();
```

23.2.3.3 Class template `stack`   [lib.stack]

1   Any sequence supporting operations `back()`, `push_back()` and `pop_back()` can be used to instantiate `stack`. In particular, `vector` (23.2.4), `list` (23.2.2) and `deque` (23.2.1) can be used.

```
    namespace std {
      template <class T, class Container = deque<T> >
      class stack {
      public:
        typedef typename Container::value_type      value_type;
        typedef typename Container::size_type        size_type;
        typedef           Container                  container_type;
      protected:
        Container c;

      public:
        explicit stack(const Container& = Container());

        bool        empty() const           { return c.empty(); }
        size_type size()    const           { return c.size(); }
        value_type&        top()            { return c.back(); }
        const value_type& top() const       { return c.back(); }
        void push(const value_type& x)      { c.push_back(x); }
        void pop()                          { c.pop_back(); }
      };

      template <class T, class Container>
        bool operator==(const stack<T, Container>& x,
                        const stack<T, Container>& y);
      template <class T, class Container>
        bool operator< (const stack<T, Container>& x,
                        const stack<T, Container>& y);
      template <class T, class Container>
        bool operator!=(const stack<T, Container>& x,
                        const stack<T, Container>& y);
      template <class T, class Container>
        bool operator> (const stack<T, Container>& x,
                        const stack<T, Container>& y);
      template <class T, class Container>
        bool operator>=(const stack<T, Container>& x,
                        const stack<T, Container>& y);
      template <class T, class Container>
        bool operator<=(const stack<T, Container>& x,
                        const stack<T, Container>& y);
    }
```

23.2.4 Class template `vector`   [lib.vector]

1   A `vector` is a kind of sequence that supports random access iterators. In addition, it supports (amortized) constant time insert and erase operations at the end; insert and erase in the middle take linear time. Storage management is handled automatically, though hints can be given to improve efficiency. The elements of a vector are stored contiguously, meaning that if v is a `vector<T, Allocator>` where T is some type other than `bool`, then it obeys the identity &v[n] == &v[0] + n for all 0 <= n < v.size().

2   A `vector` satisfies all of the requirements of a container and of a reversible container (given in two tables in 23.1) and of a sequence, including most of the optional sequence requirements (23.1.1). The exceptions are the `push_front` and `pop_front` member functions, which are not provided. Descriptions are provided here only for operations on `vector` that are not described in one of these tables or for operations where there is additional semantic information.

```
namespace std {
  template <class T, class Allocator = allocator<T> >
  class vector {
  public:
    // types:
    typedef typename Allocator::reference         reference;
    typedef typename Allocator::const_reference   const_reference;
    typedef implementation defined                iterator;         // See 23.1
    typedef implementation defined                const_iterator;   // See 23.1
    typedef implementation defined                size_type;        // See 23.1
    typedef implementation defined                difference_type;  // See 23.1
    typedef T                                     value_type;
    typedef Allocator                             allocator_type;
    typedef typename Allocator::pointer           pointer;
    typedef typename Allocator::const_pointer     const_pointer;
    typedef std::reverse_iterator<iterator>       reverse_iterator;
    typedef std::reverse_iterator<const_iterator> const_reverse_iterator;

    // 23.2.4.1 construct/copy/destroy:
    explicit vector(const Allocator& = Allocator());
    explicit vector(size_type n, const T& value = T(),
        const Allocator& = Allocator());
    template <class InputIterator>
      vector(InputIterator first, InputIterator last,
        const Allocator& = Allocator());
    vector(const vector<T,Allocator>& x);
    ~vector();
    vector<T,Allocator>& operator=(const vector<T,Allocator>& x);
    template <class InputIterator>
      void assign(InputIterator first, InputIterator last);
    void assign(size_type n, const T& u);
    allocator_type get_allocator() const;

    // iterators:
    iterator               begin();
    const_iterator         begin() const;
    iterator               end();
    const_iterator         end() const;
    reverse_iterator       rbegin();
    const_reverse_iterator rbegin() const;
    reverse_iterator       rend();
    const_reverse_iterator rend() const;
```

```
    // 23.2.4.2 capacity:
    size_type size() const;
    size_type max_size() const;
    void      resize(size_type sz, T c = T());
    size_type capacity() const;
    bool      empty() const;
    void      reserve(size_type n);

    // element access:
    reference       operator[](size_type n);
    const_reference operator[](size_type n) const;
    const_reference at(size_type n) const;
    reference       at(size_type n);
    reference       front();
    const_reference front() const;
    reference       back();
    const_reference back() const;

    // 23.2.4.3 modifiers:
    void push_back(const T& x);
    void pop_back();
    iterator insert(iterator position, const T& x);
    void     insert(iterator position, size_type n, const T& x);
    template <class InputIterator>
        void insert(iterator position,
                    InputIterator first, InputIterator last);
    iterator erase(iterator position);
    iterator erase(iterator first, iterator last);
    void     swap(vector<T,Allocator>&);
    void     clear();
};

template <class T, class Allocator>
  bool operator==(const vector<T,Allocator>& x,
                  const vector<T,Allocator>& y);
template <class T, class Allocator>
  bool operator< (const vector<T,Allocator>& x,
                  const vector<T,Allocator>& y);
template <class T, class Allocator>
  bool operator!=(const vector<T,Allocator>& x,
                  const vector<T,Allocator>& y);
template <class T, class Allocator>
  bool operator> (const vector<T,Allocator>& x,
                  const vector<T,Allocator>& y);
template <class T, class Allocator>
  bool operator>=(const vector<T,Allocator>& x,
                  const vector<T,Allocator>& y);
template <class T, class Allocator>
  bool operator<=(const vector<T,Allocator>& x,
                  const vector<T,Allocator>& y);

    // specialized algorithms:
    template <class T, class Allocator>
      void swap(vector<T,Allocator>& x, vector<T,Allocator>& y);
}
```

```
vector(const Allocator& = Allocator());
explicit vector(size_type n, const T& value = T(),
                const Allocator& = Allocator());
template <class InputIterator>
  vector(InputIterator first, InputIterator last,
         const Allocator& = Allocator());
vector(const vector<T,Allocator>& x);
```

1   **Complexity:** The constructor template <class InputIterator> vector(InputIterator
     first, InputIterator last) makes only N calls to the copy constructor of T (where N is the
     distance between first and last) and no reallocations if iterators first and last are of forward, bidi-
     rectional, or random access categories. It makes order N calls to the copy constructor of T and order
     logN reallocations if they are just input iterators.

```
template <class InputIterator>
  void assign(InputIterator first, InputIterator last);
```

2   **Effects:**

```
        erase(begin(), end());
        insert(begin(), first, last);
```

```
    void assign(size_type n, const T& t);
```

3   **Effects:**

```
        erase(begin(), end());
        insert(begin(), n, t);
```

```
    size_type capacity() const;
```

1   **Returns:** The total number of elements that the vector can hold without requiring reallocation.

```
    void reserve(size_type n);
```

2   **Effects:** A directive that informs a vector of a planned change in size, so that it can manage the storage
     allocation accordingly. After reserve(), capacity() is greater or equal to the argument of
     reserve if reallocation happens; and equal to the previous value of capacity() otherwise. Reallo-
     cation happens at this point if and only if the current capacity is less than the argument of reserve().

3   **Complexity:** It does not change the size of the sequence and takes at most linear time in the size of the
     sequence.

4   **Throws:** length_error if n > max_size().[248]

5   **Notes:** Reallocation invalidates all the references, pointers, and iterators referring to the elements in the
     sequence. It is guaranteed that no reallocation takes place during insertions that happen after a call to
     reserve() until the time when an insertion would make the size of the vector greater than the size
     specified in the most recent call to reserve().

---

[248] reserve() uses Allocator::allocate() which may throw an appropriate exception.

```
void resize(size_type sz, T c = T());
```

6   **Effects:**

```
if (sz > size())
  insert(end(), sz-size(), c);
else if (sz < size())
  erase(begin()+sz, end());
else
  ;                              // do nothing
```

23.2.4.3 vector modifiers   [lib.vector.modifiers]

```
iterator insert(iterator position, const T& x);
void    insert(iterator position, size_type n, const T& x);
template <class InputIterator>
  void insert(iterator position, InputIterator first, InputIterator last);
```

1   **Notes:** Causes reallocation if the new size is greater than the old capacity. If no reallocation happens, all
the iterators and references before the insertion point remain valid. If an exception is thrown other than
by the copy constructor or assignment operator of T there are no effects.

2   **Complexity:** If first and last are forward iterators, bidirectional iterators, or random access iterators,
the complexity is linear in the number of elements in the range [first, last) plus the distance to
the end of the vector. If they are input iterators, the complexity is proportional to the number of elements in the range [first, last) times the distance to the end of the vector.

```
iterator erase(iterator position);
iterator erase(iterator first, iterator last);
```

3   **Effects:** Invalidates all the iterators and references after the point of the erase.

4   **Complexity:** The destructor of T is called the number of times equal to the number of the elements erased,
but the assignment operator of T is called the number of times equal to the number of elements in the
vector after the erased elements.

5   **Throws:** Nothing unless an exception is thrown by the copy constructor or assignment operator of T.

23.2.4.4 vector specialized algorithms   [lib.vector.special]

```
template <class T, class Allocator>
  void swap(vector<T,Allocator>& x, vector<T,Allocator>& y);
```

1   **Effects:**

```
x.swap(y);
```

23.2.5 Class vector<bool>   [lib.vector.bool]

1   To optimize space allocation, a specialization of vector for bool elements is provided:

```
namespace std {
  template <class Allocator> class vector<bool, Allocator> {
  public:
    // types:
    typedef bool                                 const_reference;
    typedef implementation defined               iterator;          // See 23.1
    typedef implementation defined               const_iterator;  // See 23.1
    typedef implementation defined               size_type;         // See 23.1
    typedef implementation defined               difference_type;// See 23.1
    typedef bool                                 value_type;
    typedef Allocator                            allocator_type;
    typedef implementation defined               pointer;
    typedef implementation defined               const_pointer;
    typedef std::reverse_iterator<iterator>      reverse_iterator;
    typedef std::reverse_iterator<const_iterator> const_reverse_iterator;

    // bit reference:
    class reference {
     friend class vector;
     reference();
    public:
     ~reference();
      operator bool() const;
      reference& operator=(const bool x);
      reference& operator=(const reference& x);
      void flip();                    // flips the bit
    };

    // construct/copy/destroy:
    explicit vector(const Allocator& = Allocator());
    explicit vector(size_type n, const bool& value = bool(),
                const Allocator& = Allocator());
    template <class InputIterator>
      vector(InputIterator first, InputIterator last,
        const Allocator& = Allocator());
    vector(const vector<bool,Allocator>& x);
    ~vector();
    vector<bool,Allocator>& operator=(const vector<bool,Allocator>& x);
    template <class InputIterator>
      void assign(InputIterator first, InputIterator last);
    void assign(size_type n, const T& t);
    allocator_type get_allocator() const;

    // iterators:
    iterator               begin();
    const_iterator         begin() const;
    iterator               end();
    const_iterator         end() const;
    reverse_iterator       rbegin();
    const_reverse_iterator rbegin() const;
    reverse_iterator       rend();
    const_reverse_iterator rend() const;
```

```
    // capacity:
    size_type size() const;
    size_type max_size() const;
    void      resize(size_type sz, bool c = false);
    size_type capacity() const;
    bool      empty() const;
    void      reserve(size_type n);

    // element access:
    reference       operator[](size_type n);
    const_reference operator[](size_type n) const;
    const_reference at(size_type n) const;
    reference       at(size_type n);
    reference       front();
    const_reference front() const;
    reference       back();
    const_reference back() const;

    // modifiers:
    void push_back(const bool& x);
    void pop_back();
    iterator insert(iterator position, const bool& x);
    void     insert (iterator position, size_type n, const bool& x);
    template <class InputIterator>
        void insert(iterator position,
                    InputIterator first, InputIterator last);

    iterator erase(iterator position);
    iterator erase(iterator first, iterator last);
    void swap(vector<bool,Allocator>&);
    static void swap(reference x, reference y);
    void flip();                    // flips all bits
    void clear();
};

template <class Allocator>
  bool operator==(const vector<bool,Allocator>& x,
                  const vector<bool,Allocator>& y);
template <class Allocator>
  bool operator< (const vector<bool,Allocator>& x,
                  const vector<bool,Allocator>& y);
template <class Allocator>
  bool operator!=(const vector<bool,Allocator>& x,
                  const vector<bool,Allocator>& y);
template <class Allocator>
  bool operator> (const vector<bool,Allocator>& x,
                  const vector<bool,Allocator>& y);
template <class Allocator>
  bool operator>=(const vector<bool,Allocator>& x,
                  const vector<bool,Allocator>& y);
template <class Allocator>
  bool operator<=(const vector<bool,Allocator>& x,
                  const vector<bool,Allocator>& y);

// specialized algorithms:
template <class Allocator>
  void swap(vector<bool,Allocator>& x, vector<bool,Allocator>& y);
}
```

2   `reference` is a class that simulates the behavior of references of a single bit in `vector<bool>`.

23.3 Associative containers   [lib.associative]

1   Headers `<map>` and `<set>`:

Header `<map>` synopsis

```
namespace std {
  template <class Key, class T, class Compare = less<Key>,
            class Allocator = allocator<pair<const Key, T> > >
    class map;
  template <class Key, class T, class Compare, class Allocator>
    bool operator==(const map<Key,T,Compare,Allocator>& x,
                    const map<Key,T,Compare,Allocator>& y);
  template <class Key, class T, class Compare, class Allocator>
    bool operator<  (const map<Key,T,Compare,Allocator>& x,
                    const map<Key,T,Compare,Allocator>& y);
  template <class Key, class T, class Compare, class Allocator>
    bool operator!=(const map<Key,T,Compare,Allocator>& x,
                    const map<Key,T,Compare,Allocator>& y);
  template <class Key, class T, class Compare, class Allocator>
    bool operator>  (const map<Key,T,Compare,Allocator>& x,
                    const map<Key,T,Compare,Allocator>& y);
  template <class Key, class T, class Compare, class Allocator>
    bool operator>=(const map<Key,T,Compare,Allocator>& x,
                    const map<Key,T,Compare,Allocator>& y);
  template <class Key, class T, class Compare, class Allocator>
    bool operator<=(const map<Key,T,Compare,Allocator>& x,
                    const map<Key,T,Compare,Allocator>& y);
  template <class Key, class T, class Compare, class Allocator>
    void swap(map<Key,T,Compare,Allocator>& x,
              map<Key,T,Compare,Allocator>& y);

  template <class Key, class T, class Compare = less<Key>,
            class Allocator = allocator<pair<const Key, T> > >
    class multimap;
  template <class Key, class T, class Compare, class Allocator>
    bool operator==(const multimap<Key,T,Compare,Allocator>& x,
                    const multimap<Key,T,Compare,Allocator>& y);
  template <class Key, class T, class Compare, class Allocator>
    bool operator<  (const multimap<Key,T,Compare,Allocator>& x,
                    const multimap<Key,T,Compare,Allocator>& y);
  template <class Key, class T, class Compare, class Allocator>
    bool operator!=(const multimap<Key,T,Compare,Allocator>& x,
                    const multimap<Key,T,Compare,Allocator>& y);
  template <class Key, class T, class Compare, class Allocator>
    bool operator>  (const multimap<Key,T,Compare,Allocator>& x,
                    const multimap<Key,T,Compare,Allocator>& y);
  template <class Key, class T, class Compare, class Allocator>
    bool operator>=(const multimap<Key,T,Compare,Allocator>& x,
                    const multimap<Key,T,Compare,Allocator>& y);
  template <class Key, class T, class Compare, class Allocator>
    bool operator<=(const multimap<Key,T,Compare,Allocator>& x,
                    const multimap<Key,T,Compare,Allocator>& y);
  template <class Key, class T, class Compare, class Allocator>
    void swap(multimap<Key,T,Compare,Allocator>& x,
              multimap<Key,T,Compare,Allocator>& y);
}
```

Header `<set>` synopsis

```
namespace std {
  template <class Key, class Compare = less<Key>,
            class Allocator = allocator<Key> >
    class set;
  template <class Key, class Compare, class Allocator>
    bool operator==(const set<Key,Compare,Allocator>& x,
                    const set<Key,Compare,Allocator>& y);
  template <class Key, class Compare, class Allocator>
    bool operator<  (const set<Key,Compare,Allocator>& x,
                    const set<Key,Compare,Allocator>& y);
  template <class Key, class Compare, class Allocator>
    bool operator!=(const set<Key,Compare,Allocator>& x,
                    const set<Key,Compare,Allocator>& y);
  template <class Key, class Compare, class Allocator>
    bool operator>  (const set<Key,Compare,Allocator>& x,
                    const set<Key,Compare,Allocator>& y);
  template <class Key, class Compare, class Allocator>
    bool operator>=(const set<Key,Compare,Allocator>& x,
                    const set<Key,Compare,Allocator>& y);
  template <class Key, class Compare, class Allocator>
    bool operator<=(const set<Key,Compare,Allocator>& x,
                    const set<Key,Compare,Allocator>& y);
  template <class Key, class Compare, class Allocator>
    void swap(set<Key,Compare,Allocator>& x,
              set<Key,Compare,Allocator>& y);

  template <class Key, class Compare = less<Key>,
            class Allocator = allocator<Key> >
    class multiset;
  template <class Key, class Compare, class Allocator>
    bool operator==(const multiset<Key,Compare,Allocator>& x,
                    const multiset<Key,Compare,Allocator>& y);
  template <class Key, class Compare, class Allocator>
    bool operator<  (const multiset<Key,Compare,Allocator>& x,
                    const multiset<Key,Compare,Allocator>& y);
  template <class Key, class Compare, class Allocator>
    bool operator!=(const multiset<Key,Compare,Allocator>& x,
                    const multiset<Key,Compare,Allocator>& y);
  template <class Key, class Compare, class Allocator>
    bool operator>  (const multiset<Key,Compare,Allocator>& x,
                    const multiset<Key,Compare,Allocator>& y);
  template <class Key, class Compare, class Allocator>
    bool operator>=(const multiset<Key,Compare,Allocator>& x,
                    const multiset<Key,Compare,Allocator>& y);
  template <class Key, class Compare, class Allocator>
    bool operator<=(const multiset<Key,Compare,Allocator>& x,
                    const multiset<Key,Compare,Allocator>& y);
  template <class Key, class Compare, class Allocator>
    void swap(multiset<Key,Compare,Allocator>& x,
              multiset<Key,Compare,Allocator>& y);
}
```

23.3.1 Class template map   [lib.map]

1   A map is a kind of associative container that supports unique keys (contains at most one of each key value)
       and provides for fast retrieval of values of another type T based on the keys. The map class supports bidi-
       rectional iterators.

2   A map satisfies all of the requirements of a container and of a reversible container (23.1) and of an associa-
       tive container (23.1.2). A map also provides most operations described in (23.1.2) for unique keys. This
       means that a map supports the a_uniq operations in (23.1.2) but not the a_eq operations. For a
       map<Key,T> the key_type is Key and the value_type is pair<const Key,T>. Descriptions
       are provided here only for operations on map that are not described in one of those tables or for operations
       where there is additional semantic information.

```
namespace std {
  template <class Key, class T, class Compare = less<Key>,
            class Allocator = allocator<pair<const Key, T> > >
  class map {
  public:
    // types:
    typedef Key                                 key_type;
    typedef T                                   mapped_type;
    typedef pair<const Key, T>                  value_type;
    typedef Compare                             key_compare;
    typedef Allocator                           allocator_type;
    typedef typename Allocator::reference       reference;
    typedef typename Allocator::const_reference const_reference;
    typedef implementation defined              iterator;          // See 23.1
    typedef implementation defined              const_iterator;    // See 23.1
    typedef implementation defined              size_type;         // See 23.1
    typedef implementation defined              difference_type;   // See 23.1
    typedef typename Allocator::pointer         pointer;
    typedef typename Allocator::const_pointer   const_pointer;
    typedef std::reverse_iterator<iterator>     reverse_iterator;
    typedef std::reverse_iterator<const_iterator> const_reverse_iterator;

    class value_compare
      : public binary_function<value_type,value_type,bool> {
    friend class map;
    protected:
      Compare comp;
      value_compare(Compare c) : comp(c) {}
    public:
      bool operator()(const value_type& x, const value_type& y) const {
        return comp(x.first, y.first);
      }
    };

    // 23.3.1.1 construct/copy/destroy:
    explicit map(const Compare& comp = Compare(),
                 const Allocator& = Allocator());
    template <class InputIterator>
      map(InputIterator first, InputIterator last,
          const Compare& comp = Compare(), const Allocator& = Allocator());
    map(const map<Key,T,Compare,Allocator>& x);
    ~map();
    map<Key,T,Compare,Allocator>&
      operator=(const map<Key,T,Compare,Allocator>& x);
    allocator_type get_allocator() const;
```

```
// iterators:
iterator              begin();
const_iterator        begin() const;
iterator              end();
const_iterator        end() const;
reverse_iterator      rbegin();
const_reverse_iterator rbegin() const;
reverse_iterator      rend();
const_reverse_iterator rend() const;

// capacity:
bool      empty() const;
size_type size() const;
size_type max_size() const;

// 23.3.1.2 element access:
T& operator[](const key_type& x);

// modifiers:
pair<iterator, bool> insert(const value_type& x);
iterator             insert(iterator position, const value_type& x);
template <class InputIterator>
  void insert(InputIterator first, InputIterator last);

void      erase(iterator position);
size_type erase(const key_type& x);
void      erase(iterator first, iterator last);
void swap(map<Key,T,Compare,Allocator>&);
void clear();

// observers:
key_compare   key_comp() const;
value_compare value_comp() const;

// 23.3.1.3 map operations:
iterator       find(const key_type& x);
const_iterator find(const key_type& x) const;
size_type      count(const key_type& x) const;

iterator       lower_bound(const key_type& x);
const_iterator lower_bound(const key_type& x) const;
iterator       upper_bound(const key_type& x);
const_iterator upper_bound(const key_type& x) const;

pair<iterator,iterator>
    equal_range(const key_type& x);
pair<const_iterator,const_iterator>
    equal_range(const key_type& x) const;
};
```

```
template <class Key, class T, class Compare, class Allocator>
  bool operator==(const map<Key,T,Compare,Allocator>& x,
                  const map<Key,T,Compare,Allocator>& y);
template <class Key, class T, class Compare, class Allocator>
  bool operator< (const map<Key,T,Compare,Allocator>& x,
                  const map<Key,T,Compare,Allocator>& y);
template <class Key, class T, class Compare, class Allocator>
  bool operator!=(const map<Key,T,Compare,Allocator>& x,
                  const map<Key,T,Compare,Allocator>& y);
template <class Key, class T, class Compare, class Allocator>
  bool operator> (const map<Key,T,Compare,Allocator>& x,
                  const map<Key,T,Compare,Allocator>& y);
template <class Key, class T, class Compare, class Allocator>
  bool operator>=(const map<Key,T,Compare,Allocator>& x,
                  const map<Key,T,Compare,Allocator>& y);
template <class Key, class T, class Compare, class Allocator>
  bool operator<=(const map<Key,T,Compare,Allocator>& x,
                  const map<Key,T,Compare,Allocator>& y);

// specialized algorithms:
template <class Key, class T, class Compare, class Allocator>
  void swap(map<Key,T,Compare,Allocator>& x,
            map<Key,T,Compare,Allocator>& y);
}
```

23.3.1.1 map constructors, copy, and assignment   [lib.map.cons]

```
explicit map(const Compare& comp = Compare(),
             const Allocator& = Allocator());
```

1 **Effects:** Constructs an empty map using the specified comparison object and allocator.

2 **Complexity:** Constant.

```
template <class InputIterator>
  map(InputIterator first, InputIterator last,
      const Compare& comp = Compare(), const Allocator& = Allocator());
```

3 **Effects:** Constructs an empty map using the specified comparison object and allocator, and inserts elements from the range [first, last).

4 **Complexity:** Linear in N if the range [first, last) is already sorted using comp and otherwise N log N, where N is last - first.

23.3.1.2 map element access   [lib.map.access]

```
T& operator[](const key_type& x);
```

1 **Returns:** (*((insert(make_pair(x, T()))).first)).second.

23.3.1.3 map operations   [lib.map.ops]

```
iterator       find(const key_type& x);
const_iterator find(const key_type& x) const;
```

```
iterator        lower_bound(const key_type& x);
const_iterator  lower_bound(const key_type& x) const;


iterator        upper_bound(const key_type& x);
const_iterator  upper_bound(const key_type &x) const;


pair<iterator, iterator>
  equal_range(const key_type &x);
pair<const_iterator, const_iterator>
  equal_range(const key_type& x) const;
```

1   The find, lower_bound, upper_bound and equal_range member functions each have two versions, one const and the other non-const. In each case the behavior of the two functions is identical except that the const version returns a const_iterator and the non-const version an iterator (23.1.2).

23.3.1.4 map specialized algorithms [lib.map.special]

```
template <class Key, class T, class Compare, class Allocator>
  void swap(map<Key,T,Compare,Allocator>& x,
            map<Key,T,Compare,Allocator>& y);
```

1   **Effects:**

```
x.swap(y);
```

23.3.2 Class template multimap [lib.multimap]

1   A multimap is a kind of associative container that supports equivalent keys (possibly containing multiple copies of the same key value) and provides for fast retrieval of values of another type T based on the keys. The multimap class supports bidirectional iterators.

2   A multimap satisfies all of the requirements of a container and of a reversible container (23.1) and of an associative container (23.1.2). A multimap also provides most operations described in (23.1.2) for equal keys. This means that a multimap supports the a_eq operations in (23.1.2) but not the a_uniq operations. For a multimap<Key,T> the key_type is Key and the value_type is pair<const Key,T>. Descriptions are provided here only for operations on multimap that are not described in one of those tables or for operations where there is additional semantic information.

```
namespace std {
  template <class Key, class T, class Compare = less<Key>,
            class Allocator = allocator<pair<const Key, T> > >
  class multimap {
  public:
    // types:
    typedef Key                                   key_type;
    typedef T                                     mapped_type;
    typedef pair<const Key,T>                     value_type;
    typedef Compare                               key_compare;
    typedef Allocator                             allocator_type;
    typedef typename Allocator::reference         reference;
    typedef typename Allocator::const_reference   const_reference;
    typedef implementation defined                iterator;        // See 23.1
    typedef implementation defined                const_iterator;  // See 23.1
    typedef implementation defined                size_type;       // See 23.1
    typedef implementation defined                difference_type; // See 23.1
    typedef typename Allocator::pointer           pointer;
    typedef typename Allocator::const_pointer     const_pointer;
    typedef std::reverse_iterator<iterator>       reverse_iterator;
    typedef std::reverse_iterator<const_iterator> const_reverse_iterator;

    class value_compare
      : public binary_function<value_type,value_type,bool> {
    friend class multimap;
    protected:
      Compare comp;
      value_compare(Compare c) : comp(c) {}
    public:
      bool operator()(const value_type& x, const value_type& y) const {
        return comp(x.first, y.first);
      }
    };

    // construct/copy/destroy:
    explicit multimap(const Compare& comp = Compare(),
                      const Allocator& = Allocator());
    template <class InputIterator>
      multimap(InputIterator first, InputIterator last,
               const Compare& comp = Compare(),
               const Allocator& = Allocator());
    multimap(const multimap<Key,T,Compare,Allocator>& x);
    ~multimap();
    multimap<Key,T,Compare,Allocator>&
      operator=(const multimap<Key,T,Compare,Allocator>& x);
    allocator_type get_allocator() const;

    // iterators:
    iterator               begin();
    const_iterator         begin() const;
    iterator               end();
    const_iterator         end() const;
    reverse_iterator       rbegin();
    const_reverse_iterator rbegin() const;
    reverse_iterator       rend();
    const_reverse_iterator rend() const;
```

```
// capacity:
bool          empty() const;
size_type     size() const;
size_type     max_size() const;

// modifiers:
iterator insert(const value_type& x);
iterator insert(iterator position, const value_type& x);
template <class InputIterator>
  void insert(InputIterator first, InputIterator last);

void      erase(iterator position);
size_type erase(const key_type& x);
void      erase(iterator first, iterator last);
void swap(multimap<Key,T,Compare,Allocator>&);
void clear();

// observers:
key_compare    key_comp() const;
value_compare  value_comp() const;

// map operations:
iterator       find(const key_type& x);
const_iterator find(const key_type& x) const;
size_type      count(const key_type& x) const;

iterator       lower_bound(const key_type& x);
const_iterator lower_bound(const key_type& x) const;
iterator       upper_bound(const key_type& x);
const_iterator upper_bound(const key_type& x) const;

pair<iterator,iterator>
  equal_range(const key_type& x);
pair<const_iterator,const_iterator>
  equal_range(const key_type& x) const;
};

template <class Key, class T, class Compare, class Allocator>
  bool operator==(const multimap<Key,T,Compare,Allocator>& x,
                  const multimap<Key,T,Compare,Allocator>& y);
template <class Key, class T, class Compare, class Allocator>
  bool operator< (const multimap<Key,T,Compare,Allocator>& x,
                  const multimap<Key,T,Compare,Allocator>& y);
template <class Key, class T, class Compare, class Allocator>
  bool operator!=(const multimap<Key,T,Compare,Allocator>& x,
                  const multimap<Key,T,Compare,Allocator>& y);
template <class Key, class T, class Compare, class Allocator>
  bool operator> (const multimap<Key,T,Compare,Allocator>& x,
                  const multimap<Key,T,Compare,Allocator>& y);
template <class Key, class T, class Compare, class Allocator>
  bool operator>=(const multimap<Key,T,Compare,Allocator>& x,
                  const multimap<Key,T,Compare,Allocator>& y);
template <class Key, class T, class Compare, class Allocator>
  bool operator<=(const multimap<Key,T,Compare,Allocator>& x,
                  const multimap<Key,T,Compare,Allocator>& y);
```

```
// specialized algorithms:
template <class Key, class T, class Compare, class Allocator>
  void swap(multimap<Key,T,Compare,Allocator>& x,
            multimap<Key,T,Compare,Allocator>& y);
}
```

23.3.2.1 `multimap` constructors   [lib.multimap.cons]

```
explicit multimap(const Compare& comp = Compare(),
                  const Allocator& = Allocator());
```

1   **Effects:** Constructs an empty `multimap` using the specified comparison object and allocator.
2   **Complexity:** Constant.

```
template <class InputIterator>
  multimap(InputIterator first, InputIterator last,
           const Compare& comp = Compare(),
           const Allocator& = Allocator()0;
```

3   **Effects:** Constructs an empty `multimap` using the specified comparison object and allocator, and inserts
     elements from the range [*first*, *last*).
4   **Complexity:** Linear in *N* if the range [*first*, *last*). is already sorted using *comp* and otherwise *N*
     log N, where *N* is *last - first*.

23.3.2.2 `multimap` operations   [lib.multimap.ops]

```
iterator       find(const key_type &x);
const_iterator find(const key_type& x) const;


iterator       lower_bound(const key_type& x);
const_iterator lower_bound(const key_type& x) const;


pair<iterator, iterator>
  equal_range(const key_type& x);
pair<const_iterator, const_iterator>
  equal_range(const_key_type& x) const;
```

1   The `find`, `lower_bound`, `upper_bound`, and `equal_range` member functions each have two ver-
     sions, one const and one non-const. In each case the behavior of the two versions is identical except that
     the const version returns a `const_iterator` and the non-const version an `iterator` (23.1.2).

23.3.2.3 `multimap` specialized algorithms   [lib.multimap.special]

```
template <class Key, class T, class Compare, class Allocator>
  void swap(multimap<Key,T,Compare,Allocator>& x,
            multimap<Key,T,Compare,Allocator>& y);
```

1   **Effects:**

```
x.swap(y);
```

23.3.3 Class template set   [lib.set]

1   A set is a kind of associative container that supports unique keys (contains at most one of each key value) and provides for fast retrieval of the keys themselves. Class set supports bidirectional iterators.

2   A set satisfies all of the requirements of a container and of a reversible container (23.1), and of an associative container (23.1.2). A set also provides most operations described in (23.1.2) for unique keys. This means that a set supports the a_uniq operations in (23.1.2) but not the a_eq operations. For a set<Key> both the key_type and value_type are Key. Descriptions are provided here only for operations on set that are not described in one of these tables and for operations where there is additional semantic information.

```
namespace std {
  template <class Key, class Compare = less<Key>,
            class Allocator = allocator<Key> >
  class set {
  public:
    // types:
    typedef Key                                   key_type;
    typedef Key                                   value_type;
    typedef Compare                               key_compare;
    typedef Compare                               value_compare;
    typedef Allocator                             allocator_type;
    typedef typename Allocator::reference         reference;
    typedef typename Allocator::const_reference   const_reference;
    typedef implementation defined                iterator;        // See 23.1
    typedef implementation defined                const_iterator;  // See 23.1
    typedef implementation defined                size_type;       // See 23.1
    typedef implementation defined                difference_type; // See 23.1
    typedef typename Allocator::pointer           pointer;
    typedef typename Allocator::const_pointer     const_pointer;
    typedef std::reverse_iterator<iterator>       reverse_iterator;
    typedef std::reverse_iterator<const_iterator> const_reverse_iterator;

    // 23.3.3.1 construct/copy/destroy:
    explicit set(const Compare& comp = Compare(),
                 const Allocator& = Allocator());
    template <class InputIterator>
      set(InputIterator first, InputIterator last,
          const Compare& comp = Compare(), const Allocator& = Allocator());
    set(const set<Key,Compare,Allocator>& x);
    ~set();
    set<Key,Compare,Allocator>& operator=
      (const set<Key,Compare,Allocator>& x);
    allocator_type get_allocator() const;

    // iterators:
    iterator                begin();
    const_iterator          begin() const;
    iterator                end();
    const_iterator          end() const;
    reverse_iterator        rbegin();
    const_reverse_iterator  rbegin() const;
    reverse_iterator        rend();
    const_reverse_iterator  rend() const;
```

```
// capacity:
bool          empty() const;
size_type     size() const;
size_type     max_size() const;

// modifiers:
pair<iterator,bool> insert(const value_type& x);
iterator            insert(iterator position, const value_type& x);
template <class InputIterator>
    void insert(InputIterator first, InputIterator last);

void      erase(iterator position);
size_type erase(const key_type& x);
void      erase(iterator first, iterator last);
void swap(set<Key,Compare,Allocator>&);
void clear();

// observers:
key_compare   key_comp() const;
value_compare value_comp() const;

// set operations:
iterator  find(const key_type& x) const;
size_type count(const key_type& x) const;

iterator  lower_bound(const key_type& x) const;
iterator  upper_bound(const key_type& x) const;
pair<iterator,iterator> equal_range(const key_type& x) const;
};

template <class Key, class Compare, class Allocator>
  bool operator==(const set<Key,Compare,Allocator>& x,
                  const set<Key,Compare,Allocator>& y);
template <class Key, class Compare, class Allocator>
  bool operator< (const set<Key,Compare,Allocator>& x,
                  const set<Key,Compare,Allocator>& y);
template <class Key, class Compare, class Allocator>
  bool operator!=(const set<Key,Compare,Allocator>& x,
                  const set<Key,Compare,Allocator>& y);
template <class Key, class Compare, class Allocator>
  bool operator> (const set<Key,Compare,Allocator>& x,
                  const set<Key,Compare,Allocator>& y);
template <class Key, class Compare, class Allocator>
  bool operator>=(const set<Key,Compare,Allocator>& x,
                  const set<Key,Compare,Allocator>& y);
template <class Key, class Compare, class Allocator>
  bool operator<=(const set<Key,Compare,Allocator>& x,
                  const set<Key,Compare,Allocator>& y);

// specialized algorithms:
template <class Key, class Compare, class Allocator>
  void swap(set<Key,Compare,Allocator>& x,
            set<Key,Compare,Allocator>& y);
}
```

23.3.3.1 `set` constructors, copy, and assignment [lib.set.cons]

```
explicit set(const Compare& comp = Compare(),
             const Allocator& = Allocator());
```

1 **Effects:** Constructs an empty set using the specified comparison objects and allocator.

2 **Complexity:** Constant.

```
template <class InputIterator>
  set(InputIterator first, last,
      const Compare& comp = Compare(), const Allocator& = Allocator());
```

3 **Effects:** Constructs an empty `set` using the specified comparison object and allocator, and inserts elements from the range [*first*, *last*).

4 **Complexity:** Linear in N if the range [*first*, *last*) is already sorted using *comp* and otherwise N *log N*, where N is *last - first*.

23.3.3.2 `set` specialized algorithms [lib.set.special]

```
template <class Key, class Compare, class Allocator>
  void swap(set<Key,Compare,Allocator>& x,
            set<Key,Compare,Allocator>& y);
```

1 **Effects:**

```
x.swap(y);
```

23.3.4 Class template `multiset` [lib.multiset]

1 A `multiset` is a kind of associative container that supports equivalent keys (possibly contains multiple copies of the same key value) and provides for fast retrieval of the keys themselves. Class `multiset` supports bidirectional iterators.

2 A `multiset` satisfies all of the requirements of a container and of a reversible container (23.1), and of an associative container (23.1.2). `multiset` also provides most operations described in (23.1.2) for duplicate keys. This means that a `multiset` supports the a_eq operations in (23.1.2) but not the a_uniq operations. For a `multiset<Key>` both the key_type and value_type are Key. Descriptions are provided here only for operations on `multiset` that are not described in one of these tables and for operations where there is additional semantic information.

```
namespace std {
  template <class Key, class Compare = less<Key>,
            class Allocator = allocator<Key> >
  class multiset {
  public:
    // types:
    typedef Key                                key_type;
    typedef Key                                value_type;
    typedef Compare                            key_compare;
    typedef Compare                            value_compare;
    typedef Allocator                          allocator_type;
    typedef typename Allocator::reference      reference;
    typedef typename Allocator::const_reference const_reference;
    typedef implementation defined             iterator;        // See 23.1
    typedef implementation defined             const_iterator;  // See 23.1
    typedef implementation defined             size_type;       // See 23.1
    typedef implementation defined             difference_type; // See 23.1
    typedef typename Allocator::pointer        pointer;
    typedef typename Allocator::const_pointer  const_pointer;
    typedef std::reverse_iterator<iterator>    reverse_iterator;
    typedef std::reverse_iterator<const_iterator> const_reverse_iterator;

    // construct/copy/destroy:
    explicit multiset(const Compare& comp = Compare(),
                      const Allocator& = Allocator());
    template <class InputIterator>
      multiset(InputIterator first, InputIterator last,
               const Compare& comp = Compare(),
               const Allocator& = Allocator());
    multiset(const multiset<Key,Compare,Allocator>& x);
    ~multiset();
    multiset<Key,Compare,Allocator>&
        operator=(const multiset<Key,Compare,Allocator>& x);
    allocator_type get_allocator() const;

    // iterators:
    iterator               begin();
    const_iterator         begin() const;
    iterator               end();
    const_iterator         end() const;
    reverse_iterator       rbegin();
    const_reverse_iterator rbegin() const;
    reverse_iterator       rend();
    const_reverse_iterator rend() const;

    // capacity:
    bool        empty() const;
    size_type   size() const;
    size_type   max_size() const;

    // modifiers:
    iterator insert(const value_type& x);
    iterator insert(iterator position, const value_type& x);
    template <class InputIterator>
      void insert(InputIterator first, InputIterator last);
```

```
void      erase(iterator position);
size_type erase(const key_type& x);
void      erase(iterator first, iterator last);
void swap(multiset<Key,Compare,Allocator>&);
void clear();

// observers:
key_compare   key_comp() const;
value_compare value_comp() const;

// set operations:
iterator  find(const key_type& x) const;
size_type count(const key_type& x) const;

iterator  lower_bound(const key_type& x) const;
iterator  upper_bound(const key_type& x) const;
pair<iterator,iterator> equal_range(const key_type& x) const;
};

template <class Key, class Compare, class Allocator>
  bool operator==(const multiset<Key,Compare,Allocator>& x,
                  const multiset<Key,Compare,Allocator>& y);
template <class Key, class Compare, class Allocator>
  bool operator< (const multiset<Key,Compare,Allocator>& x,
                  const multiset<Key,Compare,Allocator>& y);
template <class Key, class Compare, class Allocator>
  bool operator!=(const multiset<Key,Compare,Allocator>& x,
                  const multiset<Key,Compare,Allocator>& y);
template <class Key, class Compare, class Allocator>
  bool operator> (const multiset<Key,Compare,Allocator>& x,
                  const multiset<Key,Compare,Allocator>& y);
template <class Key, class Compare, class Allocator>
  bool operator>=(const multiset<Key,Compare,Allocator>& x,
                  const multiset<Key,Compare,Allocator>& y);
template <class Key, class Compare, class Allocator>
  bool operator<=(const multiset<Key,Compare,Allocator>& x,
                  const multiset<Key,Compare,Allocator>& y);

// specialized algorithms:
template <class Key, class Compare, class Allocator>
  void swap(multiset<Key,Compare,Allocator>& x,
            multiset<Key,Compare,Allocator>& y);
}
```

23.3.4.1 multiset constructors   [lib.multiset.cons]

```
explicit multiset(const Compare& comp = Compare(),
                  const Allocator& = Allocator());
```

1   **Effects:** Constructs an empty set using the specified comparison object and allocator.
2   **Complexity:** Constant.

```
template <class InputIterator>
  multiset(InputIterator first, last,
           const Compare& comp = Compare(), const Allocator& = Allocator());
```

3   **Effects:** Constructs an empty `multiset` using the specified comparison object and allocator, and inserts
       elements from the range [`first, last`).

4   **Complexity:** Linear in *N* if the range [`first, last`) is already sorted using *comp* and otherwise *N*
       log N, where *N* is `last - first`.

23.3.4.2 `multiset` specialized algorithms   [lib.multiset.special]

```
template <class Key, class Compare, class Allocator>
  void swap(multiset<Key,Compare,Allocator>& x,
            multiset<Key,Compare,Allocator>& y);
```

1   **Effects:**

```
        x.swap(y);
```

23.3.5 Class template `bitset`   [lib.template.bitset]

Header `<bitset>` synopsis

```
#include <cstddef>              // for size_t
#include <string>
#include <stdexcept>            // for invalid_argument,
                                //       out_of_range, overflow_error
#include <iosfwd>               // for istream, ostream
namespace std {
  template <size_t N> class bitset;

  // 23.3.5.3 bitset operations:
  template <size_t N>
    bitset<N> operator&(const bitset<N>&, const bitset<N>&);
  template <size_t N>
    bitset<N> operator|(const bitset<N>&, const bitset<N>&);
  template <size_t N>
    bitset<N> operator^(const bitset<N>&, const bitset<N>&);
  template <class charT, class traits, size_t N>
    basic_istream<charT, traits>&
    operator>>(basic_istream<charT, traits>& is, bitset<N>& x);
  template <class charT, class traits, size_t N>
    basic_ostream<charT, traits>&
    operator<<(basic_ostream<charT, traits>& os, const bitset<N>& x);
}
```

1   The header `<bitset>` defines a class template and several related functions for representing and manipu-
       lating fixed-size sequences of bits.

```
namespace std {
  template<size_t N> class bitset {
  public:
    // bit reference:
    class reference {
      friend class bitset;
      reference();
    public:
      ~reference();
      reference& operator=(bool x);             // for b[i] = x;
      reference& operator=(const reference&);   // for b[i] = b[j];
      bool operator~() const;                   // flips the bit
      operator bool() const;                    // for x = b[i];
      reference& flip();                        // for b[i].flip();
    };

    // 23.3.5.1 constructors:
    bitset();
    bitset(unsigned long val);
    template<class charT, class traits, class Allocator>
      explicit bitset(
        const basic_string<charT,traits,Allocator>& str,
        typename basic_string<charT,traits,Allocator>::size_type pos = 0,
        typename basic_string<charT,traits,Allocator>::size_type n =
          basic_string<charT,traits,Allocator>::npos);

    // 23.3.5.2 bitset operations:
    bitset<N>& operator&=(const bitset<N>& rhs);
    bitset<N>& operator|=(const bitset<N>& rhs);
    bitset<N>& operator^=(const bitset<N>& rhs);
    bitset<N>& operator<<=(size_t pos);
    bitset<N>& operator>>=(size_t pos);
    bitset<N>& set();
    bitset<N>& set(size_t pos, int val = true);
    bitset<N>& reset();
    bitset<N>& reset(size_t pos);
    bitset<N>  operator~() const;
    bitset<N>& flip();
    bitset<N>& flip(size_t pos);

    // element access:
    bool operator[](size_t pos) const;          // for b[i];
    reference operator[](size_t pos);           // for b[i];

    unsigned long  to_ulong() const;
    template <class charT, class traits, class Allocator>
      basic_string<charT, traits, Allocator> to_string() const;
    size_t count() const;
    size_t size()  const;
    bool operator==(const bitset<N>& rhs) const;
    bool operator!=(const bitset<N>& rhs) const;
    bool test(size_t pos) const;
    bool any() const;
    bool none() const;
    bitset<N> operator<<(size_t pos) const;
    bitset<N> operator>>(size_t pos) const;
  };
}
```

2   The template class `bitset<N>` describes an object that can store a sequence consisting of a fixed number of bits, *N*.

3   Each bit represents either the value zero (reset) or one (set). To *toggle* a bit is to change the value zero to one, or the value one to zero. Each bit has a non-negative position *pos*. When converting between an object of class `bitset<N>` and a value of some integral type, bit position *pos* corresponds to the *bit value* `1 << pos`. The integral value corresponding to two or more bits is the sum of their bit values.

4   The functions described in this subclause can report three kinds of errors, each associated with a distinct exception:

— an *invalid-argument* error is associated with exceptions of type `invalid_argument` (19.1.3);

— an *out-of-range* error is associated with exceptions of type `out_of_range` (19.1.5);

— an *overflow* error is associated with exceptions of type `overflow_error` (19.1.8).

23.3.5.1 `bitset` constructors   **[lib.bitset.cons]**

```
bitset();
```

1   **Effects:** Constructs an object of class `bitset<N>`, initializing all bits to zero.

```
bitset(unsigned long val);
```

2   **Effects:** Constructs an object of class `bitset<N>`, initializing the first *M* bit positions to the corresponding bit values in `val`. *M* is the smaller of *N* and the value `CHAR_BIT * sizeof (unsigned long)`.[249]
     If *M* < *N*, remaining bit positions are initialized to zero.

```
template <class charT, class traits, class Allocator>
explicit
bitset(const basic_string<charT, traits, Allocator>& str,
       typename basic_string<charT, traits, Allocator>::size_type pos = 0,
       typename basic_string<charT, traits, Allocator>::size_type n =
         basic_string<charT, traits, Allocator>::npos);
```

3   **Requires:** *pos* <= `str.size()`.
4   **Throws:** `out_of_range` if *pos* > `str.size()`.
5   **Effects:** Determines the effective length `rlen` of the initializing string as the smaller of *n* and `str.size() - pos`.
     The function then throws `invalid_argument` if any of the `rlen` characters in `str` beginning at position *pos* is other than 0 or 1.
     Otherwise, the function constructs an object of class `bitset<N>`, initializing the first *M* bit positions to values determined from the corresponding characters in the string `str`. *M* is the smaller of *N* and `rlen`.

6   An element of the constructed string has value zero if the corresponding character in `str`, beginning at position *pos*, is 0. Otherwise, the element has the value one. Character position *pos* + *M* - 1 corresponds to bit position zero. Subsequent decreasing character positions correspond to increasing bit positions.

7   If *M* < *N*, remaining bit positions are initialized to zero.

---
[249] The macro `CHAR_BIT` is defined in `<climits>` (18.2).

23.3.5.2 `bitset` members [lib.bitset.members]

```
bitset<N>& operator&=(const bitset<N>& rhs);
```

1   **Effects:** Clears each bit in `*this` for which the corresponding bit in `rhs` is clear, and leaves all other bits unchanged.

2   **Returns:** `*this`.

```
bitset<N>& operator|=(const bitset<N>& rhs);
```

3   **Effects:** Sets each bit in `*this` for which the corresponding bit in `rhs` is set, and leaves all other bits unchanged.

4   **Returns:** `*this`.

```
bitset<N>& operator^=(const bitset<N>& rhs);
```

5   **Effects:** Toggles each bit in `*this` for which the corresponding bit in `rhs` is set, and leaves all other bits unchanged.

6   **Returns:** `*this`.

```
bitset<N>& operator<<=(size_t pos);
```

7   **Effects:** Replaces each bit at position `I` in `*this` with a value determined as follows:

   — If `I < pos`, the new value is zero;

   — If `I >= pos`, the new value is the previous value of the bit at position `I - pos`.

8   **Returns:** `*this`.

```
bitset<N>& operator>>=(size_t pos);
```

9   **Effects:** Replaces each bit at position `I` in `*this` with a value determined as follows:

   — If `pos >= N - I`, the new value is zero;

   — If `pos < N - I`, the new value is the previous value of the bit at position `I + pos`.

10 **Returns:** `*this`.

```
bitset<N>& set();
```

11 **Effects:** Sets all bits in `*this`.

12 **Returns:** `*this`.

```
bitset<N>& set(size_t pos, int val = 1);
```

13 **Requires:** `pos is valid`

14 **Throws:** `out_of_range` if `pos` does not correspond to a valid bit position.

15 **Effects:** Stores a new value in the bit at position `pos` in `*this`. If `val` is nonzero, the stored value is one, otherwise it is zero.

16 **Returns:** `*this`.

```
bitset<N>& reset();
```

17 **Effects:** Resets all bits in `*this`.

18 **Returns:** `*this`.

```
bitset<N>& reset(size_t pos);
```

19 **Requires:** pos is valid
20 **Throws:** out_of_range if *pos* does not correspond to a valid bit position.
21 **Effects:** Resets the bit at position *pos* in *this.
22 **Returns:** *this.

```
bitset<N> operator~() const;
```

23 **Effects:** Constructs an object *x* of class bitset<N> and initializes it with *this.
24 **Returns:** *x*.flip().

```
bitset<N>& flip();
```

25 **Effects:** Toggles all bits in *this.
26 **Returns:** *this.

```
bitset<N>& flip(size_t pos);
```

27 **Requires:** pos is valid
28 **Throws:** out_of_range if *pos* does not correspond to a valid bit position.
29 **Effects:** Toggles the bit at position *pos* in *this.
30 **Returns:** *this.

```
unsigned long to_ulong() const;
```

31 **Throws:** overflow_error if the integral value *x* corresponding to the bits in *this cannot be represented as type unsigned long.
32 **Returns:** *x*.

```
template <class charT, class traits, class Allocator>
basic_string<charT, traits, Allocator> to_string() const;
```

33 **Effects:** Constructs a string object of the appropriate type and initializes it to a string of length N characters. Each character is determined by the value of its corresponding bit position in *this. Character position $N - 1$ corresponds to bit position zero. Subsequent decreasing character positions correspond to increasing bit positions. Bit value zero becomes the character 0, bit value one becomes the character 1.
34 **Returns:** The created object.

```
size_t count() const;
```

35 **Returns:** A count of the number of bits set in *this.

```
size_t size() const;
```

36 **Returns:** N.

```
bool operator==(const bitset<N>& rhs) const;
```

37 **Returns:** A nonzero value if the value of each bit in *this equals the value of the corresponding bit in *rhs*.

```
bool operator!=(const bitset<N>& rhs) const;
```

38   **Returns:** A nonzero value if `!(*this == rhs)`.

```
bool test(size_t pos) const;
```

39   **Requires:** `pos is valid`
40   **Throws:** `out_of_range` if *pos* does not correspond to a valid bit position.
41   **Returns:** `true` if the bit at position *pos* in `*this` has the value one.

```
bool any() const;
```

42   **Returns:** `true` if any bit in `*this` is one.

```
bool none() const;
```

43   **Returns:** `true` if no bit in `*this` is one.

```
bitset<N> operator<<(size_t pos) const;
```

44   **Returns:** `bitset<N>(*this) <<= pos`.

```
bitset<N> operator>>(size_t pos) const;
```

45   **Returns:** `bitset<N>(*this) >>= pos`.

```
bool operator[](size_t pos) const;
```

46   **Requires:** *pos* is valid.
47   **Throws:** nothing.
48   **Returns:** `test(pos)`.

```
bitset<N>::reference operator[](size_t pos);
```

49   **Requires:** *pos* is valid.
50   **Throws:** nothing.
51   **Returns:** An object of type `bitset<N>::reference` such that `(*this)[pos] == this->test(pos)`, and such that `(*this)[pos] = val` is equivalent to `this->set(pos, val)`.

23.3.5.3 `bitset` operators   [lib.bitset.operators]

```
bitset<N> operator&(const bitset<N>& lhs, const bitset<N>& rhs);
```

1   **Returns:** `bitset<N>(lhs) &= rhs`.

```
bitset<N> operator|(const bitset<N>& lhs, const bitset<N>& rhs);
```

2   **Returns:** `bitset<N>(lhs) |= rhs`.

```
bitset<N> operator^(const bitset<N>& lhs, const bitset<N>& rhs);
```

3   **Returns:** `bitset<N>(lhs) ^= rhs`.

```
template <class charT, class traits, size_t N>
  basic_istream<charT, traits>&
  operator>>(basic_istream<charT, traits>& is, bitset<N>& x);
```

4   A formatted input function (27.6.1.2).

5   **Effects:** Extracts up to N (single-byte) characters from *is*. Stores these characters in a temporary object
       str of type string, then evaluates the expression x = bitset<N>(*str*). Characters are
       extracted and stored until any of the following occurs:

       — N characters have been extracted and stored;

       — end-of-file occurs on the input sequence;

       — the next input character is neither 0 or 1 (in which case the input character is not extracted).

6   If no characters are stored in *str*, calls *is*.setstate(ios::failbit) (which may throw
       ios_base::failure (27.4.4.3).

7   **Returns:** *is*.

```
template <class charT, class traits, size_t N>
  basic_ostream<charT, traits>&
  operator<<(basic_ostream<charT, traits>& os, const bitset<N>& x);
```

8   **Returns:** *os* << *x*.template to_string<charT,traits,allocator<charT> >()
       (27.6.2.5).

24   Iterators library   [lib.iterators]

1   This clause describes components that C++ programs may use to perform iterations over containers (clause 23), streams (27.6), and stream buffers (27.5).

2   The following subclauses describe iterator requirements, and components for iterator primitives, predefined iterators, and stream iterators, as summarized in Table 70:

Table 70—Iterators library summary

Subclause	Header(s)
24.1 Requirements	
24.3 Iterator primitives	
24.4 Predefined iterators	`<iterator>`
24.5 Stream iterators	

24.1 Iterator requirements   [lib.iterator.requirements]

1   Iterators are a generalization of pointers that allow a C++ program to work with different data structures (containers) in a uniform manner. To be able to construct template algorithms that work correctly and efficiently on different types of data structures, the library formalizes not just the interfaces but also the semantics and complexity assumptions of iterators. All iterators i support the expression *i, resulting in a value of some class, enumeration, or built-in type T, called the *value type* of the iterator. All iterators i for which the expression (*i).m is well-defined, support the expression i->m with the same semantics as (*i).m. For every iterator type X for which equality is defined, there is a corresponding signed integral type called the *difference type* of the iterator.

2   Since iterators are an abstraction of pointers, their semantics is a generalization of most of the semantics of pointers in C++. This ensures that every function template that takes iterators works as well with regular pointers. This International Standard defines five categories of iterators, according to the operations defined on them: *input iterators*, *output iterators*, *forward iterators*, *bidirectional iterators* and *random access iterators*, as shown in Table 71.

Table 71—Relations among iterator categories

Random access	→ Bidirectional	→ Forward	→ Input
			→ Output

3   Forward iterators satisfy all the requirements of the input and output iterators and can be used whenever either kind is specified; Bidirectional iterators also satisfy all the requirements of the forward iterators and can be used whenever a forward iterator is specified; Random access iterators also satisfy all the requirements of bidirectional iterators and can be used whenever a bidirectional iterator is specified.

4   Besides its category, a forward, bidirectional, or random access iterator can also be *mutable* or *constant* depending on whether the result of the expression *i behaves as a reference or as a reference to a constant. Constant iterators do not satisfy the requirements for output iterators, and the result of the expression *i (for constant iterator i) cannot be used in an expression where an lvalue is required.

5   Just as a regular pointer to an array guarantees that there is a pointer value pointing past the last element of the array, so for any iterator type there is an iterator value that points past the last element of a corresponding container. These values are called *past-the-end* values. Values of an iterator i for which the expression *i is defined are called *dereferenceable*. The library never assumes that past-the-end values are dereferenceable. Iterators can also have singular values that are not associated with any container. [*Example:* After the declaration of an uninitialized pointer x (as with int* x;), x must always be assumed to have a singular value of a pointer.] Results of most expressions are undefined for singular values; the only exception is an assignment of a non-singular value to an iterator that holds a singular value. In this case the singular value is overwritten the same way as any other value. Dereferenceable values are always non-singular.

6   An iterator j is called *reachable* from an iterator i if and only if there is a finite sequence of applications of the expression ++i that makes i == j. If j is reachable from i, they refer to the same container.

7   Most of the library's algorithmic templates that operate on data structures have interfaces that use ranges. A *range* is a pair of iterators that designate the beginning and end of the computation. A range [i, i) is an empty range; in general, a range [i, j) refers to the elements in the data structure starting with the one pointed to by i and up to but not including the one pointed to by j. Range [i, j) is valid if and only if j is reachable from i. The result of the application of functions in the library to invalid ranges is undefined.

8   All the categories of iterators require only those functions that are realizable for a given category in constant time (amortized). Therefore, requirement tables for the iterators do not have a complexity column.

9   In the following sections, a and b denote values of X, n denotes a value of the difference type Distance, u, tmp, and m denote identifiers, r denotes a value of X&, t denotes a value of value type T.

24.1.1 Input iterators   **[lib.input.iterators]**

1   A class or a built-in type X satisfies the requirements of an input iterator for the value type T if the following expressions are valid, where U is the type of any specified member of type T, as shown in Table 72.

2   In Table 72, the term *the domain of* == is used in the ordinary mathematical sense to denote the set of values over which == is (required to be) defined. This set can change over time. Each algorithm places additional requirements on the domain of == for the iterator values it uses. These requirements can be inferred from the uses that algorithm makes of == and !=. [*Example:* the call find(a,b,x) is defined only if the value of a has the property *p* defined as follows: b has property p and a value i has property *p* if (*i==x) or if (*i!=x and ++i has property *p*).]

Table 72—Input iterator requirements

operation	type	semantics, pre/post-conditions
`X u(a);`	`X`	post: `u` is a copy of `a` A destructor is assumed to be present and accessible.
`u = a;`	`X&`	result: `u` post: `u` is a copy of `a`
`a == b`	convertible to `bool`	`==` is an equivalence relation over its domain.
`a != b`	convertible to `bool`	`bool(a==b) != bool(a!=b)` over the domain of `==`
`*a`	convertible to `T`	pre: `a` is dereferenceable. If `a==b` and `(a,b)` is in the domain of `==` then `*a` is equivalent to `*b`.
`a->m`		pre: `(*a).m` is well-defined Equivalent to `(*a).m`
`++r`	`X&`	pre: `r` is dereferenceable. post: `r` is dereferenceable or `r` is past-the-end. post: any copies of the previous value of `r` are no longer required either to be dereferenceable or to be in the domain of `==`.
`(void)r++`		equivalent to `(void)++r`
`*r++`	`T`	`{ T tmp = *r; ++r; return tmp; }`

3   [*Note:* For input iterators, `a == b` does not imply `++a == ++b`. (Equality does not guarantee the substitution property or referential transparency.) Algorithms on input iterators should never attempt to pass through the same iterator twice. They should be *single pass* algorithms. *Value type T is not required to be an Assignable type (23.1).* These algorithms can be used with istreams as the source of the input data through the `istream_iterator` class.]

24.1.2 Output iterators   [lib.output.iterators]

1   A class or a built-in type `X` satisfies the requirements of an output iterator if `X` is an Assignable type (23.1) and also the following expressions are valid, as shown in Table 73:

Table 73—Output iterator requirements

expression	return type	operational semantics	assertion/note pre/post-condition
`X(a)`			`a = t` is equivalent to `X(a) = t`. note: a destructor is assumed.
`X u(a);` `X u = a;`			
`*a = t`	result is not used		
`++r`	`X&`		`&r == &++r`.
`r++`	convertible to `const X&`	`{ X tmp = r;` `  ++r;` `  return tmp; }`	
`*r++ = t`	result is not used		

2   [*Note:* The only valid use of an `operator*` is on the left side of the assignment statement. *Assignment through the same value of the iterator happens only once.* Algorithms on output iterators should never attempt to pass through the same iterator twice. They should be *single pass* algorithms. Equality and inequality might not be defined. Algorithms that take output iterators can be used with ostreams as the destination for placing data through the `ostream_iterator` class as well as with insert iterators and insert pointers. *—end note*]

24.1.3 Forward iterators   [lib.forward.iterators]

1   A class or a built-in type X satisfies the requirements of a forward iterator if the following expressions are valid, as shown in Table 74:

Table 74—Forward iterator requirements

expression	return type	operational semantics	assertion/note pre/post-condition
`X u;`			note: `u` might have a singular value. note: a destructor is assumed.
`X()`			note: `X()` might be singular.
`X(a)`			`a == X(a).`
`X u(a);` `X u = a;`		`X u; u = a;`	post: `u == a.`
`a == b`	convertible to `bool`		`==` is an equivalence relation.
`a != b`	convertible to `bool`	`!(a == b)`	
`r = a`	`X&`		post: r == a.
`*a`	`T&`		pre: `a` is dereferenceable. `a == b` implies `*a == *b`. If X is mutable, `*a = t` is valid.
`a->m`	`U&`	`(*a).m`	pre: `(*a).m` is well-defined.
`++r`	`X&`		pre: `r` is dereferenceable. post: `r` is dereferenceable or `r` is past-the-end. `r == s` and `r` is dereferenceable implies `++r == ++s`. `&r == &++r`.

`r++`	convertible to `const X&`	`{ X tmp = r;`
		`++r;`
		`return tmp; }`	

`*r++`	`T&`		

— If a and b are equal, then either a and b are both dereferenceable or else neither is dereferenceable.

— If a and b are both dereferenceable, then a `==` b if and only if `*a` and `*b` are the same object.

2   [*Note:* The condition that a `==` b implies `++a == ++b` (which is not true for input and output iterators) and the removal of the restrictions on the number of the assignments through the iterator (which applies to output iterators) allows the use of multi-pass one-directional algorithms with forward iterators. —*end note*]

24.1.4 Bidirectional iterators   **[lib.bidirectional.iterators]**

1   A class or a built-in type X satisfies the requirements of a bidirectional iterator if, in addition to satisfying the requirements for forward iterators, the following expressions are valid as shown in Table 75:

Table 75—Bidirectional iterator requirements (in addition to forward iterator)

expression	return type	operational semantics	assertion/note pre/post-condition
`--r`	`X&`		pre: there exists `s` such that `r == ++s`. post: `s` is dereferenceable. `--(++r) == r`. `--r == --s` implies `r == s`. `&r == &--r`.

`r--`	convertible to `const X&`	`{ X tmp = r;`
		`  --r;`
		`  return tmp; }`	

`*r--`	convertible to `T`		

2   [*Note:* Bidirectional iterators allow algorithms to move iterators backward as well as forward. —*end note*]

24.1.5 Random access iterators   [lib.random.access.iterators]

1   A class or a built-in type `X` satisfies the requirements of a random access iterator if, in addition to satisfying the requirements for bidirectional iterators, the following expressions are valid as shown in Table 76:

Table 76—Random access iterator requirements (in addition to bidirectional iterator)

expression	return type	operational semantics	assertion/note pre/post-condition

`r += n`	`X&`	`{ Distance m =`
		`n;`
		`  if (m >= 0)`
		`    while (m--)`
		`++r;`
		`  else`
		`    while (m++)`
		`--r;`
		`  return r; }`	

`a + n`
 	
`n + a`
	`X`	`{ X tmp = a;`
		`  return tmp +=`
		`n; }`
			`a + n == n + a.`

`r -= n`	`X&`	`return r += -n;`	

`a - n`	`X`	`{ X tmp = a;`
		`  return tmp -=`
		`n; }`	

`b - a`	`Distance`	`(a<b)?`
		`distance(a,b):`
		`-distance(b,a)`
			pre: there exists a value n of `Distance` such that a `+ n == b. b == a +` `(b - a).`

`a[n]`	convertible to T	`*(a + n)`	
`a < b`	convertible to `bool`	`b - a > 0`	< is a total ordering relation
`a > b`	convertible to bool	`b < a`	> is a total ordering relation opposite to <.
`a >= b`	convertible to bool	`!(a < b)`	
`a <= b`	convertible to bool	`!(a > b)`	

24.2 Header `<iterator>` synopsis [lib.iterator.synopsis]

```
namespace std {
  // 24.3, primitives:
  template<class Iterator> struct iterator_traits;
  template<class T> struct iterator_traits<T*>;

  template<class Category, class T, class Distance = ptrdiff_t,
           class Pointer = T*, class Reference = T&> struct iterator;

  struct input_iterator_tag {};
  struct output_iterator_tag {};
  struct forward_iterator_tag: public input_iterator_tag {};
  struct bidirectional_iterator_tag: public forward_iterator_tag {};
  struct random_access_iterator_tag: public bidirectional_iterator_tag {};
```

```
// 24.3.4, iterator operations:
template <class InputIterator, class Distance>
  void advance(InputIterator& i, Distance n);
template <class InputIterator>
  typename iterator_traits<InputIterator>::difference_type
  distance(InputIterator first, InputIterator last);

// 24.4, predefined iterators:
template <class Iterator> class reverse_iterator;

template <class Iterator>
  bool operator==(
    const reverse_iterator<Iterator>& x,
    const reverse_iterator<Iterator>& y);
template <class Iterator>
  bool operator<(
    const reverse_iterator<Iterator>& x,
    const reverse_iterator<Iterator>& y);
template <class Iterator>
  bool operator!=(
    const reverse_iterator<Iterator>& x,
    const reverse_iterator<Iterator>& y);
template <class Iterator>
  bool operator>(
    const reverse_iterator<Iterator>& x,
    const reverse_iterator<Iterator>& y);
template <class Iterator>
  bool operator>=(
    const reverse_iterator<Iterator>& x,
    const reverse_iterator<Iterator>& y);
template <class Iterator>
  bool operator<=(
    const reverse_iterator<Iterator>& x,
    const reverse_iterator<Iterator>& y);

template <class Iterator>
  typename reverse_iterator<Iterator>::difference_type operator-(
    const reverse_iterator<Iterator>& x,
    const reverse_iterator<Iterator>& y);
template <class Iterator>
  reverse_iterator<Iterator>
    operator+(
      typename reverse_iterator<Iterator>::difference_type n,
      const reverse_iterator<Iterator>& x);

template <class Container> class back_insert_iterator;
template <class Container>
  back_insert_iterator<Container> back_inserter(Container& x);

template <class Container> class front_insert_iterator;
template <class Container>
  front_insert_iterator<Container> front_inserter(Container& x);

template <class Container> class insert_iterator;
template <class Container, class Iterator>
  insert_iterator<Container> inserter(Container& x, Iterator i);
```

```
                // 24.5, stream iterators:
                template <class T, class charT = char, class traits = char_traits<charT>,
                    class Distance = ptrdiff_t>
                class istream_iterator;
                template <class T, class charT, class traits, class Distance>
                  bool operator==(const istream_iterator<T,charT,traits,Distance>& x,
                                  const istream_iterator<T,charT,traits,Distance>& y);
                template <class T, class charT, class traits, class Distance>
                  bool operator!=(const istream_iterator<T,charT,traits,Distance>& x,
                                  const istream_iterator<T,charT,traits,Distance>& y);

                template <class T, class charT = char, class traits = char_traits<charT> >
                    class ostream_iterator;

                template<class charT, class traits = char_traits<charT> >
                  class istreambuf_iterator;
                template <class charT, class traits>
                  bool operator==(const istreambuf_iterator<charT,traits>& a,
                                  const istreambuf_iterator<charT,traits>& b);
                template <class charT, class traits>
                  bool operator!=(const istreambuf_iterator<charT,traits>& a,
                                  const istreambuf_iterator<charT,traits>& b);

                template <class charT, class traits = char_traits<charT> >
                  class ostreambuf_iterator;
            }
```

24.3 Iterator primitives   [lib.iterator.primitives]

1   To simplify the task of defining iterators, the library provides several classes and functions:

24.3.1 Iterator traits   [lib.iterator.traits]

1   To implement algorithms only in terms of iterators, it is often necessary to determine the value and difference types that correspond to a particular iterator type. Accordingly, it is required that if `Iterator` is the
type of an iterator, the types

```
        iterator_traits<Iterator>::difference_type
        iterator_traits<Iterator>::value_type
        iterator_traits<Iterator>::iterator_category
```

be defined as the iterator's difference type, value type and iterator category, respectively. In the case of an
output iterator, the types

```
        iterator_traits<Iterator>::difference_type
        iterator_traits<Iterator>::value_type
```

are both defined as `void`.

2   The template `iterator_traits<Iterator>` is defined as

```
        template<class Iterator> struct iterator_traits {
          typedef typename Iterator::difference_type difference_type;
          typedef typename Iterator::value_type value_type;
          typedef typename Iterator::pointer pointer;
          typedef typename Iterator::reference reference;
          typedef typename Iterator::iterator_category iterator_category;
        };
```

It is specialized for pointers as

```
template<class T> struct iterator_traits<T*> {
  typedef ptrdiff_t difference_type;
  typedef T value_type;
  typedef T* pointer;
  typedef T& reference;
  typedef random_access_iterator_tag iterator_category;
};
```

and for pointers to const as

```
template<class T> struct iterator_traits<const T*> {
  typedef ptrdiff_t difference_type;
  typedef T value_type;
  typedef const T* pointer;
  typedef const T& reference;
  typedef random_access_iterator_tag iterator_category;
};
```

[*Note:* If there is an additional pointer type __far such that the difference of two __far is of type long, an implementation may define

```
template<class T> struct iterator_traits<T __far*> {
  typedef long difference_type;
  typedef T value_type;
  typedef T __far* pointer;
  typedef T __far& reference;
  typedef random_access_iterator_tag iterator_category;
};
```

—*end note*]

3   [*Example:* To implement a generic reverse function, a C++ program can do the following:

```
template <class BidirectionalIterator>
void reverse(BidirectionalIterator first, BidirectionalIterator last) {
  typename iterator_traits<BidirectionalIterator>::difference_type n =
          distance(first, last);
  --n;
  while(n > 0) {
      typename iterator_traits<BidirectionalIterator>::value_type
              tmp = *first;
      *first++ = *--last;
      *last = tmp;
      n -= 2;
  }
}
```

—*end example*]

24.3.2 Basic iterator   [lib.iterator.basic]

1   The iterator template may be used as a base class to ease the definition of required types for new iterators.

```
namespace std {
  template<class Category, class T, class Distance = ptrdiff_t,
         class Pointer = T*, class Reference = T&>
  struct iterator {
      typedef T           value_type;
      typedef Distance    difference_type;
      typedef Pointer     pointer;
      typedef Reference   reference;
      typedef Category    iterator_category;
  };
}
```

24.3.3 Standard iterator tags   [lib.std.iterator.tags]

1   It is often desirable for a function template specialization to find out what is the most specific category of
    its iterator argument, so that the function can select the most efficient algorithm at compile time. To facili-
    tate this, the library introduces *category tag* classes which are used as compile time tags for algorithm
    selection.   They   are: input_iterator_tag,   output_iterator_tag,
    forward_iterator_tag,   bidirectional_iterator_tag   and
    random_access_iterator_tag.   For   every   iterator   of   type   Iterator,
    iterator_traits<Iterator>::iterator_category must be defined to be the most specific
    category tag that describes the iterator's behavior.

```
namespace std {
  struct input_iterator_tag {};
  struct output_iterator_tag {};
  struct forward_iterator_tag: public input_iterator_tag {};
  struct bidirectional_iterator_tag: public forward_iterator_tag {};
  struct random_access_iterator_tag: public bidirectional_iterator_tag {};
}
```

2   [*Example:* For a program-defined iterator BinaryTreeIterator, it could be included into the bidirec-
    tional iterator category by specializing the iterator_traits template:

```
template<class T> struct iterator_traits<BinaryTreeIterator<T> > {
  typedef ptrdiff_t difference_type;
  typedef T value_type;
  typedef T* pointer;
  typedef T& reference;
  typedef bidirectional_iterator_tag iterator_category;
};
```

Typically,   however,   it   would   be   easier   to   derive   BinaryTreeIterator<T>   from
iterator<bidirectional_iterator_tag,T,ptrdiff_t,T*,T&>.   —*end example*]

3   [*Example:* If evolve() is well defined for bidirectional iterators, but can be implemented more efficiently
    for random access iterators, then the implementation is as follows:

```
template <class BidirectionalIterator>
inline void
 evolve(BidirectionalIterator first, BidirectionalIterator last) {
   evolve(first, last,
     typename iterator_traits<BidirectionalIterator>::iterator_category());
 }
```

```
template <class BidirectionalIterator>
void evolve(BidirectionalIterator first, BidirectionalIterator last,
            bidirectional_iterator_tag) {
                                    // ... more generic, but less efficient algorithm
}

template <class RandomAccessIterator>
void evolve(RandomAccessIterator first, RandomAccessIterator last,
    random_access_iterator_tag) {
                                    // ... more efficient, but less generic algorithm
}
```

—*end example*]

4   [*Example:* If a C++ program wants to define a bidirectional iterator for some data structure containing
     `double` and such that it works on a large memory model of the implementation, it can do so with:

```
class MyIterator :
  public iterator<bidirectional_iterator_tag, double, long, T*, T&> {
                                    // code implementing ++, etc.
};
```

5   Then there is no need to specialize the `iterator_traits` template. —*end example*]

24.3.4 Iterator operations   [lib.iterator.operations]

1   Since only random access iterators provide + and - operators, the library provides two function templates
     `advance` and `distance`. These function templates use + and - for random access iterators (and are,
     therefore, constant time for them); for input, forward and bidirectional iterators they use ++ to provide lin-
     ear time implementations.

```
template <class InputIterator, class Distance>
  void advance(InputIterator& i, Distance n);
```

2   **Requires:** n may be negative only for random access and bidirectional iterators.

3   **Effects:** Increments (or decrements for negative n) iterator reference i by n.

```
template<class InputIterator>
    typename iterator_traits<InputIterator>::difference_type
        distance(InputIterator first, InputIterator last);
```

4   **Effects:** Returns the number of increments or decrements needed to get from `first` to `last`.

5   **Requires:** `last` must be reachable from `first`.

24.4 Predefined iterators   [lib.predef.iterators]

24.4.1 Reverse iterators   [lib.reverse.iterators]

1   Bidirectional and random access iterators have corresponding reverse iterator adaptors that iterate through
     the data structure in the opposite direction. They have the same signatures as the corresponding iterators.
     The fundamental relation between a reverse iterator and its corresponding iterator i is established by the
     identity: `&*(reverse_iterator(i)) == &*(i - 1)`.

2   This mapping is dictated by the fact that while there is always a pointer past the end of an array, there might
     not be a valid pointer before the beginning of an array.

24.4.1.1 Class template `reverse_iterator`   [lib.reverse.iterator]

```
namespace std {
  template <class Iterator>
  class reverse_iterator : public
        iterator<typename iterator_traits<Iterator>::iterator_category,
                 typename iterator_traits<Iterator>::value_type,
                 typename iterator_traits<Iterator>::difference_type,
                 typename iterator_traits<Iterator>::pointer,
                 typename iterator_traits<Iterator>::reference> {
  protected:
    Iterator current;
  public:
    typedef Iterator
        iterator_type;
    typedef typename iterator_traits<Iterator>::difference_type
        difference_type;
    typedef typename iterator_traits<Iterator>::reference
        reference;
    typedef typename iterator_traits<Iterator>::pointer
        pointer;

    reverse_iterator();
    explicit reverse_iterator(Iterator x);
    template <class U> reverse_iterator(const reverse_iterator<U>& u);

    Iterator base() const;        // explicit
    reference operator*() const;
    pointer   operator->() const;

    reverse_iterator& operator++();
    reverse_iterator  operator++(int);
    reverse_iterator& operator--();
    reverse_iterator  operator--(int);

    reverse_iterator  operator+ (difference_type n) const;
    reverse_iterator& operator+=(difference_type n);
    reverse_iterator  operator- (difference_type n) const;
    reverse_iterator& operator-=(difference_type n);
    reference operator[](difference_type n) const;
  };

  template <class Iterator>
    bool operator==(
      const reverse_iterator<Iterator>& x,
      const reverse_iterator<Iterator>& y);

  template <class Iterator>
    bool operator<(
      const reverse_iterator<Iterator>& x,
      const reverse_iterator<Iterator>& y);

  template <class Iterator>
    bool operator!=(
      const reverse_iterator<Iterator>& x,
      const reverse_iterator<Iterator>& y);
```

```
template <class Iterator>
  bool operator>(
    const reverse_iterator<Iterator>& x,
    const reverse_iterator<Iterator>& y);

template <class Iterator>
  bool operator>=(
    const reverse_iterator<Iterator>& x,
    const reverse_iterator<Iterator>& y);

template <class Iterator>
  bool operator<=(
    const reverse_iterator<Iterator>& x,
    const reverse_iterator<Iterator>& y);

template <class Iterator>
  typename reverse_iterator<Iterator>::difference_type operator-(
    const reverse_iterator<Iterator>& x,
    const reverse_iterator<Iterator>& y);

template <class Iterator>
  reverse_iterator<Iterator> operator+(
    typename reverse_iterator<Iterator>::difference_type n,
    const reverse_iterator<Iterator>& x);
}
```

24.4.1.2 `reverse_iterator` requirements   [lib.reverse.iter.requirements]

1   The template parameter `Iterator` shall meet all the requirements of a Bidirectional Iterator (24.1.4).

2   Additionally, `Iterator` shall meet the requirements of a Random Access Iterator (24.1.5) if any of the members `operator+` (24.4.1.3.7), `operator-` (24.4.1.3.9), `operator+=` (24.4.1.3.8), `operator-=` (24.4.1.3.10), `operator[]` (24.4.1.3.11), or the global operators `operator<` (24.4.1.3.13), `operator>` (24.4.1.3.15), `operator<=` (24.4.1.3.17), `operator>=` (24.4.1.3.16), `operator-` (24.4.1.3.18) or `operator+` (24.4.1.3.19). is referenced in a way that requires instantiation (14.7.1).

24.4.1.3 `reverse_iterator` operations   [lib.reverse.iter.ops]

24.4.1.3.1 `reverse_iterator` constructor   [lib.reverse.iter.cons]

```
explicit reverse_iterator(Iterator x);
```

1   **Effects:** Initializes current with *x*.

```
template <class U> reverse_iterator(const reverse_iterator<U> &u);
```

2   **Effects:** Initializes current with u.current.

24.4.1.3.2 Conversion   [lib.reverse.iter.conv]

```
Iterator base() const;                     // explicit
```

1   **Returns:** current

24.4.1.3.3 operator* [lib.reverse.iter.op.star]

```
reference operator*() const;
```

1   **Effects:**

```
Iterator tmp = current;
return *--tmp;
```

24.4.1.3.4 operator-> [lib.reverse.iter.opref]

```
pointer operator->() const;
```

1   **Effects:**

```
return &(operator*());
```

24.4.1.3.5 operator++ [lib.reverse.iter.op++]

```
reverse_iterator& operator++();
```

1   **Effects:** --current;
2   **Returns:** *this

```
reverse_iterator operator++(int);
```

3   **Effects:**

```
reverse_iterator tmp = *this;
--current;
return tmp;
```

24.4.1.3.6 operator-- [lib.reverse.iter.op--]

```
reverse_iterator& operator--();
```

1   **Effects:** ++current
2   **Returns:** *this

```
reverse_iterator operator--(int);
```

3   **Effects:**

```
reverse_iterator tmp = *this;
++current;
return tmp;
```

24.4.1.3.7 operator+ [lib.reverse.iter.op+]

```
reverse_iterator
operator+(typename reverse_iterator<Iterator>::difference_type n) const;
```

1   **Returns:** reverse_iterator(current-n)

24.4.1.3.8 operator+=   [lib.reverse.iter.op+=]

```
reverse_iterator&
operator+=(typename reverse_iterator<Iterator>::difference_type n);
```

1   **Effects:** current -= n;
2   **Returns:** *this

24.4.1.3.9 operator-   [lib.reverse.iter.op-]

```
reverse_iterator
operator-(typename reverse_iterator<Iterator>::difference_type n) const;
```

1   **Returns:** reverse_iterator(current+n)

24.4.1.3.10 operator-=   [lib.reverse.iter.op-=]

```
reverse_iterator&
operator-=(typename reverse_iterator<Iterator>::difference_type n);
```

1   **Effects:** current += n;
2   **Returns:** *this

24.4.1.3.11 operator[]   [lib.reverse.iter.opindex]

```
reference
operator[](typename reverse_iterator<Iterator>::difference_type n) const;
```

1   **Returns:** current[-n-1]

24.4.1.3.12 operator==   [lib.reverse.iter.op==]

```
template <class Iterator>
  bool operator==(
    const reverse_iterator<Iterator>& x,
    const reverse_iterator<Iterator>& y);
```

1   **Returns:** x.current == y.current

24.4.1.3.13 operator<   [lib.reverse.iter.op<]

```
template <class Iterator>
  bool operator<(
    const reverse_iterator<Iterator>& x,
    const reverse_iterator<Iterator>& y);
```

1   **Returns:** x.current > y.current

24.4.1.3.14 operator!=   [lib.reverse.iter.op!=]

```
template <class Iterator>
  bool operator!=(
    const reverse_iterator<Iterator>& x,
    const reverse_iterator<Iterator>& y);
```

1   **Returns:** x.current != y.current

24.4.1.3.15 operator> [lib.reverse.iter.op>]

```
template <class Iterator>
  bool operator>(
    const reverse_iterator<Iterator>& x,
    const reverse_iterator<Iterator>& y);
```

1   **Returns:** x.current < y.current

24.4.1.3.16 operator>= [lib.reverse.iter.op>=]

```
template <class Iterator>
  bool operator>=(
    const reverse_iterator<Iterator>& x,
    const reverse_iterator<Iterator>& y);
```

1   **Returns:** x.current <= y.current

24.4.1.3.17 operator<= [lib.reverse.iter.op<=]

```
template <class Iterator>
  bool operator<=(
    const reverse_iterator<Iterator>& x,
    const reverse_iterator<Iterator>& y);
```

1   **Returns:** x.current >= y.current

24.4.1.3.18 operator- [lib.reverse.iter.opdiff]

```
template <class Iterator>
  typename reverse_iterator<Iterator>::difference_type operator-(
    const reverse_iterator<Iterator>& x,
    const reverse_iterator<Iterator>& y);
```

1   **Returns:** y.current - x.current

24.4.1.3.19 operator+ [lib.reverse.iter.opsum]

```
template <class Iterator>
  reverse_iterator<Iterator> operator+(
    typename reverse_iterator<Iterator>::difference_type n,
    const reverse_iterator<Iterator>& x);
```

1   **Returns:** reverse_iterator<Iterator> (x.current - n)

24.4.2 Insert iterators [lib.insert.iterators]

1   To make it possible to deal with insertion in the same way as writing into an array, a special kind of iterator adaptors, called *insert iterators*, are provided in the library. With regular iterator classes,
```
while (first != last) *result++ = *first++;
```

2   causes a range [first, last) to be copied into a range starting with result. The same code with result being an insert iterator will insert corresponding elements into the container. This device allows all of the copying algorithms in the library to work in the *insert mode* instead of the regular overwrite mode.

3   An insert iterator is constructed from a container and possibly one of its iterators pointing to where insertion takes place if it is neither at the beginning nor at the end of the container. Insert iterators satisfy the requirements of output iterators. operator* returns the insert iterator itself. The assignment operator=(const T& x) is defined on insert iterators to allow writing into them, it inserts x right

before where the insert iterator is pointing. In other words, an insert iterator is like a cursor pointing into the container where the insertion takes place. `back_insert_iterator` inserts elements at the end of a container, `front_insert_iterator` inserts elements at the beginning of a container, and `insert_iterator` inserts elements where the iterator points to in a container. `back_inserter`, `front_inserter`, and `inserter` are three functions making the insert iterators out of a container.

24.4.2.1 Class template `back_insert_iterator` [lib.back.insert.iterator]

```
namespace std {
  template <class Container>
  class back_insert_iterator :
      public iterator<output_iterator_tag,void,void,void,void> {
  protected:
    Container* container;

  public:
    typedef Container container_type;
    explicit back_insert_iterator(Container& x);
    back_insert_iterator<Container>&
      operator=(typename Container::const_reference value);

    back_insert_iterator<Container>& operator*();
    back_insert_iterator<Container>& operator++();
    back_insert_iterator<Container>  operator++(int);
  };

  template <class Container>
    back_insert_iterator<Container> back_inserter(Container& x);
}
```

24.4.2.2 `back_insert_iterator` operations [lib.back.insert.iter.ops]

24.4.2.2.1 `back_insert_iterator` constructor [lib.back.insert.iter.cons]

```
explicit back_insert_iterator(Container& x);
```

1   **Effects:** Initializes `container` with &*x*.

24.4.2.2.2 `back_insert_iterator::operator=` [lib.back.insert.iter.op=]

```
back_insert_iterator<Container>&
  operator=(typename Container::const_reference value);
```

1   **Effects:** `container->push_back(value);`
2   **Returns:** `*this`.

24.4.2.2.3 `back_insert_iterator::operator*` [lib.back.insert.iter.op*]

```
back_insert_iterator<Container>& operator*();
```

1   **Returns:** `*this`.

24.4.2.2.4 back_insert_iterator::operator++ [lib.back.insert.iter.op++]

```
back_insert_iterator<Container>& operator++();
back_insert_iterator<Container>  operator++(int);
```

1 **Returns:** *this.

24.4.2.2.5 back_inserter [lib.back.inserter]

```
template <class Container>
  back_insert_iterator<Container> back_inserter(Container& x);
```

1 **Returns:** back_insert_iterator<Container>(x).

24.4.2.3 Class template front_insert_iterator [lib.front.insert.iterator]

```
namespace std {
  template <class Container>
  class front_insert_iterator :
      public iterator<output_iterator_tag,void,void,void,void> {
  protected:
    Container* container;

  public:
    typedef Container container_type;
    explicit front_insert_iterator(Container& x);
    front_insert_iterator<Container>&
      operator=(typename Container::const_reference value);

    front_insert_iterator<Container>& operator*();
    front_insert_iterator<Container>& operator++();
    front_insert_iterator<Container>  operator++(int);
  };

  template <class Container>
    front_insert_iterator<Container> front_inserter(Container& x);
}
```

24.4.2.4 front_insert_iterator operations [lib.front.insert.iter.ops]

24.4.2.4.1 front_insert_iterator constructor [lib.front.insert.iter.cons]

```
explicit front_insert_iterator(Container& x);
```

1 **Effects:** Initializes container with &*x*.

24.4.2.4.2 front_insert_iterator::operator= [lib.front.insert.iter.op=]

```
front_insert_iterator<Container>&
  operator=(typename Container::const_reference value);
```

1 **Effects:** container->push_front(value);
2 **Returns:** *this.

24.4.2.4.3 `front_insert_iterator::operator*`   **[lib.front.insert.iter.op*]**

```
front_insert_iterator<Container>& operator*();
```

1   **Returns:** `*this`.

24.4.2.4.4 `front_insert_iterator::operator++`   **[lib.front.insert.iter.op++]**

```
front_insert_iterator<Container>& operator++();
front_insert_iterator<Container>  operator++(int);
```

1   **Returns:** `*this`.

24.4.2.4.5 `front_inserter`   **[lib.front.inserter]**

```
template <class Container>
  front_insert_iterator<Container> front_inserter(Container& x);
```

1   **Returns:** `front_insert_iterator<Container>(x)`.

24.4.2.5 Class template `insert_iterator`   **[lib.insert.iterator]**

```
namespace std {
  template <class Container>
  class insert_iterator :
      public iterator<output_iterator_tag,void,void,void,void> {
  protected:
    Container* container;
    typename Container::iterator iter;

  public:
    typedef Container container_type;
    insert_iterator(Container& x, typename Container::iterator i);
    insert_iterator<Container>&
      operator=(typename Container::const_reference value);

    insert_iterator<Container>& operator*();
    insert_iterator<Container>& operator++();
    insert_iterator<Container>& operator++(int);
  };

  template <class Container, class Iterator>
    insert_iterator<Container> inserter(Container& x, Iterator i);
}
```

24.4.2.6 `insert_iterator` operations   **[lib.insert.iter.ops]**

24.4.2.6.1 `insert_iterator` constructor   **[lib.insert.iter.cons]**

```
insert_iterator(Container& x, typename Container::iterator i);
```

1   **Effects:** Initializes `container` with `&x` and `iter` with `i`.

24.4.2.6.2 insert_iterator::operator=   [lib.insert.iter.op=]

```
insert_iterator<Container>&
  operator=(typename Container::const_reference value);
```

1   **Effects:**

```
    iter = container->insert(iter, value);
    ++iter;
```

2   **Returns:** `*this`.

24.4.2.6.3 insert_iterator::operator*   [lib.insert.iter.op*]

```
insert_iterator<Container>& operator*();
```

1   **Returns:** `*this`.

24.4.2.6.4 insert_iterator::operator++   [lib.insert.iter.op++]

```
insert_iterator<Container>& operator++();
insert_iterator<Container>& operator++(int);
```

1   **Returns:** `*this`.

24.4.2.6.5 inserter   [lib.inserter]

```
template <class Container, class Inserter>
  insert_iterator<Container> inserter(Container& x, Inserter i);
```

1   **Returns:** `insert_iterator<Container>(x,typename Container::iterator(i))`.

24.5 Stream iterators   [lib.stream.iterators]

1   To make it possible for algorithmic templates to work directly with input/output streams, appropriate iterator-like class templates are provided.

2   [*Example:*

```
partial_sum_copy(istream_iterator<double, char>(cin),
  istream_iterator<double, char>(),
  ostream_iterator<double, char>(cout, "\n"));
```

reads a file containing floating point numbers from `cin`, and prints the partial sums onto `cout`.
—*end example*]

24.5.1 Class template istream_iterator   [lib.istream.iterator]

1   `istream_iterator` reads (using `operator>>`) successive elements from the input stream for which it was constructed. After it is constructed, and every time ++ is used, the iterator reads and stores a value of `T`. If the end of stream is reached (`operator void*()` on the stream returns `false`), the iterator becomes equal to the *end-of-stream* iterator value. The constructor with no arguments `istream_iterator()` always constructs an end of stream input iterator object, which is the only legitimate iterator to be used for the end condition. The result of `operator*` on an end of stream is not defined. For any other iterator value a `const T&` is returned. The result of `operator->` on an end of stream is not defined. For any other iterator value a `const T*` is returned. It is impossible to store things into istream iterators. The main peculiarity of the istream iterators is the fact that ++ operators are not equality preserving, that is, `i == j` does not guarantee at all that `++i == ++j`. Every time ++ is used a new value is read.

2   The practical consequence of this fact is that istream iterators can be used only for one-pass algorithms, which actually makes perfect sense, since for multi-pass algorithms it is always more appropriate to use in-memory data structures.

3   Two end-of-stream iterators are always equal. An end-of-stream iterator is not equal to a non-end-of-stream iterator. Two non-end-of-stream iterators are equal when they are constructed from the same stream.

```
namespace std {
  template <class T, class charT = char, class traits = char_traits<charT>,
      class Distance = ptrdiff_t>
  class istream_iterator:
    public iterator<input_iterator_tag, T, Distance, const T*, const T&> {
  public:
    typedef charT char_type;
    typedef traits traits_type;
    typedef basic_istream<charT,traits> istream_type;
    istream_iterator();
    istream_iterator(istream_type& s);
    istream_iterator(const istream_iterator<T,charT,traits,Distance>& x);
   ~istream_iterator();

    const T& operator*() const;
    const T* operator->() const;
    istream_iterator<T,charT,traits,Distance>& operator++();
    istream_iterator<T,charT,traits,Distance>  operator++(int);
  private:
    //basic_istream<charT,traits>* in_stream;           exposition only
    //T value;                                          exposition only
  };

  template <class T, class charT, class traits, class Distance>
    bool operator==(const istream_iterator<T,charT,traits,Distance>& x,
                    const istream_iterator<T,charT,traits,Distance>& y);
  template <class T, class charT, class traits, class Distance>
    bool operator!=(const istream_iterator<T,charT,traits,Distance>& x,
                    const istream_iterator<T,charT,traits,Distance>& y);
}
```

24.5.1.1 `istream_iterator` constructors and destructor [lib.istream.iterator.cons]

```
istream_iterator();
```

1   **Effects:** Constructs the end-of-stream iterator.

```
istream_iterator(istream_type& s);
```

2   **Effects:** Initializes *in_stream* with *s*. *value* may be initialized during construction or the first time it is referenced.

```
istream_iterator(const istream_iterator<T,charT,traits,Distance>& x);
```

3   **Effects:** Constructs a copy of *x*.

```
~istream_iterator();
```

4   **Effects:** The iterator is destroyed.

24.5.1.2 `istream_iterator` operations   [lib.istream.iterator.ops]

```
const T& operator*() const;
```

1   **Returns:** *value*

```
const T* operator->() const;
```

2   **Returns:** &(operator*())

```
istream_iterator<T,charT,traits,Distance>& operator++();
```

3   **Effects:** **in_stream* >> *value*
4   **Returns:** *this

```
istream_iterator<T,charT,traits,Distance>& operator++(int);
```

5   **Effects:**

```
istream_iterator<T,charT,traits,Distance> tmp = *this;
*in_stream >> value;
return (tmp);
```

```
template <class T, class charT, class traits, class Distance>
  bool operator==(const istream_iterator<T,charT,traits,Distance> &x,
                  const istream_iterator<T,charT,traits,Distance> &y);
```

6   **Returns:** (x.*in_stream* == y.*in_stream*)

24.5.2 Class template `ostream_iterator`   [lib.ostream.iterator]

1   `ostream_iterator` writes (using `operator<<`) successive elements onto the output stream from
which it was constructed. If it was constructed with `char*` as a constructor argument, this string, called a
delimiter string, is written to the stream after every T is written. It is not possible to get a value out of the
output iterator. Its only use is as an output iterator in situations like

```
while (first != last) *result++ = *first++;
```

2   `ostream_iterator` is defined as:

```
namespace std {
  template <class T, class charT = char, class traits = char_traits<charT> >
  class ostream_iterator:
    public iterator<output_iterator_tag, void, void, void, void> {
  public:
    typedef charT char_type;
    typedef traits traits_type;
    typedef basic_ostream<charT,traits> ostream_type;
    ostream_iterator(ostream_type& s);
    ostream_iterator(ostream_type& s, const charT* delimiter);
    ostream_iterator(const ostream_iterator<T,charT,traits>& x);
    ~ostream_iterator();
    ostream_iterator<T,charT,traits>& operator=(const T& value);
```

```
      ostream_iterator<T,charT,traits>& operator*();
      ostream_iterator<T,charT,traits>& operator++();
      ostream_iterator<T,charT,traits>& operator++(int);
    private:
      //  basic_ostream<charT,traits>* out_stream;     exposition only
      //  const char* delim;                           exposition only
    };
  }
```

24.5.2.1 `ostream_iterator` constructors and destructor   [lib.ostream.iterator.cons.des]

```
      ostream_iterator(ostream_type& s);
```

1   **Effects:** Initializes *out_stream* with *s* and *delim* with null.

```
      ostream_iterator(ostream_type& s, const charT* delimiter);
```

2   **Effects:** Initializes *out_stream* with *s* and *delim* with `delimiter`.

```
      ostream_iterator(const ostream_iterator& x);
```

3   **Effects:** Constructs a copy of *x*.

```
      ~ostream_iterator();
```

4   **Effects:** The iterator is destroyed.

24.5.2.2 `ostream_iterator` operations   [lib.ostream.iterator.ops]

```
      ostream_iterator& operator=(const T& value);
```

1   **Effects:**

```
        *out_stream << value;
        if(delim != 0) *out_stream << delim;
        return (*this);
```

```
      ostream_iterator& operator*();
```

2   **Returns:** `*this`

```
      ostream_iterator& operator++();
      ostream_iterator& operator++(int);
```

3   **Returns:** `*this`

24.5.3 Class template `istreambuf_iterator`   [lib.istreambuf.iterator]

```
  namespace std {
    template<class charT, class traits = char_traits<charT> >
    class istreambuf_iterator
      : public iterator<input_iterator_tag, charT,
                        typename traits::off_type, charT*, charT&> {
    public:
      typedef charT                         char_type;
      typedef traits                        traits_type;
      typedef typename traits::int_type     int_type;
      typedef basic_streambuf<charT,traits> streambuf_type;
      typedef basic_istream<charT,traits>   istream_type;
```

```
      class proxy;                                // exposition only

    public:
      istreambuf_iterator() throw();
      istreambuf_iterator(istream_type& s) throw();
      istreambuf_iterator(streambuf_type* s) throw();
      istreambuf_iterator(const proxy& p) throw();
      charT operator*() const;
      istreambuf_iterator<charT,traits>& operator++();
      proxy operator++(int);
      bool equal(istreambuf_iterator& b) const;
    private:
      streambuf_type* sbuf_;      exposition only
    };

  template <class charT, class traits>
    bool operator==(const istreambuf_iterator<charT,traits>& a,
                    const istreambuf_iterator<charT,traits>& b);

  template <class charT, class traits>
    bool operator!=(const istreambuf_iterator<charT,traits>& a,
                    const istreambuf_iterator<charT,traits>& b);
}
```

1   The class template `istreambuf_iterator` reads successive *characters* from the streambuf for which it was constructed. `operator*` provides access to the current input character, if any. Each time `operator++` is evaluated, the iterator advances to the next input character. If the end of stream is reached (streambuf_type::sgetc() returns `traits::eof()`), the iterator becomes equal to the *end of stream* iterator value. The default constructor `istreambuf_iterator()` and the constructor `istreambuf_iterator(0)` both construct an end of stream iterator object suitable for use as an end-of-range.

2   The result of `operator*()` on an end of stream is undefined. For any other iterator value a `char_type` value is returned. It is impossible to assign a character via an input iterator.

3   Note that in the input iterators, ++ operators are not *equality preserving*, that is, i == j does not guarantee at all that ++i == ++j. Every time ++ is evaluated a new value is used.

4   The practical consequence of this fact is that an `istreambuf_iterator` object can be used only for *one-pass algorithms*. Two end of stream iterators are always equal. An end of stream iterator is not equal to a non-end of stream iterator.

24.5.3.1 Class template `istreambuf_iterator::proxy`   [lib.istreambuf.iterator::proxy]

```
  namespace std {
    template <class charT, class traits = char_traits<charT> >
    class istreambuf_iterator<charT, traits>::proxy {
      charT keep_;
      basic_streambuf<charT,traits>* sbuf_;
      proxy(charT c,
            basic_streambuf<charT,traits>* sbuf);
        : keep_(c), sbuf_(sbuf) {}
    public:
      charT operator*() { return keep_; }
    };
  }
```

1   Class `istreambuf_iterator<charT,traits>::proxy` is for exposition only. An implementation is permitted to provide equivalent functionality without providing a class with this name. Class `istreambuf_iterator<charT,traits>::proxy` provides a temporary placeholder as the return value of the post-increment operator (`operator++`). It keeps the character pointed to by the previous value of the iterator for some possible future access to get the character.

24.5.3.2 `istreambuf_iterator` constructors   [lib.istreambuf.iterator.cons]

```
istreambuf_iterator() throw();
```

1   **Effects:** Constructs the end-of-stream iterator.

```
istreambuf_iterator(basic_istream<charT,traits>& s) throw();
istreambuf_iterator(basic_streambuf<charT,traits>* s) throw();
```

2   **Effects:** Constructs an `istreambuf_iterator<>` that uses the `basic_streambuf<>` object `*(s.rdbuf())`, or `*s`, respectively. Constructs an end-of-stream iterator if `s.rdbuf()` is null.

```
istreambuf_iterator(const proxy& p) throw();
```

3   **Effects:** Constructs a `istreambuf_iterator<>` that uses the `basic_streambuf<>` object pointed to by the `proxy` object's constructor argument *p*.

24.5.3.3 `istreambuf_iterator::operator*`   [lib.istreambuf.iterator::op*]

```
charT operator*() const
```

1   **Returns:** The character obtained via the `streambuf` member ***sbuf_*** `->sgetc()`.

24.5.3.4 `istreambuf_iterator::operator++`   [lib.istreambuf.iterator::op++]

```
istreambuf_iterator<charT,traits>&
    istreambuf_iterator<charT,traits>::operator++();
```

1   **Effects:** ***sbuf_*** `->sbumpc()`.
2   **Returns:** `*this`.

```
proxy istreambuf_iterator<charT,traits>::operator++(int);
```

3   **Returns:** `proxy(` ***sbuf_*** `->sbumpc(), sbuf_)`.

24.5.3.5 `istreambuf_iterator::equal`   [lib.istreambuf.iterator::equal]

```
bool equal(istreambuf_iterator<charT,traits>& b) const;
```

1   **Returns:** `true` if and only if both iterators are at end-of-stream, or neither is at end-of-stream, regardless of what `streambuf` object they use.

24.5.3.6 `operator==`   [lib.istreambuf.iterator::op==]

```
template <class charT, class traits>
  bool operator==(const istreambuf_iterator<charT,traits>& a,
                  const istreambuf_iterator<charT,traits>& b);
```

1   **Returns:** *a*.`equal(`*b*`)`.

24.5.3.7 operator!= [lib.istreambuf.iterator::op!=]

```
template <class charT, class traits>
  bool operator!=(const istreambuf_iterator<charT,traits>& a,
                  const istreambuf_iterator<charT,traits>& b);
```

1   **Returns:** !a.equal(b).

24.5.4 Class template ostreambuf_iterator [lib.ostreambuf.iterator]

```
namespace std {
  template <class charT, class traits = char_traits<charT> >
  class ostreambuf_iterator:
    public iterator<output_iterator_tag, void, void, void, void> {
  public:
    typedef charT                          char_type;
    typedef traits                         traits_type;
    typedef basic_streambuf<charT,traits> streambuf_type;
    typedef basic_ostream<charT,traits>   ostream_type;

  public:
    ostreambuf_iterator(ostream_type& s) throw();
    ostreambuf_iterator(streambuf_type* s) throw();
    ostreambuf_iterator& operator=(charT c);

    ostreambuf_iterator& operator*();
    ostreambuf_iterator& operator++();
    ostreambuf_iterator& operator++(int);
    bool failed() const throw();

  private:
    streambuf_type* sbuf_;        exposition only

  };
}
```

1   The class template ostreambuf_iterator writes successive *characters* onto the output stream from which it was constructed. It is not possible to get a character value out of the output iterator.

24.5.4.1 ostreambuf_iterator constructors [lib.ostreambuf.iter.cons]

```
ostreambuf_iterator(ostream_type& s) throw();
```

1   **Requires:** s.rdbuf() is not null.
2   **Effects:** : *sbuf_*(s.rdbuf()) {}

```
ostreambuf_iterator(streambuf_type* s) throw();
```

2a **Requires:** s is not null.
3   **Effects:** : *sbuf_*(s) {}

```
ostreambuf_iterator<charT,traits>&
  operator=(charT c);
```

1 **Effects:** If `failed()` yields `false`, calls *sbuf_*`->sputc(c)`; otherwise has no effect.

2 **Returns:** `*this`.

```
ostreambuf_iterator<charT,traits>& operator*();
```

3 **Returns:** `*this`.

```
ostreambuf_iterator<charT,traits>& operator++();
ostreambuf_iterator<charT,traits>& operator++(int);
```

4 **Returns:** `*this`.

```
bool failed() const throw();
```

5 **Returns:** `true` if in any prior use of member `operator=`, the call to *sbuf_*`->sputc()` returned `traits::eof()`; or `false` otherwise.

25 Algorithms library   [lib.algorithms]

1   This clause describes components that C++ programs may use to perform algorithmic operations on containers (clause 23) and other sequences.

2   The following subclauses describe components for non-modifying sequence operation, modifying sequence operations, sorting and related operations, and algorithms from the ISO C library, as summarized in Table 77:

Table 77—Algorithms library summary

Subclause	Header(s)
25.1 Non-modifying sequence operations	
25.2 Mutating sequence operations	`<algorithm>`
25.3 Sorting and related operations	
25.4 C library algorithms	`<cstdlib>`

Header `<algorithm>` synopsis

```
namespace std {
  // 25.1, non-modifying sequence operations:
  template<class InputIterator, class Function>
    Function for_each(InputIterator first, InputIterator last, Function f);
  template<class InputIterator, class T>
    InputIterator find(InputIterator first, InputIterator last,
                       const T& value);
  template<class InputIterator, class Predicate>
    InputIterator find_if(InputIterator first, InputIterator last,
                          Predicate pred);
  template<class ForwardIterator1, class ForwardIterator2>
    ForwardIterator1
      find_end(ForwardIterator1 first1, ForwardIterator1 last1,
               ForwardIterator2 first2, ForwardIterator2 last2);
  template<class ForwardIterator1, class ForwardIterator2,
           class BinaryPredicate>
    ForwardIterator1
      find_end(ForwardIterator1 first1, ForwardIterator1 last1,
               ForwardIterator2 first2, ForwardIterator2 last2,
               BinaryPredicate pred);

  template<class ForwardIterator1, class ForwardIterator2>
    ForwardIterator1
      find_first_of(ForwardIterator1 first1, ForwardIterator1 last1,
                    ForwardIterator2 first2, ForwardIterator2 last2);
  template<class ForwardIterator1, class ForwardIterator2,
           class BinaryPredicate>
    ForwardIterator1
      find_first_of(ForwardIterator1 first1, ForwardIterator1 last1,
                    ForwardIterator2 first2, ForwardIterator2 last2,
                    BinaryPredicate pred);
```

```
template<class ForwardIterator>
  ForwardIterator adjacent_find(ForwardIterator first,
                                ForwardIterator last);
template<class ForwardIterator, class BinaryPredicate>
  ForwardIterator adjacent_find(ForwardIterator first,
      ForwardIterator last, BinaryPredicate pred);

template<class InputIterator, class T>
  typename iterator_traits<InputIterator>::difference_type
    count(InputIterator first, InputIterator last, const T& value);
template<class InputIterator, class Predicate>
  typename iterator_traits<InputIterator>::difference_type
    count_if(InputIterator first, InputIterator last, Predicate pred);

template<class InputIterator1, class InputIterator2>
  pair<InputIterator1, InputIterator2>
    mismatch(InputIterator1 first1, InputIterator1 last1,
             InputIterator2 first2);
template
 <class InputIterator1, class InputIterator2, class BinaryPredicate>
  pair<InputIterator1, InputIterator2>
    mismatch(InputIterator1 first1, InputIterator1 last1,
      InputIterator2 first2, BinaryPredicate pred);

template<class InputIterator1, class InputIterator2>
  bool equal(InputIterator1 first1, InputIterator1 last1,
             InputIterator2 first2);
template
 <class InputIterator1, class InputIterator2, class BinaryPredicate>
  bool equal(InputIterator1 first1, InputIterator1 last1,
             InputIterator2 first2, BinaryPredicate pred);

template<class ForwardIterator1, class ForwardIterator2>
  ForwardIterator1 search
    (ForwardIterator1 first1, ForwardIterator1 last1,
     ForwardIterator2 first2, ForwardIterator2 last2);
template<class ForwardIterator1, class ForwardIterator2,
         class BinaryPredicate>
  ForwardIterator1 search
    (ForwardIterator1 first1, ForwardIterator1 last1,
     ForwardIterator2 first2, ForwardIterator2 last2,
                       BinaryPredicate pred);
template<class ForwardIterator, class Size, class T>
  ForwardIterator  search_n(ForwardIterator first, ForwardIterator last,
                            Size count, const T& value);
template
 <class ForwardIterator, class Size, class T, class BinaryPredicate>
  ForwardIterator1 search_n(ForwardIterator first, ForwardIterator last,
                            Size count, const T& value,
                            BinaryPredicate pred);
```

```
// 25.2, modifying sequence operations:
// 25.2.1, copy:
template<class InputIterator, class OutputIterator>
  OutputIterator copy(InputIterator first, InputIterator last,
                      OutputIterator result);
template<class BidirectionalIterator1, class BidirectionalIterator2>
  BidirectionalIterator2
    copy_backward
      (BidirectionalIterator1 first, BidirectionalIterator1 last,
       BidirectionalIterator2 result);

// 25.2.2, swap:
template<class T> void swap(T& a, T& b);
template<class ForwardIterator1, class ForwardIterator2>
  ForwardIterator2 swap_ranges(ForwardIterator1 first1,
      ForwardIterator1 last1, ForwardIterator2 first2);
template<class ForwardIterator1, class ForwardIterator2>
  void iter_swap(ForwardIterator1 a, ForwardIterator2 b);

template<class InputIterator, class OutputIterator, class UnaryOperation>
  OutputIterator transform(InputIterator first, InputIterator last,
                           OutputIterator result, UnaryOperation op);
template<class InputIterator1, class InputIterator2, class OutputIterator,
         class BinaryOperation>
  OutputIterator transform(InputIterator1 first1, InputIterator1 last1,
                           InputIterator2 first2, OutputIterator result,
                           BinaryOperation binary_op);

template<class ForwardIterator, class T>
  void replace(ForwardIterator first, ForwardIterator last,
               const T& old_value, const T& new_value);
template<class ForwardIterator, class Predicate, class T>
  void replace_if(ForwardIterator first, ForwardIterator last,
                  Predicate pred, const T& new_value);
template<class InputIterator, class OutputIterator, class T>
  OutputIterator replace_copy(InputIterator first, InputIterator last,
                              OutputIterator result,
                              const T& old_value, const T& new_value);
template<class Iterator, class OutputIterator, class Predicate, class T>
  OutputIterator replace_copy_if(Iterator first, Iterator last,
                                 OutputIterator result,
                                 Predicate pred, const T& new_value);

template<class ForwardIterator, class T>
  void fill(ForwardIterator first, ForwardIterator last, const T& value);
template<class OutputIterator, class Size, class T>
  void fill_n(OutputIterator first, Size n, const T& value);

template<class ForwardIterator, class Generator>
  void generate(ForwardIterator first, ForwardIterator last,
                Generator gen);
template<class OutputIterator, class Size, class Generator>
  void generate_n(OutputIterator first, Size n, Generator gen);
```

```
template<class ForwardIterator, class T>
  ForwardIterator remove(ForwardIterator first, ForwardIterator last,
                         const T& value);
template<class ForwardIterator, class Predicate>
  ForwardIterator remove_if(ForwardIterator first, ForwardIterator last,
                            Predicate pred);
template<class InputIterator, class OutputIterator, class T>
  OutputIterator remove_copy(InputIterator first, InputIterator last,
                             OutputIterator result, const T& value);
template<class InputIterator, class OutputIterator, class Predicate>
  OutputIterator remove_copy_if(InputIterator first, InputIterator last,
                                OutputIterator result, Predicate pred);

template<class ForwardIterator>
  ForwardIterator unique(ForwardIterator first, ForwardIterator last);
template<class ForwardIterator, class BinaryPredicate>
  ForwardIterator unique(ForwardIterator first, ForwardIterator last,
                         BinaryPredicate pred);
template<class InputIterator, class OutputIterator>
  OutputIterator unique_copy(InputIterator first, InputIterator last,
                             OutputIterator result);
template<class InputIterator, class OutputIterator, class BinaryPredicate>
  OutputIterator unique_copy(InputIterator first, InputIterator last,
                             OutputIterator result, BinaryPredicate pred);

template<class BidirectionalIterator>
  void reverse(BidirectionalIterator first, BidirectionalIterator last);
template<class BidirectionalIterator, class OutputIterator>
  OutputIterator reverse_copy(BidirectionalIterator first,
                              BidirectionalIterator last,
                              OutputIterator result);

template<class ForwardIterator>
  void rotate(ForwardIterator first, ForwardIterator middle,
              ForwardIterator last);
template<class ForwardIterator, class OutputIterator>
  OutputIterator rotate_copy
    (ForwardIterator first, ForwardIterator middle,
     ForwardIterator last, OutputIterator result);

template<class RandomAccessIterator>
  void random_shuffle(RandomAccessIterator first,
                      RandomAccessIterator last);
template<class RandomAccessIterator, class RandomNumberGenerator>
  void random_shuffle(RandomAccessIterator first,
                      RandomAccessIterator last,
                      RandomNumberGenerator& rand);

// 25.2.12, partitions:
template<class BidirectionalIterator, class Predicate>
  BidirectionalIterator partition(BidirectionalIterator first,
                                  BidirectionalIterator last,
                                  Predicate pred);
template<class BidirectionalIterator, class Predicate>
  BidirectionalIterator stable_partition(BidirectionalIterator first,
                                         BidirectionalIterator last,
                                         Predicate pred);
```

```
// 25.3, sorting and related operations:
// 25.3.1, sorting:
template<class RandomAccessIterator>
  void sort(RandomAccessIterator first, RandomAccessIterator last);
template<class RandomAccessIterator, class Compare>
  void sort(RandomAccessIterator first, RandomAccessIterator last,
            Compare comp);

template<class RandomAccessIterator>
  void stable_sort(RandomAccessIterator first, RandomAccessIterator last);
template<class RandomAccessIterator, class Compare>
  void stable_sort(RandomAccessIterator first, RandomAccessIterator last,
                   Compare comp);

template<class RandomAccessIterator>
  void partial_sort(RandomAccessIterator first,
                    RandomAccessIterator middle,
                    RandomAccessIterator last);
template<class RandomAccessIterator, class Compare>
  void partial_sort(RandomAccessIterator first,
                    RandomAccessIterator middle,
                    RandomAccessIterator last, Compare comp);
template<class InputIterator, class RandomAccessIterator>
  RandomAccessIterator
    partial_sort_copy(InputIterator first, InputIterator last,
                      RandomAccessIterator result_first,
                      RandomAccessIterator result_last);
template<class InputIterator, class RandomAccessIterator, class Compare>
  RandomAccessIterator
    partial_sort_copy(InputIterator first, InputIterator last,
                      RandomAccessIterator result_first,
                      RandomAccessIterator result_last,
                      Compare comp);

template<class RandomAccessIterator>
  void nth_element(RandomAccessIterator first, RandomAccessIterator nth,
                   RandomAccessIterator last);
template<class RandomAccessIterator, class Compare>
  void nth_element(RandomAccessIterator first, RandomAccessIterator nth,
                   RandomAccessIterator last, Compare comp);

// 25.3.3, binary search:
template<class ForwardIterator, class T>
  ForwardIterator lower_bound(ForwardIterator first, ForwardIterator last,
                              const T& value);
template<class ForwardIterator, class T, class Compare>
  ForwardIterator lower_bound(ForwardIterator first, ForwardIterator last,
                              const T& value, Compare comp);

template<class ForwardIterator, class T>
  ForwardIterator upper_bound(ForwardIterator first, ForwardIterator last,
                              const T& value);
template<class ForwardIterator, class T, class Compare>
  ForwardIterator upper_bound(ForwardIterator first, ForwardIterator last,
                              const T& value, Compare comp);
```

```
template<class ForwardIterator, class T>
  pair<ForwardIterator, ForwardIterator>
    equal_range(ForwardIterator first, ForwardIterator last,
                const T& value);
template<class ForwardIterator, class T, class Compare>
  pair<ForwardIterator, ForwardIterator>
    equal_range(ForwardIterator first, ForwardIterator last,
                const T& value, Compare comp);


template<class ForwardIterator, class T>
  bool binary_search(ForwardIterator first, ForwardIterator last,
                     const T& value);
template<class ForwardIterator, class T, class Compare>
  bool binary_search(ForwardIterator first, ForwardIterator last,
                     const T& value, Compare comp);


// 25.3.4, merge:
template<class InputIterator1, class InputIterator2, class OutputIterator>
  OutputIterator merge(InputIterator1 first1, InputIterator1 last1,
                       InputIterator2 first2, InputIterator2 last2,
                       OutputIterator result);
template<class InputIterator1, class InputIterator2, class OutputIterator,
         class Compare>
  OutputIterator merge(InputIterator1 first1, InputIterator1 last1,
                       InputIterator2 first2, InputIterator2 last2,
                       OutputIterator result, Compare comp);


template<class BidirectionalIterator>
  void inplace_merge(BidirectionalIterator first,
                     BidirectionalIterator middle,
                     BidirectionalIterator last);
template<class BidirectionalIterator, class Compare>
  void inplace_merge(BidirectionalIterator first,
                     BidirectionalIterator middle,
                     BidirectionalIterator last, Compare comp);


// 25.3.5, set operations:
template<class InputIterator1, class InputIterator2>
  bool includes(InputIterator1 first1, InputIterator1 last1,
                InputIterator2 first2, InputIterator2 last2);
template<class InputIterator1, class InputIterator2, class Compare>
  bool includes
     (InputIterator1 first1, InputIterator1 last1,
      InputIterator2 first2, InputIterator2 last2, Compare comp);


template<class InputIterator1, class InputIterator2, class OutputIterator>
  OutputIterator set_union(InputIterator1 first1, InputIterator1 last1,
                           InputIterator2 first2, InputIterator2 last2,
                           OutputIterator result);
template<class InputIterator1, class InputIterator2, class OutputIterator,
         class Compare>
  OutputIterator set_union(InputIterator1 first1, InputIterator1 last1,
                           InputIterator2 first2, InputIterator2 last2,
                           OutputIterator result, Compare comp);
```

```
template<class InputIterator1, class InputIterator2, class OutputIterator>
  OutputIterator set_intersection
      (InputIterator1 first1, InputIterator1 last1,
       InputIterator2 first2, InputIterator2 last2,
       OutputIterator result);
template<class InputIterator1, class InputIterator2, class OutputIterator,
         class Compare>
  OutputIterator set_intersection
      (InputIterator1 first1, InputIterator1 last1,
       InputIterator2 first2, InputIterator2 last2,
       OutputIterator result, Compare comp);

template<class InputIterator1, class InputIterator2, class OutputIterator>
  OutputIterator set_difference
      (InputIterator1 first1, InputIterator1 last1,
       InputIterator2 first2, InputIterator2 last2,
       OutputIterator result);
template<class InputIterator1, class InputIterator2, class OutputIterator,
         class Compare>
  OutputIterator set_difference
      (InputIterator1 first1, InputIterator1 last1,
       InputIterator2 first2, InputIterator2 last2,
       OutputIterator result, Compare comp);

template<class InputIterator1, class InputIterator2, class OutputIterator>
  OutputIterator
    set_symmetric_difference(InputIterator1 first1, InputIterator1 last1,
                             InputIterator2 first2, InputIterator2 last2,
                             OutputIterator result);
template<class InputIterator1, class InputIterator2, class OutputIterator,
         class Compare>
  OutputIterator
    set_symmetric_difference(InputIterator1 first1, InputIterator1 last1,
                             InputIterator2 first2, InputIterator2 last2,
                             OutputIterator result, Compare comp);

// 25.3.6, heap operations:
template<class RandomAccessIterator>
  void push_heap(RandomAccessIterator first, RandomAccessIterator last);
template<class RandomAccessIterator, class Compare>
  void push_heap(RandomAccessIterator first, RandomAccessIterator last,
                 Compare comp);

template<class RandomAccessIterator>
  void pop_heap(RandomAccessIterator first, RandomAccessIterator last);
template<class RandomAccessIterator, class Compare>
  void pop_heap(RandomAccessIterator first, RandomAccessIterator last,
                Compare comp);

template<class RandomAccessIterator>
  void make_heap(RandomAccessIterator first, RandomAccessIterator last);
template<class RandomAccessIterator, class Compare>
  void make_heap(RandomAccessIterator first, RandomAccessIterator last,
                 Compare comp);
```

```
template<class RandomAccessIterator>
  void sort_heap(RandomAccessIterator first, RandomAccessIterator last);
template<class RandomAccessIterator, class Compare>
  void sort_heap(RandomAccessIterator first, RandomAccessIterator last,
                 Compare comp);
```

// 25.3.7, minimum and maximum:
```
template<class T> const T& min(const T& a, const T& b);
template<class T, class Compare>
  const T& min(const T& a, const T& b, Compare comp);
template<class T> const T& max(const T& a, const T& b);
template<class T, class Compare>
  const T& max(const T& a, const T& b, Compare comp);

template<class ForwardIterator>
  ForwardIterator min_element
    (ForwardIterator first, ForwardIterator last);
template<class ForwardIterator, class Compare>
  ForwardIterator min_element(ForwardIterator first, ForwardIterator last,
                              Compare comp);
template<class ForwardIterator>
  ForwardIterator max_element
    (ForwardIterator first, ForwardIterator last);
template<class ForwardIterator, class Compare>
  ForwardIterator max_element(ForwardIterator first, ForwardIterator last,
                              Compare comp);

template<class InputIterator1, class InputIterator2>
  bool lexicographical_compare
      (InputIterator1 first1, InputIterator1 last1,
       InputIterator2 first2, InputIterator2 last2);
template<class InputIterator1, class InputIterator2, class Compare>
  bool lexicographical_compare
      (InputIterator1 first1, InputIterator1 last1,
       InputIterator2 first2, InputIterator2 last2,
       Compare comp);
```

// 25.3.9, permutations
```
template<class BidirectionalIterator>
  bool next_permutation(BidirectionalIterator first,
                        BidirectionalIterator last);
template<class BidirectionalIterator, class Compare>
  bool next_permutation(BidirectionalIterator first,
                        BidirectionalIterator last, Compare comp);
template<class BidirectionalIterator>
  bool prev_permutation(BidirectionalIterator first,
                        BidirectionalIterator last);
template<class BidirectionalIterator, class Compare>
  bool prev_permutation(BidirectionalIterator first,
                        BidirectionalIterator last, Compare comp);
}
```

3   All of the algorithms are separated from the particular implementations of data structures and are parameterized by iterator types. Because of this, they can work with program-defined data structures, as long as these data structures have iterator types satisfying the assumptions on the algorithms.

4   Throughout this clause, the names of template parameters are used to express type requirements. If an algorithm's template parameter is `InputIterator`, `InputIterator1`, or `InputIterator2`, the actual template argument shall satisfy the requirements of an input iterator (24.1.1). If an algorithm's

template parameter is `OutputIterator`, `OutputIterator1`, or `OutputIterator2`, the actual template argument shall satisfy the requirements of an output iterator (24.1.2). If an algorithm's template parameter is `ForwardIterator`, `ForwardIterator1`, or `ForwardIterator2`, the actual template argument shall satisfy the requirements of a forward iterator (24.1.3). If an algorithm's template parameter is `BidirectionalIterator`, `BidirectionalIterator1`, or `BidirectionalIterator2`, the actual template argument shall satisfy the requirements of a bidirectional iterator (24.1.4). If an algorithm's template parameter is `RandomAccessIterator`, `RandomAccessIterator1`, or `RandomAccessIterator2`, the actual template argument shall satisfy the requirements of a random-access iterator (24.1.5).

5   If an algorithm's **Effects** section says that a value pointed to by any iterator passed as an argument is modified, then that algorithm has an additional type requirement: The type of that argument shall satisfy the requirements of a mutable iterator (24.1). [*Note:* this requirement does not affect arguments that are declared as `OutputIterator`, `OutputIterator1`, or `OutputIterator2`, because output iterators must always be mutable. —*end note*]

6   Both in-place and copying versions are provided for certain algorithms.[250] When such a version is provided for *algorithm* it is called *algorithm_copy*. Algorithms that take predicates end with the suffix `_if` (which follows the suffix `_copy`).

7   The `Predicate` parameter is used whenever an algorithm expects a function object that when applied to the result of dereferencing the corresponding iterator returns a value testable as `true`. In other words, if an algorithm takes `Predicate pred` as its argument and *first* as its iterator argument, it should work correctly in the construct `if (pred(*first)){...}`. The function object `pred` shall not apply any non-constant function through the dereferenced iterator. This function object may be a pointer to function, or an object of a type with an appropriate function call operator.

8   The `BinaryPredicate` parameter is used whenever an algorithm expects a function object that when applied to the result of dereferencing two corresponding iterators or to dereferencing an iterator and type T when T is part of the signature returns a value testable as `true`. In other words, if an algorithm takes `BinaryPredicate binary_pred` as its argument and *first1* and *first2* as its iterator arguments, it should work correctly in the construct `if (binary_pred(*first1, *first2)){...}`. `BinaryPredicate` always takes the first iterator type as its first argument, that is, in those cases when T *value* is part of the signature, it should work correctly in the context of `if (binary_pred(*first1, value)){...}`. *binary_pred* shall not apply any non-constant function through the dereferenced iterators.

9   In the description of the algorithms operators + and - are used for some of the iterator categories for which they do not have to be defined. In these cases the semantics of a+n is the same as that of

```
{ X tmp = a;
  advance(tmp, n);
  return tmp;
}
```

and that of b-a is the same as of

```
return distance(a, b);
```

---

[250] The decision whether to include a copying version was usually based on complexity considerations. When the cost of doing the operation dominates the cost of copy, the copying version is not included. For example, `sort_copy` is not included because the cost of sorting is much more significant, and users might as well do `copy` followed by `sort`.

25.1 Non-modifying sequence operations   **[lib.alg.nonmodifying]**

25.1.1 For each   **[lib.alg.foreach]**

```
template<class InputIterator, class Function>
    Function for_each(InputIterator first, InputIterator last, Function f);
```

1   **Effects:** Applies f to the result of dereferencing every iterator in the range $[first, \ last)$, starting from $first$ and proceeding to $last \ - \ 1$.
2   **Returns:** f.
3   **Complexity:** Applies f exactly $last \ - \ first$ times.
4   **Notes:** If f returns a result, the result is ignored.

25.1.2 Find   **[lib.alg.find]**

```
template<class InputIterator, class T>
    InputIterator find(InputIterator first, InputIterator last,
                       const T& value);

template<class InputIterator, class Predicate>
    InputIterator find_if(InputIterator first, InputIterator last,
                          Predicate pred);
```

1   **Requires:** Type T is EqualityComparable (20.1.1).
2   **Returns:** The first iterator i in the range $[first, \ last)$ for which the following corresponding conditions hold: *i == $value$, $pred$(*i) != false. Returns $last$ if no such iterator is found.
3   **Complexity:** At most $last \ - \ first$ applications of the corresponding predicate.

25.1.3 Find End   **[lib.alg.find.end]**

```
template<class ForwardIterator1, class ForwardIterator2>
    ForwardIterator1
        find_end(ForwardIterator1 first1, ForwardIterator1 last1,
                 ForwardIterator2 first2, ForwardIterator2 last2);

template<class ForwardIterator1, class ForwardIterator2,
         class BinaryPredicate>
    ForwardIterator1
        find_end(ForwardIterator1 first1, ForwardIterator1 last1,
                 ForwardIterator2 first2, ForwardIterator2 last2,
                 BinaryPredicate pred);
```

1   **Effects:** Finds a subsequence of equal values in a sequence.
2   **Returns:** The last iterator i in the range $[first1, \ last1 \ - \ (last2-first2))$ such that for any non-negative integer n < $(last2-first2)$, the following corresponding conditions hold: *(i+n) == *($first2$+n), $pred$(*(i+n),*($first2$+n)) != false. Returns $last1$ if no such iterator is found.
3   **Complexity:** At most $(last2 \ - \ first2) \ * \ (last1 \ - \ first1 \ - \ (last2 \ - \ first2) \ + \ 1)$ applications of the corresponding predicate.

25.1.4 Find First **[lib.alg.find.first.of]**

```
template<class ForwardIterator1, class ForwardIterator2>
  ForwardIterator1
    find_first_of(ForwardIterator1 first1, ForwardIterator1 last1,
                  ForwardIterator2 first2, ForwardIterator2 last2);

template<class ForwardIterator1, class ForwardIterator2,
         class BinaryPredicate>
  ForwardIterator1
    find_first_of(ForwardIterator1 first1, ForwardIterator1 last1,
                  ForwardIterator2 first2, ForwardIterator2 last2,
                  BinaryPredicate pred);
```

1 **Effects:** Finds an element that matches one of a set of values.

2 **Returns:** The first iterator i in the range [*first1*, *last1*) such that for some iterator j in the range [*first2*, *last2*) the following conditions hold: *i == *j, pred(*i,*j) != false. Returns *last1* if no such iterator is found.

3 **Complexity:** At most (*last1-first1*) * (*last2-first2*) applications of the corresponding predicate.

25.1.5 Adjacent find   [lib.alg.adjacent.find]

```
template<class ForwardIterator>
  ForwardIterator adjacent_find(ForwardIterator first, ForwardIterator last);

template<class ForwardIterator, class BinaryPredicate>
  ForwardIterator adjacent_find(ForwardIterator first, ForwardIterator last,
                                BinaryPredicate pred);
```

1 **Returns:** The first iterator i such that both i and i + 1 are in the range [*first*, *last*) for which the following corresponding conditions hold: *i == *(i + 1), pred(*i, *(i + 1)) != false. Returns *last* if no such iterator is found.

2 **Complexity:** Exactly find(*first*, *last*, *value*) - *first* applications of the corresponding predicate.

25.1.6 Count   [lib.alg.count]

```
template<class InputIterator, class T>
  typename iterator_traits<InputIterator>::difference_type
    count(InputIterator first, InputIterator last, const T& value);

template<class InputIterator, class Predicate>
  typename iterator_traits<InputIterator>::difference_type
    count_if(InputIterator first, InputIterator last, Predicate pred);
```

1 **Requires:** Type T is EqualityComparable (20.1.1).

2 **Effects:** Returns the number of iterators i in the range [*first*, *last*) for which the following corresponding conditions hold: *i == *value*, pred(*i) != false.

3 **Complexity:** Exactly *last* - *first* applications of the corresponding predicate.

25.1.7 Mismatch [lib.mismatch]

```
template<class InputIterator1, class InputIterator2>
  pair<InputIterator1, InputIterator2>
    mismatch(InputIterator1 first1, InputIterator1 last1,
             InputIterator2 first2);

template<class InputIterator1, class InputIterator2,
         class BinaryPredicate>
  pair<InputIterator1, InputIterator2>
    mismatch(InputIterator1 first1, InputIterator1 last1,
             InputIterator2 first2, BinaryPredicate pred);
```

1   **Returns:** A pair of iterators i and j such that j == *first2* + (i - *first1*) and i is the first iterator in the range [*first1*, *last1*) for which the following corresponding conditions hold:

```
!(*i == *(first2 + (i - first1)))
pred(*i, *(first2 + (i - first1))) == false
```

Returns the pair *last1* and *first2* + (*last1* - *first1*) if such an iterator i is not found.

2   **Complexity:** At most *last1* - *first1* applications of the corresponding predicate.

25.1.8 Equal [lib.alg.equal]

```
template<class InputIterator1, class InputIterator2>
  bool equal(InputIterator1 first1, InputIterator1 last1,
             InputIterator2 first2);

template<class InputIterator1, class InputIterator2,
         class BinaryPredicate>
  bool equal(InputIterator1 first1, InputIterator1 last1,
             InputIterator2 first2, BinaryPredicate pred);
```

1   **Returns:** true if for every iterator i in the range [*first1*, *last1*) the following corresponding conditions hold: *i == *(first2 + (i - first1)), pred(*i, *(first2 + (i - first1))) != false. Otherwise, returns false.

2   **Complexity:** At most *last1* - *first1* applications of the corresponding predicate.

25.1.9 Search [lib.alg.search]

```
template<class ForwardIterator1, class ForwardIterator2>
  ForwardIterator1
    search(ForwardIterator1 first1, ForwardIterator1 last1,
           ForwardIterator2 first2, ForwardIterator2 last2);

template<class ForwardIterator1, class ForwardIterator2,
         class BinaryPredicate>
  ForwardIterator1
    search(ForwardIterator1 first1, ForwardIterator1 last1,
           ForwardIterator2 first2, ForwardIterator2 last2,
           BinaryPredicate pred);
```

1   **Effects:** Finds a subsequence of equal values in a sequence.

2   **Returns:** The first iterator i in the range [*first1*, last1 - (*last2* - *first2*)) such that for any non-negative integer n less than *last2* - first2 the following corresponding conditions hold: *(i + n) == *(first2 + n), pred(*(i + n), *(first2 + n)) != false. Returns *last1* if no such iterator is found.

3   **Complexity:** At most (*last1* - *first1*) * (*last2* - *first2*) applications of the corresponding predicate.

```
template<class ForwardIterator, class Size, class T>
  ForwardIterator
    search_n(ForwardIterator first, ForwardIterator last, Size count,
             const T& value);

template<class ForwardIterator, class Size, class T,
         class BinaryPredicate>
  ForwardIterator
    search_n(ForwardIterator first, ForwardIterator last, Size count,
             const T& value, BinaryPredicate pred);
```

4   **Requires:** Type T is EqualityComparable (20.1.1), type Size is convertible to integral type (4.7, 12.3).

5   **Effects:** Finds a subsequence of equal values in a sequence.

6   **Returns:** The first iterator i in the range [*first*, *last* - *count*) such that for any non-negative integer n less than count the following corresponding conditions hold: *(i + n) == *value*, pred(*(i + n),*value*) != false. Returns *last* if no such iterator is found.

7   **Complexity:** At most (*last1* - *first1*) * *count* applications of the corresponding predicate.

25.2 Mutating sequence operations   [lib.alg.modifying.operations]

25.2.1 Copy   [lib.alg.copy]

```
template<class InputIterator, class OutputIterator>
  OutputIterator copy(InputIterator first, InputIterator last,
                      OutputIterator result);
```

1   **Effects:** Copies elements in the range [*first*, *last*) into the range [*result*, *result* + (*last* - *first*)) starting from *first* and proceeding to *last*. For each non-negative integer $n <$ (*last*-*first*), performs *(result + n) = *(first + n).

2   **Returns:** *result* + (*last* - *first*).

3   **Requires:** result shall not be in the range [*first*, *last*).

4   **Complexity:** Exactly *last* - *first* assignments.

```
template<class BidirectionalIterator1, class BidirectionalIterator2>
  BidirectionalIterator2
    copy_backward(BidirectionalIterator1 first,
                  BidirectionalIterator1 last,
                  BidirectionalIterator2 result);
```

5   **Effects:** Copies elements in the range [*first*, *last*) into the range [*result* - (*last* - *first*), *result*) starting from *last* - 1 and proceeding to *first*.[251] For each positive integer n <= (*last* - *first*), performs *(result - n) = *(last - n).

6   **Requires:** *result* shall not be in the range [*first*, *last*).

7   **Returns:** *result* - (*last* - *first*).

8   **Complexity:** Exactly *last* - *first* assignments.

---

[251] copy_backward (_lib.copy.backward_) should be used instead of copy when *last* is in the range [*result* - (*last* - *first*), *result*).

25.2.2 Swap [lib.alg.swap]

```
template<class T> void swap(T& a, T& b);
```

1 **Requires:** Type T is CopyConstructible (20.1.3) and Assignable (23.1).

2 **Effects:** Exchanges values stored in two locations.

```
template<class ForwardIterator1, class ForwardIterator2>
  ForwardIterator2
    swap_ranges(ForwardIterator1 first1, ForwardIterator1 last1,
                ForwardIterator2 first2);
```

3 **Effects:** For each non-negative integer n < (*last1* - *first1*) performs: swap(*(*first1* + n), *(*first2* + n)).

4 **Requires:** The two ranges [*first1*, *last1*) and [*first2*, *first2* + (*last1* - *first1*)) shall not overlap.

5 **Returns:** *first2* + (*last1* - *first1*).

6 **Complexity:** Exactly *last1* - *first1* swaps.

```
template<class ForwardIterator1, class ForwardIterator2>
  void iter_swap(ForwardIterator1 a, ForwardIterator2 b);
```

7 **Effects:** Exchanges the values pointed to by the two iterators a and b.

25.2.3 Transform [lib.alg.transform]

```
template<class InputIterator, class OutputIterator,
         class UnaryOperation>
  OutputIterator
    transform(InputIterator first, InputIterator last,
              OutputIterator result, UnaryOperation op);

template<class InputIterator1, class InputIterator2,
         class OutputIterator, class BinaryOperation>
  OutputIterator
    transform(InputIterator1 first1, InputIterator1 last1,
              InputIterator2 first2, OutputIterator result,
              BinaryOperation binary_op);
```

1 **Effects:** Assigns through every iterator i in the range [*result*, *result* + (*last1* - *first1*)) a new corresponding value equal to op(*(*first1* + (i - *result*)) or binary_op(*(*first1* + (i - *result*)), *(*first2* + (i - *result*))).

2 **Requires:** *op* and *binary_op* shall not have any side effects.

3 **Returns:** *result* + (*last1* - *first1*).

4 **Complexity:** Exactly *last1* - *first1* applications of *op* or *binary_op*

5 **Notes:** *result* may be equal to *first* in case of unary transform, or to *first1* or *first2* in case of binary transform.

25.2.4 Replace [lib.alg.replace]

```
template<class ForwardIterator, class T>
  void replace(ForwardIterator first, ForwardIterator last,
               const T& old_value, const T& new_value);

template<class ForwardIterator, class Predicate, class T>
  void replace_if(ForwardIterator first, ForwardIterator last,
                  Predicate pred, const T& new_value);
```

1 **Requires:** Type T is Assignable (23.1) (and, for `replace()`, EqualityComparable (20.1.1)).

2 **Effects:** Substitutes elements referred by the iterator i in the range [*first*, *last*) with *new_value*, when the following corresponding conditions hold: `*i == old_value`, `pred(*i) != false`.

3 **Complexity:** Exactly *last - first* applications of the corresponding predicate.

```
template<class InputIterator, class OutputIterator, class T>
  OutputIterator
    replace_copy(InputIterator first, InputIterator last,
                 OutputIterator result,
                 const T& old_value, const T& new_value);

template<class Iterator, class OutputIterator, class Predicate, class T>
  OutputIterator
    replace_copy_if(Iterator first, Iterator last,
                    OutputIterator result,
                    Predicate pred, const T& new_value);
```

4 **Requires:** Type T is Assignable (23.1) (and, for `replace_copy()`, EqualityComparable (20.1.1). The ranges [*first*, *last*) and [*result*, *result* + (*last* - *first*)) shall not overlap.

5 **Effects:** Assigns to every iterator i in the range [*result*, *result* + (*last* - *first*)) either *new_value* or `*(first + (i - result))` depending on whether the following corresponding conditions hold:
`*(first + (i - result)) == old_value`, `pred(*(first + (i - result))) != false`.

6 **Returns:** *result* + (*last* - *first*).

7 **Complexity:** Exactly *last - first* applications of the corresponding predicate.

25.2.5 Fill [lib.alg.fill]

```
template<class ForwardIterator, class T>
  void fill(ForwardIterator first, ForwardIterator last, const T& value);

template<class OutputIterator, class Size, class T>
  void fill_n(OutputIterator first, Size n, const T& value);
```

1 **Requires:** Type T is Assignable (23.1), Size is convertible to an integral type (4.7, 12.3).

2 **Effects:** Assigns value through all the iterators in the range [*first*, *last*) or [*first*, *first* + *n*).

3 **Complexity:** Exactly *last - first* (or *n*) assignments.

25.2.6 Generate [lib.alg.generate]

```
template<class ForwardIterator, class Generator>
  void generate(ForwardIterator first, ForwardIterator last,
                Generator gen);

template<class OutputIterator, class Size, class Generator>
  void generate_n(OutputIterator first, Size n, Generator gen);
```

1 **Effects:** Invokes the function object *gen* and assigns the return value of *gen* though all the iterators in the range [*first*, *last*) or [*first*, *first* + *n*).

2 **Requires:** *gen* takes no arguments, Size is convertible to an integral type (4.7, 12.3).

3 **Complexity:** Exactly *last - first* (or *n*) invocations of *gen* and assignments.

25.2.7 Remove [lib.alg.remove]

```
template<class ForwardIterator, class T>
  ForwardIterator remove(ForwardIterator first, ForwardIterator last,
                         const T& value);

template<class ForwardIterator, class Predicate>
  ForwardIterator remove_if(ForwardIterator first, ForwardIterator last,
                            Predicate pred);
```

1 **Requires:** Type T is EqualityComparable (20.1.1).

2 **Effects:** Eliminates all the elements referred to by iterator i in the range [*first*, *last*) for which the following corresponding conditions hold: `*i == value`, `pred(*i) != false`.

3 **Returns:** The end of the resulting range.

4 **Notes:** Stable: the relative order of the elements that are not removed is the same as their relative order in the original range.

5 **Complexity:** Exactly *last - first* applications of the corresponding predicate.

```
template<class InputIterator, class OutputIterator, class T>
  OutputIterator
    remove_copy(InputIterator first, InputIterator last,
                OutputIterator result, const T& value);

template<class InputIterator, class OutputIterator, class Predicate>
  OutputIterator
    remove_copy_if(InputIterator first, InputIterator last,
                   OutputIterator result, Predicate pred);
```

6 **Requires:** Type T is EqualityComparable (20.1.1). The ranges [*first*, *last*) and [*result*, *result+(last-first)*)) shall not overlap.

7 **Effects:** Copies all the elements referred to by the iterator i in the range [*first*, *last*) for which the following corresponding conditions do not hold: `*i == value`, `pred(*i) != false`.

8 **Returns:** The end of the resulting range.

9 **Complexity:** Exactly *last - first* applications of the corresponding predicate.

10 **Notes:** Stable: the relative order of the elements in the resulting range is the same as their relative order in the original range.

25.2.8 Unique [lib.alg.unique]

```
template<class ForwardIterator>
  ForwardIterator unique(ForwardIterator first, ForwardIterator last);

template<class ForwardIterator, class BinaryPredicate>
  ForwardIterator unique(ForwardIterator first, ForwardIterator last,
                         BinaryPredicate pred);
```

1 **Effects:** Eliminates all but the first element from every consecutive group of equal elements referred to by the iterator i in the range [*first*, *last*) for which the following corresponding conditions hold: `*i == *(i - 1)` or `pred(*i, *(i - 1)) != false`

2 **Returns:** The end of the resulting range.

3 **Complexity:** If the range (*last - first*) is not empty, exactly (*last - first*) - 1 applications of the corresponding predicate, otherwise no applications of the predicate.

```
template<class InputIterator, class OutputIterator>
  OutputIterator
    unique_copy(InputIterator first, InputIterator last,
                OutputIterator result);

template<class InputIterator, class OutputIterator,
         class BinaryPredicate>
  OutputIterator
    unique_copy(InputIterator first, InputIterator last,
                OutputIterator result, BinaryPredicate pred);
```

4   **Requires:** The ranges [`first`, `last`) and [`result`, `result`+(`last`-`first`)) shall not overlap.

5   **Effects:** Copies only the first element from every consecutive group of equal elements referred to by the iterator i in the range [`first`, `last`) for which the following corresponding conditions hold: `*i == *(i - 1)` or *pred*(`*i`, `*(i - 1)`) `!= false`

6   **Returns:** The end of the resulting range.

7   **Complexity:** Exactly `last - first` applications of the corresponding predicate.

25.2.9 Reverse   [lib.alg.reverse]

```
template<class BidirectionalIterator>
  void reverse(BidirectionalIterator first, BidirectionalIterator last);
```

1   **Effects:** For each non-negative integer i `<= (last - first)/2`, applies iter_swap to all pairs of iterators `first + i`, `(last - i) - 1`.

2   **Complexity:** Exactly `(last - first)/2` swaps.

```
template<class BidirectionalIterator, class OutputIterator>
  OutputIterator
    reverse_copy(BidirectionalIterator first,
                 BidirectionalIterator last, OutputIterator result);
```

3   **Effects:** Copies the range [`first`, `last`) to the range [`result`, `result + (last - first`)) such that for any non-negative integer i `< (last - first)` the following assignment takes place: `*(result + (last - first) - i) = *(first + i)`

4   **Requires:** The ranges [`first`, `last`) and [`result`, `result + (last - first`)) shall not overlap.

5   **Returns:** `result + (last - first)`.

6   **Complexity:** Exactly `last - first` assignments.

25.2.10 Rotate   [lib.alg.rotate]

```
template<class ForwardIterator>
  void rotate(ForwardIterator first, ForwardIterator middle,
              ForwardIterator last);
```

1   **Effects:** For each non-negative integer i `< (last - first)`, places the element from the position `first + i` into position `first + (i + (last - middle)) % (last - first)`.

2   **Notes:** This is a left rotate.

3   **Requires:** [`first`, `middle`) and [`middle`, `last`) are valid ranges.

4   **Complexity:** At most `last - first` swaps.

```
template<class ForwardIterator, class OutputIterator>
  OutputIterator
    rotate_copy(ForwardIterator first, ForwardIterator middle,
                ForwardIterator last, OutputIterator result);
```

5   **Effects:** Copies the range [*first*, *last*) to the range [*result*, *result* + (*last* - *first*)) such that for each non-negative integer i < (*last* - *first*) the following assignment takes place: *(*result* + i) = *(*first* + (i + (*middle* - *first*)) % (*last* - *first*))

6   **Returns:** *result* + (*last* - *first*).

7   **Requires** The ranges [*first*, *last*) and [*result*, *result* + (*last* - *first*)) shall not overlap.

8   **Complexity:** Exactly *last* - *first* assignments.

25.2.11 Random shuffle   [lib.alg.random.shuffle]

```
template<class RandomAccessIterator>
  void random_shuffle(RandomAccessIterator first,
                      RandomAccessIterator last);

template<class RandomAccessIterator, class RandomNumberGenerator>
  void random_shuffle(RandomAccessIterator first,
                      RandomAccessIterator last,
                      RandomNumberGenerator& rand);
```

1   **Effects:** Shuffles the elements in the range [*first*, *last*) with uniform distribution.

2   **Complexity:** Exactly (*last* - *first*) - 1 swaps.

3   **Notes:** random_shuffle() can take a particular random number generating function object *rand* such that if *n* is an argument for *rand*, with a positive value, that has type iterator_traits<RandomAccessIterator>::difference_type, then *rand*(*n*) returns a randomly chosen value, which lies in the interval [0, *n*), and which has a type that is convertible to iterator_traits<RandomAccessIterator>::difference_type.

25.2.12 Partitions   [lib.alg.partitions]

```
template<class BidirectionalIterator, class Predicate>
  BidirectionalIterator
    partition(BidirectionalIterator first,
              BidirectionalIterator last, Predicate pred);
```

1   **Effects:** Places all the elements in the range [*first*, *last*) that satisfy *pred* before all the elements that do not satisfy it.

2   **Returns:** An iterator i such that for any iterator j in the range [*first*, i), *pred*(*j) != false, and for any iterator k in the range [i, *last*), *pred*(*j) == false.

3   **Complexity:** At most (*last* - *first*)/2 swaps. Exactly *last* - *first* applications of the predicate are done.

```
template<class BidirectionalIterator, class Predicate>
  BidirectionalIterator
    stable_partition(BidirectionalIterator first,
                     BidirectionalIterator last, Predicate pred);
```

4   **Effects:** Places all the elements in the range [*first*, *last*) that satisfy *pred* before all the elements that do not satisfy it.

5   **Returns:** An iterator i such that for any iterator j in the range [*first*, i), *pred*(*j) != false, and for any iterator k in the range [i, *last*), *pred*(*j) == false. The relative order of the elements in both groups is preserved.

6 **Complexity:** At most $(last - first) * \log(last - first)$ swaps, but only linear number of swaps if there is enough extra memory. Exactly $last - first$ applications of the predicate.

25.3 Sorting and related operations   **[lib.alg.sorting]**

1 All the operations in 25.3 have two versions: one that takes a function object of type `Compare` and one that uses an `operator<`.

2 `Compare` is used as a function object which returns `true` if the first argument is less than the second, and `false` otherwise. `Compare` *comp* is used throughout for algorithms assuming an ordering relation. It is assumed that `comp` will not apply any non-constant function through the dereferenced iterator.

3 For all algorithms that take `Compare`, there is a version that uses `operator<` instead. That is, `comp(*i, *j) != false` defaults to `*i < *j != false`. For the algorithms to work correctly, *comp* has to induce a strict weak ordering on the values.

4 The term *strict* refers to the requirement of an irreflexive relation (`!comp(x, x)` for all x), and the term *weak* to requirements that are not as strong as those for a total ordering, but stronger than those for a partial ordering. If we define `equiv(a, b)` as `!comp(a, b) && !comp(b, a)`, then the requirements are that `comp` and `equiv` both be transitive relations:

— `comp(a, b) && comp(b, c)` implies `comp(a, c)`

— `equiv(a, b) && equiv(b, c)` implies `equiv(a, c)` [*Note:* Under these conditions, it can be shown that

— `equiv` is an equivalence relation

— `comp` induces a well-defined relation on the equivalence classes determined by `equiv`

— The induced relation is a strict total ordering. *—end note*]

5 A sequence is *sorted with respect to a comparator* *comp* if for any iterator `i` pointing to the sequence and any non-negative integer `n` such that `i + n` is a valid iterator pointing to an element of the sequence, `comp(*(i + n), *i) == false`.

6 In the descriptions of the functions that deal with ordering relationships we frequently use a notion of equivalence to describe concepts such as stability. The equivalence to which we refer is not necessarily an `operator==`, but an equivalence relation induced by the strict weak ordering. That is, two elements a and b are considered equivalent if and only if `!(a < b) && !(b < a)`.

25.3.1 Sorting   **[lib.alg.sort]**

25.3.1.1 `sort`   **[lib.sort]**

```
template<class RandomAccessIterator>
  void sort(RandomAccessIterator first, RandomAccessIterator last);

template<class RandomAccessIterator, class Compare>
  void sort(RandomAccessIterator first, RandomAccessIterator last,
            Compare comp);
```

1 **Effects:** Sorts the elements in the range $[first, last)$.

2 **Complexity:** Approximately N *log* N (where N == $last - first$) comparisons on the average.[252]

---

[252] If the worst case behavior is important `stable_sort()` (25.3.1.2) or `partial_sort()` (25.3.1.3) should be used.

25.3.1.2 stable_sort [lib.stable.sort]

```
template<class RandomAccessIterator>
  void stable_sort(RandomAccessIterator first, RandomAccessIterator last);

template<class RandomAccessIterator, class Compare>
  void stable_sort(RandomAccessIterator first, RandomAccessIterator last,
                   Compare comp);
```

1 **Effects:** Sorts the elements in the range [*first*, *last*).

2 **Complexity:** It does at most $N (log N)^2$ (where N == *last* - *first*) comparisons; if enough extra memory is available, it is $N \; log \; N$.

3 **Notes:** Stable: the relative order of the equivalent elements is preserved.

25.3.1.3 partial_sort [lib.partial.sort]

```
template<class RandomAccessIterator>
  void partial_sort(RandomAccessIterator first,
                    RandomAccessIterator middle,
                    RandomAccessIterator last);

template<class RandomAccessIterator, class Compare>
  void partial_sort(RandomAccessIterator first,
                    RandomAccessIterator middle,
                    RandomAccessIterator last,
                    Compare comp);
```

1 **Effects:** Places the first *middle* - *first* sorted elements from the range [*first*, *last*) into the range [*first*, *middle*). The rest of the elements in the range [*middle*, *last*) are placed in an unspecified order.

2 **Complexity:** It takes approximately (*last* - *first*) * log(*middle* - *first*) comparisons.

25.3.1.4 partial_sort_copy [lib.partial.sort.copy]

```
template<class InputIterator, class RandomAccessIterator>
  RandomAccessIterator
    partial_sort_copy(InputIterator first, InputIterator last,
                      RandomAccessIterator result_first,
                      RandomAccessIterator result_last);

template<class InputIterator, class RandomAccessIterator,
         class Compare>
  RandomAccessIterator
    partial_sort_copy(InputIterator first, InputIterator last,
                      RandomAccessIterator result_first,
                      RandomAccessIterator result_last,
                      Compare comp);
```

1 **Effects:** Places the first min(*last* - *first*, *result_last* - *result_first*) sorted elements into the range [*result_first*, *result_first* + min(*last* - *first*, *result_last* - *result_first*)).

2 **Returns:** The smaller of: *result_last* or *result_first* + (*last* - *first*)

3 **Complexity:** Approximately (*last* - *first*) * log(min(*last* - *first*, *result_last* - *result_first*)) comparisons.

25.3.2 Nth element [lib.alg.nth.element]

```
template<class RandomAccessIterator>
  void nth_element(RandomAccessIterator first, RandomAccessIterator nth,
                   RandomAccessIterator last);

template<class RandomAccessIterator, class Compare>
  void nth_element(RandomAccessIterator first, RandomAccessIterator nth,
                   RandomAccessIterator last,  Compare comp);
```

1   After `nth_element` the element in the position pointed to by `nth` is the element that would be in that position if the whole range were sorted. Also for any iterator i in the range `[first, nth)` and any iterator j in the range `[nth, last)` it holds that: `!(*i > *j)` or `comp(*j, *i) == false`.

2   **Complexity:** Linear on average.

25.3.3 Binary search [lib.alg.binary.search]

1   All of the algorithms in this section are versions of binary search and assume that the sequence being searched is in order according to the implied or explicit comparison function. They work on non-random access iterators minimizing the number of comparisons, which will be logarithmic for all types of iterators. They are especially appropriate for random access iterators, because these algorithms do a logarithmic number of steps through the data structure. For non-random access iterators they execute a linear number of steps.

25.3.3.1 `lower_bound` [lib.lower.bound]

```
template<class ForwardIterator, class T>
  ForwardIterator
    lower_bound(ForwardIterator first, ForwardIterator last,
                const T& value);

template<class ForwardIterator, class T, class Compare>
  ForwardIterator
    lower_bound(ForwardIterator first, ForwardIterator last,
                const T& value, Compare comp);
```

1   **Requires:** Type T is `LessThanComparable` (20.1.2).

2   **Effects:** Finds the first position into which value can be inserted without violating the ordering.

3   **Returns:** The furthermost iterator i in the range `[first, last]` such that for any iterator j in the range `[first, i)` the following corresponding conditions hold: `*j < value` or `comp(*j, value) != false`

4   **Complexity:** At most `log(last - first) + 1` comparisons.

25.3.3.2 `upper_bound` [lib.upper.bound]

```
template<class ForwardIterator, class T>
  ForwardIterator
    upper_bound(ForwardIterator first, ForwardIterator last,
                const T& value);

template<class ForwardIterator, class T, class Compare>
  ForwardIterator
    upper_bound(ForwardIterator first, ForwardIterator last,
                const T& value, Compare comp);
```

1   **Requires:** Type T is `LessThanComparable` (20.1.2).

2 **Effects:** Finds the furthermost position into which value can be inserted without violating the ordering.

3 **Returns:** The furthermost iterator i in the range [*first*, *last*) such that for any iterator j in the range [*first*, i) the following corresponding conditions hold: !(value < *j) or *comp*(*value*, *j*) == false

4 **Complexity:** At most log(*last* - *first*) + 1 comparisons.

25.3.3.3 `equal_range`   **[lib.equal.range]**

```
template<class ForwardIterator, class T>
  pair<ForwardIterator, ForwardIterator>
    equal_range(ForwardIterator first,
                ForwardIterator last, const T& value);

template<class ForwardIterator, class T, class Compare>
  pair<ForwardIterator, ForwardIterator>
    equal_range(ForwardIterator first,
                ForwardIterator last, const T& value,
                Compare comp);
```

1 **Requires:** Type T is LessThanComparable (20.1.2).

2 **Effects:** Finds the largest subrange [i, j) such that the value can be inserted at any iterator k in it without violating the ordering. k satisfies the corresponding conditions: !(*k < value) && !(value < *k) or *comp*(*k*, *value*) == false && *comp*(*value*, *k*) == false.

3 **Complexity:** At most 2 * log(*last* - *first*) + 1 comparisons.

25.3.3.4 `binary_search`   **[lib.binary.search]**

```
template<class ForwardIterator, class T>
  bool binary_search(ForwardIterator first, ForwardIterator last,
                     const T& value);

template<class ForwardIterator, class T, class Compare>
  bool binary_search(ForwardIterator first, ForwardIterator last,
                     const T& value, Compare comp);
```

1 **Requires:** Type T is LessThanComparable (20.1.2).

2 **Returns:** true if there is an iterator i in the range [*first*, *last*) that satisfies the corresponding conditions: !(*i < value) && !(value < *i) or *comp*(*i*, *value*) == false && *comp*(*value*, *i*) == false.

3 **Complexity:** At most log(*last* - *first*) + 2 comparisons.

25.3.4 Merge   **[lib.alg.merge]**

```
template<class InputIterator1, class InputIterator2,
         class OutputIterator>
  OutputIterator
    merge(InputIterator1 first1, InputIterator1 last1,
          InputIterator2 first2, InputIterator2 last2,
          OutputIterator result);

template<class InputIterator1, class InputIterator2,
         class OutputIterator, class Compare>
  OutputIterator
    merge(InputIterator1 first1, InputIterator1 last1,
          InputIterator2 first2, InputIterator2 last2,
          OutputIterator result, Compare comp);
```

1   **Effects:** Merges two sorted ranges [*first1*, *last1*) and [*first2*, *last2*) into the range
     [*result*, *result* + (*last1* - *first1*) + (*last2* - *first2*)).

2   The resulting range shall not overlap with either of the original ranges. The list will be sorted in non-
     decreasing order according to the ordering defined by *comp*; that is, for every iterator i in [*first*,
     last) other than *first*, the condition *i < *(i - 1) or *comp*(*i, *(i - 1)) will be false.

3   **Returns:** *result* + (*last1* - *first1*) + (*last2* - *first2*).

4   **Complexity:** At most (*last1* - *first1*) + (*last2* - *first2*) - 1 comparisons.

5   **Notes:** Stable: for equivalent elements in the two ranges, the elements from the first range always precede
     the elements from the second.

```
template<class BidirectionalIterator>
  void inplace_merge(BidirectionalIterator first,
                     BidirectionalIterator middle,
                     BidirectionalIterator last);

template<class BidirectionalIterator, class Compare>
  void inplace_merge(BidirectionalIterator first,
                     BidirectionalIterator middle,
                     BidirectionalIterator last, Compare comp);
```

6   **Effects:** Merges two sorted consecutive ranges [*first*, *middle*) and [middle, *last*), putting
     the result of the merge into the range [*first*, *last*). The resulting range will be in non-decreasing
     order; that is, for every iterator i in [*first*, *last*) other than *first*, the condition *i < *(i -
     1) or, respectively, *comp*(*i, *(i - 1)) will be false.

7   **Complexity:** When enough additional memory is available, (*last* - *first*) - 1 comparisons. If no
     additional memory is available, an algorithm with complexity N *log* N (where N is equal to *last* -
     first) may be used.

8   **Notes:** Stable: for equivalent elements in the two ranges, the elements from the first range always precede
     the elements from the second.

25.3.5 Set operations on sorted structures   [lib.alg.set.operations]

1   This section defines all the basic set operations on sorted structures. They also work with multisets
     (23.3.4) containing multiple copies of equivalent elements. The semantics of the set operations are general-
     ized to multisets in a standard way by defining union() to contain the maximum number of occur-
     rences of every element, intersection() to contain the minimum, and so on.

25.3.5.1 includes   [lib.includes]

```
template<class InputIterator1, class InputIterator2>
  bool includes(InputIterator1 first1, InputIterator1 last1,
                InputIterator2 first2, InputIterator2 last2);

template<class InputIterator1, class InputIterator2, class Compare>
  bool includes(InputIterator1 first1, InputIterator1 last1,
                InputIterator2 first2, InputIterator2 last2,
                Compare comp);
```

1   **Returns:** true if every element in the range [*first2*, *last2*) is contained in the range [*first1*,
     last1). Returns false otherwise.

2   **Complexity:** At most 2 * ((*last1* - *first1*) + (*last2* - *first2*)) - 1 comparisons.

25.3.5.2 set_union

```
template<class InputIterator1, class InputIterator2,
        class OutputIterator>
  OutputIterator
    set_union(InputIterator1 first1, InputIterator1 last1,
              InputIterator2 first2, InputIterator2 last2,
              OutputIterator result);

template<class InputIterator1, class InputIterator2,
        class OutputIterator, class Compare>
  OutputIterator
    set_union(InputIterator1 first1, InputIterator1 last1,
              InputIterator2 first2, InputIterator2 last2,
              OutputIterator result, Compare comp);
```

1 **Effects:** Constructs a sorted union of the elements from the two ranges; that is, the set of elements that are present in one or both of the ranges.

2 **Requires:** The resulting range shall not overlap with either of the original ranges.

3 **Returns:** The end of the constructed range.

4 **Complexity:** At most 2 * ((*last1* - *first1*) + (*last2* - *first2*)) - 1 comparisons.

5 **Notes:** Stable: if an element is present in both ranges, the one from the first range is copied.

25.3.5.3 set_intersection

```
template<class InputIterator1, class InputIterator2,
        class OutputIterator>
  OutputIterator
    set_intersection(InputIterator1 first1, InputIterator1 last1,
                     InputIterator2 first2, InputIterator2 last2,
                     OutputIterator result);

template<class InputIterator1, class InputIterator2,
        class OutputIterator, class Compare>
  OutputIterator
    set_intersection(InputIterator1 first1, InputIterator1 last1,
                     InputIterator2 first2, InputIterator2 last2,
                     OutputIterator result, Compare comp);
```

1 **Effects:** Constructs a sorted intersection of the elements from the two ranges; that is, the set of elements that are present in both of the ranges.

2 **Requires:** The resulting range shall not overlap with either of the original ranges.

3 **Returns:** The end of the constructed range.

4 **Complexity:** At most 2 * ((*last1* - *first1*) + (*last2* - *first2*)) - 1 comparisons.

5 **Notes:** Stable, that is, if an element is present in both ranges, the one from the first range is copied.

25.3.5.4 set_difference

```
template<class InputIterator1, class InputIterator2,
         class OutputIterator>
  OutputIterator
    set_difference(InputIterator1 first1, InputIterator1 last1,
                   InputIterator2 first2, InputIterator2 last2,
                   OutputIterator result);

template<class InputIterator1, class InputIterator2,
         class OutputIterator, class Compare>
  OutputIterator
    set_difference(InputIterator1 first1, InputIterator1 last1,
                   InputIterator2 first2, InputIterator2 last2,
                   OutputIterator result, Compare comp);
```

1   **Effects:** Copies the elements of the range [`first1`, `last1`) which are not present in the range
     [`first2`, `last2`) to the range beginning at `result`. The elements in the constructed range are
     sorted.

2   **Requires:** The resulting range shall not overlap with either of the original ranges.

3   **Returns:** The end of the constructed range.

4   **Complexity:** At most 2 * ((`last1` - `first1`) + (`last2` - `first2`)) - 1 comparisons.

25.3.5.5 set_symmetric_difference   [lib.set.symmetric.difference]

```
template<class InputIterator1, class InputIterator2,
         class OutputIterator>
  OutputIterator
    set_symmetric_difference(InputIterator1 first1, InputIterator1 last1,
                             InputIterator2 first2, InputIterator2 last2,
                             OutputIterator result);

template<class InputIterator1, class InputIterator2,
         class OutputIterator, class Compare>
  OutputIterator
    set_symmetric_difference(InputIterator1 first1, InputIterator1 last1,
                             InputIterator2 first2, InputIterator2 last2,
                             OutputIterator result, Compare comp);
```

1   **Effects:** Copies the elements of the range [`first1`, `last1`) which are not present in the range
     [`first2`, `last2`), and the elements of the range [`first2`, `last2`) which are not present in
     the range [`first1`, `last1`) to the range beginning at `result`. The elements in the constructed
     range are sorted.

2   **Requires:** The resulting range shall not overlap with either of the original ranges.

3   **Returns:** The end of the constructed range.

4   **Complexity:** At most 2 * ((`last1` - `first1`) + (`last2` - `first2`)) - 1 comparisons.

25.3.6 Heap operations   [lib.alg.heap.operations]

1   A *heap* is a particular organization of elements in a range between two random access iterators [a, b).
     Its two key properties are:

     (1) There is no element greater than *a in the range and

     (2) *a may be removed by pop_heap(), or a new element added by push_heap(), in *O(log* N) time.

2   These properties make heaps useful as priority queues.

3   make_heap() converts a range into a heap and sort_heap() turns a heap into a sorted sequence.

25.3.6.1 push_heap   **[lib.push.heap]**

```
template<class RandomAccessIterator>
  void push_heap(RandomAccessIterator first, RandomAccessIterator last);

template<class RandomAccessIterator, class Compare>
  void push_heap(RandomAccessIterator first, RandomAccessIterator last,
                 Compare comp);
```

1   **Requires:** The range [*first*, last - 1) shall be a valid heap.

2   **Effects:** Places the value in the location *last* - 1 into the resulting heap [*first*, *last*).

3   **Complexity:** At most log(*last* - *first*) comparisons.

25.3.6.2 pop_heap   **[lib.pop.heap]**

```
template<class RandomAccessIterator>
  void pop_heap(RandomAccessIterator first, RandomAccessIterator last);

template<class RandomAccessIterator, class Compare>
  void pop_heap(RandomAccessIterator first, RandomAccessIterator last,
                Compare comp);
```

1   **Requires:** The range [*first*, *last*) shall be a valid heap.

2   **Effects:** Swaps the value in the location *first* with the value in the location *last* - 1 and makes [*first*, last - 1) into a heap.

3   **Complexity:** At most 2 * log(*last* - *first*) comparisons.

25.3.6.3 make_heap   **[lib.make.heap]**

```
template<class RandomAccessIterator>
  void make_heap(RandomAccessIterator first, RandomAccessIterator last);

template<class RandomAccessIterator, class Compare>
  void make_heap(RandomAccessIterator first, RandomAccessIterator last,
                 Compare comp);
```

1   **Effects:** Constructs a heap out of the range [*first*, *last*).

2   **Complexity:** At most 3 * (*last* - *first*) comparisons.

25.3.6.4 sort_heap   **[lib.sort.heap]**

```
template<class RandomAccessIterator>
  void sort_heap(RandomAccessIterator first, RandomAccessIterator last);

template<class RandomAccessIterator, class Compare>
  void sort_heap(RandomAccessIterator first, RandomAccessIterator last,
                 Compare comp);
```

1   **Effects:** Sorts elements in the heap [*first*, *last*).

2   **Complexity:** At most N *log* N comparisons (where N == *last* - *first*).

3   **Notes:** Not stable.

25.3.7 Minimum and maximum [lib.alg.min.max]

```
template<class T> const T& min(const T& a, const T& b);
template<class T, class Compare>
  const T& min(const T& a, const T& b, Compare comp);
```

1   **Requires:** Type T is LessThanComparable (20.1.2) and CopyConstructible (20.1.3).
2   **Returns:** The smaller value.
3   **Notes:** Returns the first argument when the arguments are equivalent.

```
template<class T> const T& max(const T& a, const T& b);
template<class T, class Compare>
  const T& max(const T& a, const T& b, Compare comp);
```

4   **Requires:** Type T is LessThanComparable (20.1.2) and CopyConstructible (20.1.3).
5   **Returns:** The larger value.
6   **Notes:** Returns the first argument when the arguments are equivalent.

```
template<class ForwardIterator>
  ForwardIterator min_element(ForwardIterator first, ForwardIterator last);

template<class ForwardIterator, class Compare>
  ForwardIterator min_element(ForwardIterator first, ForwardIterator last,
                              Compare comp);
```

7   **Returns:** The first iterator i in the range [*first*, *last*) such that for any iterator j in the range
    [*first*, *last*) the following corresponding conditions hold: !(*j < *i) or *comp*(*j, *i)
    == false. Returns *last* if *first* == *last*.
8   **Complexity:** Exactly max((*last* - *first*) - 1, 0) applications of the corresponding comparisons.

```
template<class ForwardIterator>
  ForwardIterator max_element(ForwardIterator first, ForwardIterator last);
template<class ForwardIterator, class Compare>
  ForwardIterator max_element(ForwardIterator first, ForwardIterator last,
                              Compare comp);
```

9   **Returns:** The first iterator i in the range [*first*, *last*) such that for any iterator j in the range
    [*first*, *last*) the following corresponding conditions hold: !(*i < *j) or *comp*(*i, *j)
    == false. Returns *last* if *first* == *last*.
10 **Complexity:** Exactly max((*last* - *first*) - 1, 0) applications of the corresponding comparisons.

25.3.8 Lexicographical comparison [lib.alg.lex.comparison]

```
template<class InputIterator1, class InputIterator2>
  bool
    lexicographical_compare(InputIterator1 first1, InputIterator1 last1,
                            InputIterator2 first2, InputIterator2 last2);

template<class InputIterator1, class InputIterator2, class Compare>
  bool
    lexicographical_compare(InputIterator1 first1, InputIterator1 last1,
                            InputIterator2 first2, InputIterator2 last2,
                            Compare comp);
```

1   **Returns:** true if the sequence of elements defined by the range [*first1*, *last1*) is lexicographically less than the sequence of elements defined by the range [*first2*, *last2*).
    Returns false otherwise.

2   **Complexity:** At most `2*min((last1 - first1), (last2 - first2))` applications of the corresponding comparison.

3   **Notes:** If two sequences have the same number of elements and their corresponding elements are equivalent, then neither sequence is lexicographically less than the other. If one sequence is a prefix of the other, then the shorter sequence is lexicographically less than the longer sequence. Otherwise, the lexicographical comparison of the sequences yields the same result as the comparison of the first corresponding pair of elements that are not equivalent.

```
for ( ; first1 != last1 && first2 != last2 ; ++first1, ++first2) {
  if (*first1 < *first2) return true;
  if (*first2 < *first1) return false;
}
return first1 == last1 && first2 != last2;
```

25.3.9 Permutation generators   [lib.alg.permutation.generators]

```
template<class BidirectionalIterator>
  bool next_permutation(BidirectionalIterator first,
                        BidirectionalIterator last);

template<class BidirectionalIterator, class Compare>
  bool next_permutation(BidirectionalIterator first,
                        BidirectionalIterator last, Compare comp);
```

1   **Effects:** Takes a sequence defined by the range `[first, last)` and transforms it into the next permutation. The next permutation is found by assuming that the set of all permutations is lexicographically sorted with respect to `operator<` or `comp`. If such a permutation exists, it returns `true`. Otherwise, it transforms the sequence into the smallest permutation, that is, the ascendingly sorted one, and returns `false`.

2   **Complexity:** At most `(last - first)/2` swaps.

```
template<class BidirectionalIterator>
  bool prev_permutation(BidirectionalIterator first,
                        BidirectionalIterator last);

template<class BidirectionalIterator, class Compare>
  bool prev_permutation(BidirectionalIterator first,
                        BidirectionalIterator last, Compare comp);
```

3   **Effects:** Takes a sequence defined by the range `[first, last)` and transforms it into the previous permutation. The previous permutation is found by assuming that the set of all permutations is lexicographically sorted with respect to `operator<` or `comp`.

4   **Returns:** `true` if such a permutation exists. Otherwise, it transforms the sequence into the largest permutation, that is, the descendingly sorted one, and returns `false`.

5   **Complexity:** At most `(last - first)/2` swaps.

25.4 C library algorithms   [lib.alg.c.library]

1   Header `<cstdlib>` (partial, Table 78):

Table 78—Header `<cstdlib>` synopsis

Type	Name(s)	
Functions:	bsearch	qsort

2   The contents are the same as the Standard C library header <stdlib.h> with the following exceptions:

3   The function signature:

```
bsearch(const void *, const void *, size_t, size_t,
        int (*)(const void *, const void *));
```

is replaced by the two declarations:

```
extern "C" void *bsearch(const void *key, const void *base,
                    size_t nmemb, size_t size,
                    int (*compar)(const void *, const void *));
extern "C++" void *bsearch(const void *key, const void *base,
                    size_t nmemb, size_t size,
                    int (*compar)(const void *, const void *));
```

both of which have the same behavior as the original declaration.

4   The function signature:

```
qsort(void *, size_t, size_t,
        int (*)(const void *, const void *));
```

is replaced by the two declarations:

```
extern "C" void qsort(void* base, size_t nmemb, size_t size,
                int (*compar)(const void*, const void*));
extern "C++" void qsort(void* base, size_t nmemb, size_t size,
                int (*compar)(const void*, const void*));
```

[*Note:* Because the function argument *compar*() may throw an exception, bsearch() and qsort() are allowed to propagate the exception (17.4.4.8). —*end note*]

SEE ALSO: ISO C subclause 7.10.5.

26 Numerics library [lib.numerics]

1   This clause describes components that C++ programs may use to perform seminumerical operations.

2   The following subclauses describe components for complex number types, numeric (*n*-at-a-time) arrays, generalized numeric algorithms, and facilities included from the ISO C library, as summarized in Table 79:

Table 79—Numerics library summary

Subclause	Header(s)
26.1 Requirements	
26.2 Complex numbers	`<complex>`
26.3 Numeric arrays	`<valarray>`
26.4 Generalized numeric operations	`<numeric>`
26.5 C library	`<cmath>` `<cstdlib>`

26.1 Numeric type requirements [lib.numeric.requirements]

1   The `complex` and `valarray` components are parameterized by the type of information they contain and manipulate. A C++ program shall instantiate these components only with a type T that satisfies the following requirements:[253]

— *T* is not an abstract class (it has no pure virtual member functions);

— *T* is not a reference type;

— *T* is not cv-qualified;

— If *T* is a class, it has a public default constructor;

— If *T* is a class, it has a public copy constructor with the signature `T::T(const T&)`

— If *T* is a class, it has a public destructor;

— If *T* is a class, it has a public assignment operator whose signature is either
`T& T::operator=(const T&)` or `T& T::operator=(T)`

— If *T* is a class, its assignment operator, copy and default constructors, and destructor shall correspond to each other in the following sense: Initialization of raw storage using the default constructor, followed by assignment, is semantically equivalent to initialization of raw storage using the copy constructor. Destruction of an object, followed by initialization of its raw storage using the copy constructor, is semantically equivalent to assignment to the original object.
[*Note:* This rule states that there shall not be any subtle differences in the semantics of initialization versus assignment. This gives an implementation considerable flexibility in how arrays are initialized.
[*Example:* An implementation is allowed to initialize a `valarray` by allocating storage using the `new` operator (which implies a call to the default constructor for each element) and then assigning each element its value. Or the implementation can allocate raw storage and use the copy constructor to initialize each element. —*end example*]

---

[253] In other words, value types. These include built-in arithmetic types, pointers, the library class `complex`, and instantiations of `valarray` for value types.

If the distinction between initialization and assignment is important for a class, or if it fails to satisfy any of the other conditions listed above, the programmer should use vector (23.2.4) instead of valarray for that class; —*end note*]

— If T is a class, it does not overload unary operator&.

2   If any operation on T throws an exception the effects are undefined.

3   In addition, many member and related functions of valarray<T> can be successfully instantiated and will exhibit well-defined behavior if and only if T satisfies additional requirements specified for each such member or related function.

4   [*Example:* It is valid to instantiate valarray<*complex*>, but operator>() will not be successfully instantiated for valarray<*complex*> operands, since complex does not have any ordering operators. —*end example*]

26.2 Complex numbers   [lib.complex.numbers]

1   The header <complex> defines a class template, and numerous functions for representing and manipulating complex numbers.

2   The effect of instantiating the template complex for any type other than float, double or long double is unspecified.

3   If the result of a function is not mathematically defined or not in the range of representable values for its type, the behavior is undefined.

26.2.1 Header <complex> synopsis   [lib.complex.synopsis]

```
namespace std {
  template<class T> class complex;
  template<> class complex<float>;
  template<> class complex<double>;
  template<> class complex<long double>;

  // 26.2.6 operators:
  template<class T>
    complex<T> operator+(const complex<T>&, const complex<T>&);
  template<class T> complex<T> operator+(const complex<T>&, const T&);
  template<class T> complex<T> operator+(const T&, const complex<T>&);

  template<class T> complex<T> operator-
    (const complex<T>&, const complex<T>&);
  template<class T> complex<T> operator-(const complex<T>&, const T&);
  template<class T> complex<T> operator-(const T&, const complex<T>&);

  template<class T> complex<T> operator*
    (const complex<T>&, const complex<T>&);
  template<class T> complex<T> operator*(const complex<T>&, const T&);
  template<class T> complex<T> operator*(const T&, const complex<T>&);

  template<class T> complex<T> operator/
    (const complex<T>&, const complex<T>&);
  template<class T> complex<T> operator/(const complex<T>&, const T&);
  template<class T> complex<T> operator/(const T&, const complex<T>&);

  template<class T> complex<T> operator+(const complex<T>&);
  template<class T> complex<T> operator-(const complex<T>&);
```

```
template<class T> bool operator==
  (const complex<T>&, const complex<T>&);
template<class T> bool operator==(const complex<T>&, const T&);
template<class T> bool operator==(const T&, const complex<T>&);

template<class T> bool operator!=(const complex<T>&, const complex<T>&);
template<class T> bool operator!=(const complex<T>&, const T&);
template<class T> bool operator!=(const T&, const complex<T>&);

template<class T, class charT, class traits>
basic_istream<charT, traits>&
operator>>(basic_istream<charT, traits>&, complex<T>&);

template<class T, class charT, class traits>
basic_ostream<charT, traits>&
operator<<(basic_ostream<charT, traits>&, const complex<T>&);

// 26.2.7 values:

template<class T> T real(const complex<T>&);
template<class T> T imag(const complex<T>&);

template<class T> T abs(const complex<T>&);
template<class T> T arg(const complex<T>&);
template<class T> T norm(const complex<T>&);

template<class T> complex<T> conj(const complex<T>&);
template<class T> complex<T> polar(const T& rho, const T& theta = 0);

// 26.2.8 transcendentals:
template<class T> complex<T> cos  (const complex<T>&);
template<class T> complex<T> cosh (const complex<T>&);
template<class T> complex<T> exp  (const complex<T>&);
template<class T> complex<T> log  (const complex<T>&);
template<class T> complex<T> log10(const complex<T>&);

template<class T> complex<T> pow(const complex<T>&, int);
template<class T> complex<T> pow(const complex<T>&, const T&);
template<class T> complex<T> pow(const complex<T>&, const complex<T>&);
template<class T> complex<T> pow(const T&, const complex<T>&);

template<class T> complex<T> sin  (const complex<T>&);
template<class T> complex<T> sinh (const complex<T>&);
template<class T> complex<T> sqrt (const complex<T>&);
template<class T> complex<T> tan  (const complex<T>&);
template<class T> complex<T> tanh (const complex<T>&);
}
```

26.2.2 Class template complex   **[lib.complex]**

```
namespace std {
  template<class T>
  class complex {
  public:
    typedef T value_type;

    complex(const T& re = T(), const T& im = T());
    complex(const complex&);
    template<class X> complex(const complex<X>&);

    T real() const;
    T imag() const;

    complex<T>& operator= (const T&);
    complex<T>& operator+=(const T&);
    complex<T>& operator-=(const T&);
    complex<T>& operator*=(const T&);
    complex<T>& operator/=(const T&);

    complex& operator=(const complex&);
    template<class X> complex<T>& operator= (const complex<X>&);
    template<class X> complex<T>& operator+=(const complex<X>&);
    template<class X> complex<T>& operator-=(const complex<X>&);
    template<class X> complex<T>& operator*=(const complex<X>&);
    template<class X> complex<T>& operator/=(const complex<X>&);
  };

}
```

1   The class `complex` describes an object that can store the Cartesian components, `real()` and `imag()`, of
a complex number.

26.2.3 `complex` specializations   [lib.complex.special]

```
template<> class complex<float> {
public:
  typedef float value_type;

  complex(float re = 0.0f, float im = 0.0f);
  explicit complex(const complex<double>&);
  explicit complex(const complex<long double>&);

  float real() const;
  float imag() const;

  complex<float>& operator= (float);
  complex<float>& operator+=(float);
  complex<float>& operator-=(float);
  complex<float>& operator*=(float);
  complex<float>& operator/=(float);

  complex<float>& operator=(const complex<float>&);
  template<class X> complex<float>& operator= (const complex<X>&);
  template<class X> complex<float>& operator+=(const complex<X>&);
  template<class X> complex<float>& operator-=(const complex<X>&);
  template<class X> complex<float>& operator*=(const complex<X>&);
  template<class X> complex<float>& operator/=(const complex<X>&);
};
```

```
template<> class complex<double> {
public:
  typedef double value_type;

  complex(double re = 0.0, double im = 0.0);
  complex(const complex<float>&);
  explicit complex(const complex<long double>&);

  double real() const;
  double imag() const;

  complex<double>& operator= (double);
  complex<double>& operator+=(double);
  complex<double>& operator-=(double);
  complex<double>& operator*=(double);
  complex<double>& operator/=(double);

  complex<double>& operator=(const complex<double>&);
  template<class X> complex<double>& operator= (const complex<X>&);
  template<class X> complex<double>& operator+=(const complex<X>&);
  template<class X> complex<double>& operator-=(const complex<X>&);
  template<class X> complex<double>& operator*=(const complex<X>&);
  template<class X> complex<double>& operator/=(const complex<X>&);
};

template<> class complex<long double> {
public:
  typedef long double value_type;

  complex(long double re = 0.0L, long double im = 0.0L);
  complex(const complex<float>&);
  complex(const complex<double>&);

  long double real() const;
  long double imag() const;

  complex<long double>& operator=(const complex<long double>&);
  complex<long double>& operator= (long double);
  complex<long double>& operator+=(long double);
  complex<long double>& operator-=(long double);
  complex<long double>& operator*=(long double);
  complex<long double>& operator/=(long double);

  template<class X> complex<long double>& operator= (const complex<X>&);
  template<class X> complex<long double>& operator+=(const complex<X>&);
  template<class X> complex<long double>& operator-=(const complex<X>&);
  template<class X> complex<long double>& operator*=(const complex<X>&);
  template<class X> complex<long double>& operator/=(const complex<X>&);
};
```

26.2.4 `complex` member functions [lib.complex.members]

```
template<class T> complex(const T& re = T(), const T& im = T());
```

1 **Effects:** Constructs an object of class `complex`.

2 **Postcondition:** `real() == re && imag() == im`.

26.2.5 `complex` member operators [lib.complex.member.ops]

```
template <class T> complex<T>& operator+=(const T& rhs);
```

1 **Effects:** Adds the scalar value *rhs* to the real part of the complex value `*this` and stores the result in the real part of `*this`, leaving the imaginary part unchanged.

2 **Returns:** `*this`.

```
template <class T> complex<T>& operator-=(const T& rhs);
```

3 **Effects:** Subtracts the scalar value *rhs* from the real part of the complex value `*this` and stores the result in the real part of `*this`, leaving the imaginary part unchanged.

4 **Returns:** `*this`.

```
template <class T> complex<T>& operator*=(const T& rhs);
```

5 **Effects:** Multiplies the scalar value *rhs* by the complex value `*this` and stores the result in `*this`.

6 **Returns:** `*this`.

```
template <class T> complex<T>& operator/=(const T& rhs);
```

7 **Effects:** Divides the scalar value *rhs* into the complex value `*this` and stores the result in `*this`.

8 **Returns:** `*this`.

```
template<class T> complex<T>& operator+=(const complex<T>& rhs);
```

9 **Effects:** Adds the complex value *rhs* to the complex value `*this` and stores the sum in `*this`.

10 **Returns:** `*this`.

```
template<class T> complex<T>& operator-=(const complex<T>& rhs);
```

11 **Effects:** Subtracts the complex value *rhs* from the complex value `*this` and stores the difference in `*this`.

12 **Returns:** `*this`.

```
template<class T> complex<T>& operator*=(const complex<T>& rhs);
```

13 **Effects:** Multiplies the complex value *rhs* by the complex value `*this` and stores the product in `*this`.

14 **Returns:** `*this`.

```
template<class T> complex<T>& operator/=(const complex<T>& rhs);
```

15 **Effects:** Divides the complex value *rhs* into the complex value `*this` and stores the quotient in `*this`.

16 **Returns:** `*this`.

26.2.6 complex non-member operations [lib.complex.ops]

```
template<class T> complex<T> operator+(const complex<T>& lhs);
```

1   **Notes:** unary operator.
2   **Returns:** complex<T>(lhs).

```
template<class T>
  complex<T> operator+(const complex<T>& lhs, const complex<T>& rhs);
template<class T> complex<T> operator+(const complex<T>& lhs, const T& rhs);
template<class T> complex<T> operator+(const T& lhs, const complex<T>& rhs);
```

3   **Returns:** complex<T>(lhs) += rhs.

```
template<class T> complex<T> operator-(const complex<T>& lhs);
```

4   **Notes:** unary operator.
5   **Returns:** complex<T>(-lhs.real(),-lhs.imag()).

```
template<class T>
  complex<T> operator-(const complex<T>& lhs, const complex<T>& rhs);
template<class T> complex<T> operator-(const complex<T>& lhs, const T& rhs);
template<class T> complex<T> operator-(const T& lhs, const complex<T>& rhs);
```

6   **Returns:** complex<T>(lhs) -= rhs.

```
template<class T>
  complex<T> operator*(const complex<T>& lhs, const complex<T>& rhs);
template<class T> complex<T> operator*(const complex<T>& lhs, const T& rhs);
template<class T> complex<T> operator*(const T& lhs, const complex<T>& rhs);
```

7   **Returns:** complex<T>(lhs) *= rhs.

```
template<class T>
  complex<T> operator/(const complex<T>& lhs, const complex<T>& rhs);
template<class T> complex<T> operator/(const complex<T>& lhs, const T& rhs);
template<class T> complex<T> operator/(const T& lhs, const complex<T>& rhs);
```

8   **Returns:** complex<T>(lhs) /= rhs.

```
template<class T>
  bool operator==(const complex<T>& lhs, const complex<T>& rhs);
template<class T> bool operator==(const complex<T>& lhs, const T& rhs);
template<class T> bool operator==(const T& lhs, const complex<T>& rhs);
```

9   **Returns:** lhs.real() == rhs.real() && lhs.imag() == rhs.imag().
10 **Notes:** The imaginary part is assumed to be T(), or 0.0, for the T arguments.

```
template<class T>
  bool operator!=(const complex<T>& lhs, const complex<T>& rhs);
template<class T> bool operator!=(const complex<T>& lhs, const T& rhs);
template<class T> bool operator!=(const T& lhs, const complex<T>& rhs);
```

11 **Returns:** rhs.real() != lhs.real() || rhs.imag() != lhs.imag().

```
template<class T, class charT, class traits>
basic_istream<charT, traits>&
operator>>(basic_istream<charT, traits>& is, complex<T>& x);
```

12   **Effects:** Extracts a complex number *x* of the form: u, (u), or (u,v), where u is the real part and v is the imaginary part (27.6.1.2).

13   **Requires:** The input values be convertible to T.

        If bad input is encountered, calls *is*.setstate(ios::failbit) (which may throw ios::failure (27.4.4.3).

14   **Returns:** *is*.

14a   **Notes:** This extraction is performed as a series of simpler extractions. Therefore, the skipping of white-space is specified to be the same for each of the simpler extractions.

```
template<class T, class charT, class traits>
basic_ostream<charT, traits>&
operator<<(basic_ostream<charT, traits>& o, const complex<T>& x);
```

15   **Effects:** inserts the complex number *x* onto the stream *o* as if it were implemented as follows:

```
template<class T, class charT, class traits>
basic_ostream<charT, traits>&
operator<<(basic_ostream<charT, traits>& o, const complex<T>& x)
{
        basic_ostringstream<charT, traits> s;
        s.flags(o.flags());
        s.imbue(o.getloc());
        s.precision(o.precision());
        s << '(' << x.real() << "," << x.imag() << ')';
        return o << s.str();
}
```

26.2.7 `complex` value operations   [lib.complex.value.ops]

```
template<class T> T real(const complex<T>& x);
```

1   **Returns:** *x*.real().

```
template<class T> T imag(const complex<T>& x);
```

2   **Returns:** *x*.imag().

```
template<class T> T abs(const complex<T>& x);
```

3   **Returns:** the magnitude of *x*.

```
template<class T> T arg(const complex<T>& x);
```

4   **Returns:** the phase angle of *x*, or *atan2(imag(x), real(x))*.

```
template<class T> T norm(const complex<T>& x);
```

5   **Returns:** the squared magnitude of *x*.

```
template<class T> complex<T> conj(const complex<T>& x);
```

6   **Returns:** the complex conjugate of x.

```
template<class T> complex<T> polar(const T& rho, const T& theta = 0);
```

7   **Returns:** the `complex` value corresponding to a complex number whose magnitude is `rho` and whose phase angle is `theta`.

26.2.8 `complex` transcendentals   [lib.complex.transcendentals]

```
template<class T> complex<T> cos(const complex<T>& x);
```

1   **Returns:** the complex cosine of x.

```
template<class T> complex<T> cosh(const complex<T>& x);
```

2   **Returns:** the complex hyperbolic cosine of x.

```
template<class T> complex<T> exp(const complex<T>& x);
```

3   **Returns:** the complex base e exponential of x.

```
template<class T> complex<T> log(const complex<T>& x);
```

4   **Notes:** the branch cuts are along the negative real axis.

5   **Returns:** the complex natural (base e) logarithm of x, in the range of a strip mathematically unbounded along the real axis and in the interval [-i times pi, i times pi] along the imaginary axis. When x is a negative real number, `imag(log(x))` is pi.

```
template<class T> complex<T> log10(const complex<T>& x);
```

6   **Notes:** the branch cuts are along the negative real axis.

7   **Returns:** the complex common (base 10)logarithm of x, defined as `log(x)/log(10)`.

```
template<class T> complex<T> pow(const complex<T>& x, int y);
template<class T>
  complex<T> pow(const complex<T>& x, const complex<T>& y);
template<class T> complex<T> pow  (const complex<T>& x, const T& y);
template<class T> complex<T> pow  (const T& x, const complex<T>& y);
```

8   **Notes:** the branch cuts are along the negative real axis.

9   **Returns:** the complex power of base x raised to the y–th power, defined as `exp(y*log(x))`. The value returned for `pow(0,0)` is implementation-defined.

```
template<class T> complex<T> sin  (const complex<T>& x);
```

10   **Returns:** the complex sine of x.

```
template<class T> complex<T> sinh (const complex<T>& x);
```

11   **Returns:** the complex hyperbolic sine of x.

```
template<class T> complex<T> sqrt (const complex<T>& x);
```

12   **Notes:** the branch cuts are along the negative real axis.

13   **Returns:** the complex square root of x, in the range of the right half-plane. If the argument is a negative real number, the value returned lies on the positive imaginary axis.

```
template<class T> complex<T> tan  (const complex<T>& x);
```

14   **Returns:** the complex tangent of *x*.

```
template<class T> complex<T> tanh (const complex<T>& x);
```

15   **Returns:** the complex hyperbolic tangent of *x*.

26.3 Numeric arrays   **[lib.numarray]**

26.3.1 Header `<valarray>` synopsis   **[lib.valarray.synopsis]**

```
namespace std {
  template<class T> class valarray;       // An array of type T
  class slice;                            // a BLAS-like slice out of an array
  template<class T> class slice_array;
  class gslice;                           // a generalized slice out of an array
  template<class T> class gslice_array;
  template<class T> class mask_array;     // a masked array
  template<class T> class indirect_array; // an indirected array

  template<class T> valarray<T> operator*
    (const valarray<T>&, const valarray<T>&);
  template<class T> valarray<T> operator* (const valarray<T>&, const T&);
  template<class T> valarray<T> operator* (const T&, const valarray<T>&);

  template<class T> valarray<T> operator/
    (const valarray<T>&, const valarray<T>&);
  template<class T> valarray<T> operator/ (const valarray<T>&, const T&);
  template<class T> valarray<T> operator/ (const T&, const valarray<T>&);

  template<class T> valarray<T> operator%
    (const valarray<T>&, const valarray<T>&);
  template<class T> valarray<T> operator% (const valarray<T>&, const T&);
  template<class T> valarray<T> operator% (const T&, const valarray<T>&);

  template<class T> valarray<T> operator+
    (const valarray<T>&, const valarray<T>&);
  template<class T> valarray<T> operator+ (const valarray<T>&, const T&);
  template<class T> valarray<T> operator+ (const T&, const valarray<T>&);

  template<class T> valarray<T> operator-
    (const valarray<T>&, const valarray<T>&);
  template<class T> valarray<T> operator- (const valarray<T>&, const T&);
  template<class T> valarray<T> operator- (const T&, const valarray<T>&);

  template<class T> valarray<T> operator^
    (const valarray<T>&, const valarray<T>&);
  template<class T> valarray<T> operator^ (const valarray<T>&, const T&);
  template<class T> valarray<T> operator^ (const T&, const valarray<T>&);

  template<class T> valarray<T> operator&
    (const valarray<T>&, const valarray<T>&);
  template<class T> valarray<T> operator& (const valarray<T>&, const T&);
  template<class T> valarray<T> operator& (const T&, const valarray<T>&);
```

```
template<class T> valarray<T> operator|
  (const valarray<T>&, const valarray<T>&);
template<class T> valarray<T> operator| (const valarray<T>&, const T&);
template<class T> valarray<T> operator| (const T&, const valarray<T>&);

template<class T> valarray<T> operator<<
  (const valarray<T>&, const valarray<T>&);
template<class T> valarray<T> operator<<(const valarray<T>&, const T&);
template<class T> valarray<T> operator<<(const T&, const valarray<T>&);

template<class T> valarray<T> operator>>
  (const valarray<T>&, const valarray<T>&);
template<class T> valarray<T> operator>>(const valarray<T>&, const T&);
template<class T> valarray<T> operator>>(const T&, const valarray<T>&);

template<class T> valarray<bool> operator&&
  (const valarray<T>&, const valarray<T>&);
template<class T> valarray<bool> operator&&(const valarray<T>&, const T&);
template<class T> valarray<bool> operator&&(const T&, const valarray<T>&);

template<class T> valarray<bool> operator||
  (const valarray<T>&, const valarray<T>&);
template<class T> valarray<bool> operator||(const valarray<T>&, const T&);
template<class T> valarray<bool> operator||(const T&, const valarray<T>&);

template<class T>
  valarray<bool> operator==(const valarray<T>&, const valarray<T>&);
template<class T> valarray<bool> operator==(const valarray<T>&, const T&);
template<class T> valarray<bool> operator==(const T&, const valarray<T>&);
template<class T>
  valarray<bool> operator!=(const valarray<T>&, const valarray<T>&);
template<class T> valarray<bool> operator!=(const valarray<T>&, const T&);
template<class T> valarray<bool> operator!=(const T&, const valarray<T>&);

template<class T>
  valarray<bool> operator< (const valarray<T>&, const valarray<T>&);
template<class T> valarray<bool> operator< (const valarray<T>&, const T&);
template<class T> valarray<bool> operator< (const T&, const valarray<T>&);
template<class T>
  valarray<bool> operator> (const valarray<T>&, const valarray<T>&);
template<class T> valarray<bool> operator> (const valarray<T>&, const T&);
template<class T> valarray<bool> operator> (const T&, const valarray<T>&);
template<class T>
  valarray<bool> operator<=(const valarray<T>&, const valarray<T>&);
template<class T> valarray<bool> operator<=(const valarray<T>&, const T&);
template<class T> valarray<bool> operator<=(const T&, const valarray<T>&);
template<class T>
  valarray<bool> operator>=(const valarray<T>&, const valarray<T>&);
template<class T> valarray<bool> operator>=(const valarray<T>&, const T&);
template<class T> valarray<bool> operator>=(const T&, const valarray<T>&);

template<class T> valarray<T> abs  (const valarray<T>&);
template<class T> valarray<T> acos (const valarray<T>&);
template<class T> valarray<T> asin (const valarray<T>&);
template<class T> valarray<T> atan (const valarray<T>&);
```

```
      template<class T> valarray<T> atan2
        (const valarray<T>&, const valarray<T>&);
      template<class T> valarray<T> atan2(const valarray<T>&, const T&);
      template<class T> valarray<T> atan2(const T&, const valarray<T>&);

      template<class T> valarray<T> cos   (const valarray<T>&);
      template<class T> valarray<T> cosh  (const valarray<T>&);
      template<class T> valarray<T> exp   (const valarray<T>&);
      template<class T> valarray<T> log   (const valarray<T>&);
      template<class T> valarray<T> log10 (const valarray<T>&);

      template<class T> valarray<T> pow(const valarray<T>&, const valarray<T>&);
      template<class T> valarray<T> pow(const valarray<T>&, const T&);
      template<class T> valarray<T> pow(const T&, const valarray<T>&);

      template<class T> valarray<T> sin   (const valarray<T>&);
      template<class T> valarray<T> sinh  (const valarray<T>&);
      template<class T> valarray<T> sqrt  (const valarray<T>&);
      template<class T> valarray<T> tan   (const valarray<T>&);
      template<class T> valarray<T> tanh  (const valarray<T>&);
  }
```

1   The header `<valarray>` defines five class templates (`valarray`, `slice_array`, `gslice_array`, `mask_array`, and `indirect_array`), two classes (`slice` and `gslice`), and a series of related function templates for representing and manipulating arrays of values.

2   The `valarray` array classes are defined to be free of certain forms of aliasing, thus allowing operations on these classes to be optimized.

3   Any function returning a `valarray<T>` is permitted to return an object of another type, provided all the const member functions of `valarray<T>` are also applicable to this type. This return type shall not add more than two levels of template nesting over the most deeply nested argument type.[254]

4   Implementations introducing such replacement types shall provide additional functions and operators as follows:

— for every function taking a `const valarray<T>&`, identical functions taking the replacement types shall be added;

— for every function taking two `const valarray<T>&` arguments, identical functions taking every combination of `const valarray<T>&` and replacement types shall be added.

5   In particular, an implementation shall allow a `valarray<T>` to be constructed from such replacement types and shall allow assignments and computed assignments of such types to `valarray<T>`, `slice_array<T>`, `gslice_array<T>`, `mask_array<T>` and `indirect_array<T>` objects.

6   These library functions are permitted to throw a `bad_alloc` (18.4.2.1) exception if there are not sufficient resources available to carry out the operation. Note that the exception is not mandated.

---

[254] Clause B recommends a minimum number of recursively nested template instantiations. This requirement thus indirectly suggests a minimum allowable complexity for valarray expressions.

```
namespace std {
  template<class T> class valarray {
  public:
    typedef T value_type;

    // 26.3.2.1 construct/destroy:
    valarray();
    explicit valarray(size_t);
    valarray(const T&, size_t);
    valarray(const T*, size_t);
    valarray(const valarray&);
    valarray(const slice_array<T>&);
    valarray(const gslice_array<T>&);
    valarray(const mask_array<T>&);
    valarray(const indirect_array<T>&);
    ~valarray();

    // 26.3.2.2 assignment:
    valarray<T>& operator=(const valarray<T>&);
    valarray<T>& operator=(const T&);
    valarray<T>& operator=(const slice_array<T>&);
    valarray<T>& operator=(const gslice_array<T>&);
    valarray<T>& operator=(const mask_array<T>&);
    valarray<T>& operator=(const indirect_array<T>&);

    // 26.3.2.3 element access:
    T             operator[](size_t) const;
    T&            operator[](size_t);

    // 26.3.2.4 subset operations:
    valarray<T>        operator[](slice) const;
    slice_array<T>     operator[](slice);
    valarray<T>        operator[](const gslice&) const;
    gslice_array<T>    operator[](const gslice&);
    valarray<T>        operator[](const valarray<bool>&) const;
    mask_array<T>      operator[](const valarray<bool>&);
    valarray<T>        operator[](const valarray<size_t>&) const;
    indirect_array<T>  operator[](const valarray<size_t>&);

    // 26.3.2.5 unary operators:
    valarray<T> operator+() const;
    valarray<T> operator-() const;
    valarray<T> operator~() const;
    valarray<bool> operator!() const;

    // 26.3.2.6 computed assignment:
    valarray<T>& operator*= (const T&);
    valarray<T>& operator/= (const T&);
    valarray<T>& operator%= (const T&);
    valarray<T>& operator+= (const T&);
    valarray<T>& operator-= (const T&);
    valarray<T>& operator^= (const T&);
    valarray<T>& operator&= (const T&);
    valarray<T>& operator|= (const T&);
    valarray<T>& operator<<=(const T&);
    valarray<T>& operator>>=(const T&);
```

```
valarray<T>& operator*= (const valarray<T>&);
valarray<T>& operator/= (const valarray<T>&);
valarray<T>& operator%= (const valarray<T>&);
valarray<T>& operator+= (const valarray<T>&);
valarray<T>& operator-= (const valarray<T>&);
valarray<T>& operator^= (const valarray<T>&);
valarray<T>& operator|= (const valarray<T>&);
valarray<T>& operator&= (const valarray<T>&);
valarray<T>& operator<<=(const valarray<T>&);
valarray<T>& operator>>=(const valarray<T>&);

// 26.3.2.7 member functions:
size_t size() const;

T    sum() const;
T    min() const;
T    max() const;

valarray<T> shift (int) const;
valarray<T> cshift(int) const;
valarray<T> apply(T func(T)) const;
valarray<T> apply(T func(const T&)) const;
void resize(size_t sz, T c = T());
  };
}
```

1   The class template `valarray<T>` is a one-dimensional smart array, with elements numbered sequentially from zero. It is a representation of the mathematical concept of an ordered set of values. The illusion of higher dimensionality may be produced by the familiar idiom of computed indices, together with the powerful subsetting capabilities provided by the generalized subscript operators.[255]

2   An implementation is permitted to qualify any of the functions declared in `<valarray>` as `inline`.

26.3.2.1 `valarray` constructors   [lib.valarray.cons]

```
valarray();
```

1   **Effects:** Constructs an object of class `valarray<T>`,[256] which has zero length until it is passed into a library function as a modifiable lvalue or through a non-constant `this` pointer.[257]

```
explicit valarray(size_t);
```

2   The array created by this constructor has a length equal to the value of the argument. The elements of the array are constructed using the default constructor for the instantiating type *T*.

---

[255] The intent is to specify an array template that has the minimum functionality necessary to address aliasing ambiguities and the proliferation of temporaries. Thus, the `valarray` template is neither a matrix class nor a field class. However, it is a very useful building block for designing such classes.

[256] For convenience, such objects are referred to as ''arrays'' throughout the remainder of 26.3.

[257] This default constructor is essential, since arrays of `valarray` are likely to prove useful. There shall also be a way to change the size of an array after initialization; this is supplied by the semantics of the `resize` member function.

```
valarray(const .T&, size_t);
```

3   The array created by this constructor has a length equal to the second argument. The elements of the array
     are initialized with the value of the first argument.

```
valarray(const T*, size_t);
```

4   The array created by this constructor has a length equal to the second argument n. The values of the ele-
     ments of the array are initialized with the first n values pointed to by the first argument.[258] If the value of
     the second argument is greater than the number of values pointed to by the first argument, the behavior is
     undefined.

```
valarray(const valarray<T>&);
```

5   The array created by this constructor has the same length as the argument array. The elements are initial-
     ized with the values of the corresponding elements of the argument array.[259]

```
valarray(const slice_array<T>&);
valarray(const gslice_array<T>&);
valarray(const mask_array<T>&);
valarray(const indirect_array<T>&);
```

6   These conversion constructors convert one of the four reference templates to a `valarray`.

```
~valarray();
```

7   The destructor is applied to every element of `*this`; an implementation may return all allocated memory.

26.3.2.2 `valarray` assignment   **[lib.valarray.assign]**

```
valarray<T>& operator=(const valarray<T>&);
```

1   Each element of the `*this` array is assigned the value of the corresponding element of the argument array.
     The resulting behavior is undefined if the length of the argument array is not equal to the length of the
     `*this` array.

```
valarray<T>& operator=(const T&);
```

2   The scalar assignment operator causes each element of the `*this` array to be assigned the value of the
     argument.

```
valarray<T>& operator=(const slice_array<T>&);
valarray<T>& operator=(const gslice_array<T>&);
valarray<T>& operator=(const mask_array<T>&);
valarray<T>& operator=(const indirect_array<T>&);
```

3   These operators allow the results of a generalized subscripting operation to be assigned directly to a
     `valarray`.

---

[258] This constructor is the preferred method for converting a C array to a `valarray` object.

[259] This copy constructor creates a distinct array rather than an alias. Implementations in which arrays share storage are permitted,
but they shall implement a copy-on-reference mechanism to ensure that arrays are conceptually distinct.

4   If the value of an element in the left hand side of a valarray assignment operator depends on the value of
     another element in that left hand side, the resulting behavior is undefined.

26.3.2.3 `valarray` element access   [lib.valarray.access]

```
T  operator[](size_t) const;
T& operator[](size_t);
```

1   When applied to a constant array, the subscript operator returns the value of the corresponding element of
     the array. When applied to a non-constant array, the subscript operator returns a reference to the corre-
     sponding element of the array.

2   Thus, the expression (a[i] = q, a[i]) == q evaluates as true for any non-constant
     valarray<T> a, any T q, and for any size_t i such that the value of i is less than the length of a.

3   The expression &a[i+j] == &a[i] + j evaluates as true for all size_t i and size_t j such
     that i+j is less than the length of the non-constant array a.

4   Likewise, the expression &a[i] != &b[j] evaluates as true for any two non-constant arrays a and b
     and for any size_t i and size_t j such that i is less than the length of a and j is less than the length
     of b. This property indicates an absence of aliasing and may be used to advantage by optimizing compil-
     ers.[260]

5   The reference returned by the subscript operator for a non-constant array is guaranteed to be valid until the
     member function resize(size_t, T) (26.3.2.7) is called for that array or until the lifetime of that
     array ends, whichever happens first.

6   If the subscript operator is invoked with a size_t argument whose value is not less than the length of the
     array, the behavior is undefined.

26.3.2.4 `valarray` subset operations   [lib.valarray.sub]

```
valarray<T>        operator[](slice) const;
slice_array<T>     operator[](slice);
valarray<T>        operator[](const gslice&) const;
gslice_array<T>    operator[](const gslice&);
valarray<T>        operator[](const valarray<bool>&) const;
mask_array<T>      operator[](const valarray<bool>&);
valarray<T>        operator[](const valarray<size_t>&) const;
indirect_array<T> operator[](const valarray<size_t>&);
```

1   Each of these operations returns a subset of the array. The const-qualified versions return this subset as a
     new valarray. The non-const versions return a class template object which has reference semantics to
     the original array.

---

[260] Compilers may take advantage of inlining, constant propagation, loop fusion, tracking of pointers obtained from operator
new, and other techniques to generate efficient valarrays.

26.3.2.5 **valarray** unary operators

```
valarray<T> operator+() const;
valarray<T> operator-() const;
valarray<T> operator˜() const;
valarray<bool> operator!() const;
```

1   Each of these operators may only be instantiated for a type T to which the indicated operator can be applied and for which the indicated operator returns a value which is of type T (*bool* for *operator!*) or which may be unambiguously converted to type T (*bool* for *operator!*).

2   Each of these operators returns an array whose length is equal to the length of the array. Each element of the returned array is initialized with the result of applying the indicated operator to the corresponding element of the array.

26.3.2.6 **valarray** computed assignment

```
valarray<T>& operator*= (const valarray<T>&);
valarray<T>& operator/= (const valarray<T>&);
valarray<T>& operator%= (const valarray<T>&);
valarray<T>& operator+= (const valarray<T>&);
valarray<T>& operator-= (const valarray<T>&);
valarray<T>& operator^= (const valarray<T>&);
valarray<T>& operator&= (const valarray<T>&);
valarray<T>& operator|= (const valarray<T>&);
valarray<T>& operator<<=(const valarray<T>&);
valarray<T>& operator>>=(const valarray<T>&);
```

1   Each of these operators may only be instantiated for a type T to which the indicated operator can be applied. Each of these operators performs the indicated operation on each of its elements and the corresponding element of the argument array.

2   The array is then returned by reference.

3   If the array and the argument array do not have the same length, the behavior is undefined. The appearance of an array on the left hand side of a computed assignment does *not* invalidate references or pointers.

4   If the value of an element in the left hand side of a valarray computed assignment operator depends on the value of another element in that left hand side, the resulting behavior is undefined.

```
valarray<T>& operator*= (const T&);
valarray<T>& operator/= (const T&);
valarray<T>& operator%= (const T&);
valarray<T>& operator+= (const T&);
valarray<T>& operator-= (const T&);
valarray<T>& operator^= (const T&);
valarray<T>& operator&= (const T&);
valarray<T>& operator|= (const T&);
valarray<T>& operator<<=(const T&);
valarray<T>& operator>>=(const T&);
```

5   Each of these operators may only be instantiated for a type T to which the indicated operator can be applied.

6   Each of these operators applies the indicated operation to each element of the array and the non-array argument.

7   The array is then returned by reference.

8   The appearance of an array on the left hand side of a computed assignment does *not* invalidate references or pointers to the elements of the array.

26.3.2.7 `valarray` member functions   [lib.valarray.members]

```
size_t size() const;
```

1   This function returns the number of elements in the array.

```
T sum() const;
```

This function may only be instantiated for a type T to which `operator+=` can be applied. This function returns the sum of all the elements of the array.

2   If the array has length 0, the behavior is undefined. If the array has length 1, `sum()` returns the value of element 0. Otherwise, the returned value is calculated by applying `operator+=` to a copy of an element of the array and all other elements of the array in an unspecified order.

```
T min() const;
```

3   This function returns the minimum value contained in `*this`. The value returned for an array of length 0 is undefined. For an array of length 1, the value of element 0 is returned. For all other array lengths, the determination is made using `operator<`.

```
T max() const;
```

4   This function returns the maximum value contained in `*this`. The value returned for an array of length 0 is undefined. For an array of length 1, the value of element 0 is returned. For all other array lengths, the determination is made using `operator<`.

```
valarray<T> shift(int n) const;
```

5   This function returns an object of class `valarray<T>` of length `size()`, each of whose elements I is `(*this)[`I`+n]` if I`+n` is non-negative and less than `size()`, otherwise `T()`. Thus if element zero is taken as the leftmost element, a positive value of n shifts the elements left n places, with zero fill.

6   [*Example:* If the argument has the value -2, the first two elements of the result will be constructed using the default constructor; the third element of the result will be assigned the value of the first element of the argument; etc. —*end example*]

```
valarray<T> cshift(int n) const;
```

7   This function returns an object of class `valarray<T>`, of length `size()`, each of whose elements I is `(*this)[(`I`+n)%size()]`. Thus, if element zero is taken as the leftmost element, a positive value of n shifts the elements circularly left n places.

```
valarray<T> apply(T func(T)) const;
valarray<T> apply(T func(const T&)) const;
```

8   These functions return an array whose length is equal to the array. Each element of the returned array is assigned the value returned by applying the argument function to the corresponding element of the array.

```
void resize(size_t sz, T c = T());
```

9   This member function changes the length of the *this array to sz and then assigns to each element the
     value of the second argument. Resizing invalidates all pointers and references to elements in the array.

26.3.3 valarray non-member operations   [lib.valarray.nonmembers]

26.3.3.1 valarray binary operators   [lib.valarray.binary]

```
template<class T> valarray<T> operator*
    (const valarray<T>&, const valarray<T>&);
template<class T> valarray<T> operator/
    (const valarray<T>&, const valarray<T>&);
template<class T> valarray<T> operator%
    (const valarray<T>&, const valarray<T>&);
template<class T> valarray<T> operator+
    (const valarray<T>&, const valarray<T>&);
template<class T> valarray<T> operator-
    (const valarray<T>&, const valarray<T>&);
template<class T> valarray<T> operator^
    (const valarray<T>&, const valarray<T>&);
template<class T> valarray<T> operator&
    (const valarray<T>&, const valarray<T>&);
template<class T> valarray<T> operator|
    (const valarray<T>&, const valarray<T>&);
template<class T> valarray<T> operator<<
    (const valarray<T>&, const valarray<T>&);
template<class T> valarray<T> operator>>
    (const valarray<T>&, const valarray<T>&);
```

1   Each of these operators may only be instantiated for a type T to which the indicated operator can be applied
     and for which the indicated operator returns a value which is of type T or which can be unambiguously con-
     verted to type T.

2   Each of these operators returns an array whose length is equal to the lengths of the argument arrays. Each
     element of the returned array is initialized with the result of applying the indicated operator to the corre-
     sponding elements of the argument arrays.

3   If the argument arrays do not have the same length, the behavior is undefined.

```
template<class T> valarray<T> operator* (const valarray<T>&, const T&);
template<class T> valarray<T> operator* (const T&, const valarray<T>&);
template<class T> valarray<T> operator/ (const valarray<T>&, const T&);
template<class T> valarray<T> operator/ (const T&, const valarray<T>&);
template<class T> valarray<T> operator% (const valarray<T>&, const T&);
template<class T> valarray<T> operator% (const T&, const valarray<T>&);
template<class T> valarray<T> operator+ (const valarray<T>&, const T&);
template<class T> valarray<T> operator+ (const T&, const valarray<T>&);
template<class T> valarray<T> operator- (const valarray<T>&, const T&);
template<class T> valarray<T> operator- (const T&, const valarray<T>&);
template<class T> valarray<T> operator^ (const valarray<T>&, const T&);
template<class T> valarray<T> operator^ (const T&, const valarray<T>&);
template<class T> valarray<T> operator& (const valarray<T>&, const T&);
template<class T> valarray<T> operator& (const T&, const valarray<T>&);
template<class T> valarray<T> operator| (const valarray<T>&, const T&);
template<class T> valarray<T> operator| (const T&, const valarray<T>&);
template<class T> valarray<T> operator<<(const valarray<T>&, const T&);
template<class T> valarray<T> operator<<(const T&, const valarray<T>&);
template<class T> valarray<T> operator>>(const valarray<T>&, const T&);
template<class T> valarray<T> operator>>(const T&, const valarray<T>&);
```

4   Each of these operators may only be instantiated for a type T to which the indicated operator can be applied and for which the indicated operator returns a value which is of type T or which can be unambiguously converted to type T.

5   Each of these operators returns an array whose length is equal to the length of the array argument. Each element of the returned array is initialized with the result of applying the indicated operator to the corresponding element of the array argument and the non-array argument.

26.3.3.2 `valarray` logical operators   [lib.valarray.comparison]

```
template<class T> valarray<bool> operator==
    (const valarray<T>&, const valarray<T>&);
template<class T> valarray<bool> operator!=
    (const valarray<T>&, const valarray<T>&);
template<class T> valarray<bool> operator<
    (const valarray<T>&, const valarray<T>&);
template<class T> valarray<bool> operator>
    (const valarray<T>&, const valarray<T>&);
template<class T> valarray<bool> operator<=
    (const valarray<T>&, const valarray<T>&);
template<class T> valarray<bool> operator>=
    (const valarray<T>&, const valarray<T>&);
template<class T> valarray<bool> operator&&
    (const valarray<T>&, const valarray<T>&);
template<class T> valarray<bool> operator||
    (const valarray<T>&, const valarray<T>&);
```

1   Each of these operators may only be instantiated for a type T to which the indicated operator can be applied and for which the indicated operator returns a value which is of type $bool$ or which can be unambiguously converted to type $bool$.

2   Each of these operators returns a $bool$ array whose length is equal to the length of the array arguments. Each element of the returned array is initialized with the result of applying the indicated operator to the corresponding elements of the argument arrays.

3   If the two array arguments do not have the same length, the behavior is undefined.

```
template<class T> valarray<bool> operator==(const valarray<T>&, const T&);
template<class T> valarray<bool> operator==(const T&, const valarray<T>&);
template<class T> valarray<bool> operator!=(const valarray<T>&, const T&);
template<class T> valarray<bool> operator!=(const T&, const valarray<T>&);
template<class T> valarray<bool> operator< (const valarray<T>&, const T&);
template<class T> valarray<bool> operator< (const T&, const valarray<T>&);
template<class T> valarray<bool> operator> (const valarray<T>&, const T&);
template<class T> valarray<bool> operator> (const T&, const valarray<T>&);
template<class T> valarray<bool> operator<=(const valarray<T>&, const T&);
template<class T> valarray<bool> operator<=(const T&, const valarray<T>&);
template<class T> valarray<bool> operator>=(const valarray<T>&, const T&);
template<class T> valarray<bool> operator>=(const T&, const valarray<T>&);
template<class T> valarray<bool> operator&&(const valarray<T>&, const T&);
template<class T> valarray<bool> operator&&(const T&, const valarray<T>&);
template<class T> valarray<bool> operator||(const valarray<T>&, const T&);
template<class T> valarray<bool> operator||(const T&, const valarray<T>&);
```

4   Each of these operators may only be instantiated for a type T to which the indicated operator can be applied and for which the indicated operator returns a value which is of type $bool$ or which can be unambiguously converted to type $bool$.

5   Each of these operators returns a $bool$ array whose length is equal to the length of the array argument. Each element of the returned array is initialized with the result of applying the indicated operator to the corresponding element of the array and the non-array argument.

26.3.3.3 valarray transcendentals   [lib.valarray.transcend]

```
template<class T> valarray<T> abs  (const valarray<T>&);
template<class T> valarray<T> acos (const valarray<T>&);
template<class T> valarray<T> asin (const valarray<T>&);
template<class T> valarray<T> atan (const valarray<T>&);
template<class T> valarray<T> atan2
    (const valarray<T>&, const valarray<T>&);
template<class T> valarray<T> atan2(const valarray<T>&, const T&);
template<class T> valarray<T> atan2(const T&, const valarray<T>&);
template<class T> valarray<T> cos  (const valarray<T>&);
template<class T> valarray<T> cosh (const valarray<T>&);
template<class T> valarray<T> exp  (const valarray<T>&);
template<class T> valarray<T> log  (const valarray<T>&);
template<class T> valarray<T> log10(const valarray<T>&);
template<class T> valarray<T> pow
    (const valarray<T>&, const valarray<T>&);
template<class T> valarray<T> pow  (const valarray<T>&, const T&);
template<class T> valarray<T> pow  (const T&, const valarray<T>&);
template<class T> valarray<T> sin  (const valarray<T>&);
template<class T> valarray<T> sinh (const valarray<T>&);
template<class T> valarray<T> sqrt (const valarray<T>&);
template<class T> valarray<T> tan  (const valarray<T>&);
template<class T> valarray<T> tanh (const valarray<T>&);
```

1   Each of these functions may only be instantiated for a type T to which a unique function with the indicated name can be applied. This function shall return a value which is of type T or which can be unambiguously converted to type T.

26.3.4 Class `slice` [lib.class.slice]

```
namespace std {
  class slice {
  public:
    slice();
    slice(size_t, size_t, size_t);

    size_t start() const;
    size_t size() const;
    size_t stride() const;
  };
}
```

1 The `slice` class represents a BLAS-like slice from an array. Such a slice is specified by a starting index, a length, and a stride.[261]

26.3.4.1 `slice` constructors [lib.cons.slice]

```
slice();
slice(size_t start, size_t length, size_t stride);
slice(const slice&);
```

1 The default constructor for `slice` creates a `slice` which specifies no elements. A default constructor is provided only to permit the declaration of arrays of slices. The constructor with arguments for a slice takes a start, length, and stride parameter.

2 [*Example:* `slice(3, 8, 2)` constructs a slice which selects elements 3, 5, 7, ... 17 from an array. —*end example*]

26.3.4.2 `slice` access functions [lib.slice.access]

```
size_t start() const;
size_t size() const;
size_t stride() const;
```

1 These functions return the start, length, or stride specified by a `slice` object.

26.3.5 Class template `slice_array` [lib.template.slice.array]

---

[261] BLAS stands for *Basic Linear Algebra Subprograms*. C++ programs may instantiate this class. See, for example, Dongarra, Du Croz, Duff, and Hammerling: *A set of Level 3 Basic Linear Algebra Subprograms*; Technical Report MCS–P1–0888, Argonne National Laboratory (USA), Mathematics and Computer Science Division, August, 1988.

```
namespace std {
  template <class T> class slice_array {
  public:
    typedef T value_type;

    void operator=  (const valarray<T>&) const;
    void operator*= (const valarray<T>&) const;
    void operator/= (const valarray<T>&) const;
    void operator%= (const valarray<T>&) const;
    void operator+= (const valarray<T>&) const;
    void operator-= (const valarray<T>&) const;
    void operator^= (const valarray<T>&) const;
    void operator&= (const valarray<T>&) const;
    void operator|= (const valarray<T>&) const;
    void operator<<=(const valarray<T>&) const;
    void operator>>=(const valarray<T>&) const;

    void operator=(const T&);
    ~slice_array();
  private:
    slice_array();
    slice_array(const slice_array&);
    slice_array& operator=(const slice_array&);
  };
}
```

1   The `slice_array` template is a helper template used by the `slice` subscript operator

```
slice_array<T> valarray<T>::operator[](slice);
```

It has reference semantics to a subset of an array specified by a `slice` object.

2   [*Example:* The expression a[slice(1, 5, 3)] = b; has the effect of assigning the elements of b to a slice of the elements in a. For the slice shown, the elements selected from a are 1, 4, ..., 13. —*end example*]

3   [*Note:* C++ programs may not instantiate `slice_array`, since all its constructors are private. It is intended purely as a helper class and should be transparent to the user. —*end note*]

26.3.5.1 `slice_array` constructors   **[lib.cons.slice.arr]**

```
slice_array();
slice_array(const slice_array&);
```

1   The `slice_array` template has no public constructors. These constructors are declared to be private. These constructors need not be defined.

26.3.5.2 `slice_array` assignment   **[lib.slice.arr.assign]**

```
void         operator=(const valarray<T>&) const;
slice_array& operator=(const slice_array&);
```

1   The second of these two assignment operators is declared private and need not be defined. The first has reference semantics, assigning the values of the argument array elements to selected elements of the `valarray<T>` object to which the `slice_array` object refers.

26.3.5.3 `slice_array` computed assignment   **[lib.slice.arr.comp.assign]**

```
void operator*= (const valarray<T>&) const;
void operator/= (const valarray<T>&) const;
void operator%= (const valarray<T>&) const;
void operator+= (const valarray<T>&) const;
void operator-= (const valarray<T>&) const;
void operator^= (const valarray<T>&) const;
void operator&= (const valarray<T>&) const;
void operator|= (const valarray<T>&) const;
void operator<<=(const valarray<T>&) const;
void operator>>=(const valarray<T>&) const;
```

1   These computed assignments have reference semantics, applying the indicated operation to the elements of the argument array and selected elements of the `valarray<T>` object to which the `slice_array` object refers.

26.3.5.4 `slice_array` fill function   **[lib.slice.arr.fill]**

```
void operator=(const T&);
```

1   This function has reference semantics, assigning the value of its argument to the elements of the `valarray<T>` object to which the `slice_array` object refers.

26.3.6 The `gslice` class   **[lib.class.gslice]**

```
namespace std {
  class gslice {
  public:
    gslice();
    gslice(size_t s, const valarray<size_t>& l, const valarray<size_t>& d);

    size_t           start() const;
    valarray<size_t> size() const;
    valarray<size_t> stride() const;
  };
}
```

1   This class represents a generalized slice out of an array. A `gslice` is defined by a starting offset (s), a set of lengths (l_j), and a set of strides (d_j). The number of lengths shall equal the number of strides.

2   A `gslice` represents a mapping from a set of indices (i_j), equal in number to the number of strides, to a single index k. It is useful for building multidimensional array classes using the `valarray` template, which is one-dimensional. The set of one-dimensional index values specified by a `gslice` are $k = s + \sum_j i_j d_j$ where the multidimensional indices i_j range in value from 0 to $l_{ij} - 1$.

3   [*Example:* The `gslice` specification

```
start  = 3
length = {2, 4, 3}
stride = {19, 4, 1}
```

yields the sequence of one-dimensional indices

$$k = 3 + (0,1) \times 19 + (0,1,2,3) \times 4 + (0,1,2) \times 1$$

which are ordered as shown in the following table:

$$(i_0, \ i_1, \ i_2, \ k) \ =$$

```
(0,  0,  0,  3),
(0,  0,  1,  4),
(0,  0,  2,  5),
(0,  1,  0,  7),
(0,  1,  1,  8),
(0,  1,  2,  9),
(0,  2,  0,  11),
(0,  2,  1,  12),
(0,  2,  2,  13),
(0,  3,  0,  15),
(0,  3,  1,  16),
(0,  3,  2,  17),
(1,  0,  0,  22),
(1,  0,  1,  23),
...
(1,  3,  2,  36)
```

That is, the highest-ordered index turns fastest. —*end example*]

4   It is possible to have degenerate generalized slices in which an address is repeated.

5   [*Example:* If the stride parameters in the previous example are changed to {1, 1, 1}, the first few elements of the resulting sequence of indices will be

```
(0,  0,  0,  3),
(0,  0,  1,  4),
(0,  0,  2,  5),
(0,  1,  0,  4),
(0,  1,  1,  5),
(0,  1,  2,  6),
...
```

—*end example*]

6   If a degenerate slice is used as the argument to the non-const version of operator[] (const gslice&), the resulting behavior is undefined.

26.3.6.1 gslice constructors [lib.gslice.cons]

```
gslice();
gslice(size_t start, const valarray<size_t>& lengths,
                     const valarray<size_t>& strides);
gslice(const gslice&);
```

1   The default constructor creates a gslice which specifies no elements. The constructor with arguments builds a gslice based on a specification of start, lengths, and strides, as explained in the previous section.

26.3.6.2 gslice access functions [lib.gslice.access]

```
size_t            start() const;
valarray<size_t> size() const;
valarray<size_t> stride() const;
```

These access functions return the representation of the start, lengths, or strides specified for the gslice.

26.3.7 Class template `gslice_array` [lib.template.gslice.array]

```
namespace std {
  template <class T> class gslice_array {
  public:
    typedef T value_type;

    void operator=  (const valarray<T>&) const;
    void operator*= (const valarray<T>&) const;
    void operator/= (const valarray<T>&) const;
    void operator%= (const valarray<T>&) const;
    void operator+= (const valarray<T>&) const;
    void operator-= (const valarray<T>&) const;
    void operator^= (const valarray<T>&) const;
    void operator&= (const valarray<T>&) const;
    void operator|= (const valarray<T>&) const;
    void operator<<=(const valarray<T>&) const;
    void operator>>=(const valarray<T>&) const;

    void operator=(const T&);
    ~gslice_array();
  private:
    gslice_array();
    gslice_array(const gslice_array&);
    gslice_array& operator=(const gslice_array&);
  };
}
```

1   This template is a helper template used by the `slice` subscript operator

```
gslice_array<T> valarray<T>::operator[](const gslice&);
```

It has reference semantics to a subset of an array specified by a `gslice` object.

2   Thus, the expression `a[gslice(1, length, stride)]` = b has the effect of assigning the elements of b to a generalized slice of the elements in a.

3   [*Note:* C++ programs may not instantiate `gslice_array`, since all its constructors are private. It is intended purely as a helper class and should be transparent to the user. —*end note*]

26.3.7.1 `gslice_array` constructors [lib.gslice.array.cons]

```
gslice_array();
gslice_array(const gslice_array&);
```

1   The `gslice_array` template has no public constructors. It declares the above constructors to be private. These constructors need not be defined.

26.3.7.2 `gslice_array` assignment [lib.gslice.array.assign]

```
void operator=(const valarray<T>&) const;
gslice_array& operator=(const gslice_array&);
```

1   The second of these two assignment operators is declared private and need not be defined. The first has reference semantics, assigning the values of the argument array elements to selected elements of the `valarray<T>` object to which the `gslice_array` refers.

26.3.7.3 `gslice_array` computed assignment **[lib.gslice.array.comp.assign]**

```
void operator*= (const valarray<T>&) const;
void operator/= (const valarray<T>&) const;
void operator%= (const valarray<T>&) const;
void operator+= (const valarray<T>&) const;
void operator-= (const valarray<T>&) const;
void operator^= (const valarray<T>&) const;
void operator&= (const valarray<T>&) const;
void operator|= (const valarray<T>&) const;
void operator<<=(const valarray<T>&) const;
void operator>>=(const valarray<T>&) const;
```

1   These computed assignments have reference semantics, applying the indicated operation to the elements of the argument array and selected elements of the `valarray<T>` object to which the `gslice_array` object refers.

26.3.7.4 `gslice_array` fill function   [lib.gslice.array.fill]

```
void operator=(const T&);
```

1   This function has reference semantics, assigning the value of its argument to the elements of the `valarray<T>` object to which the `gslice_array` object refers.

26.3.8 Class template `mask_array`   [lib.template.mask.array]

```
namespace std {
  template <class T> class mask_array {
  public:
    typedef T value_type;

    void operator=  (const valarray<T>&) const;
    void operator*= (const valarray<T>&) const;
    void operator/= (const valarray<T>&) const;
    void operator%= (const valarray<T>&) const;
    void operator+= (const valarray<T>&) const;
    void operator-= (const valarray<T>&) const;
    void operator^= (const valarray<T>&) const;
    void operator&= (const valarray<T>&) const;
    void operator|= (const valarray<T>&) const;
    void operator<<=(const valarray<T>&) const;
    void operator>>=(const valarray<T>&) const;

    void operator=(const T&);
    ~mask_array();
  private:
    mask_array();
    mask_array(const mask_array&);
    mask_array& operator=(const mask_array&);
  };
}
```

1   This template is a helper template used by the mask subscript operator:
```
mask_array<T> valarray<T>::operator[](const valarray<bool>&).
```
It has reference semantics to a subset of an array specified by a boolean mask. Thus, the expression `a[mask] = b;` has the effect of assigning the elements of b to the masked elements in a (those for which the corresponding element in `mask` is `true`.)

2   [*Note:* C++ programs may not declare instances of mask_array, since all its constructors are private. It is intended purely as a helper class, and should be transparent to the user. —*end note*]

26.3.8.1 mask_array constructors   [lib.mask.array.cons]

```
mask_array();
mask_array(const mask_array&);
```

1   The mask_array template has no public constructors. It declares the above constructors to be private. These constructors need not be defined.

26.3.8.2 mask_array assignment   [lib.mask.array.assign]

```
void operator=(const valarray<T>&) const;
mask_array& operator=(const mask_array&);
```

1   The second of these two assignment operators is declared private and need not be defined. The first has reference semantics, assigning the values of the argument array elements to selected elements of the valarray<T> object to which it refers.

26.3.8.3 mask_array computed assignment   [lib.mask.array.comp.assign]

```
void operator*= (const valarray<T>&) const;
void operator/= (const valarray<T>&) const;
void operator%= (const valarray<T>&) const;
void operator+= (const valarray<T>&) const;
void operator-= (const valarray<T>&) const;
void operator^= (const valarray<T>&) const;
void operator&= (const valarray<T>&) const;
void operator|= (const valarray<T>&) const;
void operator<<=(const valarray<T>&) const;
void operator>>=(const valarray<T>&) const;
```

1   These computed assignments have reference semantics, applying the indicated operation to the elements of the argument array and selected elements of the valarray<T> object to which the mask object refers.

26.3.8.4 mask_array fill function   [lib.mask.array.fill]

```
void operator=(const T&);
```

This function has reference semantics, assigning the value of its argument to the elements of the valarray<T> object to which the mask_array object refers.

26.3.9 Class template `indirect_array` [lib.template.indirect.array]

```
namespace std {
  template <class T> class indirect_array {
  public:
    typedef T value_type;

    void operator=  (const valarray<T>&) const;
    void operator*= (const valarray<T>&) const;
    void operator/= (const valarray<T>&) const;
    void operator%= (const valarray<T>&) const;
    void operator+= (const valarray<T>&) const;
    void operator-= (const valarray<T>&) const;
    void operator^= (const valarray<T>&) const;
    void operator&= (const valarray<T>&) const;
    void operator|= (const valarray<T>&) const;
    void operator<<=(const valarray<T>&) const;
    void operator>>=(const valarray<T>&) const;

    void operator=(const T&);
    ~indirect_array();
  private:
    indirect_array();
    indirect_array(const indirect_array&);
    indirect_array& operator=(const indirect_array&);
  };
}
```

1   This template is a helper template used by the indirect subscript operator
```
    indirect_array<T> valarray<T>::operator[](const valarray<size_t>&).
```
It has reference semantics to a subset of an array specified by an `indirect_array`. Thus the expression `a[indirect] = b;` has the effect of assigning the elements of b to the elements in a whose indices appear in `indirect`.

2   [*Note:* C++ programs may not declare instances of `indirect_array`, since all its constructors are private. It is intended purely as a helper class, and should be transparent to the user. *—end note*]

26.3.9.1 `indirect_array` constructors [lib.indirect.array.cons]

```
    indirect_array();
    indirect_array(const indirect_array&);
```

The `indirect_array` template has no public constructors. The constructors listed above are private. These constructors need not be defined.

26.3.9.2 `indirect_array` assignment [lib.indirect.array.assign]

```
    void operator=(const valarray<T>&) const;
    indirect_array& operator=(const indirect_array&);
```

1   The second of these two assignment operators is declared private and need not be defined. The first has reference semantics, assigning the values of the argument array elements to selected elements of the `valarray<T>` object to which it refers.

2   If the `indirect_array` specifies an element in the `valarray<T>` object to which it refers more than once, the behavior is undefined.

3   [*Example:*

```
int addr[] = {2, 3, 1, 4, 4};
valarray<size_t> indirect(addr, 5);
valarray<double> a(0., 10), b(1., 5);
a[indirect] = b;
```

results in undefined behavior since element 4 is specified twice in the indirection.   —*end example*]

26.3.9.3 `indirect_array` computed assignment   [lib.indirect.array.comp.assign]

```
void operator*= (const valarray<T>&) const;
void operator/= (const valarray<T>&) const;
void operator%= (const valarray<T>&) const;
void operator+= (const valarray<T>&) const;
void operator-= (const valarray<T>&) const;
void operator^= (const valarray<T>&) const;
void operator&= (const valarray<T>&) const;
void operator|= (const valarray<T>&) const;
void operator<<=(const valarray<T>&) const;
void operator>>=(const valarray<T>&) const;
```

1   These computed assignments have reference semantics, applying the indicated operation to the elements of the argument array and selected elements of the `valarray<T>` object to which the `indirect_array` object refers.

2   If the `indirect_array` specifies an element in the `valarray<T>` object to which it refers more than once, the behavior is undefined.

26.3.9.4 `indirect_array` fill function   [lib.indirect.array.fill]

```
void operator=(const T&);
```

1   This function has reference semantics, assigning the value of its argument to the elements of the `valarray<T>` object to which the `indirect_array` object refers.

26.4 Generalized numeric operations   [lib.numeric.ops]

Header `<numeric>` synopsis

```
namespace std {
  template <class InputIterator, class T>
    T accumulate(InputIterator first, InputIterator last, T init);
  template <class InputIterator, class T, class BinaryOperation>
    T accumulate(InputIterator first, InputIterator last, T init,
                 BinaryOperation binary_op);

  template <class InputIterator1, class InputIterator2, class T>
    T inner_product(InputIterator1 first1, InputIterator1 last1,
                    InputIterator2 first2, T init);
  template <class InputIterator1, class InputIterator2, class T,
            class BinaryOperation1, class BinaryOperation2>
    T inner_product(InputIterator1 first1, InputIterator1 last1,
                    InputIterator2 first2, T init,
                    BinaryOperation1 binary_op1,
                    BinaryOperation2 binary_op2);
```

```
        template <class InputIterator, class OutputIterator>
          OutputIterator partial_sum(InputIterator first,
                                     InputIterator last,
                                     OutputIterator result);
        template <class InputIterator, class OutputIterator,
                  class BinaryOperation>
          OutputIterator partial_sum(InputIterator first,
                                     InputIterator last,
                                     OutputIterator result,
                                     BinaryOperation binary_op);

        template <class InputIterator, class OutputIterator>
          OutputIterator adjacent_difference(InputIterator first,
                                             InputIterator last,
                                             OutputIterator result);
        template <class InputIterator, class OutputIterator,
                  class BinaryOperation>
          OutputIterator adjacent_difference(InputIterator first,
                                             InputIterator last,
                                             OutputIterator result,
                                             BinaryOperation binary_op);
      }
```

1   The requirements on the types of algorithms' arguments that are described in the introduction to clause 25 also apply to the following algorithms.

26.4.1 Accumulate [lib.accumulate]

```
        template <class InputIterator, class T>
          T accumulate(InputIterator first, InputIterator last, T init);
        template <class InputIterator, class T, class BinaryOperation>
          T accumulate(InputIterator first, InputIterator last, T init,
                       BinaryOperation binary_op);
```

1   **Effects:** Computes its result by initializing the accumulator acc with the initial value $init$ and then modifies it with $acc = acc + *i$ or $acc = binary\_op(acc, *i)$ for every iterator i in the range $[first, last)$ in order.[262]

2   **Requires:** T must meet the requirements of CopyConstructible (20.1.3) and Assignable (23.1) types. binary_op shall not cause side effects.

---

[262] accumulate is similar to the APL reduction operator and Common Lisp reduce function, but it avoids the difficulty of defining the result of reduction on an empty sequence by always requiring an initial value.

26.4.2 Inner product [lib.inner.product]

```
template <class InputIterator1, class InputIterator2, class T>
  T inner_product(InputIterator1 first1, InputIterator1 last1,
                  InputIterator2 first2, T init);
template <class InputIterator1, class InputIterator2, class T,
          class BinaryOperation1, class BinaryOperation2>
  T inner_product(InputIterator1 first1, InputIterator1 last1,
                  InputIterator2 first2, T init,
                  BinaryOperation1 binary_op1,
                  BinaryOperation2 binary_op2);
```

1 **Effects:** Computes its result by initializing the accumulator acc with the initial value init and then modifying it with acc = acc + (*i1) * (*i2) or acc = binary_op1(acc, binary_op2(*i1, *i2)) for every iterator i1 in the range [first, last) and iterator i2 in the range [first2, first2 + (last - first)) in order.

2 **Requires:** T must meet the requirements of CopyConstructible (20.1.3) and Assignable (23.1) types. binary_op1 and binary_op2 shall not cause side effects.

26.4.3 Partial sum [lib.partial.sum]

```
template <class InputIterator, class OutputIterator>
  OutputIterator
    partial_sum(InputIterator first, InputIterator last,
                OutputIterator result);
template
  <class InputIterator, class OutputIterator, class BinaryOperation>
    OutputIterator
      partial_sum(InputIterator first, InputIterator last,
                  OutputIterator result, BinaryOperation binary_op);
```

1 **Effects:** Assigns to every element referred to by iterator i in the range [result, result + (last - first)) a value correspondingly equal to

((...(*first + *(first + 1)) + ...) + *(first + (i - result)))

or

binary_op(binary_op(..., binary_op(*first, *(first + 1)),...), *(first + (i - result)))

2 **Returns:** result + (last - first).

3 **Complexity:** Exactly (last - first) - 1 applications of binary_op.

4 **Requires:** binary_op is expected not to have any side effects.

5 **Notes:** result may be equal to first.

26.4.4 Adjacent difference [lib.adjacent.difference]

```
template <class InputIterator, class OutputIterator>
  OutputIterator
    adjacent_difference(InputIterator first, InputIterator last,
                        OutputIterator result);
template
  <class InputIterator, class OutputIterator, class BinaryOperation>
    OutputIterator
      adjacent_difference(InputIterator first, InputIterator last,
                          OutputIterator result,
                          BinaryOperation binary_op);
```

1 **Effects:** Assigns to every element referred to by iterator i in the range [result + 1, result + (last - first)) a value correspondingly equal to

*(first + (i - result)) - *(first + (i - result) - 1)

or

```
binary_op(*(first + (i - result)), *(first + (i - result) - 1)).
result gets the value of *first.
```

2   **Requires:** `binary_op` shall not have any side effects.

3   **Notes:** `result` may be equal to `first`.

4   **Returns:** `result + (last - first)`.

5   **Complexity:** Exactly `(last - first) - 1` applications of `binary_op`.

26.5 C Library   [lib.c.math]

1   Tables 80 and 81 describe headers `<cmath>` and `<cstdlib>` (`abs()`, `div()`, `rand()`, `srand()`), respectively.

Table 80—Header `<cmath>` synopsis

Type	Name(s)			
Macro:	HUGE_VAL			
Functions:				
acos	cos	fmod	modf	tan
asin	cosh	frexp	pow	tanh
atan	exp	ldexp	sin	
atan2	fabs	log	sinh	
ceil	floor	log10	sqrt	

Table 81—Header `<cstdlib>` synopsis

Type	Name(s)	
Macros:	RAND_MAX	
Types:	div_t	ldiv_t
Functions:		
abs	labs	srand
div	ldiv	rand

2   The contents of these headers are the same as the Standard C library headers `<math.h>` and `<stdlib.h>` respectively, with the following additions:

3   In addition to the `int` versions of certain math functions in `<cstdlib>`, C++ adds `long` overloaded versions of these functions, with the same semantics.

4   The added signatures are:

```
long    abs(long);              // labs()
ldiv_t div(long, long);         // ldiv()
```

5   In addition to the `double` versions of the math functions in `<cmath>`, C++ adds `float` and `long double` overloaded versions of these functions, with the same semantics.

6   The added signatures are:

```
float abs   (float);
float acos  (float);
float asin  (float);
float atan  (float);
float atan2 (float, float);
float ceil  (float);
float cos   (float);
float cosh  (float);
float exp   (float);
float fabs  (float);
float floor (float);
float fmod  (float, float);
float frexp (float, int*);
float ldexp (float, int);
float log   (float);
float log10 (float);
float modf  (float, float*);
float pow   (float, float);
float pow   (float, int);
float sin   (float);
float sinh  (float);
float sqrt  (float);
float tan   (float);
float tanh  (float);


double abs(double);                    // fabs()
double pow(double, int);


long double abs   (long double);
long double acos  (long double);
long double asin  (long double);
long double atan  (long double);
long double atan2 (long double, long double);
long double ceil  (long double);
long double cos   (long double);
long double cosh  (long double);
long double exp   (long double);
long double fabs  (long double);
long double floor (long double);
long double fmod  (long double, long double);
long double frexp (long double, int*);
long double ldexp (long double, int);
long double log   (long double);
long double log10 (long double);
long double modf  (long double, long double*);
long double pow   (long double, long double);
long double pow   (long double, int);
long double sin   (long double);
long double sinh  (long double);
long double sqrt  (long double);
long double tan   (long double);
long double tanh  (long double);
```

SEE ALSO: ISO C subclauses 7.5, 7.10.2, 7.10.6.

27   Input/output library   [lib.input.output]

1   This clause describes components that C++ programs may use to perform input/output operations.

2   The following subclauses describe requirements for stream parameters, and components for forward declarations of iostreams, predefined iostreams objects, base iostreams classes, stream buffering, stream formatting and manipulators, string streams, and file streams, as summarized in Table 82:

Table 82—Input/output library summary

Subclause	Header(s)
27.1 Requirements	
27.2 Forward declarations	`<iosfwd>`
27.3 Standard iostream objects	`<iostream>`
27.4 Iostreams base classes	`<ios>`
27.5 Stream buffers	`<streambuf>`
27.6 Formatting and manipulators	`<istream>` `<ostream>` `<iomanip>`
27.7 String streams	`<sstream>` `<cstdlib>`
27.8 File streams	`<fstream>` `<cstdio>` `<cwchar>`

27.1   Iostreams requirements   [lib.iostreams.requirements]

27.1.1   Imbue Limitations   [lib.iostream.limits.imbue]
No function described in clause 27 except for `ios_base::imbue` causes any instance of `basic_ios::imbue` or `basic_streambuf::imbue` to be called. If any user function called from a function declared in clause 27 or as an overriding virtual function of any class declared in clause 27 calls `imbue`, the behavior is undefined.

27.1.2   Positioning Type Limitations   [lib.iostreams.limits.pos]
The classes of clause 27 with template arguments `charT` and `traits` behave as described if `traits::pos_type` and `traits::off_type` are `streampos` and `streamoff` respectively. Except as noted explicitly below, their behavior when `traits::pos_type` and `traits::off_type` are other types is implementation-defined.

27.2   Forward declarations   [lib.iostream.forward]

Header `<iosfwd>` synopsis

```
namespace std {
  template<class charT> class char_traits;
  template<> class char_traits<char>;
  template<> class char_traits<wchar_t>;
```

```
template<class T> class allocator;

template <class charT, class traits = char_traits<charT> >
  class basic_ios;

template <class charT, class traits = char_traits<charT> >
  class basic_streambuf;

template <class charT, class traits = char_traits<charT> >
  class basic_istream;

template <class charT, class traits = char_traits<charT> >
  class basic_ostream;

template <class charT, class traits = char_traits<charT> >
  class basic_iostream;

template <class charT, class traits = char_traits<charT>,
          class Allocator = allocator<charT> >
  class basic_stringbuf;

template <class charT, class traits = char_traits<charT>,
          class Allocator = allocator<charT> >
  class basic_istringstream;

template <class charT, class traits = char_traits<charT>,
          class Allocator = allocator<charT> >
  class basic_ostringstream;

template <class charT, class traits = char_traits<charT>,
          class Allocator = allocator<charT> >
  class basic_stringstream;

template <class charT, class traits = char_traits<charT> >
  class basic_filebuf;

template <class charT, class traits = char_traits<charT> >
  class basic_ifstream;

template <class charT, class traits = char_traits<charT> >
  class basic_ofstream;

template <class charT, class traits = char_traits<charT> >
  class basic_fstream;

template <class charT, class traits = char_traits<charT> >
  class istreambuf_iterator;

template <class charT, class traits = char_traits<charT> >
  class ostreambuf_iterator;

typedef basic_ios<char>        ios;
typedef basic_ios<wchar_t>     wios;

typedef basic_streambuf<char> streambuf;
typedef basic_istream<char>   istream;
typedef basic_ostream<char>   ostream;
typedef basic_iostream<char>  iostream;
```

```
        typedef basic_stringbuf<char>      stringbuf;
        typedef basic_istringstream<char> istringstream;
        typedef basic_ostringstream<char> ostringstream;
        typedef basic_stringstream<char>   stringstream;

        typedef basic_filebuf<char>  filebuf;
        typedef basic_ifstream<char> ifstream;
        typedef basic_ofstream<char> ofstream;
        typedef basic_fstream<char>  fstream;

        typedef basic_streambuf<wchar_t> wstreambuf;
        typedef basic_istream<wchar_t>   wistream;
        typedef basic_ostream<wchar_t>   wostream;
        typedef basic_iostream<wchar_t>  wiostream;

        typedef basic_stringbuf<wchar_t>     wstringbuf;
        typedef basic_istringstream<wchar_t> wistringstream;
        typedef basic_ostringstream<wchar_t> wostringstream;
        typedef basic_stringstream<wchar_t>  wstringstream;

        typedef basic_filebuf<wchar_t>  wfilebuf;
        typedef basic_ifstream<wchar_t> wifstream;
        typedef basic_ofstream<wchar_t> wofstream;
        typedef basic_fstream<wchar_t>  wfstream;

        template <class state> class fpos;
        typedef fpos<char_traits<char>::state_type>    streampos;
        typedef fpos<char_traits<wchar_t>::state_type> wstreampos;

    }
```

1   Default template arguments are described as appearing both in `<iosfwd>` and in the synopsis of other headers but it is well-formed to include both `<iosfwd>` and one or more of the other headers.[263]

2   [*Note:* The class template specialization `basic_ios<charT,traits>` serves as a virtual base class for the class templates `basic_istream`, `basic_ostream`, and class templates derived from them. `basic_iostream` is a class template derived from both `basic_istream<charT,traits>` and `basic_ostream<charT,traits>`.

3   The class template specialization `basic_streambuf<charT,traits>` serves as a base class for template classes `basic_stringbuf` and `basic_filebuf`.

4   The class template specialization `basic_istream<charT,traits>` serves as a base class for template classes `basic_istringstream` and `basic_ifstream`

5   The class template specialization `basic_ostream<charT,traits>` serves as a base class for template classes `basic_ostringstream` and `basic_ofstream`

6   The class template specialization `basic_iostream<charT,traits>` serves as a base class for template classes `basic_stringstream` and `basic_fstream`.

7   Other typedefs define instances of class templates specialized for `char` or `wchar_t` types.

8   Specializations of the class template `fpos` are used for specifying file position information.

---

[263] It is the implementation's responsibility to implement headers so that including `<iosfwd>` and other headers does not violate the rules about multiple occurences of default arguments.

9   The types streampos and wstreampos are used for positioning streams specialized on char and wchar_t respectively.

10   This synopsis suggests a circularity between streampos and char_traits<char>. An implementation can avoid this circularity by substituting equivalent types. One way to do this might be

```
template<class stateT> class fpos { ... };      // depends on nothing
typedef ... _STATE;                 // implementation private declaration of stateT

typedef fpos<_STATE> streampos;

template<> struct char_traits<char> {
   typedef streampos
 pos_type;
   // ...
}
```

     —*end note*]

27.3 Standard iostream objects   [lib.iostream.objects]

Header <iostream> synopsis

```
namespace std {
  extern istream cin;
  extern ostream cout;
  extern ostream cerr;
  extern ostream clog;

  extern wistream wcin;
  extern wostream wcout;
  extern wostream wcerr;
  extern wostream wclog;
}
```

1   The header <iostream> declares objects that associate objects with the standard C streams provided for by the functions declared in <cstdio> (27.8.2).

2   Mixing operations on corresponding wide- and narrow-character streams follows the same semantics as mixing such operations on FILEs, as specified in Amendment 1 of the ISO C standard. The objects are constructed, and the associations are established at some time prior to or during first time an object of class ios_base::Init is constructed, and in any case before the body of main begins execution.[264] The objects are *not* destroyed during program execution.[265]

27.3.1 Narrow stream objects   [lib.narrow.stream.objects]

```
istream cin;
```

1   The object cin controls input from a stream buffer associated with the object stdin, declared in <cstdio>.

2   After the object cin is initialized, cin.tie() returns &cout. Its state is otherwise the same as required for basic_ios<char>::init (27.4.4.1).

---

[264] If it is possible for them to do so, implementations are encouraged to initialize the objects earlier than required.
[265] Constructors and destructors for static objects can access these objects to read input from stdin or write output to stdout or stderr.

```
ostream cout;
```

3   The object `cout` controls output to a stream buffer associated with the object `stdout`, declared in `<cstdio>` (27.8.2).

```
ostream cerr;
```

4   The object `cerr` controls output to a stream buffer associated with the object `stderr`, declared in `<cstdio>` (27.8.2).

5   After the object `cerr` is initialized, `cerr.flags() & unitbuf` is nonzero. Its state is otherwise the same as required for `basic_ios<char>::init` (27.4.4.1).

```
ostream clog;
```

6   The object `clog` controls output to a stream buffer associated with the object `stderr`, declared in `<cstdio>` (27.8.2).

27.3.2 Wide stream objects   [lib.wide.stream.objects]

```
wistream wcin;
```

1   The object `wcin` controls input from a stream buffer associated with the object `stdin`, declared in `<cstdio>`.

2   After the object `wcin` is initialized, `wcin.tie()` returns `&wcout`. Its state is otherwise the same as required for `basic_ios<wchar_t>::init` (27.4.4.1).

```
wostream wcout;
```

3   The object `wcout` controls output to a stream buffer associated with the object `stdout`, declared in `<cstdio>` (27.8.2).

```
wostream wcerr;
```

4   The object `wcerr` controls output to a stream buffer associated with the object `stderr`, declared in `<cstdio>` (27.8.2).

5   After the object `wcerr` is initialized, `wcerr.flags() & unitbuf` is nonzero. Its state is otherwise the same as required for `basic_ios<wchar_t>::init` (27.4.4.1).

```
wostream wclog;
```

6   The object `wclog` controls output to a stream buffer associated with the object `stderr`, declared in `<cstdio>` (27.8.2).

27.4 Iostreams base classes

Header <ios> synopsis

```
#include <iosfwd>

namespace std {
  typedef OFF_T  streamoff;
  typedef SZ_T streamsize;
  template <class stateT> class fpos;

  class ios_base;
  template <class charT, class traits = char_traits<charT> >
    class basic_ios;

// 27.4.5, manipulators:
  ios_base& boolalpha  (ios_base& str);
  ios_base& noboolalpha(ios_base& str);

  ios_base& showbase   (ios_base& str);
  ios_base& noshowbase (ios_base& str);

  ios_base& showpoint  (ios_base& str);
  ios_base& noshowpoint(ios_base& str);

  ios_base& showpos    (ios_base& str);
  ios_base& noshowpos  (ios_base& str);

  ios_base& skipws     (ios_base& str);
  ios_base& noskipws   (ios_base& str);

  ios_base& uppercase  (ios_base& str);
  ios_base& nouppercase(ios_base& str);

  ios_base& unitbuf    (ios_base& str);
  ios_base& nounitbuf  (ios_base& str);

// 27.4.5.2 adjustfield:
  ios_base& internal   (ios_base& str);
  ios_base& left       (ios_base& str);
  ios_base& right      (ios_base& str);

// 27.4.5.3 basefield:
  ios_base& dec        (ios_base& str);
  ios_base& hex        (ios_base& str);
  ios_base& oct        (ios_base& str);

// 27.4.5.4 floatfield:
  ios_base& fixed      (ios_base& str);
  ios_base& scientific (ios_base& str);
}
```

27.4.1 Types   **[lib.stream.types]**

```
typedef OFF_T streamoff;
```

1   The type `streamoff` is an implementation-defined type that satisfies the requirements of 27.4.3.2.

```
typedef SZ_T streamsize;
```

2   The type `streamsize` is a synonym for one of the signed basic integral types. It is used to represent the number of characters transferred in an I/O operation, or the size of I/O buffers.[266]

27.4.2 Class `ios_base`   **[lib.ios.base]**

```
namespace std {
  class ios_base {
  public:
    class failure;

    typedef T1 fmtflags;
    static const fmtflags boolalpha;
    static const fmtflags dec;
    static const fmtflags fixed;
    static const fmtflags hex;
    static const fmtflags internal;
    static const fmtflags left;
    static const fmtflags oct;
    static const fmtflags right;
    static const fmtflags scientific;
    static const fmtflags showbase;
    static const fmtflags showpoint;
    static const fmtflags showpos;
    static const fmtflags skipws;
    static const fmtflags unitbuf;
    static const fmtflags uppercase;
    static const fmtflags adjustfield;
    static const fmtflags basefield;
    static const fmtflags floatfield;

    typedef T2 iostate;
    static const iostate badbit;
    static const iostate eofbit;
    static const iostate failbit;
    static const iostate goodbit;

    typedef T3 openmode;
    static const openmode app;
    static const openmode ate;
    static const openmode binary;
    static const openmode in;
    static const openmode out;
    static const openmode trunc;
```

---

[266] `streamsize` is used in most places where ISO C would use `size_t`. Most of the uses of `streamsize` could use `size_t`, except for the `strstreambuf` constructors, which require negative values. It should probably be the signed type corresponding to `size_t` (which is what Posix.2 calls `ssize_t`).

```
    typedef T4 seekdir;
    static const seekdir beg;
    static const seekdir cur;
    static const seekdir end;

    class Init;

    // 27.4.2.2 fmtflags state:
    fmtflags flags() const;
    fmtflags flags(fmtflags fmtfl);
    fmtflags setf(fmtflags fmtfl);
    fmtflags setf(fmtflags fmtfl, fmtflags mask);
    void unsetf(fmtflags mask);

    streamsize precision() const;
    streamsize precision(streamsize prec);
    streamsize width() const;
    streamsize width(streamsize wide);

    // 27.4.2.3 locales:
    locale imbue(const locale& loc);
    locale getloc() const;

    // 27.4.2.5 storage:
    static int xalloc();
    long&  iword(int index);
    void*& pword(int index);

    // destructor
    virtual ~ios_base();

    // 27.4.2.6 callbacks;
    enum event { erase_event, imbue_event, copyfmt_event };
    typedef void (*event_callback)(event, ios_base&, int index);
    void register_callback(event_callback fn, int index);

    static bool sync_with_stdio(bool sync = true);

  protected:
    ios_base();

  private:
//   static int index;      exposition only
//   long* iarray;          exposition only
//   void** parray;         exposition only
  private:
    ios_base(const ios_base&);
    ios_base& operator=(const ios_base&);
  };
}
```

1   ios_base defines several member types:

— a class failure derived from exception;

— a class Init;

— three bitmask types, fmtflags, iostate, and openmode;

— an enumerated type, seekdir.

2   It maintains several kinds of data:

— state information that reflects the integrity of the stream buffer;

— control information that influences how to interpret (format) input sequences and how to generate (format) output sequences;

— additional information that is stored by the program for its private use.

3   [*Note:* For the sake of exposition, the maintained data is presented here as:

— `static int` *index*, specifies the next available unique index for the integer or pointer arrays maintained for the private use of the program, initialized to an unspecified value;

— `long*` *iarray*, points to the first element of an arbitrary-length `long` array maintained for the private use of the program;

— `void**` *parray*, points to the first element of an arbitrary-length pointer array maintained for the private use of the program. *—end note*]

27.4.2.1 Types   [lib.ios.types]

27.4.2.1.1 Class `ios_base::failure`   [lib.ios::failure]

```
namespace std {
  class ios_base::failure : public exception {
  public:
    explicit failure(const string& msg);
    virtual ~failure();
    virtual const char* what() const throw();
  };
}
```

1   The class `failure` defines the base class for the types of all objects thrown as exceptions, by functions in the iostreams library, to report errors detected during stream buffer operations.

```
explicit failure(const string& msg);
```

2   **Effects:** Constructs an object of class `failure`.
3   **Postcondition:** `strcmp(what(), msg.c_str()) == 0`

```
const char* what() const;
```

4   **Returns:** The message *msg* with which the exception was created.

27.4.2.1.2 Type `ios_base::fmtflags`   [lib.ios::fmtflags]

```
typedef T1 fmtflags;
```

1   The type `fmtflags` is a bitmask type (17.3.2.1.2). Setting its elements has the effects indicated in Table 83:

Table 83—`fmtflags` effects

Element	Effect(s) if set
boolalpha	insert and extract `bool` type in alphabetic format
dec	converts integer input or generates integer output in decimal base
fixed	generate floating-point output in fixed-point notation;
hex	converts integer input or generates integer output in hexadecimal base;
internal	adds fill characters at a designated internal point in certain generated output, or identical to `right` if no such point is designated;
left	adds fill characters on the right (final positions) of certain generated output;
oct	converts integer input or generates integer output in octal base;
right	adds fill characters on the left (initial positions) of certain generated output;
scientific	generates floating-point output in scientific notation;
showbase	generates a prefix indicating the numeric base of generated integer output;
showpoint	generates a decimal-point character unconditionally in generated floating-point output;
showpos	generates a + sign in non-negative generated numeric output;
skipws	skips leading white space before certain input operations;
unitbuf	flushes output after each output operation;
uppercase	replaces certain lowercase letters with their uppercase equivalents in generated output.

2   Type `fmtflags` also defines the constants indicated in Table 84:

Table 84—`fmtflags` constants

Constant	Allowable values
adjustfield	left | right | internal
basefield	dec | oct | hex
floatfield	scientific | fixed

27.4.2.1.3 Type `ios_base::iostate`   **[lib.ios::iostate]**

```
typedef T2 iostate;
```

1   The type `iostate` is a bitmask type (17.3.2.1.2) that contains the elements indicated in Table 85:

Table 85—`iostate` effects

Element	Effect(s) if set
badbit	indicates a loss of integrity in an input or output sequence (such as an irrecoverable read error from a file);
eofbit	indicates that an input operation reached the end of an input sequence;
failbit	indicates that an input operation failed to read the expected characters, or that an output operation failed to generate the desired characters.

2   Type `iostate` also defines the constant:

— `goodbit`, the value zero.

27.4.2.1.4 Type ios_base::openmode **[lib.ios::openmode]**

```
typedef T3 openmode;
```

1   The type openmode is a bitmask type (17.3.2.1.2). It contains the elements indicated in Table 86:

Table 86—openmode effects

Element	Effect(s) if set
app	seek to end before each write
ate	open and seek to end immediately after opening
binary	perform input and output in binary mode (as opposed to text mode)
in	open for input
out	open for output
trunc	truncate an existing stream when opening

27.4.2.1.5 Type ios_base::seekdir **[lib.ios::seekdir]**

```
typedef T4 seekdir;
```

1   The type seekdir is an enumerated type (17.3.2.1.1) that contains the elements indicated in Table 87:

Table 87—seekdir effects

Element	Meaning
beg	request a seek (for subsequent input or output) relative to the beginning of the stream
cur	request a seek relative to the current position within the sequence
end	request a seek relative to the current end of the sequence

27.4.2.1.6 Class ios_base::Init **[lib.ios::Init]**

```
namespace std {
  class ios_base::Init {
  public:
    Init();
    ~Init();
  private:
//  static int init_cnt;   exposition only
  };
}
```

1   The class Init describes an object whose construction ensures the construction of the eight objects declared in <iostream> (27.3) that associate file stream buffers with the standard C streams provided for by the functions declared in <cstdio> (27.8.2).

2   For the sake of exposition, the maintained data is presented here as:

— static int *init_cnt*, counts the number of constructor and destructor calls for class Init, initialized to zero.

```
Init();
```

3   **Effects:** Constructs an object of class Init. If *init_cnt* is zero, the function stores the value one in *init_cnt*, then constructs and initializes the objects cin, cout, cerr, clog (27.3.1), wcin, wcout, wcerr, and wclog (27.3.2). In any case, the function then adds one to the value stored in *init_cnt*.

```
~Init();
```

4   **Effects:** Destroys an object of class Init. The function subtracts one from the value stored in *init_cnt* and, if the resulting stored value is one, calls cout.flush(), cerr.flush(), clog.flush(), wcout.flush(), wcerr.flush(), wclog.flush().

27.4.2.2 ios_base fmtflags state functions   [lib.fmtflags.state]

```
fmtflags flags() const;
```

1   **Returns:** The format control information for both input and output.

```
fmtflags flags(fmtflags fmtfl);
```

2   **Postcondition:** *fmtfl* == flags().
3   **Returns:** The previous value of flags().

```
fmtflags setf(fmtflags fmtfl);
```

4   **Effects:** Sets *fmtfl* in flags().
5   **Returns:** The previous value of flags().

```
fmtflags setf(fmtflags fmtfl, fmtflags mask);
```

6   **Effects:** Clears *mask* in flags(), sets *fmtfl* & *mask* in flags().
7   **Returns:** The previous value of flags().

```
void unsetf(fmtflags mask);
```

8   **Effects:** Clears *mask* in flags().

```
streamsize precision() const;
```

9   **Returns:** The precision to generate on certain output conversions.

```
streamsize precision(streamsize prec);
```

10   **Postcondition:** *prec* == precision().
11   **Returns:** The previous value of precision().

```
streamsize width() const;
```

12   **Returns:** The minimum field width (number of characters) to generate on certain output conversions.

```
streamsize width(streamsize wide);
```

13   **Postcondition:** *wide* == width().
14   **Returns:** The previous value of width().

27.4.2.3 ios_base locale functions   [lib.ios.base.locales]

```
locale imbue(const locale& loc);
```

1   **Effects:**   Calls   each   registered   callback   pair   `(fn,index)`   (27.4.2.6)   as
     `(*fn)(imbue_event,*this,index)` at such a time that a call to `ios_base::getloc()`
     from within `fn` returns the new locale value `loc`.

2   **Returns:** The previous value of `getloc()`.

3   **Postcondition:** `loc == getloc()`.

```
locale getloc() const;
```

4   **Returns:** If no locale has been imbued, a copy of the global C++ locale, `locale()`, in effect at the time of
     construction. Otherwise, returns the imbued locale, to be used to perform locale-dependent input and
     output operations.

27.4.2.4 ios_base static members   [lib.ios.members.static]

```
bool sync_with_stdio(bool sync = true);
```

1   **Returns:** `true` if the standard iostream objects (27.3) are synchronized and otherwise returns `false`.
     The first time it is called, the function returns `true`.

2   **Effects:** If any input or output operation has occurred using the standard streams prior to the call, the effect
     is implementation-defined. Otherwise, called with a false argument, it allows the standard streams to
     operate independently of the standard C streams.

27.4.2.5 ios_base storage functions   [lib.ios.base.storage]

```
static int xalloc();
```

1   **Returns:** `index ++`.

```
long& iword(int idx);
```

2   **Effects:** If `iarray` is a null pointer, allocates an array of `long` of unspecified size and stores a pointer to
     its first element in `iarray`. The function then extends the array pointed at by `iarray` as necessary to
     include the element `iarray[idx]`. Each newly allocated element of the array is initialized to zero.
     The reference returned is invalid after any other operations on the object.[267] However, the value of the
     storage referred to is retained, so that until the next call to `copyfmt`, calling `iword` with the same
     index yields another reference to the same value. If the function fails[268] and `*this` is a base sub-
     object of a `basic_ios<>` object or sub-object, the effect is equivalent to calling
     `basic_ios<>::setstate(badbit)` on the derived object (which may throw `failure`).

3   **Returns:** On success `iarray[idx]`. On failure, a valid `long&` initialized to 0.

```
void* & pword(int idx);
```

4   **Effects:** If `parray` is a null pointer, allocates an array of pointers to `void` of unspecified size and stores a
     pointer to its first element in `parray`. The function then extends the array pointed at by `parray` as
     necessary to include the element `parray[idx]`. Each newly allocated element of the array is initial-
     ized to a null pointer. The reference returned is invalid after any other operations on the object. How-
     ever, the value of the storage referred to is retained, so that until the next call to `copyfmt`, calling
     `pword` with the same index yields another reference to the same value. If the function fails[269] and

---

[267] An implementation is free to implement both the integer array pointed at by `iarray` and the pointer array pointed at by `parray`
as sparse data structures, possibly with a one-element cache for each.
[268] for example, because it cannot allocate space.
[269] for example, because it cannot allocate space.

`*this` is a base sub-object of a `basic_ios<>` object or sub-object, the effect is equivalent to calling `basic_ios<>::setstate(badbit)` on the derived object (which may throw `failure`).

5 **Returns:** On success `parray[idx]`. On failure a valid `void*&` initialized to 0.

6 **Notes:** After a subsequent call to `pword(int)` for the same object, the earlier return value may no longer be valid.

27.4.2.6 `ios_base` callbacks [lib.ios.base.callback]

```
void register_callback(event_callback fn, int index);
```

1 **Effects:** Registers the pair (`fn`, `index`) such that during calls to `imbue()` (27.4.2.3), `copyfmt()`, or `~ios_base()` (27.4.2.7), the function `fn` is called with argument `index`. Functions registered are called when an event occurs, in opposite order of registration. Functions registered while a callback function is active are not called until the next event.

2 **Requires:** The function `fn` shall not throw exceptions.

3 **Notes:** Identical pairs are not merged. A function registered twice will be called twice.

27.4.2.7 `ios_base` constructors/destructors [lib.ios.base.cons]

```
ios_base();
```

1 **Effects:** Each `ios_base` member has an indeterminate value after construction. These members must be initialized by calling `basic_ios::init`. If an `ios_base` object is destroyed before these initializations have taken place, the behavior is undefined.

```
~ios_base()
```

2 **Effects:** Destroys an object of class `ios_base`. Calls each registered callback pair (`fn`, `index`) (27.4.2.6) as `(*fn)(erase_event,*this,index)` at such time that any `ios_base` member function called from within `fn` has well defined results.

27.4.3 Class template `fpos` [lib.fpos]

```
namespace std {
  template <class stateT> class fpos {
  public:
    // 27.4.3.1 Members
    stateT state() const;
    void state(stateT);
  private;
//   stateT st;    exposition only
  };
}
```

27.4.3.1 `fpos` Members [lib.fpos.members]

```
void state(stateT s);
```

1 **Effects:** Assign `s` to `st`.

```
stateT state();
```

2 **Returns:** Current value of `st`.

27.4.3.2 `fpos` requirements

1 Operations specified in Table 88 are permitted. In that table,

— `P` refers to an instance of `fpos`,

— `p` and `q` refer to an values of type `P`,

— `O` refers to type `streamoff`,

— `o` refers to a value of type `streamoff`,

— `sz` refers to a value of type `streamsize` and

— `i` refers to a value of type `int`.

Table 88—Position type requirements

expression	return type	operational semantics	assertion/note pre/post-condition
`P(i)`			`p == P(i)` note: a destructor is assumed.
`P p(i);` `P p = i;`			post: `p == P(i)`.
`P(o)`	`fpos`	converts from offset	
`O(p)`	`OFF_T`	converts to offset	`P(O(p)) == p`
`p == q`	convertible to `bool`		`==` is an equivalence relation
`p != q`	convertible to `bool`	`!(p==q)`	
`q = p + o` `p += o`	`fpos`	`+` offset	`q-o == p`
`q = p - o` `p -= o`	`fpos`	`-` offset	`q+o == p`
`o = p - q`	`OFF_T`	distance	`q+o == p`
`streamsize(o)` `O(sz)`	`streamsize` `OFF_T`	converts converts	`streamsize(O(sz)) == sz` `streamsize(O(sz)) == sz`

[*Note:* Every implementation is required to supply overloaded operators on `fpos` objects to satisfy the requirements of 27.4.3.2. It is unspecified whether these operators are members of `fpos`, global operators, or provided in some other way. —*end note*]

2 Stream operations that return a value of type `traits::pos_type` return `P(O(-1))` as an invalid value to signal an error. If this value is used as an argument to any `istream`, `ostream`, or `streambuf` member that accepts a value of type `traits::pos_type` then the behavior of that function is undefined.

27.4.4 Class template `basic_ios`

```
namespace std {
  template <class charT, class traits = char_traits<charT> >
  class basic_ios : public ios_base {
  public:

    // Types:
    typedef charT                     char_type;
    typedef typename traits::int_type int_type;
    typedef typename traits::pos_type pos_type;
    typedef typename traits::off_type off_type;
    typedef traits                    traits_type;

    operator void*() const;
    bool operator!() const;
    iostate rdstate() const;
    void clear(iostate state = goodbit);
    void setstate(iostate state);
    bool good() const;
    bool eof()  const;
    bool fail() const;
    bool bad()  const;

    iostate exceptions() const;
    void exceptions(iostate except);

    // 27.4.4.1 Constructor/destructor:
    explicit basic_ios(basic_streambuf<charT,traits>* sb);
    virtual ~basic_ios();

    // 27.4.4.2 Members:
    basic_ostream<charT,traits>* tie() const;
    basic_ostream<charT,traits>* tie(basic_ostream<charT,traits>* tiestr);

    basic_streambuf<charT,traits>* rdbuf() const;
    basic_streambuf<charT,traits>* rdbuf(basic_streambuf<charT,traits>* sb);

    basic_ios& copyfmt(const basic_ios& rhs);

    char_type fill() const;
    char_type fill(char_type ch);

    // 27.4.2.3 locales:
    locale imbue(const locale& loc);

    char      narrow(char_type c, char dfault) const;
    char_type widen(char c) const;

  protected:
    basic_ios();
    void init(basic_streambuf<charT,traits>* sb);

  private:
    basic_ios(const basic_ios& );           // not defined
    basic_ios& operator=(const basic_ios&);    // not defined
  };
}
```

27.4.4.1 `basic_ios` constructors   **[lib.basic.ios.cons]**

```
explicit basic_ios(basic_streambuf<charT,traits>* sb);
```

1   **Effects:** Constructs an object of class `basic_ios`, assigning initial values to its member objects by calling `init(sb)`.

```
basic_ios();
```

2   **Effects:** Constructs an object of class `basic_ios` (27.4.2.7) leaving its member objects uninitialized. The object must be initialized by calling its `init` member function. If it is destroyed before it has been initialized the behavior is undefined.

```
~basic_ios();
```

2a   **Notes:** The destructor does not destroy `rdbuf()`.

```
void init(basic_streambuf<charT,traits>* sb);
```

3   **Postconditions:** The postconditions of this function are indicated in Table 89:

Table 89—`basic_ios::init()` effects

Element	Value
`rdbuf()`	sb
`tie()`	0
`rdstate()`	`goodbit` if *sb* is not a null pointer, otherwise `badbit`.
`exceptions()`	`goodbit`
`flags()`	`skipws	dec`
`width()`	0
`precision()`	6
`fill()`	`widen(' ');`
`getloc()`	a copy of the value returned by `locale()`
iarray	a null pointer
parray	a null pointer

27.4.4.2 Member functions   **[lib.basic.ios.members]**

```
basic_ostream<charT,traits>* tie() const;
```

1   **Returns:** An output sequence that is *tied* to (synchronized with) the sequence controlled by the stream buffer.

```
basic_ostream<charT,traits>* tie(basic_ostream<charT,traits>* tiestr);
```

2   **Postcondition:** *tiestr* == `tie()`.
3   **Returns:** The previous value of `tie()`.

```
basic_streambuf<charT,traits>* rdbuf() const;
```

4   **Returns:** A pointer to the `streambuf` associated with the stream.

```
basic_streambuf<charT,traits>* rdbuf(basic_streambuf<charT,traits>* sb);
```

5   **Postcondition:** *sb* == rdbuf().
6   **Effects:** Calls clear().
7   **Returns:** The previous value of rdbuf().

```
// 27.4.2.3 locales:
locale imbue(const locale& loc);
```

8   **Effects:**   Calls   ios_base::imbue(*loc*)   (27.4.2.3)   and   if   rdbuf()!=0   then
     rdbuf()->pubimbue(*loc*) (27.5.2.2.1).
9   **Returns:** The prior value of ios_base::imbue().

```
char narrow(char_type c, char dfault) const;
```

10   **Returns:** use_facet< ctype<char_type> >(getloc()).narrow(*c*,*dfault*)

```
char_type widen(char c) const;
```

11   **Returns:** use_facet< ctype<char_type> >(getloc()).widen(*c*)

```
char_type fill() const;
```

12   **Returns:** The character used to pad (fill) an output conversion to the specified field width.

```
char_type fill(char_type fillch);
```

13   **Postcondition:** *fillch* == fill()
14   **Returns:** The previous value of fill().

```
basic_ios& copyfmt(const basic_ios& rhs);
```

15   **Effects:** Assigns to the member objects of *this the corresponding member objects of *rhs*, except that:

     — rdstate() and rdbuf() are left unchanged;

     — exceptions() is altered last by calling exceptions(*rhs.except*).

     — The contents of arrays pointed at by pword and iword are copied not the pointers themselves.[270]

16   If any newly stored pointer values in *this point at objects stored outside the object *rhs*, and those
     objects are destroyed when *rhs* is destroyed, the newly stored pointer values are altered to point at newly
     constructed copies of the objects.

17   Before copying any parts of *rhs*, calls each registered callback pair (*fn*,*index*) as
     (*fn*)(erase_event,*this,*index*). After all parts but exceptions() have been replaced,
     calls each callback pair that was copied from *rhs* as (*fn*)(copy_event,*this,*index*).
18   **Notes:** The second pass permits a copied pword value to be zeroed, or its referent deep copied or refer-
     ence counted or have other special action taken.
19   **Returns:** *this.

---

[270] This suggests an infinite amount of copying, but the implementation can keep track of the maximum element of the arrays that is
non-zero.

27.4.4.3 basic_ios iostate flags functions [lib.iostate.flags]

```
operator void*() const;
```

1 **Returns:** If `fail()` then a null pointer; otherwise some non-null pointer to indicate success.

```
bool operator!() const;
```

2 **Returns:** `fail()`.

```
iostate rdstate() const;
```

3 **Returns:** The error state of the stream buffer.

```
void clear(iostate state = goodbit);
```

4 **Postcondition:** If `rdbuf()!=0` then `state == rdstate();` otherwise `rdstate()==state|ios_base::badbit`.

5 **Effects:** If `(rdstate() & exceptions()) == 0`, returns. Otherwise, the function throws an object `fail` of class `basic_ios::failure` (27.4.2.1.1), constructed with implementation-defined argument values.

```
void setstate(iostate state);
```

6 **Effects:** Calls `clear(rdstate() | state)` (which may throw `basic_ios::failure` (27.4.2.1.1)).

```
bool good() const;
```

7 **Returns:** `rdstate() == 0`

```
bool eof() const;
```

8 **Returns:** `true` if `eofbit` is set in `rdstate()`.

```
bool fail() const;
```

9 **Returns:** `true` if `failbit` or `badbit` is set in `rdstate()`.[271]

```
bool bad() const;
```

10 **Returns:** `true` if `badbit` is set in `rdstate()`.

```
iostate exceptions() const;
```

11 **Returns:** A mask that determines what elements set in `rdstate()` cause exceptions to be thrown.

```
void exceptions(iostate except);
```

12 **Postcondition:** `except == exceptions()`.
13 **Effects:** Calls `clear(rdstate())`.

---

[271] Checking `badbit` also for `fail()` is historical practice.

27.4.5.1 `fmtflags` manipulators

[lib.fmtflags.manip]

```
ios_base& boolalpha(ios_base& str);
```

1   **Effects:** Calls *str*`.setf(ios_base::boolalpha)`.
2   **Returns:** *str*.

```
ios_base& noboolalpha(ios_base& str);
```

3   **Effects:** Calls *str*`.unsetf(ios_base::boolalpha)`.
4   **Returns:** *str*.

```
ios_base& showbase(ios_base& str);
```

5   **Effects:** Calls *str*`.setf(ios_base::showbase)`.
6   **Returns:** *str*.

```
ios_base& noshowbase(ios_base& str);
```

7   **Effects:** Calls *str*`.unsetf(ios_base::showbase)`.
8   **Returns:** *str*.

```
ios_base& showpoint(ios_base& str);
```

9   **Effects:** Calls *str*`.setf(ios_base::showpoint)`.
10   **Returns:** *str*.

```
ios_base& noshowpoint(ios_base& str);
```

11   **Effects:** Calls *str*`.unsetf(ios_base::showpoint)`.
12   **Returns:** *str*.

```
ios_base& showpos(ios_base& str);
```

13   **Effects:** Calls *str*`.setf(ios_base::showpos)`.
14   **Returns:** *str*.

```
ios_base& noshowpos(ios_base& str);
```

15   **Effects:** Calls *str*`.unsetf(ios_base::showpos)`.
16   **Returns:** *str*.

```
ios_base& skipws(ios_base& str);
```

17   **Effects:** Calls *str*`.setf(ios_base::skipws)`.
18   **Returns:** *str*.

```
ios_base& noskipws(ios_base& str);
```

19   **Effects:** Calls *str*`.unsetf(ios_base::skipws)`.
20   **Returns:** *str*.

```
ios_base& uppercase(ios_base& str);
```

21 **Effects:** Calls *str*.setf(ios_base::uppercase).
22 **Returns:** *str*.

```
ios_base& nouppercase(ios_base& str);
```

23 **Effects:** Calls *str*.unsetf(ios_base::uppercase).
24 **Returns:** *str*.

```
ios_base& unitbuf(ios_base& str);
```

25 **Effects:** Calls *str*.setf(ios_base::unitbuf).
26 **Returns:** *str*.

```
ios_base& nounitbuf(ios_base& str);
```

27 **Effects:** Calls *str*.unsetf(ios_base::unitbuf).
28 **Returns:** *str*.

27.4.5.2 `adjustfield` manipulators   [lib.adjustfield.manip]

```
ios_base& internal(ios_base& str);
```

1 **Effects:** Calls *str*.setf(ios_base::internal, ios_base::adjustfield).
2 **Returns:** *str*.

```
ios_base& left(ios_base& str);
```

3 **Effects:** Calls *str*.setf(ios_base::left, ios_base::adjustfield).
4 **Returns:** *str*.

```
ios_base& right(ios_base& str);
```

5 **Effects:** Calls *str*.setf(ios_base::right, ios_base::adjustfield).
6 **Returns:** *str*.

27.4.5.3 `basefield` manipulators   [lib.basefield.manip]

```
ios_base& dec(ios_base& str);
```

1 **Effects:** Calls *str*.setf(ios_base::dec, ios_base::basefield).
2 **Returns:** *str*.

```
ios_base& hex(ios_base& str);
```

3 **Effects:** Calls *str*.setf(ios_base::hex, ios_base::basefield).
4 **Returns:** *str*.

---

272) The function signature dec(ios_base&) can be called by the function signature basic_ostream& stream::operator<<(ios_base& (*)(ios_base&)) to permit expressions of the form cout << dec to change the format flags stored in cout.

```
ios_base& oct(ios_base& str);
```

5   **Effects:** Calls *str*.setf(ios_base::oct, ios_base::basefield).
6   **Returns:** *str*.

27.4.5.4 `floatfield` manipulators   [lib.floatfield.manip]

```
ios_base& fixed(ios_base& str);
```

1   **Effects:** Calls *str*.setf(ios_base::fixed, ios_base::floatfield).
2   **Returns:** *str*.

```
ios_base& scientific(ios_base& str);
```

3   **Effects:** Calls *str*.setf(ios_base::scientific, ios_base::floatfield).
4   **Returns:** *str*.

27.5 Stream buffers   [lib.stream.buffers]

Header <`streambuf`> synopsis

```
namespace std {
  template <class charT, class traits = char_traits<charT> >
    class basic_streambuf;
  typedef basic_streambuf<char>    streambuf;
  typedef basic_streambuf<wchar_t> wstreambuf;
}
```

1   The header <`streambuf`> defines types that control input from and output to *character* sequences.

27.5.1 Stream buffer requirements   [lib.streambuf.reqts]

1   Stream buffers can impose various constraints on the sequences they control. Some constraints are:

— The controlled input sequence can be not readable.

— The controlled output sequence can be not writable.

— The controlled sequences can be associated with the contents of other representations for character sequences, such as external files.

— The controlled sequences can support operations *directly* to or from associated sequences.

— The controlled sequences can impose limitations on how the program can read characters from a sequence, write characters to a sequence, put characters back into an input sequence, or alter the stream position.

2   Each sequence is characterized by three pointers which, if non-null, all point into the same charT array object. The array object represents, at any moment, a (sub)sequence of characters from the sequence. Operations performed on a sequence alter the values stored in these pointers, perform reads and writes directly to or from associated sequences, and alter ''the stream position'' and conversion state as needed to maintain this subsequence relationship. The three pointers are:

— the *beginning pointer,* or lowest element address in the array (called *xbeg* here);

— the *next pointer,* or next element address that is a current candidate for reading or writing (called *xnext* here);

— the *end pointer,* or first element address beyond the end of the array (called *xend* here).

3   The following semantic constraints shall always apply for any set of three pointers for a sequence, using the pointer names given immediately above:

— If *xnext* is not a null pointer, then *xbeg* and *xend* shall also be non-null pointers into the same charT array, as described above; otherwise, *xbeg* and *xend* shall also be null.

— If *xnext* is not a null pointer and *xnext* < *xend* for an output sequence, then a *write position* is available. In this case, **xnext* shall be assignable as the next element to write (to put, or to store a character value, into the sequence).

— If *xnext* is not a null pointer and *xbeg* < *xnext* for an input sequence, then a *putback position* is available. In this case, *xnext*[-1] shall have a defined value and is the next (preceding) element to store a character that is put back into the input sequence.

— If *xnext* is not a null pointer and *xnext* < *xend* for an input sequence, then a *read position* is available. In this case, **xnext* shall have a defined value and is the next element to read (to get, or to obtain a character value, from the sequence).

27.5.2 Class template `basic_streambuf<charT,traits>`   [lib.streambuf]

```
namespace std {
  template <class charT, class traits = char_traits<charT> >
  class basic_streambuf {
  public:

    // Types:
    typedef charT                    char_type;
    typedef typename traits::int_type int_type;
    typedef typename traits::pos_type pos_type;
    typedef typename traits::off_type off_type;
    typedef traits                   traits_type;

    virtual ~basic_streambuf();

    // 27.5.2.2.1 locales:
    locale   pubimbue(const locale& loc);
    locale   getloc() const;

    // 27.5.2.2.2 buffer and positioning:
    basic_streambuf<char_type,traits>*
            pubsetbuf(char_type* s, streamsize n);
    pos_type pubseekoff(off_type off, ios_base::seekdir way,
                      ios_base::openmode which =
                          ios_base::in | ios_base::out);
    pos_type pubseekpos(pos_type sp,
                      ios_base::openmode which =
                          ios_base::in | ios_base::out);
    int      pubsync();

    // Get and put areas:
    // 27.5.2.2.3 Get area:
    streamsize in_avail();
    int_type snextc();
    int_type sbumpc();
    int_type sgetc();
    streamsize sgetn(char_type* s, streamsize n);
```

```
        // 27.5.2.2.4 Putback:
        int_type sputbackc(char_type c);
        int_type sungetc();

        // 27.5.2.2.5 Put area:
        int_type   sputc(char_type c);
        streamsize sputn(const char_type* s, streamsize n);

    protected:
        basic_streambuf();

        // 27.5.2.3.1 Get area:
        char_type* eback() const;
        char_type* gptr()  const;
        char_type* egptr() const;
        void       gbump(int n);
        void       setg(char_type* gbeg, char_type* gnext, char_type* gend);

        // 27.5.2.3.2 Put area:
        char_type* pbase() const;
        char_type* pptr() const;
        char_type* epptr() const;
        void       pbump(int n);
        void       setp(char_type* pbeg, char_type* pend);

        // 27.5.2.4 virtual functions:
        // 27.5.2.4.1 Locales:
        virtual void imbue(const locale& loc);

        // 27.5.2.4.2 Buffer management and positioning:
        virtual basic_streambuf<char_type,traits>*
                     setbuf(char_type* s, streamsize n);
        virtual pos_type seekoff(off_type off, ios_base::seekdir way,
                ios_base::openmode which = ios_base::in | ios_base::out);
        virtual pos_type seekpos(pos_type sp,
                ios_base::openmode which = ios_base::in | ios_base::out);
        virtual int      sync();

        // 27.5.2.4.3 Get area:
        virtual streamsize showmanyc();
        virtual streamsize xsgetn(char_type* s, streamsize n);
        virtual int_type   underflow();
        virtual int_type   uflow();

        // 27.5.2.4.4 Putback:
        virtual int_type   pbackfail(int_type c = traits::eof());

        // 27.5.2.4.5 Put area:
        virtual streamsize xsputn(const char_type* s, streamsize n);
        virtual int_type   overflow (int_type c = traits::eof());
    };
}
```

1   The class template `basic_streambuf<charT,traits>` serves as an abstract base class for deriving
various *stream buffers* whose objects each control two *character sequences*:

— a character *input sequence*;

— a character *output sequence*.

2   [*Note:* This paragraph is intentionally empty. —*end note*]

3   [*Note:* This paragraph is intentionally empty. —*end note*]

27.5.2.1 `basic_streambuf` constructors   [lib.streambuf.cons]

```
basic_streambuf();
```

1   **Effects:** Constructs an object of class `basic_streambuf<charT,traits>` and initializes:[273]

— all its pointer member objects to null pointers,

— the `getloc()` member to a copy the global locale, `locale()`, at the time of construction.

2   **Notes:** Once the `getloc()` member is initialized, results of calling locale member functions, and of members of facets so obtained, can safely be cached until the next time the member `imbue` is called.

```
~basic_streambuf();
```

3   **Effects:** None.

27.5.2.2 `basic_streambuf` public member functions   [lib.streambuf.members]

27.5.2.2.1 Locales   [lib.streambuf.locales]

```
locale pubimbue(const locale& loc);
```

1   **Postcondition:** *loc* == `getloc()`.
2   **Effects:** Calls `imbue(loc)`.
3   **Returns:** Previous value of `getloc()`.

```
locale getloc() const;
```

4   **Returns:** If `pubimbue()` has ever been called, then the last value of *loc* supplied, otherwise the current global locale, `locale()`, in effect at the time of construction. If called after `pubimbue()` has been called but before `pubimbue` has returned (i.e. from within the call of `imbue()`) then it returns the previous value.

27.5.2.2.2 Buffer management and positioning   [lib.streambuf.buffer]

```
basic_streambuf<char_type,traits>* pubsetbuf(char_type* s, streamsize n);
```

1   **Returns:** `setbuf(s,n)`.

```
pos_type pubseekoff(off_type off, ios_base::seekdir way,
                    ios_base::openmode which = ios_base::in | ios_base::out);
```

2   **Returns:** `seekoff(off,way,which)`.

```
pos_type pubseekpos(pos_type sp,
                    ios_base::openmode which = ios_base::in | ios_base::out);
```

3   **Returns:** `seekpos(sp,which)`.

---

[273] The default constructor is protected for class `basic_streambuf` to assure that only objects for classes derived from this class may be constructed.

```
int pubsync();
```

4   **Returns:** sync().

27.5.2.2.3 Get area   [lib.streambuf.pub.get]

```
streamsize in_avail();
```

1   **Returns:** If a read position is available, returns egptr() - gptr(). Otherwise returns
     showmanyc() (27.5.2.4.3).

```
int_type snextc();
```

2   **Effects:** Calls sbumpc().
3   **Returns:** if that function returns traits::eof(), returns traits::eof(). Otherwise, returns
     sgetc().

```
int_type sbumpc();
```

4   **Returns:** If the input sequence read position is not available, returns uflow(). Otherwise, returns
     traits::to_int_type(*gptr()) and increments the next pointer for the input sequence.

```
int_type sgetc();
```

5   **Returns:** If the input sequence read position is not available, returns underflow(). Otherwise, returns
     traits::to_int_type(*gptr()).

```
streamsize sgetn(char_type* s, streamsize n);
```

6   **Returns:** xsgetn(s, n).

27.5.2.2.4 Putback   [lib.streambuf.pub.pback]

```
int_type sputbackc(char_type c);
```

1   **Returns:** If the input sequence putback position is not available, or if traits::eq(c, gptr()[-1])
     is false, returns pbackfail(traits::to_int_type(c)). Otherwise, decrements the next
     pointer for the input sequence and returns traits::to_int_type(*gptr()).

```
int_type sungetc();
```

2   **Returns:** If the input sequence putback position is not available, returns pbackfail(). Otherwise,
     decrements   the   next   pointer   for   the   input   sequence   and   returns
     traits::to_int_type(*gptr()).

27.5.2.2.5 Put area   [lib.streambuf.pub.put]

```
int_type sputc(char_type c);
```

1   **Returns:**   If   the   output   sequence   write   position   is   not   available,   returns
     overflow(traits::to_int_type(c)). Otherwise, stores c at the next pointer for the output
     sequence, increments the pointer, and returns traits::to_int_type(c).

```
streamsize sputn(const char_type* s, streamsize n);
```

2   **Returns:** xsputn(*s*, *n*).

27.5.2.3 `basic_streambuf` protected member functions   [lib.streambuf.protected]

27.5.2.3.1 Get area access   [lib.streambuf.get.area]

```
char_type* eback() const;
```

1   **Returns:** The beginning pointer for the input sequence.

```
char_type* gptr() const;
```

2   **Returns:** The next pointer for the input sequence.

```
char_type* egptr() const;
```

3   **Returns:** The end pointer for the input sequence.

```
void gbump(int n);
```

4   **Effects:** Adds *n* to the next pointer for the input sequence.

```
void setg(char_type* gbeg, char_type* gnext, char_type* gend);
```

5   **Postconditions:** *gbeg* == eback(), *gnext* == gptr(), and *gend* == egptr().

27.5.2.3.2 Put area access   [lib.streambuf.put.area]

```
char_type* pbase() const;
```

1   **Returns:** The beginning pointer for the output sequence.

```
char_type* pptr() const;
```

2   **Returns:** The next pointer for the output sequence.

```
char_type* epptr() const;
```

3   **Returns:** The end pointer for the output sequence.

```
void pbump(int n);
```

4   **Effects:** Adds *n* to the next pointer for the output sequence.

```
void setp(char_type* pbeg, char_type* pend);
```

5   **Postconditions:** *pbeg* == pbase(), *pbeg* == pptr(), and *pend* == epptr().

27.5.2.4 `basic_streambuf` virtual functions   [lib.streambuf.virtuals]

27.5.2.4.1 Locales   **[lib.streambuf.virt.locales]**

```
void imbue(const locale&)
```

1   **Effects:** Change any translations based on locale.

2   **Notes:** Allows the derived class to be informed of changes in locale at the time they occur. Between invocations of this function a class derived from streambuf can safely cache results of calls to locale functions and to members of facets so obtained.

3   **Default behavior:** Does nothing.

27.5.2.4.2 Buffer management and positioning   **[lib.streambuf.virt.buffer]**

```
basic_streambuf* setbuf(char_type* s, streamsize n);
```

1   **Effects:** Performs an operation that is defined separately for each class derived from basic_streambuf in this clause (27.7.1.3, 27.8.1.4).

2   **Default behavior:** Does nothing. Returns this.

```
pos_type seekoff(off_type off, ios_base::seekdir way,
                 ios_base::openmode which
                 = ios_base::in | ios_base::out);
```

3   **Effects:** Alters the stream positions within one or more of the controlled sequences in a way that is defined separately for each class derived from basic_streambuf in this clause (27.7.1.3, 27.8.1.4).

4   **Default behavior:** Returns pos_type(off_type(-1)).

```
pos_type seekpos(pos_type sp,
                 ios_base::openmode which
                 = ios_base::in | ios_base::out);
```

5   **Effects:** Alters the stream positions within one or more of the controlled sequences in a way that is defined separately for each class derived from basic_streambuf in this clause (27.7.1, 27.8.1.1).

6   **Default behavior:** Returns pos_type(off_type(-1)).

```
int sync();
```

7   **Effects:** Synchronizes the controlled sequences with the arrays. That is, if pbase() is non-null the characters between pbase() and pptr() are written to the controlled sequence. The pointers may then be reset as appropriate.

8   **Returns:** -1 on failure. What constitutes failure is determined by each derived class (27.8.1.4).

9   **Default behavior:** Returns zero.

27.5.2.4.3 Get area   **[lib.streambuf.virt.get]**

```
streamsize showmanyc();[274]
```

1   **Returns:** an estimate of the number of characters available in the sequence, or -1. If it returns a positive value, then successive calls to underflow() will not return traits::eof() until at least that number of characters have been extracted from the stream. If showmanyc() returns -1, then calls to underflow() or uflow() will fail.[275]

2   **Default behavior:** Returns zero.

---

[274] The morphemes of showmanyc are "es-how-many-see", not "show-manic".

[275] underflow or uflow might fail by throwing an exception prematurely. The intention is not only that the calls will not return eof() but that they will return "immediately."

3   **Notes:** Uses `traits::eof()`.

         streamsize xsgetn(char_type* s, streamsize n);

4   **Effects:** Assigns up to *n* characters to successive elements of the array whose first element is designated
     by *s*. The characters assigned are read from the input sequence as if by repeated calls to `sbumpc()`.
     Assigning stops when either *n* characters have been assigned or a call to `sbumpc()` would return
     `traits::eof()`.

5   **Returns:** The number of characters assigned.[276]

6   **Notes:** Uses `traits::eof()`.

         int_type underflow();

7   **Notes:** The public members of `basic_streambuf` call this virtual function only if `gptr()` is null or
     `gptr() >= egptr()`

8   **Returns:** `traits::to_int_type(c)`, where *c* is the first *character* of the *pending sequence*, without
     moving the input sequence position past it. If the pending sequence is null then the function returns
     `traits::eof()` to indicate failure.

9   The *pending sequence* of characters is defined as the concatenation of:

     a) If `gptr()` is non- NULL, then the `egptr() - gptr()` characters starting at `gptr()`, otherwise
         the empty sequence.

     b) Some sequence (possibly empty) of characters read from the input sequence.

10   The *result character* is

     a) If the pending sequence is non-empty, the first character of the sequence.

     b) If the pending sequence is empty then the next character that would be read from the input sequence.

11   The *backup sequence* is defined as the concatenation of:

     a) If `eback()` is null then empty,

     b) Otherwise the `gptr() - eback()` characters beginning at `eback()`.

12   **Effects:** The function sets up the `gptr()` and `egptr()` satisfying one of:

     a) If the pending sequence is non-empty, `egptr()` is non-null and `egptr() - gptr()` characters
         starting at `gptr()` are the characters in the pending sequence

     b) If the pending sequence is empty, either `gptr()` is null or `gptr()` and `egptr()` are set to the same
         non-NULL pointer.

13   If `eback()` and `gptr()` are non-null then the function is not constrained as to their contents, but the
     "usual backup condition" is that either:

     a) If the backup sequence contains at least `gptr() - eback()` characters, then the `gptr() -
         eback()` characters starting at `eback()` agree with the last `gptr() - eback()` characters of the
         backup sequence.

     b) Or the *n* characters starting at `gptr() - n` agree with the backup sequence (where *n* is the length of
         the backup sequence)

14   **Default behavior:** Returns `traits::eof()`.

---

[276] Classes derived from `basic_streambuf` can provide more efficient ways to implement `xsgetn()` and `xsputn()` by overriding these definitions from the base class.

```
int_type uflow();
```

15   **Requires:** The constraints are the same as for `underflow()`, except that the result character is trans-
      ferred from the pending sequence to the backup sequence, and the pending sequence may not be empty
      before the transfer.

16   **Default behavior:** Calls `underflow()`. If `underflow()` returns `traits::eof()`, returns
      `traits::eof()`. Otherwise, returns the value of `traits::to_int_type(*gptr())` and
      increment the value of the next pointer for the input sequence.

17   **Returns:** `traits::eof()` to indicate failure.

27.5.2.4.4 Putback   [lib.streambuf.virt.pback]

```
int_type pbackfail(int_type c = traits::eof());
```

1   **Notes:** The public functions of `basic_streambuf` call this virtual function only when `gptr()` is null,
      `gptr()` == `eback()`, or `traits::eq(traits::to_char_type(c),gptr()[-1])`
      returns `false`. Other calls shall also satisfy that constraint.
      The *pending sequence* is defined as for `underflow()`, with the modifications that

      — If `traits::eq_int_type(c,traits::eof())` returns `true`, then the input sequence is
        backed up one character before the pending sequence is determined.

      — If `traits::eq_int_type(c,traits::eof())` return false, then `c` is prepended. Whether the
        input sequence is backed up or modified in any other way is unspecified.

2   **Postcondition:** On return, the constraints of `gptr()`, `eback()`, and `pptr()` are the same as for
      `underflow()`.

3   **Returns:** `traits::eof()` to indicate failure. Failure may occur because the input sequence could not
      be backed up, or if for some other reason the pointers could not be set consistent with the constraints.
      `pbackfail()` is called only when put back has really failed.
      Returns some value other than `traits::eof()` to indicate success.

4   **Default behavior:** Returns `traits::eof()`.

27.5.2.4.5 Put area   [lib.streambuf.virt.put]

```
streamsize xsputn(const char_type* s, streamsize n);
```

1   **Effects:** Writes up to *n* characters to the output sequence as if by repeated calls to `sputc(c)`. The char-
      acters written are obtained from successive elements of the array whose first element is designated by *s*.
      Writing stops when either *n* characters have been written or a call to `sputc(c)` would return
      `traits::eof()`.

2   **Returns:** The number of characters written.

```
int_type overflow(int_type c = traits::eof());
```

3   **Effects:** Consumes some initial subsequence of the characters of the *pending sequence*. The pending
      sequence is defined as the concatenation of

      a) if `pbase()` is NULL then the empty sequence otherwise, `pptr()` - `pbase()` characters beginning
          at `pbase()`.

      b) if `traits::eq_int_type(c,traits::eof())` returns `true`, then the empty sequence other-
          wise, the sequence consisting of `c`.

4   **Notes:** The member functions `sputc()` and `sputn()` call this function in case that no room can be
      found in the put buffer enough to accomodate the argument character sequence.

5   **Requires:** Every overriding definition of this virtual function shall obey the following constraints:

      1) The effect of consuming a character on the associated output sequence is specified[277]

      _____
      [277] That is, for each class derived from an instance of `basic_streambuf` in this clause (27.7.1, 27.8.1.1), a specification of how
      consuming a character effects the associated output sequence is given. There is no requirement on a program-defined class.

2) Let r be the number of characters in the pending sequence not consumed. If r is non-zero then pbase() and pptr() must be set so that: pptr() - pbase() == r and the r characters starting at pbase() are the associated output stream. In case r is zero (all characters of the pending sequence have been consumed) then either pbase() is set to NULL, or pbase() and pptr() are both set to the same non-NULL value.

3) The function may fail if either appending some character to the associated output stream fails or if it is unable to establish pbase() and pptr() according to the above rules.

6 **Returns:** traits::eof() or throws an exception if the function fails.
Otherwise, returns some value other than traits::eof() to indicate success.[278]

7 **Default behavior:** Returns traits::eof().

27.6 Formatting and manipulators [lib.iostream.format]

Header <istream> synopsis

```
namespace std {
  template <class charT, class traits = char_traits<charT> >
    class basic_istream;
  typedef basic_istream<char>    istream;
  typedef basic_istream<wchar_t> wistream;

  template <class charT, class traits = char_traits<charT> >
    class basic_iostream;
  typedef basic_iostream<char>    iostream;
  typedef basic_iostream<wchar_t> wiostream;

  template <class charT, class traits>
    basic_istream<charT,traits>& ws(basic_istream<charT,traits>& is);
}
```

Header <ostream> synopsis

```
namespace std {
  template <class charT, class traits = char_traits<charT> >
    class basic_ostream;
  typedef basic_ostream<char>    ostream;
  typedef basic_ostream<wchar_t> wostream;

  template <class charT, class traits>
    basic_ostream<charT,traits>& endl(basic_ostream<charT,traits>& os);
  template <class charT, class traits>
    basic_ostream<charT,traits>& ends(basic_ostream<charT,traits>& os);
  template <class charT, class traits>
    basic_ostream<charT,traits>& flush(basic_ostream<charT,traits>& os);
}
```

---

[278] Typically, overflow returns c to indicate success, except when traits::eq_int_type(c,traits::eof()) returns true, in which case it returns traits::not_eof(c).

Header <iomanip> synopsis

```
namespace std {
    // Types T1, T2, ... are unspecified implementation types
    T1 resetiosflags(ios_base::fmtflags mask);
    T2 setiosflags  (ios_base::fmtflags mask);
    T3 setbase(int base);
    template<charT> T4 setfill(charT c);
    T5 setprecision(int n);
    T6 setw(int n);
}
```

27.6.1 Input streams   [lib.input.streams]

1   The header <istream> defines two types and a function signature that control input from a stream buffer.

27.6.1.1 Class template `basic_istream`   [lib.istream]

```
namespace std {
  template <class charT, class traits = char_traits<charT> >
  class basic_istream : virtual public basic_ios<charT,traits> {
  public:
  // Types (inherited from basic_ios (27.4.4)):
    typedef charT                    char_type;
    typedef typename traits::int_type int_type;
    typedef typename traits::pos_type pos_type;
    typedef typename traits::off_type off_type;
    typedef traits                   traits_type;

    // 27.6.1.1.1 Constructor/destructor:
    explicit basic_istream(basic_streambuf<charT,traits>* sb);
    virtual ~basic_istream();

    // 27.6.1.1.2 Prefix/suffix:
    class sentry;

    // 27.6.1.2 Formatted input:
    basic_istream<charT,traits>& operator>>
        (basic_istream<charT,traits>& (*pf)(basic_istream<charT,traits>&));
    basic_istream<charT,traits>& operator>>
        (basic_ios<charT,traits>& (*pf)(basic_ios<charT,traits>&));
    basic_istream<charT,traits>& operator>>
        (ios_base& (*pf)(ios_base&));

    basic_istream<charT,traits>& operator>>(bool& n);
    basic_istream<charT,traits>& operator>>(short& n);
    basic_istream<charT,traits>& operator>>(unsigned short& n);
    basic_istream<charT,traits>& operator>>(int& n);
    basic_istream<charT,traits>& operator>>(unsigned int& n);
    basic_istream<charT,traits>& operator>>(long& n);
    basic_istream<charT,traits>& operator>>(unsigned long& n);
    basic_istream<charT,traits>& operator>>(float& f);
    basic_istream<charT,traits>& operator>>(double& f);
    basic_istream<charT,traits>& operator>>(long double& f);

    basic_istream<charT,traits>& operator>>(void*& p);
    basic_istream<charT,traits>& operator>>
        (basic_streambuf<char_type,traits>* sb);
```

```
                // 27.6.1.3 Unformatted input:
                streamsize gcount() const;
                int_type get();
                basic_istream<charT,traits>& get(char_type& c);
                basic_istream<charT,traits>& get(char_type* s, streamsize n);
                basic_istream<charT,traits>& get(char_type* s, streamsize n,
                                char_type delim);
                basic_istream<charT,traits>& get(basic_streambuf<char_type,traits>& sb);
                basic_istream<charT,traits>& get(basic_streambuf<char_type,traits>& sb,
                                char_type delim);

                basic_istream<charT,traits>& getline(char_type* s, streamsize n);
                basic_istream<charT,traits>& getline(char_type* s, streamsize n,
                                char_type delim);

                basic_istream<charT,traits>& ignore
                    (streamsize n = 1, int_type delim = traits::eof());
                int_type                    peek();
                basic_istream<charT,traits>& read    (char_type* s, streamsize n);
                streamsize                  readsome(char_type* s, streamsize n);

                basic_istream<charT,traits>& putback(char_type c);
                basic_istream<charT,traits>& unget();
                int sync();

                pos_type tellg();
                basic_istream<charT,traits>& seekg(pos_type);
                basic_istream<charT,traits>& seekg(off_type, ios_base::seekdir);
            };

            // 27.6.1.2.3 character extraction templates:
            template<class charT, class traits>
                basic_istream<charT,traits>& operator>>(basic_istream<charT,traits>&,
                                                charT&);
            template<class traits>
                basic_istream<char,traits>& operator>>(basic_istream<char,traits>&,
                                                unsigned char&);
            template<class traits>
                basic_istream<char,traits>& operator>>(basic_istream<char,traits>&,
                                                signed char&);

            template<class charT, class traits>
                basic_istream<charT,traits>& operator>>(basic_istream<charT,traits>&,
                                                charT*);
            template<class traits>
                basic_istream<char,traits>& operator>>(basic_istream<char,traits>&,
                                                unsigned char*);
            template<class traits>
                basic_istream<char,traits>& operator>>(basic_istream<char,traits>&,
                                                signed char*);
        }
```

1   The class `basic_istream` defines a number of member function signatures that assist in reading and interpreting input from sequences controlled by a stream buffer.

2   Two groups of member function signatures share common properties: the *formatted input functions* (or *extractors*) and the *unformatted input functions*. Both groups of input functions are described as if they obtain (or *extract*) input *characters* by calling `rdbuf()->sbumpc()` or `rdbuf()->sgetc()`. They may use other public members of `istream`.

3   If rdbuf()->sbumpc() or rdbuf()->sgetc() returns traits::eof(), then the input function, except as explicitly noted otherwise, completes its actions and does setstate(eofbit), which may throw ios_base::failure (27.4.4.3), before returning.

4   If one of these called functions throws an exception, then unless explicitly noted otherwise, the input function sets badbit in error state. If badbit is on in exceptions(), the input function rethrows the exception without completing its actions, otherwise it does not throw anything and proceeds as if the called function had returned a failure indication.

27.6.1.1.1 basic_istream constructors   [lib.istream.cons]

```
explicit basic_istream(basic_streambuf<charT,traits>* sb);
```

1   **Effects:** Constructs an object of class basic_istream, assigning initial values to the base class by calling basic_ios::init(sb) (27.4.4.1).

2   **Postcondition:** gcount() == 0

```
virtual ~basic_istream();
```

3   **Effects:** Destroys an object of class basic_istream.
4   **Notes:** Does not perform any operations of rdbuf().

27.6.1.1.2 Class basic_istream::sentry   [lib.istream::sentry]

```
namespace std {
  template <class charT,class traits = char_traits<charT> >
  class basic_istream<charT,traits>::sentry {
    typedef traits traits_type;
//  bool ok_;   exposition only
  public:
    explicit sentry(basic_istream<charT,traits>& is, bool noskipws = false);
    ~sentry();
    operator bool() const { return ok_; }
  private:
    sentry(const sentry&); //   not defined
    sentry& operator=(const sentry&); //   not defined
  };
}
```

1   The class sentry defines a class that is responsible for doing exception safe prefix and suffix operations.

```
explicit sentry(basic_istream<charT,traits>& is, bool noskipws = false);
```

2   **Effects:** If is.good() is true, prepares for formatted or unformatted input. First, if is.tie() is not a null pointer, the function calls is.tie()->flush() to synchronize the output sequence with any associated external C stream. Except that this call can be suppressed if the put area of is.tie() is empty. Further an implementation is allowed to defer the call to flush until a call of is->rdbuf()->underflow occurs. If no such call occurs before the sentry object is destroyed, the call to flush may be eliminated entirely.[279] If noskipws is zero and is.flags() & ios_base::skipws is nonzero, the function extracts and discards each character as long as the next available input character c is a whitespace character. If is.rdbuf()->sbumpc() or is.rdbuf()->sgetc() returns traits::eof(), the function calls setstate(failbit | eofbit) (which may throw ios_base::failure).

---

[279] This will be possible only in functions that are part of the library. The semantics of the constructor used in user code is as specified.

3 **Notes:** The constructor `explicit sentry(basic_istream<charT,traits>& is, bool noskipws = false)` uses the currently imbued locale in *is* , to determine whether the next input character is whitespace or not.

4 To decide if the character *c* is a whitespace character, the constructor performs "as if" it executes the following code fragment:

```
const ctype<charT>& ctype = use_facet<ctype<charT> >(is.getloc());
if (ctype.is(ctype.space,c)!=0)
    // c is a whitespace character.
```

5 If, after any preparation is completed, *is*.`good()` is true, *ok_* `!= false` otherwise, *ok_* `== false`. During preparation, the constructor may call `setstate(failbit)` (which may throw `ios_base::failure` (27.4.4.3))[280]

6 [*Note:* This paragraph is intentionally empty. —*end note*]

```
~sentry();
```

7 **Effects:** None.

```
operator bool() const;
```

8 **Effects:** Returns *ok_* .

27.6.1.2 Formatted input functions [lib.istream.formatted]

27.6.1.2.1 Common requirements [lib.istream.formatted.reqmts]

1 Each formatted input function begins execution by constructing an object of class `sentry` with the `noskipws` (second) argument `false`. If the `sentry` object returns `true`, when converted to a value of type `bool`, the function endeavors to obtain the requested input. If an exception is thrown during input then `ios::badbit` is turned on[281] in `*this`'s error state. If `(exceptions()&badbit) != 0` then the exception is rethrown. In any case, the formatted input function destroys the `sentry` object. If no exception has been thrown, it returns `*this`.

27.6.1.2.2 Arithmetic Extractors [lib.istream.formatted.arithmetic]

```
operator>>(short& val);
operator>>(unsigned short& val);
operator>>(int& val);
operator>>(unsigned int& val);
operator>>(long& val);
operator>>(unsigned long& val);
operator>>(float& val);
operator>>(double& val);
operator>>(long double& val);
operator>>(bool& val);
operator>>(void*& val);
```

As in the case of the inserters, these extractors depend on the locale's `num_get<>` (22.2.2.1) object to perform parsing the input stream data. These extractors behave as formatted input functions (as described in 27.6.1.2.1). After a sentry object is constructed, the conversion occurs as if performed by the following code fragment:

---

[280] The sentry constructor and destructor can also perform additional implementation-dependent operations.

[281] This is done without causing an `ios::failure` to be thrown.

```
typedef num_get< charT,istreambuf_iterator<charT,traits> > numget;
iostate err = 0;
use_facet< numget >(loc).get(*this, 0, *this, err, val);
setstate(err);
```

In the above fragment, `loc` stands for the private member of the `basic_ios` class. [*Note:* The first argument provides an object of the `istreambuf_iterator` class which is an iterator pointed to an input stream. It bypasses istreams and uses streambufs directly. —*end note*] Class `locale` relies on this type as its interface to `istream`, so that it does not need to depend directly on `istream`.

27.6.1.2.3 `basic_istream::operator>>`   [lib.istream::extractors]

```
basic_istream<charT,traits>& operator>>
    (basic_istream<charT,traits>& (*pf)(basic_istream<charT,traits>&))
```

0a   **Effects:** None. This extractor does not behave as a formatted input function (as described in 27.6.1.2.1.)
1   **Returns:** `pf(*this)`.[282]

```
basic_istream<charT,traits>& operator>>
    (basic_ios<charT,traits>& (*pf)(basic_ios<charT,traits>&));
```

2   **Effects:** Calls `pf(*this)`. This extractor does not behave as a formatted input function (as described in 27.6.1.2.1).

3   **Returns:** `*this`.

```
basic_istream<charT,traits>& operator>>
    (ios_base& (*pf)(ios_base&));
```

4   **Effects:** Calls `pf(*this)`.[283] This extractor does not behave as a formatted input function (as described in 27.6.1.2.1).

5   **Returns:** `*this`.

```
template<class charT, class traits>
  basic_istream<charT,traits>& operator>>(basic_istream<charT,traits>& in,
                                           charT* s);
template<class traits>
  basic_istream<char,traits>& operator>>(basic_istream<char,traits>& in,
                                          unsigned char* s);
template<class traits>
  basic_istream<char,traits>& operator>>(basic_istream<char,traits>& in,
                                          signed char* s);
```

6   **Effects:** Behaves like a formatted input member (as described in 27.6.1.2.1) of *in*. After a `sentry` object is constructed, `operator>>` extracts characters and stores them into successive locations of an array whose first element is designated by *s*. If `width()` is greater than zero, *n* is `width()`. Otherwise *n* is the the number of elements of the largest array of `char_type` that can store a terminating `charT()`. *n* is the maximum number of characters stored.

7   Characters are extracted and stored until any of the following occurs:

   — *n*-1 characters are stored;

   — end of file occurs on the input sequence;

   — `ct.is(ct.space,c)` is true for the next available input character *c*; where *ct* is `use_facet<ctype<charT> >(in.getloc())`.

---
[282] See, for example, the function signature ws (`basic_istream&`) (27.6.1.4).
[283] See, for example, the function signature dec (`ios_base&`) (27.4.5.3).

Operator>> then stores a null byte (charT()) in the next position, which may be the first position if no characters were extracted. operator>> then calls width(0).

8   If the function extracted no characters, it calls setstate(failbit), which may throw ios_base::failure (27.4.4.3).

9   **Returns:** in.

```
template<class charT, class traits>
  basic_istream<charT,traits>& operator>>(basic_istream<charT,traits>& in,
                                          charT& c);
template<class traits>
  basic_istream<char,traits>& operator>>(basic_istream<char,traits>& in,
                                         unsigned char& c);
template<class traits>
  basic_istream<char,traits>& operator>>(basic_istream<char,traits>& in,
                                         signed char& c);
```

10   **Effects:** Behaves like a formatted input member (as described in 27.6.1.2.1) of *in*. After a sentry object is constructed a character is extracted from *in*, if one is available, and stored in c. Otherwise, the function calls *in*.setstate(failbit).

11   **Returns:** in.

```
basic_istream<charT,traits>& operator>>
    (basic_streambuf<charT,traits>* sb);
```

12   **Effects:** Behaves as a formatted input function (as described in 27.6.1.2.1). If *sb* is null, calls setstate(failbit), which may throw ios_base::failure (27.4.4.3). After a sentry object is constructed, extracts characters from *this and inserts them in the output sequence controlled by *sb*. Characters are extracted and inserted until any of the following occurs:

— end-of-file occurs on the input sequence;

— inserting in the output sequence fails (in which case the character to be inserted is not extracted);

— an exception occurs (in which case the exception is caught).

13   If the function inserts no characters, it calls setstate(failbit), which may throw ios_base::failure (27.4.4.3). If it inserted no characters because it caught an exception thrown while extracting characters from *sb* and failbit is on in exceptions() (27.4.4.3), then the caught exception is rethrown.

14   **Returns:** *this.

27.6.1.3 Unformatted input functions   [lib.istream.unformatted]

1   Each unformatted input function begins execution by constructing an object of class sentry with the default argument noskipws (second) argument true. If the sentry object returns true, when converted to a value of type bool, the function endeavors to obtain the requested input. If an exception is thrown during input then ios::badbit is turned on[284] in *this's error state. (Exceptions thrown from basic_ios<>::clear() are not caught or rethrown.) If (exceptions()&badbit) != 0 then the exception is rethrown. It also counts the number of characters extracted. If no exception has been thrown it ends by storing the count in a member object and returning the value specified. In any event the sentry object is destroyed before leaving the unformatted input function.

---

[284] This is done without causing an ios::failure to be thrown.

```
streamsize gcount() const;
```

1a **Effects:** None. This member function does not behave as an unformatted input function (as described in 27.6.1.3, paragraph 1).

2 **Returns:** The number of characters extracted by the last unformatted input member function called for the object.

```
int_type get();
```

3 **Effects:** Behaves as an unformatted input function (as described in 27.6.1.3, paragraph 1). After constructing a sentry object, extracts a character c, if one is available. Otherwise, the function calls `setstate(failbit)`, which may throw `ios_base::failure` (27.4.4.3),

4 **Returns:** c if available, otherwise `traits::eof()`.

```
basic_istream<charT,traits>& get(char_type& c);
```

5 **Effects:** Behaves as an unformatted input function (as described in 27.6.1.3, paragraph 1). After constructing a sentry object, extracts a character, if one is available, and assigns it to c.[285] Otherwise, the function calls `setstate(failbit)` (which may throw `ios_base::failure` (27.4.4.3)).

6 **Returns:** `*this`.

```
basic_istream<charT,traits>& get(char_type*  s, streamsize n,
                  char_type delim );
```

7 **Effects:** Behaves as an unformatted input function (as described in 27.6.1.3, paragraph 1). After constructing a sentry object, extracts characters and stores them into successive locations of an array whose first element is designated by s.[286] Characters are extracted and stored until any of the following occurs:

— n - 1 characters are stored;

— end-of-file occurs on the input sequence (in which case the function calls `setstate(eofbit)`);

— c == $delim$ for the next available input character c (in which case c is not extracted).

8 If the function stores no characters, it calls `setstate(failbit)` (which may throw `ios_base::failure` (27.4.4.3)). In any case, it then stores a null character into the next successive location of the array.

9 **Returns:** `*this`.

```
basic_istream<charT,traits>& get(char_type*  s, streamsize n)
```

10 **Effects:** Calls `get(s,n,widen('\n'))`

11 **Returns:** Value returned by the call.

```
basic_istream<charT,traits>& get(basic_streambuf<char_type,traits>& sb,
                  char_type delim );
```

12 **Effects:** Behaves as an unformatted input function (as described in 27.6.1.3, paragraph 1). After constructing a sentry object, extracts characters and inserts them in the output sequence controlled by sb. Characters are extracted and inserted until any of the following occurs:

— end-of-file occurs on the input sequence;

— inserting in the output sequence fails (in which case the character to be inserted is not extracted);

— c == $delim$ for the next available input character c (in which case c is not extracted);

---

[285] Note that this function is not overloaded on types `signed char` and `unsigned char`.
[286] Note that this function is not overloaded on types `signed char` and `unsigned char`.

— an exception occurs (in which case, the exception is caught but not rethrown).

13   If the function inserts no characters, it calls `setstate(failbit)`, which may throw `ios_base::failure` (27.4.4.3).

14   **Returns:** `*this`.

```
basic_istream<charT,traits>& get(basic_streambuf<char_type,traits>& sb);
```

15   **Effects:** Calls `get(s,n,widen('\n'))`

16   **Returns:** Value returned by the call.

```
basic_istream<charT,traits>& getline(char_type* s, streamsize n,
                            char_type delim);
```

17   **Effects:** Behaves as an unformatted input function (as described in 27.6.1.3, paragraph 1). After constructing a sentry object, extracts characters and stores them into successive locations of an array whose first
element is designated by s.[287] Characters are extracted and stored until one of the following occurs:

1) end-of-file occurs on the input sequence (in which case the function calls `setstate(eofbit)`);

2) `c == delim` for the next available input character c (in which case the input character is extracted but
not stored);[288]

3) `n - 1` characters are stored (in which case the function calls `setstate(failbit)`).

18   These conditions are tested in the order shown.[289]

19   If the function extracts no characters, it calls `setstate(failbit)` (which may throw
`ios_base::failure` (27.4.4.3)).[290]

20   In any case, it then stores a null character (using `charT()`) into the next successive location of the array.

21   **Returns:** `*this`.

22   [*Example:*

---

287) Note that this function is not overloaded on types `signed char` and `unsigned char`.

288) Since the final input character is "extracted," it is counted in the `gcount()`, even though it is not stored.

289) This allows an input line which exactly fills the buffer, without setting `failbit`. This is different behavior than the historical AT&T implementation.

290) This implies an empty input line will not cause `failbit` to be set.

```
#include <iostream>

int main()
{
  using namespace std;
  const int line_buffer_size = 100;

  char buffer[line_buffer_size];
  int line_number = 0;
  while (cin.getline(buffer, line_buffer_size, '\n') || cin.gcount()) {
    int count = cin.gcount();
    if (cin.eof())
      cout << "Partial final line";     // cin.fail() is false
    else if (cin.fail()) {
      cout << "Partial long line";
      cin.clear(cin.rdstate() & ~ios::failbit);
    } else {
      count--;                          // Don't include newline in count
      cout << "Line " << ++line_number;
    }
    cout << " (" << count << " chars): " << buffer << endl;
  }
}
```

—end example]

```
basic_istream<charT,traits>& getline(char_type* s, streamsize n);
```

23   **Returns:** getline(s, n, widen('\n'))

```
basic_istream<charT,traits>&
    ignore(streamsize n = 1, int_type delim = traits::eof());
```

24   **Effects:** Behaves as an unformatted input function (as described in 27.6.1.3, paragraph 1). After constructing a sentry object, extracts characters and discards them. Characters are extracted until any of the following occurs:

— if n != numeric_limits<streamsize>::max() (18.2.1), n characters are extracted

— end-of-file occurs on the input sequence (in which case the function calls setstate(eofbit),
which may throw ios_base::failure (27.4.4.3));

— c == delim for the next available input character c (in which case c is extracted).

25   **Notes:** The last condition will never occur if delim == traits::eof().
26   **Returns:** *this.

```
int_type peek();
```

26a **Effects:** Behaves as an unformatted input function (as described in 27.6.1.3, paragraph 1). After constructing a sentry object, reads but does not extract the current input character.
27   **Returns:** traits::eof() if good() is false. Otherwise, returns rdbuf()->sgetc().

```
basic_istream<charT,traits>& read(char_type* s, streamsize n);
```

28   **Effects:** Behaves as an unformatted input function (as described in 27.6.1.3, paragraph 1). After constructing a sentry object, if !good() calls setstate(failbit) which may throw an exception, and
return. Otherwise extracts characters and stores them into successive locations of an array whose first
element is designated by s.[291] Characters are extracted and stored until either of the following occurs:

---
[291] Note that this function is not overloaded on types signed char and unsigned char.

— *n* characters are stored;

— end-of-file occurs on the input sequence (in which case the function calls `setstate(failbit|eofbit)`, which may throw `ios_base::failure` (27.4.4.3)).

29   **Returns:** `*this`.

```
streamsize readsome(char_type* s, streamsize n);
```

30   **Effects:** Behaves as an unformatted input function (as described in 27.6.1.3, paragraph 1). After constructing a sentry object, if `!good()` calls `setstate(failbit)` which may throw an exception, and return. Otherwise extracts characters and stores them into successive locations of an array whose first element is designated by `s`. If `rdbuf()->in_avail()` `==` `-1`, calls `setstate(eofbit)` (which may throw `ios_base::failure` (27.4.4.3)), and extracts no characters;

— If `rdbuf()->in_avail()` `==` `0`, extracts no characters

— If `rdbuf()->in_avail()` `>` `0`, extracts `min(rdbuf()->in_avail(),n))`.

31   **Returns:** The number of characters extracted.

```
basic_istream<charT,traits>& putback(char_type c);
```

32   **Effects:** Behaves as an unformatted input function (as described in 27.6.1.3, paragraph 1). After constructing a sentry object, if `!good()` calls `setstate(failbit)` which may throw an exception, and return. If `rdbuf()` is not null, calls `rdbuf->sputbackc()`. If `rdbuf()` is null, or if `sputbackc()` returns `traits::eof()`, calls `setstate(badbit)` (which may throw `ios_base::failure` (27.4.4.3)). [*Note:* this function extracts no characters, so the value returned by the next call to `gcount()` is 0. —*end note*]

33   **Returns:** `*this`.

```
basic_istream<charT,traits>& unget();
```

34   **Effects:** Behaves as an unformatted input function (as described in 27.6.1.3, paragraph 1). After constructing a sentry object, if `!good()` calls `setstate(failbit)` which may throw an exception, and return. If `rdbuf()` is not null, calls `rdbuf()->sungetc()`. If `rdbuf()` is null, or if `sungetc()` returns `traits::eof()`, calls `setstate(badbit)` (which may throw `ios_base::failure` (27.4.4.3)). [*Note:* this function extracts no characters, so the value returned by the next call to `gcount()` is 0. —*end note*]

35   **Returns:** `*this`.

```
int sync();
```

36   **Effects:** Behaves as an unformatted input function (as described in 27.6.1.3, paragraph 1), except that it does not count the number of characters extracted and does not affect the value returned by subsequent calls to `gcount()`. After constructing a sentry object, if `rdbuf()` is a null pointer, returns -1 . Otherwise, calls `rdbuf()->pubsync()` and, if that function returns -1 calls `setstate(badbit)` (which may throw `ios_base::failure` (27.4.4.3), and returns -1. Otherwise, returns zero.

```
pos_type tellg();
```

36a   **Effects:** Behaves as an unformatted input function (as described in 27.6.1.3, paragraph 1), except that it does not count the number of characters extracted and does not affect the value returned by subsequent calls to `gcount()`.

37   **Returns:** After constructing a sentry object, if `fail()` `!=` `false`, returns `pos_type(-1)` to indicate failure. Otherwise, returns `rdbuf()->pubseekoff(0, cur, in)`.

```
basic_istream<charT,traits>& seekg(pos_type pos);
```

38 **Effects:** Behaves as an unformatted input function (as described in 27.6.1.3, paragraph 1), except that it does not count the number of characters extracted and does not affect the value returned by subsequent calls to gcount(). After constructing a sentry object, if fail() != true, executes rdbuf()->pubseekpos(*pos*). In case of failure, the function calls setstate(failbit) (which may throw ios_base::failure).

39 **Returns:** *this.

```
basic_istream<charT,traits>& seekg(off_type& off, ios_base::seekdir dir);
```

40 **Effects:** Behaves as an unformatted input function (as described in 27.6.1.3, paragraph 1), except that it does not count the number of characters extracted and does not affect the value returned by subsequent calls to gcount(). After constructing a sentry object, if fail() != true, executes rdbuf()->pubseekoff(*off*, *dir*).

41 **Returns:** *this.

27.6.1.4 Standard `basic_istream` manipulators [lib.istream.manip]

```
namespace std {
  template <class charT, class traits>
    basic_istream<charT,traits>& ws(basic_istream<charT,traits>& is);
}
```

1 **Effects:** Extracts characters as long as the next available character c is whitespace or until there are no more characters in the sequence. Whitespace characters are distinguished with the same criterion as used by sentry::sentry (27.6.1.1.2). If ws stops extracting characters because there are no more available it sets eofbit, but not failbit.

2 **Returns:** *is*.

27.6.1.5 Class template `basic_iostream` [lib.iostreamclass]

```
namespace std {
  template <class charT, class traits = char_traits<charT> >
  class basic_iostream :
    public basic_istream<charT,traits>,
    public basic_ostream<charT,traits> {
  public:
    // constructor/destructor
    explicit basic_iostream(basic_streambuf<charT,traits>* sb);
    virtual ~basic_iostream();
  };
}
```

1 The class basic_iostream inherits a number of functions that allow reading input and writing output to sequences controlled by a stream buffer.

27.6.1.5.1 `basic_iostream` constructors [lib.iostream.cons]

```
explicit basic_iostream(basic_streambuf<charT,traits>* sb);
```

1 **Effects** Constructs an object of class basic_iostream, assigning initial values to the base classes by calling basic_istream<charT,traits>(*sb*) (27.6.1.1) and basic_ostream<charT,traits>(*sb*) (27.6.2.1)

2 **Postcondition:** rdbuf()==sb and gcount()==0.

27.6.1.5.2 basic_iostream destructor   **[lib.iostream.dest]**

```
virtual ~basic_iostream();
```

1   **Effects:** Destroys an object of class basic_iostream.

2   **Notes:** Does not perform any operations on rdbuf().

27.6.2 Output streams   **[lib.output.streams]**

1   The header <ostream> defines a type and several function signatures that control output to a stream
buffer.

27.6.2.1 Class template basic_ostream   **[lib.ostream]**

```
namespace std {
  template <class charT, class traits = char_traits<charT> >
  class basic_ostream : virtual public basic_ios<charT,traits> {
  public:
  // Types (inherited from basic_ios (27.4.4)):
    typedef charT                    char_type;
    typedef typename traits::int_type int_type;
    typedef typename traits::pos_type pos_type;
    typedef typename traits::off_type off_type;
    typedef traits                   traits_type;

    // 27.6.2.2 Constructor/destructor:
    explicit basic_ostream(basic_streambuf<char_type,traits>* sb);
    virtual ~basic_ostream();

    // 27.6.2.3 Prefix/suffix:
    class sentry;

    // 27.6.2.5 Formatted output:
    basic_ostream<charT,traits>& operator<<
        (basic_ostream<charT,traits>& (*pf)(basic_ostream<charT,traits>&));
    basic_ostream<charT,traits>& operator<<
        (basic_ios<charT,traits>& (*pf)(basic_ios<charT,traits>&));
    basic_ostream<charT,traits>& operator<<
        (ios_base& (*pf)(ios_base&));

    basic_ostream<charT,traits>& operator<<(bool n);
    basic_ostream<charT,traits>& operator<<(short n);
    basic_ostream<charT,traits>& operator<<(unsigned short n);
    basic_ostream<charT,traits>& operator<<(int n);
    basic_ostream<charT,traits>& operator<<(unsigned int n);
    basic_ostream<charT,traits>& operator<<(long n);
    basic_ostream<charT,traits>& operator<<(unsigned long n);
    basic_ostream<charT,traits>& operator<<(float f);
    basic_ostream<charT,traits>& operator<<(double f);
    basic_ostream<charT,traits>& operator<<(long double f);

    basic_ostream<charT,traits>& operator<<(const void* p);
    basic_ostream<charT,traits>& operator<<
        (basic_streambuf<char_type,traits>* sb);

    // 27.6.2.6 Unformatted output:
    basic_ostream<charT,traits>& put(char_type c);
    basic_ostream<charT,traits>& write(const char_type* s, streamsize n);
```

```
basic_ostream<charT,traits>& flush();

// 27.6.2.4 seeks:
pos_type tellp();
basic_ostream<charT,traits>& seekp(pos_type);
basic_ostream<charT,traits>& seekp(off_type, ios_base::seekdir);
};
```

```
// 27.6.2.5.4 character inserters
template<class charT, class traits>
basic_ostream<charT,traits>& operator<<(basic_ostream<charT,traits>&,
                                        charT);
template<class charT, class traits>
basic_ostream<charT,traits>& operator<<(basic_ostream<charT,traits>&,
                                        char);
// specialization
template<class traits>
    basic_ostream<char,traits>& operator<<(basic_ostream<char,traits>&,
                                           char);
// signed and unsigned
template<class traits>
    basic_ostream<char,traits>& operator<<(basic_ostream<char,traits>&,
                                           signed char);
template<class traits>
    basic_ostream<char,traits>& operator<<(basic_ostream<char,traits>&,
                                           unsigned char)

template<class charT, class traits>
    basic_ostream<charT,traits>& operator<<(basic_ostream<charT,traits>&,
                                            const charT*);
template<class charT, class traits>
    basic_ostream<charT,traits>& operator<<(basic_ostream<charT,traits>&,
                                            const char*);
// partial specializationss
template<class traits>
    basic_ostream<char,traits>& operator<<(basic_ostream<char,traits>&,
                                           const char*);
// signed and unsigned
template<class traits>
    basic_ostream<char,traits>& operator<<(basic_ostream<char,traits>&,
                                           const signed char*);
template<class traits>
    basic_ostream<char,traits>& operator<<(basic_ostream<char,traits>&,
                                           const unsigned char*);

}
```

1   The class `basic_ostream` defines a number of member function signatures that assist in formatting and writing output to output sequences controlled by a stream buffer.

2   Two groups of member function signatures share common properties: the *formatted output functions* (or *inserters*) and the *unformatted output functions*. Both groups of output functions generate (or *insert*) output *characters* by actions equivalent to calling `rdbuf()->sputc(int_type)`. They may use other public members of `basic_ostream` except that they do not invoke any virtual members of `rdbuf()` except `overflow()`.

3   If one of these called functions throws an exception, then unless explicitly noted otherwise the output function set `badbit` in error state. If `badbit` is on in `exceptions()`, the output function rethrows the exception without completing its actions, otherwise it does not throw anything and treat as an error.

27.6.2.2 basic_ostream constructors **[lib.ostream.cons]**

```
explicit basic_ostream(basic_streambuf<charT,traits>* sb);
```

1   **Effects:** Constructs an object of class `basic_ostream`, assigning initial values to the base class by calling `basic_ios<charT,traits>::init(sb)` (27.4.4.1).

2   **Postcondition:** `rdbuf() == sb`.

```
virtual ~basic_ostream();
```

3   **Effects:** Destroys an object of class `basic_ostream`.

4   **Notes:** Does not perform any operations on `rdbuf()`.

27.6.2.3 Class basic_ostream::sentry   [lib.ostream::sentry]

```
namespace std {
  template <class charT,class traits = char_traits<charT> >
  class basic_ostream<charT,traits>::sentry {
//  bool ok_;   exposition only
  public:
    explicit sentry(basic_ostream<charT,traits>& os);
    ~sentry();
    operator bool() const { return ok_; }
  private:
    sentry(const sentry&); //  not defined
    sentry& operator=(const sentry&); //  not defined
  };
}
```

1   The class `sentry` defines a class that is responsible for doing exception safe prefix and suffix operations.

```
explicit sentry(basic_ostream<charT,traits>& os);
```

2   If `os.good()` is nonzero, prepares for formatted or unformatted output. If `os.tie()` is not a null pointer, calls `os.tie()->flush()`.[292]

3   If, after any preparation is completed, `os.good()` is true, `ok_ == true` otherwise, `ok_ == false`. During preparation, the constructor may call `setstate(failbit)` (which may throw `ios_base::failure` (27.4.4.3))[293]

```
~sentry();
```

4   If `((os.flags() & ios_base::unitbuf) && !uncaught_exception())` is true, calls `os.flush()`.

```
operator bool();
```

5   **Effects:** Returns `ok_`.

---

[292] The call `os.tie()->flush()` does not necessarily occur if the function can determine that no synchronization is necessary.
[293] The `sentry` constructor and destructor can also perform additional implementation-dependent operations.

27.6.2.4 `basic_ostream` seek members   **[lib.ostream.seeks]**

```
pos_type tellp();
```

1   **Returns:** if `fail() != false`, returns `pos_type(-1)` to indicate failure. Otherwise, returns `rdbuf()->pubseekoff(0, cur, out)`.

```
basic_ostream<charT,traits>& seekp(pos_type& pos);
```

2   **Effects:** If `fail() != true`, executes `rdbuf()->pubseekpos(pos)`. In case of failure, the function calls `setstate(failbit)` (which may throw `ios_base::failure`).

3   **Returns:** `*this`.

```
basic_ostream<charT,traits>& seekp(off_type& off, ios_base::seekdir dir);
```

4   **Effects:** If `fail() != true`, executes `rdbuf()->pubseekoff(off, dir)`.

5   **Returns:** `*this`.

27.6.2.5 Formatted output functions   **[lib.ostream.formatted]**

27.6.2.5.1 Common requirements   **[lib.ostream.formatted.reqmts]**

1   Each formatted output function begins execution by constructing an object of class `sentry`. If this object returns `true` when converted to a value of type `bool`, the function endeavors to generate the requested output. If the generation fails, then the formatted output function does `setstate(ios::failbit)`, which might throw an exception. If an exception is thrown during output, then `ios::badbit` is turned on[294] in `*this`'s error state. If `(exceptions()&badbit) != 0` then the exception is rethrown. Whether or not an exception is thrown, the `sentry` object is destroyed before leaving the formatted output function. If no exception is thrown, the result of the formattted output function is `*this`.

2   The descriptions of the individual formatted output operations describe how they perform output and do not mention the `sentry` object.

27.6.2.5.2 Arithmetic Inserters   **[lib.ostream.inserters.arithmetic]**

```
operator<<(bool val);
operator<<(short val);
operator<<(unsigned short val);
operator<<(int val);
operator<<(unsigned int val);
operator<<(long val);
operator<<(unsigned long val);
operator<<(float val);
operator<<(double val);
operator<<(long double val);
operator<<(const void* val);
```

1   **Effects:** The classes `num_get<>` and `num_put<>` handle locale-dependent numeric formatting and parsing. These inserter functions use the imbued `locale` value to perform numeric formatting. These inserters behave as formatted output functions (as described in 27.6.2.5.1). After the sentry object is constructed, the conversion occurs as if it performed the following code fragment:

```
bool failed =
    use_facet< num_put<charT,ostreambuf_iterator<charT,traits> > >(getloc()).
        put(*this, *this, fill(), val). failed();
```

The first argument provides an object of the `ostreambuf_iterator<>` class which is an iterator

---

[294] without causing an `ios::failure` to be thrown.

for class basic_ostream<>. It bypasses `ostreams` and uses `streambufs` directly. Class `locale` relies on these types as its interface to iostreams, since for flexibility it has been abstracted away from direct dependence on `ostream`. The second parameter is a reference to the base subobject of type `ios_base`. It provides formatting specifications such as field width, and a locale from which to obtain other facets. If `failed` is `true` then does `setstate(badbit)`, which may throw an exception, and returns.

2 **Returns:** `*this`.

27.6.2.5.3 `basic_ostream::operator<<` [lib.ostream.inserters]

```
basic_ostream<charT,traits>& operator<<
    (basic_ostream<charT,traits>& (*pf)(basic_ostream<charT,traits>&))
```

0a **Effects:** None. Does not behave as a formatted output function (as described in 27.6.2.5.1).
1 **Returns:** pf(`*this`).[295]

```
basic_ostream<charT,traits>& operator<<
    (basic_ios<charT,traits>& (*pf)(basic_ios<charT,traits>&))
```

2 **Effects:** Calls pf(`*this`). This inserter does not behave as a formatted output function (as described in 27.6.2.5.1).
3 **Returns:** `*this`.[296]

```
basic_ostream<charT,traits>& operator<<
    (ios_base& (*pf)(ios_base&))
```

4 **Effects:** Calls pf(`*this`). This inserter does not behave as a formatted output function (as described in 27.6.2.5.1).
5 **Returns:** `*this`.

```
basic_ostream<charT,traits>& operator<<
    (basic_streambuf<charT,traits>* sb);
```

6 **Effects:** Behaves as a formatted output function (as described in 27.6.2.5.1). After the sentry object is constructed, if `sb` is null calls `setstate(badbit)` (which may throw `ios_base::failure`).

7 Gets characters from `sb` and inserts them in `*this`. Characters are read from `sb` and inserted until any of the following occurs:

— end-of-file occurs on the input sequence;

— inserting in the output sequence fails (in which case the character to be inserted is not extracted);

— an exception occurs while getting a character from `sb`.

8 If the function inserts no characters, it calls `setstate(failbit)` (which may throw `ios_base::failure` (27.4.4.3)). If an exception was thrown while extracting a character, the function set `failbit` in error state, and if `failbit` is on in `exceptions()` the caught exception is rethrown.
9 **Returns:** `*this`.

---

[295] See, for example, the function signature `endl(basic_ostream&)` (27.6.2.7).
[296] See, for example, the function signature `dec(ios_base&)` (27.4.5.3).

27.6.2.5.4 Character inserter function templates   [lib.ostream.inserters.character]

```
template<class charT, class traits>
  basic_ostream<charT,traits>& operator<<(basic_ostream<charT,traits>& out,
                                          charT c);
template<class charT, class traits>
  basic_ostream<charT,traits>& operator<<(basic_ostream<charT,traits>& out,
                                          char c);
// specialization
template<class traits>
  basic_ostream<char,traits>& operator<<(basic_ostream<char,traits>& out,
                                         char c);
// signed and unsigned
template<class traits>
  basic_ostream<char,traits>& operator<<(basic_ostream<char,traits>& out,
                                         signed char c);
template<class traits>
  basic_ostream<char,traits>& operator<<(basic_ostream<char,traits>& out,
                                         unsigned char c);
```

1   **Effects:** Behaves like a formatted inserter (as described in 27.6.2.5.1) of *out*. After a `sentry` object is constructed it inserts characters. In case *c* has type `char` and the character type of the stream is not `char`, then the character to be inserted is *out*.`widen(c)`; otherwise the character is c[297]. Padding is determined as described in 22.2.2.2.2. `width(0)` is called. The insertion character and any required padding are inserted into *out*.

2   **Returns:** *out*

```
template<class charT, class traits>
  basic_ostream<charT,traits>& operator<<(basic_ostream<charT,traits>& out,
                                          const charT* s);
template<class charT, class traits>
  basic_ostream<charT,traits>& operator<<(basic_ostream<charT,traits>& out,
                                          const char* s);
template<class traits>
  basic_ostream<char,traits>& operator<<(basic_ostream<char,traits>& out,
                                         const char* s);
template<class traits>
  basic_ostream<char,traits>& operator<<(basic_ostream<char,traits>& out,
                                         const signed char* s);
template<class traits>
  basic_ostream<char,traits>& operator<<(basic_ostream<char,traits>& out,
                                         const unsigned char* s);
```

3   **Requires:** *s* is non-null.

4   **Effects:** Behaves like an formatted inserter (as described in 27.6.2.5.1) of *out*. After a `sentry` object is constructed it inserts characters. The number of characters starting at *s* to be inserted is `traits::length(s)`. Padding is determined as described in 22.2.2.2.2. The `traits::length(s)` characters starting at *s* are widened using *out*.`widen` (27.4.4.2). The widened characters and any required padding are inserted into *out*. Calls `width(0)`.

5   **Returns:** *out*

---

[297] In case the insertion is into a `char` stream, `widen(c)` will usually be *c*.

27.6.2.6 Unformatted output functions [lib.ostream.unformatted]

1   Each unformatted output function begins execution by constructing an object of class `sentry`. If this object returns `true`, while converting to a value of type `bool`, the function endeavors to generate the requested output. If an exception is thrown during output, then `ios::badbit` is turned on[297a] in `*this`'s error state. If `(exceptions() & badbit) != 0` then the exception is rethrown. In any case, the unformatted output function ends by destroying the sentry object, then, if no exception was thrown, returning the value specified for the unformatted output function.

```
basic_ostream<charT,traits>& put(char_type c);
```

2   **Effects:** Behaves as an unformatted output function (as described in 27.6.2.6, paragraph 1). After constructing a sentry object, inserts the character c, if possible.[298]

3   Otherwise, calls `setstate(badbit)` (which may throw `ios_base::failure` (27.4.4.3)).

4   **Returns:** `*this`.

```
basic_ostream& write(const char_type* s, streamsize n);
```

5   **Effects:** Behaves as an unformatted output function (as described in 27.6.2.6, paragraph 1). After constructing a sentry object, obtains characters to insert from successive locations of an array whose first element is designated by s.[299] Characters are inserted until either of the following occurs:

— n characters are inserted;

— inserting in the output sequence fails (in which case the function calls `setstate(badbit)`, which may throw `ios_base::failure` (27.4.4.3)).

6   **Returns:** `*this`.

```
basic_ostream& flush();
```

7   If `rdbuf()` is not a null pointer, calls `rdbuf()->pubsync()`. If that function returns -1 calls `setstate(badbit)` (which may throw `ios_base::failure` (27.4.4.3)). Does not behave as an unformatted output function (as described in 27.6.2.6, paragraph 1).

8   **Returns:** `*this`.

27.6.2.7 Standard `basic_ostream` manipulators [lib.ostream.manip]

```
namespace std {
  template <class charT, class traits>
    basic_ostream<charT,traits>& endl(basic_ostream<charT,traits>& os);
}
```

1   **Effects:** Calls `os.put(os.widen('\n') )`, then `os.flush()`.

2   **Returns:** `os`.[300]

[297a] without causing an `ios::failure` to be thrown.
[298] Note that this function is not overloaded on types `signed char` and `unsigned char`.
[299] Note that this function is not overloaded on types `signed char` and `unsigned char`.
[300] The effect of executing `cout << endl` is to insert a newline character in the output sequence controlled by `cout`, then synchronize it with any external file with which it might be associated.

```
namespace std {
  template <class charT, class traits>
    basic_ostream<charT,traits>& ends(basic_ostream<charT,traits>& os);
}
```

3   **Effects:** Inserts a null character into the output sequence: calls *os*.put(charT()).

4   **Returns:** *os*.

```
namespace std {
  template <class charT, class traits>
    basic_ostream<charT,traits>& flush(basic_ostream<charT,traits>& os);
}
```

5   **Effects:** Calls *os*.flush().

6   **Returns:** *os*.

27.6.3 Standard manipulators   **[lib.std.manip]**

1   The header <iomanip> defines a type and several related functions that use this type to provide extractors and inserters that alter information maintained by class ios_base and its derived classes.

2   The type designated *smanip* in each of the following function descriptions is implementation-specified and may be different for each function.

> *smanip* resetiosflags(ios_base::fmtflags *mask*);

3   **Returns:** An object *s* of unspecified type such that if out is an (instance of) basic_ostream then the expression out<<*s* behaves as if f(*s*) were called, and if in is an (instance of) basic_istream then the expression in>>*s* behaves as if f(*s*) were called. Where f can be defined as:[301]

```
ios_base& f(ios_base& str, ios_base::fmtflags mask)
{
  // reset specified flags
  str.setf(ios_base::fmtflags(0), mask);
  return str;
}
```

The expression out<<*s* has type ostream& and value out. The expression in>>*s* has type istream& and value in.

> *smanip* setiosflags(ios_base::fmtflags *mask*);

4   **Returns:** An object *s* of unspecified type such that if out is an (instance of) basic_ostream then the expression out<<*s* behaves as if f(*s*) were called, in is an (instance of) basic_istream then the expression in>>*s* behaves as if f(*s*) were called. Where f can be defined as:

```
ios_base& f(ios_base& str, ios_base::fmtflags mask)
{
  // set specified flags
  str.setf(mask);
  return str;
}
```

The expression out<<*s* has type ostream& and value out. The expression in>>*s* has type istream& and value in.

---

[301] The expression cin >> resetiosflags(ios_base::skipws) clears ios_base::skipws in the format flags stored in the istream object cin (the same as cin >> noskipws), and the expression cout << resetiosflags(ios_base::showbase) clears ios_base::showbase in the format flags stored in the ostream object cout (the same as cout << noshowbase).

> *smanip* setbase(int *base*);

5   **Returns:** An object *s* of unspecified type such that if out is an (instance of) basic_ostream then the expression out<<*s* behaves as if f(*s*) were called, in is an (instance of) basic_istream then the expression in>>*s* behaves as if f(*s*) were called. Where f can be defined as:

```
ios_base& f(ios_base& str, int base)
{
  // set basefield
  str.setf(base ==  8 ? ios_base::oct :
           base == 10 ? ios_base::dec :
           base == 16 ? ios_base::hex :
              ios_base::fmtflags(0), ios_base::basefield);
  return str;
}
```

The expression out<<*s* has type ostream& and value out. The expression in>>*s* has type istream& and value in.

> *smanip* setfill(char_type *c*);

6   **Returns:** An object *s* of unspecified type such that if out is (or is derived from) basic_ostream<charT,traits> and *c* has type charT then the expression out<<*s* behaves as if f(*s*) were called, where f can be defined as:

```
template<class charT, class traits>
basic_ios<charT,traits>& f(basic_ios<charT,traits>& str, charT c)
{
  // set fill character
  str.fill(c);
  return str;
}
```

The expression out<<*s* has type ostream& and value out.

> *smanip* setprecision(int *n*);

7   **Returns:** An object *s* of unspecified type such that if out is an (instance of) basic_ostream then the expression out<<*s* behaves as if f(*s*) were called, in is an (instance of) basic_istream then the expression in>>*s* behaves as if f(*s*) were called. Where f can be defined as:

```
ios_base& f(ios_base& str, int n)
{
  // set precision
  str.precision(n);
  return str;
}
```

The expression out<<*s* has type ostream& and value out. The expression in>>*s* has type istream& and value in.

> *smanip* setw(int *n*);

8   **Returns:** An object *s* of unspecified type such that if out is an (instance of) basic_ostream then the expression out<<*s* behaves as if f(*s*) were called, in is an (instance of) basic_istream then the expression in>>*s* behaves as if f(*s*) were called. Where f can be defined as:

```
ios_base& f(ios_base& str, int n)
{
  // set width
  str.width(n);
  return str;
}
```

The expression out<<s has type ostream& and value out. The expression in>>s has type istream& and value in.

27.7 String-based streams   [lib.string.streams]

1   The header <sstream> defines four class templates and six types, that associate stream buffers with objects of class basic_string, as described in 21.2.

Header <sstream> synopsis

```
namespace std {
  template <class charT, class traits = char_traits<charT>,
            class Allocator = allocator<charT> >
    class basic_stringbuf;

  typedef basic_stringbuf<char>    stringbuf;
  typedef basic_stringbuf<wchar_t> wstringbuf;

  template <class charT, class traits = char_traits<charT>,
            class Allocator = allocator<charT> >
    class basic_istringstream;

  typedef basic_istringstream<char>    istringstream;
  typedef basic_istringstream<wchar_t> wistringstream;

  template <class charT, class traits = char_traits<charT>,
            class Allocator = allocator<charT> >
    class basic_ostringstream;
  typedef basic_ostringstream<char>    ostringstream;
  typedef basic_ostringstream<wchar_t> wostringstream;

  template <class charT, class traits = char_traits<charT>,
            class Allocator = allocator<charT> >
    class basic_stringstream;
  typedef basic_stringstream<char>    stringstream;
  typedef basic_stringstream<wchar_t> wstringstream;
}
```

27.7.1 Class template basic_stringbuf   [lib.stringbuf]

```
namespace std {
  template <class charT, class traits = char_traits<charT>,
            class Allocator = allocator<charT> >
  class basic_stringbuf : public basic_streambuf<charT,traits> {
  public:
    typedef charT                   char_type;
    typedef typename traits::int_type int_type;
    typedef typename traits::pos_type pos_type;
    typedef typename traits::off_type off_type;
    typedef traits                   traits_type;
```

```
// 27.7.1.1 Constructors:
explicit basic_stringbuf(ios_base::openmode which
                         = ios_base::in | ios_base::out);
explicit basic_stringbuf
    (const basic_string<charT,traits,Allocator>& str,
     ios_base::openmode which = ios_base::in | ios_base::out);

// 27.7.1.2 Get and set:
basic_string<charT,traits,Allocator> str() const;
void                  str(const basic_string<charT,traits,Allocator>& s);

protected:
// 27.7.1.3 Overridden virtual functions:
virtual int_type    underflow();
virtual int_type    pbackfail(int_type c = traits::eof());
virtual int_type    overflow (int_type c = traits::eof());
virtual  basic_streambuf<charT,traits>* setbuf(charT*, streamsize);


virtual pos_type    seekoff(off_type off, ios_base::seekdir way,
                            ios_base::openmode which
                            = ios_base::in | ios_base::out);
virtual pos_type    seekpos(pos_type sp,
                            ios_base::openmode which
                            = ios_base::in | ios_base::out);

private:
//   ios_base::openmode mode;        exposition only
};
}
```

1   The class `basic_stringbuf` is derived from `basic_streambuf` to associate possibly the input sequence and possibly the output sequence with a sequence of arbitrary *characters*. The sequence can be initialized from, or made available as, an object of class `basic_string`.

2   For the sake of exposition, the maintained data is presented here as:

— `ios_base::openmode` *mode*, has `in` set if the input sequence can be read, and `out` set if the output sequence can be written.

27.7.1.1 `basic_stringbuf` constructors   [lib.stringbuf.cons]

```
explicit basic_stringbuf(ios_base::openmode which =
                         ios_base::in | ios_base::out);
```

1   **Effects:** Constructs an object of class `basic_stringbuf`, initializing the base class with `basic_streambuf()` (27.5.2.1), and initializing *mode* with *which*.

2   **Notes:** The function allocates no array object.

```
explicit basic_stringbuf(const basic_string<charT,traits,Allocator>& str,
                ios_base::openmode which = ios_base::in | ios_base::out);
```

3   **Effects:** Constructs an object of class `basic_stringbuf`, initializing the base class with `basic_streambuf()` (27.5.2.1), and initializing *mode* with *which*. Then copies the content of *str* into the `basic_stringbuf` underlying character sequence and initializes the input and output sequences according to *which*. If *which* & `ios_base::out` is true, initializes the output sequence with the underlying sequence. If *which* & `ios_base::in` is true, initializes the input sequence with the underlying sequence.

4   **Postconditions:** `str() == ` *`str`*.

27.7.1.2 Member functions [lib.stringbuf.members]

```
basic_string<charT,traits,Allocator> str() const;
```

1   **Returns:** A `basic_string` object whose content is equal to the `basic_stringbuf` underlying character sequence. If the buffer is only created in input mode, the underlying character sequence is equal to the input sequence; otherwise, it is equal to the output sequence. In case of an empty underlying character sequence, the function returns `basic_string<charT,traits,Allocator>()`.

```
void str(const basic_string<charT,traits,Allocator>& s);
```

2   **Effects:** If the `basic_stringbuf`'s underlying character sequence is not empty, deallocates it. Then copies the content of *s* into the `basic_stringbuf` underlying character sequence and initializes the input and output sequences according to the mode stored when creating the `basic_stringbuf` object. If `(mode&ios_base::out)` is `true`, then initializes the output sequence with the underlying sequence. If `(mode&ios_base::in)` is `true`, then initializes the input sequence with the underlying sequence.

3   **Postcondition:** `str() == ` *`s`*.

27.7.1.3 Overridden virtual functions [lib.stringbuf.virtuals]

```
int_type underflow();
```

1   **Returns:** If the input sequence has a read position available, returns `traits::to_int_type(*gptr())`.
Otherwise, returns `traits::eof()`.

```
int_type pbackfail(int_type c = traits::eof());
```

2   **Effects:** Puts back the character designated by *c* to the input sequence, if possible, in one of three ways:

— If `traits::eq_int_type(c,traits::eof())` returns `false` and if the input sequence has a putback position available, and if `traits::eq(to_char_type(c),gptr()[-1])` returns `true`, assigns `gptr() - 1` to `gptr()`.
Returns: *c*.

— If `traits::eq_int_type(c,traits::eof())` returns `false` and if the input sequence has a putback position available, and if *mode* `&` *`ios_base::out`* is nonzero, assigns *c* to `*--gptr()`.
Returns: *c*.

— If `traits::eq_int_type(c,traits::eof())` returns `true` and if the input sequence has a putback position available, assigns `gptr() - 1` to `gptr()`.
Returns: `traits::not_eof(c)`.

3   **Returns:** `traits::eof()` to indicate failure.

4   **Notes:** If the function can succeed in more than one of these ways, it is unspecified which way is chosen.

```
int_type overflow(int_type c = traits::eof());
```

5   **Effects:** Appends the character designated by *c* to the output sequence, if possible, in one of two ways:

— If `traits::eq_int_type(c,traits::eof())` returns `false` and if either the output sequence has a write position available or the function makes a write position available (as described below), the function calls `sputc(c)`.
Signals success by returning *c*.

— If `traits::eq_int_type(c,traits::eof())` returns `true`, there is no character to append.
Signals success by returning a value other than `traits::eof()`.

6   **Notes:** The function can alter the number of write positions available as a result of any call.

7   **Returns:** `traits::eof()` to indicate failure.

8   **Notes:** The function can make a write position available only if (*mode* `& ios_base::out) != 0`. To make a write position available, the function reallocates (or initially allocates) an array object with a sufficient number of elements to hold the current array object (if any), plus at least one additional write position. If (*mode* `& ios_base::in) != 0`, the function alters the read end pointer `egptr()` to point just past the new write position (as does the write end pointer `epptr()`).

```
pos_type seekoff(off_type off, ios_base::seekdir way,
                 ios_base::openmode which
               = ios_base::in | ios_base::out);
```

10   **Effects:** Alters the stream position within one of the controlled sequences, if possible, as indicated in Table 90:

Table 90—`seekoff` positioning

Conditions	Result
(*which* `& basic_ios::in) != 0`	positions the input sequence
(*which* `& basic_ios::out) != 0`	positions the output sequence
(*which* `& (basic_ios::in | basic_ios::out)) == (basic_ios::in | basic_ios::out)` and *way* == either `basic_ios::beg` or `basic_ios::end`	positions both the input and the output sequences
Otherwise	the positioning operation fails.

11   For a sequence to be positioned, if its next pointer (either `gptr()` or `pptr()`) is a null pointer, the positioning operation fails. Otherwise, the function determines *newoff* as indicated in Table 91:

Table 91—`newoff` values

Condition	`newoff` Value
way == `basic_ios::beg`	0
way == `basic_ios::cur`	the next pointer minus the beginning pointer (*xnext* - *xbeg*).
way == `basic_ios::end`	the end pointer minus the beginning pointer (*xend* - *xbeg*)

12   _ If (*newoff* + *off*) < 0, or (*xend* - *xbeg*) < (*newoff* + *off*), the positioning operation fails. Otherwise, the function assigns *xbeg* + *newoff* + *off* to the next pointer *xnext*.

13   **Returns:** `pos_type(`*newoff*`)`, constructed from the resultant offset *newoff* (of type `off_type`), that stores the resultant stream position, if possible. If the positioning operation fails, or if the constructed object cannot represent the resultant stream position, the return value is `pos_type(off_type(-1))`.

```
pos_type seekpos(pos_type sp, ios_base::openmode which
                = ios_base::in | ios_base::out);
```

14   **Effects:** Alters the stream position within the controlled sequences, if possible, to correspond to the stream position stored in *sp* (as described below).

— If (*which* & basic_ios::in) != 0, positions the input sequence.

— If (*which* & basic_ios::out) != 0, positions the output sequence.

— If *sp* is an invalid stream position, or if the function positions neither sequence, the positioning operation fails. If *sp* has not been obtained by a previous successful call to one of the positioning functions(seekoff, seekpos, tellg, tellp) the effect is undefined.

15   **Returns:** *sp* to indicate success, or pos_type(off_type(-1)) to indicate failure.

```
basic_streambuf<charT,traits>* setbuf(charT* s, streamsize n);
```

16   **Effects:** implementation-defined, except that setbuf(0,0) has no effect.
17   **Returns:** this.

27.7.2 Class template `basic_istringstream`   [lib.istringstream]

```
namespace std {
  template <class charT, class traits = char_traits<charT>,
          class Allocator = allocator<charT> >
  class basic_istringstream : public basic_istream<charT,traits> {
  public:
    typedef charT                    char_type;
    typedef typename traits::int_type int_type;
    typedef typename traits::pos_type pos_type;
    typedef typename traits::off_type off_type;
    typedef traits                    traits_type;

    // 27.7.2.1 Constructors:
    explicit basic_istringstream(ios_base::openmode which = ios_base::in);
    explicit basic_istringstream(
                const basic_string<charT,traits,Allocator>& str,
                ios_base::openmode which = ios_base::in);

    // 27.7.2.2 Members:
    basic_stringbuf<charT,traits,Allocator>* rdbuf() const;

    basic_string<charT,traits,Allocator> str() const;
    void str(const basic_string<charT,traits,Allocator>& s);
  private:
  //  basic_stringbuf<charT,traits,Allocator> sb;    exposition only
    };
}
```

1   The class basic_istringstream<charT,traits,Allocator> supports reading objects of class basic_string<charT,traits,Allocator>.   It   uses   a basic_stringbuf<charT,traits,Allocator> object to control the associated storage. For the sake of exposition, the maintained data is presented here as:

— *sb*, the stringbuf object.

27.7.2.1 `basic_istringstream` **constructors** **[lib.istringstream.cons]**

```
explicit basic_istringstream(ios_base::openmode which = ios_base::in);
```

1   **Effects:** Constructs an object of class `basic_istringstream<charT,traits>`, initializing the base class with `basic_istream(&sb)` and initializing `sb` with `basic_stringbuf<charT,traits,Allocator>(which|ios_base::in))` (27.7.1.1).

```
explicit basic_istringstream(
                const basic_string<charT,traits,allocator>& str,
                ios_base::openmode which = ios_base::in);
```

2   **Effects:** Constructs an object of class `basic_istringstream<charT,traits>`, initializing the base class with `basic_istream(&sb)` and initializing `sb` with `basic_stringbuf<charT,traits,Allocator>(str, which | ios_base::in))` (27.7.1.1).

27.7.2.2 Member functions [lib.istringstream.members]

```
basic_stringbuf<charT,traits,Allocator>* rdbuf() const;
```

1   **Returns:** `(basic_stringbuf<charT,traits,Allocator>*)&sb`.

```
basic_string<charT,traits,Allocator> str() const;
```

2   **Returns:** `rdbuf()->str()`.[302]

```
void str(const basic_string<charT,traits,Allocator>& s);
```

3   **Effects:** Calls `rdbuf()->str(s)`.

27.7.3 Class `basic_ostringstream` [lib.ostringstream]

```
namespace std {
    template <class charT, class traits = char_traits<charT>,
            class Allocator = allocator<charT> >
    class basic_ostringstream : public basic_ostream<charT,traits> {
    public:

        // Types:
        typedef charT               char_type;
        typedef typename traits::int_type int_type;
        typedef typename traits::pos_type pos_type;
        typedef typename traits::off_type off_type;
        typedef traits              traits_type;

        // 27.7.3.1 Constructors/destructor:
        explicit basic_ostringstream(ios_base::openmode which = ios_base::out);
        explicit basic_ostringstream(
                        const basic_string<charT,traits,Allocator>& str,
                        ios_base::openmode which = ios_base::out);

        // 27.7.3.2 Members:
        basic_stringbuf<charT,traits,Allocator>* rdbuf() const;
```

---

[302] `rdbuf()` is never NULL because it always returns the private `object`.

```
      basic_string<charT,traits,Allocator> str() const;
      void    str(const basic_string<charT,traits,Allocator>& s);
    private:
// basic_stringbuf<charT,traits,Allocator> sb;     exposition only
    };
}
```

1   The class basic_ostringstream<charT,traits,Allocator> supports writing objects of class
     basic_string<charT,traits,Allocator>. It uses a basic_stringbuf object to control the
     associated storage. For the sake of exposition, the maintained data is presented here as:

     — sb, the stringbuf object.

27.7.3.1 basic_ostringstream constructors   [lib.ostringstream.cons]

```
      explicit basic_ostringstream(ios_base::openmode which = ios_base::out);
```

1   **Effects:** Constructs an object of class basic_ostringstream, initializing the base class with
     basic_ostream(&sb)   and   initializing   sb   with
     basic_stringbuf<charT,traits,Allocator>(which | ios_base::out))
     (27.7.1.1).

```
      explicit basic_ostringstream(
                    const basic_string<charT,traits,Allocator>& str,
                    ios_base::openmode which = ios_base::out);
```

2   **Effects:** Constructs an object of class basic_ostringstream<charT,traits>, initializing the
     base   class   with   basic_ostream(&sb)   and   initializing   sb   with
     basic_stringbuf<charT,traits,Allocator>(str,   which | ios_base::out))
     (27.7.1.1).

27.7.3.2 Member functions   [lib.ostringstream.members]

```
      basic_stringbuf<charT,traits,Allocator>* rdbuf() const;
```

1   **Returns:** (basic_stringbuf<charT,traits,Allocator>*)&sb.

```
      basic_string<charT,traits,Allocator> str() const;
```

2   **Returns:** rdbuf()->str().[303]

```
      void str(const basic_string<charT,traits,Allocator>& s);
```

3   **Effects:** Calls rdbuf()->str(s).

27.7.4 Class template basic_stringstream   [lib.stringstream]

```
      namespace std {
        template <class charT, class traits = char_traits<charT>,
                class Allocator = allocator<charT> >
        class basic_stringstream
          : public basic_iostream<charT,traits> {
        public:
```

---

[303] rdbuf() is never NULL because it always returns the private object.

```
// Types
typedef charT                      char_type;
typedef typename traits::int_type  int_type;
typedef typename traits::pos_type  pos_type;
typedef typename traits::off_type  off_type;
typedef traits                     traits_type;

// constructors/destructors
explicit basic_stringstream(
    ios_base::openmode which = ios_base::out|ios_base::in);
explicit basic_stringstream(
    const basic_string<charT,traits,Allocator>& str,
    ios_base::openmode which = ios_base::out|ios_base::in);

// Members:
basic_stringbuf<charT,traits,Allocator>* rdbuf() const;
basic_string<charT,traits,Allocator> str() const;
void str(const basic_string<charT,traits,Allocator>& str);

  private:
// basic_stringbuf<charT, traits> sb;  exposition only
  };
}
```

1   The class template `basic_stringstream<charT,traits>` supports reading and writing from objects of class `basic_string<charT,traits,Allocator>`. It uses a `basic_stringbuf<charT,traits,Allocator>` object to control the associated sequence. For the sake of exposition, the maintained data is presented here as

— *sb*, the `stringbuf` object.

27.7.5 basic_stringstream constructors   [lib.stringstream.cons]

```
explicit basic_stringstream(
    ios_base::openmode which = ios_base::out|ios_base::in);
```

1   **Effects:** Constructs an object of class `basic_stringstream<charT,traits>`, initializing the base class with `basic_iostream(&sb)` and initializing *sb* with `basic_stringbuf<charT,traits,Allocator>(which)`.

```
explicit basic_stringstream(
    const basic_string<charT,traits,Allocator>& str,
    ios_base::openmode which = ios_base::out|ios_base::in);
```

2   **Effects:** Constructs an object of class `basic_stringstream<charT,traits>`, initializing the base class with `basic_iostream(&sb)` and initializing *sb* with `basic_stringbuf<charT,traits,Allocator>(str,which)`.

27.7.6 Member functions   [lib.stringstream.members]

```
basic_stringbuf<charT,traits,Allocator>* rdbuf() const;
```

1   **Returns:** `&sb`

```
basic_string<charT,traits,Allocator> str() const;
```

2   **Returns:** rdbuf()->str().[304]

```
void str(const basic_string<charT,traits,Allocator>& str);
```

3   **Effects:** Calls rdbuf()->str(str).

27.8 File-based streams   [lib.file.streams]

27.8.1 File streams   [lib.fstreams]

1   The header <fstream> defines four class templates and six types that associate stream buffers with files and assist reading and writing files.

Header <fstream> synopsis

```
namespace std {
  template <class charT, class traits = char_traits<charT> >
    class basic_filebuf;
  typedef basic_filebuf<char>    filebuf;
  typedef basic_filebuf<wchar_t> wfilebuf;

  template <class charT, class traits = char_traits<charT> >
    class basic_ifstream;
  typedef basic_ifstream<char>    ifstream;
  typedef basic_ifstream<wchar_t> wifstream;

  template <class charT, class traits = char_traits<charT> >
    class basic_ofstream;
  typedef basic_ofstream<char>    ofstream;
  typedef basic_ofstream<wchar_t> wofstream;

  template <class charT, class traits = char_traits<charT> >
    class basic_fstream;
  typedef basic_fstream<char>    fstream;
  typedef basic_fstream<wchar_t> wfstream;
}
```

2   In this subclause, the type name *FILE* refers to the type FILE defined in <cstdio> (27.8.2).[305]

— **File** A File provides an external source/sink stream whose *underlaid character type* is char (byte).[306]

— **Multibyte character and Files** A File provides byte sequences. So the streambuf (or its derived classes) treats a file as the external source/sink byte sequence. In a large character set environment, multibyte character sequences are held in files. In order to provide the contents of a file as wide character sequences, wide-oriented filebuf, namely wfilebuf should convert wide character sequences.

---

[304] rdbuf() is never NULL because it always returns the private object.
[305] In C FILE must be a typedef. In C++ it may be a typedef or other type name.
[306] A File is a sequence of multibyte characters. In order to provide the contents as a wide character sequence, filebuf should convert between wide character sequences and multibyte character sequences.

27.8.1.1 Class template `basic_filebuf` **[lib.filebuf]**

```
namespace std {
  template <class charT, class traits = char_traits<charT> >
  class basic_filebuf : public basic_streambuf<charT,traits> {
  public:
    typedef charT                    char_type;
    typedef typename traits::int_type int_type;
    typedef typename traits::pos_type pos_type;
    typedef typename traits::off_type off_type;
    typedef traits                   traits_type;

    // 27.8.1.2 Constructors/destructor:
    basic_filebuf();
    virtual ~basic_filebuf();

    // 27.8.1.3 Members:
    bool is_open() const;
    basic_filebuf<charT,traits>* open
        (const char* s, ios_base::openmode mode);
    basic_filebuf<charT,traits>* close();

  protected:
    // 27.8.1.4 Overridden virtual functions:
    virtual streamsize showmanyc();
    virtual int_type underflow();
    virtual int_type uflow();
    virtual int_type pbackfail(int_type c = traits::eof());
    virtual int_type overflow (int_type c = traits::eof());

    virtual basic_streambuf<charT,traits>*
                    setbuf(char_type* s, streamsize n);
    virtual pos_type seekoff(off_type off, ios_base::seekdir way,
                       ios_base::openmode which
                          = ios_base::in | ios_base::out);
    virtual pos_type seekpos(pos_type sp, ios_base::openmode which
                          = ios_base::in | ios_base::out);
    virtual int     sync();
    virtual void    imbue(const locale& loc);
  };
}
```

1   The class `basic_filebuf<charT,traits>` associates both the input sequence and the output sequence with a file.

2   The restrictions on reading and writing a sequence controlled by an object of class `basic_filebuf<charT,traits>` are the same as for reading and writing with the Standard C library FILEs.

3   In particular:

— If the file is not open for reading the input sequence cannot be read.

— If the file is not open for writing the output sequence cannot be written.

— A joint file position is maintained for both the input sequence and the output sequence.

4   An instance of `basic_filebuf` behaves as described in 27.8.1.1 provided `traits::pos_type` is `fpos<traits::state_type>`. Otherwise the behavior is undefined.

5   In order to support file I/O and multibyte/wide character conversion, conversions are performed using members of a facet, referred to as *a_codecvt* in following sections, obtained ''as if'' by

```
codecvt<charT,char,typename traits::state_type> a_codecvt =
    use_facet<codecvt<charT,char,typename traits::state_type> >(getloc());
```

27.8.1.2 `basic_filebuf` constructors   [lib.filebuf.cons]

```
basic_filebuf();
```

1   **Effects:** Constructs an object of class `basic_filebuf<charT,traits>`, initializing the base class with `basic_streambuf<charT,traits>()` (27.5.2.1).

2   **Postcondition:** `is_open() == false`.

```
virtual ~basic_filebuf();
```

3   **Effects:** Destroys an object of class `basic_filebuf<charT,traits>`. Calls `close()`.

27.8.1.3 Member functions   [lib.filebuf.members]

```
bool is_open() const;
```

1   **Returns:** `true` if a previous call to `open` succeeded (returned a non-null value) and there has been no intervening call to close.

```
basic_filebuf<charT,traits>* open(
    const char* s,
    ios_base::openmode mode );
```

2   **Effects:** If `is_open() != false`, returns a null pointer. Otherwise, initializes the `filebuf` as required.

It then opens a file, if possible, whose name is the NTBS *s* (''as if'' by calling `std::fopen(s,modstr)`).

The NTBS *modstr* is determined from *mode* & ~`ios_base::ate` as indicated in Table 92:

Table 92—File open modes

ios_base Flag combination					**stdio** equivalent
binary	in	out	trunc	app	
		+			`"w"`
		+		+	`"a"`
		+	+		`"w"`
	+				`"r"`
	+	+			`"r+"`
	+	+	+		`"w+"`
+		+			`"wb"`
+		+		+	`"ab"`
+		+	+		`"wb"`
+	+				`"rb"`
+	+	+			`"r+b"`
+	+	+	+		`"w+b"`

If *mode* is not some combination of flags shown in the table then the open fails.

3   If the open operation succeeds and (*mode* & ios_base::ate) != 0, positions the file to the end
("as if" by calling std::fseek(*file*,0,SEEK_END)).[307]

4   If the repositioning operation fails, calls close() and returns a null pointer to indicate failure.

5   **Returns:** this if successful, a null pointer otherwise.

```
basic_filebuf<charT,traits>* close();
```

6   **Effects:** If is_open() == false, returns a null pointer. If a put area exists, calls overflow(EOF)
to flush characters. If the last virtual member function called on *this (between underflow,
overflow, seekoff, and seekpos) was overflow then calls *a_codecvt*.unshift (possibly
several times) to determine a termination sequence, inserts those characters and calls
overflow(EOF) again. Finally it closes the file ("as if" by calling std::fclose(*file*)).[308] If
any of the calls to overflow or std::fclose fails then close fails.

7   **Returns:** this on success, a null pointer otherwise.

8   **Postcondition:** is_open() == false.

27.8.1.4 Overridden virtual functions   [lib.filebuf.virtuals]

```
streamsize showmanyc();
```

1   **Effects:** Behaves the same as basic_streambuf::showmanyc() (27.5.2.4).

2   **Notes:** An implementation might well provide an overriding definition for this function signature if it can
determine that more characters can be read from the input sequence.

```
int_type underflow();
```

3   **Effects:** Behaves according to the description of basic_streambuf<charT,traits>::
underflow(), with the specialization that a sequence of characters is read from the input sequence
"as if" by reading from the associated file into an internal buffer (extern_buf) and then "as if"
doing

```
char    extern_buf[XSIZE];
char*   extern_end;
charT   intern_buf[ISIZE];
charT*  intern_end;
codecvt_base::result r =
    a_codecvt.in(st, extern_buf, extern_buf+XSIZE, extern_end,
                     intern_buf, intern_buf+ISIZE, intern_end);
```

This must be done in such a way that the class can recover the position (fpos_t) corresponding to
each character between intern_buf and intern_end. If the value of r indicates that
a_codecvt.in() ran out of space in intern_buf, retry with a larger intern_buf.

```
int_type uflow();
```

4   **Effects:** Behaves according to the description of basic_streambuf<charT,traits>::
uflow(), with the specialization that a sequence of characters is read from the input with the same
method as used by underflow.

---

[307] The macro SEEK_END is defined, and the function signatures fopen(const char_type*, const char_type*) and
fseek(FILE*, long, int) are declared, in <cstdio> (27.8.2).
[308] The function signature fclose(FILE*) is declared in <cstdio> (27.8.2).

```
int_type pbackfail(int_type c = traits::eof());
```

5   **Effects:** Puts back the character designated by c to the input sequence, if possible, in one of three ways:

— If `traits::eq_int_type(c,traits::eof())` returns `false` and if the function makes a put-back position available and if `traits::eq(to_char_type(c),gptr()[-1])` returns `true`, decrements the next pointer for the input sequence, `gptr()`.
Returns: c.

— If `traits::eq_int_type(c,traits::eof())` returns `false` and if the function makes a put-back position available, and if the function is permitted to assign to the putback position, decrements the next pointer for the input sequence, and stores c there.
Returns: c.

— If `traits::eq_int_type(c,traits::eof())` returns `true`, and if either the input sequence has a putback position available or the function makes a putback position available, decrements the next pointer for the input sequence, `gptr()`.
Returns: `traits::not_eof(c)`.

6   **Returns:** `traits::eof()` to indicate failure.

7   **Notes:** If `is_open() == false`, the function always fails.
The function does not put back a character directly to the input sequence.
If the function can succeed in more than one of these ways, it is unspecified which way is chosen. The function can alter the number of putback positions available as a result of any call.

```
int_type overflow(int_type c = traits::eof());
```

8   **Effects:**   Behaves   according   to   the   description   of
`basic_streambuf<charT,traits>::overflow(c)`, except that the behavior of "consuming characters" is performed by first coverting "as if" by:

```
charT* b = pbase();
charT* p = pptr();
charT* end;
char   xbuf[XSIZE];
char*  xbuf_end;
codecvt_base::result r =
         a_codecvt.out(st, b, p, end, xbuf, xbuf+XSIZE, xbuf_end);
```

and then

— If `r == codecvt_base::error` then fail.

— If `r == codecvt_base::noconv` then output characters from b up to (and not including) p.

— If `r == codecvt_base::partial` then output to the file characters from `xbuf` up to `xbuf_end`, and repeat using characters from end to p. If output fails, fail (without repeating).

— Otherwise output from xbuf to xbuf_end, and fail if output fails. At this point if b `!=` p and b `==` end (buf isn't large enough) then increase `BSIZE` and repeat from the beginning.

9   **Returns:** `traits::not_eof(c)` to indicate success, and `traits::eof()` to indicate failure. If `is_open() == false`, the function always fails.

```
basic_streambuf* setbuf(char_type* s, streamsize n);
```

10   **Effects:** If `setbuf(0,0)` is called on a stream before any I/O has occured on that stream, the stream becomes unbuffered. Otherwise the results are implementation-defined. "Unbuffered" means that `pbase()` and `pptr()` always return null and output to the file should appear as soon as possible.

```
pos_type seekoff(off_type off, ios_base::seekdir way,
                 ios_base::openmode which
                 = ios_base::in | ios_base::out);
```

11 **Effects:** Let *width* denote *a_codecvt*.encoding(). If is_open() == false, or *off* != 0 && *width* <= 0, then the positioning operation fails. Otherwise, if *way* != basic_ios::cur or *off* != 0, and if the last operation was output, then update the output sequence and write any unshift sequence. Next, seek to the new position: if *width* > 0, call std::fseek(*file*, *width* * *off*, *whence*), otherwise call std::fseek(*file*, 0, *whence*).

12 **Notes:** "The last operation was output" means either the last virtual operation was overflow or the put buffer is non-empty. "Write any unshift sequence" means, if *width* if less than zero then call *a_codecvt*.unshift(st, xbuf, xbuf+XSIZE, xbuf_end) and output the resulting unshift sequence. The function determines one of three values for the argument *whence*, of type int, as indicated in Table 93:

Table 93—seekoff **effects**

way **Value**	stdio **Equivalent**
basic_ios::beg	SEEK_SET
basic_ios::cur	SEEK_CUR
basic_ios::end	SEEK_END

13 **Returns:** a newly constructed pos_type object that stores the resultant stream position, if possible. If the positioning operation fails, or if the object cannot represent the resultant stream position, returns pos_type(off_type(-1)).

```
pos_type seekpos(pos_type sp, ios_base::openmode which
                 = ios_base::in | ios_base::out);
```

Alters the file position, if possible, to correspond to the position stored in *sp* (as described below).

— if (*which*&ios_base::in)!=0, set the file position to *sp*, then update the input sequence

— if (*which*&ios_base::out)!=0, then update the output sequence, write any unshift sequence, and set the file position to *sp*.

14 If *sp* is an invalid stream position, or if the function positions neither sequence, the positioning operation fails. If *sp* has not been obtained by a previous successful call to one of the positioning functions (seekoff or seekpos) on the same file the effects are undefined.

15 **Returns:** *sp* on success. Otherwise returns pos_type(off_type(-1)).

```
int sync();
```

16 **Effects:** If a put area exists, calls filebuf::overflow to write the characters to the file. If a get area exists, the effect is implementation-defined.

```
void imbue(const locale& loc);
```

17 **Precondition:** If the file is not positioned at its beginning and the encoding of the current locale as determined by *a_codecvt*.encoding() is state-dependent (22.2.1.5.2) then that facet is the same as the corresponding facet of *loc*.

18 **Effects:** Causes characters inserted or extracted after this call to be converted according to *loc* until another call of imbue.

19 **Note:** This may require reconversion of previously converted characters. This in turn may require the implementation to be able to reconstruct the original contents of the file.

27.8.1.5 Class template `basic_ifstream`   [lib.ifstream]

```
namespace std {
  template <class charT, class traits = char_traits<charT> >
  class basic_ifstream : public basic_istream<charT,traits> {
  public:
    typedef charT                     char_type;
    typedef typename traits::int_type int_type;
    typedef typename traits::pos_type pos_type;
    typedef typename traits::off_type off_type;
    typedef traits                    traits_type;

    // 27.8.1.6 Constructors:
    basic_ifstream();
    explicit basic_ifstream(const char* s,
                            ios_base::openmode mode = ios_base::in);

    // 27.8.1.7 Members:
    basic_filebuf<charT,traits>* rdbuf() const;

    bool is_open();
    void open(const char* s, ios_base::openmode mode = ios_base::in);
    void close();
  private:
//  basic_filebuf<charT,traits> sb;          exposition only
  };
}
```

1   The class `basic_ifstream<charT,traits>` supports reading from named files. It uses a `basic_filebuf<charT,traits>` object to control the associated sequence. For the sake of exposition, the maintained data is presented here as:

— *sb*, the `filebuf` object.

27.8.1.6 `basic_ifstream` constructors   [lib.ifstream.cons]

```
basic_ifstream();
```

1   **Effects:** Constructs an object of class `basic_ifstream<charT,traits>`, initializing the base class with `basic_istream(&sb)` and initializing *sb* with `basic_filebuf<charT,traits>()` (27.6.1.1.1, 27.8.1.2).

```
explicit basic_ifstream
        (const char* s, ios_base::openmode mode = ios_base::in);
```

2   **Effects:** Constructs an object of class `basic_ifstream`, initializing the base class with `basic_istream(&sb)` and initializing *sb* with `basic_filebuf<charT,traits>()` (27.6.1.1.1, 27.8.1.2), then calls `rdbuf()->open(s,mode|in)`.[309] If that function returns a null pointer, calls `setstate(failbit)`, (which may throw `ios_base::failure`).

---
[309] `rdbuf()` is never NULL because it always returns the private `object`.

27.8.1.7 Member functions **[lib.ifstream.members]**

```
basic_filebuf<charT,traits>* rdbuf() const;
```

1   **Returns:** (basic_filebuf<charT,traits>*)&*sb*.

```
bool is_open();
```

2   **Returns:** rdbuf()->is_open().[310]

```
void open(const char* s, ios_base::openmode mode = ios_base::in);
```

3   **Effects:** Calls rdbuf()->open(*s*, *mode*|in). If that function returns a null pointer, calls setstate(failbit) (which may throw ios_base::failure (27.4.4.3)).[310a]

```
void close();
```

4   **Effects:** Calls rdbuf()->close() and, if that function returns false, calls setstate(failbit) (which may throw ios_base::failure (27.4.4.3)).

27.8.1.8 Class template `basic_ofstream`   [lib.ofstream]

```
namespace std {
  template <class charT, class traits = char_traits<charT> >
  class basic_ofstream : public basic_ostream<charT,traits> {
  public:
    typedef charT                    char_type;
    typedef typename traits::int_type int_type;
    typedef typename traits::pos_type pos_type;
    typedef typename traits::off_type off_type;
    typedef traits                   traits_type;

    // 27.8.1.9 Constructors:
    basic_ofstream();
    explicit basic_ofstream(const char* s,
                            ios_base::openmode mode
                              = ios_base::out);

    // 27.8.1.10 Members:
    basic_filebuf<charT,traits>* rdbuf() const;

    bool is_open();
    void open(const char* s, ios_base::openmode mode = ios_base::out);
    void close();
  private:
//  basic_filebuf<charT,traits> sb;        exposition only
  };
}
```

1   The class basic_ofstream<charT,traits> supports writing to named files. It uses a basic_filebuf<charT,traits> object to control the associated sequence. For the sake of exposition, the maintained data is presented here as:

— *sb*, the filebuf object.

---

[310] rdbuf() is never NULL because it always returns the private object.
[310a] A successful open does not change the error state.

27.8.1.9 `basic_ofstream` constructors   [lib.ofstream.cons]

```
basic_ofstream();
```

1   **Effects:** Constructs an object of class `basic_ofstream<charT,traits>`, initializing the base class
     with `basic_ostream(&sb)` and initializing `sb` with `basic_filebuf<charT,traits>()`
     (27.6.2.2, 27.8.1.2).

```
explicit basic_ofstream
        (const char* s, ios_base::openmode mode = ios_base::out);
```

2   **Effects:** Constructs an object of class `basic_ofstream<charT,traits>`, initializing the base class
     with `basic_ostream(&sb)` and initializing `sb` with `basic_filebuf<charT,traits>()`
     (27.6.2.2, 27.8.1.2), then calls `rdbuf()->open(s, mode|out)`.[311] If that function returns a null
     pointer, calls `setstate(failbit)`, (which may throw `ios_base::failure`).

27.8.1.10 Member functions   [lib.ofstream.members]

```
basic_filebuf<charT,traits>* rdbuf() const;
```

1   **Returns:** `(basic_filebuf<charT,traits>*)&sb`.

```
bool is_open();
```

2   **Returns:** `rdbuf()->is_open()`.

```
void open(const char* s, ios_base::openmode mode = ios_base::out);
```

3   **Effects:** Calls `rdbuf()->open(s,mode|out)`. If that function returns a null pointer, calls
     `setstate(failbit)` (which may throw `ios_base::failure` (27.4.4.3)).[311a]

```
void close();
```

4   **Effects:** Calls `rdbuf()->close()` and, if that function fails (returns a null pointer), calls
     `setstate(failbit)` (which may throw `ios_base::failure` (27.4.4.3)).

27.8.1.11 Class template `basic_fstream`   [lib.fstream]

```
namespace std {
  template <class charT, class traits=char_traits<charT> >
  class basic_fstream
    : public basic_iostream<charT,traits> {

  public:
    typedef charT                    char_type;
    typedef typename traits::int_type int_type;
    typedef typename traits::pos_type pos_type;
    typedef typename traits::off_type off_type;
    typedef traits                   traits_type;

    // constructors/destructor
    basic_fstream();
    explicit basic_fstream(
        const char* s,
        ios_base::openmode mode = ios_base::in|ios_base::out);
```

---

[311] `rdbuf()` is never NULL because it always returns the private `filebuf` object.
[311a] A successful open does not change the error state.

```
        // Members:
        basic_filebuf<charT,traits>* rdbuf() const;
        bool is_open();
        void open(
            const char* s,
            ios_base::openmode mode = ios_base::in|ios_base::out);
        void close();

    private:
        // basic_filebuf<charT,traits> sb; exposition only
    };
}
```

1   The class template `basic_fstream<charT,traits>` supports reading and writing from named files.
    It uses a `basic_filebuf<charT,traits>` object to control the associated sequences. For the sake
    of exposition, the maintained data is presented here as:

— *sb*, the `basic_filebuf` object.

27.8.1.12 `basic_fstream` constructors   [lib.fstream.cons]

```
    basic_fstream();
```

1   **Effects:** Constructs an object of class `basic_fstream<charT,traits>`, initializing the base class
    with `basic_iostream(&sb)` and initializing *sb* with `basic_filebuf<charT,traits>()`.

```
    explicit basic_fstream(const char* s, ios_base::openmode mode);
```

2   **Effects:** Constructs an object of class `basic_fstream<charT,traits>`, initializing the base class
    with `basic_iostream(&sb)` and initializing *sb* with `basic_filebuf<charT,traits>()`.
    Then calls `rdbuf()->open(s,mode)`. If that function returns a null pointer, calls
    `setstate(failbit)` (which may throw `ios_base::failure`).

27.8.1.13 Member functions   [lib.fstream.members]

```
    basic_filebuf<charT,traits>* rdbuf() const;
```

1   **Returns:** &*sb*

```
    bool is_open();
```

2   **Returns:** `rdbuf()->is_open()`.

```
    void open(const char* s, ios_base::openmode mode);
```

3   **Effects:** Calls `rdbuf()->open(s,mode)`, If that function returns a null pointer, calls
    `setstate(failbit)`, (which may throw `ios_base::failure`). (27.4.4.3))

```
    void close();
```

4   **Effects:** Calls `rdbuf()->close()` and, if that function returns `false`, calls
    `setstate(failbit)` (27.4.4.3) (which may throw `ios_base::failure`).

1   Table 94 describes header <cstdio>.

Table 94—Header <cstdio> synopsis

Type					Name(s)
Macros:					
BUFSIZ	FOPEN_MAX	SEEK_CUR	TMP_MAX	_IONBF	stdout
EOF	L_tmpnam	SEEK_END	_IOFBF	stderr	
FILENAME_MAX	NULL <cstdio>	SEEK_SET	_IOLBF	stdin	
Types:	FILE	fpos_t	size_t <cstdio>		
Functions:					
clearerr	fgets	fscanf	gets	rename	tmpfile
fclose	fopen	fseek	perror	rewind	tmpnam
feof	fprintf	fsetpos	printf	scanf	ungetc
ferror	fputc	ftell	putc	setbuf	vfprintf
fflush	fputs	fwrite	putchar	setvbuf	vprintf
fgetc	fread	getc	puts	sprintf	vsprintf
fgetpos	freopen	getchar	remove	sscanf	

SEE ALSO: ISO C subclause 7.9, Amendment 1 subclause 4.6.2.

(informative)

Grammar summary

1   This summary of C++ syntax is intended to be an aid to comprehension. It is not an exact statement of the language. In particular, the grammar described here accepts a superset of valid C++ constructs. Disambiguation rules (6.8, 7.1, 10.2) must be applied to distinguish expressions from declarations. Further, access control, ambiguity, and type rules must be used to weed out syntactically valid but meaningless constructs.

A.1 Keywords [gram.key]

1   New context-dependent keywords are introduced into a program by `typedef` (7.1.3), namespace (7.3.1), class (clause 9), enumeration (7.2), and `template` (clause 14) declarations.

typedef-name:
        identifier

namespace-name:
        original-namespace-name
        namespace-alias

original-namespace-name:
        identifier

namespace-alias:
        identifier

class-name:
        identifier
        template-id

enum-name:
        identifier

template-name:
        identifier

Note that a *typedef-name* naming a class is also a *class-name* (9.1).

A.2 Lexical conventions [gram.lex]

hex-quad:
        hexadecimal-digit hexadecimal-digit hexadecimal-digit hexadecimal-digit

universal-character-name:
        \u *hex-quad*
        \U *hex-quad hex-quad*

preprocessing-token:
> *header-name*
> *identifier*
> *pp-number*
> *character-literal*
> *string-literal*
> *preprocessing-op-or-punc*
> each non-white-space character that cannot be one of the above

token:
> *identifier*
> *keyword*
> *literal*
> *operator*
> *punctuator*

header-name:
> *<h-char-sequence>*
> *"q-char-sequence"*

h-char-sequence:
> *h-char*
> *h-char-sequence h-char*

h-char:
> any member of the source character set except
> > new-line and >

q-char-sequence:
> *q-char*
> *q-char-sequence q-char*

q-char:
> any member of the source character set except
> > new-line and "

pp-number:
> *digit*
> *. digit*
> *pp-number digit*
> *pp-number nondigit*
> *pp-number* e *sign*
> *pp-number* E *sign*
> *pp-number .*

identifier:
> *nondigit*
> *identifier nondigit*
> *identifier digit*

nondigit: one of
> *universal-character-name*
> ```
> _ a b c d e f g h i j k l m
>   n o p q r s t u v w x y z
>   A B C D E F G H I J K L M
>   N O P Q R S T U V W X Y Z
> ```

digit : one of
    0 1 2 3 4 5 6 7 8 9

preprocessing-op-or-punc : one of

{	}	[	]	#	##	(	)	
<:	:>	<%	%>	%:	%:%:	;	:	...
new	delete	?	::	.	.*			
+	-	*	/	%	^	&	|	~
!	=	<	>	+=	-=	*=	/=	%=
^=	&=	|=	<<	>>	>>=	<<=	==	!=
<=	>=	&&	||	++	--	,	->*	->
and	and_eq	bitand	bitor	compl	not	not_eq		
or	or_eq	xor	xor_eq					

literal:
> *integer-literal*
> *character-literal*
> *floating-literal*
> *string-literal*
> *boolean-literal*

integer-literal:
> *decimal-literal integer-suffix$_{opt}$*
> *octal-literal integer-suffix$_{opt}$*
> *hexadecimal-literal integer-suffix$_{opt}$*

decimal-literal:
> *nonzero-digit*
> *decimal-literal digit*

octal-literal:
> 0
> *octal-literal octal-digit*

hexadecimal-literal:
> 0x *hexadecimal-digit*
> 0X *hexadecimal-digit*
> *hexadecimal-literal hexadecimal-digit*

nonzero-digit: one of
    1 2 3 4 5 6 7 8 9

octal-digit: one of
    0 1 2 3 4 5 6 7

hexadecimal-digit: one of
    0 1 2 3 4 5 6 7 8 9
    a b c d e f
    A B C D E F

integer-suffix:
> *unsigned-suffix long-suffix$_{opt}$*
> *long-suffix unsigned-suffix$_{opt}$*

unsigned-suffix: one of
    u U

long-suffix: one of
      l L

character-literal:
      ' *c-char-sequence* '
      L' *c-char-sequence* '

c-char-sequence:
      c-char
      c-char-sequence c-char

c-char:
      any member of the source character set except
            the single-quote ' , backslash \, or new-line character
      escape-sequence
      universal-character-name

escape-sequence:
      simple-escape-sequence
      octal-escape-sequence
      hexadecimal-escape-sequence

simple-escape-sequence: one of
      \' \" \? \\
      \a \b \f \n \r \t \v

octal-escape-sequence:
      \ *octal-digit*
      \ *octal-digit octal-digit*
      \ *octal-digit octal-digit octal-digit*

hexadecimal-escape-sequence:
      \x *hexadecimal-digit*
      hexadecimal-escape-sequence hexadecimal-digit

floating-literal:
      fractional-constant exponent-part$_{opt}$ floating-suffix$_{opt}$
      digit-sequence exponent-part floating-suffix$_{opt}$

fractional-constant:
      digit-sequence$_{opt}$. *digit-sequence*
      digit-sequence .

exponent-part:
      e *sign$_{opt}$ digit-sequence*
      E *sign$_{opt}$ digit-sequence*

sign: one of
      + -

digit-sequence:
      digit
      digit-sequence digit

floating-suffix: one of
      f l F L

string-literal:
        "*s-char-sequence$_{opt}$*"
        L"*s-char-sequence$_{opt}$*"

s-char-sequence:
        s-char
        s-char-sequence s-char

s-char:
        any member of the source character set except
                the double-quote ", backslash \, or new-line character
        escape-sequence
        universal-character-name

boolean-literal:
        `false`
        `true`

A.3 Basic concepts   **[gram.basic]**

translation-unit:
        declaration-seq$_{opt}$

A.4 Expressions   **[gram.expr]**

primary-expression:
        literal
        `this`
        (*expression*)
        id-expression

id-expression:
        unqualified-id
        qualified-id

unqualified-id:
        identifier
        operator-function-id
        conversion-function-id
        ˜ *class-name*
        template-id

qualified-id:
        `::`$_{opt}$ *nested-name-specifier* `template`$_{opt}$ *unqualified-id*
        `::` *identifier*
        `::` *operator-function-id*
        `::` *template-id*

nested-name-specifier:
        class-or-namespace-name `::` *nested-name-specifier$_{opt}$*
        class-or-namespace-name `::` `template` *nested-name-specifier*

class-or-namespace-name:
        class-name
        namespace-name

postfix-expression:
>   *primary-expression*
>   *postfix-expression* [*expression*]
>   *postfix-expression* (*expression-list$_{opt}$*)
>   *simple-type-specifier* (*expression-list$_{opt}$*)
>   typename :: $_{opt}$ *nested-name-specifier identifier* (*expression-list$_{opt}$*)
>   typename :: $_{opt}$ *nested-name-specifier* template$_{opt}$ *template-id* (*expression-list$_{opt}$*)
>   *postfix-expression* . template$_{opt}$ *id-expression*
>   *postfix-expression* -> template$_{opt}$ *id-expression*
>   *postfix-expression* . *pseudo-destructor-name*
>   *postfix-expression* -> *pseudo-destructor-name*
>   *postfix-expression* ++
>   *postfix-expression* --
>   dynamic_cast < *type-id* > (*expression*)
>   static_cast < *type-id* > (*expression*)
>   reinterpret_cast < *type-id* > (*expression*)
>   const_cast < *type-id* > (*expression*)
>   typeid (*expression*)
>   typeid (*type-id*)

expression-list:
>   *assignment-expression*
>   *expression-list* , *assignment-expression*

pseudo-destructor-name:
>   :: $_{opt}$ *nested-name-specifier$_{opt}$ type-name* :: ~ *type-name*
>   :: $_{opt}$ *nested-name-specifier* template *template-id* :: ~ *type-name*
>   :: $_{opt}$ *nested-name-specifier$_{opt}$* ~ *type-name*

unary-expression:
>   *postfix-expression*
>   ++ *cast-expression*
>   -- *cast-expression*
>   *unary-operator cast-expression*
>   sizeof *unary-expression*
>   sizeof (*type-id*)
>   *new-expression*
>   *delete-expression*

unary-operator: one of
>   * & + - ! ~

new-expression:
>   :: $_{opt}$ new *new-placement$_{opt}$ new-type-id new-initializer$_{opt}$*
>   :: $_{opt}$ new *new-placement$_{opt}$* (*type-id*) *new-initializer$_{opt}$*

new-placement:
>   (*expression-list*)

new-type-id:
>   *type-specifier-seq new-declarator$_{opt}$*

new-declarator:
>   *ptr-operator new-declarator$_{opt}$*
>   *direct-new-declarator*

direct-new-declarator:
        [*expression*]
        direct-new-declarator [*constant-expression*]

new-initializer:
        (*expression-list$_{opt}$*)

delete-expression:
        : :$_{opt}$ delete *cast-expression*
        : :$_{opt}$ delete [ ] *cast-expression*

cast-expression:
        unary-expression
        (*type-id*) *cast-expression*

pm-expression:
        cast-expression
        pm-expression .* *cast-expression*
        pm-expression ->* *cast-expression*

multiplicative-expression:
        pm-expression
        multiplicative-expression * *pm-expression*
        multiplicative-expression / *pm-expression*
        multiplicative-expression % *pm-expression*

additive-expression:
        multiplicative-expression
        additive-expression + *multiplicative-expression*
        additive-expression - *multiplicative-expression*

shift-expression:
        additive-expression
        shift-expression << *additive-expression*
        shift-expression >> *additive-expression*

relational-expression:
        shift-expression
        relational-expression < *shift-expression*
        relational-expression > *shift-expression*
        relational-expression <= *shift-expression*
        relational-expression >= *shift-expression*

equality-expression:
        relational-expression
        equality-expression == *relational-expression*
        equality-expression != *relational-expression*

and-expression:
        equality-expression
        and-expression & *equality-expression*

exclusive-or-expression:
        and-expression
        exclusive-or-expression ^ *and-expression*

inclusive-or-expression:
> *exclusive-or-expression*
> *inclusive-or-expression* | *exclusive-or-expression*

logical-and-expression:
> *inclusive-or-expression*
> *logical-and-expression* && *inclusive-or-expression*

logical-or-expression:
> *logical-and-expression*
> *logical-or-expression* || *logical-and-expression*

conditional-expression:
> *logical-or-expression*
> *logical-or-expression* ? *expression* : *assignment-expression*

assignment-expression:
> *conditional-expression*
> *logical-or-expression* *assignment-operator* *assignment-expression*
> *throw-expression*

assignment-operator : one of
> = *= /= %= += -= >>= <<= &= ^= |=

expression:
> *assignment-expression*
> *expression* , *assignment-expression*

constant-expression:
> *conditional-expression*

A.5 Statements   [gram.stmt.stmt]

statement:
> *labeled-statement*
> *expression-statement*
> *compound-statement*
> *selection-statement*
> *iteration-statement*
> *jump-statement*
> *declaration-statement*
> *try-block*

labeled-statement:
> *identifier* : *statement*
> case *constant-expression* : *statement*
> default : *statement*

expression-statement:
> $expression_{opt}$;

compound-statement:
> { $statement\text{-}seq_{opt}$ }

statement-seq:
> *statement*
> *statement-seq* *statement*

selection-statement:
>   if (*condition*) *statement*
>   if (*condition*) *statement* else *statement*
>   switch (*condition*) *statement*

condition:
>   *expression*
>   *type-specifier-seq declarator* = *assignment-expression*

iteration-statement:
>   while (*condition*) *statement*
>   do *statement* while (*expression*) ;
>   for (*for-init-statement condition$_{opt}$* ; *expression$_{opt}$*) *statement*

for-init-statement:
>   *expression-statement*
>   *simple-declaration*

jump-statement:
>   break ;
>   continue ;
>   return *expression$_{opt}$* ;
>   goto *identifier* ;

declaration-statement:
>   *block-declaration*

A.6 Declarations [gram.dcl.dcl]

declaration-seq:
>   *declaration*
>   *declaration-seq declaration*

declaration:
>   *block-declaration*
>   *function-definition*
>   *template-declaration*
>   *explicit-instantiation*
>   *explicit-specialization*
>   *linkage-specification*
>   *namespace-definition*

block-declaration:
>   *simple-declaration*
>   *asm-definition*
>   *namespace-alias-definition*
>   *using-declaration*
>   *using-directive*

simple-declaration:
>   *decl-specifier-seq$_{opt}$ init-declarator-list$_{opt}$* ;

decl-specifier:
>   *storage-class-specifier*
>   *type-specifier*
>   *function-specifier*
>   friend
>   typedef

decl-specifier-seq:
>   *decl-specifier-seq$_{opt}$ decl-specifier*

storage-class-specifier:
>   auto
>   register
>   static
>   extern
>   mutable

function-specifier:
>   inline
>   virtual
>   explicit

typedef-name:
>   *identifier*

type-specifier:
>   *simple-type-specifier*
>   *class-specifier*
>   *enum-specifier*
>   *elaborated-type-specifier*
>   *cv-qualifier*

simple-type-specifier:
>   ::$_{opt}$ *nested-name-specifier$_{opt}$ type-name*
>   ::$_{opt}$ *nested-name-specifier* template *template-id*
>   char
>   wchar_t
>   bool
>   short
>   int
>   long
>   signed
>   unsigned
>   float
>   double
>   void

type-name:
>   *class-name*
>   *enum-name*
>   *typedef-name*

elaborated-type-specifier:
>   *class-key* ::$_{opt}$ *nested-name-specifier$_{opt}$ identifier*
>   *class-key* ::$_{opt}$ *nested-name-specifier$_{opt}$ template$_{opt}$ template-id*
>   enum ::$_{opt}$ *nested-name-specifier$_{opt}$ identifier*
>   typename ::$_{opt}$ *nested-name-specifier identifier*
>   typename ::$_{opt}$ *nested-name-specifier template$_{opt}$ template-id*

enum-name:
>   *identifier*

enum-specifier:
>   `enum` *identifier*$_{opt}$ { *enumerator-list*$_{opt}$ }

enumerator-list:
>   *enumerator-definition*
>   *enumerator-list* , *enumerator-definition*

enumerator-definition:
>   *enumerator*
>   *enumerator* = *constant-expression*

enumerator:
>   *identifier*

namespace-name:
>   *original-namespace-name*
>   *namespace-alias*

original-namespace-name:
>   *identifier*

namespace-definition:
>   *named-namespace-definition*
>   *unnamed-namespace-definition*

named-namespace-definition:
>   *original-namespace-definition*
>   *extension-namespace-definition*

original-namespace-definition:
>   `namespace` *identifier* { *namespace-body* }

extension-namespace-definition:
>   `namespace` *original-namespace-name* { *namespace-body* }

unnamed-namespace-definition:
>   `namespace` { *namespace-body* }

namespace-body:
>   *declaration-seq*$_{opt}$

namespace-alias:
>   *identifier*

namespace-alias-definition:
>   `namespace` *identifier* = *qualified-namespace-specifier* ;

qualified-namespace-specifier:
>   `::`$_{opt}$ *nested-name-specifier*$_{opt}$ *namespace-name*

using-declaration:
>   `using` `typename`$_{opt}$ `::`$_{opt}$ *nested-name-specifier unqualified-id* ;
>   `using` `::` *unqualified-id* ;

using-directive:
>   `using` `namespace` `::`$_{opt}$ *nested-name-specifier*$_{opt}$ *namespace-name* ;

asm-definition:
> asm (*string-literal*) ;

linkage-specification:
> extern *string-literal* { *declaration-seq*_{opt} }
> extern *string-literal* *declaration*

A.7 Declarators

init-declarator-list:
> *init-declarator*
> *init-declarator-list* , *init-declarator*

init-declarator:
> *declarator* *initializer*$_{opt}$

declarator:
> *direct-declarator*
> *ptr-operator declarator*

direct-declarator:
> *declarator-id*
> *direct-declarator* (*parameter-declaration-clause*) *cv-qualifier-seq*$_{opt}$ *exception-specification*$_{opt}$
> *direct-declarator* [*constant-expression*$_{opt}$]
> (*declarator*)

ptr-operator:
> * *cv-qualifier-seq*$_{opt}$
> &
> : :$_{opt}$ *nested-name-specifier* * *cv-qualifier-seq*$_{opt}$

cv-qualifier-seq:
> *cv-qualifier* *cv-qualifier-seq*$_{opt}$

cv-qualifier:
> const
> volatile

declarator-id:
> *id-expression*
> : :$_{opt}$ *nested-name-specifier*$_{opt}$ *type-name*

type-id:
> *type-specifier-seq* *abstract-declarator*$_{opt}$

type-specifier-seq:
> *type-specifier type-specifier-seq*$_{opt}$

abstract-declarator:
> *ptr-operator abstract-declarator*$_{opt}$
> *direct-abstract-declarator*

direct-abstract-declarator:
> *direct-abstract-declarator*$_{opt}$
> > (*parameter-declaration-clause*) *cv-qualifier-seq*$_{opt}$ *exception-specification*$_{opt}$
> *direct-abstract-declarator*$_{opt}$ [*constant-expression*$_{opt}$]
> (*abstract-declarator*)

parameter-declaration-clause:
    parameter-declaration-list$_{opt}$ $\cdots_{opt}$
    parameter-declaration-list , $\cdots$

parameter-declaration-list:
    parameter-declaration
    parameter-declaration-list , *parameter-declaration*

parameter-declaration:
    decl-specifier-seq declarator
    decl-specifier-seq declarator = *assignment-expression*
    decl-specifier-seq abstract-declarator$_{opt}$
    decl-specifier-seq abstract-declarator$_{opt}$ = *assignment-expression*

function-definition:
    decl-specifier-seq$_{opt}$ declarator ctor-initializer$_{opt}$ function-body
    decl-specifier-seq$_{opt}$ declarator function-try-block

function-body:
    compound-statement

initializer:
    = *initializer-clause*
    (*expression-list*)

initializer-clause:
    assignment-expression
    { *initializer-list* $,_{opt}$ }
    { }

initializer-list:
    initializer-clause
    initializer-list , *initializer-clause*

A.8 Classes [gram.class]

class-name:
    identifier
    template-id

class-specifier:
    class-head { *member-specification$_{opt}$* }

class-head:
    class-key identifier$_{opt}$ base-clause$_{opt}$
    class-key nested-name-specifier identifier base-clause$_{opt}$
    class-key nested-name-specifier$_{opt}$ template-id base-clause$_{opt}$

class-key:
    `class`
    `struct`
    `union`

member-specification:
    member-declaration member-specification$_{opt}$
    access-specifier : *member-specification$_{opt}$*

member-declaration:
> *decl-specifier-seq$_{opt}$ member-declarator-list$_{opt}$* ;
> *function-definition* ; $_{opt}$
> : : $_{opt}$ *nested-name-specifier* template$_{opt}$ *unqualified-id* ;
> *using-declaration*
> *template-declaration*

member-declarator-list:
> *member-declarator*
> *member-declarator-list* , *member-declarator*

member-declarator:
> *declarator pure-specifier$_{opt}$*
> *declarator constant-initializer$_{opt}$*
> *identifier$_{opt}$* : *constant-expression*

pure-specifier:
> = 0

constant-initializer:
> = *constant-expression*

A.9 Derived classes   [gram.class.derived]

base-clause:
> : *base-specifier-list*

base-specifier-list:
> *base-specifier*
> *base-specifier-list* , *base-specifier*

base-specifier:
> ::$_{opt}$ *nested-name-specifier$_{opt}$ class-name*
> *virtual access-specifier$_{opt}$* ::$_{opt}$ *nested-name-specifier$_{opt}$ class-name*
> *access-specifier virtual$_{opt}$* ::$_{opt}$ *nested-name-specifier$_{opt}$ class-name*

access-specifier:
> private
> protected
> public

A.10 Special member functions   [gram.special]

conversion-function-id:
> operator *conversion-type-id*

conversion-type-id:
> *type-specifier-seq conversion-declarator$_{opt}$*

conversion-declarator:
> *ptr-operator conversion-declarator$_{opt}$*

ctor-initializer:
> : *mem-initializer-list*

mem-initializer-list:
        mem-initializer
        mem-initializer , *mem-initializer-list*

mem-initializer:
        mem-initializer-id (*expression-list$_{opt}$*)

mem-initializer-id:
        : :$_{opt}$ *nested-name-specifier$_{opt}$ class-name*
        identifier

A.11 Overloading [gram.over]

operator-function-id:
        `operator` *operator*
        `operator` *operator* < *template-argument-list$_{opt}$* >

operator: one of
    `new`   `delete`   `new[]`   `delete[]`
    `+`   `-`   `*`   `/`   `%`   `^`   `&`   `|`   `~`
    `!`   `=`   `<`   `>`   `+=`   `-=`   `*=`   `/=`   `%=`
    `^=`   `&=`   `|=`   `<<`   `>>`   `>>=`   `<<=`   `==`   `!=`
    `<=`   `>=`   `&&`   `||`   `++`   `--`   `,`   `->*`   `->`
    `()`   `[]`

A.12 Templates [gram.temp]

template-declaration :
        `export`$_{opt}$ `template` < *template-parameter-list* > *declaration*

template-parameter-list :
        template-parameter
        template-parameter-list , *template-parameter*

template-parameter:
        type-parameter
        parameter-declaration

type-parameter:
        `class` *identifier$_{opt}$*
        `class` *identifier$_{opt}$* = *type-id*
        `typename` *identifier$_{opt}$*
        `typename` *identifier$_{opt}$* = *type-id*
        `template` < *template-parameter-list* > `class` *identifier$_{opt}$*
        `template` < *template-parameter-list* > `class` *identifier$_{opt}$* = *id-expression*

template-id :
        template-name < *template-argument-list$_{opt}$* >

template-name :
        identifier

template-argument-list :
        template-argument
        template-argument-list , *template-argument*

template-argument :
> *assignment-expression*
> *type-id*
> *id-expression*

explicit-instantiation :
> `template` *declaration*

explicit-specialization :
> `template < >` *declaration*

A.13 Exception handling   [gram.except]

try-block:
> `try` *compound-statement handler-seq*

function-try-block:
> `try` *ctor-initializer$_{opt}$ function-body handler-seq*

handler-seq:
> *handler handler-seq$_{opt}$*

handler:
> `catch` (*exception-declaration*) *compound-statement*

exception-declaration:
> *type-specifier-seq declarator*
> *type-specifier-seq abstract-declarator*
> *type-specifier-seq*
> . . .

throw-expression:
> `throw` *assignment-expression$_{opt}$*

exception-specification:
> `throw` (*type-id-list$_{opt}$*)

type-id-list:
> *type-id*
> *type-id-list* , *type-id*

A.14 Preprocessing directives   [gram.cpp]

preprocessing-file:
> *group$_{opt}$*

group:
> *group-part*
> *group group-part*

group-part:
> *pp-tokens$_{opt}$ new-line*
> *if-section*
> *control-line*

if-section:
> *if-group elif-groups$_{opt}$ else-group$_{opt}$ endif-line*

if-group:

        `# if`   *constant-expression new-line group$_{opt}$*
        `# ifdef`   *identifier new-line group$_{opt}$*
        `# ifndef` *identifier new-line group$_{opt}$*

elif-groups:

        elif-group
        elif-groups elif-group

elif-group:

        `# elif`   *constant-expression new-line group$_{opt}$*

else-group:

        `# else`   *new-line group$_{opt}$*

endif-line:

        `# endif`   *new-line*

control-line:

        `# include` *pp-tokens new-line*
        `# define` *identifier replacement-list new-line*
        `# define` *identifier lparen identifier-list$_{opt}$) replacement-list new-line*
        `# undef`   *identifier new-line*
        `# line`   *pp-tokens new-line*
        `# error`   *pp-tokens$_{opt}$ new-line*
        `# pragma` *pp-tokens$_{opt}$ new-line*
        `#`   *new-line*

lparen:

        the left-parenthesis character without preceding white-space

replacement-list:

        pp-tokens$_{opt}$

pp-tokens:

        preprocessing-token
        pp-tokens preprocessing-token

new-line:

        the new-line character

Annex B [limits]
(informative)
Implementation quantities

1 Because computers are finite, C++ implementations are inevitably limited in the size of the programs they can successfully process. Every implementation shall document those limitations where known. This documentation may cite fixed limits where they exist, say how to compute variable limits as a function of available resources, or say that fixed limits do not exist or are unknown.

2 The limits may constrain quantities that include those described below or others. The bracketed number following each quantity is recommended as the minimum for that quantity. However, these quantities are only guidelines and do not determine compliance.

— Nesting levels of compound statements, iteration control structures, and selection control structures [256].

— Nesting levels of conditional inclusion [256].

— Pointer, array, and function declarators (in any combination) modifying an arithmetic, structure, union, or incomplete type in a declaration [256].

— Nesting levels of parenthesized expressions within a full expression [256].

— Number of characters in an internal identifier or macro name [1 024].

— Number of characters in an external identifier [1 024].

— External identifiers in one translation unit [65 536].

— Identifiers with block scope declared in one block [1 024].

— Macro identifiers simultaneously defined in one translation unit [65 536].

— Parameters in one function definition [256].

— Arguments in one function call [256].

— Parameters in one macro definition [256].

— Arguments in one macro invocation [256].

— Characters in one logical source line [65 536].

— Characters in a character string literal or wide string literal (after concatenation) [65 536].

— Size of an object [262 144].

— Nesting levels for #include files [256].

— Case labels for a switch statement (excluding those for any nested switch statements) [16 384].

— Data members in a single class, structure, or union [16 384].

— Enumeration constants in a single enumeration [4 096].

— Levels of nested class, structure, or union definitions in a single *struct-declaration-list* [256].

— Functions registered by atexit() [32].

— Direct and indirect base classes [16 384].

— Direct base classes for a single class [1 024].

— Members declared in a single class [4 096].

— Final overriding virtual functions in a class, accessible or not [16 384].

— Direct and indirect virtual bases of a class [1 024].

— Static members of a class [1 024].

— Friend declarations in a class [4 096].

— Access control declarations in a class [4 096].

— Member initializers in a constructor definition [6 144].

— Scope qualifications of one identifier [256].

— Nested external specifications [1 024].

— Template arguments in a template declaration [1 024].

— Recursively nested template instantiations [17].

— Handlers per `try` block [256].

— Throw specifications on a single function declaration [256].

Annex C [diff]
(informative)
Compatibility

1   The subclauses of this subclause list the differences between C++ and ISO C, by the chapters of this document.

C.1.1 Clause 2: lexical conventions [diff.lex]

2.3

Change: C++ style comments (/ /) are added
A pair of slashes now introduce a one-line comment.
Rationale: This style of comments is a useful addition to the language.
Effect on original feature: Change to semantics of well-defined feature. A valid ISO C expression containing a division operator followed immediately by a C-style comment will now be treated as a C++ style comment. For example:

```
{
    int a = 4;
    int b = 8                        //* divide by a*/ a;
    +a;
}
```

Difficulty of converting: Syntactic transformation. Just add white space after the division operator.
How widely used: The token sequence / /* probably occurs very seldom.

2.11

Change: New Keywords
New keywords are added to C++; see 2.11.
Rationale: These keywords were added in order to implement the new semantics of C++.
Effect on original feature: Change to semantics of well-defined feature. Any ISO C programs that used any of these keywords as identifiers are not valid C++ programs.
Difficulty of converting: Syntactic transformation. Converting one specific program is easy. Converting a large collection of related programs takes more work.
How widely used: Common.

2.13.2

Change: Type of character literal is changed from `int` to `char`
Rationale: This is needed for improved overloaded function argument type matching. For example:

```
int function( int i );
int function( char c );

function( 'x' );
```

It is preferable that this call match the second version of function rather than the first.

Effect on original feature: Change to semantics of well-defined feature. ISO C programs which depend on

```
sizeof('x') == sizeof(int)
```

will not work the same as C++ programs.

Difficulty of converting: Simple.

How widely used: Programs which depend upon `sizeof('x')` are probably rare.

Subclause _lex.string:

Change: String literals made const
The type of a string literal is changed from "array of `char`" to "array of `const char`." The type of a wide string literal is changed from "array of `wchar_t`" to "array of `const wchar_t`."

Rationale: This avoids calling an inappropriate overloaded function, which might expect to be able to modify its argument.

Effect on original feature: Change to semantics of well-defined feature.

Difficulty of converting: Simple syntactic transformation, because string literals can be converted to `char*`; (4.2). The most common cases are handled by a new but deprecated standard conversion:

```
char* p = "abc";            // valid in C, deprecated in C++
char* q = expr ? "abc" : "de";   // valid in C, invalid in C++
```

How widely used: Programs that have a legitimate reason to treat string literals as pointers to potentially modifiable memory are probably rare.

C.1.2 Clause 3: basic concepts   [diff.basic]

3.1

Change: C++ does not have "tentative definitions" as in C
E.g., at file scope,

```
int i;
int i;
```

is valid in C, invalid in C++. This makes it impossible to define mutually referential file-local static objects, if initializers are restricted to the syntactic forms of C. For example,

```
struct X { int i; struct X *next; };

static struct X a;
static struct X b = { 0, &a };
static struct X a = { 1, &b };
```

Rationale: This avoids having different initialization rules for built-in types and user-defined types.

Effect on original feature: Deletion of semantically well-defined feature.

Difficulty of converting: Semantic transformation. In C++, the initializer for one of a set of mutually-referential file-local static objects must invoke a function call to achieve the initialization.

How widely used: Seldom.

3.3

Change: A `struct` is a scope in C++, not in C

Rationale: Class scope is crucial to C++, and a struct is a class.

Effect on original feature: Change to semantics of well-defined feature.

Difficulty of converting: Semantic transformation.

How widely used: C programs use `struct` extremely frequently, but the change is only noticeable when `struct`, enumeration, or enumerator names are referred to outside the `struct`. The latter is probably rare.

3.5 [also 7.1.5]

Change: A name of file scope that is explicitly declared `const`, and not explicitly declared `extern`, has internal linkage, while in C it would have external linkage

Rationale: Because `const` objects can be used as compile-time values in C++, this feature urges programmers to provide explicit initializer values for each `const`. This feature allows the user to put `const` objects in header files that are included in many compilation units.

Effect on original feature: Change to semantics of well-defined feature.

Difficulty of converting: Semantic transformation

How widely used: Seldom

3.6

Change: Main cannot be called recursively and cannot have its address taken

Rationale: The main function may require special actions.

Effect on original feature: Deletion of semantically well-defined feature

Difficulty of converting: Trivial: create an intermediary function such as `mymain(argc, argv)`.

How widely used: Seldom

3.9

Change: C allows "compatible types" in several places, C++ does not

For example, otherwise-identical `struct` types with different tag names are "compatible" in C but are distinctly different types in C++.

Rationale: Stricter type checking is essential for C++.

Effect on original feature: Deletion of semantically well-defined feature.

Difficulty of converting: Semantic transformation. The "typesafe linkage" mechanism will find many, but not all, of such problems. Those problems not found by typesafe linkage will continue to function properly, according to the "layout compatibility rules" of this International Standard.

How widely used: Common.

4.10

Change: Converting `void*` to a pointer-to-object type requires casting

```
char a[10];
void *b=a;
void foo() {
char *c=b;
}
```

ISO C will accept this usage of pointer to void being assigned to a pointer to object type. C++ will not.

Rationale: C++ tries harder than C to enforce compile-time type safety.

Effect on original feature: Deletion of semantically well-defined feature.

Difficulty of converting: Could be automated. Violations will be diagnosed by the C++ translator. The fix is to add a cast For example:

```
char *c = (char *) b;
```

How widely used: This is fairly widely used but it is good programming practice to add the cast when assigning pointer-to-void to pointer-to-object. Some ISO C translators will give a warning if the cast is not used.

4.10

Change: Only pointers to non-const and non-volatile objects may be implicitly converted to `void*`
Rationale: This improves type safety.
Effect on original feature: Deletion of semantically well-defined feature.
Difficulty of converting: Could be automated. A C program containing such an implicit conversion from (e.g.) pointer-to-const-object to void* will receive a diagnostic message. The correction is to add an explicit cast.
How widely used: Seldom.

C.1.3 Clause 5: expressions   [diff.expr]

5.2.2

Change: Implicit declaration of functions is not allowed
Rationale: The type-safe nature of C++.
Effect on original feature: Deletion of semantically well-defined feature. Note: the original feature was labeled as "obsolescent" in ISO C.
Difficulty of converting: Syntactic transformation. Facilities for producing explicit function declarations are fairly widespread commercially.
How widely used: Common.

5.3.3, 5.4

Change: Types must be declared in declarations, not in expressions
In C, a sizeof expression or cast expression may create a new type. For example,

```
p = (void*)(struct x {int i;} *)0;
```

declares a new type, struct x .
Rationale: This prohibition helps to clarify the location of declarations in the source code.
Effect on original feature: Deletion of a semantically well-defined feature.
Difficulty of converting: Syntactic transformation.
How widely used: Seldom.

5.16, 5.17, 5.18

Change: The result of a conditional expression, an assignment expression, or a comma expression may be an lvalue
Rationale: C++ is an object-oriented language, placing relatively more emphasis on lvalues. For example, functions may return lvalues.
Effect on original feature: Change to semantics of well-defined feature. Some C expressions that implicitly rely on lvalue-to-rvalue conversions will yield different results. For example,

```
char arr[100];
sizeof(0, arr)
```

yields `100` in C++ and `sizeof(char*)` in C.
Difficulty of converting: Programs must add explicit casts to the appropriate rvalue.
How widely used: Rare.

C.1.4 Clause 6: statements   [diff.stat]

6.4.2, 6.6.4 (`switch` **and** `goto` **statements**)

Change: It is now invalid to jump past a declaration with explicit or implicit initializer (except across entire block not entered)
Rationale: Constructors used in initializers may allocate resources which need to be de-allocated upon leaving the block. Allowing jump past initializers would require complicated run-time determination of allocation. Furthermore, any use of the uninitialized object could be a disaster. With this simple compile-time rule, C++ assures that if an initialized variable is in scope, then it has assuredly been initialized.
Effect on original feature: Deletion of semantically well-defined feature.
Difficulty of converting: Semantic transformation.
How widely used: Seldom.

6.6.3

Change: It is now invalid to return (explicitly or implicitly) from a function which is declared to return a value without actually returning a value
Rationale: The caller and callee may assume fairly elaborate return-value mechanisms for the return of class objects. If some flow paths execute a return without specifying any value, the implementation must embody many more complications. Besides, promising to return a value of a given type, and then not returning such a value, has always been recognized to be a questionable practice, tolerated only because very-old C had no distinction between void functions and int functions.
Effect on original feature: Deletion of semantically well-defined feature.
Difficulty of converting: Semantic transformation. Add an appropriate return value to the source code, e.g. zero.
How widely used: Seldom. For several years, many existing C implementations have produced warnings in this case.

C.1.5 Clause 7: declarations   [diff.dcl]

7.1.1

Change: In C++, the `static` or `extern` specifiers can only be applied to names of objects or functions Using these specifiers with type declarations is illegal in C++. In C, these specifiers are ignored when used on type declarations. Example:

```
static struct S {            // valid C, invalid in C++
int i;
// ...
};
```

Rationale: Storage class specifiers don't have any meaning when associated with a type. In C++, class members can be defined with the `static` storage class specifier. Allowing storage class specifiers on type declarations could render the code confusing for users.
Effect on original feature: Deletion of semantically well-defined feature.

Difficulty of converting: Syntactic transformation.
How widely used: Seldom.

7.1.3

Change: A C++ typedef name must be different from any class type name declared in the same scope (except if the typedef is a synonym of the class name with the same name). In C, a typedef name and a struct tag name declared in the same scope can have the same name (because they have different name spaces)
Example:

```
typedef struct name1 { /*...*/ } name1;          // valid C and C++
struct name { /*...*/ };
typedef int name;                    // valid C, invalid C++
```

Rationale: For ease of use, C++ doesn't require that a type name be prefixed with the keywords `class`, `struct` or `union` when used in object declarations or type casts. Example:

```
class name { /*...*/ };
name i;                      // i has type class name
```

Effect on original feature: Deletion of semantically well-defined feature.
Difficulty of converting: Semantic transformation. One of the 2 types has to be renamed.
How widely used: Seldom.

7.1.5 [see also 3.5]

Change: const objects must be initialized in C++ but can be left uninitialized in C
Rationale: A const object cannot be assigned to so it must be initialized to hold a useful value.
Effect on original feature: Deletion of semantically well-defined feature.
Difficulty of converting: Semantic transformation.
How widely used: Seldom.

7.1.5 (type specifiers)

Change: Banning implicit int
In C++ a *decl-specifier-seq* must contain a *type-specifier*. In the following example, the left-hand column presents valid C; the right-hand column presents equivalent C++:

```
void f(const parm);           void f(const int parm);
const n = 3;                  const int n = 3;
main()                        int main()
   /* ... */                     /* ... */
```

Rationale: In C++, implicit int creates several opportunities for ambiguity between expressions involving function-like casts and declarations. Explicit declaration is increasingly considered to be proper style. Liaison with WG14 (C) indicated support for (at least) deprecating implicit int in the next revision of C.
Effect on original feature: Deletion of semantically well-defined feature.
Difficulty of converting: Syntactic transformation. Could be automated.
How widely used: Common.

7.2

Change: C++ objects of enumeration type can only be assigned values of the same enumeration type. In C, objects of enumeration type can be assigned values of any integral type

Example:

```
enum color { red, blue, green };
color c = 1;                          // valid C, invalid C++
```

Rationale: The type-safe nature of C++.

Effect on original feature: Deletion of semantically well-defined feature.

Difficulty of converting: Syntactic transformation. (The type error produced by the assignment can be automatically corrected by applying an explicit cast.)

How widely used: Common.

7.2

Change: In C++, the type of an enumerator is its enumeration. In C, the type of an enumerator is `int`.

Example:

```
enum e { A };
sizeof(A) == sizeof(int)        // in C
sizeof(A) == sizeof(e)          // in C++
/* and sizeof(int) is not necessary equal to sizeof(e) */
```

Rationale: In C++, an enumeration is a distinct type.

Effect on original feature: Change to semantics of well-defined feature.

Difficulty of converting: Semantic transformation.

How widely used: Seldom. The only time this affects existing C code is when the size of an enumerator is taken. Taking the size of an enumerator is not a common C coding practice.

C.1.6 Clause 8: declarators   [diff.decl]

8.3.5

Change: In C++, a function declared with an empty parameter list takes no arguments.
In C, an empty parameter list means that the number and type of the function arguments are unknown"

Example:

```
int f();                              // means int f(void)    in C++
                                      //     int f(unknown) in C
```

Rationale: This is to avoid erroneous function calls (i.e. function calls with the wrong number or type of arguments).

Effect on original feature: Change to semantics of well-defined feature. This feature was marked as "obsolescent" in C.

Difficulty of converting: Syntactic transformation. The function declarations using C incomplete declaration style must be completed to become full prototype declarations. A program may need to be updated further if different calls to the same (non-prototype) function have different numbers of arguments or if the type of corresponding arguments differed.

How widely used: Common.

8.3.5 [see 5.3.3]

Change: In C++, types may not be defined in return or parameter types. In C, these type definitions are allowed

Example:

```
void f( struct S { int a; } arg ) {}        // valid C, invalid C++
enum E { A, B, C } f() {}                    // valid C, invalid C++
```

Rationale: When comparing types in different compilation units, C++ relies on name equivalence when C relies on structural equivalence. Regarding parameter types: since the type defined in an parameter list would be in the scope of the function, the only legal calls in C++ would be from within the function itself.
Effect on original feature: Deletion of semantically well-defined feature.
Difficulty of converting: Semantic transformation. The type definitions must be moved to file scope, or in header files.
How widely used: Seldom. This style of type definitions is seen as poor coding style.

8.4

Change: In C++, the syntax for function definition excludes the "old-style" C function. In C, "old-style" syntax is allowed, but deprecated as "obsolescent."
Rationale: Prototypes are essential to type safety.
Effect on original feature: Deletion of semantically well-defined feature.
Difficulty of converting: Syntactic transformation.
How widely used: Common in old programs, but already known to be obsolescent.

8.5.2

Change: In C++, when initializing an array of character with a string, the number of characters in the string (including the terminating '\0') must not exceed the number of elements in the array. In C, an array can be initialized with a string even if the array is not large enough to contain the string terminating '\0'
Example:

```
char array[4] = "abcd";              // valid C, invalid C++
```

Rationale: When these non-terminated arrays are manipulated by standard string routines, there is potential for major catastrophe.
Effect on original feature: Deletion of semantically well-defined feature.
Difficulty of converting: Semantic transformation. The arrays must be declared one element bigger to contain the string terminating '\0'.
How widely used: Seldom. This style of array initialization is seen as poor coding style.

C.1.7 Clause 9: classes   [diff.class]

9.1 [see also 7.1.3]

Change: In C++, a class declaration introduces the class name into the scope where it is declared and hides any object, function or other declaration of that name in an enclosing scope. In C, an inner scope declaration of a struct tag name never hides the name of an object or function in an outer scope
Example:

```
int x[99];
void f()
{
        struct x { int a; };
        sizeof(x);   /* size of the array in C     */
        /* size of the struct in C++ */
}
```

Rationale: This is one of the few incompatibilities between C and C++ that can be attributed to the new C++ name space definition where a name can be declared as a type and as a nontype in a single scope causing the nontype name to hide the type name and requiring that the keywords class, struct, union or enum be used to refer to the type name. This new name space definition provides important notational conveniences to C++ programmers and helps making the use of the user-defined types as similar as possible to the use of built-in types. The advantages of the new name space definition were judged to outweigh by far the incompatibility with C described above.

Effect on original feature: Change to semantics of well-defined feature.

Difficulty of converting: Semantic transformation. If the hidden name that needs to be accessed is at global scope, the :: C++ operator can be used. If the hidden name is at block scope, either the type or the struct tag has to be renamed.

How widely used: Seldom.

9.7

Change: In C++, the name of a nested class is local to its enclosing class. In C the name of the nested class belongs to the same scope as the name of the outermost enclosing class

Example:

```
struct X {
        struct Y { /* ... */ } y;
};
struct Y yy;                            // valid C, invalid C++
```

Rationale: C++ classes have member functions which require that classes establish scopes. The C rule would leave classes as an incomplete scope mechanism which would prevent C++ programmers from maintaining locality within a class. A coherent set of scope rules for C++ based on the C rule would be very complicated and C++ programmers would be unable to predict reliably the meanings of nontrivial examples involving nested or local functions.

Effect on original feature: Change of semantics of well-defined feature.

Difficulty of converting: Semantic transformation. To make the struct type name visible in the scope of the enclosing struct, the struct tag could be declared in the scope of the enclosing struct, before the enclosing struct is defined. Example:

```
struct Y;                              // struct Y and struct X are at the same scope
struct X {
        struct Y { /* ... */ } y;
};
```

All the definitions of C struct types enclosed in other struct definitions and accessed outside the scope of the enclosing struct could be exported to the scope of the enclosing struct. Note: this is a consequence of the difference in scope rules, which is documented in 3.3.

How widely used: Seldom.

9.9

Change: In C++, a typedef name may not be redefined in a class declaration after being used in the declaration

Example:

```
typedef int I;
struct S {
        I i;
        int I;                         // valid C, invalid C++
};
```

Rationale: When classes become complicated, allowing such a redefinition after the type has been used can create confusion for C++ programmers as to what the meaning of 'I' really is.

Effect on original feature: Deletion of semantically well-defined feature.

Difficulty of converting: Semantic transformation. Either the type or the struct member has to be renamed.
How widely used: Seldom.

C.1.8 Clause 12: special member functions   [diff.special]

12.8 (copying class objects)

Change: Copying volatile objects
The implicitly-declared copy constructor and implicitly-declared copy assignment operator cannot make a copy of a volatile lvalue. For example, the following is valid in ISO C:

```
struct X { int i; };
struct X x1, x2;
volatile struct X x3 = {0};
x1 = x3;                    // invalid C++
x2 = x3;                    // also invalid C++
```

Rationale: Several alternatives were debated at length. Changing the parameter to `volatile const X&` would greatly complicate the generation of efficient code for class objects. Discussion of providing two alternative signatures for these implicitly-defined operations raised unanswered concerns about creating ambiguities and complicating the rules that specify the formation of these operators according to the bases and members.
Effect on original feature: Deletion of semantically well-defined feature.
Difficulty of converting: Semantic transformation. If volatile semantics are required for the copy, a user-declared constructor or assignment must be provided. If non-volatile semantics are required, an explicit `const_cast` can be used.
How widely used: Seldom.

C.1.9 Clause 16: preprocessing directives   [diff.cpp]

16.8 (predefined names)

Change: Whether `__STDC__` is defined and if so, what its value is, are implementation-defined
Rationale: C++ is not identical to ISO C. Mandating that `__STDC__` be defined would require that translators make an incorrect claim. Each implementation must choose the behavior that will be most useful to its marketplace.
Effect on original feature: Change to semantics of well-defined feature.
Difficulty of converting: Semantic transformation.
How widely used: Programs and headers that reference `__STDC__` are quite common.

C.2 Standard C library   [diff.library]

1   This subclause summarizes the contents of the C++ Standard library included from the Standard C library. It also summarizes the explicit changes in definitions, declarations, or behavior from the ISO/IEC 9899:1990 and ISO/IEC 9899:1990/DAM 1 noted in other subclauses (17.4.1.2, 18.1, 21.4).

2   The C++ Standard library provides 54 standard macros from the C library, as shown in Table 95.

3   The header names (enclosed in < and >) indicate that the macro may be defined in more than one header. All such definitions are equivalent (3.2).

Table 95—Standard Macros

assert	HUGE_VAL	NULL <cstring>	SIGILL	va_arg
BUFSIZ	LC_ALL	NULL <ctime>	SIGINT	va_end
CLOCKS_PER_SEC	LC_COLLATE	NULL <cwchar>	SIGSEGV	va_start
EDOM	LC_CTYPE	offsetof	SIGTERM	WCHAR_MAX
EOF	LC_MONETARY	RAND_MAX	SIG_DFL	WCHAR_MIN
ERANGE	LC_NUMERIC	SEEK_CUR	SIG_ERR	WEOF <cwchar>
errno	LC_TIME	SEEK_END	SIG_IGN	WEOF <cwctype>
EXIT_FAILURE	L_tmpnam	SEEK_SET	stderr	_IOFBF
EXIT_SUCCESS	MB_CUR_MAX	setjmp	stdin	_IOLBF
FILENAME_MAX	NULL <cstddef>	SIGABRT	stdout	_IONBF
FOPEN_MAX	NULL <cstdio>	SIGFPE	TMP_MAX	

4   The C++ Standard library provides 45 standard values from the C library, as shown in Table 96:

Table 96—Standard Values

CHAR_BIT	FLT_DIG	INT_MIN	MB_LEN_MAX
CHAR_MAX	FLT_EPSILON	LDBL_DIG	SCHAR_MAX
CHAR_MIN	FLT_MANT_DIG	LDBL_EPSILON	SCHAR_MIN
DBL_DIG	FLT_MAX	LDBL_MANT_DIG	SHRT_MAX
DBL_EPSILON	FLT_MAX_10_EXP	LDBL_MAX	SHRT_MIN
DBL_MANT_DIG	FLT_MAX_EXP	LDBL_MAX_10_EXP	UCHAR_MAX
DBL_MAX	FLT_MIN	LDBL_MAX_EXP	UINT_MAX
DBL_MAX_10_EXP	FLT_MIN_10_EXP	LDBL_MIN	ULONG_MAX
DBL_MAX_EXP	FLT_MIN_EXP	LDBL_MIN_10_EXP	USHRT_MAX
DBL_MIN	FLT_RADIX	LDBL_MIN_EXP	
DBL_MIN_10_EXP	FLT_ROUNDS	LONG_MAX	
DBL_MIN_EXP	INT_MAX	LONG_MIN	

5   The C++ Standard library provides 19 standard types from the C library, as shown in Table 97:

Table 97—Standard Types

clock_t	ldiv_t	size_t <cstdio>	wctrans_t
div_t	mbstate_t	size_t <cstring>	wctype_t
FILE	ptrdiff_t	size_t <ctime>	wint_t <cwchar>
fpos_t	sig_atomic_t	time_t	wint_t <cwctype>
jmp_buf	size_t <cstddef>	va_list	

6   The C++ Standard library provides 2 standard structures from the C library, as shown in Table 98:

Table 98—Standard Structs

lconv	tm

7   The C++ Standard library provides 209 standard functions from the C library, as shown in Table 99:

Table 99—Standard Functions

abort	fmod	isupper	mktime	strftime	wcrtomb
abs	fopen	iswalnum	modf	strlen	wcscat
acos	fprintf	iswalpha	perror	strncat	wcschr
asctime	fputc	iswcntrl	pow	strncmp	wcscmp
asin	fputs	iswctype	printf	strncpy	wcscoll
atan	fputwc	iswdigit	putc	strpbrk	wcscpy
atan2	fputws	iswgraph	putchar	strrchr	wcscspn
atexit	fread	iswlower	puts	strspn	wcsftime
atof	free	iswprint	putwc	strstr	wcslen
atoi	freopen	iswpunct	putwchar	strtod	wcsncat
atol	frexp	iswspace	qsort	strtok	wcsncmp
bsearch	fscanf	iswupper	raise	strtol	wcsncpy
btowc	fseek	iswxdigit	rand	strtoul	wcspbrk
calloc	fsetpos	isxdigit	realloc	strxfrm	wcsrchr
ceil	ftell	labs	remove	swprintf	wcsrtombs
clearerr	fwide	ldexp	rename	swscanf	wcsspn
clock	fwprintf	ldiv	rewind	system	wcsstr
cos	fwrite	localeconv	scanf	tan	wcstod
cosh	fwscanf	localtime	setbuf	tanh	wcstok
ctime	getc	log	setlocale	time	wcstol
difftime	getchar	log10	setvbuf	tmpfile	wcstombs
div	getenv	longjmp	signal	tmpnam	wcstoul
exit	gets	malloc	sin	tolower	wcsxfrm
exp	getwc	mblen	sinh	toupper	wctob
fabs	getwchar	mbrlen	sprintf	towctrans	wctomb
fclose	gmtime	mbrtowc	sqrt	towlower	wctrans
feof	isalnum	mbsinit	srand	towupper	wctype
ferror	isalpha	mbsrtowcs	sscanf	ungetc	wmemchr
fflush	iscntrl	mbstowcs	strcat	ungetwc	wmemcmp
fgetc	isdigit	mbtowc	strchr	vfprintf	wmemcpy
fgetpos	isgraph	memchr	strcmp	vfwprintf	wmemmove
fgets	islower	memcmp	strcoll	vprintf	wmemset
fgetwc	isprint	memcpy	strcpy	vsprintf	wprintf
fgetws	ispunct	memmove	strcspn	vswprintf	wscanf
floor	isspace	memset	strerror	vwprintf	

C.2.1 Modifications to headers   [diff.mods.to.headers]

1   For compatibility with the Standard C library, the C++ Standard library provides the 18 *C headers* (D.5), but their use is deprecated in C++.

C.2.2 Modifications to definitions   **[diff.mods.to.definitions]**

C.2.2.1 Type `wchar_t`   **[diff.wchar.t]**

1   `wchar_t` is a keyword in this International Standard (2.11). It does not appear as a type name defined in any of `<cstddef>`, `<cstdlib>`, or `<cwchar>` (21.4).

C.2.2.2 Header `<iso646.h>`   **[diff.header.iso646.h]**

1   The tokens `and`, `and_eq`, `bitand`, `bitor`, `compl`, `not_eq`, `not`, `or`, `or_eq`, `xor`, and `xor_eq` are keywords in this International Standard (2.11). They do not appear as macro names defined in `<ciso646>`.

C.2.2.3 Macro `NULL`   **[diff.null]**

1   The macro `NULL`, defined in any of `<clocale>`, `<cstddef>`, `<cstdio>`, `<cstdlib>`, `<cstring>`, `<ctime>`, or `<cwchar>`, is an implementation-defined C++ null pointer constant in this International Standard (18.1).

C.2.3 Modifications to declarations   **[diff.mods.to.declarations]**

1   Header `<cstring>`: The following functions have different declarations:

— `strchr`

— `strpbrk`

— `strrchr`

— `strstr`

— `memchr`

2   21.4 describes the changes.

C.2.4 Modifications to behavior   **[diff.mods.to.behavior]**

1   Header `<cstdlib>`: The following functions have different behavior:

— `atexit`

— `exit`

— `abort`

18.3 describes the changes.

2   Header `<csetjmp>`: The following functions have different behavior:

— `longjmp`

18.7 describes the changes.

C.2.4.1 Macro `offsetof(`*type, member-designator*`)`   **[diff.offsetof]**

1   The macro `offsetof`, defined in `<cstddef>`, accepts a restricted set of *type* arguments in this International Standard. 18.1 describes the change.

C.2.4.2 Memory allocation functions   [diff.malloc]

1   The functions `calloc`, `malloc`, and `realloc` are restricted in this International Standard. 20.4.6
describes the changes.

Annex D   [depr]
(normative)
Compatibility features

1   This clause describes features of the C++ Standard that are specified for compatibility with existing implementations.

2   These are deprecated features, where *deprecated* is defined as: Normative for the current edition of the Standard, but not guaranteed to be part of the Standard in future revisions.

D.1 Increment operator with `bool` operand   [depr.incr.bool]

1   The use of an operand of type `bool` with the ++ operator is deprecated (see 5.3.2 and 5.2.6).

D.2 static keyword   [depr.static]

1   The use of the `static` keyword is deprecated when declaring objects in namespace scope (see 3.3.5).

D.3 Access declarations   [depr.access.dcl]

1   Access declarations are deprecated (see 11.3).

D.4 Implicit conversion from const strings   [depr.string]

1   The implicit conversion from const to non-const qualification for string literals (4.2) is deprecated.

D.5 Standard C library headers   [depr.c.headers]

1   For compatibility with the Standard C library, the C++ Standard library provides the 18 *C headers*, as shown in Table 100:

Table 100—C Headers

`<assert.h>`	`<iso646.h>`	`<setjmp.h>`	`<stdio.h>`	`<wchar.h>`
`<ctype.h>`	`<limits.h>`	`<signal.h>`	`<stdlib.h>`	`<wctype.h>`
`<errno.h>`	`<locale.h>`	`<stdarg.h>`	`<string.h>`	
`<float.h>`	`<math.h>`	`<stddef.h>`	`<time.h>`	

2   Every C header, each of which has a name of the form *name*.h, behaves as if each name placed in the Standard library namespace by the corresponding *cname* header is also placed within the namespace scope of the namespace `std` and is followed by an explicit *using-declaration* (7.3.3).

3   [*Example:* The header `<cstdlib>` provides its declarations and definitions within the namespace `std`. The header `<stdlib.h>` makes these available also in the global namespace, much as in the C Standard. —*end example*]

1   The following member names are in addition to names specified in clause 27:

```
namespace std {
  class ios_base {
  public:
    typedef T1   io_state;
    typedef T2 open_mode;
    typedef T3   seek_dir;
    typedef OFF_T  streamoff;
    typedef POS_T  streampos;
    // remainder unchanged
  };
}
```

2   The type `io_state` is a synonym for an integer type (indicated here as *T1*) that permits certain member functions to overload others on parameters of type `iostate` and provide the same behavior.

3   The type `open_mode` is a synonym for an integer type (indicated here as *T2*) that permits certain member functions to overload others on parameters of type `openmode` and provide the same behavior.

4   The type `seek_dir` is a synonym for an integer type (indicated here as *T3*) that permits certain member functions to overload others on parameters of type `seekdir` and provide the same behavior.

5   The type `streamoff` is an implementation-defined type that satisfies the requirements of type *OFF_T* (27.4.1).

6   The type `streampos` is an implementation-defined type that satisfies the requirements of type *POS_T* (27.2).

7   An implementation may provide the following additional member function, which has the effect of calling `sbumpc()` (27.5.2.2.3):

```
namespace std {
  template<class charT, class traits = char_traits<charT> >
  class basic_streambuf {
  public:
    void stossc();
    // remainder unchanged
  };
}
```

8   An implementation may provide the following member functions that overload signatures specified in clause 27:

```
namespace std {
  template<class charT, class Traits> class basic_ios {
  public:
    void clear(io_state state);
    void setstate(io_state state);
    void exceptions(io_state);
    // remainder unchanged
  };

  class ios_base {
  public:
    // remainder unchanged
  };
```

```
template<class charT, class traits = char_traits<charT> >
class basic_streambuf {
public:
  pos_type pubseekoff(off_type off, ios_base::seek_dir way,
            ios_base::open_mode which = ios_base::in | ios_base::out);
  pos_type pubseekpos(pos_type sp,
            ios_base::open_mode which);
  // remainder unchanged
};

template <class charT, class traits = char_traits<charT> >
class basic_filebuf : public basic_streambuf<charT,traits> {
public:
  basic_filebuf<charT,traits>* open
      (const char* s, ios_base::open_mode mode);
  // remainder unchanged
};

template <class charT, class traits = char_traits<charT> >
class basic_ifstream : public basic_istream<charT,traits> {
public:
  void open(const char* s, ios_base::open_mode mode);
  // remainder unchanged
};

template <class charT, class traits = char_traits<charT> >
class basic_ofstream : public basic_ostream<charT,traits> {
public:
  void open(const char* s, ios_base::open_mode mode);
  // remainder unchanged
};

}
```

9   The effects of these functions is to call the corresponding member function specified in clause 27.

D.7 `char*` streams   [depr.str.strstreams]

1   The header `<strstream>` defines three types that associate stream buffers with character array objects
and assist reading and writing such objects.

D.7.1 Class `strstreambuf`   [depr.strstreambuf]

```
namespace std {
  class strstreambuf : public basic_streambuf<char> {
  public:
    explicit strstreambuf(streamsize alsize_arg = 0);
    strstreambuf(void* (*palloc_arg)(size_t), void (*pfree_arg)(void*));
    strstreambuf(char* gnext_arg, streamsize n, char* pbeg_arg = 0);
    strstreambuf(const char* gnext_arg, streamsize n);

    strstreambuf(signed char* gnext_arg, streamsize n,
                 signed char* pbeg_arg = 0);
    strstreambuf(const signed char* gnext_arg, streamsize n);
    strstreambuf(unsigned char* gnext_arg, streamsize n,
                 unsigned char* pbeg_arg = 0);
    strstreambuf(const unsigned char* gnext_arg, streamsize n);
```

```
        virtual ~strstreambuf();

        void   freeze(bool freezefl = true);
        char*  str();
        int    pcount();

    protected:
        virtual int_type overflow (int_type c = EOF);
        virtual int_type pbackfail(int_type c = EOF);
        virtual int_type underflow();
        virtual pos_type seekoff(off_type off, ios_base::seekdir way,
                          ios_base::openmode which
                          = ios_base::in | ios_base::out);
        virtual pos_type seekpos(pos_type sp, ios_base::openmode which
                          = ios_base::in | ios_base::out);
        virtual streambuf* setbuf(char* s, streamsize n);

    private:
//   typedef T1 strstate;                         exposition only
//   static const strstate allocated;             exposition only
//   static const strstate constant;              exposition only
//   static const strstate dynamic;               exposition only
//   static const strstate frozen;                exposition only
//   strstate strmode;                            exposition only
//   streamsize alsize;                           exposition only
//   void* (*palloc)(size_t);                     exposition only
//   void (*pfree)(void*);                        exposition only
    };
}
```

1   The class `strstreambuf` associates the input sequence, and possibly the output sequence, with an object of some *character* array type, whose elements store arbitrary values. The array object has several attributes.

2   [*Note:* For the sake of exposition, these are represented as elements of a bitmask type (indicated here as *T1*) called `strstate`. The elements are:

— `allocated`, set when a dynamic array object has been allocated, and hence should be freed by the destructor for the `strstreambuf` object;

— `constant`, set when the array object has `const` elements, so the output sequence cannot be written;

— `dynamic`, set when the array object is allocated (or reallocated) as necessary to hold a character sequence that can change in length;

— `frozen`, set when the program has requested that the array object not be altered, reallocated, or freed. —*end note*]

3   [*Note:* For the sake of exposition, the maintained data is presented here as:

— `strstate strmode`, the attributes of the array object associated with the `strstreambuf` object;

— `int alsize`, the suggested minimum size for a dynamic array object;

— `void* (*palloc)(size_t)`, points to the function to call to allocate a dynamic array object;

— `void (*pfree)(void*)`, points to the function to call to free a dynamic array object. —*end note*]

4   Each object of class `strstreambuf` has a *seekable area*, delimited by the pointers *seeklow* and *seekhigh*. If *gnext* is a null pointer, the seekable area is undefined. Otherwise, *seeklow* equals *gbeg* and *seekhigh* is either *pend*, if *pend* is not a null pointer, or *gend*.

D.7.1.1 `strstreambuf` constructors [depr.strstreambuf.cons]

```
explicit strstreambuf(streamsize alsize_arg = 0);
```

1 **Effects:** Constructs an object of class `strstreambuf`, initializing the base class with `streambuf()`. The postconditions of this function are indicated in Table 101:

Table 101—`strstreambuf(streamsize)` effects

Element	Value
`strmode`	`dynamic`
`alsize`	`alsize_arg`
`palloc`	a null pointer
`pfree`	a null pointer

```
strstreambuf(void* (*palloc_arg)(size_t), void (*pfree_arg)(void*));
```

2 **Effects:** Constructs an object of class `strstreambuf`, initializing the base class with `streambuf()`. The postconditions of this function are indicated in Table 102:

Table 102—`strstreambuf(void* (*)(size_t),void (*)(void*)` effects

Element	Value
`strmode`	`dynamic`
`alsize`	an unspecified value
`palloc`	`palloc_arg`
`pfree`	`pfree_arg`

```
strstreambuf(char* gnext_arg, streamsize n, char *pbeg_arg = 0);
strstreambuf(signed char* gnext_arg, streamsize n,
                                    signed char *pbeg_arg = 0);
strstreambuf(unsigned char* gnext_arg, streamsize n,
                                    unsigned char *pbeg_arg = 0);
```

3 **Effects:** Constructs an object of class `strstreambuf`, initializing the base class with `streambuf()`. The postconditions of this function are indicated in Table 103:

Table 103—`strstreambuf(charT*,streamsize,charT*)` effects

Element	Value
`strmode`	0
`alsize`	an unspecified value
`palloc`	a null pointer
`pfree`	a null pointer

4 *gnext_arg* shall point to the first element of an array object whose number of elements N is determined as follows:

— If $n > 0$, N is n.

— If $n == 0$, N is `std::strlen(gnext_arg)`.

— If $n < 0$, N is `INT_MAX`.[312]

---
[312] The function signature `strlen(const char*)` is declared in `<cstring>`. (21.4). The macro `INT_MAX` is defined in `<climits>` (18.2).

5   If `pbeg_arg` is a null pointer, the function executes:

     setg(*gnext_arg, gnext_arg, gnext_arg + N*);

6   Otherwise, the function executes:

     setg(*gnext_arg, gnext_arg, pbeg_arg*);
     setp(*pbeg_arg, pbeg_arg + N*);

```
strstreambuf(const char* gnext_arg, streamsize n);
strstreambuf(const signed char* gnext_arg, streamsize n);
strstreambuf(const unsigned char* gnext_arg, streamsize n);
```

7   **Effects:** Behaves the same as `strstreambuf((char*)`*gnext_arg*`,`*n*`)`, except that the constructor also sets *constant* in *strmode*.

```
virtual ~strstreambuf();
```

8   **Effects:** Destroys an object of class `strstreambuf`. The function frees the dynamically allocated array object only if *strmode* `&` *allocated* `!=` `0` and *strmode* `&` *frozen* `==` `0`. (_lib.strstreambuf.virtuals_ describes how a dynamically allocated array object is freed.)

D.7.1.2 Member functions   [depr.strstreambuf.members]

```
void freeze(bool freezefl = true);
```

1   **Effects:** If *strmode* `&` *dynamic* is non-zero, alters the freeze status of the dynamic array object as follows:

— If *freezefl* is `true`, the function sets *frozen* in *strmode*.

— Otherwise, it clears *frozen* in `strmode`.

```
char* str();
```

2   **Effects:** Calls `freeze()`, then returns the beginning pointer for the input sequence, *gbeg*.
3   **Notes:** The return value can be a null pointer.

```
int pcount() const;
```

4   **Effects:** If the next pointer for the output sequence, *pnext*, is a null pointer, returns zero. Otherwise, returns the current effective length of the array object as the next pointer minus the beginning pointer for the output sequence, *pnext* - *pbeg*.

D.7.1.3 `strstreambuf` overridden virtual functions   [depr.strstreambuf.virtuals]

```
int_type overflow(int_type c = EOF);
```

1   **Effects:** Appends the character designated by *c* to the output sequence, if possible, in one of two ways:

— If *c* `!=` EOF and if either the output sequence has a write position available or the function makes a write position available (as described below), assigns *c* to `*`*pnext*`++`.
Returns `(unsigned char)`*c*.

— If *c* `==` EOF, there is no character to append.
Returns a value other than EOF.

2   Returns EOF to indicate failure.
3   **Notes:** The function can alter the number of write positions available as a result of any call.
To make a write position available, the function reallocates (or initially allocates) an array object with a sufficient number of elements *n* to hold the current array object (if any), plus at least one additional

write position. How many additional write positions are made available is otherwise unspecified.[313] If *palloc* is not a null pointer, the function calls (*palloc)(n) to allocate the new dynamic array object. Otherwise, it evaluates the expression new charT[n]. In either case, if the allocation fails, the function returns EOF. Otherwise, it sets *allocated* in *strmode*.

4   To free a previously existing dynamic array object whose first element address is *p*: If *pfree* is not a null pointer, the function calls (*pfree)(p). Otherwise, it evaluates the expression delete[] *p*.

5   If *strmode* & *dynamic* == 0, or if *strmode* & *frozen* != 0, the function cannot extend the array (reallocate it with greater length) to make a write position available.

        int_type pbackfail(int_type c = EOF);

6   Puts back the character designated by *c* to the input sequence, if possible, in one of three ways:

   — If *c* != EOF, if the input sequence has a putback position available, and if (char)*c* == *gnext*[-1], assigns *gnext* - 1 to *gnext*.
   Returns *c*.

   — If *c* != EOF, if the input sequence has a putback position available, and if *strmode* & *constant* is zero, assigns *c* to *--gnext*.
   Returns *c*.

   — If *c* == EOF and if the input sequence has a putback position available, assigns *gnext* - 1 to *gnext*.
   Returns a value other than EOF.

7   Returns EOF to indicate failure.

8   **Notes:** If the function can succeed in more than one of these ways, it is unspecified which way is chosen. The function can alter the number of putback positions available as a result of any call.

        int_type underflow();

9   **Effects:** Reads a character from the *input sequence*, if possible, without moving the stream position past it, as follows:

   — If the input sequence has a read position available, the function signals success by returning (unsigned char)*gnext*.

   — Otherwise, if the current write next pointer *pnext* is not a null pointer and is greater than the current read end pointer *gend*, makes a *read position* available by: assigning to *gend* a value greater than *gnext* and no greater than *pnext*.
   Returns (unsigned char)*gnext*.

10   Returns EOF to indicate failure.

11   **Notes:** The function can alter the number of read positions available as a result of any call.

        pos_type seekoff(off_type off, seekdir way, openmode which = in | out);

12   **Effects:** Alters the stream position within one of the controlled sequences, if possible, as indicated in Table 104:

---
[313] An implementation should consider *alsize* in making this decision.

Table 104—`seekoff` **positioning**

Conditions	Result
(`which` & `ios::in`) `!= 0`	positions the input sequence
(`which` & `ios::out`) `!= 0`	positions the output sequence
(`which` & (`ios::in` | `ios::out`)) `==` (`ios::in` | `ios::out`)) and `way ==` either `ios::beg` or `ios::end`	positions both the input and the output sequences
Otherwise	the positioning operation fails.

13   For a sequence to be positioned, if its next pointer is a null pointer, the positioning operation fails. Otherwise, the function determines `newoff` as indicated in Table 105:

Table 105—`newoff` **values**

Condition	`newoff` Value
`way == ios::beg`	0
`way == ios::cur`	the next pointer minus the beginning pointer (`xnext` - `xbeg`)
`way == ios::end`	`seekhigh` minus the beginning pointer (`seekhigh` - `xbeg`)
If (`newoff + off`) `<` (`seeklow` - `xbeg`), or (`seekhigh` - `xbeg`) `<` (`newoff + off`)	the positioning operation fails

14   Otherwise, the function assigns `xbeg` + `newoff` + `off` to the next pointer `xnext`.

15   **Returns:** `pos_type`(`newoff`), constructed from the resultant offset `newoff` (of type `off_type`), that stores the resultant stream position, if possible. If the positioning operation fails, or if the constructed object cannot represent the resultant stream position, the return value is `pos_type(off_type(-1))`.

```
pos_type seekpos(pos_type sp, ios_base::openmode which
               = ios_base::in | ios_base::out);
```

16   **Effects:** Alters the stream position within one of the controlled sequences, if possible, to correspond to the stream position stored in `sp` (as described below).

— If (`which` & `ios::in`) `!= 0`, positions the input sequence.

— If (`which` & `ios::out`) `!= 0`, positions the output sequence.

— If the function positions neither sequence, the positioning operation fails.

17   For a sequence to be positioned, if its next pointer is a null pointer, the positioning operation fails. Otherwise, the function determines `newoff` from `sp.offset()`:

— If `newoff` is an invalid stream position, has a negative value, or has a value greater than (`seekhigh` - `seeklow`), the positioning operation fails

— Otherwise, the function adds `newoff` to the beginning pointer `xbeg` and stores the result in the next pointer *xnext*.

18 **Returns:** `pos_type(newoff)`, constructed from the resultant offset *newoff* (of type `off_type`), that stores the resultant stream position, if possible. If the positioning operation fails, or if the constructed object cannot represent the resultant stream position, the return value is `pos_type(off_type(-1))`.

```
streambuf<char>* setbuf(char* s, streamsize n);
```

19 **Effects:** Implementation defined, except that `setbuf(0, 0)` has no effect.

D.7.2 Class `istrstream` [depr.istrstream]

```
namespace std {
  class istrstream : public basic_istream<char> {
  public:
    explicit istrstream(const char* s);
    explicit istrstream(char* s);
    istrstream(const char* s, streamsize n);
    istrstream(char* s, streamsize n);
    virtual ~istrstream();

    strstreambuf* rdbuf() const;
    char *str();
  private:
//  strstreambuf sb;      exposition only
  };
}
```

1 The class `istrstream` supports the reading of objects of class `strstreambuf`. It supplies a `strstreambuf` object to control the associated array object. For the sake of exposition, the maintained data is presented here as:

— *sb*, the `strstreambuf` object.

D.7.2.1 `istrstream` constructors [depr.istrstream.cons]

```
explicit istrstream(const char* s);
explicit istrstream(char* s);
```

1 **Effects:** Constructs an object of class `istrstream`, initializing the base class with `istream(&sb)` and initializing *sb* with `strstreambuf(s,0))`. *s* shall designate the first element of an NTBS.

```
istrstream(const char* s, streamsize n);
```

2 **Effects:** Constructs an object of class `istrstream`, initializing the base class with `istream(&sb)` and initializing *sb* with `strstreambuf(s,n))`. *s* shall designate the first element of an array whose length is *n* elements, and *n* shall be greater than zero.

D.7.2.2 Member functions [depr.istrstream.members]

```
strstreambuf* rdbuf() const;
```

1 **Returns:** `(strstreambuf*)&sb`.

```
        char* str();
```

2   **Returns:** `rdbuf()->str()`.

D.7.3 Class `ostrstream`   [depr.ostrstream]

```
namespace std {
  class ostrstream : public basic_ostream<char> {
  public:
    ostrstream();
    ostrstream(char* s, int n, ios_base::openmode mode = ios_base::out);
    virtual ~ostrstream();

    strstreambuf* rdbuf() const;
    void freeze(bool freezefl = true);
    char* str();
    int pcount() const;
  private:
//  strstreambuf sb;       exposition only
  };
}
```

1   The class `ostrstream` supports the writing of objects of class `strstreambuf`. It supplies a `strstreambuf` object to control the associated array object. For the sake of exposition, the maintained data is presented here as:

— *sb*, the `strstreambuf` object.

D.7.3.1 `ostrstream` constructors   [depr.ostrstream.cons]

```
        ostrstream();
```

1   **Effects:** Constructs an object of class `ostrstream`, initializing the base class with `ostream(&sb)` and initializing *sb* with `strstreambuf()`.

```
        ostrstream(char* s, int n, ios_base::openmode mode = ios_base::out);
```

2   **Effects:** Constructs an object of class `ostrstream`, initializing the base class with `ostream(&sb)`, and initializing *sb* with one of two constructors:

— If (*mode* & `app`) `== 0`, then *s* shall designate the first element of an array of *n* elements. The constructor is `strstreambuf(s, n, s)`.

— If (*mode* & `app`) `!= 0`, then *s* shall designate the first element of an array of *n* elements that contains an NTBS whose first element is designated by *s*. The constructor is `strstreambuf(s, n, s + std::strlen(s))`.[314]

---

[314] The function signature `strlen(const char*)` is declared in `<cstring>` (21.4).

D.7.3.2 Member functions   [depr.ostrstream.members]

```
strstreambuf* rdbuf() const;
```

1   **Returns:** (strstreambuf*)&*sb*.

```
void freeze(bool freezefl = true);
```

2   **Effects:** Calls rdbuf()->freeze(*freezefl*).

```
char* str();
```

3   **Returns:** rdbuf()->str().

```
int pcount() const;
```

4   **Returns:** rdbuf()->pcount().

D.7.4 Class **strstream**   [depr.strstream]

```
namespace std {
  class strstream
    : public basic_iostream<char> {
  public:
    // Types
    typedef char                                char_type;
    typedef typename char_traits<char>::int_type int_type;
    typedef typename char_traits<char>::pos_type pos_type;
    typedef typename char_traits<char>::off_type off_type;

    // consturctors/destructor
    strstream();
    strstream(char* s, int n,
              ios_base::openmode mode = ios_base::in|ios_base::out);
    virtual ~strstream();

    // Members:
    strstreambuf* rdbuf() const;
    void freeze(bool freezefl = true);
    int pcount() const;
    char* str();

  private:
    // strstreambuf sb; exposition only
  };
}
```

1   The class strstream supports reading and writing from objects of classs strstreambuf. It supplies a strstreambuf object to control the associated array object. For the sake of exposition, the maintained data is presented here as

— *sb*, the strstreambuf object.

D.7.4.1 `strstream` constructors   **[depr.strstream.cons]**

```
strstream();
```

1   **Effects:** Constructs an object of class `strstream`, initializing the base class with `iostream(&sb)`.

```
strstream(char* s, int n,
          ios_base::openmode mode = ios_base::in|ios_base::out);
```

2   **Effects:** Constructs an object of class `strstream`, initializing the base class with `iostream(&sb)` and initializing `sb` with one of the two constructors:

— If ($mode$ & `app`) `==` 0, then s shall designate the first element of an array of n elements. The constructor is `strstreambuf(s,n,s)`.

— If ($mode$ & `app`) `!=` 0, then s shall designate the first element of an array of n elements that contains an NTBS whose first element is designated by s. The constructor is `strstreambuf(s,n,s+std::strlen(s))`.

D.7.4.2 `strstream` destructor   **[depr.strstream.dest]**

```
virtual ~strstream()
```

1   **Effects:** Destroys an object of class `strstream`.

```
strstreambuf* rdbuf() const;
```

2   **Returns:** `&sb`.

D.7.4.3 `strstream` operations   **[depr.strstream.oper]**

```
void freeze(bool freezefl = true);
```

1   **Effects:** Calls `rdbuf()->freeze(freezefl)`.

```
char* str();
```

2   **Returns:** `rdbuf()->str()`.

```
int pcount() const;
```

3   **Returns:** `rdbuf()->pcount()`.

Annex E   [extendid]
(normative)
Universal-character-names

1   This clause lists the complete set of hexadecimal code values that are valid in universal-character-names in C++ identifiers (2.10).

2   This table is reproduced unchanged from ISO/IEC PDTR 10176, produced by ISO/IEC JTC1/SC22/WG20, except that the ranges 0041–005a and 0061–007a designate the upper and lower case English alphabets, which are part of the basic source character set, and are not repeated in the table below.

Latin: 00c0–00d6, 00d8–00f6, 00f8–01f5, 01fa–0217, 0250–02a8, 1e00–1e9a, 1ea0–1ef9

Greek: 0384, 0388–038a, 038c, 038e–03a1, 03a3–03ce, 03d0–03d6, 03da, 03dc, 03de, 03e0, 03e2–03f3, 1f00–1f15, 1f18–1f1d, 1f20–1f45, 1f48–1f4d, 1f50–1f57, 1f59, 1f5b, 1f5d, 1f5f–1f7d, 1f80–1fb4, 1fb6–1fbc, 1fc2–1fc4, 1fc6–1fcc, 1fd0–1fd3, 1fd6–1fdb, 1fe0–1fec, 1ff2–1ff4, 1ff6–1ffc

Cyrillic: 0401–040d, 040f–044f, 0451–045c, 045e–0481, 0490–04c4, 04c7–04c8, 04cb–04cc, 04d0–04eb, 04ee–04f5, 04f8–04f9

Armenian: 0531–0556, 0561–0587

Hebrew: 05d0–05ea, 05f0–05f4

Arabic: 0621–063a, 0640–0652, 0670–06b7, 06ba–06be, 06c0–06ce, 06e5–06e7

Devanagari: 0905–0939, 0958–0962

Bengali: 0985–098c, 098f–0990, 0993–09a8, 09aa–09b0, 09b2, 09b6–09b9, 09dc–09dd, 09df–09e1, 09f0–09f1

Gurmukhi: 0a05–0a0a, 0a0f–0a10, 0a13–0a28, 0a2a–0a30, 0a32–0a33, 0a35–0a36, 0a38–0a39, 0a59–0a5c, 0a5e

Gujarati: 0a85–0a8b, 0a8d, 0a8f–0a91, 0a93–0aa8, 0aaa–0ab0, 0ab2–0ab3, 0ab5–0ab9, 0ae0

Oriya: 0b05–0b0c, 0b0f–0b10, 0b13–0b28, 0b2a–0b30, 0b32–0b33, 0b36–0b39, 0b5c–0b5d, 0b5f–0b61

Tamil: 0b85–0b8a, 0b8e–0b90, 0b92–0b95, 0b99–0b9a, 0b9c, 0b9e–0b9f, 0ba3–0ba4, 0ba8–0baa, 0bae–0bb5, 0bb7–0bb9

Telugu: 0c05–0c0c, 0c0e–0c10, 0c12–0c28, 0c2a–0c33, 0c35–0c39, 0c60–0c61

Kannada: 0c85–0c8c, 0c8e–0c90, 0c92–0ca8, 0caa–0cb3, 0cb5–0cb9, 0ce0–0ce1

Malayalam: 0d05–0d0c, 0d0e–0d10, 0d12–0d28, 0d2a–0d39, 0d60–0d61

Thai: 0e01–0e30, 0e32–0e33, 0e40–0e46, 0e4f–0e5b

Lao: 0e81–0e82, 0e84, 0e87, 0e88, 0e8a, 0e8d, 0e94–0e97, 0e99–0e9f, 0ea1–0ea3, 0ea5, 0ea7, 0eaa, 0eab, 0ead–0eb0, 0eb2, 0eb3, 0ebd, 0ec0–0ec4, 0ec6

Georgian: 10a0–10c5, 10d0–10f6

Hiragana: 3041–3094, 309b–309e

Katakana: 30a1–30fe

Bopmofo: 3105–312c

Hangul: 1100–1159, 1161–11a2, 11a8–11f9

CJK Unified Ideographs: f900–fa2d, fb1f–fb36, fb38–fb3c, fb3e, fb40–fb41, fb42–fb44, fb46–fbb1, fbd3–fd3f, fd50–fd8f, fd92–fdc7, fdf0–fdfb, fe70–fe72, fe74, fe76–fefc, ff21–ff3a, ff41–ff5a, ff66–ffbe, ffc2–ffc7, ffca–ffcf, ffd2–ffd7, ffda–ffdc, 4e00–9fa5

Index

J

X

Z